PACIFIC WINDS
AND CURRENTS

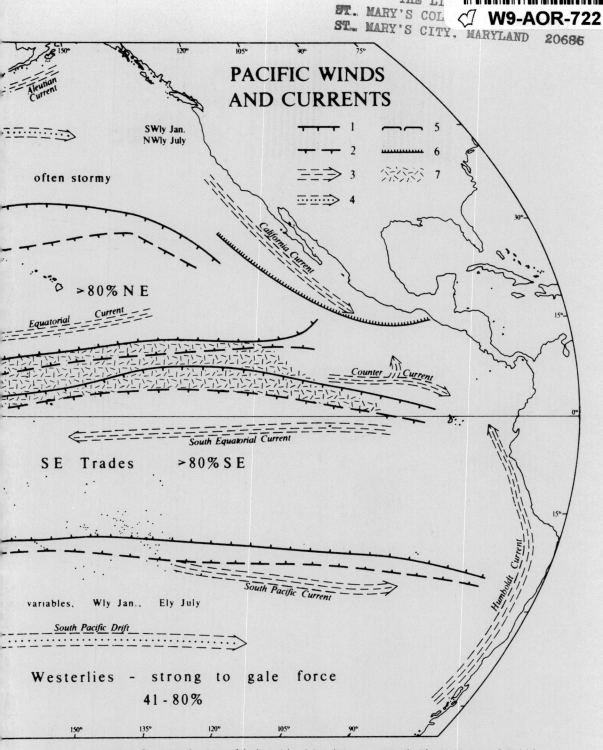

150°   120°   105°   90°   75°   30°   15°   0°   15°

Aleutian Current

SWly Jan.
NWly July

often stormy

1   5
2   6
3   7
4

>80% N E

Equatorial   Current

California Current

Counter   Current

South Equatorial Current

S E Trades   >80% S E

Humboldt Current

South Pacific Current

variables, Wly Jan., Ely July

South Pacific Drift

Westerlies - strong to gale force
41 - 80%

150°   135°   120°   105°   90°

Compiled from *Fiziko-Geograficheskiy Atlas Mira* (Moscow 1964), Plates 40–1, and British Admiralty Charts 5215, 5216. Base map by courtesy of American Geographical Society, New York.

Monopolists and Freebooters

By the same author

Burma Setting, 1943

The Compass of Geography, 1953

India and Pakistan: A general and regional geography, 1954, 3rd ed. (revised with A. T. A. Learmonth) 1967; translated into Russian 1957 as *Indiya i Pakistan*

Australia, New Zealand and the Pacific, 1956, 3rd ed. 1969

The Fijian People: Economic Problems and Prospects, 1959: translated into Fijian as *Na Kawa I Taukei*

Let Me Enjoy: Essays, partly geographical, 1965

Australia, 1968

The Pacific since Magellan: I. The Spanish Lake, 1979

Edited Works

The Changing Map of Asia (jointly with W. G. East), 1950, 5th ed. 1971

Peter Dillon of Vanikoro: Chevalier of the South Seas, by J. W. Davidson, 1975

The Pacific since Magellan, Volume II

Monopolists and Freebooters

O. H. K. Spate

'the good old rule
Sufficeth them, the simple plan
That they should take, who have the power,
And they should keep who can.'

UNIVERSITY OF MINNESOTA PRESS

MINNEAPOLIS

Published by the University of Minnesota Press,
2037 University Avenue Southeast, Minneapolis MN 55414

Printed in Australia

ISBN 0-8166-1121-0

The University of Minnesota
is an equal opportunity
educator and employer.

For B

the shadow was dark, but we entered it hand in hand
and though it was dark, it was warmed by the warmth of love

Preface

The reception of *The Spanish Lake* has been more than kind, even in quarters whose response I awaited with some trepidation, knowing my limitations in certain fields.

Monopolists and Freebooters, as its title may suggest, deals mainly with the actions of Europeans, often *inter se*, on the shores and waters of the Pacific or even in their home bases, since political decisions in Amsterdam, London, Madrid, Paris, and St Petersburg motivated enterprises on the opposite face of the globe. I trust that the opening chapters of the next volume will go a good way to offset this Eurocentric cast, which is not adopted by design but inherent in the theme: a disregard of non-European values is certainly no part of my general philosophy. The fact remains that the naming and the delimiting of the Ocean, and the (imperfect) bonding of the diverse sectors of its margins into an entity which can be summed up in the term 'Pacific' has been essentially a European, or Euroamerican, work. But not wholly so: apart from the great marginal civilisations, in Asia and America, the Polynesian saga lies central to the concept of Oceania as a cultural realm, and I hope to do justice to this achievement in my next instalment.

It must be confessed that this volume lacks the unity given to its predecessor by the theme of Iberian domination and, I may hope, to its successor by that of the geographical and commercial opening of the vast expanse of the Oceanic waters. From 1600 to about 1750 is the Dark Age of Pacific historiography, and a coherent overview has to be pieced together from scrappy materials, and this without imposing an extraneous pattern upon events. Since much of the actual course of events is unfamiliar to English readers, there is a good deal of direct narrative in this volume, but I have tried to present incidents in relation to a wider background. Some are linked by the search for knowledge, though the inspiration to this was more often than not geopolitical rather than disinterested. There is also a fascination in detecting the strange and indirect linkages whereby, for instance, the natural irascibility of a British Commodore, faced with the natural hauteur of a Viceroy of the Celestial Empire, contributed to the building of a stereotype which was to bedevil Euro-Chinese relations for two centuries; or the grog-induced melancholy of a British privateer, only by accident of timing not sailing under the colours of the House of Austria, found its avatar in that archetypal image of Romanticism, the Albatross. If I have now and then succumbed to the seduction of an intriguing by-way, this temptation has been resisted more often than the reader may realise: the story of the *Wager* could have been six or ten times longer, and still only an outline.

A generalist work such as this, with so wide a scope both in space and time, inevitably has its errors, whether of commission or omission; I am gratified that the reviewers of *The Spanish Lake* found, or at least revealed, so few. More important than error of detail (unless to a degree which implies unscholarly carelessness) is the inevitable simplification of complex processes, the built-in handicap of the generalist. It is like cartography: one cannot be more accurate than the scale permits. On small-scale maps of wide areas, the width of roads and rivers is grossly exaggerated, and archipelagoes are reduced to blobs and dots. One can at least strive not to place a city on the wrong side of the river, and to keep the co-ordinates of place and time accurate, so that the general outlines are fair enough; and I trust that I have, in general, succeeded in so doing.

One point in the organisation of the book calls for comment: it is in effect double-ended. The more general narrative comes up to about 1760, but the story of the Philippines and Spanish America is carried on till the end of the century and, for Pacific Peru and Chile, even to Independence. For this I could cite the highly respectable precedent of Vincent Harlow, on specifically the same point. The essential reason is that while on the strictly Oceanic facies there is a break of continuity in the 1760s, no such break is possible for the Spanish colonial polity. On the open Ocean, a new and essentially different phase begins with the circum-navigations of 1764–9, from Byron to Bougainville—expeditions oriented to the acquisition of knowledge, albeit for geopolitical advantage, and directly organised by the State. But in the Spanish Indies a process of conscious change was continuous through the century, at least from Alberoni in 1719 till the death of Carlos III in 1788 and indeed for some years after that, and cannot be arbitrarily split. Such Pacific voyaging as the Spaniards did carry out is detachable from the general evolution of their polity, and better treated as part of the great opening after Byron or, for the northern voyages, as part of the sparring for geopolitical advantage which followed the opening of the North Pacific fur trade as a result of Cook's third voyage, and the Russian push into mainland Alaska.

I have also indulged myself, rather less legitimately, in two or three pages of 'prospective epilogue', in the manner of the hard-pressed examinee who desperate-ly jots down the heads of what he would have said: for it is obvious that my chronological reach has exceeded my grasp, and references to subsequent volumes may express a lively hope rather than an assured conviction. As one passes seventy, Time's wingèd chariot becomes damnably noisy.

The last paragraph of the preface to *The Spanish Lake* still stands: 'How much the execution of such a work falls short of his ideal, only its author can truly know; he alone also knows both its drudgeries and its delights. The drudgeries have been lightened, the delights immeasurably enhanced, by the constant loving kindness of my wife.'

O.H.K.S.

Canberra
14 October 1981

Acknowledgements

Though they are no longer with us, I think I must still place first my gratitude for the inspiration of my friends Jim Davidson and Armando Cortesão.

My debts to that 'magnificent support for scholarship', The Australian National University, increase—materially through the continuation of a Visiting Fellowship, morally through the continued interest and encouragement of Professor Gavan Daws, head of the Department of Pacific and South-East Asian History; Professor Wang Gungwu, Director of the Research School of Pacific Studies, and his successor Professor R. Gerard Ward; and Professor Anthony Low, the Vice-Chancellor. Harry Maude has cheered me on from his busy retirement, Bob Langdon and Tony Reid still feed me from their private libraries, and Norah Forster with references. Until her departure from Canberra, Robyn Savory brought more than normal enthusiasm to the typing, a tradition carried on by Pat Gilbert, Helen Hookey, and Julie Gordon. Once again Pat Croft has given meticulous care to the editing of the text, and Keith Mitchell has turned my crude drafts into works of cartographic art. And so many friends in the Tea Room of the Coombs Building have matched my Pacific ardours with their endurances.

Outside the ANU, I must thank H.E. Sr Carlos Fernández-Shaw, the Ambassador of Spain in Australia, for his interest and help; Dr Alan Frost of La Trobe University and his wife Isabel for their generous hospitality; Father Michael Cooper SJ of Sophia University, Tokyo, for continued assistance on Japanese matters; and Dorothy Prescott of the Map Room in the National Library of Australia. My thanks are also due to Mr N. Israel of Amsterdam, Sr José Ventura Reja of the Escuela de Estudios Hispano-Americanos, Seville, and Dr Howard Fry of James Cook University, Townsville.

I have had always courteous assistance from staff members of the following Libraries: in Australia, the ANU and National Libraries in Canberra, the Mitchell and the New South Wales Public Libraries in Sydney, the La Trobe University and the Victorian State Libraries in Melbourne; and in the United States, the University of California and the Bancroft Libraries in Berkeley.

Scholars who have kindly answered specific queries are acknowledged individually in the notes, but I must mention in particular Dr Helen Wallis, in charge of the map collections of The British Library, not least for introducing me to Don Vicente Memije. I owe much to the exciting symposium on 'Captain James Cook and His Times' held at Simon Fraser University, Vancouver, in 1978 and so magnificently organised by Professor Phyllis Autry: the only conference, to my recollection, after which I left *none* of the papers in the hotel wastepaper basket.

Contents

Maps

Plates

Preliminary Data

1. BIBLIOGRAPHICAL

References

For a work cited more than once, the full title, with place and date of publication, is given at first citation in each chapter, with a short title in brackets: R. H. Fisher, *Bering's Voyages: Whither and Why* (Seattle 1977) [*Bering*]. Where paperback editions have been used, the name of the series is given: W. Dampier, *A New Voyage Round the World* (Dover ed., New York 1968). The original date of reprinted works, if not given in the text, is indicated in the notes, but where several places of publication appear on a title page, only the first is normally shown. It is worth noting that when the place of publication is Berkeley, this normally implies the University of California Press; Amsterdam, N. Israel; Harmondsworth, Penguin or Pelican.

Occasionally a very cumbersome title or sub-title has been slightly shortened, and in journal articles sub-titles are omitted when they seem to add nothing.

Abbreviations

A few often-cited works are referred to by author's or editor's name only:

Beaglehole	J. C. Beaglehole, *The Journals of Captain James Cook on his Voyages of Discovery*, Hakluyt Society Extra Series 34–7, Cambridge:
	I. *The Voyage of the* Endeavour, *1768–1771* (1955, reprint with addenda and corrigenda 1968)
	II. *The Voyage of the* Resolution *and* Adventure, *1772–1775* (1961, reprint 1969)
	III. *The Voyage of the* Resolution *and* Discovery, *1776–1780* (1967)
	IV. *The Life of Captain James Cook* (London 1974)
Blair & Robertson	E. H. Blair and J. A. Robertson (eds.), *The Philippine Islands 1493–1803*[*–1898*], 55 volumes (Cleveland 1903–9, reprint Manila c. 1962)
Burney	J. Burney, *A Chronological History of Discoveries in the South Sea or Pacific Ocean* (London 1803–17, reprint Amsterdam 1967)
Dermigny	L. Dermigny, *La Chine et l'Occident: Le Commerce à Canton au XVIIIe Siècle 1719–1833* (Paris 1964)

Fernández Duro   C. Fernández Duro, *La Armada Española desde la Unión de las Coronas de Castilla y León* (Madrid 1895–1903)

Spate   O. H. K. Spate, *The Pacific since Magellan: I. The Spanish Lake* (Canberra 1979)

Abbreviations for periodicals and series are self-explanatory, except for:

AEA   *Anuario de Estudios Americanos* (Seville), 1944

HAHR   *Hispanic American Historical Review*, 1918+

HS 1st   Publications of the Hakluyt Society, First Series 1847–99,
(2nd) Ser.   Second Series 1899+ (serial number also given)

MM   *The Mariner's Mirror*, 1911+

NCMH   *The New Cambridge Modern History:*

      III. *The Counter-Reformation and Price Revolution, 1559–1610* (1968)

      IV. *The Decline of Spain and the Thirty Years' War, 1609–1648/59* (1970)

      VI. *The Rise of Great Britain and Russia, 1688–1715/25* (1971)

      VII. *The Old Regime, 1713–1763* (1957)

      VIII. *The American and French Revolutions, 1763–1793* (1965)

Chartered Companies:

EIC   East India Company
RCF   Real Compañía de Filipinas
SSC   South Sea Company
VOC   Vereenigde Oost-Indische Compagnie
WIC   West-Indische Compagnie

General

Translations are by myself, except when quoted from previously Englished works, as acknowledged in the notes or made clear by context.

It seems impossible to compile a short select bibliography which would not be invidious, and a full formal bibliography would give equal weight to the most diversely valuable items, unless it were expanded into a *catalogue raisonné* of enormous length, adding little or nothing worthwhile to the comments in the notes.

Only rarely, and then by reason of non-availability of the specific works, have quotations cited from other authors been accepted unchecked; but I have indicated by whom I have been led to a particular work. For any inadvertent omission of such ackowledgement, I offer my apologies.

2. GENERAL

Dates

Dates are given in New Style, except for events at sea on Dutch ships up to 1700, British to 1752, and Russian throughout the volume; by 1752, when Great Britain changed from the Julian to the Gregorian calendar, Old Style was eleven days behind new. Occasionally I have specified OS or NS for emphasis.

Times for shipboard events are in 'ship time', the day running for twenty-four hours from noon on the previous day by civil time; thus from midnight to noon on 1 April is the first of the month by both ship and civil time, but at noon ship time moves to 2 April.

Units of distance

Although the metric system is used in this book, distances are often given in leagues, since for its period the league was the unit most commonly used for distances at sea, and indeed the general Spanish usage on land as well. The 'sea league', Portuguese in origin and reckoned at $17\frac{1}{2}$ to a degree of latitude, was 4 Roman miles (3.2 nautical miles or approximately 3.7 statute miles, or 5.9 km); the Spanish league, reckoned at $16\frac{2}{3}$ to a degree, was about 5.6 km.

The 'miles' in Dutch accounts are old German miles, 5358 m (3.35 English statute miles), but increasingly from 1617 the new value of W. Snellius, 7158 m (4.47 English miles), was used.

It is worth remembering that the mean length of a degree of latitude (or of longitude on the Equator) is 60 nautical miles, roughly 69 statute miles or 111 km.

Money

The most important monetary unit referred to in this volume is the Spanish *peso de ocho reales*. Actual coinage was in *reales* or in multiples or subdivisions of them, but in the Spanish Indies there was also a good deal of uncoined silver bullion used in exchange. The pesos of eight reales were the famous 'pieces of eight' of romantic fiction, but buccaneers and privateers seem more often to have reckoned their loot, anticipated or realised, in 'dollars'; as 'Mexican dollars', pesos of eight reales had a great role in international exchange, especially in East Asia, which lasted far into the nineteenth century.

Very roughly indeed, for the period of this volume,

$£1 = 4\frac{1}{2}$ dollars = 2 Dutch florins = 20 French livres.

(Source: H. Furber, *Rival Empires of Trade in the Orient, 1660–1800* (Minneapolis 1976), 276.)

Given the great inflation of our century, and the vastly changed conditions of economic life, it is pointless to attempt the conversion of sums of money into modern equivalents. The figures in pesos and other units given in this volume are thus given for what they are worth, and that is as indices or orders of magnitude.

Non-English names and terms

Spellings of place-names usually conform to those in *Webster's Geographical Dictionary* or are those of my sources. Accents are given for Spanish names except those in such common use in English that this seems pedantic; thus they are omitted for Darien, Peru and Panama (strictly Daríen, El Perú, Panamá) but kept for less well-known places such as Córdoba and Tucumán. For the same reason the definite article is omitted from such names as El Callao, El Perú. Accents are of course retained in quotations, personal names, and titles of books and articles.

Russian names in general follow the more modern sources used, but I have tried to maintain consistency; thus Chirikov is always so spelt and not Chirikoff, Chirigof, or Tchirikof. It would be anachronistic in the extreme to use the recently promulgated Chinese transliteration in seventeenth or eighteenth century contexts, but the new equivalents for all Chinese names used are given in an appendix, for which I am indebted to my colleague Professor Wang Gungwu.

Titles of rank are given as in the original language, e.g. 'Marqués de Cañete', 'Duc d'Orléans'; similarly for foreign sovereigns: Isabel Farnese, Fernando VII, not Elizabeth and Ferdinand. For the Felipes of Spain, this would be mere pedantry, since they are so well known as Philips in writings in English. One might perhaps say as much for Carlos III, but one would like to maintain a distinction between two such wildly different contemporaries as Charles II, 'the Merry Monarch', and Carlos II, 'the Bewitched'. Maurice of Nassau and Peter the Great are of course totally naturalised in English.

Spanish terms such as *corregidor*, Japanese such as *daimyo*, Russian such as *ostrog*, are italicised at their first appearance, thereafter in Roman. Their meaning is given (sometimes by context) at first appearance or main treatment, and this can be found from the index.

Shipping tonnages

The earlier evolution of shipping tonnage has been discussed in the Preliminary Data to the first volume of this work (xxii–xxiv); what follows refers specifically to British ships.

Before 1773, a ship's tonnage generally meant 'tons burden', much the same as carrying capacity or deadweight tonnage, expressed in units of 40 cu. ft (1.13 m³) which ultimately derived from the tun (French *tonneau*) used in the medieval Bordeaux wine trade. Measurement tonnage, derived from the ship's length multiplied by her beam multiplied by the depth of her hold and then divided by 100 (later 94), or a similar but rather more refined formula, was used as 'a basis for the shipwright's selling price, and in government contracts', and it was not until after compulsory registration of shipping was introduced in 1786 that the old 'tons burden' was completely replaced by measurement or register tons (Davis, 7). In the seventeenth century, the deadweight tonnage of most English ships would have been about three-quarters of their tonnage by measurement, but by 1775 carrying capacity would more often than not exceed measured tonnage.

Except in the Levant and East India trades, a 'large' merchantman of the early seventeenth century would have been about 200 tons; by George II's day, 300–400. The loss off Java, on its maiden voyage, of the EIC's giant *Trade's Increase* of 1609 (1293 measurement tons, 950–1000 tons burden) emphasised the need to spread risks by using smaller ships of 300–500 tons, and the EIC also took to hiring almost all the vessels it used. By the end of the century East Indiamen were around 500–700 tons, and only in 1767 was the *Trade's Increase* surpassed. For many years, however, the EIC regularly registered its ships at a standard figure of 498 or 499 tons, though some were much larger; the suggestion that this was because they were legally bound to carry a chaplain on ships over 500 tons seems more picturesque than adequate, and Davis (262) offers no explanation. For all this see R. Davis, *The Rise of the English Shipping Industry in the Seventeenth and Eighteenth Centuries* (Newton Abbot 1962), 7, 74–8, 86–7, 98, 258–62, 472–3.

Plates

Every effort has been made to trace the owners of the copyright in the plates; any omission is inadvertent and will be willingly rectified.

'Photo ANU' in Plate captions indicates that the prints were prepared in the Instructional Resources Unit, Australian National University.

Special usages

'Straits' unless otherwise stated or clearly implied by context means the Straits of Magellan; 'Cape', the Cape of Good Hope; 'Islands' (except for named groups such as the Falkland Islands), those of Oceania; 'Isthmus', the Isthmus of Panama or Darien. 'Galleon' or 'Galleons' when given an initial capital refers to those on the Manila-Acapulco run, as distinct from galleons in general. Strictly speaking the name 'Juan Fernández' is that of the group of Chilean islands comprising Mas-a-Tierra ('Nearer land'), Santa Clara, and Mas Afuera ('Further out'), of which only the first is inhabited; but in normal usage, both ancient and modern, the term unless qualified always signifies Mas-a-Tierra alone, and is so used here. A distinction is maintained between the shores of oceans or seas and the coasts of landmasses.

Chapter 1

THE DUTCH IRRUPTION

We sailed the Southern Sea, where the Spaniard spied our trail,
And brought the King's ships up to fight us tooth and nail . . .
The Spanish Commandant, Rodrigo de Mendoza,
Was loth to know us there or to approach us closer . . .
The fortress Acapulco did pay us toll and tax
In numbers of fat cattle, ripe fruits in well-filled sacks . . .
Then further on we passed Manila's Strait with speed
And entering the bay in triumph took our meed
Of tribute from the Dons . . . and God, so ends our story,
Did grant us this, wherefore to Him be praise and glory.

This brisk ballad forms a down-to-earth gloss on the famous Christmas message of Jan Pieterszoon Coen to his Amsterdam Directors, who managed (in his view, mismanaged) the affairs of the Vereenigde Oost-Indische Compagnie: 'we cannot carry on trade without war nor war without trade.' Coen, a Bismarckian blood-and-iron man, was the Albuquerque or Clive of Dutch domination in Asia, and his terse formula is as neat and pithy a rationale of mercantile imperialism as could be found. It sets the leitmotiv for half a century of the most complex conflict imaginable, conflict at once commercial, military, national, and ideological, moving from one side of the Pacific to the other, from Malacca through Formosa to Nagasaki; linked too with arenas beyond our purview, in the Persian Gulf and off Surat, in Ceylon and Mozambique, in Angola and Brazil: our own is not the first 'global century'. On the Pacific margins of Asia, the interlocking struggles involved Dutch and Iberian, Macaonese and Manileños, Jesuits and Franciscans; Japanese and Chinese; Ming and Manchu; Atchenese, Javanese, Buginese, Moluccans, Makassars; freebooters Asian or European or Eurasian, with one remarkable independent man, Cheng Ch'eng-kung, known to Europeans as Coxinga. The major European protagonists were the Hollanders and Castilians, but the English also had their role (on this stage a minor one), and there were French and Danes in the wings.

The necessities of narrative obviously impose some artificial separation of these intertwining themes; Procrustes had it easier: he had only to stretch or chop, not to shape or dovetail. But this is the common lot of the historian, whose skills must often exceed those of the circus rider: each must manage six horses at once, but at least the equestrian's mounts are all racing at the same speed in the same direction. Which is usually about the last thing that can be said of human affairs, at least in the short term and not *sub specie aeternitatis*. I shall endeavour first to construct a

'Ode in Honour of these Fresh Navigations', in J. A. J. Villiers (ed.), *The East and West Indian Mirror* (London 1906), 6–8.

coherent narrative of events, reserving to a later chapter most comment and analysis of consequences.

The entry of the Dutch

The geostrategic position in eastern Asia had by the 1580s changed considerably from that of half a century earlier, when the Treaty of Zaragoza (1529) had left the Portuguese firmly implanted in the Moluccas. Their murder of Sultan Hairun of Ternate in 1570 led to a general revolt under his son Baabullah, and they were driven from that most important of the Spice Islands, though they retained a footing in Amboyna and, after 1578, a fort in Tidore. But their hold was precarious. The Moluccas were after all 'a monsoon away from Malacca and yet another from Goa',[1] and after the Union of the Crowns in 1580 there was a much nearer Iberian base at Manila. It is not true, as is often stated or implied, that the Spaniards gave no aid to the Portuguese, now through the Union exposed to Dutch attack; though their succours were often ineffective. Indeed, six months before Macao formally accepted Philip II as Philip I of Portugal, the Governor of the Philippines, Gonzalo Ronquillo de Peñalosa, was writing to the King that he would soon be in possession of Ternate; true, the Portuguese had not asked for help, but help would be sent.[2] Neither Ronquillo's expedition of 1582 nor Santiago de Vera's of 1585 had any luck, and that of Gomez Pérez Dasmariñas in 1593, though on a large scale (over 900 Spaniards), ended abruptly when his Chinese rowers—paid men, not slaves, but unwillingly conscripted, and mistreated—rose on the second night out and killed him. A further project by Dasmariñas's son Luis was diverted to a wild adventure in Cambodia.[3] At this point the whole situation was transformed by the advent of another European power, in much more solid force than the single-ship raids of the earlier heretics Drake and Cavendish.

Philip II's embargoes and seizures on Dutch traders in Iberian ports (1585, 1595) probably merely forced on an extrusion of Dutch trading that was bound to come. Attempts, Dutch and English, to find a way to the riches of the East by the northern passages were abortive, but an already active mercantile interest was much enhanced by the detailed information brought back by Jan Huyghen van Linschoten, who had made very good use of his years as a clerk with the Portuguese at Goa, and whose massive *Itinerario* was a mine of commercial and political intelligence, a best-seller and a 'must' for the so far frustrated merchantry of Holland and Zeeland. There was also some misinformation, notably that Java would be a good place for 'trafique, without any impeachment, for that the Portingales came not thether', which was a factor in the initial Dutch concentration on that island.[4]

The first fleet sent out by the 'Company of Far Lands', with Cornelis Houtman as chief merchant, sailed on 2 April 1595: four ships, including the *Duyfken* which eleven years later was to make the first definitely known European sighting of Australia. Bantam (Banten) was reached in June 1596: internal dissension, Portuguese intrigues, the standard 'fault of the Dutch, Offering too little and asking too much',[5] all but ruined trading operations; two-thirds of the crews were lost, and the profits were dubious. The Company's second fleet of eight ships, under the firmer control of Jacob van Neck, made much more rapid passages, and by tact (assisted by hostilities between Bantam and the Portuguese) traded with success. Van Neck himself, with four ships, was back home in July 1599, fifteen months against Houtman's twenty-nine; meanwhile, detachments under Wybrand van Warwyck and Jacob van Heemskerck had reached the Spiceries: Amboyna, Banda, Ternate. All ships were back by September 1600, and now there was no dubiety about the financial gain: profits were 400 per cent, and the rush was on. Companies mushroomed; twenty-two ships sailed east in 1598, and although eight were lost, no fewer than sixty-five vessels in fourteen fleets went out in 1601.[6]

The confusion of companies soon led to co-ordination in the great VOC, 'Jan Compagnie', founded in 1602. The VOC's directorate, the Heeren XVII, reflected the power-structure of the Netherlands themselves: eight were from Amsterdam, which supplied nearly 60 per cent of the initial capital, and four from Zeeland. They were given a 21-years monopoly of Dutch trade between the Cape of Good Hope and the Straits of Magellan, and authority to build fortresses, to make treaties and war—'in principle', of course, defensive war, but the principle soon wore thin: already in 1603 instructions were given to 'Attack the Spanish and Portuguese wherever you find them.'[7] Though at times distrustful on both sides, relations with the Netherlands States-General were much closer than those between the English government and the VOC's English opposite number, the East India Company, founded two years earlier: the whole operation was an extension of the Netherlands War of Liberation to the East, a powerful counter-attack aimed at a main source of Iberian revenues. The VOC was much more heavily capitalised than the EIC—about £540,000, eight times the English investment—and it soon abandoned the system of separate ventures for each voyage.[8] Although 'such shifts as a pretence to prior occupation' (Drakes's!) were not likely to be taken seriously by the Hollanders, the slightly elder EIC definitely took second place, though a more respectable one than is implied by Furnivall's phrase that the English 'follow[ed] the Dutch around the archipelago, pursuing them like gadflies'.[9]

The facts of life in the Eastern Seas led to a polity in which mercantilism and militarism were inextricably mixed, and with Coen's appointment as Governor-General in 1618 and next year his founding, in circumstances at once desperate and farcical, of the great fortified base at Batavia (at Jacatra, now Jakarta),[10] the Hollanders were established as an aggressive and ruthless power; though aggression was tempered by a canny balancing of resources and advantages, and there were no extravagant forays such as those of the Spaniards in Cambodia and Siam. Domination was by no means sudden or complete; but one by one the great centres of indigenous trade were isolated or gathered in, until in 1667-9 the fall of Makassar, a wealthy emporium of what to the Dutch was smuggling, set the seal on VOC monopoly: the principles of Grotius's *Mare Liberum* did not apply East of Suez or the Cape. Indigenous traders remained active or even flourishing, but increasingly they survived as mere feeders or in the less worth-while interstices of the system or on its remotest frontiers, as providing local shipping on bottomry charters, and probably also as a front for illicit trade by officials of the great companies. Despite these important survivals, the Dutch eventually wrought a far greater revolution than that of the Portuguese.

There was also a French Compagnie des Indes Orientales, founded in 1604 and destined to have a bewildering progeny of successors; but although one voyage made 400 per cent, on the whole French activity, then and later, was somewhat spasmodic. Imperial or 'Ostend' companies were active at times, as were the Danes (especially at Makassar); but Dutch interlopers also used Danish colours or front men. In effect, though trades and wars were multi-angular, well before 1619 the Dutch were the great challenging power, the Iberians forced onto a difficult defensive.[11]

Private raids: Mahu-Cordes and van Noort

The Dutch first reached East Asia by the Cape of Good Hope, but they were not long in following the Magellanic way: in 1598 two fleets left Rotterdam for the Straits, those of Jaques Mahu and Simon de Cordes, and of Oliver van Noort. The former sailed in June and consisted of five ships, the largest of 500–600 tons: *Hoop*, *Geloof*, *Liefde*, *Trouw*, and the yacht or pinnace *Blijde Boodschap*—that is, *Hope*, *Faith*, *Charity*, *Fidelity*, and *Glad Tidings*; but they relied less on these well-sounding moral virtues than on a heavy armament of between 107 and 135 guns, 20,000 pounds of powder, hundreds of small arms, equipment for 'arming certain natives against the Spaniards', and materials for fortification.[12] They also carried six English pilots (one had been with Cavendish, one was Will Adams, later famous in Japan), eight French gunners, and the liberal supply of thirty English musicians, out of a total complement of between 450 and 500. They were poorly provisioned, but for 8000 gallons of wine.

The Atlantic passage was long and muddled, and plagued by scurvy; Mahu died and de Cordes took command. They took five months in passing the Straits, and when they emerged into the South Sea (4 September 1599) were scattered by the usual gales. The *Trouw* was forced back into the Straits and did not get out again into the Pacific until December; the *Geloof* lost faith and returned to Holland, her skipper, Sebald de Weert, sighting and giving his name to some islands which were probably outliers of the Falklands. The remaining three stumbled into a large-scale Araucanian revolt, in which Valdivia had been overrun; this was double-edged, since although advance warnings of the Dutch had been scouted in Peru, the rising meant that there was unusual Spanish military activity in southern Chile. The Dutch played a double game: in contact with 'natives' they too often fired first and asked afterwards, while the Araucanians on their part did not always make nice distinctions between white men: de Cordes was killed in an opposed landing. With the Spaniards, the Hollanders tried to pass themselves off as loyal subjects of King Philip, even offering to fight the 'Indian dogs'; but this thin pretence was exploded in December, when the *Blijde Boodschap*, over-shooting the rendezvous at Mocha and Santa Maria, gave herself up at Valparaiso, on good terms. Interrogation of her skipper, Dirck Gerritzoon Pomp (known as 'China'—he had been in Japan with the Portuguese) gave away the hostile intent, and the Spaniards naturally disowned the agreement.

Their reaction was prompt: a large galleon was held at Callao, four more (with the seized *Blijde Boodschap*) were to lie off-shore some 200 km southwards to wait for news or to intercept any northwards move by the pirates, while on 1 January 1600 two galleons and a patache, with 300 soldiers, sailed from Callao to seek out the enemy. Already, however, after some ambiguous relations with the Spaniards at Santa Maria, the *Hoop* and *Liefde* had revictualled and left the coast on 27 November. The *Trouw* did not make Chiloé until March 1600; her people deceived the local Spaniards by offering armed aid against the Indians, with whom they were in secret contact; they actually joined the Araucanians in taking and looting Castro, but the little town was retaken with heavy loss to the Hollanders. The survivors set out for the Spice Islands, reaching them late in the year, but on 3 January 1601 the Portuguese took the ship at Tidore and killed most of the remaining crew.

As for the other two, the *Hoop* was lost in a storm, perhaps north of Hawaii; the *Liefde* struggled on, to reach Japan on 11 April 1600, with only a quarter of her original crew of 110 still alive and only five fit to stand on their feet. She still had a mixed cargo of cloth and trinkets for 'natives', and good store of arms and ammunition, and these we may be sure were appreciated: they are said, doubtfully, to have played a part in Ieyasu's decisive victory at Sekigahara in October. Apart from a detailed chart of the Straits brought back by the *Geloof*, the sole gain of this wretched expedition was the good repute thus acquired in Japan, and enhanced by the tact and skills of Will Adams. This contributed to the favourable reception of the ensuing Dutch ventures to that Empire.[13]

Olivier van Noort, a Rotterdam tavern-keeper, and probably before that an old hand at privateering, enlisted enough support to equip two ships for an avowedly freebooting venture, though seemingly with some sort of authorisation from the Stadtholder Maurice of Nassau. He sailed on 2 July 1598, and in September was joined off the English coast by two Amsterdammers; again he had an English chief pilot, one Melis, who had been through the Straits with Cavendish: the occasion for a very cock-a-hoop marginal note by the patriotic Samuel Purchas.[14] The Atlantic stage, like Mahu's, was marked by topsy-turvy navigation, scurvy, and brushes with the Portuguese on both sides of the Ocean; in one of these, on Principe in the Gulf of Guinea, Melis was 'suddenly and treacherously slaine' by Portuguese or Blacks. The four ships did not reach Magellan's Cabo Virgenes, at the entrance to the Straits, until 4 November 1599, and then were four months passing through to the South Sea. They 'found no foot prints of [Sarmiento's] late Philip-Citie' but did meet the *Geloof* and hear of the troubles of de Cordes's ships: 'Thus hard newes,

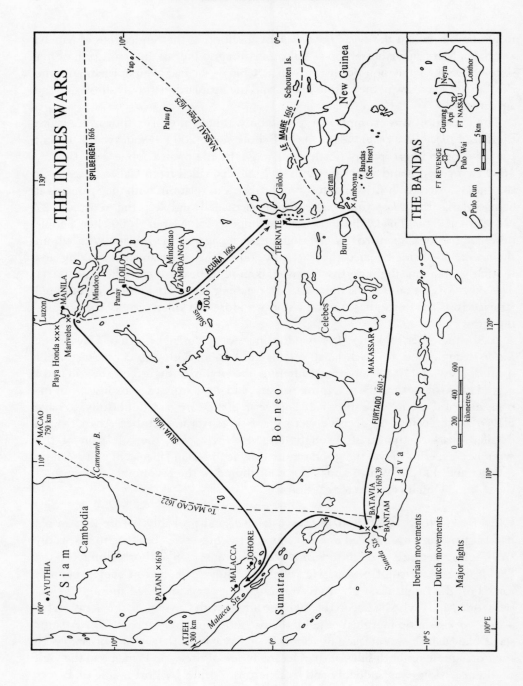

storms, and mutinies ended this moneth and yeare', van Noort's Vice-Admiral being marooned *pour encourager les autres*. On the last of February 1600 they entered the South Sea, to be as usual separated by storms. Although Melis's notes proved useful, the new Vice-Admiral, in the *Hendrick Frederick* (the largest ship, 350 tons), failed to rendezvous at Mocha or Santa Maria, and after cruising far to the north and taking a couple of prizes near Cano Island, sailed across to Ternate, where the ship ran aground and was sold to the Sultan.[15]

At Valparaiso van Noort himself took two ships (but their gold had been thrown overboard) and sailed on up the coast, but the Spaniards had of course been thoroughly roused by de Cordes. Their patrols to the south had failed to make contact—van Noort was still in the Straits—and attention was turned to northern waters. In May 1600 five ships were sent out from Callao under the Viceroy's nephew Juan de Velasco; one, *La Visitación*, was also known as *La Inglesa*, being in fact Richard Hawkins's old *Dainty* taken in 1594. Velasco convoyed the silver fleet to Panama and then went on to Acapulco, reporting that he 'had counted the stones along the coast', and as far as Cabo San Lucar; but in September he and his own ship were lost by storm or wreck. Steps had been taken to warn the Manila Galleons to keep well away from the cape, where either van Noort or the *Hendrick Frederick* were expected to lie in wait for them; but the latter had left the Nicaraguan coast while Velasco was off San Lucar, and van Noort had given up the game much earlier.[16] On his cruise north from Valparaiso he had failed to make prizes, 'Ships built for that Sea . . . outstripping the Hollanders exceedingly', and he also failed to sight Cocos Island, which may have been meant as a rendezvous. Fearing inter-ception, he decided on 20 May to sail for the Ladrones, reaching Guam on 15 September; a month later he was in the Philippines, burning villages on mere suspicion of unfriendly acts and taking a few trivial prizes, Chinese or local pro-visioners. These were easy pickings, but now the Dutch were to face tougher work.

They resolved to lie off the entrance to Manila Bay, 'in expectation of the Japonian [really Chinese] ships'. In Manila itself, where the raiders were taken for English, the Governor Francisco Tello de Guzman was at a loss: the local forces, land and sea, were committed in the south, against Sulu and Mindanao. Under the judge of the Audiencia, Antonio de Morga (whose account does not minimise his own role), the out-port of Cavite was put into a state of defence, while within it such ships as could be found were fitted out: the *capitana* (flagship) *San Diego* and the recently launched *San Bartolomeo*, with some small auxiliaries. Both larger ships, of some 300 tons each, were armed with eleven guns, with hundreds of hastily mobilised fighting men against a few score Hollanders. On 13 December 1600 Morga sallied forth, and next day engaged van Noort off Mariveles Island—now better known as Corregidor. The fighting was savage: Morga in the *San Diego* boarded the Dutch flagship *Mauritius* and all but took her, but she caught fire (van Noort is said to have rallied his disheartened crew by threatening to blow her up)

Figure 2. THE INDIES WARS. Compiled from literary sources; routes approximate only.

and the *San Diego* sheered off to avoid the flames. Lightly built and not meant for war, she was leaking badly and soon foundered, the Dutch 'in their inhumane feritie to the swimming remainders of the enemie, entertaining them with Pikes, Shot . . .' (Plate I). The badly shaken *Mauritius* fled, while Morga and his survivors camped out on the little island of Fortuna. Meantime, the *San Bartolomeo* had taken the *Eendracht*, a mere pinnace with only a score or two of men; most of the prisoners were garrotted as 'thieves, pirates and murderers'.

Van Noort made for Brunei, where he traded with Patani merchants, finding Chinese linen much preferred to Dutch. But on New Year's Day 1601 he was given notice to quit, by an attempted attack by a hundred praus, and made his way out of the archipelago by the Bali Straits. On 27 August he was back in Rotterdam, with only forty-five of his original 248 men. The voyage was to all intents merely piratical, and even as such a total failure,[17] but for the distinction of being the first Dutch circumnavigation of the globe.

The Iberian revanche: Acuña and Silva

Countermeasures to the Dutch incursion were vigorous, but the Spaniards were hampered by internal preoccupations in the Philippines, such as Chinese revolts and Moro wars. Externally, it was logistically difficult to co-ordinate joint Spanish and Portuguese action, and this was even more difficult later on when Batavia had become a firm base and a great arsenal: the Dutch were now operating on interior lines, and the Belgic Lion was couched to strike at Malacca, Manila, or the Moluccas (Fig. 2). Probably as much difficulty stemmed from ineradicable Luso-Castilian jealousies; co-operation was only now and then whole-hearted. Nevertheless, before Batavia was founded the Dutch were at the end of enormously long lines of communication, whether by the Indian Ocean or *a fortiori* by the Pacific. In the long run, though Malacca fell, both Macao and Manila survived; but the former was as it were cut off from really organic connection with the homeland and had to find a new symbiosis, while the latter was barred from any effective outreach, except eastwards into the Marianas. The Dutch eventually secured the dominion over the trade of these East Asian seas, and they, not the King of Portugal (even with Spain added), really deserved the proud title assumed a century earlier by King Manuel—'Lord of the Conquest, Navigation, and Commerce of India'.

Within the Philippines, the ceaseless small wars against the Moros of the south were a constant drain; and nearer home the Spaniards were always, naturally enough, suspicious of the Sangleys, the Chinese traders and artisans of the Parian at Manila, virtually a self-governing colony within the colony. In 1598 Governor Tello was planning to cast guns on a Chinese model, and 'after they are finished I shall not fail to go to China to attack the Sangleys'—the old dream; but next year he

Plate I. THE FIGHT OFF MARIVELES. The sinking of Morga's flagship by Olivier van Noort's *Mauritius*: the 'inhumane feritie' of the Dutch is made clear. From Antonio de Morga, *The Philippine Islands*, by courtesy of the Hakluyt Society. Photo ANU.

had lowered his sights and was using the most ludicrous economic arguments in favour of getting rid of the Parian. Fears were heightened in 1603 by the mysterious visit of three Mandarins, ostensibly seeking a mythical golden mountain; they gave great offence by executing their own justice on their countrymen. After their departure the Spaniards began to tighten security and the Sangleys in turn became fearful, being especially alarmed by Spanish moves to enlist the support of the Japanese community. Finally, in October, the Parian rose in arms; the former Governor Luis Pérez Dasmariñas and most of his company were killed in an early action, but recklessly determined assaults on Manila itself were defeated. Reinforcements came from the south, neighbouring Indians (especially the Pampangans who made very good soldiers) were rallied to the Spanish cause, and the Sangleys were forced into the hills and hunted down. According to Governor Pedro de Acuña, something like 15,000 were slaughtered, mainly by the Indios and the Japanese, and other estimates were double.

But the problem could not be solved by killing: Morga lamented that 'When the whole business was over the city found itself in distress, for since there were no Sangleys there was nothing to eat and no shoes to wear. . . .'[18] Acuña took a more enlarged view: 'If we are cut off from China the many ordinary dangers cannot be overcome . . . if the trade with China should fail, in no wise could this country be maintained',[19] and after all many Chinese merchants 'of better conduct' had kept the peace. There were fears of reprisals from the mainland, and hurried diplomatic reassurances were sent via Macao; but the Imperial authorities were not much concerned with these low fellows who had basely deserted their homeland for gain. Confidence was restored and trade began again, with thirteen Chinese ships in one fleet in May 1604. Immigration was theoretically restricted to 1500 a year with a maximum of 6000 residents; but Chinese pertinacity combined with Spanish needs and insouciance to rebuild the Parian, and in its next rising (1639) over 20,000 were said to have been slain.

The Sangleys crushed, Acuña was free to turn to the Dutch menace. To begin with this affected primarily the Portuguese; van Noort's appearance off Manila was a mere foray, and a fiasco at that. But in the south Steven van der Hagen had negotiated a formal treaty with Amboyna, in the fraudulent name of 'King' Maurice,[20] as early as 1600; there were Dutch trading posts there and in the Bandas and Ternate, while the VOC's first fleet had been allowed to build a stone factory at Bantam (1603), the first serious lodgement. Soon after Cornelis Houtman's departure a squadron sent from Goa in search of him had tried, in direct disobedience to its orders, to terrorise the Bantamese away from any dealings with the heretics; the result was failure, with the loss of two ships. A much larger expedition—six or eight galleons, perhaps a score of galliots, with 1300 combatants—sailed from Malacca under Andrés Furtado de Mendonça 'to put an end to the navigation of the Hollanders . . . their commerce being injurious to the service of God and of his Majesty'; it was roughly handled off Bantam by an inferior Dutch fleet, on Christmas Day 1601. Both parties made for Amboyna, where the Dutch ships scattered on minor trading visits; Furtado was able to subdue the island, and called on Manila for help in reducing Ternate. Aids were sent from the Sulu front, but Furtado called off the campaign, alleging shortages: the Portuguese had been seriously depleted both in numbers and morale. Apart from the success at Amboyna (short-lived), the net results were the strengthening of Ternate, and its alliance with the Dutch; a weakening of the Spanish in Sulu and Mindanao; and probably some ill-feeling on their part towards the Portuguese, despite Furtado's polite praises of the Spanish officers.[21] The pattern was to be repeated.

At this point the Dutch seemed in a rapid ascendant: in its first three years the VOC sent out thirty-eight heavily-armed ships. In 1605 van der Hagen took the small Portuguese fort at Amboyna, almost without effort; the Ambonese accepted the suzerainty of the Netherlands States-General and bound themselves to sell cloves only to the VOC, as the Bandanese had already done for nutmegs: tiny beginning of a giant monopoly. Tidore also was taken; but now there was a check. An attack on Malacca, jointly with the Sultan of Johore and with the aim of making it the main Dutch base in the Indies, was a failure, and the Sultan, who had ancestral claims to that city himself and whose support was half-hearted at best, cooled off. Johore and Bantam were too independent and unpredictable for either to be suitable as a central seat of Dutch power, so the Hollanders shifted their interest to the weaker Jacatra.[22] And meanwhile their standing in the Moluccas had been subverted by a counter-offensive from Manila.

This was launched, and led in person, by Pedro de Acuña, and consisted of nearly forty assorted craft, carrying over 1400 Iberians (including 800 troops from New Spain) and seventy-five guns; but only five ships were of any size. Acuña sailed from Iloilo (Panay) early in 1606 and was off Ternate towards the end of March. There he found only one Dutch ship, whose thirty well-handled heavy guns beat off the heterogeneous flotilla; Acuña avoided a set combat, but went on to Tidore and rallied its Sultan to the old alliance made by Loaysa's men nearly eighty years ago. The Dutch ship having left, he returned to Ternate and took it rapidly and with little loss; the Sultan and many of his family were carried off to Manila as hostages, a piece of policy which caused bitter resentment in the Moluccas.[23] The Dutch admiral Cornelis Matelief, who had led the Malacca attack, arrived with eight ships about May 1607; but Acuña had left a garrison of 600, too strongly emplaced to be easily evicted, and Matelief's instructions to proceed to China on a (fruitless) trade mission prevented him from doing more than leaving a small fort on Ternate. This managed to hold out until relief came, but Matelief's successor Paulus van Caerden lost two ships in a storm and in September was himself taken prisoner.

The Spanish success seemed complete. In May 1606 Acuña had returned to a great reception in Manila: a reconquest and indeed more, a specifically Spanish conquest: therefore not conducive to good Luso-Castilian relations. But the triumph was fragile: Fernández Duro points up its fundamental weakness:

Little is gained by clearing the bush if the roots are left in the

soil. The occupation of outlying islands without a navy to
maintain them was bound to be ephemeral. Did not a single 30-gun
ship show what the feeble Filipino craft were worth? Because the
banner of Castile was planted in the Moluccas, did the Dutch cease to
be lords of the sea?[24]

The struggle went on, a sort of maritime guerrilla amongst the lovely but scarcely
idyllic islands, with shifting advantages to either party, and confusing alternations
between Malacca and the Spiceries, and indeed from side to side of the Pacific itself.
The Twelve Years' Truce of 1609 between the Iberian Crowns and the Netherlands States-General made hardly any difference; true, the Dutch were to be
allowed to trade with princes and peoples outside the rule of Philip III and II, but
the network of old and new alliances and agreements between the local potentates
and the Europeans left ample room for 'interpretation', and as much from *amour
propre* as anything else the Iberians delayed or evaded implementation—thus
playing directly into the hands of the Dutch as the better-found and more aggressive party.[25] The Spanish conquest of the Moluccas left the Ternateans with no
option but to go along with the VOC, which by 1610 had forts in Ternate, Makian,
Motir, and Bachan—all the Spice Islands but for Tidore, though the Iberians still
held on to that island and had a toe-hold on Ternate, receiving an unexpected
reinforcement from Peru—a launch and twenty men left there by Torres on his
voyage from Espíritu Santo to Manila.[26]

But the Dutch also could miscalculate and over-extend, and—particularly in the
Banda Islands—their insistence on the strict legal execution of their one-sided and
forcibly imposed contracts, and a general ruthless highhandedness, gave occasion
for local recalcitrance, abetted by English intrigue. Conversely, the murder of the
Dutch Admiral Verhoeff on Neyra, one of the Bandas, afforded a pretext for outright annexation of the island in 1609, the first formal territorial acquisition by the
VOC. In the west the stalemate continued: the Portuguese could not be dislodged
from Malacca, but as a rule were bottled up in the Straits—quite as much by the
able Iskander Muda of Atjeh as by Dutch power. But it is significant that while the
Dutch were able to attack Malacca, Macao, and Manila Bay (though failing in all
but the first), the Iberians were never able even to project a campaign against
Batavia.

The Hollanders now carried the war to Manila Bay itself, more formally and in
greater force than in van Noort's raid. After the Moluccan reconquest, and the
return of two ships and other resources to New Spain, the only naval forces left in
the Philippines were locally built, usually only *fregatas* and galleys, perhaps adequate
for coping with Moro praus but no match for heavy Dutch ships, of which henceforth there were always several around the Spiceries. Except when the Manila
Galleons happened to be in port, the sighting of Dutch sails from Mariveles nearly
always meant that the Spaniards had to improvise some sort of fleet from scratch;
which they did with remarkable success, fortune seeming to favour the brave—and
improvident.

In 1609 a squadron under Francis Wittert, who had helped restore the Dutch position in the Moluccas, cruised looting along the Panay coast, and in November appeared off Cavite.[27] A few weeks earlier the place had been utterly defenceless: there were only four ships and one galley, all useless, and Morga's batteries had been allowed to decay in the normal Spanish manner. But the new Governor, Juan de Silva, was a man of Acuña's stamp, and did wonders to turn Cavite, in Fernández Duro's words, into 'a simulacrum of a stronghold'; Wittert was greeted by so sustained a cannonade that he stood off. For the next five months he blockaded the Bay, taking forty or fifty Chinese junks; he considered taking their silks to Japan and offering Ieyasu guns and ships for the conquest of the Philippines, or at least opening a Japanese trade. Meanwhile, unobserved by the Dutch, Silva worked frantically to build or repair ships, cast guns, and secure Sangley friendship—a task eased by the Dutch depredations on their shipping. By mid-April he had a respectable little fleet, two ships of over twenty guns each and two smaller ones, and on the 24th he fell upon the Dutch, who were apparently preoccupied with taking on their Chinese loot and refitting. In this, the first of the three battles of Playa Honda, three of Wittert's ships were taken and himself killed; on his body were found the orders for departure in a week's time. Silva took much silk and specie and, even more valuable, seventy guns and a great deal of munitions and marine stores, while the victory had an important moral effect in the Indies: after this, Dutch armadas seemed not so invincible after all.

The euphoria did not last. In 1611 Silva attacked Gilolo, with some success; but in 1614 renewed Dutch threats led him to project a great joint offensive against the Moluccas from Manila and from Malacca, or indeed Goa, despite the manifest logistic difficulties of co-ordinating fleet movements in monsoon seas and from exterior bases. The booty of Playa Honda enabled him to build three galleons of up to 800 tons, and he had been reinforced by five caravels and 600 men sent from Spain, under Portuguese command, by the Cape of Good Hope, ships and men in bad shape after the long voyage; but even with this enlarged fleet Silva was by himself still inferior to the Dutch.[28] In response to his appeals, the Viceroy at Goa sent out in May 1615 four large galleons and 300 to 400 soldiers. Their voyage was grossly mismanaged. Scores of slaves were surreptitiously shipped aboard, so that the ships were fearfully overcrowded; they took 102 days instead of the normal month to reach Malacca, and such was the privation, disease, dissension and mutinous disorder that some of their own people said that 'God is punishing Yndia and the Portuguese nation, which alone has more slaves than any other nation in the world'.[29] The fleet, with additions from that city, was first beaten up by the Atjehnese and then, in December, destroyed by a Dutch force: on the one side, disorder, indiscipline, defeat in detail; on the other, Muslim-'Lutheran' co-operation more effective than that of Catholic with Catholic.[30]

Silva had meanwhile managed to gather a really strong force at Cavite: ten large ships (the capitana with forty-six guns), five smaller ones, and the usual congeries of lighter units; altogether he had 300 guns and over 5000 men, including a tough

Japanese contingent. This force was ready at the end of 1615; hearing nothing of or from the Portuguese, and rightly surmising that they were in serious trouble with the Dutch and Atjehnese, Silva sailed for Malacca to seek them out, and then to sweep east *viribus unitis*. On the approach of this unexpectedly substantial armament the Dutch blockaders of Malacca sensibly withdrew; but on 19 April 1616 Juan de Silva died of fever in that city, and with him died the hope of a united offensive against the heretic intruders.

His body was taken back to Manila, and only a few ships were sent on to the Moluccas. The Portuguese had failed him, lamentably and completely; there were suspicions, probably well-founded, that their ill-conduct was due to Acuña's conduct in so blatantly making over the traditionally Lusian Moluccas into virtually a Castilian possession.

Moreover, the great effort had left Manila defenceless and indeed almost unmanned, to meet a new threat which Silva could not have foreseen. Only a month or so after he had cleared Manila Bay, four Dutch ships and two pinnaces entered, and lay off the city for a fortnight unharmed and unmolested, leaving in their own time and of their own volition. They had come across that South Sea which in the preceding century had been a Spanish lake, and on their way they had menaced Callao and Acapulco as well as now threatening Manila: for the first time the eastern and the western shores of the Pacific were linked by martial actions more substantial than the raids of Drake, Cavendish, van Noort.

Official assault: Joris van Spilbergen

This fleet was no mere private excursion like its predecessors, English and Dutch: it was commissioned by the States-General and Prince Maurice, and was in part designed to reassert the VOC's exclusive rights to passage by the Straits of Magellan, since dissidents like Isaac Le Maire were arguing that as the Company had failed to use its privilege, others—meaning of course himself—should be allowed to try.[31] The expedition was much more solidly organised than those of Mahu and van Noort, and placed under the highly professional and competent command of Joris van Spilbergen, a fighting seaman of much experience whose powers of leadership are shown by his very interesting battle instructions, and even more by the fact that (with one minor exception) his fleet held together throughout the voyage; and this was a rarity indeed.[32]

Van Spilbergen left Texel on 8 August 1614, with two 600-ton 28-gun ships, *Groote Sonne* and *Groote Manne*, two of 400 tons and 24 guns, *Morgensterre* and *Aeolus*, plus two yachts or pinnaces, carrying altogether 800 men, about half of them trained soldiers.[33] The Atlantic voyage had the standard features of scurvy and skirmishes in Brazil, but apart from an attempt at mutiny in Patagonia (also

Plate II. ACAPULCO. D and E, the 'numbers of fat cattle, ripe fruits in well-filled sacks' of the ballad; I 'a wonderful fish'. From *The East and West Indian Mirror*, by courtesy of the Hakluyt Society. Photo ANU.

standard) there was little dissension. The fleet spent three weeks beating on and off Cabo Virgenes, but finally entered the Straits on 28 March 1615, and after all the ships (but for the one desertion, the yacht *Meeuwe*) had rendezvoused on the same day in Cordes Bay, they passed into the South Sea on 6 May: a remarkably quick passage, probably aided by the very good illustrated rutter brought back by Jan Outghersz of Mahu's *Geloof*.[34] By 23 May they were at Isla Mocha, where relations with the Indians ('of good morals, and almost equal to Christians') were friendly, and made less friendly contacts with the Spaniards at Santa Maria, where the little town was burnt. Here van Spilbergen heard that two big galleons and a patache were in search of him, and he and his council resolved themselves to seek out the enemy in Concepción, Valparaiso, or Arica.

As usual, warning had reached Lima—early in 1614, long before van Spilbergen sailed—and, also as usual, was at first discounted. Realistically, it should no longer have been possible to rely on the assumptions of the Viceroy Luis de Velasco in 1597, that the enemy's ignorance and 'the opposition of the country and the weather' on the southern approaches were more of a defence than any local forces; but the weakness of Cordes and van Noort and their poor state when they reached Chile still gave some plausibility to this view that any intruders by the Straits would be too exhausted to be really dangerous. Since Drake and Cavendish, the convoy for the silver ships to Panama had been instituted; but after all, their raids were a long way back, and the recent failures of Richard Hawkins and the Dutchmen were more in mind; to cite Fernández Duro again, the latest foray was always regarded as the last.[35] There was some anxiety in 1600, when Velasco realised that an 'Armada del Mar del Sur' of only four ships could not at once defend Callao and patrol the distant southern coast, while despite an offer of three pays in advance and no risks, he could enlist only fifty recruits for the sea service. He demanded that three or four galleons should be sent out by the Straits; but then the danger passed—seemingly—and in 1604 Velasco professed that his fleet was fine and adequate. His successor Montesclaros found none of the ships fit for serious service; he ordered two small galleons to be built at Guayaquil and made some reforms, somewhat offset by the fact that the General of the Armada, his nephew Rodrigo de Mendoza, led a smuggling ring.

In time of threat, the Armada could be called upon to perform three functions: convoy to Panama; guard on Callao, the nerve-centre of the whole coast; patrol in the south to keep up communications with Chile and to intercept intruders. Even were its nominal establishment complete, it would hardly have been capable of fulfilling these tasks against an enemy of any strength; and since the Treasury was at all times most reluctant to sanction expenditure on local defence, it is safe to say that throughout its history the Armada was only momentarily (if indeed ever) at full strength. As a rule it was miserably below establishment, in number of units, armament, and especially in maintenance and manning: 'the Viceregal fleet showed signs of life only when our waters were infested by the corsairs'.[36] Naval defence was also most seriously impeded by the northwards set of winds and currents along the coast: if the Armada were held back to guard Callao and the Panama convoy, all the long southern coast—far too long to be effectively fortified or garrisoned, even had the money been available—would lie open to devastation; if it were sent well forward, it might be evaded, if not beaten, and then even the north, with its heart at Callao, would be exposed. And the fleet was too small to be safely divided.

Plate III. CAPE HORN. Bearing NE from 600 metres; by courtesy of Mr William Rhodes Hervey Jr, Balboa Beach, California.

In November 1614 Montesclaros received false news of Dutch ships in Valdivia, which had not been reoccupied after the Araucanian sack in 1599. He risked splitting his forces, keeping one small ship at Callao, sending three to collect the silver at Arica and take it to Panama, and two galleons and a patache under Rodrigo de Mendoza to carry the administrative subsidy to Chile and patrol as far as Isla Mocha and Valdivia. Mendoza sailed on 29 December and naturally found no enemy; van Spilbergen was still in Brazilian waters. The Panama squadron picked up the silver in April 1615 and left Callao for the Isthmus on 12 May, safely out of harm's way but also out of the way of harming the Dutch. A month later Montesclaros heard of the sacking of Santa Maria; by this time, after a skirmish at Valparaiso, van Spilbergen was quietly watering at Quintero Bay; early in July the Dutch looked into Arica and found no ships and no silver. With the usual Spanish energy in confused last-minute crises, Montesclaros and Mendoza had scraped and patched up a fleet of sorts, and the stage was set for the first formal fleet action in American Pacific waters.

Mendoza had only two King's ships, one of them, the *Santa Ana*, just built and very hard to manoeuvre; his capitana had only twenty-four guns, and even with the addition of five hastily-armed merchantmen, he had only about half the Dutch minimum of 112 cannon, though his soldiers outnumbered the Dutch by perhaps two to one: a disparity well provided for in van Spilbergen's battle orders. The fleet sailed on 12 July; the Dutch were met with off Cañete, about 150 km southeast of Callao. On the afternoon of the 17th contact was made: the *almirante* Pedro Alvarez de Pulgar, an experienced seaman who should have been first not second in command, wanted to wait until the scattered Spanish ships came together. Mendoza admitted the sense of this, but he was afraid of Viceregal and public opinion if the Dutch got away in the night, and was encouraged by the corregidor of Cañete, who sent a message that the enemy, seen through a telescope,[37] appeared battered and weak, and should be attacked at once. There was a bitter and confused night action; considering the scratch nature of ships and crews, the King's ships fought remarkably well, though the merchantmen took little or no part. At dawn the Dutch were together; of the Spanish, the two Royal ships were trapped to windward, the others safe to leeward—and towards refuge in Callao. Mendoza managed to get away to Pisco; Pulgar refused to strike or to leave the *Santa Ana*, and went down with her.

There followed an anticlimax. Callao had been stripped, left with only two small guns and one big cannon, which was too heavy to mount on the ships and too rusty to fire more than a few rounds. Montesclaros himself lent a hand in trench-digging, and when van Spilbergen entered the port there was a fine show of defence, banners and trumpets and countermarching, so that the Dutch thought that there were eight companies of horse and 4000 foot. The numbers were there, 3000 or more, but miserably trained and armed and low in morale. However, the big cannon, worked by a Franciscan Father, got off two or three shots, one of which nearly sank the yacht *Jager*, and the bluff worked. In any case, van Spilbergen's ultimate objective was the East Indies and his program did not include extensive land operations. The Dutch lay off to blockade, but the small local craft were too nimble—only one was taken to replace the lost *Meeuwe*. After four days van Spilbergen sailed again, taking careful coastal profiles and occasionally landing; Antonio de Morga, on his way to take over the Audiencia of Quito, narrowly escaped capture,[38] and Paita, that luckless town, was burnt. In August the fleet stood over for New Spain.

Meanwhile Montesclaros built a small work on the Callao waterfront and mounted a few guns, pending the arrival of his successor Esquilache, who had sailed from Panama in August with the returning convoy and was also lucky not to fall in with van Spilbergen. It was left to Esquilache to build three forts at Callao and to set on foot a small permanent force of 500 men. There were proposals for arming all merchantmen and for insisting on all-Spanish crews, not the usual mixed gangs of Blacks and mestizos; for building eight or ten galleons in Spain, so that the Armada del Mar del Sur should be strong enough to cope with its three-fold task—too costly; for building as many locally—not enough skilled builders; later on, even for taking the silver to Panama by oared galleys. In the event, by 1621 Esquilache managed to build up the Armada to three large and four small ships, but fiscal constraints forced him to farm out their maintenance to contractors, who used the ships for their own purposes.[39] For a few years after 1615 there were no raids, one could relax, and there was always *mañana*. . . .

Van Spilbergen sought but failed to find Cocos Island, which one of his crew said was very good for revictualling; it is possible that the *Hendrick Frederick* had been there, and as we have seen, van Noort had looked for it, also in vain.[40] Early in September the Callao prize was lost by tempest, all the crew being saved, and on the 20th they sighted New Spain. Heavy seas made landing impossible, and by this time they were badly in need of provisions: it was decided to enter Acapulco and if need were to take them by force. There was no need—although the town had been warned long before, and its strength raised from three to seventeen guns and from forty to 400 men, only the most token resistance was offered. After a few ill-aimed shots from the recently begun castle, friendly relations were established—much to the relief of the Dutch, who admitted (to themselves only) that a real defence would have made things very difficult. Courtesies were exchanged, and prisoners against provisions, all in an atmosphere of fiesta (11–18 October); but this visit at least settled the long-debated question of the fortification of Acapulco: the sketchy defences of 1615 had become the strong Castillo de San Diego by 1617.[41]

The next stop was not so idyllic. Near Zacatula they took a pearler, with four guns, and added her to the fleet; her captain escaped and brought news of the pirate to Sebastián Vizcaíno, who had been sent with 200 soldiers to guard Salagua (Manzanillo) and Navidad.[42] Van Spilbergen's prisoners from the pearler told him that provisions were plentiful at Salagua and that only two or three Spaniards lived thereabouts, and the Dutch might have walked into the trap had not Vizcaíno's men, lying in ambush inland, left bootprints all over the beach. Put on their guard, the Dutch landed with white flags but 200 strong; the resulting combat, dismissed by van Spilbergen as not much more than a skirmish, was reported by Vizcaíno as a notable victory. Since a few days later the Dutch found Navidad deserted, Vizcaíno having retreated through it, his version is more than doubtful.

On 20 November, near Cabo Corrientes, the council decided to wait off San Lucar for the Manila Galleon, but the plan was abandoned on the grounds that it would have been warned to keep well off-shore. Warning was in fact sent but apparently not received, for when on 2 December van Spilbergen set course for the Ladrones, he missed the Galleon by only a few days; indeed, two days later the Dutch thought they saw her, but the 'sail' turned out to be only Roca Partida in the Revillagigedo Islands. The passage to Guam, reached on 23 January 1616, was uneventful, and by the end of February van Spilbergen was off Manila Bay.

The timing was lucky: Silva's great fleet had only recently sailed and Manila and

Cavite were defenceless. No doubt murmuring *silent leges inter arma*, the legal
gentlemen of the Audiencia, as in Morga's day, 'put aside their togas and girded on
their swords', but were reduced to sifting the waste-heaps around the old foundry
to collect scrap metal for gun-casting.[43] Van Spilbergen spent ten days in the Bay,
provisioning himself from Chinese sampans, and then decided that rather than wait
for the arrival of the silk-laden junks from China, it would be 'more advisable for
the common weal' to go to Ternate 'to aid and succour our countrymen there in
accordance with the tenour of our commission'; a decision fortunate for the
Manileños but pointing a striking contrast between the VOC's discipline and that
under the Spanish Crown. He reached Ternate on 29 March, and in July was
ordered to Java by the Governor-General, Laurens Reael. At Jacatra he heard of
Silva's death and met Jacob Le Maire, whose report of a new passage into the South
Sea was greeted with sceptical hostility. Thence van Spilbergen set forth for home;
Le Maire was sent with him but died at sea. On 1 July 1617, van Spilbergen arrived
in Zeeland: the fifth circumnavigator, the first to sail half-way round the world
with a whole fleet well in hand.[44]

Le Maire and the 'niew Zuyd Zee'

The monopoly of the VOC was not universally popular in the Netherlands; in
particular, it was challenged by Isaac Le Maire, a refugee from the Catholic and still
Spanish southern provinces and an old hand at company promoting. His Brabant
Company was one of those merging to form the VOC, whose board he joined; but
his fellow directors were far too cautious to fall in with his grandiose ideas, which
included fortifying the Straits and conquering the Spanish holdings in Pacific
America. In 1605 Le Maire withdrew from the VOC, selling out in the boom after
the first successful voyage; later, when stocks were falling at the news of Acuña's
counter-attack, he speculated to depress them further and 'thus earned himself the
dubious reputation of being the first to instigate a bear raid in a capital market'. One
may suspect that rigging the market had been tried before, but Isaac does seem a
pioneer who would have been quite at home in the New York of the Erie
Railroad War or the Paris of Panama.[45] In 1609 he launched a 'Remonstrance' to
the States-General against the VOC, which was rejected after much in-fighting.

However, by 1614 he persuaded the States to issue a decree giving citizens who
found *new* 'passages, harbours, or lands' the privilege of the first four voyages to
them,[46] and Prince Maurice to grant his 'Austral Company'—a designedly
indefinite title—rights to visit 'Tartary, China, Japan, East India, Terra Australis, and
the islands in the South Sea'—Quiros's memorials were at last falling on fertile soil,
though hardly the ground he would have wished. The VOC's charter gave it the
monopoly of voyages by the Cape or by the Straits: there was here a legal loophole,

Plate IV. HOORN ISLANDS. Probably Singave Bay on Futuna. A and B, the two 'Kings'; C, the
Dutch drum and trumpet voluntary for the 'Kings' (but note the earlier shooting at left); D, kava being prepared. From *The East and West Indian Mirror*, by courtesy of the Hakluyt Society. Photo ANU.

should there prove to be also a physical one. By diligent study Le Maire convinced himself that such a loophole did indeed exist, a passage beyond Magellan's: had not Magellan himself surmised Tierra del Fuego to be an island? and did not Hondius in 1589 draw upon Drake's voyage to show, however hesitantly, a great belt of open sea between Tierra del Fuego and Terra Australis?[47]

Le Maire enlisted the support of Willem Corneliszoon Schouten, who had thrice been to the East Indies and who also believed in the likelihood of a new passage; financial support came largely from Schouten's home town Hoorn in North Holland, doubtless resentful of the dominance of Amsterdam. Two well-found ships were equipped, the *Eendracht* ('Unity' or 'Concord', an oft-repeated name) of 220 tons and 19 guns, the *Hoorn* of 110 and 8, amply provided with small boats for inshore work. The crews were only sixty-five and twenty-two respectively, for an exploring rather than a marauding voyage, and they must have been well-picked, for there was no mutiny. There was also relatively little scurvy, an immunity probably owed to the thousands of lemons they got in Sierra Leone in exchange for beads and knives. Schouten was skipper of the *Eendracht*, Isaac Le Maire's son Jacob supercargo and in general control. That the voyage is often referred to as Schouten's is probably due to Jacob Le Maire's death at sea and to sharp practice by the VOC, which seized his journal and in 1618 secured publication of Schouten's, which though based on Jacob's log played down the role of the Le Maires. When Isaac regained his son's journal, he published it with his own Magellanic studies (1622), and the reprinting of the 1618 account in the *East and West Indian Mirror* replaced Schouten's name in the title with Le Maire's.[48]

They were given a civic send-off from Hoorn, and cleared Texel on 14 June 1615; the destination of the voyage was kept secret until they had been at sea for four and a half months, when the crews were encouraged by the reading of one of Quiros's glowing memorials on Terra Australis.[49] On 6 December they reached Port Desire, a favourite halt from Cavendish onwards as its tidal range made it a good place to careen. The *Eendracht* was soon cleaned, but *Hoorn* was heavily infested with weed, and while this was being burned off she caught fire and became a total loss but for her ironwork.[50] The now solitary *Eendracht* left the port on 13 January 1616 and by the 20th was south of the latitude of Cabo Virgenes, at the entrance to the Straits of Magellan; four days later her people saw a rugged coast, but there was a way through: 'to the more easterly land, which was very high and perilous ... we gave the name of Staten-landt', a name it still bears, as does the adjacent Strait that of Le Maire. Although claims have been made that one of the ships of Alonso de Camargo's expedition passed through the Strait and wintered in 1540 on the southern coast of Tierra del Fuego, this is extremely unlikely; but even were it so, as Riesenberg says 'Small attention was given to unsuccessful ships limping back home' and her journal was lost in the archives and not printed until 1879.[51] If 'discovery' means placing new information on accessible record, the discoverers of the passage were Le Maire and Schouten, as they were in all probability the first Europeans to see it.

The more so as, instead of returning to Europe, the Dutch followed through. After passing the new Strait

> we then ran southward that night with a heavy roll from the
> south-west and very blue water, from which we opined and were
> certain that we had open and deep water on the weatherside, not
> doubting but that it was the great South Sea, whereat we were very
> glad, holding that a way had been discovered which until then had
> been unknown to man, as we afterwards found to be the truth.[52]

On the 29th they found some 'barren grey rocks' which they called the Barneveldt Islands, and in the evening again saw land to their right: 'it consisted entirely of high mountains covered with snow, which we called the Cape of Hoorn'; really an island jutting out into a rocky head 400 metres high. A far cry from the little port on the flat shore of the Zuider Zee, and one may feel that the English form 'the Horn' fittingly expresses both the physical and the symbolic nature of this last great headland of the Americas. A day or two later there could be no question but that they were in the open South Sea, the 'niew Zuyd Zee' of Le Maire's portrait, and all through February they sailed a northerly course. Today the names of Drake and Le Maire are linked on a seaway which was to become, though not until many decades had elapsed, one of the great channels of maritime trade. The next phase of the voyage was also notable, the one genuine voyage of Oceanic exploration between Quiros and Tasman. On 1 March they sighted Juan Fernández, but were unable to land, 'to the very great pain and sorrow of the sick ... but God gives relief', though not very quickly. They continued to the northwest and then, between 15 and 20°S, bore west in search of Terra Australis (Fig. 4). The first landfall, on 10 April, was Pukapuka, probably Magellan's San Pablo; during the next week they saw several of the northern Tuamotus (Fig. 18)—the atolls of Takaroa and Takapoto ('Sonder grondt' or Bottomless Island, since they found no anchorage), Manihi or Ahe ('Waterlandt'), Rangiroa ('Vlieghen' or Fly Island).[53] The absence of swells in the Tuamotus suggested that a mainland—Terra Australis?—might be near to the south, an opinion which was to influence the planning of Roggeveen's voyage a century later. At Takapoto first contacts were friendly enough, but the 'thievish folk' pulled out nails from the officers' cabins, and a landing party was menaced and opened fire. A few days later a double canoe failed to stop for a shot across its bows—the maritime code had not reached Oceania; one of its people was wounded by musketry and some may have drowned, but after this show of power a frightened amity prevailed; the little vessel was 'wonderful to behold' and very handy 'from which-ever quarter the wind blew'. In May they found more islands, Tafahi, Niuatobatabu and Niuafou ('Cocos', 'Verraders' or Traitors, 'Goede Hope'), northern outliers of the Tonga group. At first provisions were readily traded, but the swarms of canoes made the Dutch nervous, and the visit ended with stone-throwing replied to 'with muskets and three guns (charged with musket balls and old nails) ... We calculated that some of them forgot to go home at all. ...'. One sickens.

There was now some debate about the proper course. Le Maire was convinced that they were near Quiros's South Land and wished to push on westwards; in fact, at Goede Hope (Niuafou) they were almost due east of Espíritu Santo, Quiros's Terra Austrialia, and had they pursued this course might well have come to it, or possibly have fallen in with Vanua Levu in Fiji, rather to the south of the direct course. But Schouten was afraid of being embayed on the unknown and presumably perilous south coast of New Guinea, held there by the steady easterly winds, a not unreasonable apprehension; and as the skipper responsible for the ship, and the most seasoned navigator, he made his will prevail. They edged north, and on 19 May saw two high islands, Futuna and Alofi, which they called the Hoornse Eylanden, a name which they still bear as a group, in English or French forms. Here there was at first some violence, six islanders being killed, but after this the fortnight's stay was a happy one; there was much trading and mutual entertainment, the island 'kings' being especially taken by the Dutch drums and trumpets; but when they offered kava, 'our men . . . had more than enough at the sight of it'.[54]

Leaving these hospitable islands, which Le Maire took to be the Solomons,[55] they bore north and then west, sighting Nukumanu and the Tauu ('Marcken'), Green, and Feni Islands north of the true Solomons, and on 25 May came upon a land 'high and green, very beautiful to behold', which they thought was New Guinea but was actually New Ireland. Attempts to trade led to menaces and more firing, some of the victims being wantonly killed as they tried to swim ashore. The Dutch ran along the coast and early in July reached the Admiralties, discovered by Saavedra in 1528–9, and then New Guinea itself. This they coasted, alternately trading and shooting their way through, until, like Torres on the south coast ten years earlier, they met people who had Chinese porcelain, 'so that we presumed that Christian vessels had been there, especially as they were not so curious about our ship.' They named Schouten Island (Biak and Supiori) and rounding Gilolo came on 17 September to Ternate, where they were well received by Laurens Reael. Here also was van Spilbergen's *Morgensterre*, which Reael considered sending out for Terra Australis; but the project lapsed.[56] Finally the *Eendracht* reached Jacatra towards the end of October; only three men had been lost, an amazing record for such a voyage not only in that but in any time. But the Hollanders had left behind them many dead Islanders.

On the last day of October, Jan Pieterszoon Coen also arrived at Jacatra, where he was President. Vastly different from the easy-going Reael, he was not likely to be swayed by the fact that he was a Hoorn man himself. He flatly refused to admit that a new passage had been found; one suspects that even if he had believed it, he would not have let himself be bound down by the mere letter of the VOC's charter; he seized the *Eendracht*, giving an inventory, and took into VOC service all of her people who were willing; Jacob Le Maire and Schouten were shipped for home with van Spilbergen, the former dying on 22 December 1616, soon after sailing. But old Isaac, who amidst his lusty speculations and agitations had begotten twenty-two children, was not to be so bowed down by grief for the loss of one of them as to give up the fight. He took suit against the mighty Company for the return of his property, including his son's journal; and won, with costs.

Postscript: the Nodals in the far South

Within fifteen months of van Spilbergen's return, bringing the news of Le Maire's new passage, the Galician brothers Bartolomé and Gonzalo García de Nodal were despatched by the Council of the Indies 'for the discovery of the new Strait of San Vicente and the reconnaissance of that of Magellan'.[57] This can scarcely be a coincidence, though in their account the brothers give no hint of any earlier discovery.[58] It might indeed be thought a lapse in Spanish security that their journal was published so soon as 1621; but perhaps the speed and efficiency of their voyage were thought so creditable that prestige prevailed over security; or perhaps, since the passage was already known to the heretics, publication might serve to reassert Spanish claims in Magellanica.

The Nodals had joined the Spanish navy in 1590 as volunteers, aged sixteen and twelve, and were not cast down by the fate of the Armada two years earlier; by 1618 they had a splendid sailing and fighting record, having taken seventy-six enemy ships, English, Dutch, French, or Barbary pirate, while their journal shows them to have been exceptionally good navigators and observers. They fitted out two caravels,[59] each of 80 tons, 4 guns, and 40 men; the crews were all Portuguese, and pressed men, though they received ten pays in advance.

They sailed from Lisbon on 27 September 1618, and on 15 November were at Rio de Janeiro. The captains did not altogether trust their conscript crews, and on arrival the men were jailed to prevent desertions—but as humanely as possible, not under gratings in the calaboose! A little later an appeal to patriotism, fortified by the threat that any deserter caught would be hanged without confession, brought them round, and volunteers replaced the handful who for one reason or another had to be left behind. The caravels had a very low freeboard, and the local experts said that to get the timber and fit the bulwarks essential for the turbulent southern seas would take a whole month, perhaps two; the Nodals got out the timber with their own men and finished the job in ten days, remarking with just pride that this was 'one of the smartest pieces of work that was done during the voyage.' They left Rio on 6 December and on 6 January 1619 were near 'port de Sire', anchoring inside Cabo Virgenes on the 15th. Like so many others, they were at once blown out again, and unlike so many others, at once decided to press on down the east coast of Tierra del Fuego.

On 22 January they made the new Strait, with great rejoicing. They named it San Vicente, after the patron of Lisbon (whose day it was), and anchored in a good bay on the Tierra del Fuego side—Puerto del Buen Suceso: an appropriate name both for the event and as being that of one of the caravels. After passing through the Strait they met adverse currents and winds, but nothing like the frightful tempests that had battered Drake. They sighted Cape Horn, which they called San Ildefonso, making its latitude 55°50'S, only 9' out, a much better observation than that of Schouten and Le Maire, who put it at 57°48', an error of 165 km. Some bare rocky crags, even further out than Cape Horn, were named for their cosmographer (whom they did not much need) the Islas de Diego Ramirez, a name which, like that of Puerto del Buen Suceso, survives on today's charts. By 25 February the caravels were off Cabo Deseado. The Straits were passed in fifteen days, and after a fortnight's refreshment at Pernambuco (Recife) they reached Cabo San Vicente on 7 July. Here Gonzalo landed to report to the royal Court, then at Lisbon; two days later Bartolomé crossed San Lucar bar.

This was the first circumnavigation of Tierra del Fuego. The whole voyage, out and back, had taken only nine months and twelve days: 'a period which, in the present [1810] state of navigation, would be reckoned very short for the perform-ance of such a voyage, and was then unprecedented'[60]—many a Dutch and English ship took longer just to reach Cabo Virgenes. The ships had never once separated, and except for one man hanged at Rio for plotting mutiny, there was not a single death. Rapid as the voyage was, it was not scamped; the Nodals brought back careful and clear sailing directions, and paid unusual attention to tidal observations. Their conduct of the voyage was indeed a model of decision and efficiency; but they fell victims to the general slackness which was creeping over Spanish naval affairs: the Spain of Philip III was not that of Philip II.

The Nodals went back to Atlantic convoy work; the silver fleets from Vera Cruz and Puerto Bello were supposed, by the rules and by common sense, to rendezvous at Habana in March, so as to sail for Spain before summer brought the hurricane season. The returning Armada of 1622 was badly mismanaged, and on 5 September was hardly out of Habana when it was caught in a violent hurricane: Bartolomé and Gonzalo de Nodal, both in their forties, went down with their ships. One wishes that their name had been linked with those of Drake and Le Maire on the charts of Magellanic waters.

Chapter 2

FROM CONFLICT TO STASIS, 1618–48

> Your Honours should know by experience that trade
> in Asia must be driven and maintained under the
> protection and favour of Your Honours' own weapons,
> and that the weapons must be paid for by the profits
> from the trade; so that we cannot carry on trade
> without war nor war without trade.

The Coen imperium

For neither the first time nor the last in the history of empires, the rise of the Dutch power in Asia was marked by tension between the metropolitan directors and the 'Forward School' of their agents in the field. The Heeren XVII in comfortable Amsterdam were sober, cautious, generally pacific, and vaguely humanitarian, so far as that was compatible with profits; like the Spanish Crown in the Indies, they would have preferred to commit injustice equitably.[1] The agents, with exceptions, were less scrupulous, and least of all Jan Pieterszoon Coen. In 1618, impressed by the clarity and force of his policy memoranda, the Directors appointed him Governor-General, and willy-nilly gave rein to his arrogant vision, relentless energy, and extreme ruthlessness. Although he produced contorted lawyers' pleadings to legitimise a Dutch hegemony, it is clear that Coen's ultimate (or perhaps his first) argument was that of the epigraph to this volume—'the good old rule, the simple plan'—and he had no doubt that, if they would use it, his country-men had the power both to get and to keep, provided there was not too much nonsense about fair play.[2]

Coen's vision ran to limited territorial holdings, settled by Dutch colonists who would be allowed to carry on intra-Asian trade, eliminating both rival Europeans and indigenous merchants and shipmen: a policy of Thorough. Ancillary servile colonists could be obtained, by force if need be, from China and other parts of Asia. So manned, a vast commercial empire could be set up, ranging from Aden to Ormuz and to Nagasaki, bringing the commodities of all Asia to the great entrepôt at Batavia,[3] there to be exchanged for spices and pepper. The long-distance trade to Europe would be reserved for the VOC and 'limited to a few ships a year, but these would be ships laden with cargo worth millions'. Forceful as the policy was, there were flaws; as Laurens Reael pointed out, if the 'Indians' were to be so utterly dispossessed, 'you would not find any profit in it, for on empty seas, in empty countries and with dead people little profit can be earned.'[4] The Heeren XVII

Coen to Heeren XVII from Bantam, 27 Dec. 1614, cited in C. R. Boxer, *The Dutch Seaborne Empire 1600–1800* (London 1973), 107.

looked on the project askance; although, or because, the local 'country trade' was becoming more and more 'the base of Dutch fortunes', the proposal to cut out the VOC's monopoly in the region itself was startling, and the capital and recurrent costs of such a vast colonising scheme would be enormous; and in fact Coen's financial results compared unfavourably with those under the milder sway of Anthonio van Diemen.[5] Moreover, throughout Coen's first term as Governor-General (1618–23), his plans were bedevilled by his tangled relations with the English, for most of the period his nominal allies but always regarded by him as dastardly interlopers.

The plan called for the capture of Macao and (with the aid of Japanese mercenaries) the Philippines, although before he took over from Reael, Coen had disapproved of the latter's sending sixteen ships directly against Manila, preferring to use them for the Malacca blockade or between Manila and China. In the event, the Manila expedition was beaten off in the second battle of Playa Honda (April 1617), a very tough fight in which the Dutch lost several good ships.[6] Nevertheless, the Philippines remained as it were under a loose siege, and after 1619 the Dutch had English assistance under the mis-called 'Treaty of Defence' between the two.

Macao, a prime objective, seemed an easy one. Coen launched his attack in 1622 with an exceptionally well-mounted force, so carefully organised that he wrote to the Heeren XVII regretting his inability to lead 'so magnificent an expedition' in person; his letter crossed one of theirs saying that the project was 'clean contrary to our previous determination', there being enough costly wars on hand. Two English ships had been blockading the port with two Dutch; so confident was Coen that he refused the English any share in the anticipated booty, whereupon they declined any share in the fighting. Even so, when the Dutch attacked on St John Baptist's Day (24 June), they had thirteen ships and a landing force of 700 or 800 Europeans (plus Bandanese and a few Japanese) against a town whose Portuguese and Eurasian population was about the same number—and many of these were absent for the annual market at Canton. The Chinese had not allowed much fortification, only two batteries and a half-finished citadel.

Opposition was probably stiffer than had been expected, but the landing was making progress when a shot from a Jesuit-aimed bombard blew up a barrel of powder, and before the Dutch could consolidate their bridgehead a spirited counter-attack completely routed them, with heavy loss in men and *matériel*. The Portuguese and Eurasian defenders were outnumbered three or four to one, and a major share of the credit for a handsome victory was owed to their black slaves, many of whom were emancipated on the field. As Boxer remarks, this was the only battle ever fought between Europeans on Chinese soil, and it was largely won by men (and at least one woman) of another colour.[7]

The defeated Dutch retired to the Pescadores, which had been named by Coen as an alternative target. Here they built a fort at Penghu, using forced Chinese labour, and set out on a vicious harrying of the mainland coast and its shipping, designed to

Plate V. JAN PIETERSZOON COEN. By courtesy of the Westfriesch Museum, Hoorn, Netherlands.

force Chinese merchants to this new base, and to secure trading rights from the Imperial authorities. After two years the folly of this brutal policy was apparent, and Chinese demands for the restitution of the islands were backed up by 150 war-junks and 4000 men. The Pescadores were given up, and the next move was to Formosa, whither the fort was removed stone by stone;[8] meanwhile the fortifica-tion of Macao went on apace. Coen had more success against his English allies.

The English intervention

Although the Portuguese and the Dutch were the first Europeans to establish a maritime power in the Eastern Seas (the Spanish at Manila being maritime only by the link with Acapulco), the Hollanders had been anticipated by the English so far as sporadic reconnaissance went. Drake and Cavendish had taken the Magellanic way, with 'wayside financing . . . in the form of plundering Peru', but the use of the Cape route for normal trading voyages was inhibited by lack of ships with large enough pay-load in proportion to crew, and by ignorance. After the Armada large shipping was more readily available, and in 1587 Drake's capture of a home-bound Portuguese carrack in the Azores yielded not only a lucrative material booty but papers with valuable trade secrets. The voyages of Fenton and Wood were mis-carriages, but in 1592—three or four years before Cornelis Houtman—James Lancaster reached the Straits of Malacca by the Indian Ocean with the *Edward Bonaventure*, the one remaining of his three ships. Short-handed from scurvy, she was lost in the West Indies on the return, and Lancaster with a handful of survivors reached England in a Dieppe privateer. The commercial loss was total, but the gain in experience and contacts considerable, the more so as Lancaster had been admir-ably tactful in keeping only Portuguese prizes, releasing Asian-owned captures.[9]

The EIC was two years older than the VOC, but its impact in Asia took longer to become really effective. For one thing, its organisation was relatively antiquated, on the whole looser and with less centralised on-the-spot control in the Indies; though private trading by their officials was rampant in both Companies, the VOC's servants seem to have been under a firmer discipline. Initially at least, the EIC retained some of the characteristics of a merchants' guild rather than those of an impersonal trading corporation; certainly until 1612 each voyage was a separate venture, leading to competition between their respective factors in the Indies.[10] As a powerful weapon in the struggle against Spain, the VOC had much the stronger government backing; from 1604 England was at peace with Spain, and James I and VI's attempts at appeasement all round, however morally creditable in a Christian Prince, hampered the EIC in its relations with both Iberians and Hollanders. Commercially, the English government was opposed to the export of silver, of which in any case the Dutch, themselves bullionist but permitting the export of specie, had larger stocks as the result of their trading with the enemy, a traffic highly anomalous by modern notions but vital to both parties. But trade in Asia could not be carried on without silver, or in the Archipelago without Indian cottons and other Asian goods which in turn had to be bought with silver; and the staple

English export, woollen cloth, was an obvious drug on any tropical market. Nevertheless, while the English role was minor, it was not negligible: in the 1620s they had about a third as many ships in the Indies as the Dutch, a great improvement, relatively and absolutely, over the first decade of the century.[11]

The EIC's first voyage, again under Lancaster, traded successfully at Atjeh and Bantam in 1602, all four ships reaching England with good cargoes, mostly pepper, only to find the market glutted. The second, under Henry Middleton in 1604–6, saw the beginnings of Anglo-Dutch friction. At Bantam the Hollanders were friendly and helpful enough, but Middleton went on to Amboyna where he was equally well received by the Portuguese—and a Dutch fleet arrived and took their fort, warning the English off. Much the same happened in the Moluccas where the Dutch and Ternateans took Tidore in Middleton's presence and the English were charged, possibly correctly, with selling munitions to the Portuguese defenders: with five sets of conflicting interests (Ternatean, Tidorean, Iberian, Dutch, English) the inevitable latent tension became on occasion overt, though the courtesies were as yet preserved.[12] On the third voyage (1607–10) William Keeling was at Banda at the time of Verhoeff's murder, and made an unsuccessful bid to forestall the Hollanders by securing 'the formall delivering of Banda ... to his Majestie of England'; the visit of David Middleton in the next year nearly led to open hostilities.[13] The pattern was set: in the years between Lancaster's first and second voyages, the Dutch had ranged widely through the Archipelago, and apart from Atjeh and Bantam and (much more dubiously) Ternate, could claim to be first on the ground. Any intrusion was bound to be resented, more or less forcefully.

The Hollanders claimed not just a mere priority of arrival, but also rights from their expenditure of blood and treasure against the till recently common enemy, Spain. Except in Banda and Amboyna, they had not yet succeeded in enforcing monopoly treaties on the local rulers, but they were obviously trending that way, while the conclusion of the Twelve Years' Truce with Spain would enable them to devote more resources to the Indies. In the fluctuant conditions of trade with adroit Chinese and Muslim merchants, and with princes not always possessed of good Calvinist burgher ideas on the sanctity of contracts, there was ample room for English influence or, from the Dutch point of view, English intrigue. What the English saw as conflicts of commercial interest to which the Dutch over-reacted, the latter saw as ugly incidents threatening the basis of their hard-won power. Of course, except in the most acute phases of the conflict, there could be united fronts when serious clashes with the 'Indians' were imminent, and neither official rivalry at the top nor frequent waterfront brawls at the bottom precluded mutual good offices at the local level: not only drinking parties, but the carriage of mail and so on, while later on the agents of each company were only too willing to oblige their opposite numbers in remitting home their illicit gains from private trade.[14] But serious conflict was inherent in the situation.

In 1613 the EIC's John Jourdain, recognised by Coen as his most dangerous rival, stoutly defied the Dutch in Ceram, after an exceedingly acrimonious interview between the two tough-minded men. By 1616 there was open war over Pulo Run and Pulo Wai in the Bandas, where on Jourdain's instructions Nathaniel Courthope had formally accepted the cession of the little islands, hoisted English colours, and built batteries: Run was held against Dutch attacks until 1620, which did not save the Bandanese from virtual extirpation at Coen's hands. In Java, the English had co-operated with the Rajah of Jacatra in the siege of the Dutch fort there, and with a local naval superiority had beaten off Coen's relieving fleet from Amboyna at the end of 1618. The success was brief: the English fleet divided, Coen returned in strength, and in July 1619 Jourdain was trapped by a superior Dutch force at Patani and killed, very likely by treachery, while negotiating.[15] With Coen now Governor-General, the stage was set for a struggle of elimination; but policy decisions made in Europe intervened.

From 'Alliance' to 'Massacre'

The Twelve Years' Truce was nearing its end. In the Netherlands, these were the years of the great Remonstrant and Contra-Remonstrant controversy, ending in the triumph of hard-line Orangism and Calvinism by Prince Maurice's *coup d'état* of 1618. In Spain, the same year saw the fall of Philip III's disastrously feckless favourite Lerma, which raised hope of better things; the King had not long to live, and his son, who succeeded in March 1621 as Philip IV, was already in the wings, a livelier man than his father and with a far more able and dynamic favourite, the Count-Duke Olivares. Spanish pride and Calvinist intransigence were both resurgent; between the two, tentative moves for a renewal of the Truce were fated.[16]

As early as 1611 the EIC had petitioned for support from the Crown in negotiations to redress 'sundry notorious wrongs & injuryous Courses at the hands of the *Hollanders*', and Robert Middleton, a cousin of Sir Henry, had visited Amsterdam to discuss grievances. As a result, conferences were held in London in 1613 and The Hague in 1615, with representatives both of the Companies and the governments; as might be expected with Hugo Grotius explaining that the freedom of the seas, so classically defended in his *Mare Liberum*, had to be restricted by the chains of contracts, the disputations were both subtle and wide-ranging.[17] They were also inconclusive. The Dutch harped constantly on the fact that trade in Asia was not like trade in Europe, it had to be defended by arms and this was expensive; it was not fair that they should bear the costs of warships and fortresses while the English came along only to share the profits. Moreover, they were in honour bound to protect the local princes and peoples against their Iberian oppressors, for which their tight monopolistic contracts were no more than a fair return. The English, as well as they might, scouted this specious argument, and insisted on what they claimed to be the Grotian principles of freedom to trade—*Mare Liberum* had been published, anonymously, in 1609, and Grotius may have been piqued to find himself quoted against himself. They also refused to be dragged into war against

Spain, which King James (who had always the Spanish Marriage in mind) would not allow.

After the failure of the second conference, there were desultory diplomatic moves, until in 1618 the position sharpened. News trickled in of actual Anglo-Dutch hostilities in the Indies, while in the Netherlands the religious quarrel, intimately bound up with social and political antipathies, came to a head with Maurice's coup on the high-flying Calvinist side, the judicial murder of Johan van Oldenbarneveldt (who had been largely responsible for the Truce), and the imprisonment of Grotius, whose all-too-obvious superiority in legal learning, and immoderate pertinacity in its display, had irritated the English in the conferences. In this, the first year of the Thirty Years' War, the international situation was darkening, and Maurice urgently needed the continuing support of King James. Hence a settlement of the Indies dispute was essential, and to this end new negotiations were initiated in England early in 1619.

By mid-year agreement was reached. Various proposals for an actual union of the Companies had been made since 1611, but these were put aside in favour of an 'accord' for twenty years.[18] This avoided the awkward problem of joint capitalisation, and the well-warranted fear of the English that 'In case of joyning, if it be upon equall Terms, the Art and Industry of their People will wear out ours'.[19] It opened the Indies trade to both parties, with concerted price fixing both for sale and purchase. The EIC was to have one-third of the import and export trade in the Moluccas, Bandas, and Amboyna, and one-half the pepper. There was to be a fleet of ten warships from each Company, with alternating command, controlled by a joint 'Council of Defence'; it would seem that the English were after all to be drawn into war with the Iberians, glossed over by the double-talk of 'defence'. The main gap was that the question of new English forts in the Moluccas could not be resolved; somewhat inconsistently with their former stance, the English claimed that they would be necessary, against *inter alia* the Spaniards, the Dutch arguing that under the new arrangements they would be superfluous. The matter was left in abeyance for three years, in which time it became academic.

Obviously, this was a European solution signally out of key with the realities in the field; and there was still ample room for dispute even given the greatest good will on the part of the executants. This was lacking on both sides, and most particularly on Coen's part. By a singular coincidence, John Jourdain was killed on the same day that King James ratified the accord.

In the Indies, the English had rallied from their disasters, and Martin Pring, returning from India with a strong fleet to confront Coen at Bantam, found that they were allies. Coen had written to the Heeren XVII in terms in which the sorrow barely concealed the anger—they had hastily taken an English viper into their bosoms—but for the time being there was nothing to be done but to go through with this forced alliance. It is not surprising that the achievements of the 'Fleet of Defence', a misnomer if ever there was one, were slight. Coen was careful

not to let the English in on any schemes of new conquest, as we have seen at Macao; but they took part in the blockade of Manila.

Indeed, at this time the situation in the Philippines was critical: Silva's ship-building drive had severely strained the economy; Lorenzo de Zuazola's fleet from Spain, to come by the Cape and on which much hope was placed, had been wrecked at the start by tempest on the Andalusian coast; vague ideas of co-operation with the English were dashed by news of the accord. There was even serious debate in Spain on the advisability of abandoning the islands, or exchanging them with the Portuguese for Brazil, which would have come to much the same thing.[20] However, the Anglo-Dutch alliance soon dissolved in recrimination, and before this the blockade was raised in May 1622. Two years later a renewed Dutch attack was repulsed in a third battle of Playa Honda, and by 1626 the Archbishop of Manila could write that the Dutch 'have allowed us to breathe this year'.[21] Hostilities were shifting northwards to Formosa, southwards to Sulu and Mindanao.

It is over-picturesque to think of the EIC as 'the poor man's version' of the VOC,[22] but the plain fact was that it had not the resources in ships or money to meet its commitments under the alliance, and the effort to do so severely over-extended it.[23] Coen, whose action in detail was one of obstruction and even sabotage, almost certainly counted on this in advance; at any rate, it provided him with the excuse to resume the conquest of the Bandas and Amboyna, and the enforcement of the nutmeg monopoly there, with a complete disregard of English interests and indeed rights. So great was the strain on the EIC that by 1622–3 its inability to fulfil its allotted role in the joint venture was openly admitted, and indeed was being translated into a general retreat—accompanied it is true by a concentration on India proper. The factories in Japan and at Patani and Ayuthia in Siam were closed as unprofitable, and around the end of 1622 it was decided to withdraw from the Spiceries themselves. The famous or infamous 'Massacre of Amboyna' in March 1623—rather judicial murders than massacre in the normal acceptance of the term—was thus not the occasion for this withdrawal, rather a bloody epilogue which served for decades, whenever occasion arose, to embitter Anglo-Dutch relations; as late as 1673 it was put on the London stage as war propaganda, by no less a writer than John Dryden.[24]

English feeling on the spot was naturally bitter; there was wild talk of joining with the Portuguese 'to root the bloody Dutch out of the Indies', and in fact in 1635 and 1636 English captains helped the Portuguese by taking cannon cast at Macao to beleaguered Goa, through the Dutch blockade of Malacca Straits.[25] But the EIC was too weak to take a hard line; its Batavian headquarters were withdrawn to Lagoendi in the Straits of Sunda, but disease and Malay attacks soon forced a return to Batavia, now under Coen's milder successor Pieter de Carpentier; after

Plate VI. MANILA. D, Cavite; note the Chinese junks and sampans. From *The East and West Indian Mirror,* by courtesy of the Hakluyt Society. Photo ANU.

Coen arrived for a second term in 1627, the EIC settled down once more in Bantam—a reminder that the withdrawal was by no means total. Although in a sense the Amboyna affair may symbolise what became in effect a *de facto* and informal delimitation of spheres of exploitation in Asia, the English in India proper and the Dutch in Indonesia, the division was as yet far from clear cut.[26] Informal co-operation against the Portuguese continued in the Indian Ocean, and there were still opportunities for the EIC in the Archipelago. The cutting adrift from the VOC gave an opening to trade with the independent 'smuggling' emporium of Makassar, and in fact the peak period of the English clove trade was probably in the 1630s. After this the trade dwindled as the Dutch enforced a lower profile on Makassar and, in the fifties, pursued their policy of ruthless destruction of clove trees not under their direct control, although this was far from complete until their final reckoning with Makassar in 1667–9. There remained however the important trade in pepper, which the Dutch could not so readily control: it was more widely grown in the southern islands (and in India), and, as a vine not a tree, it was probably more difficult to eradicate; for decades the EIC retained a large share of the trade, and until 1680 all comers could readily obtain pepper at still independent Bantam. But Drake's dream in the Moluccas was dissipated, the Japanese venture had failed, and as yet the EIC had gained no footing in the direct China trade.

Trans-Pacific interlude: the 'Nassau Fleet'

Van Spilbergen's expedition, though made in time of truce with Spain, had the legitimate motives of reasserting the VOC's rights to the Magellanic route against other Dutchmen and of reinforcing the Company in the East Indies, where *de facto* the Truce did not run, and his attacks on Callao and Acapulco were incidental and not pressed. After him, the Spanish holdings on the eastern Pacific shores were left in peace for nearly a decade. The formal expiry of the Truce, however, 'freed the subjects of both countries from the small portion of restraint to which some respect for a convention, never well observed, had made them submit',[27] and an expedition was now mounted with objectives going beyond mere raiding; they included the formation, with the aid of Indian or slave risings, of a Dutch military and trading base in Peru or Chile. The fleet, commissioned by Prince Maurice and the States-General, was commanded by Jacques l'Hermite, and was not only the most powerful armament yet seen in the South Sea but probably the strongest ever known in the Pacific proper under sail: eleven ships, five of them of 600 tons or over, carrying 1600 men of whom 1000 or more were available for landing, and over 290 guns, many of them heavy.[28] It was also the first armed entry into the Ocean by the new route around the Horn and, significantly, one of its pilots had been with the Nodals.[29]

This 'Nassau Fleet' sailed in late April 1623 and took nine months to reach Fuegian waters; much of this time was spent in refreshing, especially with citrus fruit, in the Cape Verdes, Sierra Leone, and Annabon.[30] In the first half of February 1624 they discovered Hermite Island and Nassau Gulf to the north of it; the Horn was thus found to be detached from Tierra del Fuego, though their chart shows it not as an island of itself but as a cape of the larger one (Hermite) just found.[31] As usual, the fleet was scattered after entering the South Sea, but in April all the ships rendezvoused at Juan Fernández, whence they made directly for central Peru. On the morning of 5 May they were sighted off Mala, between Cañete and Callao, and next day the Viceroy Marqués de Guadalcázar received the news at a bull-fight held to celebrate the safe despatch to Panama of the silver convoy—8,000,000 pesos—only three days before.

Since van Spilbergen's raid, there had been the usual relaxed neglect of defence, despite a false report in April 1623—just before l'Hermite sailed—of fifteen sail, suspected to be Dutch, off Chile. But nothing had come of this, and l'Hermite broke away from precedent by not creeping up the coast, so that the surprise was complete. Two warships and most of the best men had been sent with the silver, and Callao was left with only the *Nuestra Señora de Loreto* (most of her forty guns unmounted), one or two pataches, and a variety of trading vessels which could not be armed. Guadalcázar was no soldier, but when the first shock was over he rallied in the usual Spanish manner, distributing cannon to vital points from Ancon north to Pachacamac south of Callao, and helping to mount the *pièce de résistance*, a royal culverin weighing over four tons, with his own hands—an almost compulsory viceregal gesture. More to the point, he supplemented his 300 or so troops with a heterogeneous volunteer force—privately paid levies, clergy and students, freed Blacks—until he had some 4600 men under arms. A dozen or so small oared vessels were got together, and a barge carrying three or four heavy pieces for dismasting fire; it would not be too easy for the Dutch to raid inshore.[32] But it is very doubtful if these scratch forces could have stood up to nearly 300 guns and 1100 trained landing troops had the Hollanders pressed the attack home.

In fact, they failed to act with any resolution. L'Hermite, who had been ill ever since they left Sierra Leone in September, died on 17 May, and his successor Hugo Schapenham, 'a man of sweet disposition', seems to have been no leader. An attempt at landing in force failed owing to heavy surf, and two attacks on Pisco were repulsed: everywhere the Spaniards were ready. The barge and small craft prevented the enemy from getting at the *Loreto*, and numerous minor skirmishes in the bay were indecisive. The Dutch confined themselves to blockading, burning coastal shipping, a successful but profitless raid by a detachment on Guayaquil, and the brutal mass hanging or drowning of prisoners after exchange was refused. Scurvy was rife and morale low; after a hundred weary days they raised the blockade and sailed for Puna; a second attack on Guayaquil was a failure. A decision was taken to make for New Spain to intercept the Manila Galleon, with some vague intention of returning later to Chile. Despite losses by scurvy and combat, the fleet was intact and had still over 1300 men, so this decision can hardly have been more than temporising to save face.

After careening and watering at Puna and Ancon, the fleet sailed in mid-September and sighted New Spain on 20 October; a week later it was at Acapulco.

The rudimentary Castle of San Diego of van Spilbergen's days was now complete and strongly armed, and the Governor not so forthcoming as his predecessor; even a watering-party was driven off from Puerto del Marqués. The Dutch were in no mood to try conclusions; by this time desertion was setting in, and there was no sign of the Galleon. On 1 November they left Acapulco, by the end of the month any idea of operations in American waters was given over, and the fleet set course for Guam, which it reached on 25 February 1625. Going on towards the Spice Islands, it made on 15 February what was possibly the first European sighting of Yap,[33] and soon after met with the VOC forces in the Moluccas. At the end of August the Nassau Fleet was at Batavia, where it was split up.

'Thus cheaply were the Spaniards freed from the most formidable armament that at any time before or since threatened their possessions in the *South Sea*.'[34] The only legacy of this irresolute and inept Nassau Fleet was an enhanced and more scientific attention to the fortifications of Callao and Lima; and, ironically, until the last days of Spanish rule the only attacks on these works were those of neglect, the undermining sea, and earthquakes.[35] The once-more decayed walls of Callao were a refuge for the citizens when the town was flooded by the 1687 quake, and after the greater disaster of 1746, when much of Lima was destroyed and Callao again swept by a tsunami, the massive fortress of Real Felipe was built, to stand a long and bitter siege in 1824–6 and to dominate the waterfront of Callao to this day. There have been blockades and operations in the harbour during the War of Independence and by the Chileans in the War of the Pacific (1879–83), but in both cases Callao fell to attack from the land. By a grotesque paradox, the only real attack on its fortifications from the sea was the futile bombardment of 1866, a last arrogant and inconsequential assertion of Spanish power.[36]

The Dutch in the North Pacific: Fries

For two decades from the third battle of Playa Honda (1624) there was stalemate in the Philippines proper; the Spaniards could never feel quite secure, the Hollanders could not force a decision. Dutch commitments in Asia were of course not confined to Indonesia: the VOC was active in the Indian Ocean, where the Portuguese holds in Ceylon could be reduced only by hard fighting, and more peaceably around the Bay of Bengal and in Siam and Annam. Much was still to do in Indonesia, even in Java itself, where the able and ambitious Sultan Agung of Mataram was forging a power which bade fair to dominate the whole island. Indeed, Coen's second term as Governor-General (1627–9) ended with his death from cholera in a Batavia under close siege by the Mataram forces, and although the menace receded—armies big enough to destroy the well-fortified Dutch were too big to be subsisted—and in fact brought renewed Bantamese friendship with the Company, Agung's hostility remained an irritant and a threat.[37] Coen's successors, of whom the most notable were Hendrik Brouwer (1632–6) and Anthonio van Diemen (1636–45), had to cope with revolts in Ceram and Buton (off Celebes) and in 1637 forced Makassar to acknowledge the VOC's rights in the Moluccas, including the right to destroy Makassarese ships illicitly trading there.[38] There were still Spanish forts and some local skirmishing in the Moluccas,[39] while the Spaniards were not expelled from Formosa until 1642. The final eviction of the Portuguese from Nagasaki in 1638–40 left the Hollanders as the only Europeans allowed to trade in Japan, albeit under the most severe restrictions, and hence much Dutch effort went north.

In respect of the Portuguese at least, van Diemen's hands were freed not only by their expulsion from Japan but more importantly by the fall of Malacca. That city had withstood thirty-five years of constant threat and frequent direct attacks by Atjehnese, Johoreans, and Dutch; after a most gallant final defence, it at last succumbed in January 1641; it is true that Lusian resilience forged a working alliance which enabled them to 'keep Macassar for their Malacca',[40] but a constant direct burden on Dutch resources was eliminated. Malacca fell less than two months after a beautifully executed coup in Lisbon restored the independence of Portugal, which secured a ten years' truce with the Netherlands. Shipping was thus released from the blockades of Malacca and Goa, and van Diemen was able to devote resources to far-flung explorations in two opposite directions. One of these efforts resumed the northern search for Rica de Oro and Rica de Plata, dropped by the Spaniards after Vizcaíno's failure in 1611–12 (Fig. 3); the other, to the south and east, resulted in the most important voyage of Pacific discovery between Quiros and the great opening of the Ocean in the eighteenth century—Abel Janszoon Tasman's wide sweep around Australia and New Guinea in 1642–3 (Fig. 4).

The voyage of Matthijs Hendrickszoon Quast and Tasman in 1639 produced the first systematic reports on the Volcano and Bonin groups (Kazan Retto, Ogasawara-gunto respectively), but despite two long probes east of Japan, one reaching as far as 175°W, it was otherwise fruitless. The second had as objectives not only the ever-elusive isles of gold and silver, but also the opening of trade with Tartary and Cathay, thought to be approachable from north of Japan and inhabited by civilised people. It had more substantial results than the first, though their interpretation contributed to the 'mercurial cartographical vicissitudes' of the Sea of Okhotsk region, whose outlines were not finally stabilised until Sakhalin was demonstrated to be insular by a Russo-British game of hide-and-seek during the Crimean War.[41] Two ships, the *Castricum* and the *Breskens*, under Maarten Gerritszoon Fries (often called (de) Vries), left Batavia in February 1643 and Ternate on 4 April; on 20 May they lost touch off 'Ongaluckich' or Unlucky Island (Hachijo Shima, 290 km south of Tokyo). The *Breskens* may have reached Simushir in the mid-Kurils, but about the end of July her skipper and some of his officers were incautious enough to land in northern Honshu; they were not ill-treated, but closely interrogated, and not released until December.

Meanwhile Fries in the *Castricum* had sailed quietly up the east coast of Japan, making friendly contacts with fishermen and the crews of trading junks, who warned his people that it was 'no good in the north'. There was a good deal of fog

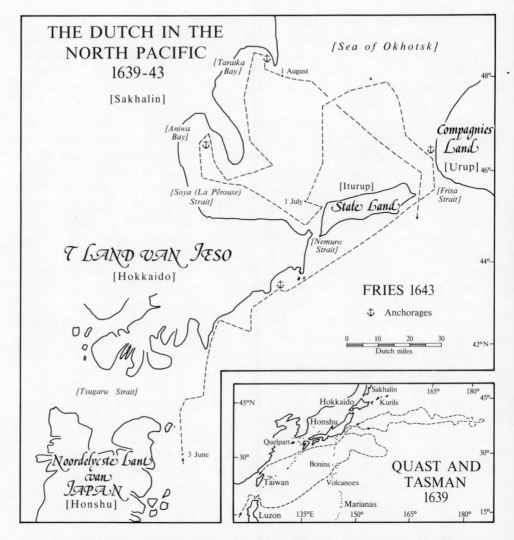

Figure 3. THE DUTCH IN THE NORTH PACIFIC 1639–43. Main map based on anonymous contemporary chart, Plate VI in P. Teleki, *Atlas zur Geschichte der Kartographie der Japanesischen Inseln* (Budapest 1909); inset on Fig. 17 in H. Friis (ed.), *The Pacific Basin* (New York 1967), by courtesy of American Geographical Society.

and they were careful to avoid embayment in the presumed bight between Japan and Yezo or Eso—that is, Honshu and Hokkaido; early in June they met their first Ainu on the latter island, and got on very well with them. In mid-June they saw Kunashir, Iturup ('Staten Landt'), and Urup, which last Fries named Compagnie Landt, thinking it a possible projection of America. Like Gamaland, Compagnie Landt was to spread and contract across the North Pacific like an amoeba, sometimes dwindling almost to nothing, sometimes 'ballooning like a mini-continent', a great bridge between Japan and America; so late as 1960 Urup appears as 'Kompaneyskiy' on British Admiralty Chart 5215.

The *Castricum*'s people ate and drank on Compagnie Landt, going through formal acts of possession and making themselves pleasant to the Ainu: relations seem to have been almost idyllic. Fries now passed through Frisa (= Fries) Strait, between Iturup and Urup, and pressed north into the Sea of Okhotsk, until towards the end of June he was driven south to Hokkaido. Making his way north again, he anchored in Taraika (Terpeniya) Bay on the east coast of Sakhalin, where the people indulged in snowballing—in July—from a still unthawed drift on the beach; this was their farthest north. Coming south again, Fries entered Aniwa Bay—the putative eponym of 'Anian'—but did not recognise the separation of Sakhalin and Hokkaido by the Soya or La Pérouse Strait. He also missed the Nemuro and Yekateriny Straits separating Hokkaido from Kunashir and Kunashir from Iturup, and so re-entered the main Pacific by his original passage through Friza Strait. These errors, rather pardonable considering the fogs which beset the voyage in these latitudes, contributed to the enormous cartographical confusion of the next hundred years or so. After a further and of course futile sally eastwards seeking Rica de Oro, reaching perhaps as far as 180°, Fries returned to Japan, meeting the *Breskens* off Kyushu, and was back in Batavia by mid-December. His voyage, significant though it was, overlapped with and historically was overshadowed by that of Abel Tasman in waters far to the south.

For the sake of completeness mention should be made of the first substantial European contact with Korea. There may have been some Jesuits with Hideyoshi's armies, but if so it is surprising that they left no record; and three Dutchmen who landed in the country in 1627 were detained there. One of them lived to interpret for the survivors of the Nagasaki-bound ship *Sparwer*, wrecked on Quelpart (Cheju or Saishu) Island in 1653. The surviving crew were taken to the mainland, and thirteen years later eight of them succeeded in escaping and reaching Nagasaki; the account of the supercargo Hendrik Hamel, sketchy as it was, 'gave the West its first direct knowledge of Korea's government, social institutions, and way of life.'[42] Korea remained, however, even more tightly closed than China or Japan until the 1870s.

Intra-Pacific excursus: Abel Tasman

The preliminaries to Tasman's voyage must be sought in the largely accidental revelation of a great South Land—perhaps Terra Australis at last Cognita?—lying south of New Guinea. As early as 10 April 1602, just three weeks after the VOC had been chartered, the yacht *Duyfken* had been sent from Banda to ascertain whether there was any trade between Ceram and New Guinea.[43] The findings were negative, but in 1605, now under VOC orders, the *Duyfken* returned to the search, crossing from the Papuan coast near False Cape on Frederik Hendrik Island to make the first unequivocally documented European sighting of Australia, at the Pennefather River on the eastern shores of the Gulf of Carpentaria; but there is circumstantial evidence for Portuguese knowledge of the northwest coast, and quite possibly also the coasts of Queensland and New South Wales, in the 1520s. The *Duyfken*'s skipper, Willem Janszoon, coasted south to Cape Keerweer ('Turnagain'), about 250 km south of Endeavour Strait, then back north to Prince of Wales Island and New Guinea; there was no suspicion of the strait through which Torres was to pass a few months later. In 1623 Jan Carstenz with the *Pera* and *Arnhem* followed up this first reconnaissance, extending the *Duyfken*'s findings some way south, and again missing Torres Strait—excusably, since he found himself in what seemed a 'shallow bight', a maze of reefs and shoals—although by this time the Dutch were suspecting the existence of a passage, from Iberian maps.[44] The *Arnhem*, which had separated, crossed the Gulf of Carpentaria to find the northeastern extremities of what is now Arnhem Land. In 1636 a third voyage, beginning under the command of Gerrit Pool (who was killed by Papuans), found the Cobourg Peninsula, in northwest Arnhem Land, and Melville Island.

The results of these voyages were not encouraging. Both the countries and the peoples seen were poor; the second European-bestowed name in Australia was Vliege Baij, 'Fly Bay', thus setting a note repeated by irritated travellers from that day to this. There had been many fights with the inhabitants on either shore, and the question of a connection between New Guinea and the land to the south remained unanswered. Equally barren in a commercial sense, but more spectacular in their long-term effects, were accidental landfalls to the west and south.

These accidents, however, stemmed from a deliberate shift in sailing routes.[45] In 1610 Hendrik Brouwer represented to the Heeren XVII that there would be advantage in using the nearly constant westerly winds found south of the Cape of Good Hope as a route to the Indies, bypassing the Portuguese-dominated Mozambique Channel, or, should this be avoided by sailing east of Madagascar, the often difficult traverse of the Southeast Trades. Brouwer was allowed to try, and by going east as far as the estimated longitude of the Sunda Straits he made the passage in six months, perhaps half the normal period by the old routes, and his experience was confirmed by other captains. By 1616–17 this course was formally laid down for VOC captains; by making the standard Dutch entry into the Indies well to the east of Malacca, it probably contributed to the locational advantages of Batavia.

The orders were to sail at least 1000 miles in 35–44°S before turning northwards. This stretch of at least 5300 km, perhaps over 7000,[46] would bring ships quite close to Australia, and longitude estimation being what it was, sooner or later some skipper would be bound to sail too far before beginning his northing, and so to bump into the continent. The first to do so was Dirck Hartog in the *Eendracht*, who on 25 October 1616 came upon the extreme western point of Australia, the island still known by his name, where he left an inscribed pewter plate to be found eighty-one years later by his compatriot Willem de Vlamingh.[47] Other landfalls in the next few years included the wreck of the English ship *Tryall* on the Monte

Bello Islands, north of Dirck Hartog's, in 1622; the discovery in the same year of the southwest corner of the continent, named Leeuwins Land for the ship making it (the Cape itself was named by Matthew Flinders). Five years later Pieter Nuyts in the *Gulden Zeepaerd* filled in the coast of the Great Australian Bight for some 1450 km east of Cape Leeuwin, as far as the Nuyts Archipelago off Ceduna, South Australia. Finally, in 1629 the bare reefs of Houtman Abrolhos, off the present Geraldton, saw a grotesque orgy of mutiny and massacre of their fellows by some of the survivors of the wrecked *Batavia*, followed by a bloody retribution when the commander, François Pelsaert, returned from a boat voyage to Batavia, in the nick of time for the loyalist party.[48]

By 1640, then, the Dutch had an outline knowledge, with gaps, of the Australian coast from Northwest Cape southabout almost to Eyre Peninsula, and of segments of the coast of Arnhem Land and the shores of the Gulf of Carpentaria. True, most of the lands seen were jungly, or more often arid, and as such repellent; and in Dutch eyes the people, utterly devoid not only of 'civility' but more importantly of riches, were no less so. But this was merely the selvedge of a vast landmass, which should surely repay more intensive searches.

The first move was projected by Coen, in instructions for two ships which he proposed to send out in 1622: they were to make the new coast in 32–33°S and follow it down to 50°, if it went so far. The first emphasis was on 'obtaining a full and accurate knowledge of the true bearing and conformation of the said land'— Coen had been much impressed by the implications for VOC ships of the *Tryall*'s wreck—but of course the nature, productions, and trading opportunities of the country were to be investigated. Extreme caution was to be used with the natives 'to prevent sudden traitorous surprises, the like of which, sad to say, have but too often been met with'; but care should also be taken to offer 'no molestation from our men', which is a little difficult to square with the recommendation to get hold, 'by adroit management or other means', of some persons, preferably boys or girls, to 'be brought up here and turned to useful purpose in the said quarters'. There is a pleasing contrast in van Diemen's later instructions to Pool and Tasman: one has 'need to be patient and long-suffering, noways quick to fly out'—badly needed advice!—and kidnapping was discouraged.[49]

This project lapsed, and it was not until 1642—after peace feelers from Goa, but a little before news of truce with Portugal had reached Batavia—'that the Governor-General and Councillors took the resolution—and they could do so "without cutting down the means for customary trade and war" '—of sending two ships on protracted southern exploration.[50] These were the *Heemskerck* of 120 tons and the smaller fluyt *Zeehaen*, with a total complement of 110. They were under the command of Abel Janszoon Tasman, who had been in northern waters with Quast and had a good deal of Indies experience; chief pilot was Frans Jacobszoon Visscher, who had survived the Nassau Fleet and possessed, in Beaglehole's words, 'a first-rate planning mind.'[51]

The design was basically Visscher's: it was to sail from Batavia to Dutch-occupied Mauritius and thence south to 52–54°S, then eastwards as far as or even beyond the estimated longitude of the Solomons, which Visscher equated with Le Maire's discoveries from Cocos (Tafahi, northern Tongas) to the Horne Islands. Going northwards with the Southeast Trades, they were to coast New Guinea on the north as far as Gilolo; somewhere hereabouts passages should be found to reach the south coast of the island and the Gulf of Carpentaria. The final task would be to join up the discrete stretches of coast already found between Cape Keerweer and Willems River, which was in Dirck Hartog's Eendrachtsland, just south of Exmouth Gulf. This was certainly an ambitious program, and in fact the last phase was in the upshot left over for Tasman's second voyage; but his instructions in 1642 gave the option of turning north in the longitude of the SS Peter and Francis Islands (Nuyts Archipelago), to see if the coast discovered by the *Gulden Zeepaerd* linked up with Cape Keerweer. There were the usual careful provisions covering discipline, relations with the natives, commercial observations, and taking possession.

The stated objective of the first part of the program was 'the better to be assured of a passage from the Indian into the South Sea, for finding after this conveniently a short passage to Chile', presumably by using the Westerlies which could be presumed to blow in the Pacific as in the Indian Ocean. It should not be overlooked that at this very time the pioneer of the new Westerlies route, Hendrik Brouwer, was engaged, for the West India Company, in a descent on Chile designed to establish a Dutch foothold there; and in reporting Tasman's sailing to the Heeren XVII, van Diemen and his Council indulged in great hopes: the voyage would bring certainty on the hardly doubtful possibility of a shorter and more commodious route to Chile, and

> Should its result prove such a route practicable, which God in his
> mercy grant, the Company will be enabled to do great things with
> the Chileses . . . to snatch rich booty from the Castilian in the West
> Indies, who will never dream of such a thing.[52]

Tasman sailed from Batavia on 14 August 1642, and after a month refitting at Mauritius (twice as long as expected), the ships reached their farthest south, 49°04′, on 6 November. Seas were violent, with hail and snow, and on Visscher's advice it was decided to sail eastwards, first in 44° and then in 40, for another 105° of longitude: on his reckoning, this should bring them east of the longitude of the Solomons and into the Southeast Trades, giving fair sailing for those islands and New Guinea. The new course brought them on 24 November (civil time) to 'the first land in the South Sea', which was named in honour of van Diemen (Fig. 4); a century and a half later Matthew Flinders gave two of the mountains first sighted the names of Mt Heemskerk and Mt Zeehan. They sailed past the much-indented south coast, finding no anchorage until 1 December, after rounding the modern Tasman Peninsula to North Bay. Detailed charts and coastal profiles were drawn, but land exploration was perfunctory. A shore excursion led by Visscher saw no inhabitants, though voices were heard, and smokes and notched trees were seen. On the 3rd Visscher and other officers were sent to take possession, but rising seas enforced an attenuated ceremony: the carpenter, whose feelings are not recorded, was ordered to swim ashore and plant a marked stake and the flag. Westerly winds prevented them from following the coast closely, and on the 5th they bore away eastwards. It would have been far better for the Aboriginal Tasmanians had later visitors been so easily satisfied.

Plate VII. MURDERERS' BAY. The first European sighting of New Zealand and the first depiction of Maoris, in what is now Golden Bay, South Island. From A. Dalrymple, *Voyages and Discoveries in the South Pacific Ocean*, by courtesy of Mr N. Israel, Amsterdam. Photo ANU.

Nine days later they saw 'a large high elevated land' ahead, in about 42°S, and following up the coast they anchored on the evening of 17 December close to Cape Farewell, the northwest point of New Zealand's South Island; it appeared a very fine country and was given the name of Staten Landt, for the States-General and because it might run on to join Le Maire's land of the same name. On the night of the 18th, within Cape Farewell, they saw lights ashore and heard gruff voices and blasts on an instrument sounding 'like the moors' Trumpets', to which the Dutch replied in kind—an eerie nocturnal concert; but they also looked to their weapons. Next day took place the first meeting between Maori and Pakeha, and it was not a friendly reception, one of the *Zeehaen*'s boats being deliberately rammed by a canoe and four of its people clubbed to death. The assailants got away without being hit by the Dutch fire, though later in the day the leader of another group of canoes was shot.[53] It was decided to leave this 'Murderers' Bay' (now Golden Bay) and press on; by the 20th they 'had sailed fully thirty miles [*c.* 220 km] into a bight [not far from Wanganui] not doubting we Shall find from there a passage into the open South Sea, but This turned out to our hearts' pain very much otherwise'. On Christmas Eve it was still thought that there might be a way through, the flood tide coming from southeast; but the weather on Christmas Day was dirty, and on the morrow the ships began to make their way out of the embayment. Charts derived from Visscher do indeed show an opening—hypothetical—corresponding to Cook Strait, but that in Tasman's journal has a dead end.[54]

By 4 January 1643 they had reached Cape Maria van Diemen and the Three Kings Islands, so named because, after failing to water owing to heavy surf, they sailed away on the 6th, Twelfth Night. Not a single landing had been made, hardly the way to explore commercial possibilities; but here, at the northern tip of New Zealand, great seas and swells from northeast, east and southeast indicated that there was 'an even waterway [with] nothing in the way' stretching on to Chile; so one item on the agenda could be marked off.

For thirteen days the ships held northeast, until on the 19th their people saw an island 'like 2 woman's breasts': Ata, the southernmost of the Tonga group. Here at last, on a large island they called Amsterdam 'by reason of abundance of supplies', and at Rotterdam—Tongatapu and Nomuka respectively—they met 'a good peaceful people [though] excessively lascivious wanton and thievish so that argus Eyes are scarcely enough for a person to watch out'. But all was good fellowship, though Tasman, despite his hospitable reception, thought that the people 'had the form of a man but inhuman Morals and customs'. He had to admit, however, that they showed 'men's ingenuity' in their admirable gardens and orchards, 'a pleasure to behold, giving ... a lovely pleasant aroma'; others found the Tongan ladies anything but inhuman in their morals. The Dutch took full advantage of this other Eden, demi-Paradise, spending the rest of the month in revictualling and watering. After passing the high islands of Tofua and Kao, they had their last sight of Tonga—Late—on 3 February, and set their course west for Le Maire's Cocos and Verraders, unaware that these (Tafahi and Niuatobutabu) were already left behind to the north and east.

Keeping a good lookout for these islands, they saw land in the early hours of 6 February, and by daylight 'were very concerned' to find themselves enmeshed in reefs and small islands, with breakers on all sides except to windward. There seemed no way out except 'a small place about 2 Ships length wide' and they ran through 'with great Anxiety' in only four fathoms; a very narrow escape indeed, and one must admire the understatement. The land first seen was probably Qele Levu, the

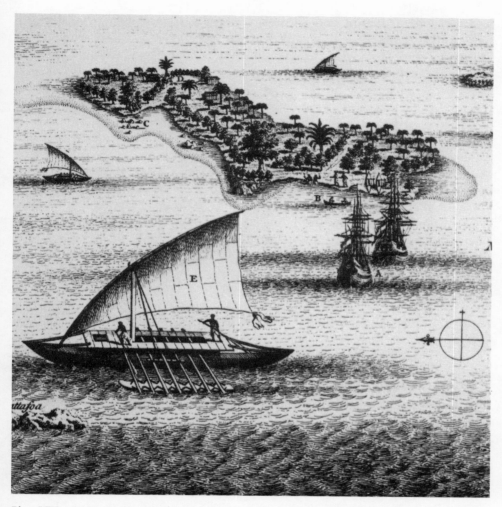

Plate VIII. TASMAN'S TONGA. Nomuka, Tasman's 'Rotterdam'; note the 'Proa under sail bringing Fruits from the other Islands.' From A. Dalrymple, *Voyages in the South Pacific Ocean*, by courtesy of Mr N. Israel, Amsterdam. Photo ANU.

extreme northeastern island of Fiji, and Tasman had driven straight across the Nanuku Reefs, his Heemskerck Shoals. The ships were still in danger, with a score of islands in sight, including Taveuni, the third largest of the group, and with the weather still rough. What could be seen of slab-sided Taveuni must have looked most uninviting; Tasman very sensibly gave up thoughts of anchoring and made north to get out of these cluttered seas, passing the eastern tip of Vanua Levu (seen as three hills or islands) and Cikobia.[55] The first European glimpse of Fiji was mighty discouraging.

Tasman and Visscher were now most unsure of their whereabouts. They did not seem in the right place for the Horne Islands, and either their own or Le Maire's longitudes seemed badly out—Tasman quotes an apposite jingle, 'guessing is missing'. It was too rough to consult with the *Zeehaen*'s officers, but those on the *Heemskerck* were faced with the old problem of Schouten and Le Maire, and came to the old decision: the risks of embayment on the unknown south coast of New Guinea dictated a course north of that island (as was anyhow laid down in their instructions), and they should therefore go north from their latitude of 15°29'S to 4 or 6°S. For ten days, however, they were forced west, going round the north of Vanua Levu (but not sighting it) and as far south as 16°30' before they could make any northing; after doing so and turning westwards again, progress was slow since they unexpectedly met westerly winds, which Tasman correctly attributed to the monsoon prevailing over the Trades.[56]

On 22 March they sighted an extensive atoll (possibly already seen by Mendaña in 1568) which Tasman named Ontong Java after a similar island-ring in the Indies. They got into Le Maire's track, seeing his Marcken and Green Islands, and on 1 April 'cabo santa Maria', a name perhaps dating back to de Retes in 1545; Tasman took it for the New Guinea mainland but it was in fact East Cape in New Ireland. He tried to find a passage southwards for Cape Keerweer, and got well down into the Bismarck Sea, within sight of New Britain; but the way through eluded him, and was left for William Dampier. After passing the string of volcanic islands from Umboi, between New Guinea and New Britain, to Karkar, the ships followed the already known north coast of the big island. By mid-May they were off its western end, where some Moluccans were met with. According to the plan, they should have been in this area by April, before the Southeast Monsoon set in; but in view of their lateness, it was decided on 24 May that the return by Cape Keerweer and Willems River being impossible, they would go on to Ceram and Batavia. The home port was reached on 15 June.

Australia had been circumnavigated, at a distance, in just ten months: a very notable voyage, without the trail of gun-smoke which hangs so heavily over other Dutch visits to the Pacific Islands. The long-term results were important—the discovery of what was to become New Zealand; the elimination from a vast sector of the South Sea of any Terra Australis Incognita; the finding, in 'Amsterdam' and 'Rotterdam', of a new and hospitable oasis for future navigators. But, quite apart from the allowable failure to carry out the last phase of the original plan, the short-term results were disappointing to the Batavia Council; although in each individual case Tasman might put up a reasonable excuse for not exploring the land he had found, the hard fact was that he had brought back no commercial information at all. In view of the actual discoveries, the Council sanctioned the promised bonus of

Figure 4. THE DUTCH IN THE SOUTH PACIFIC 1606–44. Le Maire's discoveries in the Tuamotus omitted (see Fig. 18). Tracks after H. Wallis, The Exploration of the South Sea, 1519 to 1644. Insets: Tasman in Tonga and Fiji, from his chart as given in A. Dalrymple, *Voyages and Discoveries in the South Pacific Ocean* (London 1770).

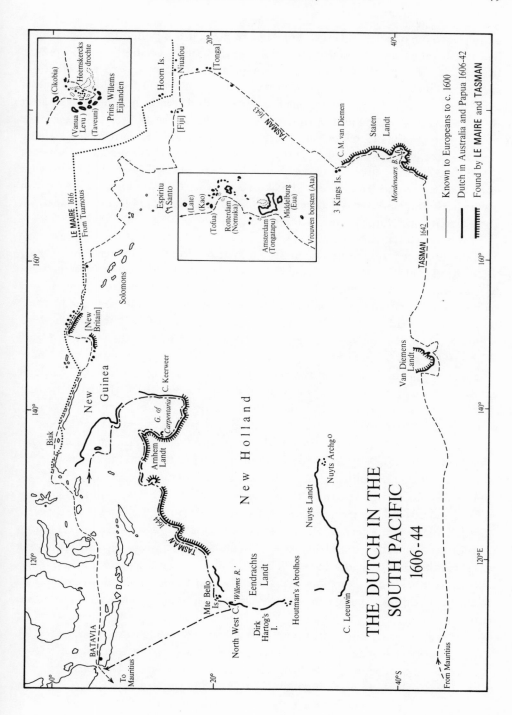

THE DUTCH IN THE
SOUTH PACIFIC
1606 - 44

Known to Europeans to c. 1600
Dutch in Australia and Papua 1606-42
Found by LE MAIRE and TASMAN

extra pay to the officers and crew, but Tasman himself was rather under a cloud. He had not been zealous enough in ascertaining the nature of the lands and people found, and had left all such questions for some more curious and conscientious successor. The Council still had hope of the Chilean passage, and proposed to follow it up with an armed expedition, but the truce of 1641 with the Portuguese, after their successful revolt against Spanish rule, was in the Indies broken almost at once by a dispute over Galle in Ceylon, where in May 1643 the Dutch received a severe check. A strong force under François Caron had to be sent thither, and this meant that little could be spared for wider forays. In the meantime, however, 'to prevent idleness' Tasman and Visscher could make a more modest expedition to the Gulf of Carpentaria and find out whether New Guinea, the Southland found by Janszoon and Carstenz, and Van Diemen's Land were connected.[57]

This voyage (January-August 1644), important in the history of Australian exploration, need not long detain us. Coastal exploration Tasman thoroughly understood, and he and Visscher did a competent job of survey from Torres Strait to south of Exmouth Gulf, but once more failed to find any passage between New Guinea and the landmass to the south, and indeed do not seem to have made much of an effort to do so. They were to some extent covered by their instructions, which expressed doubt as to the existence of a strait. More to the point, as Helen Wallis points out, is the fact that the difficulties of the passage are more apparent to a navigator approaching from the west, and were sufficient reasonably to deter anyone who had not a compelling reason to force a way through; from the east, Torres had no option but to do so, and Cook little, being short of provisions; moreover, the latter had at least a shrewd suspicion that a passage did exist, from de Brosses's or rather Vaugondy's maps in de Brosses's *Histoire des Navigations aux Terres Australes* (1756) and Dalrymple. For Tasman, the supposition was the other way.[58]

Tasman was undoubtedly an able navigator—many of his longitudes are remarkably close to the real ones, though as others are not that was perhaps a matter of luck, and he has been over-praised on this score.[59] Unlike the Nodals, he gives no impression of joy in a job well done. Certainly it took nerve, a good eye, and instant decision to dash across the Heemskerck Shoals, though admittedly the alternative was mere helpless surrender to the elements. Nevertheless, there are just too many failings to investigate likely openings for Tasman to be given full marks as an explorer, as distinct from a seaman. And this time van Diemen's report was damning:

> they secured nothing profitable, but only poor naked beach-runners,
> without rice or any noteworthy fruits, very poor, and in many places
> evil natured people . . . [he] who shall investigate what the lands give,
> must walk therein and through, for which these envoys say they had
> not enough power, in which there may be something. . . .[60]

Despite a couple of scrapes, Tasman remained employed, and well employed, in VOC service; but in more routine tasks.

Van Diemen remained anxious to follow through the reconnaissance of the Southland; in so vast an area, there must be something worth the finding. He did not live to see the response of the Heeren XVII:

> [We] see that Your Worships have again taken up the exploration of the coast of Nova Guinea . . . We do not expect great things from the continuation of such explorations, which more and more burden the Company's resources . . . These plans of Your Worships somewhat aim beyond our mark. The gold- and silver-mines that will best serve the Company's turn have already been found, which we deem our trade over the whole of India. . . .[61]

As for any Chilean proposals, they too lapsed. Although in October 1643, after Tasman's return, van Diemen was envisaging an expedition direct to Chile, by December doubts had set in. There was also the question of whether it might not infringe the West India Company's monopoly rights in America. In fact, on the day that Tasman reached his farthest south (6 November 1642), Hendrik Brouwer sailed from Texel to promote those rights in Chile.

The Chilean venture of Hendrik Brouwer

The West India Company, founded in 1621 at the end of the Twelve Years' Truce, was 'from the first intended as striking against the roots of Iberian power in the New World'.[62] Its first coup was the taking of Bahia in 1624, and although this was lost in the next year, by the mid-thirties the Dutch were solidly lodged in north-eastern Brazil, the first 'New Holland', where the genial rule of Prince Johan Maurits van Nassau-Siegen fostered a remarkable cultural centre, belatedly Renaissance, around his viceregal court at Pernambuco (now Recife) near the old Portuguese base Olinda. Truce with Portugal after the 1640 Revolution gave fallacious hopes of stability in this new base; it was time to seek out new fields of enterprise. Hendrik Brouwer, van Diemen's predecessor as Governor-General at Batavia, was now a Director of the WIC, and was put in command of an expedition to Chile.[63] Sailing with five ships from Texel in November 1642 and from Pernambuco on 15 January 1643, he was off Le Maire's Staten Landt early in March. In clear weather, it was seen to be an island, and after four days trying to pass the Strait against headwinds, Brouwer sailed round it to the east and south and found a clear passage to the South Sea. This dissolved Tasman's hypothetical continuity with his own Staten Landt, which soon received its present name of New Zealand.[64]

By the end of April, less one separated ship, they were at Chiloé and trying to make friends with the Indians, who held off despite white flags and the leaving of presents for them. A couple of trifling Spanish forts were taken and burnt, and the fleet moved on to Castro, the only place on the island of the slightest note. The town had been abandoned and fired by the inhabitants, and nothing was gained but some useful news about Indian discontents and Spanish forces in southern Chile, and the less gratifying information that gold mining had petered out since the great

Araucanian rising of 1599. However, despite their wanton devastations around Castro, the Dutch now made amicable contact with the Indians through the belated release of 'Chilese' prisoners, and plans were made for joint action against Valdivia. This was deferred owing to bad weather and Brouwer's death on 8 August, but on the 21st they sailed from 'Brouwer's Haven' at the northern tip of Chiloé.[65] The ships carried 470 Araucanians, and some Indians had been sent ahead by land to spread liberation propaganda.

Valdivia, or what had been Valdivia, was reached on 27 August; there had been 450 houses, there were still many walls, but since 1599 all had been smothered by bush. The Hollanders were well received by the local Indians, whose numbers were swelled by refugees from Spanish counter-measures, several *caciques* (chiefs) having been hanged on suspicion. Brouwer's successor, Elias Harckmans, made a speech (presumably in Spanish) to some 1200 Araucanians: after an eighty years' struggle for liberty, the Hollanders now had a Brazilian base within two months of Chile, and had come with arms to assist the valiant Chileans against the common enemy. A formal, though verbal, defensive and offensive alliance was made, and the Dutch received permission to build a fort. So far all was well; but now, 'in prudent words', they imprudently let slip a hitherto concealed major motive: the arms should be exchanged for the gold of which they had heard.[66] The caciques were shocked; they had not used the accursed metal for years, but the memory of the Spanish exactions was so bitter that 'even to hear the word *gold* pronounced was grievous to them'. Harckmans replied 'with affability' that there was no question of tribute, only of fair exchange, but the chiefs remained silent. Hoping that the Indians' desire for arms and iron would win out in time, the Dutch 'abstained from saying more on this matter, so as not to appear greedy . . . seeing that the people were intelligent and ought to be dealt with by peaceable means'.[67]

Unaware of the damage they had done themselves, the Dutch carried on with their plans: there were rumours of risings in Peru, and the Portuguese in La Plata had 'showed their teeth to the Spaniards. With all this, a conflagration could arise among the Indians, such that it might extend itself through all Chile and even to the hill of Potosí'. There were under 1500 Spanish soldiers in Chile; rumours of 2000 assembling were discounted, though it was thought that ten ships and 800 men from Brazil might be needed to make the conquest secure. However, the first flush of Araucanian enthusiasm was waning. The caciques professed themselves unable to meet the Dutch demand for live meat, since for fear of losing any surplus to Spanish raids they raised only enough for their own needs; they should have had one or two years' notice. Such supplies as did come in were scanty and irregular, and there were minor irritations on both sides. Meanwhile, the fort had been started, and as Brouwer had desired, his embalmed body was buried with some ceremony at Valdivia; only to be dug up in 1645 and burned as that of a heretic. One ship had been sent to Brazil in September, to request reinforcements; but in view of the shortage of provisions and the unwillingness of the Chileans to work for gold, it was decided to leave, to the professed regret of the Araucanians. The fleet sailed from Valdivia towards the end of October—for the first known west to east passage around the Horn—and on 28 December 1643 one of the ships reached Pernambuco, to find reinforcements ready to sail.... As James Burney remarked, the expedition had been as fruitless for the Hollanders, if not quite so discreditable, as that of the Nassau Fleet against Peru.

The rumours of a Spanish counter-attack had some basis in fact, but were premature. The Viceroy Marqués de Mancera perpended a fleet to sail in November 1643—it could be at Valdivia by January, and the Dutch could not get help from Pernambuco before March. But as usual, nothing was ready; the two galleons from Panama would need a lengthy refit, there were not enough guns to arm auxiliaries or even another two galleons at Guayaquil—all cannon had gone to the new forts at Callao, and neither Guayaquil nor Callao could be left defenceless. Perhaps a couple of the big Manila Galleons could be borrowed from New Spain, as well as arms, munitions, sailors and soldiers—these last being exceedingly difficult to recruit in Peru for 'a theatre of action so much in discredit as Chile'.[68] Mancera was relieved of his predicament by news from the south; it seemed likely that the Dutch could receive no succours from Brazil until 1645, so there was no hurry, and then later news of their withdrawal gave him the green light, and time to prepare. The armada—twelve ships, 118 heavy guns, 1800 men—left Callao on 31 December 1644. There was a typical Spanish hitch—the charts of the long narrow drowned valley leading to Valdivia were so manifestly faulty that it would be unwise for the squadron to rely on them. However, the fleet reached Valdivia on 4 February 1645, and left 700 men with thirty-five guns to refound the city and begin the fortifications which, later much elaborated, were not to see action until near the end of Spanish rule, in 1820, when a domestic enemy, the Chileans under Cochrane, took them in an action of astonishing dash.

Epilogue to the Indies wars

Meanwhile, the Philippines had some respite from direct attacks after the repulse of the Hollanders at the third battle of Playa Honda (1624); the Spanish improved the occasion by engaging in a singularly inept and disastrous expedition to Siam in 1624–6.[69] But with the Dutch installing themselves in Formosa, 'we live in anxieties', and—perhaps reflecting Olivares's project for the 'Union of Arms'—in 1632 Governor Tavora was arguing that since 'the forces of Francia, Olanda, Ynglaterra, and Dinamarca [Denmark] are united in these districts', so should be those of Portugal and Castile: Malacca and Macao should be joined to the government of Manila, and four galleons with some galleys in the Straits of Malacca could keep the Dutch hemmed in. Eleven years later men could still dream that 'if vigorous measures were taken to send four thousand men to Filipinas', the immense flow of wealth which supported the rebels in Flanders could easily be stopped at its source: better to try damming a river near its head than near the sea.[70] But still 'we live in anxieties', and not least those caused by the Sangleys, who rose again in 1639 and were again defeated with great slaughter,[71] and by the Muslims of the south.

Definite war with the Moros began in 1578 with an attack on Jolo, the chief town of Sulu; and it is still in effect going on four centuries later. From 1599 onwards there were many Moro raids on the islands south of Luzon; in 1616 they even penetrated Manila Bay and attacked the shipyards at Cavite. Four counter-attacks reached Jolo itself, but all failed to take it; a major effort by 350 Spaniards and 2000 Filipinos in 1628–9 was a miserable fiasco—the Moros were well versed in the arts of both bush warfare and bush fortification, and they had guns largely taken from the Spaniards.[72] A climax came in 1636, when Tagal, brother of a Mindanao sultan Kudarat (Corralat to the Spaniards), spent nearly eight months in and around Mindoro, reaping a rich booty, especially from the churches. On his return, however, he was caught and killed by a force from the fort at Zamboanga, strategically emplaced on the southwestern tip of Mindanao in the previous year. The Governor, Hurtado de Corcuera, now resolved to make an end to these affairs, despite the opposition of all his council except his nephew.

His first move was against Kudarat's stronghold in southwestern Mindanao. This was taken by a relatively small Spanish force in March 1637, after very tough bush fighting; Kudarat escaped into the jungle. The Zamboanga base was proving its worth; after various minor raids and reductions, making a complete circuit of the island, and a puppet-treaty with a local rajah nominally converted to the Faith, Corcuera returned to Manila in triumph from a brilliant campaign of less than four months. There remained Sulu itself, which demanded a bigger effort by 600 Spaniards and 1000 Indios; the chief town, Jolo, was reduced only by a formal siege which lasted from 4 January to 17 April 1638.[73] The Sultan Bungsu escaped, but an agreement was made with his captured wife; Corcuera left a garrison and received another triumphal reception in Manila; the welcome was not unanimous, since there were those who thought that he was neglecting the northern danger from Formosa. Nor was his victory decisive either in Mindanao or in Sulu; sporadic but often bitter fighting continued until in 1646 Jolo was evacuated in view of renewed Dutch threats to Manila; the withdrawal was accompanied by an offensive and defensive alliance between Spaniards and Moros which lasted, unremarkably, until 1647 .... Zamboanga remained as a southern bastion until in 1662 it also was abandoned when Coxinga's seizure of Formosa from the Dutch portended a new and formidable threat; this was also responsible for the final withdrawal from Tidore, where the Spaniards had retained a foothold throughout the Dutch wars.[74]

The Hollanders of course were neither ignorant of these affairs nor disinterested; they gave material aid to the Sulus and in 1645 bombarded Jolo, but were driven off. The fall of Malacca and the Portuguese truce, reluctant and fragile as it was, together with the taking of the Spanish fort on Formosa, left them free to renew direct attacks on the Philippines. When Governor Diego Fajardo arrived in June 1644, things were in a bad way; both Fajardo and the new Archbishop (who died of the effort) had to land in Cagayan and travel over the jungly hills to Manila, since the Dutch were active around the Embocadero.[75] As usual, ships were not available—they had been sent to the Moluccas—and a royal order to the Viceroy of New Spain to send men and money was too late to be of effect; such aid was normally scanty and grudging. In February 1646 news was received of a Dutch fleet of eighteen sail, against which Fajardo could initially muster only two galleons, together with another expected from Acapulco. Fortunately, the Hollanders split their forces and generally mismanaged the campaign; in a series of running fights (March to July) between the Embocadero and Cavite, the defenders inflicted severe losses with little to themselves. This was 'La Naval de Manila', celebrated by an annual festival into our own days.[76]

The last assault came in June 1647, when eleven ships under Martin Gertzen bombarded Cavite and made landings around the Bay, in one of which the Pampangan auxiliaries put up a much better showing than the Spaniards themselves. All attacks were repulsed and Gertzen himself killed: the final action in the long struggle, since the Eighty Years' War was soon to be ended by Spanish recognition, at long last, of Netherlands independence by the Treaty of Munster (1648). Oft-beleaguered Manila had saved herself, and largely by her own resources.

So far, we have been dealing with theatres of action where the Europeans could carry things with a high hand. At least after Sultan Agung's failure to take Batavia in 1629, there was no real threat, indigenous or European, to Dutch dominance in the islands eastwards from Java to the Moluccas, though it is also true that for the time being they had about reached the limits of their expansive power:

> [All] the offices of the Indies [are] taxed with one or the other
> difficulty: Amboyna with a dangerous war . . . Solor and Malacca
> with burdens and no profit . . . Taiwan seems through divers
> accidents to be oppressed by God's hand; Japan through lack of capital
> cannot accumulate any capital; and Batavia is smothering in its own
> expenses and the burdens of all the offices, besides the losses at
> sea. . . .[77]

Mataram was still independent; Atjeh, Bantam, Johore, and Makassar not only independent but commercially active; but all were thorns in Batavian flesh rather than real menaces. Tagal and Kudarat had been rather more than thorns, but by themselves could hardly have expelled Spanish power in the Philippines. But we must now turn to the northern sector, where Europeans if they were wise walked humbly, and where their moves towards trade and influence could be not only checked and manipulated but ruined by the powerful lords of the land: not only in the empires of China and Japan, but even in the apparently solid Dutch holding of Formosa.

Chapter 3

THE NORTHERN TANGLE: JAPAN AND TAIWAN

> ... our ministers have no other instructions to take [to
> Japan] except to look to the wishes of that brave, superb,
> precise nation in order to please it in everything ...
> consequently the Company's ministers frequenting the
> scrupulous state each year must above all go armed in
> modesty, humility, courtesy, and amity, being always the
> lesser ...

After Sekigahara: Ieyasu consolidates

Hideyoshi died on 18 September 1598, surviving Philip II by six days. His armies
were still in Korea, and still formidable, but now reduced to a bridgehead; had he
lived, he might well have sought to compensate this frustration by an easier
triumph over the Spaniards in the Philippines. His heir Hideyori was four years old,
and Hideyoshi's careful arrangements for the minority were strictly dependent on
the loyalty and team spirit of a number of ambitious and violent *daimyo* or feudal
magnates, a weak basis indeed. Armed factionalism was inevitable, but was crushed
for the time being in October 1600 at the great battle of Sekigahara, by Matsudaira
Motoyasu, better known as Tokugawa Ieyasu, who thereby became the master of
Japan's destiny. But the man who could wait for the bird to sing was in no hurry to
put his power at risk by too abrupt and extravagant an exercise of it.[1]

Nevertheless, he early took a decisive step by reviving the title of Shogun, which
had lapsed under Nobunaga and Hideyoshi since neither was of sufficiently high
birth to claim it. The Shogunal government, often called the *Bakufu*, was in essence
a military régime, and the Shogun, roughly a generalissimo for the defence of the
realm, was hereditary in the Tokugawa family. One is inclined to forget that all
through Japan's times of troubles there was an Emperor in the dim background, to
whom the Shogun was nominally responsible; from him Ieyasu in 1603 secured his
own appointment to the office, which in Sansom's words gave 'a so-to-speak
constitutional form to his control over the whole country', and wide military
powers. For the time, however, he prudently held these powers in reserve, and
devoted himself to a massive redistribution of fiefs—after Sekigahara there were
many daimyo to be rewarded, and more to be deprived—and to building up his
own and his family's domains, which after 1600 accounted for a quarter or even a
third of the assessed revenue of the country.[2]

'Points and Articles in the Form of General Instructions' made by the Heeren
XVII, 26 April 1650; quoted from J. C. van Leur, *Indonesian Trade and Society*
(The Hague 1955), 242. An exquisitely nice selection of adjectives!

The daimyo were divided into the Fudai or 'hereditary vassals'—connections of the Tokugawa family and the earlier adherents to Ieyasu's side—and the 'outer lords' or Tozama, opponents or neutrals who were late in submitting; these were most numerous in the north and west. Many Tozama castles were destroyed, and their lords financially weakened by forced contributions to public works and the building of Bakufu-controlled strongholds; compulsory attendance at the Shogunal Court for fixed and lengthy periods was also a financial drain on the daimyo and a means of surveillance. Ieyasu also took under direct Bakufu control five key towns, Edo (Yedo, Tokyo), Kyoto, Osaka, Sakai, and Nagasaki; he fixed his headquarters at Edo. As for the Emperor, in whose name all government was supposed to be carried on, he 'is to devote himself to learning. He must follow the teaching of the classics and uphold the tradition of poetry'.[3]

All this took time, and indeed the full development of Tokugawa institutions had to wait for Ieyasu's grandson Iemitsu (1623–51) or even later. Ieyasu himself nominally handed over the Shogunate to his son Hidetada in 1605, but he retained effective political control—the move was probably an insurance for the smooth succession of the new dynasty. There were still of course plenty of malcontents, especially the thousands of *ronin*, the now masterless retainers of dispossessed or diminished daimyo, whose occupations of private war and pillage were now gone: as Hideyori grew to manhood, they rallied to his cause. By a combination of treachery and hard fighting, Ieyasu broke their resistance: Hideyori's stronghold, Osaka Castle, was stormed in June 1615; he killed himself, and his family was savagely annihilated. A year later, almost to the day, Ieyasu himself died.

Ieyasu's expansionist phase

The 'Southern Barbarians' found little immediate change in this consolidation of power; certainly no hint of the seclusion that was to come. The daimyo of Kyushu could no longer play their own hands as freely as in the old days when a local baron could comfortably install the Portuguese at Nagasaki, making it virtually a little Jesuit city-state; but Ieyasu was anxious not only to tolerate but even to foster foreign commerce, though not on the old terms in which trade brought an alien Faith and a potential fifth column.

The first three decades of Tokugawa rule were indeed the palmy days of Japanese overseas shipping, licensed under the 'Red Seal' instituted by Hideyoshi in 1592. Originally the Red Seal ships were legally obliged to use Portuguese pilots and charts; later Dutchmen were brought in, but increasingly Japanese themselves were able to take over. The shippers to whom licences were granted were mostly merchants, especially from Hakata, but they included daimyo and Bakufu officials, Europeans and Chinese. Ieyasu himself invested in cargoes on the Great Ship from Macao and issued it with a Red Seal; and the Dutch had to allow ships under the Seal through the Manila blockade.[4] There seems to have been an average of about ten two-way voyages a year between 1604 and 1635, in sizable ships; the great majority were to Indo-China, Siam, and Manila. Exports were largely luxury craft goods, with some silver and copper, but the Philippines took some bulkier foodstuffs; by far the most important return cargo was raw or worked silk. The Japanese now offered substantial competition to European traders: a Portuguese padre reported that in 1612 the Great Ship carried only 1300 quintals of silk to Nagasaki, against 5000 quintals in Red Seal and Chinese ships.

Before Ieyasu was succeeded *de facto* as well as *de jure* by the less large-minded and less dynamic Hidetada, there was even a mild expansionism towards the south, perhaps by way of giving the Tozama daimyo of the far west some external outlet for their energies, in the manner of European Marcher Lords; this, and the desirability of outposts towards Luzon, were factors in the takeover of the Ryukyus. The alleged Japanese discovery of the Bonins in 1593 is now regarded as an eighteenth-century fabrication, but there were other avenues to the south.[5] During the 1590s, when relations between Hideyoshi and the Spaniards in Manila were extremely strained, the strategic importance of Taiwan became obvious to both parties: the Spaniards considered an expedition to the island to forestall a feared occupation by Hideyoshi as a stepping-stone to Luzon. These alarms died down, and the first decade of the new century saw a 'normalisation' of Filipino-Japanese relations. In 1609 Arima Harunobu, one of the Christian daimyo in Kyushu and connected with the Red Seal trade, received detailed orders for a reconnaissance of Taiwan, with political as well as commercial motives. The mission had no success beyond bringing back a few aboriginal captives.[6]

More important was the definitive conquest of the Ryukyus (the Lequeos of contemporary Europeans) by the Shimazu brothers, lords of Satsuma in the extreme south of Kyushu. The little kingdom, a chain of islands lying between Kyushu and Taiwan, had prospered as an entrepôt, especially when the Ming discouraged or prohibited Chinese overseas trading and after the fall of Malacca to the Portuguese; although now declining before the competition of Macao, it was still an important link between Japan and China. For a century or more it had had a rather tenuous relationship of vassalage to Satsuma; but the Shimazu had not been able to give the kingdom total protection against Hideyoshi's demands for men and supplies for his Korean war. The Ryukyuans naturally turned towards China—for instance, by giving Peking advance information of Hideyoshi's plans—while the Chinese merchant colony in the main port, Naha on Okinawa, was strong and influential. The Ryukyuan King Sho Nei was evasive in face of Satsuma pressure for a more loyal attitude, and in 1609 a small but carefully prepared expedition sailed from Kagoshima to bring him to heel. Within three months it was home again, with Sho Nei himself a prisoner.[7]

The islands then remained in a most anomalous position—anomalous at least to tidy modern European minds. Their king was vassal to Satsuma and so mediately to the Shogun, but the immemorial tribute embassies were sent to the Celestial Emperor in Peking, whether he was Ming or Manchu: these were essential if the trade to China was to continue. Basically, political and economic control rested with Satsuma, which maintained the most careful surveillance over this continuing commerce. The Ryukyus were exempt from the Shogunal edicts banning overseas ventures by Japanese, but only Ryukyuans were allowed to sail to China, and the most elaborate precautions were taken to maintain, for Chinese official eyes, the fiction of independence—even to coaching Ryukyuan merchants and seamen with model answers to parry awkward questions. To this end Satsuma positively encouraged tributary missions to China, and the island kings continued to receive investiture from Peking. The Chinese missions to Okinawa which carried out the ceremony were themselves occasions for trade—in 1719, one man listed on the mission staff as a sedan-chair bearer had in his baggage 45,000 pieces of benzoin and eighty pairs of eye-glasses![8] The Chinese Court had no real interest in these remote islands and was perfectly happy so long as the forms of overlordship were preserved; and Satsuma again was perfectly happy to have in its hands a lucrative quasi-monopoly of Japan's overseas trade, after 1639–41 shared only with the better-known trade outlet at Nagasaki. As for the Ryukyuans, they were like the cormorants 'made to catch fish which they are not permitted to swallow', and saved from economic disaster only by the introduction of the sweet potato and sugar-cane.[9]

The Franciscan missionaries who had begun to penetrate Japan in the 1590s were deterred neither by the papal bull of 1585 reserving the field to the Jesuits (it was revoked early in the next century) nor by the martyrdom of six friars and twenty converts at Nagasaki in 1597. Fray Jerónimo de Jesus (whose lay name was de Castro) OFM, who had escaped and returned in secret, was brought before Ieyasu in December 1598, no doubt expecting the stake or the cross; instead there was friendly discourse of the prospects for Spanish trade, especially to Ieyasu's home ground in Kanto—clearly he wanted a counterweight both to the Portuguese and to the concentration on Kyushu—and even of direct sailings from Japan to New Spain. For that, he would need European-style ships, and hence proposed that Spanish shipwrights should be sent to him. He sent an envoy to the new Governor at Manila, Pedro de Acuña; as might be expected, the general overture was welcome, the bland request for shipwrights another matter altogether: to accede to it would be 'giving [the Japanese] the very weapons they needed to destroy the Philippines.' Acuña naturally hedged, agreeing to send ships to Kanto but saying that anything more was beyond his powers and must be referred to Spain and to New Spain; a reply would take three years, so Ieyasu must be more patient. . . . Fray Jerónimo was told to be more careful in what he said and 'to string him along'; not inconveniently, the returning Japanese envoy was wrecked and lost on Taiwan.[10]

This promising start was jeopardised by Fray Jerónimo's death and by the misadventure of the *Espíritu Santo*, a Manila Galleon forced by tempest into a Shikoku port. The initial reception was friendly, but warned by an Augustinian padre of the plundering propensities of the locals, and alarmed by their apparently aggressive stance, her captain bethought him of the fate of the *San Felipe*, plundered only six years earlier and not far away. He forced his way out, with much firing but few casualties.[11] Ieyasu's reaction to this violent incident was extremely conciliatory; he not only ordered restitution for lost merchandise, but sent eight Red Seals to Manila for future use, while Spanish trade was exempted from the *ito wappu* or bulk-buying of imports at a fixed price (like the Filipino *pancada*) which applied to the Portuguese. Even the troublesome question of the Japanese living at Manila, whose numbers and mettlesome temper made them in Spanish eyes a menace to security, was amicably settled in 1608. Relations seemed set fair: Ieyasu was bestowing favour on the rival missions 'in accordance with their proved efficiency as decoys for foreign merchantmen'[12] and playing off Manila against Macao, to the immediate advantage of the former. He now received two new pieces for his board.

The Dutch and English at Hirado

Will Adams reached Japan in the *Liefde* in April 1600, and a month later was interviewed by Ieyasu, who chose to ignore dire Jesuit warnings based on the heavy armament of the ship. Adams's answers to his questions were much to Ieyasu's taste: yes, the English did make wars, but only with Spaniards and Portingalls, and he and the Dutch desired only such trade as those nations possessed. Adams had been apprenticed to a Thames shipbuilder, and when Ieyasu learnt this he pressed him to build a small ship. Modestly and no doubt prudently, Adams discounted his skills, but Ieyasu insisted, and the 80-ton craft proved satisfactory. No doubt it was also a relief to Ieyasu to have discussions not laced with theology. He retained Adams in his service, eventually giving him an estate near Uraga at the entrance to Tokyo Bay; but in 1605 the captain of the *Liefde*, Jacob Quaeckernaeck, was allowed to leave with a virtual invitation to the Dutch to open trade with Japan.

It was not until 1609 that they were able to take up the offer; in July of that year Jacob Specx arrived at Hirado from Patani. Hirado had suffered economically from the rise of Nagasaki, and its daimyo Matsura Hoin,[13] no friend of the Portuguese, had facilitated Quaeckernaeck's voyage to Patani on a Red Seal ship; Hirado thus became the seat of the Dutch factory. The Dutch promised to send at least one ship a year, but were unable to do so in 1610, ships meant for Japan being lost in Wittert's disastrous defeat at Playa Honda. In 1611, however, Specx, who had come to Patani to expedite matters, returned; the cargo he brought could not match Iberian offerings, but he adroitly turned the situation by picking out the best things for an embassy of thanks to Ieyasu. Largely by Adams's help, he secured a very favourable patent, which included some freedom from the interference of local officials with actual trading.[14] By 1612, when Adams had definitely replaced the Jesuit João Rodríguez as Ieyasu's most trusted interpreter, the Dutch were solidly lodged in the trade.

As early as 1580 the Muscovy Company had sent out Arthur Pet and Charles Jackman, in two tiny craft with a total complement of eighteen souls, to seek out the Northeast Passage, and John Dee's 'briefe advises' to them airily suggested that after visiting northern China 'You may have opportunitie to saile over to Japan Island, where you shall finde Christian men', including perhaps some English Jesuits. They got a little beyond Vaigach Island, south of Novaya Zembla and a far cry from Japan; apart from Adams the first English contact with Japanese was in 1605, when the great navigator John Davis was killed in a savage fight with a junk, Wako or Red Seal, off Malaya.[15] News of Adams's presence in Japan had reached England via the Dutch, and the EIC's instructions to John Saris for the first venture to Japan relied confidently on his help.[16] Saris had gone out to the Indies with Henry Middleton's voyage of 1604, and until his return home in 1609 was based in Bantam, where he was assiduous in compiling trade intelligence, including the interesting item that high on the list of priorities for Japan were 'Pictures paynted, som lasciuous, others of Stories of Warres by Sea and Land, the larger the better'. He seems to have been an unpleasant person, tactless and even arrogant, and his penchant for pornography got him into trouble on his return home;[17] but his experience and interests must have seemed to fit him for the task of opening this new field. After the event, this appears an error.

Japan was not the only objective of this, the EIC's Eighth Voyage; Saris was directed to make first for Surat, and to go farther only if full ladings could not be obtained there. He left England in April 1611 and in the Arabian Sea had highly acrimonious wrangles with Middleton, commanding the Sixth Voyage—a direct result of the system of separately-accounted voyages already given up by the VOC. It was not until 15 January 1613 that Saris left Bantam in the *Clove*, and after some unpleasant passages with the Hollanders in the Moluccas, he reached Hirado (Firando in the English accounts) on 11 June. Matsura gave him a warm welcome, and immediately sent off a messenger to find Adams, who however was neither at Edo nor on his own estate but with Ieyasu at Shizuoka on Ise Bay, so that seven weeks elapsed before he reached Hirado on 29 July.

As so often with a long-awaited meeting, the effect was disillusioning: Adams by this time was no longer a simple English seaman but a 'naturalised Japanner' and declined the proffered hospitality of his countrymen, going off to his Japanese quarters by himself, which naturally gave offence. His position as an honest broker and friend at court to all men was in fact anomalous: he had retained close relations with the Hollanders, was helpful to the Iberians in secular matters, and was greatly trusted by Ieyasu: it would not have been easy to keep his footing amidst these conflicting interests. To the English, of course, he seemed intolerably stand-offish; five days after his arrival Saris induced him to spend the night at the English house to talk business, 'but many times the Spannyard salors sent for him, with whome his better part was, but went not to them.'[18]

Nothing, however, could be done without his good offices, and on 7 August Saris and Adams set off through the Inland Sea, and a month later met Ieyasu. The interview, and one with Hidetada, went off well, the English receiving a liberal patent to trade. The Japanese version, but not the English one sent to the EIC by Saris, contained a strong hint that Ieyasu wished the English trade to be settled in

Kanto, ground for a factory being specifically offered at Edo. Adams was strongly in favour of this, and got Saris to view the harbour at Uraga, which (unlike Hirado's) was found excellent. It would also of course be much more convenient for Adams himself if the English were based near his estate. However, on his return to Hirado Saris decided to fix the factory there; suspicion of Adams, his liking for Matsura (a fellow *bon viveur*), and perhaps also 'the lure of the China Trade', for which Hirado was more handy (Fig. 5), were probably his main reasons. Commercially, the decisions to set up shop next door to the Hollanders, the EIC's most serious rivals, seems absurd.[19]

Adams had gained Ieyasu's permission to leave Japan, but changed his mind: the shipwright's apprentice now had 'a living, like unto a Lordship in England' (and a Japanese lady with it) and was a prominent man of affairs, by now habituated to a court more polished and subtle than King Jamie's; his own country could have little in comparison to offer, as was sufficiently shown by Saris's attitude to him, a marked contrast to the courtly respect to which he was now accustomed. After much haggling, he accepted a two years' contract with the EIC; in Saris's view, he was only fit to be a junk-master and an interpreter, but it was necessary to secure his services initially, since the Flemings and Spaniards were making false offers to retain him and without his bilingualism 'we [were] wholly destitute of language'. But Richard Cocks, to be left at Hirado as chief factor, was warned that on no account was Adams to be entrusted with any Company moneys. It was not long, however, before Cocks revised this unflattering opinion.[20]

The history of the factory was of a piece with this inauspicious start. Cocks was an honest man, but no driving business genius; even had he been such, it is not likely that he could have done much with the inadequate working capital of £7000. Adams and others had warned that the limited market for woollens was already saturated, and advised that China and Siam wares should be sought, especially from Patani; yet in his first letter to the Company, Cocks ingenuously remarked that

> could we gett any greate quantety of broad cloth to vent, it wold
> prove a greate matter, although at low rates; but as yet they are soe
> adicted to silks, that they do not enter into consideration of the
> benefitt of wearing cloth. But tyme may altar theyr mindes. . . .[21]

The Company persisted in sending woollens and the Japanese in wearing silk. Between 1617 and 1619, the only English ships to enter Hirado came as Dutch prizes; with the Treaty of Alliance, when Hirado was used as a base for the Manila blockade, the English did have some share in silks taken from Portuguese or Chinese shipping. After Ieyasu's death, privileges were reduced; English agents had to be withdrawn from Edo and Osaka, though they were still allowed at Nagasaki, where at various times in its short life the agency was headed not only by two Englishmen but also by an Italian, a Spaniard, a Dutchman, and 'the China Captain Whaw'—scarcely the way to run a profitable business.[22]

The factory might have been saved if adequately supplied as part of a 'single commercial unit with interdependent branches of trade', which was how the

Dutch regarded their traffic in Asia; but at this stage the EIC's criterion was by and large simply success in selling English manufactures. Attempts at building up a local trade were only sporadic; some Cambay cloths, for example, were sold as novelties, but Cocks was soon telling his agent not to stick to the recommended price but to 'sell away . . . as yoe can'.[23] The factory lasted only ten years, when it was shut down as part of the general contraction of 1623, with the Dutch left in charge of its interests in case it should be possible to start again. The total loss on the venture had not been great; but then little had been ventured. Its chief monuments were Cocks's diary, an inconsequential but fascinating picture of life as it was most oddly lived at Hirado, and his introduction from the Ryukyus of potatoes, 'a thing not planted yet in Japan.'[24]

Japan and Nueva España

The eight years (1609–16) between the Dutch establishment at Hirado and the death of Ieyasu were a period of intricate manoeuvre and intrigue, in which the concerns of various Japanese groups were involved with those of three or four foreign powers. They were marked by the first really serious moves, since the 1597 martyrdoms, in the anti-Christian backlash, which was to end in the policy of seclusion; although as long as Ieyasu was alive, these would not be taken very far. But they were also marked by the use of Japan as a base for Vizcaíno's explorations and by the most ambitious effort of pre-Meiji Japan towards forming commercial links with far distant lands, nothing less than a formal mission to New Spain and beyond. The opening year 1609 saw the wreck of the Manila Galleon *San Francisco*, carrying the ex-Governor of the Philippines Rodrigo Vivero y Velasco, and the heroic tragedy of the Macao carrack *Madre de Deus*, which stemmed from street-fighting wantonly provoked in Macao by the crew of a Red Seal ship belonging to the Christian daimyo Arima Harunobu. It was put down by the Captain-Major André Pessoa with the loss of forty-odd Japanese lives.

In July 1609 Pessoa brought the Great Ship *Madre de Deus* (or *Nossa Senhora da Graça*) to Nagasaki and at once ran into trouble with the *Bugyo* (the chief Shogunal official) Hasegawa Sahioye, a born intriguer. Things were smoothed over, since both sides needed the silk trade; but the arrival of the Japanese version of the Macao affray—naturally very different from the Portuguese—and the possibility of obtaining silk from the newly-arrived Hollanders or from the Manileños, who were actively negotiating for a direct trade, weakened Pessoa's bargaining position. The upshot of a tangle of intrigues and misunderstandings was that Ieyasu directed Arima and Hasegawa (whose sister was conveniently the Shogun's currently favourite concubine) to take Pessoa dead or alive. The Captain-Major saw the signs, and exceedingly short-handed as he was (he had only about forty Portuguese effectives when the crunch came) was ready for Arima's attack by swarms of small craft and hundreds of tough fighting men. On Twelfth Night 1610 the *Madre de Deus* had nearly fought herself out of harbour when a chance shot set her ablaze. Pessoa threw down sword and shield, took up crucifix and torch, and fired the magazine; a dramatic death which made him, paradoxically, a hero of local folklore.[25]

The loss was immense: Ieyasu, the Macaonese, and the Jesuits (who lost two years' finance for the mission) were all appalled. But it was far from certain that the Dutch and Spanish could as yet supply the silk that Japan needed—no Dutch ship had come in 1610, and the promised Manila ships to Kanto were also wanting. It was tacitly agreed that the gallant Pessoa was to be the scapegoat, and within a couple of years the trade of the Great Ship was back on the old footing, ostensibly at least; though the incident doubtless added an incentive, were one needed, to closer relations with Macao's rivals. Manila had not followed up the favourable issue of the *Espíritu Santo* affair of 1602, though one ship did set out for Kanto in 1603, only to be forced by weather into Hirado; Spanish pilots apparently feared the exposed southern coasts of Shikoku and Honshu.[26]

In 1608 Ieyasu sent an envoy to Manila, where Governor Rodrigo de Vivero was being pressed by the Manileños to reopen negotiations; the most amicable letters were exchanged, a vast contrast with the correspondence between Hideyoshi and Dasmariñas. Then in 1609 Vivero himself was wrecked on the Pacific shores east of Edo: a chance opportunity too good to be missed. Authorities differ as to whether Vivero's suggestion that Manila could send two or three ships a year, against Macao's one, influenced Ieyasu's decision to act dramatically against Pessoa, but certainly Vivero was treated with exceptional favour, and after about a year was sent on his way to Acapulco (1 August 1610) in the *San Buenventura*, built by Adams for Ieyasu; and he took with him twenty-six Japanese merchants.[27]

Sebastián Vizcaíno, whom we have met off the Californias in 1587 and 1602, strongly recommended the use of his new-found port of Monterey as a way-station for the Galleons coming to Acapulco; amongst other advantages, it would obviate the need for using Japanese ports of refuge. He was backed by the Viceroy Monterey, but the new Viceroy Montesclaros condemned the plan, which would have meant an inconvenient delay for the merchants of Mexico. He had however more objective arguments: the real need was for a harbour before the Galleons entered 'the great gulf of Nueva España', and such a port might be found in the islands of Rica de Oro and de Plata, thought to lie somewhere east of Japan. In 1608, therefore, a new Viceroy, Luis de Velasco, was ordered to send Vizcaíno to Manila, to return with two light vessels specifically to search for the islands; only if these proved unsuitable should the previous instruction to colonise Monterey be acted upon. Next year, on the intervention of Hernando de los Rios Coronel, always a stout defender of Manileño interests, Velasco was told to consider carefully whether the discovery might not be made more easily and cheaply from Luzon, and, if this seemed more likely, to remit the sum allotted for the voyage to the Governor of the Philippines.[28]

Vivero's arrival in the *San Buenventura* led Velasco to combine the search for Rica de Oro with a return mission to Japan. Vizcaíno accordingly sailed from

Acapulco in the *San Francisco* on 22 March 1611, with twenty-three of Vivero's Japanese (their potential competition was not welcome in Acapulco) and reached Uraga early in June.[29] He was well received, and made a good initial impression once compromise was reached on the question of court etiquette, agonising alike to Japanese and Spanish punctilio; he noted that the Japanese showed an interest in military arts 'equal to that of the characters in Don Quijote'. The Spaniards put on a good display, and conversely 'the liturgy of the encounters with these new-comers by the Pacific prefigured, even in detail, the activities evoked by the arrival of Perry, 242 years later.'[30] To begin with Vizcaíno claimed to have come with no motives beyond returning the twenty-three Japanese, paying for the *San Buenventura* and Vivero's debts, and generally fostering amity; but after interviews with Ieyasu and Hidetada, he requested permission to survey the coasts to find a good harbour of refuge (copies of the charts would of course be given to the Japanese), to build a replacement for the weather-worn *San Francisco*, and to do some limited trading to meet expenses. All these requests were granted, and Vizcaíno, led astray by his apparent success, now began to overplay his hand.

His own account shows him as a man possessed by an impregnable conceit, and he had not an inkling that Ieyasu and the Shogun were simply manipulating the several European interests to secure the best trading terms for Japan. Vizcaíno tried to set impossible terms for the building of the ship, and made a bitter attack on the Hollanders, mere rebels and pirates. As at this very time Adams was bear-leading Specx's mission, and as his friendship to the Iberians did not extend to their Papistry, this open attempt at exerting pressure was most inopportune; an interview between Adams and Vizcaíno by way of mediation had no effect except that the Spaniard's arrogance alienated the potential honest broker. The initial good feelings between Vizcaíno and the Shogunal court were waning on both sides, and Adams took an opportunity to warn Ieyasu about Spanish ambitions for world domination, their use of religion to form a fifth column, and more specifically of the danger of allowing a coastal survey. Ieyasu loftily replied that he was not like the English and the Dutch and had not the slightest fear of what the Spaniards might do; they could go on with their charting and their search for the isles of gold.

The coastal surveys were made, from Nagasaki to about 40°N, and Vizcaíno received vague reports of Yezo (Hokkaido) and the Ainu; he also had a second meeting with Date Masamune, the most powerful Tozama lord in the north, who, like the lords of Kyushu in the previous century, was anxious to forge his own links with the profitable foreigners. On his return to Uraga, however, Vizcaíno found that there had been very little progress on the *San Francisco*'s replacement. Disagreements were mounting, and the Spanish position was weakened by court intrigues and allegations of Christian plotting. Vizcaíno was thus forced after all to use the *San Francisco* for the fruitless search for Rica de Oro, on which he found nothing but floating pumice (September–October 1612). Ieyasu and Hidetada had given him letters for the Viceroy—not for the King; his claim to be Philip III's direct ambassador had been seen through—in the expectation that he was sailing

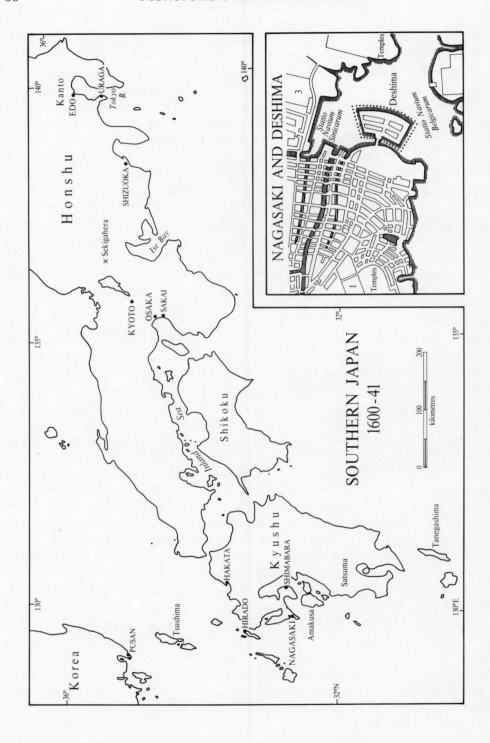

NAGASAKI AND DESHIMA

Temples

3

Statio Navium Sinicarum

Deshima

Statio Navium Belgicarum

Temples

1

SOUTHERN JAPAN
1600 - 41

0   100   200
kilometres

Honshu

Kanto

URAGA

EDO

Tokyo B.

SHIZUOKA

× Sekigahera

Ise Bay

KYOTO

OSAKA

SAKAI

Inland Sea

Shikoku

Korea

PUSAN

Tsushima

HIRADO

HAKATA

Kyushu

SHIMABARA

NAGASAKI

Amakusa

Satsuma

Tanegashima

130°

135°

140°

36°

140°

135°

130°E

32°N

36°

32°

direct to New Spain; the letters welcomed trade but made it quite clear that this welcome did not extend to missionary activities. Whatever his original intention, a damaging storm forced Vizcaíno back to Japan, where he found that in his absence the Franciscan Luis Sotelo had been assigned for despatch to New Spain on a separate embassy from the Shogun to the Viceroy—wheels within wheels. Sotelo sailed in the replacement ship, but she had been so hastily and unskilfully completed that she was lost at the very outset, and the Friar, who had been reckless in open disregard of the prohibition on public christian worship, was saved from execution only by the protection of Date Masamune.

Vizcaíno's credit at court was now in ruins, destroyed by his own fumbling and arrogance, the hostile suggestions of Adams and the Hollanders, and apparently also a whispering campaign by an unnamed Friar, probably Sotelo. He hung on desperately, no longer receiving any material support from the Shogunal court, getting deeper into debt, and longing to get away 'even with no more than water and rice', until he was unexpectedly rescued by Date Masamune, who undertook to pay for the building of a ship and the maintenance of its Spanish crew. The terms were magnanimous, but there was a flaw: Sotelo was to sail as Date's envoy to the Viceroy.

Date Masamune's embassy was directed not only to the Viceroy but also to the King of Spain and the Pope. The nominal head of the mission was Hasekura Rokuemon, with a suite of 150 or more Japanese, samurai as well as merchants— far more than Vizcaíno thought safe or proper, especially as it was far from certain that the Mexican authorities, who had sent back Vivero's twenty-three, would permit them entry. They sailed on 26 October 1613, Vizcaíno by his own account reduced to a mere passenger by Sotelo's influence with the Japanese, and reached Zacatula by 22 January 1614. Despite Vizcaíno's fears, they were feted in Mexico, and the thirty or so who went on to Europe were splendidly received in Seville, Madrid, Venice and Rome.

It is scarcely believable that an enterprise of this magnitude could have been undertaken without at least the tacit consent of Ieyasu and Hidetada. There had not been much concrete result to show for Ieyasu's dealings with the Manileños, going back to 1598, and he may well have been content to let things develop under Date's auspices, without committing his own or the Bakufu's prestige. He was also losing patience with Catholic action in Japan; a new edict of expulsion was to be issued in January 1614. As for Date and Sotelo, their motives have been neatly summed up by a Japanese historian—'a combination of those who wished to use the Kingdom of Heaven for trade, and those who wished to use trade for the Kingdom of Heaven.'[31]

Figure 5. SOUTHERN JAPAN 1600–41. Inset: NAGASAKI AND DESHIMA, adapted from map in E. Kaempfer, *A History of Japan* (London 1727). 1, Bugyo's residence; 2, prison; 3, Chinese compound.

There was scant profit for either Heaven or trade. Despite the clear if courteous warnings in the letters given to Vizcaíno, the Viceroy foolishly sent a purely Franciscan return embassy; naturally affronted, Ieyasu refused them an interview and Hidetada turned down their presents. Sotelo failed to gain the Bishopric of Eastern Japan of which he dreamed; he returned to Japan and died a martyr.[32] Publicity in Catholic Europe, clearly inspired by Sotelo, said not a word of Vizcaíno's mission but built up a grossly inflated image of Date Masamune as a great king, more wealthy and prestigious than the Shogun and the likely successor to Ieyasu—and one desirous of embracing the Faith. In fact, after the Osaka campaign, in which he was suspected of backwardness, he fell into disfavour and may have been lucky to have been allowed to live out his days in his northern fief.

On the commercial side, Luis de Velasco was now in Madrid as President of the Council of the Indies, which in June 1613 authorised one ship a year from New Spain to Japan. But this was little more than a gesture; there was apprehension at the number of Japanese who would learn the secrets of the navigation, and of course there was strong and effective pressure from Manila and Seville against any direct trade. Then Joris van Spilbergen's raid on Acapulco created panic: on Christmas Eve 1615, Richard Cocks was visited by three Spaniards from that port, who told him that the Viceregal authorities had 'made proclamecon, in payne of death, that all strangers were to avoide out of New Spaine and never retorne to trade theare any more'; and this ban was met by a Shogunal edict prohibiting, also on pain of death, any Japanese from visiting New Spain.[33] The Franciscan embassy returned to New Spain in 1617, despite the ban taking with it some Japanese; but after this the controls were tightened up. The first move towards a direct trans-Pacific link, diplomatic and commercial, between an Asian and an American country had ended in a mutual exclusion.

Towards seclusion

The Iberians still had a presence in Japan, but it was gravely weakened. Hideyoshi's expulsion order of 1587 had never been rescinded, but it was scarcely enforced, and in Ieyasu's time no foreign priest was put to death, though there were local persecutions of Japanese converts, as by Hasegawa Sahioye in Arima Harunobu's old fief; padres and Christians could still 'live in the shadow of the Ship'. In 1614, however, a more stringent edict was issued, providing *inter alia* for the deportation of all missionaries and some of their leading adherents; some forty padres, half of them Jesuits, managed to stay and work underground.[34]

The Portuguese traders were still needed, however, as they alone had direct access to Chinese silk, and the Japanese tried to keep religion and commerce in separate boxes: the heretics at Hirado had no difficulty in falling in with this. They did not confine themselves to anti-Iberian propaganda, but despite Shogunal orders to the contrary used Hirado as a base for hostilities. In August 1615 the Dutch brought in a Portuguese prize taken in Japanese waters, and later Cocks wrote that

Specx had received a friendly warning from Hasegawa Gonroku, the new Bugyo of Nagasaki and a better man than his uncle Sahioye, that Hollanders and English

> should take heed that they did not meddell with the greate ship of
> Amacon, for that the Emperor had much adventure in her. Yet I say I
> wish we might take her and then make the reconying after.[35]

English and Dutch also collaborated closely in the murky affair of Luis Flores and Pedro Zuñiga, Spanish 'merchants' taken by an English ship from a Japanese junk—a grave outrage unless the two could be shown to be mission priests. In the end they confessed to their calling and were roasted alive; Cocks and Specx had worked hard to secure their conviction; we may hope that they did not foresee the end.[36]

After Ieyasu's death in 1616, Hidetada, a narrower man, took a harder line with alien interests and influences. To begin with, all foreign shipping except Chinese was confined to Hirado and Nagasaki, a blow to the aspirations of Date Masamune in the north and Shimazu of Satsuma in the south: the later policy of seclusion was in part a matter of controlling Tozama daimyo. Then in 1622 over fifty Christians, including Flores and Zuñiga, were put to the sword or the stake at Nagasaki. This spectacle was indeed the occasion for demonstrations of sympathy by the populace of the port, so long and so closely associated with the missionary enterprise; but this in itself of course served to deepen what became a paranoid xenophobia. Next year Hidetada handed over the Shogunate to his son Iemitsu (although like Ieyasu he retained effective control until his death in 1632), and the new Shogun took a harder line still, celebrating his investiture at Edo with a mass burning of another fifty or more Christians. Iemitsu also signalised his accession by the contrast between his reception of a Siamese embassy and his refusal to allow Spanish envoys to come to Edo: it was made clear that their talk of trade was seen as a mere cover for subversion. In 1627 a Spanish squadron, sent out to counterattack the Dutch cruisers, gave real cause of offence by taking Red Seal ships off Siam. The immediate sufferers were the Macaonese; their galliots were detained at Nagasaki and their trade banned from 1628 to 1630. In Manila the Governor, Juan de Tavora, did his best to smooth things over, but the rebuff to the 1624 embassy marked the effective end of trade between the Philippines and Japan.[37]

English, Mexicans, Manileños were now eliminated; but it was still not plain sailing for the Hollanders. Although the Ming prohibition of direct trade with Japan was still in force, there was plenty of roundabout or illicit Chinese trading, while Macaonese trade was still very much alive, though after 1616 the great carracks were replaced by flotillas of handy galliots to spread risks and evade the Dutch cruisers. The Dutch lodgement in Taiwan involved them in friction with Japanese frequenting the island, and the violent Nuyts affair in 1628 led to an embargo on Dutch trade with Japan which lasted until 1632. As for part of this time the ban on Macao trade was also in force, the Red Seal ships flourished mightily.[38] But neither their activity nor the Macaonese revival was to last long.

The Red Seal shipping was the first to go. It at once depended upon and supported the Japanese trading groups in southeast Asia, and these had a large component of ronin and Christians. To the increasingly isolationist temper of the Bakufu, any contact with such unreliable elements might menace the Tokugawa peace—surely a very distant threat but, such as it was, eliminated by a series of decrees which by 1636 were draconic indeed. No Japanese ships were to leave for foreign lands, and any Japanese returning from abroad was to be put to death. Other clauses offered rewards for the denunciation of Christians and provided for the execution or banishment of children of Southern Barbarians by Japanese mothers; even correspondence between deportees and their relatives carried heavy penalties. Significantly, the same document contained restrictive commercial clauses, for instance enforcing the ito wappu and forbidding unsold goods to be left in Japanese care.[39]

This left only the Portingalls, the Hollanders, and the pettier Chinese trade. The Macao trade survived a severe credit crisis in 1635; it relied heavily on Japanese *respondencia* loans of silver (at very high rates), and these were suddenly and collusively called in.[40] With the suppression of the Red Seal trade, however, Japanese merchants and daimyo with silver on their hands had no other avenue of investment (the Dutch financed themselves), while the Macaonese were still the most reliable suppliers of raw silk, the Chinese junk trade being disrupted by Manchu inroads in the north and piracy (to which the Portuguese were less vulnerable) in the south.[41] The 1636 voyage of four galliots was thus a commercial triumph, leaving Nagasaki with nearly 7,000,000 florins' worth of silver, against cargoes worth 3,200,000 florins carried by nine Dutch ships from Hirado. But the galliots also carried back nearly 300 women and children, married or born to Portuguese, expelled under the new edict. Moreover, for the past two years the Japanese had been building the artificial island of Deshima in Nagasaki harbour. Into its narrow compass the Portuguese were now confined.

Shimabara and the end of the Macao trade

Persecution under Iemitsu was savage but intermittent: in many areas there was much sympathy with the victims amongst the general populace, and even from officials and daimyo. The maximum number of recorded martyrs in any one year was 316 in 1630, and the total between 1614 and 1650 some 5–6000 at the outside.[42] There were thousands of apostasies, but many of these were only skin-deep. The modes of execution and the tortures used to secure recantations were, however, extremely horrible, probably worse than anything carried out as deliberate policy by Church or State in the Europe of that time.

The time had not yet come for extreme measures against the Portuguese merchants as such, and indeed they were still protected; in 1632, for example, the Dutch failed in efforts to get the repeal of orders which kept their ships in Hirado until twenty days after the galliots had left Nagasaki, and three years later they were warned against interference with the flotilla, although 'the more damage we did the Portuguese on the far side of Macao, the better His Majesty would be pleased.'[43] The Portuguese owed the final ruin of their Nagasaki trade not to their European rivals but to the ferociously exploited peasantry of Amakusa and Shimabara (Fig. 5) in Kyushu.

The islands of Amakusa near Nagasaki had been Christian, at the behest of their then daimyo, since 1577, and had been held before Sekigahara by the Christian general Konishi Yukinaga; the adjacent peninsula of Shimabara had been a part of Arima Harunobu's domains until 1614. Both had been places of refuge for the Jesuit seminary and printery in Hideyoshi's day, both had since fallen into the evil hands of absentee daimyo. Moreover, these rustic areas were full of ronin and of former samurai, many of them once Christian, who since the fall of Osaka had been reduced to a poverty-stricken life on the land. There had been persecutions and mass apostasies, but also portents and prophecies of a divine Messenger who should come to resurrect the Faith: he duly appeared in the person of Masuda Shiro, son of one of Konishi's old retainers. Matsukura Shigehara of Shimabara was a particularly cruel lord, employing and apparently enjoying terrorism and torture to exact the rice tribute. The outbreak in its origins resembled a *jacquerie*; the actual incident which traditionally touched it off is strikingly reminiscent of Wat Tyler's rising in 1381—a taxgatherer's indecent outrage on a farmer's daughter. But there may well have been an organisation, Christian and ronin, behind it, and if indeed its origins were mainly economic, it at once took on religious colours—Jesus, Maria, Santiago as its war-cries, Catholic mottoes and symbols on its banners.[44]

The rising began early in December 1637 and was soon in control of Amakusa; arms were obtained largely through successful ambushes, and although an attack on Shimabara castle failed, by the end of January the insurgents—some 37,000, including 15,000 fighting men—had dug themselves in at Hara castle. Neighbouring lords raised levies to suppress them, but declined to cross their own borders without due authorisation—the Augustan peace was sapping initiative and the Bakufu's control over the feudality working too well. By the same token, the rebels made no attempt upon Nagasaki—an open town crammed with Christian sympathisers; this alone demonstrates the baselessness of the Bakufu's paranoid dread of subversion from without. Nagasaki was now made secure and the rebellion stood on the defensive, always a fatal stance for insurrection. The first government assaults on Hara were repulsed with heavy losses, including the commander; he was replaced by Matsudaira Nobotsuna, a courtier very close to Iemitsu—an appointment which indicates how badly the Bakufu was shaken by the startlingly successful resistance of a peasant rabble.

Matsudaira decided to starve the rebels out, but he also demanded aid from the Dutch not far away in Hirado. With or without some qualms, Nicholaes Koeckebacker, the head of the factory, sent guns and then a ship which bombarded Hara for a fortnight, apparently in a rather desultory way.[45] Testimonies as to the material damage done vary, but this appeal to the barbarian foreigner was a gift to the rebels' propaganda. But they were now starving, their munitions were exhausted, and on 12 April 1638 Hara was stormed. It remained only to slaughter the women and children.

And yet this was not quite a 'final solution'. The tracking-down of Christians became a fine art; the test of trampling on the Cross was introduced, and those who recanted were illogically compelled to swear to their abjurations by the Trinity and the Virgin as well as by Buddhist and Shinto deities. Not until the next century did the Bakufu relax, thinking its work was done. And yet, when Catholic priests returned to Nagasaki in the 1860s they found, or were found by, a faithful remnant who through over two centuries of persecution and isolation had contrived to maintain much of Christian practice, and more of Christian faith.[46]

All centuries, every land, have seen peasant risings bloodily suppressed; probably no other has had the international significance of Shimabara. The Bakufu was deeply shocked by the fact that its greatly superior forces had taken four months to put down a few thousand despised peasants, losing some 13,000 out of a force which rose to 100,000—a very poor showing indeed. Paradoxically, the first result of Shimabara was to put an abrupt end to maturing plans to cut off the missionary menace at its roots in Macao or Manila.

An attack on the former would of course have meant complications with China, even though the Ming government was already in deep distress between internal rebellions and Manchu inroads in the north; the memory of the rout of the Dutch in 1622 was still strong, and the city was now better fortified. Manila seemed a better option. In the 1590s Hideyoshi had seriously considered attacking the Philippines, and the scanty Spanish garrison could hardly have stood out against even a fraction of the armies which had swept through Korea. The Spaniards had shown remarkable powers of improvisation during the Dutch wars, but they had not had to meet really substantial land forces; should they have to do so, their predicament was neatly put in a Jesuit relation of 1663:

> a city where all the forts together could not call to arms 2,000
> Spaniards—and these of so many colors that not two hundred pure
> Spaniards could be picked out from them—and occupying so much
> space that for its suitable garrison it needs 6,000 soldiers.[47]

But all depended on transport for an expeditionary force, which could not be locally gathered as it could for the short crossing to Korea. Now there seemed a possibility that the Hollanders might provide shipping. Richard Cocks had suggested to influential Japanese that Luzon would be an easy conquest, and in 1630 Matsukura Shigemasa had actually sent a mission of espionage, under cover of renewed trade talks, to Manila; he proposed to conquer the island, in return for a handsome fief there. This in itself may have given the Bakufu pause: it might be hazardous to allow the Tozama lords of Kyushu to set up new and distant bases of power. In the event the Spaniards saw through the scheme and did their best to impress Matsukura's emissaries with the strength of the place; he died before they returned, and nothing was done.

The idea however was gathering strength and was carefully fostered by the Dutch. Both the Japanese and the Hollanders would of course have liked the other party to pull the chestnuts out of the fire, but at last in 1637 the Bakufu decided to commit some 10,000 men to an attack on Luzon. They called on the Dutch for support, and the Council at Hirado agreed to supply four well-armed ships and two yachts.[48] Such a combination of Dutch fire-power and Japanese manpower, even if the men were no longer the men of Korea, would have had a very good chance of capturing Manila, which had already escaped so often and so narrowly. The consequences defy speculation: for instance, the effects on European economy if the flow of silver across the Pacific had been turned back across the Atlantic, not to mention an almost certain Dutch-Japanese conflict. But in the face of Shimabara, the Bakufu lost its nerve and called off the invasion. Rarely can an obscure and failed peasant rising have had such an influence, even if a negative one, on the course of world events.

The Bakufu was now approaching a 'final solution' of the Macaonese problem. The Portuguese were allowed to trade in 1638, and borrowed heavily to do so; but the commander of the flotilla was detained in Japan and the galliots returned with the message that if any more religious arrived from Manila, any Macao ships arriving in 1639 would be burned with everything and everybody on board; since both cities were subject to the same King, both were responsible.[49] The Senate of Macao, backed by the ecclesiastical hierarchy, accordingly appealed to Manila, Philip IV, and the Pope to stop any missionaries going to Japan. The threat was conditional, there had been no formal ban on trade, and in view of the large sums owing to the Japanese, none seemed immediately likely. Despite this, the two galliots which reached Deshima in 1639 were not allowed to land goods, not even to pay off old creditors, and the Captain-Major was given a decree asserting that men and material smuggled in by Macaonese had fomented the Shimabara rebellion, which was not true. All Portuguese were henceforth banned from Japan on pain of death.

'The City of the Name of God in China' now faced ruin, but was not willing to accept it without striving for a reprieve. As a back-stop, the Crown was asked to legalise the Macao-Manila trade and to extend it to Acapulco; more immediately, the Senate secured from the Governor of the Philippines, and the Church authorities there, written assurances that no religious were to be allowed to leave for Japan. These assurances, with the city's apologetic petition, were to be taken to Japan by an embassy carrying no merchandise, and headed by four of the most respected and experienced men in Macao. They knew the risks; every soul confessed and communicated before embarking.

They reached Nagasaki on 6 July 1640, and were detained under guard at Deshima while the matter was referred to Edo. A decision was reached at once; by 1 August two commissioners had reached Nagasaki, making a record of only ten days on the road, and the envoys were summoned to hear the Shogun's answer. They dressed as for an honourable reception, but were bluntly asked why they had defied the ban: the plea that they came as ambassadors entitled to diplomatic protection was brushed aside, but since they had not come to trade but 'only to beg for something' the painful death they deserved was remitted for simple beheading. On 3 August sixty-one were executed; thirteen of the lowest of the ship's company were spared to tell the Macaonese that if King Philip himself, or even the God of the Christians, should come to Japan, his head should pay for it. With something of an old Roman spirit, the city rejoiced that its ambassadors were now ambassadors to heaven.

Even now Macao did not quite give up hope: Portuguese independence in 1640 and the consequent disengagement from Manila seemed to offer some chance of a new start.[50] It is an index of the importance of Macao to the Portuguese Crown that in 1644, with independence so recently gained and so far from secure, João IV despatched two ships from Lisbon itself, the first embassy 'from King to King'. The ambassador, Gonçalo de Siqueira de Souza, reached Macao in 1645, but his instructions did not allow him to promise that no religious should ever be allowed to go to Japan, and the Senate pointed out that this was a *sine qua non*. He had to sail to Goa to obtain Viceregal and ecclesiastical sanction to over-ride his brief, and did not arrive in Nagasaki until July 1647. His two well-armed galleons had to be treated with more respect than the single galliot of 1640, but hundreds of small craft and some 50,000 men were mobilised in and around the harbour, as in André Pessoa's day. The embassy was refused, but allowed to depart in peace. As late as 1685 the Macaonese made a last attempt at contact, by sending back some Japanese blown to the Port by a typhoon; they were thanked, but told not to try again. By this time conditions had changed: Macao itself had found new outlets, home production in Japan had reduced the demand for silks from China, and direct trade between the two countries was now legal. There was no point in further Macaonese efforts; a fascinating chapter in the annals of commerce was closed.

Deshima and 'sakoku'

François Caron, *opperhoofd* or chief of the Dutch factory in 1639–40, remarked thoughtfully that 'when it rained on the Portuguese, the Company likewise was apt to get wet'.[51] The sudden elimination of the Macao trade ruined many Japanese merchants who were creditors to the Portingalls but debtors to the Hollanders, and the depression was worsened by a sumptuary law confining the wearing of silk to the higher classes; but by 1640 Dutch trade was reviving. Caron improved on the occasion by a successful demonstration of mortar-founding at Edo (mortars could be most useful against Tozama castles) and by complicated intrigues both with and against the Chinese. There were difficulties: until 1645 copper exports were banned as war material, the ito wappu was still insisted upon, and the silk guilds of the five Bakufu-controlled towns were petitioning to have the Dutch transferred to Nagasaki, to make up for the loss of the Macao trade. Earlier, the Dutch themselves had seen advantages in this—it was a far better harbour than Hirado, a place of resort for the merchants of the other four towns (Edo, Osaka, Sakai, and Kyoto), and its Shogunal officials had more influence at Court than the Daimyo of Hirado. In the changed climate of 1640, however, they were doubtful—control would be stricter, the Bugyo of Nagasaki less open to manipulation than the Daimyo. For the time being Caron was able to stave off the threat, largely by presents to Iemitsu such as a gold-inlaid telescope.[52]

But what had begun as a perfectly reasonable apprehension of possibly disruptive alien influences was swelling into a paranoid xenophobia. Try as they might to insist on their hostility to Rome and its Jesuits and Franciscans, the Hollanders after all could not deny that they were Christians of a sort. They had warned the Bakufu of the insidious conquests of Spain and Portugal, but were their own actions in Java and the Moluccas any different? Unluckily for them, the one place where the VOC had done anything substantial towards bringing the Gospel light to the heathen was near at hand—Taiwan. A strong anti-Dutch party at Edo lost no opportunity of driving home such arguments; Caron as constantly warned Batavia against anything which might look in the least like proselytism, such as sending chaplains in their black gowns. A snap inspection of the factory, under pretence of mere curiosity, by Inouye Masashige, the chief commissioner for the extirpation of Christianity, failed to find any religious objects; but a warehouse bore above its doorway a fatal date: A.D. 1637. This was enough.

Caron was summoned to meet Inouye, who told him that the differences alleged between Catholics and Calvinists were all a pretence, the fundamentals being the same, and that all buildings dated by the Christian era must be destroyed at once. There had been no warning at all, and this was a trap—troops were at hand for a general killing should the Dutch make difficulties. Caron, experienced and wary, saw the risk; he kept his head and said simply that the Shogunal orders would be instantly obeyed: the removal of all goods to temporary cover began within an hour, though even this was hardly quick enough for Inouye. The Dutch were allowed to stay, but on new terms; for one, the opperhoofd was to be replaced annually—this meant that Caron had to leave in February 1641, a great loss at this critical time. In May, with ten days' notice, the Hollanders were moved to Nagasaki, or rather to 'that small Island, I should rather say, Prison'—Deshima.[53]

For over two centuries this was to be Japan's only window on the world, a tiny and closely-shuttered window (Fig. 5 inset). The island was only 64 metres wide with median length of 95 metres, an area of 1.25 hectares; there was one footbridge to the town, and it was surrounded by posts carrying notices forbidding approach by boats. Except for two or three months in the year, when the Dutch ships were in, there were rarely more than a score of Hollanders on the island; for their surveillance there were over 250 officials, interpreters, guards, and hangers-on, with more guards at sale times, and more cooks than people to be served. All these had to be paid for by the VOC, and high rentals were also charged. No Japanese were allowed to stay on the island at night, except (some concession to human needs) whores and concubines; as a nineteenth-century opperhoofd plaintively apologised, this was the only way in which the Dutchmen could 'procure any domestic comfort in the long nights of winter—their tea water, for instance'.[54] Conditions were initally so humiliating that in 1652 Batavia asked the Heeren XVII whether Deshima should not be given up for the sake of the national honour, but in course of time relaxations crept in; though nothing, surely, could much alleviate the intensest boredom. Even the consolations of religion, if desired, must be surreptitious; the Bible banned, there remained only the bottle and the bed.

Nevertheless, the Dutch shared only with the Chinese the import into Japan of a wide variety of goods, mainly Asian but with Western novelty or luxury items such as timepieces, optical goods, and exotic weaponry; drugs were important, including the much-valued 'unicorn horn', really that of the narwhal. To the Dutch, the country was an invaluable source of silver until its export was banned in 1668, and then of copper, 'the bride for whom we dance' and a main staple from about 1670 to 1770.[55] Such a position was worth keeping. There was only one external challenge, and that slight. In 1672–3 the EIC attempted to reopen the Japan trade, with a cargo that did not include a thread of silk. The knowledge that the Queen of England was a 'daughter of Portugal' had been obligingly passed to the Bakufu by the Dutch as early as 1663, and this was enough: nobody was allowed to land and no trade was done. The Japanese ensured that there should be no clash in their waters (the Third Anglo-Dutch War was on) and politely sent the *Return* on her way.[56] The Hollanders remained, locked on their islet.

Sakoku, the policy of seclusion, was not only a matter of excluding foreigners; its motivation was at least as much a matter of internal as of external policy. It involved severe restrictions on the Japanese themselves, notably on the rising trading class, expressed most strikingly by the limitation on shipping: no craft was to be built of greater capacity than 500 koku (909 hectolitres). This still left scope for an active coastal traffic—there were regular freight lines to supply Edo with rice from Osaka—but it did mean the end of any ocean-going merchant marine; in Murdoch's view this was perhaps the only serious loss to Japan through sakoku, at least until the advent of steam power.[57]

The basis seems not to have been primarily a generalised xenophobia, though this was certainly exhibited by some circles at some times. The Tokugawa policy was in itself intensely conservative, and its inherent distrust of change was *a fortiori* applicable to foreign-induced change. Engelbert Kaempfer, in a remarkable appreciation of what he saw as an almost Utopian polity, hit the nail on the head:

> the secular Monarchs [i.e. the Shoguns] . . . had their hands tied no
> longer, but were at liberty to do what they thought fit, to attempt
> things, *which it would be impossible to bring about in any open Country,*
> *where there is a free access and commerce,* to bring towns, burroughs,
> villages, all colleges and mutual societies . . . to the strictest order and
> regulation imaginable . . . by appointing multitudes of overseers and
> rigid Censors to have a watchful Eye over the conduct of the people. . . .[58]

The new regime had at last enforced internal peace, after generations of bloody and at times anarchic conflict; it was very fearful of any possible disturbance of the equilibrium, and the great western lords were seen as potential catalysts of disorder and clients of foreign interests, as indeed they had been. It is not without significance that when the Bakufu was eventually overthrown, a high proportion of the leaders in the Meiji restoration came from the Mori of western Honshu and the Shimazu of Satsuma.[59] Christianity by 1639 was no longer a danger, but so long as the Bakufu had not automatic control of the western ports, there seemed always a risk that it might seep in again through the ambitions of the Tozama lords of the region. The answer was a policy of Thorough, the total prohibition of all foreign contact except that direcly and strictly supervised by the Bakufu at Nagasaki.[60]

So Japan was taken out of 'the mainstream of history' (whatever that is), and this was probably not so greatly (if at all) to her disadvantage as earlier schools of European historians have assumed: India and Indonesia did not greatly gain, in their own values at least, by being forcibly dragged into the stream. For two centuries, while Europe was being wracked by a ghastly succession of conflicts from the Thirty Years' War to those of Napoleon, Japan enjoyed a peace broken only by occasional riots and more numerous peasant risings. Nor was this a mere peace of stagnation. It is true that the peasants were frightfully exploited—where were they not?—and after the Shogunate of Yoshimune (1716–45) famines and peasant revolts became more frequent, economic problems more intractable; despite Zero Population Growth, the fragile balance between numbers and production was always vulnerable to natural disasters.[61] But the country was sufficiently well endowed and diversified to support a remarkable flowering of urban life and culture—'the floating world' of the stories of Ihara Saikaku, the plays of Chikamatsu and the Kabuki drama, the glorious prints of Hiroshige, Hokusai, and Utamaro.[62] Through it all, however, ran 'the inherent contradictions in an insulated military society cultivating the insurbordinate arts of peace.'[63] Well before Perry's arrival, the Tokugawa polity was approaching crisis.

The little window on the world at Deshima was shuttered indeed, but not completely blacked out; in fact, the Dutch were formally required to submit intelligence reports on foreign affairs—those at the time of the Opium War make very interesting reading indeed. In 1720 Yoshimune repealed the prohibition on all foreign (mostly Chinese) books (imposed just in case there should be some faint reference to Christianity), and later in the century some intellectuals took eagerly to *Rangaku* ('Dutch Studies'), particularly in medicine, astronomy, botany, and military arts. A few also of the VOC's officials were men of talent and curiosity, and with at least one of them, Isaac Titsingh, opperhoofd in the 1780s, there was a true meeting of minds.[64] The Rangakusha were never more than a handful, and their views of European life were often highly distorted—'in the West, no man, not even an emperor, might have a concubine'.[65] But their enthusiasm, just as the enthusiasm for China in the West, served as a needed criticism of society; they were courageous enquirers (some went to prison for their pains) and formed an invaluable leaven: without their passion for the new learning and their display of its practical advantages, and their warnings of the dangers of isolationism, the great change after Perry might have been even more traumatic. In the long run, the value of Deshima for Japan may have been less in the mercantile than in the intellectual sphere.

The Dutch in Taiwan

Taiwan, the Formosa or Hermosa of the Iberians, on the map enjoys a magnificent strategic situation: Taipei is just half-way between Manila and Nagasaki by air-line distances, and the fertile western lowlands face the commercially active Fukien coast little over 200 kilometres away. As a base for interfering with shipping between Macao and Manila or between either city and Japan, it was obviously excellently placed. Its value to China as 'seal[ing] permanently the defense perimeter of our southeast' was pointed out in 1683 by Shih Lang, commanding the Ch'ing naval forces in Fukien.[66] Yet for most of its history the island was left singularly untouched by the activities of the great navalist powers, a reminder that the significance of location is a variable dependent on other factors than mere propinquity on a map. Only in two periods has Taiwan been a focus of power rivalry: for a hundred or so years preceding our own day, and in the sixty years between the Dutch failure at Macao and the reassertion of mainland Chinese control in 1683.

The aboriginal population was mainly proto-Malayan, but centuries of immigration from southeast China had made the island virtually a Chinese colony; but since the Ming had given over interest in overseas affairs, any official control had virtually lapsed.[67] When the Chinese evicted the Dutch from the Pescadores, they made no difficulty about the transfer to Taiwan. In 1624 the Dutch built Casteel Zeelandia on the site of the modern Anping (the port of Tainan), which became a flourishing centre for trade with Fukien, partly by Chinese ships and partly by a direct trade to Amoy, illicit but connived at by local officials.[68] This did not go unchallenged by the Spaniards. As early as 1597 Hernando de los Rios Coronel had advocated the seizure of Keelung in the north of the island, and despite some sound arguments against over-extension, Governor Fernando de Silva countered the Dutch move by building a fort at San Salvador (Keelung) in 1626, and three years later a second establishment was made at San Domingo (Tanshui). Despite warnings from Pieter Nuyts at Zeelandia, the Dutch left these settlements to stagnate in their isolation until a Chinese revolt in 1640, in which Spanish incitement was suspected, perhaps with good reason. Their first attack at Tanshui in 1641 was repulsed, but next year both San Domingo and San Salvador were taken; at this time the Spanish were heavily committed in Mindanao and Sulu, and as we have seen Governor Corcuera, who indeed thought Taiwan a liability rather than an asset, was blamed for neglecting the northern island.[69]

Taiwan's basic commercial importance was as an exchange point between China and Japan, direct trade being still banned by the Ming, and the island was greatly resorted to by Red Seal ships. Until the advent of the Dutch, this was really free trade; but the Japanese were dangerous competitors, and the VOC accordingly imposed a greatly resented 10 per cent tax. An attempt at negotiation in 1627 failed, and the returning shogunal envoy took with him sixteen Formosans who were induced to petition for Japanese annexation, a move countered by sending Nuyts to Edo with funds for judicious bribery. He left Japan with a grudge and next year, as Governor at Zeelandia, high-handedly detained two junks to spoil their trade; quite in the modern manner, some of their people seized Nuyts in his own office and threatened his life if their demands for compensation and immediate departure were not met. They had to be allowed to go, taking with them amongst other hostages Nuyts's young son. The immediate results were his recall to Batavia in disgrace and the impounding of nine Dutch ships at Hirado. The embargo on Dutch trade was not lifted until 1632, when Nuyts was sent to Japan as a scapegoat, not to be released until 1636. In that year the problem was resolved in an unexpected manner by the prohibition on any Japanese overseas trading.[70]

Opinions differ as to the general effect of Dutch rule.[71] The trade in silk and porcelain from China, as well as the more exotic local export of deer-skins, made Taiwan one of the most profitable Dutch holdings, and there was an ample labour supply for planatations of sugar-cane and for rice-growing. Under François Caron, there was even an export of coal and sulphur from mines near Keelung and Tamshui; the latter in particular was in great demand for the Ming/Manchu wars, and thirty junks loaded with it in 1644.[72] Taiwan was also the scene of a considerable evangelistic effort. With exceptions, the missionaries were often poor material poorly trained, and they had also to act as chaplains to the Hollanders and as tax-gatherers and general administrators in the countryside, while at times—especially times of anti-Christian troubles in Japan—the VOC officials were less than encouraging. Nevertheless, there were a large number of conversions, and not all of these were merely skin-deep, since in 1715 the Jesuit de Mailla (employed by the Ch'ing to survey the island) found that some aborigines still read Dutch books and retained some Christian knowledge and ceremonies.[73]

By 1652, after the suppression of another Chinese rising, the Dutch hold on Taiwan seemed more than secure: there were twenty-five military posts controlling some 300 mainly Chinese towns and villages in the lowlands, with a regular system of village headmen. By 1662 it had ceased to be: this was the first, and for generations the only, substantial territorial loss by a European power to Asians.

Coxinga's maritime kingdom

The Manchus occupied Peking in 1644; the last Ming Emperor had hanged himself, but south of the Yangtse various Ming princes or pretenders carried on the struggle against the new Ch'ing dynasty. In these confused conditions, one of the powers in the land was Cheng Chih-lung, a Fukienese adventurer generally known to Europeans by his baptismal name of Nicholas Iquan. He was well known as a trader in Macao, Manila, and Hirado, and in Taiwan and Fukien as a pirate who by 1627 dominated the whole coast from the Yangtse to the Canton estuary. The

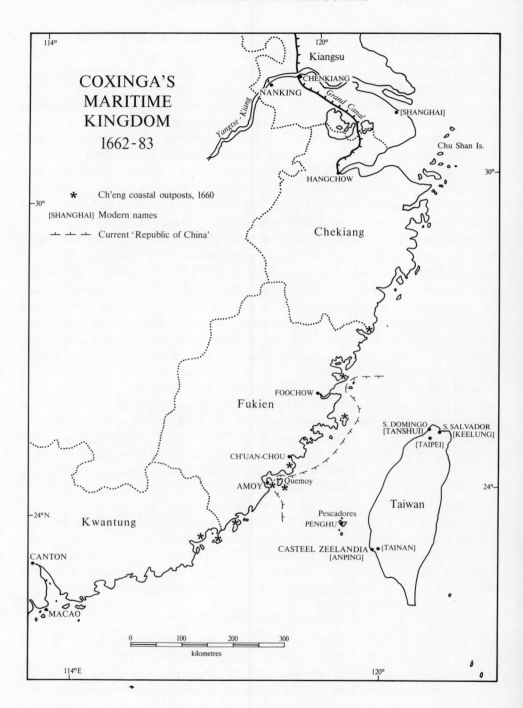

COXINGA'S
MARITIME
KINGDOM
1662-83

*   Ch'eng coastal outposts, 1660

[SHANGHAI]   Modern names

┼ ┼ ┼ ┼   Current 'Republic of China'

Ming authorities, already hard-pressed by the Manchus in the north, bought him off on the poacher-gamekeeper principle, and initially he stood by the claimant Lung-wu, who, after the Manchus took Nanking in 1645, was proclaimed Ming 'Emperor' at Foochow. Iquan's son Cheng Cheng-kung, a greater man, was born to a Japanese wife at Hirado in 1624, and in 1645 Lung-wu bestowed on the younger Cheng the title Kuo-hsing-yeh ('Lord of the Imperial Surname'), distorted by Europeans into Coxinga or Koxinga.[74]

Next year the Manchu forces pressed on to Foochow, and Cheng Chih-lung made terms (not strictly honoured) with the Ch'ing. Despite many tempting offers, Coxinga refused to follow his father, and built up a formidable power from bases on Amoy and Quemoy Islands; this was not a mere maritime guerrilla, but a well-organised military and naval command. By 1658–9 he was strong enough to take Chenkiang at the junction of the Grand Canal and the Yangtse, and to besiege Nanking itself. The city was too strong for him, however, and he had to retreat to Amoy, while the Ch'ing recaptured most of his outposts on the mainland and in their turn launched a great naval attack on Amoy. These waters were Coxinga's element, and the Ch'ing armada was shattered in June 1660; but his appeals to Japan for support produced only sympathy, while the Ming adherents in southern China had been forced away from Fukien, their last *soi-disant* Emperor fleeing to Burma in 1659. Like the Ming in the days of the Wako pirates a century earlier, the Ch'ing resorted to the desperate policy of forced evacuation of the whole littoral to cut off any support or supply. Coxinga was safe enough on his tight little islands, but could do nothing on the mainland; he turned to Taiwan, on which he had very good intelligence, including a wooden model of Casteel Zeelandia.[75]

At the end of April 1661 Coxinga entered the harbour as if it were his own, and landed 25,000 men (Pl. IX). Batavia had received many warnings, including specific ones from the Governor Frederik Coyett, and had done something to strengthen the place; but within a week the Hollanders were left with nothing but Zeelandia itself. An assault failed and Coxinga settled down to a siege. The defence was stout enough, but the Batavian reaction was inept. Coyett was under recall, and his replacement arrived to find a full-scale battle going on; he was able to get in touch with Coyett, but saw fit to proceed to Japan to revictual, without landing. Batavia now bestirred itself to send ten ships and 700 men under a lawyer, Jacob Cau, no other high official being game. Cau at least landed but decided to go to Batavia for reinforcements, or alternatively to join the Ch'ing in an attack on Coxinga's Amoy base; he did send ships to Fukien but they were scattered by tempest. It was now December; the garrison thus forsaken held out until 1 February 1662. They received the honours of war—Coxinga was running short of provisions—but Taiwan and all VOC property were yielded. Coyett was most disgracefully made

Figure 6. COXINGA'S MARITIME KINGDOM 1662–83. Holdings on mainland coast as listed in J. E. Wills, *Pepper, Guns and Parleys* (Cambridge, Mass., 1974), 16.

Plate IX. FORT ZEELANDIA: COXINGA'S ATTACK. From W. Campbell, *Formosa under the Dutch* (reprint Ch'eng-Wen Publishing Co., Taipei). Photo ANU.

the scapegoat, and with Coxinga's move to Taiwan, Cheng Chih-lung was of no more use to the Ch'ing; he was put to death in November 1661.[76]

'Pirate' or not, Coxinga had already shown himself a first-class organiser, and he now proceeded to build up a miniature Celestial Kingdom—much the same as the present 'Republic of China' (Fig. 6). The provision shortage towards the end of the campaign led him to pay special attention to agricultural settlement. But he was soon looking further afield, and Luzon was an obvious target. In 1662 he sent Fr Vittorio Ricci OP, whom he had known in Amoy, with an embassy demanding tribute. Naturally Coxinga's success against a European power lost nothing in the telling, and both the Spaniards and the Sangleys of Manila were highly excited, for opposite reasons. The embassy was in Manila for five weeks, and during this time there were serious disturbances in the Parian. These were put down partly by dissimulation and some genuine moderation, partly by force; to impress the envoys, Spanish troops were kept in reserve and Pampangans used for the action. There were also deportations, but as in Acuña's time 'All recognized our need of that nation . . . on account of our dependence upon their trade, for everything'—but not too many of that nation; the old limit of 6000 was accepted. Coxinga's demands were of course rejected, and the Spaniards devoted themselves to such preparation as they might for the expected onslaught. Early in 1663 Ricci returned, but with the unexpected news that 'Only a few days after his Lordship had placed our forces under the powerful protection of the holy archangel', Coxinga had died.[77]

The circumstances of Coxinga's death, whether through madness brought on by reverses on the Fukien coast and by family quarrels or some less sensational disease, are thickly covered by legend;[78] but his loss, before he was forty, robbed his new-born state of a dynamic, not to say daemonic, leader. His son Cheng Ching was also a man of ability, and carried on the 'nation-building' work in Taiwan. The Dutch were now eager to regain prestige, if not Taiwan itself, and in mid-1663 sent Balthasar Bort to Foochow to co-ordinate action with the Ch'ing forces; he had the strongest fleet yet sent to Chinese waters—sixteen ships, 440 guns, 1382 seamen, 1234 soldiers.[79] The situation was complex: the Dutch wanted speedy revenge, the Chinese were prepared to wait on Cheng dissension to bring about a negotiated solution, Cheng Ching or his subordinates put out tempting peace-feelers to both parties. The Dutch were not always clear on their own objectives: it might be better to let Taiwan go and concentrate on forcing the Ch'ing to open trade at Foochow; and they were utterly lost in the maze of Chinese protocol and 'face'. However, in November 1663 the Ch'ing and the Hollanders together took Amoy and Quemoy, though Cheng Ching still held two points on the coast. There were more fruitless expeditions and shady negotiations, and in 1664 Keelung was reoccupied and held until 1668; but the end result of endless double-crossing all round was that the Cheng power was confined to Taiwan, while the Dutch had a few seasons of semi-licit but always difficult trade at Foochow. Neither Chinese nor Dutch could understand the other party's principles or rules of conduct; by 1670 Batavia had wearily come to recognise that only frustration came of formal embassies, and for a few years left the trade in the hands of the 'free burghers', self-employed locally based Hollanders. This was mostly a contraband traffic in the Canton region.[80]

There was a Taiwanese *revanche* in 1674–5, when Cheng Ching took advantage of the 'Rebellion of the Three Feudatories' in Yunnan, Kwangtung, and Fukien to retake Amoy and besiege Ch'uan-chou in 1678. News of these events came to Batavia by burgher yachts bringing approaches from the rebel war-lords; conversely the Ch'ing once more saw advantage in a Dutch alliance. The English also intervened in Cheng-held Amoy and Taiwan; as a pay-back for the Dutch sabotage of the *Return*'s visit to Nagasaki, they in turn warned Cheng Ching of Dutch trading under Danish colours. But the Cheng intervention in the Rebellion of the Three Feudatories had at last roused the Ch'ing: *il faut en finir*. The EIC Directors' letter of November 1678 to Bantam sums all up: 'The warrs and revolutions that happen there will alter matters much . . . for if the Tartars recover Amoy, we can hope for no trade with China.'[81] And indeed when the Ch'ing finally took over Taiwan, the Company's factors had much difficulty in explaining away the advice—and guns—they had given Cheng Ching; a substantial bribe was needed.

The rebellion split up in mutual distrust, and by 1680 Cheng Ching was forced to abandon Amoy. When Cheng Chih-lung had made terms with the Ch'ing in 1646, one of his chief naval captains, Shih Lang, had entered their service; Coxinga had executed his family. Cheng Ching, a not unworthy son of his father, died in 1681; there was a succession dispute, and Shih Lang, now influential in the Imperial court, seized his chance. He was given command of 300 junks and 200,000 men, and in July 1683 decisively defeated the Taiwanese fleet off the Pescadores. Surrender followed quickly.

The Coxinga episode was over; had Coxinga himself lived to a normal span, it might have been much more than an episode—an Asian sea-state taking over where Hideyoshi and Ieyasu had left off. It is perhaps not entirely fanciful to see it as Asia's last chance to turn back the tide of European domination; but more probably such a maritime enterprise was too much at variance with the whole Chinese tradition, agrarian and bureaucratic, which placed the scholar and the farmer above the merchant and the warrior.[82] Once the moment was passed, each succeeding decade increased the odds in Europe's favour through her giant advances both in technology and in money power, the latter paradoxically drawn so largely from the exploitation of Asian peoples and resources.

As it was, Taiwan under the Ch'ing had an interesting internal history; but to an extent astonishing in view of its geographical location it became for Europeans virtually *terra incognita*. The Ch'ing restriction of foreign commerce to Canton was perhaps the main factor in this: until the mid-nineteenth-century opening of more northerly Treaty Ports and of Japan, main shipping routes did not pass too close. Hence outside contacts were sporadic, and did not become significant until the Opium War of 1840. For over a century and a half, the only new 'information' on Taiwan available to the West was George Psalmanazaar's splendid and elaborate hoax *An Historical and Geographical Description of Formosa* (1704) and the little less odd account by the Polish adventurer Count Benyowsky, who spent seventeen days on the island in 1771, and proposed its colonisation in a document which tells us more of the spirit of his age than of Taiwan.[83]

Chapter 4

SURVIVALS AND ARRIVALS IN EAST ASIA

> ... les merchandises ne sont pas une matière sans
> âme; elles sont solidaires de la civilisation qui
> les produit... La marchandise, quelle qu'elle soit,
> porte avec elle une philosophie practique et une
> doctrine de la vie....

The take-over of the seventeenth century

Immemorially—certainly from as far back as the contacts between the Han and the Antonine dynasties[1]—the Pacific margins of Asia had been enmeshed in a web of thalassic trade, linking them to a Europe always hankering for spices and silks, by maritime and overland routes which debouched into the Mediterranean world between the mouths of the Nile and the Don. The Spaniards opened an entirely new trans-Pacific route via the Philippines; but they had practically no merchandise of their own to distribute even had Asians wanted it (they did not), and they scarcely lifted a finger to collect their return cargoes: the Sangleys at Manila did that for them. The Portuguese also opened a completely new route to Europe, but only briefly were they able to divert the bulk of the spice trade through it: by the 1560s or 1570s as much went by the Red Sea, especially from Atjeh, as by the Cape of Good Hope.[2] In 1600 they had also a favoured position in Japan, where direct trade with China was inhibited by Ming embargoes. The Portuguese Crown claimed no monopoly except for spices and for the Macao-Nagasaki trade, which was granted or farmed out to grandees and their clientèle attached to the former city; but the 'Estado da India' did endeavour to exert control over regional shipping and to profit by customs and port duties, by a system of *cartazes* or 'navicerts'. These could be evaded—there were few ports directly in Portuguese hands, and Afonso de Albuquerque, the major architect of the system, had failed in 1513 to capture Aden, the key to the Red Sea; costs of surveillance were heavy, and the whole system was very vulnerable to corruption. Apart from spices, the 'monopoly', so far as it existed, was a racketeering one—the selling of protection, or of exemption from further extortion, on the shipping routes.[3]

Fundamentally, the Portuguese were 'late mediaevals' rather than 'early moderns' like the English and *a fortiori* the Dutch, and by that very fact—and despite their Catholic ardour—they fitted more smoothly into the less secular Asian *Weltanschauung*: 'The Portuguese colonial regime, then, did not introduce a single new economic element into the commerce of southern Asia', rather they were indirect borrowers.[4] Steensgaard is unduly picturesque when he says that 'the

---

Sylvain Levi, quoted in L. Dermigny, *Le Commerce à Canton* (Paris 1964), I.14.

85

warrior, not the merchant, became the dominant figure in the *Estado da India*'; the line between them was soon very thin, most officials and ecclesiastics being either active traders or investors in regional traffic, and Steensgaard himself goes on to say that 'the most important entrepreneurs were the officials themselves' and that the trade did not deviate from the Asian pattern.[5] Albuquerque's conscious decision to make up for paucity of manpower by miscegenation, theoretically in lawful wedlock, not only produced many picaresque characters but meant that in time the Asian posts became 'home' to many Portuguese, in contrast to their northern rivals—a point, as we have seen, well taken by Anthonio van Diemen.

From the point of view of the Portuguese State, this was a weakness—it made it harder to give up unprofitable and untenable outposts, as is witnessed by the long series of stubborn last-ditch defences from Ormuz in 1622 to Bassein in 1739.[6] But on another view, it was a strength; in places where they were long supplanted by the Dutch, such as Ceylon and Malacca, the Lusitanians have left a stronger cultural impress than their rivals. Commercially, they as it were integrated themselves into the indigenous trading complex that they had not been able to supersede, and hence the astonishing resilience of Macao after the almost simultaneous catastrophes of the fall of Malacca and the expulsion from Japan.[7]

Around 1600, then, the trade position in the East Asian seas looked relatively simple. The Portuguese held the Malacca-Macao-Nagasaki route and a good share of the spice and pepper trades from the Moluccas and Bantam; the Spaniards the Galleon trade, the great mediator between Mexican silver and Chinese silks. Carrack and Galleon were under the same Crown, but (apart from illicit trading) the link between them was in Chinese hands. Essentially, the Iberians ran the long-distance extra-Asian trade, imposed upon rather than implanted in the complex of indigenous commerce, as yet scarcely eroded. Indeed, as their links with the metropolis became more difficult to maintain (Goa itself was blockaded by the Dutch in the 1630s) the Portuguese tended to merge into this original complex.

By 1700 there had been immense changes. Portuguese and Spaniards were now overshadowed by the far more modern machines of the English and especially the Dutch East India Companies; the Portuguese indeed subsisted only marginally. There was a vast increase in the volume and value of traffic, accompanied by diversification: new commodities had become, or were on the way to becoming, staples of trade—cottons, coffee, tea, copper. The course of commerce was punctuated by dramatic political events—the 'Massacre of Amboyna'; the defeats of Iskandar Muda of Atjeh off Malacca and of Sultan Agung at Batavia, both in 1629; the long sequence of Dutch attacks on Manila; the fall of Malacca and the defensive triumph of Macao; in Japan the tragedy of Shimabara and the closure of all the country but for Deshima; the Ch'ing conquest of China and its offshoot the Coxingan feat in Taiwan; the VOC's devastation of the Spiceries and suppression of Makassar. But if the century's leitmotiv was the stubborn pursuit by the Dutch of economic hegemony, its closing decades saw two new openings in which they had little or no share: the beginnings of the China trade, in which the English were to make the running, and the arrival of the Russians on Pacific shores.

Not only was the VOC unable to shut out European competition in East Asia, but the indigenous polities themselves showed marked powers of resistance. Before tracing the growth and changes of the great mercantilist enterprises, we may glance at the fortunes of the southeast Asian trading states, still worthy of the title 'country powers'.

The survival of indigenous polities

In southeast Asia the Europeans had to come to terms with a sophisticated system of organised states; if there was no need for the suppliant approach demanded in China and eventually in Japan, neither was there 'room for the application of titles of discovery or occupation of terra nullius'.[8] Although by and large the newcomers were better found technologically (at least, and 'at least' is much, in armament), they were working with limited manpower at the extremities of enormously long lines of communication, and so initially the terms were not too unequal; even much later, 'the monopoly contracts for a particular product at a specific location ... account for only a small fraction of the business transactions involving Europeans with non-Europeans'.[9]

Trading opportunities therefore depended very much on the political behaviour both of the Europeans and of the indigenous rulers, some of whom—and not only those of China and Japan—controlled superior force. Nor were their principles and practices always compatible with Western concepts of mercantile justice and the sanctity of contract. While diplomatic style and courtesies were fully as well developed in Asia as in Europe (often indeed protocol was frustratingly intricate), and European lodgements were facilitated by the age-old custom of granting groups of alien merchants immunities sometimes amounting to self-government, there were inevitable misunderstandings and frictions. Especially awkward was the general assumption of Asian rulers that agreements were personal to themselves and did not bind their successors. From a strictly commercial point of view, however, discrepancies in aim and practice were not often great enough to drive away trade altogether.[10] Whatever may have been the Imperial stance in China, even there local officials and merchants had an eye to the main chance, and else-where pious Muslims and Hindus were as much seized of, or by, the profit motive as pious Calvinists, and had as good techniques for its satisfaction.

In the long run, the Europeans' strongest weapon was perhaps not so much in gunnery or capital or book-keeping as in their possession of a coherent policy with the one over-riding objective of trade expansion: it may be significant that the European State which gave most weight to prestige and power was France, and on the whole its commercial record was the most depressing; glory and good account-ing didn't mix. There was of course much faltering, much trial and error, in the application of policy, and eventually, through the need to secure continuity of supply on favourable terms, the single-minded pursuit of trade became entangled in political ramifications, initially undesired and often embarrassing;[11] but by then the Companies had built up greater resources to cope. In contrast, the congeries of local states (as in the break-down of late Mogul India) had no one central aim and was riddled not only by inter-state rivalries but by intra-state dynastic feuds, the two often enough running in harness. In such an 'international anarchy', the short-term advantage of securing European aid led to a long-term creeping take-over by the 'great and powerful friend', whether the EIC in India or the VOC in the Indies.

Yet the country powers maintained independent activity, often aggressive enough (especially amongst themselves), for much longer than is usually recognised: the European rise into hegemony was truly the great over-riding factor in the long run, until say the Japanese victory of 1904–5, but it was not the smooth almost automatic triumph of new forces that it tends to appear in general histories. Perhaps indeed the possibility of reversing the secular trend in Indonesia died (ironically, with Jan Pieterszoon Coen himself) when Sultan Agung failed to take Batavia in 1629, and the seal was set on the VOC's commercial dominion half a century later, with the fall of Makassar and Bantam; but for a long time yet the Dutch could not accept the risks and costs of full political control, except in very limited areas such as the environs of Batavia, Malacca, a few other bases, and the Bandas.[12]

The power of Iskandar Muda of Atjeh was also decisively checked in 1629, but at the hands not of the Dutch but of a strange alliance—the Malaccan Portuguese, Johore whose Sultan was the heritor of the royal house expelled from Malacca by the forebears of these same Portuguese, and Patani. When Malacca did fall to the Dutch, the VOC found itself enforced to protect Johore in order to contain Atjeh, despite complaints from its Malaccan factory faced by Johorean competition. Later, and paradoxically enough, the Dutch success against Makassar led to a swarming of displaced sea-rovers into Java and as far as the Malay peninsula, and this new, dynamic, and turbulent element meant that Batavia had once more to prop up Johore in an endeavour to control, cheaply, wandering piratical rajas. The kaleido-scopic political shifts need not concern us, but it is worth noting that the Buginese brought war to the very gates of Malacca in 1756–7, and as late as 1783 badly defeated a considerable Dutch fleet at Riau, off modern Singapore.[13] In a sense the toleration by the Dutch of all this political turmoil, while all the time tightening their commercial control, seems a preview of the 'informal imperialism'—taking the trading profits but not taking on the costs of governance—of the United States in much of Latin America in the present century.

European activities, then, must always be seen against this background of indigenous politics and commerce, potent factors in their own right far into the eighteenth century. Their commerce was thalassic, not oceanic; but the European-run long-distance trades of the Indian Ocean and the Pacific depended to a very great extent on the pre-existing commercial networks of the south and east Asian seas, their essential feeders. The organisational details of these indigenous trading patterns, complex and fascinating as they are, cannot be discussed at any length here—they are amply documented by van Leur and Meilink-Roelofsz—but a few salient points may be noted.

The complex of traffic was by no means a petty trade or confined to small cargoes of spices and luxuries. Malacca and the Spice Islands, for instance, had little arable land and had to be supplied with rice and other foodstuffs; hence Japara in Java, a major supplier of foodstuffs, had junks which could carry up to 400 tons, larger than the standard bulk-carriers of northwest Europe, though most local craft were smaller.[14] There has been some dispute as to whether this can be called a 'peddling trade'; certainly some of it resembles tramp trading, but as well as 'pedlars' the participants included very solid merchants, and also princes and their nobles and officials; and some in each class could command very substantial capital sums, which at times were called upon for working capital even by the great Companies. Indeed, Europeans sometimes baulked at the scale of propositions put to them: in 1628 Coxinga's father Iquan, the 'pirate' governing Amoy, offered the VOC a three-year contract to supply silk to the value of 300,000 reals a year, to be paid for partly in pepper but mostly in silver; the affair was too big for the VOC to risk it.[15] As Furber puts it, 'the "free enterprise" of individual merchants or small family groups and not the "corporation" was dominant in the eastern seas long before the Europeans arrived and remained so after their coming'; which does not mean that these groups, merchant or princely, were averse to trying their hands at corners or monopolies when conditions seemed right: we have seen Coen's horror at the 'hideous' Bantam pepper ring.[16] Financial relations between Asian and European traders were intricate, loans flowing both ways; English, Portuguese, and Danes contributed to the rise of Makassar by bottomry loans. At times the VOC itself depended on Chinese junks, or even the Macaonese, for the transport of goods from and pepper to China.[17]

Apart from the Chinese, who despite massacres at Manila (and in 1740 at Batavia) were indestructible, the leading regional trading powers after the incomplete decline of Atjeh were Bantam in Java and Makassar on Celebes (Sulawesi). Most of the Javanese rulers were too close to the seat of Dutch power and too much locked in intra-island conflicts, and hence open to manipulation by Batavia, to maintain their old external links; their once flourishing ports declined until in 1657 even Japara had to appeal for Dutch pilots to carry on petty cabotage: 'the sea is large and the Javanese cannot sail it...'.[18] But Makassar became a city of refuge: for Malays from a Johore constantly under attack by Iskandar Muda; for refugees fleeing from the ruthless devastation of the Spiceries; and for Portuguese from Malacca. It had a Portuguese colony amounting at times to some 500 souls, including the notable Francisco Vieira de Figueiredo, trading amongst other things in sandalwood from the Sundas and Timor and, when they could get them, in spices smuggled across Celebes.[19] Makassar was not only a link in Portuguese trade between the Indian Ocean, Timor, and Macao, but developed its own shipping and its own commerce.

Obviously this could not be allowed to last. By 1656 the VOC had deliberately

ruined the Moluccas as a spice supplier by the wholesale destruction of clove trees, a
sort of economic genocide to keep output down and prices (at the Amsterdam end)
up; and after a delay caused by the Luso-Dutch wars in Ceylon and Malabar, it was
Makassar's turn. The Dutch were very materially assisted, as usual, by local rivalries,
and in particular by the moral and material aid of the dynamic ruler of adjacent
Bone, Arung Palakka. The Sultan Hasanuddin put up a tough and protracted resistance, but in 1667 he was forced to accept Dutch overlordship; kicking against the
pricks, he was deposed and pensioned off two years later. The VOC was now in
control of the trade and external relations of south Sulawesi, but Arung Palakka
remained a power in the land, and in some contexts it would be hard to say which
was patron and which client. As usual on the fall of a trading kingdom, the
dispossessed dispersed into 'piracy', really a continuation of hostilities by a maritime
guerrilla which could never quite be put down. Meanwhile, the able Sultan
Abulfatah Agung had made Bantam into an entrepôt for merchants of all nations,
European or Asian, and developed his own shipping; but once again a succession
war played into Dutch hands and in 1684 Bantam had to accept strict Dutch
control. The English were expelled and had to fall back on Benculen, on the
Sumatran west coast.[20]

From now on indigenous shipping was more and more squeezed out: 'The
Dutch company used the *cartaz* far more ruthlessly against Asian shipping than did
the Portuguese ... to eliminate Asian shipping from a particular region.'[21] In the
geographical and political conditions of the east Asian seas, the supersession could
not be total—Makassar craft were trading to Kedah a century after the city's fall,
and in 1803 Flinders met some of a fleet of sixty Makassar praus fishing for trepang
(bêche-de-mer) on the Australian coast, at the northeast tip of Arnhem Land.[22] In
time, however, locally owned and run vessels were reduced to merely filling in the
decreasing gaps in the European network. Always excepting the Chinese junk
trade, the place of the Asian traders was taken over by European 'country traders',
including as one might say 'honorary Europeans' such as Armenians and Parsees
under British protection, or Asians used as front men for interlopers. Unlike the
EIC, the VOC managed to keep this local trade, feeding the main intercontinental
lines, in its own hands, the 'free burghers' of Batavia, last remnants of Coen's grand
colonising design, being allowed only a minor role.

Trade not directly connected with either of the two great Companies flourished
exceedingly, but it was in the main carried on by a motley collection of merchant
adventurers, often dubious in their origins and practices, and often indeed the
agents for illicit on-the-side activities by Company officials. They included English,
Armenians from Madras, Portuguese and their mestizos, Danes, interloping
Ostenders disguised as an 'Imperial Company' which again was often a cover for
Dutch and British speculators and smugglers, including Jacobites—a mixed bag
indeed, and their exploits a saga of skulduggery.[23] Their crews, however, were very
largely Asian or Eurasian, in every variety, and Asian merchants continued to be
very active as suppliers, agents and factors, financiers, and partners in interloping

ventures. Atjeh lingered on, with independent external connections, far into the nineteenth century; but with the fall of Makassar and Bantam the indigenous emporia, the great trading sultanates, were gone, and their glory had departed, to be thinly reflected in the tinsel show of fossil Courts like those of the Princes of the British Raj.

Some 'terms of trade'

'The trade of Asia is the foundation of commerce'[24]—in a macro-sense, this statement has been true enough since Roman times, though it should be added that in our period the world's commerce was powered by American silver. European trade with Asia was most one-sided, and this injection of silver was the only way in which it could be carried on, since the Emperor Ch'ien Lung's superb reply to Lord Macartney's embassy of 1793 was neither mere arrogance nor bargaining:

> Our celestial Empire possesses all things in prolific abundance and
> lacks no product within its borders. There is, therefore, no need to
> import the manufactures of outside barbarians. . . . But the tea and
> porcelain which the celestial Empire produces are absolute necessities
> to European nations.[25]

Much the same was true, *mutatis mutandis*, in India and the Indies.

Critical as the Euro-Asian trade has been in the growth of the world economy, it should be noted that it was only a small fraction of European commerce, and during the spice age (and even after) its real impact on the metropolitan economies was restricted. As regards production, it had little multiplier effect—that came later with the growth of mass markets for tea and cottons; earlier, indeed, Asian textile exports seriously depressed such industries as Lyons silk-weaving and Spitalfields calico-printing.[26] Later still, the pattern was reversed; with the import of raw cotton for European mills and the flood of mass-produced Manchester goods, it was the turn of Asian industries to be depressed. But of course these far-flung and exotic trades had much prestige, in part simply because they were far-flung and exotic, in part because profits—especially gross profits—could be spectacular in lines such as porcelain, silks, and spices, in which the difference between the buying price in Asia and the selling price in Europe was high, and as regards spices kept artificially high by the VOC's restriction on output. Moreover, the great Companies were political entities in Asia, and at home they were powerful moneyed corporations closely linked with governing groups. The surface of their affairs was highly visible, however designedly obscure and even murky their depths: outsiders often regarded them askance, like today's multinationals. Hence the Companies attracted attention disproportionate to the scale of their strictly commercial workings.

They were in truth massive operations on the scale of their times; yet their share of total commercial resources and operations was quantitatively surprisingly small. At a time when the total shipping of the United Netherlands was numbered in thousands of keels (most of course small), there were only about a score of big East

Indiamen, and van Leur estimated that in the 1620s the VOC's tonnage in Asian waters was only a fraction of Indonesian, though 'the significance of the centralised shipping to Europe . . . is clear.'[27] As regards tonnage and personnel, the Asian trade was dwarfed by the carrying trade in European waters and the fisheries: 'As late as 1666 it was estimated that three-fourths of the capital active on the Amsterdam bourse was engaged in the Baltic trade.'[28] For England, the figures tell a similar story even later: in the seventeenth century the tonnage needed for the East Indian trade was rather over 6 per cent of the total needed for overseas trade, and in 1771–3 it was still only 7.7 per cent. Export tonnage needs were minimal—the only export commodity calling for over 1000 tons was lead, which went out mainly as ballast but hopefully might be sold and replaced as such by saltpetre or Japanese copper. Import values in 1699–1701 were 13.1 per cent of the total, exports the lowest of any of the recognised branches of English overseas trade—2.15 per cent.[29]

What had begun with the Portuguese as overwhelmingly a spice trade changed greatly during the seventeenth century. Taking the values of VOC cargoes when shipped from Asia as a rough guide, in 1619–21 spices and pepper amounted to 74 per cent (pepper alone over 56 per cent) and the only other significant items were textiles and fibres, at this stage predominantly silk, with 16 per cent, and drugs with nearly 10. By 1699–1700 textiles, by now nearly half cotton, were over 54 per cent, spices and pepper had equal shares in 23 per cent; drugs were fairly steady, tea and coffee together 4 per cent, but sugar, which had been significant in mid-century, was again negligible. Metals, insignificant in 1619–21, were over 5 per cent by the century's end, mainly Japanese copper; saltpetre, used as ballast and in great demand in the Europe of Louis XIV's wars, about 4 per cent.[30] As for porcelain, which together with silk 'best defined the prestige of China' in European eyes, in the seventeenth century Japan was the main supplier—the Chinese industry declined massively during the Ming troubles, not reviving until after 1680, and Japan filled the breach, even producing, to Dutch orders, in Chinese styles.[31]

The reverse flow of commodities from Europe did not amount to much, although European gadgetry found a market in East Asia. Ballast lead could be sold, and in the eighteenth century there was an increase in sales of iron wares; in some regions there was a demand for military and marine stores, but there could be political objections to selling these to local warlords, unless of course 'it is to be feared that a refusal would lead them to call upon other Europeans . . . who would not fail to supply them'—a foretaste of our own age of U2s and MIGs and 'arms diplomacy'.[32] Hard pushing of European textiles rarely found a good response and often meant a loss; the intra-Asian trade in piece-goods was far greater. Until well into the eighteenth century, the major European export remained what it had been—silver. The 'desire to export at all costs, born of an economic necessity, the need to support European textile industries, and of a mental attitude, [the drive to] the Eurocentric standardisation of the world by trade', had to wait on the Industrial Revolution for its fulfilment.[33]

East Asian trade and Japan

'East India' trade was in essence a network of trades ranging from the Red Sea and the Persian Gulf to the Moluccas and Timor, held together by the very active country shipping, Asian and European, and by the European control on the long-distance runs across the Indian Ocean and the Pacific. Paradoxical as it may seem, much of this commerce hinged on a Japan that was geographically eccentric—the farthest European outreach into the Pacific—and culturally and commercially self-isolated. In a sense, Japan was a locked chest holding treasure essential to the conduct of trade, and of Europeans only the Dutch held a key; English attempts to get one were fumbling. Not only was the Deshima trade in itself perhaps the most profitable of the VOC's activities, it was also the source of precious metals, the necessary catalysts.[34]

Although in time the 'India' Companies, other than the VOC, became really China Companies, until about 1680 Japan still occupied 'a much more important place than China in the commercial strategy of the Europeans'; the seventeenth century was dominated by 'the double primacy of the Dutch presence and the Japanese magnet [*attraction*]', especially in the period 1640–80—the time of the great crisis of the Ch'ing conquest of China, and also of the worst days of that other great silver-chest, Manila, while the English were still uncertain as to their aims and methods.[35] After 1680 there is a new linkage, of the EIC with China, the Dutch virtually withdrawing, while the old China-Japan junk traffic revives; it is significant that the Dutch were late starters at Canton, and indeed had less trade there than the combined Danish and Swedish Companies.[36] As late as the 1720s, fear that the EIC's success at Canton was bringing the English closer to Japan and its copper, which in the seventeenth century was 'promoted almost to the status of a precious metal', was an argument for holding on at Deshima, despite declining profits there.[37]

It is no wonder, then, that the Japanese market was carefully nursed. Thus Chinese raw silk was valued more highly than Persian or Bengali, and the last, though cheapest of the three at source, fetched more in Europe than did Persian, and unlike Persian could be sold in Japan. But Batavia's supplies from China were indirect and irregular, and to keep the Deshima market sweet, 'Where the Dutch demand collided with demand ... in Japan, Japan was first of all taken into consideration ... the rule was introduced that the wishes of the Japan office should come before everything else...'.[38]

'Down to 1668 the stream of silver from Japan was an essential factor in the [Dutch] Company's trade in Asia'; in that year its export was banned by the Bakufu, but the VOC was able to turn to Japanese gold. In the long run, however, the restriction advantaged the English, more solidly established at Canton where the gold:silver ratio was 1:10 (at times even less) against a standard European ratio of 1:15; the benefit of exchanging silver for gold at these rates was also a motive in the French voyages to China by the South Sea, tapping the silver of Peru *en route*, during the War of the Spanish Succession.[39] Nevertheless, the VOC's unique position at Deshima enabled it to dominate the extremely important trade in Japanese copper; at least against other Europeans, though not, after 1685, against the Chinese.

Before the advent of the Dutch, Japanese copper had reached as far as Arabia, via Malacca and Bantam, and it remained largely an intra-Asian trade; for eighty years it was 'the great driving-force' of European trade in Asia, and its rise is linked with the fall in American silver output. Apart from its use for small change, for receptacles of all sorts, for implements and instruments, there was an important Asian demand for copper as a roofing material and for statues of the Buddha, small or immense.[40] Shipments to Europe began in the 1620s; profits were not as high as the Heeren XVII would have liked, but after all it doubled as ballast. It was probably this, together with the big Spanish mintage of *vellon* in the first half of that decade, which enabled Japanese copper to have some place in western markets alongside that of Sweden, far the biggest European producer. There was a check when the Japanese banned its export, from 1638 to 1645, and European copper had to be sent to Batavia. With the lifting of the ban 'the copper bars poured out' and in 1655 the Heeren XVII for the first time entered Japanese copper in their list of the most important return commodities; prices for Javanese sugar, also a return ballast, were low, and Batavia was told that it could not send too much copper. In fact, however, only about a quarter of the home orders was met—it was essential that shipments to Europe should not prejudice sales in Asia.

In 1668 the Bakufu embargoed both silver and copper, in the interests of the Japanese currency; the silver ban was permanent and gold became dearer, so that when copper was released again in 1670, it soon became dominant. In the early 1680s enhanced demand in India and low prices at Amsterdam inhibited exports to Europe; they began again in 1689, perhaps significantly the opening year of another general war in Europe. Partly under the stimulus of Indian demand, but mainly with the idea of cutting off the supply by Chinese traders to the English and other trespassers on Dutch reserves, the VOC proposed to buy up the entire copper export of Japan. It was unlucky for this projected corner that the move coincided with a massive demand from China to stabilise her copper currency.[41] The Japanese naturally refused to tie their hands, and indeed took steps to stop the copper drain—their home market, for building and coinage, was substantial—by fixing maximum export quotas, allowing the Chinese twice as much as the Dutch. The expansion of direct Sino-Japanese trade cut into the supply of silk to Manila, and offered very strong competition to the VOC in Japan itself.

Some copper was still sent to Europe when demand or price was high as a result of the wars (Swedish as well as French) and supply in Asia was good, but the latter was decreasingly the case. In 1731 the English started shipping Swedish copper to Asia; by the 1760s this was competing seriously with the VOC's supplies from Japan. Governor-General van Imhoff (1743–50) still held that 'Next to spices copper was the Company's most important article of commerce, and so the trade to

Japan exclusively ought to be carried on from this point of view'; but he also found himself impelled to send two ships direct to Acapulco to trade for silver; an initiative naturally rebuffed by the Spaniards, and also rebuked by the Heeren XVII.[42] These tangled stories of silk and copper illustrate the very real limitations within which Dutch 'hegemony' and 'monopoly' had to work, and the real strength which could be exercised by local bureaucracies and entrepreneurs.

The Netherlands' 'monopoly'

As van Leur points out, to speak of a 'Company Indies' in the first half of the seventeenth century 'would appear premature. The control of a few points on the intra-Asian trade routes had also formed the power of the Portuguese.' In 1650 the Heeren XVII issued 'Instructions for the Government in the Indies' which clearly set out three classes of trade: from directly governed factories, and conquests such as the Bandas; by forced monopoly contracts as in the Moluccas and Amboyna; and elsewhere trade freely negotiated with the rulers and 'alongside merchants of all other nations'. Already, however, the debate between Coen and Reael had fore-shadowed the more ruthless policy which by the end of the century enabled the VOC to fix at least clove and nutmeg prices completely—both the buying price in Asia and the selling price in Europe.[43]

This was not achieved simply by superior commercial techniques and resources, and was not a merely economic domination: it depended directly on superior armament and a careful selection of targets. Amboyna, the Bandas, the Moluccas were easy prey: small islands with their people concentrated on the coast, not self-sufficing in food or clothing, and (unlike the sultanates in the west of the Indies) with no naval force to speak of; and they could produce more cloves, nutmegs, and mace than the world could consume. The Company could now do 'pioneer work in the techniques of synthetic scarcities, a branch of economics which has become increasingly important.'[44] The particular technique was simply the cutting down of all clove and nutmeg trees, outside small specified areas, by armed inspections—or raids. Production of cloves was allowed only in Amboyna and nutmegs only in the Bandas, resettled on slave-plantation lines after Coen's genocidal devastations; here the number of trees was strictly controlled, while the inhabitants, officially styled 'privileged', had the privilege of selling their output and buying their needs at the Company's prices. The art of extortion has rarely been screwed up to a higher pitch. Well might we say with the Portuguese historian of a century earlier that since God made the clove, it may be accounted good—but in truth 'an apple of all discord', more to be cursed than gold itself.[45]

As we have seen, the monopoly could not be extended to pepper, and even for cloves and nutmegs its success carried the hazard of over-pricing in Europe, and hence consumer resistance. Good businessmen as they were, the Heeren XVII were of course aware of this danger and endeavoured to adjust supplies and prices accordingly; they succeeded in keeping the Amsterdam price of cloves constant from 1677 to 1744, though not without some fall in turnover.[46] There were more concealed risks: failure to revise cost structures set in the mid-seventeenth century; accounting never fully broken-down nor up-to-date, which gave an increasingly distorted picture of the VOC's financial position; the concentration of energy on attaining and maintaining the spice monopoly; complacency in its success. The Company fumbled the great opportunity afforded by the rise of the China tea trade, and 'In the eighteenth century it was the Company's misfortune to develop no adequate substitute for spices.'[47]

The system was geared to the maintenance of a static position, in a rapidly changing world; it is true that Dutch resources, strained by the long sequence of wars, could not have afforded an adventurous forward policy. Although the VOC remained dominant in the spice trade nearly until its liquidation in 1795, the writing on the wall appeared when in 1770–1 the appropriately named Pierre Poivre at last succeeded in introducing cloves and nutmegs to the Ile de France (Mauritius).[48] Meanwhile the English—Company and country traders—retained more than a negligible hold in pepper and dominated the Asia piece-goods trade and the tea of Canton. The Golden Century of the Netherlands was over.

The opening of the China trade

The supplanting of the Netherlands by Britain as the dominant sharer in the European trade with eastern Asia was essentially the work of the eighteenth century, but the beginning of this evolution, in which China replaced Japan as the magnet, belongs to the seventeenth: the foundations were laid between 1670 and 1710, when the pattern of Chinese trading was painfully learnt. At the same time the Russians were opening a new route to China, by land across Siberia, of less immediate notoriety but in the long run of no less significance in Pacific or rather global geopolitics: the Treaty of Nerchinsk, defining Sino-Russian relations for nearly two centuries, was concluded in 1689, almost mid-point between 1670 and 1710.

In the evolution of the China trade, Canton replaced Macao as the main European point of contact with China, although its position on the approaches to Canton meant that Macao retained considerable importance: as a place to pick up essential information on trading conditions up-river, as a shelter for interlopers and cover for their numerous chicaneries, and not least as a place of rest and recreation, during the off-season, for the merchants and clerks cooped up in the factories at Canton, where they were almost as closely confined as the Dutch at Deshima but (in stark contrast to Japanese amenities) without the alleviation of any female company whatsoever, Chinese or European.[49]

Initially, both English and Dutch tried to by-pass the 'barrage' of Macao, and get direct access to Chinese silks for Japan, by using Hirado as a base; later, attention turned to Taiwan and Amoy.[50] Not much came of this: we have seen the poor results of the Dutch entanglement with the Ch'ing at Amoy and Foochow and that of the English with Coxinga's heirs. Conditions along the coast were too unsettled and the new Manchu officials, unlettered military men, too much inclined to charge more than the traffic would bear. Not until the Ch'ing were in really undisturbed control, after the Rebellion of the Three Feudatories and the conquest of Taiwan, could trade be put on a regular footing; and then it was very much on Chinese terms, terms disagreeable enough to the Europeans but inescapable. In 1684 the Emperor Kang-hsi issued an edict favouring foreign trade, but in practice Peking endeavoured, successfully, to restrict it to a few points fixed as far as possible from the centre of things: in the north Kiakhta, just on the Russian side of the Mongolian border; in the south Canton—there would be no need for barbarian ships to come further up the coast. In the next century European merchants became restricted to the tiny strip (about 310 by 200 metres) of Thirteen Factory Street along the Pearl River—a narrow slit indeed through which to view the Celestial Empire.[51]

Although 'Cathay' had been an ultimate objective for attempts to discover the Northwest or Northeast Passage from John Cabot's day onwards, the first English move to open direct trade with China was Edward Fenton's voyage of 1582, sponsored by Queen Elizabeth's favourite, Leicester; a botched venture which fell to pieces in the Atlantic. In 1596 Leicester's son Sir Robert Dudley tried again, sending out three ships under Benjamin Wood. Hakluyt ends his *Principal Navigations* with the Queen's commendatory letter to 'the most puissant Governour of the great kingdome of China ... great monarke of the orientall regions of the world' and the inconclusive editorial comment, strangely plaintive for so great and robust a work, that there is no news: perhaps Wood's company has been detained by the Emperor of China, perhaps they have fallen victims to 'some treacherie ... by the Portugales of Macao, or the Spaniards of the Philippinas.' In fact, all the company except one Frenchman perished by misadventures between Malaya and Mauritius.[52]

Apart from the interloping voyage of Sir Edward Michelborne (1604–6), which got as far as Patani, where John Davis was killed in a fight with Japanese pirates, the first attempt actually to reach Chinese waters was made by the *London* in 1635— from India, in response to a 'Truce and Free Trade' arranged between the Viceroy at Goa and the EIC's President at Surat, William Methwold. The Viceroy saw the agreement as a device to run the Dutch blockade under a neutral flag; Methwold as one to get a foot inside the Chinese door. The Macaonese on the spot naturally saw through this and had no difficulty in raising impediments with the Chinese; the venture failed.

The next, and the first full-scale, English attempt also tried to capitalise on the 'Truce and Free Trade', but was not made by the EIC but by the rival Courteen Company which, alleging that the EIC had failed to make proper use of its privileges, obtained an over-generous charter from Charles I, himself an investor. The Commission to John Weddell and Nathaniel Mountney (both ex-EIC servants) had a remarkable geographical range, including Madagascar, Socotra, Japan, and both the Northeast and Northwest Passages, and authorised them to fly the Union colours.[53] In June 1637 Weddell arrived at Macao with three ships and a pinnace; but the Macaonese again were not co-operative. It was not only the fear of losing to the English the trade on which they depended for very life, but fear of the reactions of the Chinese, who had been angry enough at the arrival of the *London* two years earlier. Now there were four stranger ships in the roadstead, and hence the Senators of Macao trembled for their title in 'this city which, though it belongs to our King, the site thereof belongs to the Emperor of China.'[54] At the end of July Weddell took his ships up to The Bogue (Boca Tigris, the 'Tiger's Mouth') in the face of Chinese protests, and one of his boats, taking soundings, was fired upon but not hit.[55] He had no difficulty in taking one of the forts and beating off an attack by fireships; but meanwhile Mountney and two other merchants had been allowed into Canton, and detained there. Weddell consoled himself by burning a small town and some junks, but was deadlocked. He retired to Lintin Island and then to Macao; complicated negotiations through the Portuguese followed, and eventually the merchants were released and some trade allowed—against almost abject written apologies and a solemn promise never to return. The grandiose project was a failure.

There were other rather half-hearted and fruitless visits to Macao; despite the treaty of 1654 opening Portuguese possessions to English trade, the local authorities were as unhelpful as ever. They had good reason, since in the struggle against Cheng Ching the Manchus had adopted the old scorched littoral policy used by the Ming a century earlier, and the Portuguese secured exemption at some cost, being specifically warned against harbouring other foreign ships.[56] The EIC Directors in London still hankered after Japan and its metals, keeping up stations in Siam and Tongking in the hope of supplying her with silks; but the fiasco of the *Return*'s visit to Nagasaki in 1672 showed this to be a dead end. The local EIC officials grasped realities more quickly, and eventual success was due to them rather than to any headquarters policy.

'The real début of English trade to China' came in the 1670s when Henry Dacres, the factor at Bantam, sponsored voyages to Taiwan and Amoy, the latter temporarily held by Cheng Ching; the Directors followed rather grudgingly, and somehow the men on the spot pulled through the crisis of the Ch'ing conquest of Taiwan.[57] Trade resumed at Amoy in 1685–6, though with the usual difficulties of 'squeeze', and at the turn of the century at the Chusan Islands, erroneously thought to be the gateway to Nanking via Ningpo. 'For a few years there was confused trading to China', largely by private country ships under EIC licence. These were difficult years at home, the EIC being under violent attack which led to the chartering of a rival 'New Company' in 1698; it was this New or 'English Company' which in August 1699 made the first lodgement at Canton with the *Macclesfield*.[58] Her supercargo James Douglas rented a house at Canton for the whole season; not quite the beginning of the factory system, since consequent upon the successful voyage of their *Amphitrite* in 1698 the French had a permanent resident from that year, with some breaks between 1715 and 1735.

The *Macclesfield* was well received, selling her entire stock and contracting for almost a full lading; but it took almost nine months before Douglas could take delivery and satisfy all demands for duties and fees: the concept of 'f.o.b.' was difficult to apply. In fact, he lost the monsoon and did not sail for Chusan until July 1700. However, 'The English had now ... thrust their feet over the threshhold of the China trade, but had not yet obtained a seat at the table.'[59] With the consolidation of Ch'ing power in the south, trade became increasingly settled at Canton, a Viceregal capital, magnificently situated at the head of the great Si-kiang delta, far more wealthy and important than Amoy or *a fortiori* Chusan; in Dermigny's phrase, 'a sort of Far Eastern Amsterdam'. Twelve English ships totalling 4170 tons visited Canton in 1700–9; in 1740–9, forty-four with 21,162 tons—Company ships, plus some private country ships from Indian ports.[60]

It is difficult, or rather impossible, to give an adequate account of the complexities of trade at Canton within a small compass; and even the presentation of a few salient points must take us well into the eighteenth century.[61] The official Chinese proclamation of Canton as the sole port of entry in 1757, at least twenty years after it had supplanted other ports, merely set the seal on its extraordinary role as 'Morally, a Deshima transported from Nagasaki Roads to the banks of the Pearl River, but materially, from the amplitude of the trade and the resources it made available, a Batavia or a Calcutta.' The comparison with Deshima is significant: once more the ineluctable clash between an inward-looking polity in whose highly conservative scheme of things the merchantry held an inferior place, over against one wedded (again in Dermigny's phrase) to 'progress' as the motor-force of societies and to 'the Rights of Man and the Merchant'.[62]

This clash was compounded by an internal conflict between Imperial Peking, loftily aloof from the mundanities of trade, and the active littoral of the southwest, with its millennial tradition of overseas venturing by an enterprising merchantry, and also with badly underpaid short-tenure officials who had to supplement their salaries somehow. Hence the inordinate delays and the back-tracking of officials, their unpredictable and to the Europeans (even of that day) often outrageous demands for fees for highly artificial or indeed invisible services, the whole system of 'squeeze' which not only baffled and infuriated the alien merchants but also, as Dermigny brilliantly shows, served to undermine the Enlightenment vision (paradoxically, Jesuit-inspired) of the Celestial Empire as a pure and virtuous philosophocracy. Yet if after reading Morse's tedious detail of exaction piled upon exaction, we are tempted to agree with his remark that in the beginning the officials had not learnt how to shear the sheep without skinning it, we may also recall Baddeley's, that 'Europeans were probably shocked and grieved to find natives anywhere who could give them points' in craftiness and cheating.[63]

Certainly some things in the two societies were not totally alien. Corruption was assuredly not foreign to the Europe of that or any day, and once institutionalised, once the guide-lines are set, it can coexist with high standards of individual probity inside the system, as the reputation of the Canton Hong merchants demonstrates. Even bulk-buying by rings or guilds—the co-hong or Hong merchants—had its analogue in the Spanish pancada, not to mention the VOC's attempt to corner Japanese copper. The factory system represented a sort of 'embryonic extra-territoriality', again with European analogues of long standing such as the Hanseatic Steelyard in London itself; the institution by the Companies of Councils of their supercargoes, under a President, 'fitted in very well with the Chinese doctrine ... that a community of foreigners should have a chief or Taipan who could be held responsible for their conduct'—and with two or three thousand sailors ashore at Whampoa, below Canton itself, after months at sea, this was surely no sinecure. But while there was a certain political security, even privilege, the foreigners were enmeshed in a web of economic regulation and, to coin a word, irregulation.[64] This arose from the interposing of layers of subordinate officials between the Viceroy (approachable only in extremities), the Hoppo (*hopou*, the Imperial Commissioner of Customs), and the Chinese merchants. Everything had to be channelled through these 'Security Merchants', who fixed both buying and selling prices, were responsible for the right conduct of their European counterparts, and met the demands of the officials, who were good at thinking up new ones. The system had obviously a good deal of flexibility, if one allowed enough for unsuspected over-heads, and despite all its frustrations, it worked. That it did so was in no small part owing to the personal integrity of the leading Hong merchants.

As well as these obstacles and inconveniences more or less peculiar to the Chinese system, there were the more normal hazards of commerce, of which the chief was the lack of saleable European products:

> We cannot tell what to advise your Honours to send to these Parts,
> the natives being fond of nothing but Silver and Lead; and probably if
> the rest of your Goods were thrown overboard at Sea, your Cargoes
> home would not be much the less.[65]

It was extremely difficult to sell cloth, which was sometimes held over for years, or had to be exhanged for truck, which was against Company policy. Hence, while by law 20 per cent by value of outward cargoes should have been English products, in practice 90 per cent or more were silver until far into the eighteenth century, and only in the last thirty years or so of that century does merchandise bulk really large. In these years the opium trade was growing, although mainly in the hands of 'country traders' and largely by smuggling; it could be held—at this stage—that 'the opium trade was dangerous to the merchandise trade from England, for it turned the buying capacity of the Chinese from British merchandise to Indian opium',[66] until the increasing cheapness of Manchester goods brought a new dimension into the equation.

Return cargoes in the earlier years were largely raw silk and silk fabrics (which remained a leading branch even when import into England was legally restricted), gold, porcelain, and varying amounts of mercury, alum, and tutenague, a copper-zinc-nickel alloy. Tea in Europe was initially more of a medicine than a social beverage, and imported in very small quantities, though it was taxed in England as early as 1689. By 1702 the Directors of the London Company informed their agents that 'Tea does very much obtaine in reputacōn among persons of all qualities', and by the 1720s it formed 57 to 67 per cent by value of some home ladings.[67]

It goes without saying that the English were not allowed to monopolise the lucrative trade of this port where access was free, if not exactly welcoming, to all; the French *Amphitrite* had preceded the *Macclesfield*. The extremely high English duties on tea—they reached 119 per cent in 1784, when Pitt cut them to 12.5—were a standing invitation to smuggling, and the game was entered into by French, Danes, Swedes, and Ostenders with as much zeal as ever British merchants contrabanded in the Spanish Indies; Canton's neutrality gave smaller powers their chance. Of these the Danish and Swedish Companies were the most solid and best run. The Spanish Netherlands, with Ostend, passed into Austrian hands by the Treaty of Rastatt (1714), and the Ostenders claimed title from the Holy Roman Empire; but they included private as well as Imperial Company traders, and used Polish, Prussian, and even the ancient Burgundian colours, not to mention British captains and seamen; real fly-by-nighters, as shown by the Ostend-owned but nominally German ship which left Trieste as the *Mermaid*, became the *Phoenix* before sailing from Cadiz, and returned as the *Syrène*.[68]

The French companies (they were always changing, and their genealogies are most confusing) must rank as a major failure in Colbert's policy: his company of 1664 foundered in 1684 and the 'rump company' which succeeded it in 1685 was on the point of collapse ten years later, and lost privileges to a new China company and to Noël Danycan's St Malo-based company for the South Sea. The amount of shady work was prodigious; in Dahlgren's (too numerous) pages Danycan appears as a racketeer of heroic stature, a figure out of Frank Norris or Theodore Dreiser. The main companies were, in Hannay's phrase, 'cut flowers', showy but quickly fading; not natural growths but creatures of the State, which provided itself or extorted from unwilling investors—in one instance under threat of literal dragooning— the bulk of the capital. Unlike the EIC, which had neatly parried an attempt at participation by James I with the smooth remark that a trading partnership was below the majesty of a king, Colbert's company had Louis XIV as a major and too-active investor: its general meetings were irregular and sometimes held in the royal presence, and after 1668 the Crown nominated the directors. Trade was confused with colonising projects and prestige diplomacy, and activities were always liable to be manipulated for showy political ends; profits were often offset by heavy military expenditure. In contrast, the VOC had proudly, in fact arrogantly, proclaimed in 1644 that its holdings in Asia were not national but private property, which could be sold as the proprietors wished, were it to the King of Spain himself. Dermigny's summary is crushing: 'the style of these [merchant] oligarchies accorded better with the genius of a bourgeois republic or a plutocratic monarchy

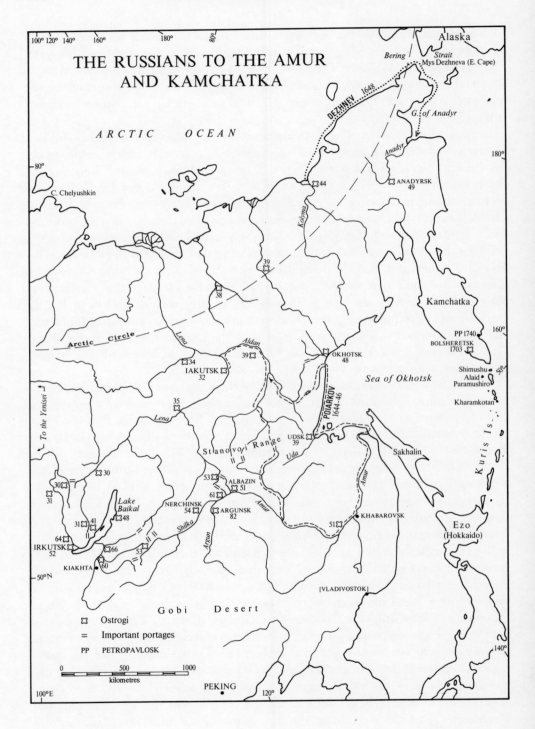

THE RUSSIANS TO THE AMUR
AND KAMCHATKA

[William III's] than with that of a kingdom too much concerned for the glory of its king.'[69]

Hence, while the French companies had some spectacular successes, they did not attain real stability—and that was limited—until well into the eighteenth century. The most interesting aspect of French activities, however, is their role (to which we shall return) in breaking into the Spanish monopoly of trade on the South American west coast and going on around the world via China: the first truly intra-Pacific commercial enterprise since the establishment of the Manila Galleon.

The Russian entry to China

Well before the maritime Europeans had established themselves at Canton, a new power, land-based and in the beginning perhaps only quasi-European, had spanned Asia, reached the Pacific, and contacted Peking. Although pioneers from Novgorod had penetrated the Urals and reached the Ob perhaps as early as the twelfth century, and Tsar Ivan III had sent an army to that river in 1499, Russian expansion into Siberia is traditionally taken as beginning with Yermak (or Ermak) about 1581–4. This was in fact the first serious lodgement, although in 1554 Tsar Ivan IV ('the Terrible'), improving on a tactical submission by a petty khan, had styled himself 'lord of all Sibir'.[70]

Yermak was a Volga river-pirate, displaced by Ivan's cleaning-up of the river, who attached himself and his band of some hundreds to the Stroganovs, a remarkable entrepreneurial family with diverse interests on the western flanks of the Urals, where they controlled in effect a 'Frontier Mark'. They obtained Ivan's permission to establish posts east of the ranges, both to protect a turbulent frontier and to expand their trade in furs. An unmistakable flavour of the *entrada* hangs over Yermak's thrust: clearly a tumultuous subject who would be less dangerous and more useful beyond the frontiers. In the event he defeated the Tatar Khan of Sibir, Kuchum, and took his capital, close to the modern Tobolsk, in 1582; he was rewarded by Ivan with a suit of elaborate armour, and was drowned in it when Kuchum counter-attacked two years later. But the Muscovites were now set on the path of one of the most rapid territorial expansions in all history, comparable only with those of the Arabs and the Mongols centuries earlier, and with the Spanish Conquista in America. They reached the Pacific at Okhotsk, 4600 km from the Urals, in sixty years—before indeed Russia had secured an outlet on either the Baltic or the Black Sea (Fig. 7).[71]

The motivation of this great *Drang nach Osten* was of course Siberia's wealth in furs, and especially the sable, 'a beast full marvellous and prolific ... a merry little beast it is, and a beautiful', which the ancients called the Golden Fleece.[72] In some aspects the expansion recalls the Conquista: 'the pioneering was done by private

Figure 7. THE RUSSIANS TO THE AMUR AND KAMCHATKA. Numbers by ostrogi indicate date of foundation, e.g. 48 = [16]48; positions and dates from maps in R. J. Kerner, *The Urge to the Sea* (Berkeley 1946).

individuals, out for what they could get, and when it was apparent that they were on to a good thing, the state followed up with the formal framework of adminis- tration', though in the remoter reaches this was at times only a thin overlay.[73] The *promyshlenniki*, the pioneer hunters-cum-traders, were and had to be exceedingly tough men, as ruthless as the Conquistadores, if less polished; and as in the Indies, the State tried to protect the natives, with very little success. In so vast and almost empty a land, control could not be rigid: smuggling was rife, and 'official graft and private brigandage ... brought about a fearful decline of the native population and woeful oppression of the survivors.' The government received tribute in furs, took a 10 per cent tax from the promyshlenniki in high quality furs, reserved the right of buying their best pelts, and monopolised the sale of sable and black fox to China.[74] The exploitation was very intensive, and good areas might be quickly depleted— itself a factor in the speed of the advance, which was also facilitated by the fragmentation and numerical weakness of the tribes scattered through the *taiga* or boreal forest.

The taiga was the home of the fur-bearers, fox and ermine as well as sable, and the great steppes south of it not only offered less attraction but were occupied by tough nomads, Tatar or Mongol, who could make head against the small Russian bands, had they sought to penetrate these regions; expansion here had to wait until the nineteenth century.[75] Moreover, the advance depended almost absolutely on the great network of rivers—Ob, Yenisei, Lena—whose long west-east reaches and tributaries provided waterways right across the continent, linked by portages which were in general low and easy, at least until the mountainous country east of the Lena was reached. The *ostrogi* or fortified posts were normally at nodal points on rivers, at confluences or commanding the debouchment of portages. Navigation was by a variety of craft, many small and crude but effective, quickly built with very little need of iron.[76]

By 1600 Moscow had a fortified route from the Kama, west of the Urals, to the Irtysh, where Tobolsk was founded as early as 1587; in two decades (1607–26) the Yenisei basin came under Muscovite control. Iakutsk (Yakutsk) on the great easterly bend of the Lena dates from 1632, Irkutsk in the rugged country around the south of Lake Baikal from twenty years later, and the Russians were poised for the last stages across the mountains to the Pacific, or south to the Amur and China (Fig. 7). Already, by about 1619, Mys Chelyushkin, the most northerly point on the Asian mainland, had been rounded.[77] The Pacific itself was reached from Iakutsk by a small party in 1639; Okhotsk was founded in 1648. These last stages, however, were extremely difficult, owing to terrain and climate in the north, and in the south, towards the Amur, to stiffer tribal resistance, eventually backed by the Manchus.

The Amur, which the Russians may have heard about as early as 1620, was explored in the mid-1640s by Vasili Poiarkov, who went from Iakutsk up the Aldan, crossed the watershed between Arctic and Pacific drainage, and sailed down the Amur and along the shores of the Sea of Okhotsk. He found none of the rumoured silver of the Amur basin, but did note the good arable land along its course. Much earlier, however—in 1608—an abortive mission had been sent from Tomsk to make contact with China, concerning which Russian ideas were bizarre. China was reported to be 'completely surrounded by a brick wall, from which it is evident that it is no large place', while even at the end of the century the cartographer Remezov could note at the mouth of the Amur that 'as far as this spot came the Tsar Alexander of Macedon, and hid a gun'.[78] Yet the first European embassy actually to reach Peking and (unlike Tomé Pires) to return safely was that of Ivan Perlin and Ondrushka Mundov in 1618–19; it brought back an offer of homage, assuredly never made, from 'Van-li Chinese Tsar'.[79] And the lower Amur was soon seen as well worth a struggle, both as a way to the sea and as a potential granary, and became a hotly disputed marchland between the two great continental empires.

The indiscriminate cruelties of Poiarkov and his successors such as Erofei Khabarov (for whom the modern city is named) ensured that the local tribal rulers, with few exceptions, much preferred to yield their allegiance to the more civil Manchus.[80] The fortunes of war fluctuated: the Russians seemed to hold the Amur in the early 1650s, but in face of nomad counter-raids and a Chinese scorched earth policy they had practically withdrawn by 1661, only to return a few years later and found, or re-found, the stronghold of Albazin on the northern bend of the river. Some effort was made towards real colonisation, not just garrisons to collect tribute and push trade, and eventually there were at least 277 peasant households between Albazin and Nerchinsk.[81] But the frontier remained incurably lawless and the Russians were at the end of their reach. Against this, the Ch'ing were unable to exert their full force owing to the demands of reconstruction in China (Poiarkov reached the Amur in the year that the Ming dynasty fell) and later the Rebellion of the Three Feudatories (1672–80), and they were also heavily involved in the task of controlling their unreliable Mongol tributaries. Hence they fell back on the scorched earth tactic, and in 1676 accepted the great Muscovite embassy led by the Wallachian diplomat and scholar Nicolai Gavrilovich Spathary.[82] He received much assistance, including advance notice of Chinese intentions, from the Jesuit interpreter Ferdinand Verbiest, and was actually allowed an audience by the Emperor, rather distant but without the kowtow. But Kang-hsi dismissed him with a message whose very terms were to be repeated by Kien-lung to Lord Macartney in 1793; the requests for a firm trade agreement were fobbed off. On his return journey Spathary tried, with little effect, to dissuade the Russians at Albazin and Nerchinsk from their violent raiding; in 1682 they set up the ostrog of Argunsk well to the south of the Amur. Kang-hsi now decided that *il faut en finir*, and by 1681–3, with the suppression of the revolt in southern China and the taking of Taiwan, his hands were free.

Kang-hsi's campaign was carefully prepared both by land and water, and by 1683 the Russian settlements were overrun, but for Albazin, which (for the time and place) was well fortified and garrisoned. It fell in 1685 but was at once reoccupied, only to be besieged again in the next year. Kang-hsi ordered the siege to be relaxed pending negotiations, and in August 1689 a new ambassador, Theodor Alexeevich Golovin, met the Chinese envoys at Nerchinsk. These were accompanied not only by the indispensable Jesuit intermediaries but by some 10,000 men, and when the negotiations broke down they decided to invest Nerchinsk. Faced by such a show of force, the Russians had no option but to accept the Chinese demand for complete withdrawal from the Amur; nevertheless, they managed to salve a great deal from this unequal treaty. Banking on Chinese geographical ignorance, they managed to interpret its terms restrictively. In the Latin text, only the rivers *quid ad Borealem plagam vergunt*—i.e. which fell into the Arctic—were to remain Russian. This would have made the entire Pacific seaboard of Siberia a no-man's-land; omitting this clause from their own text, and adding a couple of doctored touches, the Russians were able to retain as their boundary the northern watershed of the Amur basin, the Stanovoi Range.[83] Treaty or no treaty, once the Russians were at Iakutsk it is most unlikely that Ch'ing power could have stopped them from going on to Okhotsk and Kamchatka; but this sleight-of-hand helped them to fend off later Chinese pressure for demarcation, until in the nineteenth century they were again in a position to press on to the Amur itself, and this time with permanent success.

Mongolia became a closed buffer-zone, Amuria remained a virtually empty no-man's-land. The existing caravan trade to Peking shifted to a route from Irkutsk to Kiakhta on the Mongolian border, a shift formalised by the Treaty of Kiakhta (1728) which made the town as it were an inland Canton. Hence caravans crossed the Gobi Desert, taking to China furs and peltry (including beaver from Canada via England), coarse Russian and fine English woollens, linen and leather. They returned with tea (the most profitable item to the Russians), raw silk and silk fabrics, raw cotton and Nankeens, rhubarb, porcelain and Chinoiserie. Contraband trade was reckoned as at least a fifth of the total value, including all the raw silk and the best rhubarb, a valued drug in the costive Europe of the day. Opposite Kiakhta was the Chinese town of entry, Maimatschin; to complete the analogy of Canton, no women were allowed there.[84]

The Russian drive to the Pacific

Repulsed on the Amur, Russian energies turned to the northeast, where Okhotsk was already forty years old. Although this ostrog was to be a base for Russian Pacific exploration through the eighteenth century, the landward approaches were frightful: as late as the 1840s, after 'improvements', Sir George Simpson (of the Hudson's Bay Company) found the road 'more thickly strewed with [horses'] bones than any part of the plains on the Saskatchewan with those of the buffalo'.[85] Uneasy of approach, the town itself began as a miserable place, as wretched as Nombre de Dios on the Isthmus, and remained so; in 1682 it had only eight dwellings, and even when it was Bering's main base in 1726–8 there were less than a dozen households; and the port was very poor, indeed dangerous.

By sea, the Russians had reached the Pacific, or at least its extension in Bering Sea, almost simultaneously with the founding of Okhotsk. Semen Dezhnev's 1648 voyage from the mouth of the Kolyma, on the Arctic, to the Gulf of Anadyr became an article of faith in Russia, Tsarist or Soviet—the land's end of Siberia, named East Cape by Cook, was officially renamed Mys Dezhneva in 1898. The authenticity of this exploit has been assailed, especially by F. A. Golder, on grounds of the unreliability of the documents, the physical impossibility of the voyage, the vagueness of Dezhnev's *ex parte* account, and the lack of any reference until G. F. Müller published his report of it at St Petersburg in 1758. There are in fact two or three prior references to such a voyage, though not to Dezhnev by name, as well as Krasheninnikov's in 1755, which does give the name and is not mentioned by Golder although he cites his book. Golder's scepticism gained some acceptance outside Russia, but he consistently played down the pros and played up the cons, and his case could be and was badly shaken, and this without recourse to documents discovered since his time.

The voyage is perhaps less surprising than might seem, since on their Arctic littoral the Russians had developed the *koch*, a craft remarkably well adapted to coastal voyaging in icy seas. The voyage was an extension of probes eastwards from the Kolyma in search of walrus ivory, but from Dezhnev's own reports it seems likely that he did not realise that he had passed through a strait, and in fact to him the finding of a rich walrus rookery was more important than the finding of the sea route—which was not really practicable. He had the luck of an exceptionally good season; from 1649 to 1764 there were seven attempts to repeat his feat, all failures. Paradoxically, the main effect of his voyage was to deflect Russian attention away from the extreme northeast, southwards to Kamchatka. The Soviet ranking of Dezhnev alongside Columbus, da Gama, and Magellan is indeed excessive; but there can now be no doubt as to his priority on the passage from the Arctic into Bering Sea, which was not repeated, in this direction, until Nordenskiöld's voyage of 1878–9. Dezhnev's voyage stands as a remarkable feat of resolution and endurance.[86]

Siberian cartography of the century is extremely crude, but Godunov's map of 1667 definitely shows a land's end between the Arctic and the Gulf of Anadyr, and this obviously owes nothing to the Strait of Anian concept in earlier Western European maps. However, some documents and maps refer to an impassable 'Stone Nose' between Arctic and 'Amur Sea', and Soviet writers admit that 'throughout the seventeenth century and even later the question of a free sea passage from the Arctic into the Pacific Ocean remained unclear'.[87] In 1937 the remains of what is stated to be a European settlement some 300 years old were found on the Kenai Peninsula in Alaska, and this has been thought to indicate the last resting place of those in the four boats under Dezhnev's companion Fedot Alekseev, separated after rounding his cape.[88] But Kenai is on the other side of Alaska, near Anchorage, far beyond the Aleutian Peninsula, and their reaching so far seems highly improbable. It would seem more likely, as Krasheninnikov thought, that Alekseev ended somewhere in Kamchatka. There are reports of Russian visits to the Kurils in 1656, or even earlier;[89] some unrecorded party blown eastwards from these islands might better account for the Kenai find. These reports are dubious, but it is certain that the Russians had some knowledge of Kamchatka before its official 'conquest' by Vladimir Atlasov in 1697, though this was vague enough.[90]

There had been tentative approaches from Anadyrsk (Dezhnev's old camp) before Atlasov, but he penetrated far down the peninsula, probably far enough to see the volcanic cone of Alaid (nearly 2300 metres) in the northern Kurils. He also picked up a shipwrecked Japanese, Denbei, whom he took to Moscow. Denbei, the first of his nation to visit Russia, was presented to Peter the Great, baptised, and kept on as a language instructor.[91] From him and from the evidence of ceramics, fabrics, and metal wares in Kamchadal hands, Atlasov deduced the proximity of a civilised state, perhaps India. Moscow's geography was better, and the correct interpretation of Japan was made; this possible opening for trade and influence, Kamchatka's wealth in furs, and over-optimistic estimates of its potential for agricultural supplies for the Russian Far East (always dependent for grain on bulky imports over huge distances) ensured Peter's continuing interest.

For the time, however, he was deeply involved in war with Sweden and plans for St Petersburg, and resources at this remotest end of his empire were scant. Atlasov was put in charge of a second expedition, with cannon, but on his way east from Tobolsk he engaged in some river-piracy and was prosecuted for it, and so was not able to return to Kamchatka until 1707: a man too violent and extortionate even for his own Cossacks, he was murdered by them in 1711, 'and from then on there was no excess, no revolt, no insolence that they did not commit.'[92] The rebels accompanied their bloody anarchy with respectful petitions for pardon to Authority at Iakutsk, promising to make amends by finding new lands for the Tsar. In pursuance of this promise they visited Shimusu and probably Paramushiro, the first two of the Kurils: there were no furs on the first and too many hostile Ainu on the second, but they did get more news of Japan. A more official visit in 1713 confirmed that Japanese traders came as far as Kharamkotan, only three or four islands away.[93]

Administrator after administrator was sent to Kamchatka, but for two or three decades there was only the simulacrum of a stable government: several Crown officials lost their lives, to rebels, bandits, or the indigenes. The Chukchis around Anadyrsk, the Koryaks south of them, the Kamchadals in the peninsula itself, were by no means disposed to accept the benefits of civilisation through such barbarous mediators. Risings were endemic, particularly in 1714–16, and culminated in the great Kamchadal revolt of 1731. They were waged and put down with ferocity, but amongst themselves the Russians were hardly less ferocious. Clearly nothing effective could be done in Kamchatka until some order prevailed, and even Peter's writ was difficult to enforce when the chain of command ran from St Petersburg to Iakutsk and thence by the circuitous route, beset with perils both from nature and man, through Anadyrsk: 'this was of no small advantage to the commanders in their brigandry.' Between indigenous revolt and Cossack anarchy, the whole Russian position, from the Kolyma to the tip of Kamchatka, seemed at risk.[94]

Persistent efforts were therefore made to open up the obvious seaway from Okhotsk to the peninsula: they were plagued by dissension and inefficiency—a large and well-equipped expedition from Tobolsk simply fell to pieces, leaving its supplies abandoned along the road and on the Okhotsk beaches. The craft adequate to Siberian rivers and merely coastal voyages were not suited to the open sea; the first boat built at Okhotsk on western European lines, the *Okhota*, undecked as she was, eventually made the passage in summer 1716, and by 1720 the standard route to Kamchatka was by sea to Bol'sheretsk on the southwest coast.[95] Here there was an easy crossing of the peninsula to the good harbour of Avatcha Bay, where Petropavlosk was founded in 1740.

With all its crudities and violence, the Russian advance to the Pacific was an astonishing achievement; it took less than seventy years from Yermak's foray to the founding of Okhotsk, and this miserable little ostrog was the starting-point for a thrust which brought the Russian flag around the North Pacific shores as far as Fort Ross, a mere 100 km north of San Francisco, itself founded as a Spanish response to the Russian presence in America.

The trend of the century

This great Russian irruption, unchecked until the 1680s, may be seen as running counter to the general trend of the times; but the check was political, a consequence of the resurgence of Chinese power under the Ch'ing, and this resurgence itself is fully in accord with the trend to world recovery from about 1680, after the deep depressions of the middle decades of the century. To this secular movement we must now return.

It was a century in which a defeat on the very farthest frontier of Christendom —the Araucanian rising which began in 1599—could have ripples in Bohemia.[96] Some world-parallelisms speak loud and clear: the revolutionary decade of the 1640s, with civil wars or revolts in Germany, Ireland, Scotland, England, France (the Frondes, which had a republican colour at Bordeaux), Portugal, Catalonia, Naples, may be matched in Asia with the fall of the Ming and the final closure of Japan, while in the Philippines 'After 1640, there is not a single index whose evolution is not one of catastrophic and exponential decline.'[97] Similarly the 1680s and 1690s saw the beginnings of economic revival in Spain and the Philippines, Ch'ing power consummated and the first real lodgements of English trade in China, the decisive achievement of Dutch hegemony in Java; as well as the Glorious Revolution and the consolidation of money power in Britain with the founding in 1694 of the Bank of England. Moreover, there were the beginnings of a new inflow of treasure to Europe—the gold of Brazil.

The parallelisms seem too striking to be mere coincidence; yet, as the theoreticians of 'conjuncture' admit, their explanation in detail is tricky, and at times may seem questionable. The decision, disastrous for Spain as for Europe, to commit Spanish troops to the aid of the Empire at the opening of the Thirty Years' War has been linked with the 'brief resurgence of Sevillean trade between 1616 and 1619'; but this seems to consider far too curiously.[98] There are discrepancies in interpretation: Mauro classifies 1620–40 as 'positive'; Chaunu sees the trend for the Iberian Pacific as strictly conformable to that for the Sevillean Atlantic, with a sharp downwards break about 1620, and 'the maximum break of slope for all the indices ... between 1630 and 1640.' Nor, as Mauro admits, is the self-closure of Japan necessarily an index of regression.

Dermigny also sees the 1620s as a negative period in Asia: check to missionary expansion in the Philippines (i.e. to the increased affirmation of the Spanish presence), sharp falling off of entries (especially from China) to Manila, decline of English enterprise. However, the English and the Dutch reacted differently: a general retreat by the EIC, for the VOC temporary tactical retreats at some points alongside aggressive moves at others. But these differing ways of facing up to a contractionist phase B of the conjuncture were rooted in differing attitudes to the rationale of East Asian trade: the English still under the sway of 'an entirely Eurocentric mercantilism', while the Dutch—in this heirs to their long tradition as carriers in European seas—had very quickly grasped 'the unity of the economic space between Java and Japan.' Again, there seems to be some tendency to take things both ways, or better perhaps conjuncture can work both ways: if nothing much happens, that is because of the contraction of phase B; if much does happen, that is also because of the contraction, now seen as a spur to new, sometimes outlandish, enterprise in search of compensation for narrowing opportunities. So the abortive mid-century attempts at forcing trade with China—including one from Genoa—are 'the reflection of the crisis which is accentuating in the Atlantic world'; and the desperate shortfalls in silver arriving at Seville lead to an intensified search for compensating supplies of gold, silver, and copper in Asia. The crisis at the same time proliferates projects and frustrates them.[99]

As the Czech historian Polišenský remarks, by 1609–18 American treasure was more a collateral for raising credit than a real resource, 'but the legend of the silver and the flotas was still a historical reality, and even legends have their functions.' It is, however, easy to make the whole rhythm of the world hinge too exclusively on the production of the American mines; there were other factors, of demand as well as supply. Changes in the gold:silver ratio, the improvement of European credit and exchange facilities, poor harvests, demographic checks, all may well have been factors in a slackening of demand for silver. There were also, of course, objective factors in America itself—the working out of the more accessible ore-bodies, the difficulties in maintaining the mercury supply, perhaps also labour shortages; and also 'a switch in the deployment of American silver, related to changing needs [of administration and defence] in the Indies.' In J. H. Elliott's view, by the earlier decades of the seventeenth century the European and American economies were getting out of phase: 'There was a diminishing demand in the Indies for European goods, and a diminishing demand in Europe for American silver. As a result, their economies failed to complement each other as neatly as they had in earlier years.'[1] However ambivalent the detail, there can be no doubt that the vicissitudes of European commerce in the East Asian trading zone must be seen against this background of secular movements. The great rising trend of the sixteenth century suffered serious set-back in the first years of the seventeenth, and between 1640 and 1660 came a débâcle. The effort to create a world-girdling economy had overstrained the resources of Iberia in manpower, and now money power also was in a decline and could not compensate. The fall in American silver enforced drastic structural changes. Despite 'the double primacy of the Dutch presence' and Japan, the Philippines long remained an important link in the chain of the world economy;[2] but increasingly the Iberian system was overshadowed, in the end supplanted, by the Dutch and the English, with their powerful engines of expansion, the great Companies. Fiscally there was a search for alternative sources of treasure, including the ersatz precious metal, copper; later Brazilian gold. The recovery after 1680-5, which lasted about twenty years, was not a complete reversal of conjuncture, the flourishing opening of a new phase A, but it was more than a mere halt in the contraction of phase B. It was rather a period of recuperation during which bases were laid for a new period of vigorous expansion: 'the great world-wide adventure of Europe' towards a global economic unification 'was not over; it was only suspended, awaiting the illustrious achievements of the eighteenth century.'[3]

The balance: gain or drain?

How illustrious the achievements were is of course much questioned nowadays. As for the balance-sheet between Europe and Asia, any firm conclusions—for the seventeenth century at least—would indeed be rash; and in a total reckoning, moral and cultural gains and losses would have to be taken into account, though of their nature they cannot be counted: the archives hold no bills of lading for ideas. There can be no reasonable question as to the devastating effects on large sectors of Asian societies and economies in the later phases, after the Industrial Revolution (not to mention opium) had subjugated Asian markets; but this has probably too much coloured our views of earlier periods, when by and large the terms were not too unequal—indeed, sometimes slanted against the Europeans. There was the notable exception of the areas utterly ruined by Dutch restrictions of output and insistence on forced deliveries on grossly inequitable terms; unlike the Spaniards, they did not even try, for the most part, to commit inhumanities humanely. But elsewhere in Asia the economic effect was more likely to have been moderately stimulating; after all, so much of the feeding of the great long-distance trades was in Asian hands.

Again, big as the Euro-Asian trades look, imposing as their structures were by the scale of the times, they accounted for but a small fraction of total economic transactions both in Europe and Asia. Their profits came back to small circles of merchants and their associates, who reinvested in the same trade or put their money into buying lands, offices, and titles, or into conspicuous consumption; they also played a most important fiscal role, 'lending' to governments on a large scale—on the renewal of a charter, or to buy off the issue of a charter to a rival group—as well as providing an opening for taxation on their luxury imports.[4] Not until much later was there much investment in productive industry—for one thing, as we have seen, those dazzling Asian markets for European products, some arms and gadgetry apart, turned out to be simply not there. There was thus very little multiplier effect; what there was would be mainly in ship-building and armaments.[5] In the long run also, as contemporaries (not disinterested) argued, the ossified commercial bureau-cracies of the greater Companies became obstructive rather than constructive, perhaps of use mainly as providing negative examples for the theoreticians of Free Trade, and its interloping or smuggling practitioners.

Against the high gross returns must be set the costs of administration and of armed protection and aggression, as much or more against European rivals as against Asian powers. It would be quite impossible to disentangle these; and moreover the activities of the Companies themselves were shot through with undercover trading by their own officers, in collusion with interlopers of all sorts and degrees of respectability, from Armenian traders to the Imperial Ostend Company, which was little more than a front. Many of the Asian goods which came back in return for the silver were luxuries or semi-luxuries, but Europeans desperately wanted them—silks, spices, drugs, porcelain, Chinoiserie, and later that mass luxury tea—and they could be had nowhere else.

Invoice costs in Asia were low, or looked low when concealed overheads were discounted, and the true profits were very generally over-estimated. In one example which can be assessed, a profit of 300 per cent reckoned on the invoice price came down to 52 per cent when transport and other charges were taken into account; and this neglects the concealed overheads of general administration and military expenditure.[6] Given the distance from the VOC's base in Holland to Batavia, and thence to the factories scattered from the Arabian Sea to Japan, not to mention the complications of half a hundred fluctuating local currencies (and weights and measures), keeping the accounts in phase would probably have been an insuperable task, before computers. The high dividends declared by the VOC in the early eighteenth century did not really represent trading profits, although it is too much to claim them as a main cause of the decline of the Company—reserves were ample, and some of the charges against the Heeren XVII (and their opposite numbers in the EIC) were exaggerated. A general view was exceedingly difficult, though attempts in this direction were sometimes made; unprofitable factories were identified, though not so often closed down. Glamman puts up a spirited defence, claiming for example that 'The Directors were also aware of surplus and loss from season to season in each single place in Asia' (if so, probably too late!); but he also remarks that 'It is no exaggeration to say that calculations of the gross profit on each commodity was the Alpha and Omega of the Company's trade.'[7] The *gross* profit; the net could hardly be calculated.

Whatever the national accounting might come to, for the groups directly involved the gains were often immense: the Heeren XVII and their higher officials in Amsterdam and Batavia, the EIC Directors and the Nabobs of eighteenth century England, their political backers, and a host of smaller people—merchants and captains, speculators and smugglers—were scarcely penniless in the worst of times. Those outside the circle of the oligarchs and their hangers-on saw things differently, and their complaints were often bitter. The lament for the eastwards outflow of precious gold and silver in exchange for trivial and corrupting luxuries was voiced by Pliny the Elder in the first century A.D.; it was still voiced at the end of the eighteenth:

> Can one conceive of anything more monstrous than the parallel to be
> drawn between the pouring of a milliard into the Asian abyss . . . and
> the paltry result of a market for a few hundred thousands which we
> get for the products of our soil and our industry?[8]

(What would or could have been done with the milliard is a question more beyond conjecture than what song the Sirens sang.)

This was to change, drastically, with mass production in Europe and mass marketing in Asia, but that lay ahead; the turning-point would seem to lie about the middle of the eighteenth century. Meanwhile, however much individuals may have made by shaking the pagoda tree, with the turn to Empire and the more effective competition of the later eighteenth century the military and administrative charges became higher, until as Furber says, 'it may well be that the industrial revolution came . . . in the nick of time to support European conquest and rule in a large part of Asia.'[9] Long before that most decisive turn in human history, however, the great Companies of the seventeenth century may have done little for productive investment either in Europe or in Asia, and still less for general welfare: Dermigny sees them not as creators of wealth but as agencies for the levying of contributions from the producers and consumers of both continents.[10] But if not multipliers, then at least unifiers.

Profit or loss, gain or drain, may never be accurately quantifiable even in a cash sense; and how to balance against the social evil of opium the social comfort of tea? which yet was regarded by some contemporaries rather as opium for the people of Europe.[11]

Chapter 5

PRIESTS AND PEARLERS

... what has hitherto been doubted is now assured,
that there is a navigable strait to the Mar del Norte.

California is not an island but only a peninsula,
as long since very well and correctly has been said
by Fr Eusevio Francisco Kino ... the heretic Drake
is author of the lie that the Sea of California ascends
to the North Sea, wishing to discredit the ancient
Spaniards who depicted California as terra firma with
this land ...

After Tasman, very little was added to European knowledge of the Pacific in the
rest of the seventeenth century (Fig. 14). It is tempting, and may not be too fanciful,
though it must be speculative, to associate this slackening of exploration, compared
with the preceding hundred years (Fig. 13), with the contracting phase B of the
world conjuncture; be that as it may, the fact remains that there was no great
voyage of discovery in the open Pacific between Tasman in 1642 and Roggeveen
in 1722; William Dampier's explorations in 1699 were confined to New Guinea
waters. The last two decades of the century did indeed see the remarkable outburst
of buccaneering voyages into and across the Ocean, but their motives were purely,
or impurely, predatory. They followed known routes and added scarcely any new
geographical data, though they did help to spread knowledge hitherto jealously
guarded by Spain. Dampier's observations were valuable and Lionel Wafer's were
politically significant as directly serving the misdirected scheme of the Scots in
Darien, but they brought not knowledge of new lands or seas, but rather better
information about the already known. Though the buccaneers did pioneer voyages
from west to east round the Horn, the only real discoveries were Dampier's
demonstration of the insularity of New Britain and—on the opposite shores of the
Ocean—Fr Kino's demonstration of the non-insularity of California, a re-
discovery which should also have exploded the myth of the Strait of Anian, and
indeed did so in its southern versions.

The Marianas mission

If there was no true discovery in the western Pacific, the Jesuit mission to the
Ladrones or Marianas, all of which had been seen before, at least 'established their

Pedro Porter y Casanate to Viceroy of New Spain, 18 August 1651, in A. del
Portillo y Diez Sollano, *Descubrimientos en . . . California* (Madrid 1947), 281; Fr
Manuel Fuensaldana, in H. E. Bolton, *Rim of Christendom* (New York 1960),
556.

geography' more correctly (Fig. 8).[1] For over a century after Legazpi annexed the group, there was little Spanish contact except the annual visits of the Manila-bound Galleons, an abortive mission in 1595, and two wrecks on Saipan, in 1600 and 1638.[2] Cavendish and the Dutch trans-Pacific voyagers also called at Guam. The Chamorros might have rested indefinitely in their isolation, punctuated by bouts of symbiotic trading with the strangers (valuable for their iron), had it not been for the zeal of Diego Luis de Sanvitores.

This Jesuit Father had touched at Guam in 1662, and immediately resolved to bring the Gospel to these luckless heathen souls. The Philippine authorities saw no point in this: the Galleons and Guam were well enough off as they were, a view which had much to recommend it to the Spaniards, and everything to the Chamorros. Sanvitores wrote off to Philip IV and his Queen Mariana, soon to become Regent for the wretched little boy Carlos II, 'the Bewitched'; it was a happy chance that her confessor and controller, Fr Juan Everardo Nithard, was also a Jesuit. Royal pressure overcame the reasonable reluctance of officialdom, and on 15 June 1668 Sanvitores landed on Guam, coming from New Spain, and accompanied by four priests, a few laymen, and thirty-three soldiers: the proportion was ominous.[3] One of the first acts of the grateful Father was to replace the indivious name of Ladrones ('Robbers') by the more auspicious Marianas.

Initial success was almost startling; in his first year Sanvitores claimed over 13,000 baptisms. Easy come, easy go; it soon appeared that superficial compliance masked deep disquiets, which rapidly shifted to aversion. There were several factors: Chamorro society was divided into three classes, and the ruling group saw no earthly reason why, if the Gospel were so great a gift, it should be shared with commoners and serfs; the missionaries naturally tried to get rid of the 'great houses' in which bachelors lived with unmarried girls in common; and apparently most important of all, the baptism of a baby was so often followed by its death that the bereaved parents saw a causal connection. Already in 1668 the first missionary to visit Tinian was driven out, and in 1670 there was open 'rebellion' with a spirited attack on the Spanish settlement at Agana. This was repelled, but on 2 April 1672 Sanvitores himself was killed after christening a baby over the protests of its father, Matapang, who became one of the most prominent resistance leaders.

Sanvitores, compassionate as well as courageous, might have been able to hold the military men in check; after his death the mission in effect was carried forward behind a creeping barrage of sheer terrorism. José de Quiroga, Governor in 1680 and a throw-back to the earlier Conquistadores, accentuated this policy; by early 1681, death and flight to the northern islands had so depopulated Guam that there were not enough people to raise supplies for the Galleons. Quiroga went to Rota and rounded up the refugees, who were brought back and herded into large settlements, easier to control than their original scattered villages and hamlets; a procedure not unknown in our own day. By this time reports of these devastations had reached Madrid, and Quiroga was relieved by Antonio de Saravia, who turned to an apparently successful policy of conciliation. This 'gleam of sunshine' did not

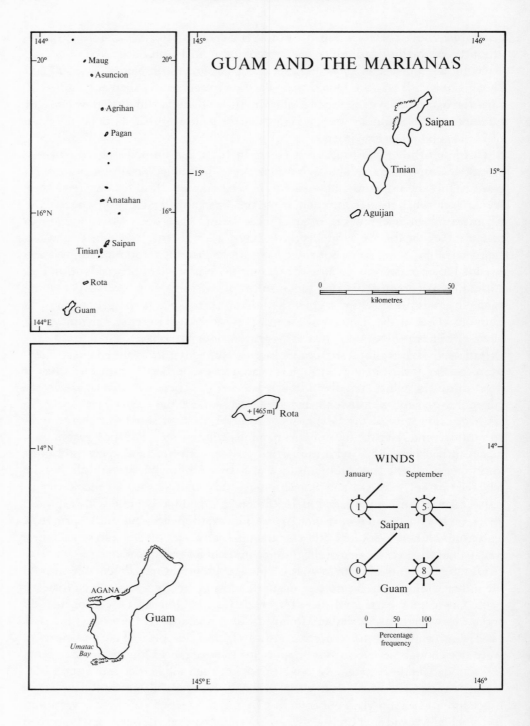

GUAM AND THE MARIANAS

last; Saravia died in 1683, and the old methods were revived. Quiroga launched an attack on Saipan, the second largest island; in his absence there was a general rising on Guam and another attack on Agana. During the stalemate which ensued, Guam was visited by the buccaneer John Eaton, who apologised to the Governor for an affray in which some Chamorros were killed, and had 'for answer, that if he had killed them all, he should have esteemed the favour the greater ... The Spanish Governor's kindness increased in proportion to the mischief done to the Indians', which mischief included cutlassing and shooting prisoners who were trying to escape by swimming, with their arms pinioned behind them.[4] Eaton's men had given the first provocation by felling coconut trees, and could hardly plead the excuse of religious zeal.

Quiroga, 'to whose finishing hand may be ascribed the total depopulation and abandonment of the Northern Islands', became Governor again, and at once engaged on the conquest of Rota and Saipan. There was no possibility of a long-sustained guerrilla on these small islands; by July 1695, after a battle on Aguijan, submission was complete, 'and these ill-fated people were thus hurried off to repeople a land once their own ... under the unrighteous assumption, that it advanced the cause of Religion.' The survivors were concentrated in a few large easily-controlled villages on Guam, 140 settlements reduced to seven. Sanvitores estimated the population of the islands at 100,000; this is agreed to be an exaggeration, but there were probably half as many. Now 'paganism had been reduced to vanishing point';[5] but by the time the Marianas were safely Christian, most of the Chamorros were safely dead: by 1710 there were only about 4000 still alive. Spanish losses were trifling, those of the Chamorros probably mainly due to the disruption of economic life—the standard burning of villages—aided by two typhoons and by epidemics, one in 1688 which was probably influenza, one of smallpox at the turn of the century.[6]

For over a century and a half the lesser islands remained empty, visited only by small parties in search of feral cattle; Anson surprised one on Tinian. Guam itself vegetated. Umatac Bay, the traditional landing-place of Magellan, had a good harbour and was an excellent watering-point; it was the standard port for the Galleons.[7] The main centre was Agana, which seems to have been an agreeable little town; but it must be remembered that the infrequent visitors would have spent weeks at sea and it would have been months since they had seen anything to remind them even faintly of European amenities. For the local Spaniards it must have been a *far niente* life, except when the Galleons were in. The Spanish introduced a wide variety of food plants and livestock and the Jesuits as usual were active agricultural entrepreneurs. When they were expelled in 1769 the

Figure 8. GUAM AND THE MARIANAS. Wind data from Fig. 67 in Naval Intelligence Division *Handbook [of the] Pacific Islands* (1945), IV.309; numerals in circles indicate percentage frequency of calms.

Augustinians took over, and the plantations were neglected; there was some economic revival under the reforming Governor Mariano Tobias in the 1770s. The pure Chamorro population, however, long continued to decline: 1318 in 1786, rising to 2628 in 1810. After that no attempt was made to separate them statistically, and 'the Chamorros as a radically mixed group' with a hispanicised but individual culture 'became a recognized entity.'[8] A new people had been born.

Theirs had been a bloody travail, the more pitiful because so needless. The islands were only a burden to Spain, of no real value unless to deny to others their use as a base for attacking the Philippines; and Anson showed that for denial to be effective, the whole chain would have had to be occupied, in more strength than she could afford. With the independence of New Spain, the colonial *raison d'être* of Guam, the refreshment of the Galleon, vanished; and as for that function, Burney deserves the last word: this was 'a purpose which for a century preceding the Mission, had been cheaply and without difficulty answered by traffic with the natives', and so it might have remained for another century and a half. *Tantum religio potuit suadere malorum*: to so great evils could religion lead.[9]

While the conquest of the Marianas was still in full swing, their christening for the Queen of Spain was matched by one for King Carlos II: in 1686 a Manila-bound Galleon strayed off course and found a large island, most likely Ulithi but perhaps Yap or Fais, and named it La Carolina. The Spaniards in the Philippines seem to have been vaguely aware of the existence of a large number of islands south of Guam, and indeed it was no new discovery. Ulithi, Yap, Fais, Palau, Ponape, Truk and several other islands had been seen by Portuguese or Spaniards between 1525 and 1565; the 'Islands of Gomes Sequeira', who sailed from the Moluccas in 1525, were a standard feature in sixteenth century maps—again probably Yap, Ulithi or Palau; and Ruy Lopez de Villalobos, coming from New Spain, had been greeted with 'Buenos dias, matelotes' at Fais in 1543. But as navigation settled into the fixed tracks of the Galleons, these earlier discoveries faded from memory. There were also drift voyages from these islands to the Philippines; the best known is that reported in 1697 by Fr Paul Clain SJ, of the twenty-nine 'Palaos' blown to Samar, who gave him the names of some thirty inhabited islands; a fine field, he thought, for the Gospel. There were Spanish visits in 1696 to Faraulep, Ulithi, and Palau (Belau); in Sharp's view these were the first firmly assured European contacts with Ulithi and Palau. But this Gospel field was to lie empty for nearly two centuries, and then the first workers were to be Protestants. Not until 1870, under the apprehension of German expansion, did Spain take any steps to make good the shadowy claim implied in the name of the Caroline Islands.[10]

Ascensión's island

One cannot doubt the good intentions of Sanvitores and his brethren, but they assuredly paved the road to hell for the Chamorros. If however the Marianas mission forms one of the darker chapters in the history of the Society of Jesus, at this same time a brighter one was being written across the Pacific. On the northern marches of New Spain the Jesuits were able to keep their Spanish coadjutors as well as their Indian converts under control; the Fathers were 'the staunchest friends of the simple Indian, so long as he remained simple'.[11] The gathering together into mission stations of scattered and in part semi-nomadic peoples did indeed lead to much loss of life by epidemics, and land which had once maintained a modest human population too often became the domain of the herds of great pastoralist grantees. In the interim, however, the missions established a protective paternalism, on the same lines as the more famous Jesuit polity in Paraguay, if not taken to such an extreme of kindly *apartheid*. In the course of their civilising evangelism, the Jesuits also cleared up a geographical mystery which had bemused cartographers through most of the seventeenth century: was California an island?

This question had really been answered in the negative before it was posed—as early as Cortés's time—only to be reopened some sixty years later by the misguided enthusiasm of the recorder of Sebastián Vizcaíno's expedition. It remained open, though it should not have been so, for at least eighty years, 1622 to 1702; and even after that there were doubters.

As we have seen, Francisco de Ulloa, sent out by Cortés in 1539, had reached the head of the Mar Vermejo—the Gulf of California—and gone up the west coast of its bounding peninsula, Baja California, beyond Cedros Island; and even without Hernando de Alarcon's entry well into the Rio Colorado in 1540 and Cabrillo's voyages of 1542–3 (probably as far as southern Oregon), this should really have settled the matter. The results of Ulloa's and Alarcon's voyages are shown on a map of 1541, which gives the real outlines remarkably well.[12] There was no question at all in the sixteenth century: Mercator, Ortelius, Hondius, Plancius, Wright and other cartographers all show Baja California as continuous with Alta, and even on very small scale reproductions of world maps the head of the Gulf and the Colorado estuary are usually readily recognisable.[13]

The concept that the Gulf of California was in fact a strait was closely linked with the concept of the 'Strait of Anian', and this, though not Drake's invention, may have caused new apprehension to the Spaniards by his carefully planted hints about his possible exit from the South Sea by an undisclosed new route. The objective of Vizcaíno's second, and official, voyage of 1602 was the exploration of the outer coast north of Cabo San Lucar, to see whether it might not afford good way-stations for the Acapulco-bound Galleons; if conditions were favourable he might go beyond Cabo Mendocino (40°75′N) to Cabo Blanco (42°50′), but if the coast trended westwards from the former cape, he was not to sail along it more than a hundred leagues. As for the Gulf, entry into it on the outwards journey was specifically barred, and even on the return he might put into it only if he still had plenty of supplies—and this was so unlikely that the proviso was virtually a prohibition. There is nothing of Anian in this, and there thus seems no warrant at all for Portillo's assertion that Vizcaíno was instructed to find the 'rear entrance [*entrada posterior*]' to the Gulf beyond Cabo Blanco. Wagner's conclusion, after his usual very

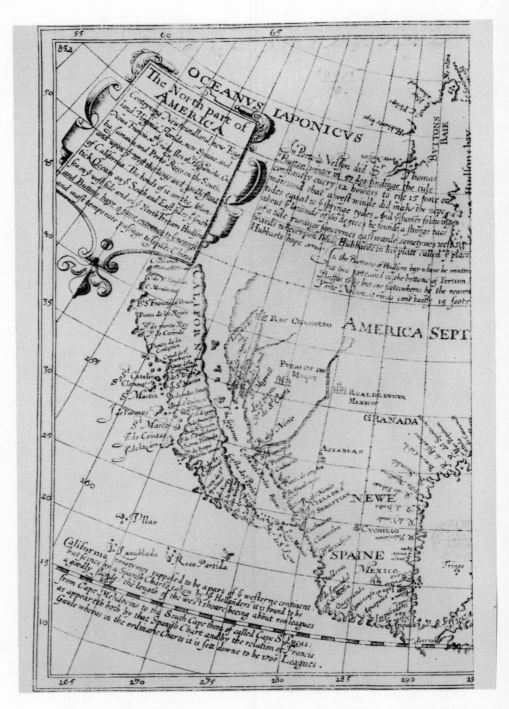

Plate X.   CALIFORNIA AN ISLAND.   Henry Briggs's map of 1625, probably from a chart by Fr Antonio de la Ascensión; for comment see text. By permission of the British Library, London.

full and careful discussion, is that 'everything goes to show that if the search for a strait was one of the objects of the expedition, it was a very minor one'.[14]

A restricted but sensible objective was not good enough for Vizcaíno's chronicler, Fr Antonio de la Ascensión. To him, Quivira and Anian were the real goals; and the river near Cabo Blanco which had been named for Martin Aguilar, one of Vizcaíno's officers, he inflated into the entrance to the Strait, which he connected with the Mar Vermejo. He also swallowed whole the tale, apparently not set down until some fifty years after the alleged event, of one Morena or Morera, who claimed to have piloted Drake through the Strait of Anian, from the Mar del Norte to the Mar del Sur, and to have been left by him near the Strait to recover his health. Morena made his way to Sombrerete (in Zacatecas), and on the way he saw to the west an arm of the sea dividing New Mexico from a great land farther west still; on its shores were white people who rode horses and fought with lance and dagger; these Fr Antonio took to be Muscovites (in Drake's day, Yermak was just crossing the Urals!). In this way Baja California became an island, and that lean and arid peninsula was blown up, by Fr Antonio's bad mathematics and vivid imagination, into a fertile realm larger than the present State of California, of course stocked with mines of gold and silver, banks of pearls and amber, and possessing, of all places, 'the loveliest of climates'.[15]

Fr Antonio was not alone responsible for this geographical blunder; the Iturbe/Cardona expedition was in the north of the Gulf in 1616, and 'confirmed' the Father's views.[16] Nevertheless, it was from Ascensión that the concept entered European cartography, and by a peculiar irony this was in the first instance through the hands of the Englishman Henry Briggs. It is a further irony that the Jesuit missionaries who exploded the myth themselves fathered it on the lies of the heretic Drake, who was entirely innocent. It is unlikely that, as Brebner suggests, the Spanish 'thought that they had corroborated the geographical knowledge of the English' as shown on the maps of Michael Lok and Sir Humphrey Gilbert. Both of these are very odd, but on Lok's map Baja California is definitely a peninsula, and while Gilbert's is perhaps ambivalent—there is a big island of sorts, perhaps not entirely cut off from the mainland—it can hardly be described as 'masking the Strait of Anian and the site of Quivira': a waterway takes off from the head of the Mar Vermejo and goes right across to the Atlantic by Houcholaga, Canada, and Saguenai, while north of Quivira the coast simply bends round into a circumpolar sea.[17]

A key document is the map published by Henry Briggs in 1625 (Plate X): this, so far as California is concerned, is based on a map sent to Spain which fell into Dutch hands en route. A legend states clearly that California was

> sometymes supposed to be a part of ye westerne continent but scince
> by a Spanish Charte taken by ye Hollanders it is found to be a goodly
> Ilande.

This chart may not be Ascensión's own work, but it clearly reflects his views, with however a gratuitous and startling amendment of the Spanish nomenclature.[18]

On the northwest of Briggs's island is 'Pº. Sʳ Francisco Draco', which is Cermeño's Bahía de San Francisco; Draco is the Latin form of the Spanish nickname for Drake—*El Draque*, the Dragon. The substitution of the heretic for the saint must have seemed a good joke—as well as staking an English claim—but it may well have saddled Drake, in Spanish eyes, with the illegitimate paternity of the island idea. California ends at Cabo Blanco, and the area immediately north of the cape is occupied by an elaborate cartouche stating that 'on yᵉ North Fretum Hudson and Buttons baye have a faire entrance to yᵉ nearest and most temperate passage to Japã and China'; the inconvenient gap of ignorance between Hudson Bay and the Pacific is neatly masked by legends. This is clearly the Anian concept, and since the map is designed to minimise the length and lower the latitude of a North-west Passage, it is difficult to see why Leighley should think that Briggs knew that the Strait of Anian did not exist.[19]

The subsequent career of this major geographical error can best be followed in Tooley's *California as an Island*, which lists a hundred and reproduces forty maps from 1625 to 1770. We need note only that the idea first became popular in England—perhaps Briggs's twist of San Francisco to Sir Francis did the trick—and by a final irony, saintliness was restored to the Bay in 1761, by the Geographer to His (Britannick) Majesty, through the inadvertent and incongruous medium of a misprint: 'Port Sᵗ [*sic*] Francis Drake *Wrongly named Port Sᵗ Francisco*'. Insularity was at first resisted in the Netherlands, then the greatest centre of map production; in the 1630s the great cartographers—Hondius, De Laet, Blaeu, Visscher—still followed the Mercator-Ortelius tradition; then they weakened. Visscher 'corrected' his maps and became a main supporter of the insular idea; Jansson accepted it in 1638 'and his influence and Visscher's was sufficient to swing the whole of European geography behind them.'[20] Peninsular California survived mainly in unrevised reprintings, and until well into the eighteenth century the insular idea prevailed: between 1715 and 1730 Van der Aa issued maps both ways, presumably on the principle that the customer is always right. Fr Antonio had done his work, though in New Spain itself his appeals for the exploitation of his 'discovery' met with little response.

Before Kino: the pearlers

Ascensión and Vizcaíno desired to see a way-station for the Galleons set up at the port which they had found (or refound, after Cermeño) and named for the Viceroy Monterey; to secure for Spain the approaches to and from Anian and Quivira, on the presumed shortest route to the Mar del Norte; and not least, in fact certainly first on Ascensión's and ostensibly so on Vizcaíno's view, to bring the pearls of the Gospel to those 'affable Indians of good disposition and well built' whom they had met. Commercial interests in New Spain were opposed to anything which might delay the Galleon's arrival at Acapulco—never mind the crew, they were used to scurvy; it could also be argued that a post so far north would be a mere hostage for English or Dutch raiders, and it was so argued, cogently, by the new Viceroy

Montesclaros, who succeeded Monterey in 1603 and sabotaged any move to develop the port favoured by his predecessor. As for Anian, whatever the apprehensions aroused by Drake and Cavendish, the arguments against Monterey applied *a fortiori* to any point farther north, and then there was the simple fact that so far no intruders had come by that so hypothetical Strait, but only from the south: in fact, the less said about it the better.[21] Remained the pearls: those which attracted the adventurers of New Spain were not spiritual, to be scattered abroad, but material, to be gathered in.

The pearl banks of the Mar Vermejo had been known since Cortés, and at least one venture in the mid-sixteenth century had yielded goodly profits. There were other voyages, licensed or illicit, and it may be recalled that Vizcaíno's first, and private, exploration in 1596 was seeking pearls. After his second in 1602–3, 'expeditions to California entered a new phase, characterised by the dominant preoccupation with pearls'.[22]

The first formal long-term pearling contract was granted to Tomás de Cardona in 1612; he and his partners claimed to have equipment by which they could obtain pearl shells from depths of twenty-five to fifty fathoms (45–90 m); the standard maximum for a diver was twelve fathoms. We know at least that they acquired highly skilled black slaves in the Caribbean. Since the shallower known banks in the Mar Vermejo had been worked out, the partners were given a licence for ten years, in both the Mar del Norte and the Mar del Sur.[23] Their operations in the Caribbean do not concern us, but by 1614 the firm was building three ships, the biggest the *San Francisco* of 200 tons, at Acapulco, despite the fact that as a ship-building port it lacked good timber. These were launched in January 1615, but were at once held in port in view of rumours of Dutch pirates entering the South Sea by the Straits of Magellan: this was of course an early warning of Joris van Spilbergen's fleet. The immediate scare once over, they sailed north under Tomás de Cardona's nephew Nicolás (as the Spanish authority Alvarez del Portillo asserts) or, as is more often stated and is perhaps more likely, under Juan de Iturbe; this was a prospecting cruise, but as soon as they had crossed from Mazatlan to Baja California they heard, from the Indians, of unknown ships. These were probably illicit Spanish pearlers, but they were naturally assumed to be Dutch, so the *San Francisco* set off to warn Acapulco and ran straight into five ships of Spilbergen's near Zacatula: the ship, its pearls, and eleven valuable black divers were taken, some Spaniards escaping to join Vizcaíno's scratch defence levy.[24] A second voyage in 1616, most likely under Juan de Iturbe, seems to have produced a fairly good haul of pearls, probably more than were reported to the officials collecting the Royal Fifth.

Partly in compensation for their losses to Spilbergen, the Cardonas were granted a new monopoly, to run for ten years from the effective establishment of a pearl fishery; colonisation in Baja California was also envisaged, and they were promised all the mercury needed to process any silver ores that might be found. Their limits ran from Tehuantepec to 38°N on both the inner and outer coasts of California (i.e.

on both sides of the peninsula); by this time the authorities seem to have accepted, on the faith of Ascensión and the Iturbe/Cardona voyage of 1616, the Anglo-Dutch geographical heresy. So in 1619 Nicolás de Cardona, who had returned to Spain, came back to make another attempt on the Gulf, this time from Panama. Again there was a scare of twelve Dutch ships coming from Peru to the Isthmus, and once more Cardona and his men were impressed for local defence—there was no Dutch fleet at large in the South Sea, but such false or premature alarms were a constant on these shores.[25] When Nicolás did get away, his last ship was wrecked at Tehuantepec, and he finally sailed for Spain in 1623.

Geographically, the Cardona voyages merely added to the confusion started by Ascensión. Cardona (whether from his own observations or Iturbe's does not matter) reported that his ships had reached 34°N, and that from one point

> it seems that the mainland is joined with that of California; however
> after having given the sails to the wind and crossed to the other shore,
> it was seen that the sea divided the lands, from which it is supposed
> that this might be the strait of Anian, or at least that it remains certain
> [*queda averiguado*] that California was a very large island and not a
> mainland.[26]

It is of course manifestly impossible that they should have reached 34°N and been certain of any such thing, since at that latitude they would have been a good 110 km up the Río Colorado; a discrepancy which does not seem to worry Portillo.

Such a monopoly as that of the Cardonas was easier to grant than to police, and there were of course attempts to break it, whether by respectable petitioning, local or family interest, or corruption; one effort, by Vizcaíno's son-in-law, seems to have been defeated not by law but by the San Blas mosquitoes. Memorials and Relations flowed in to the authorities, several from Ascensión, who kept up his propaganda for some thirty years. He seems to have enthusiastically briefed anybody who might be interested, even although in his view the Crown itself should take the matter in hand, given the strategic and commercial importance of making sure that the Gulf communicated with the Strait of Anian.

The Viceroy was directed to enquire into the advantages and modalities of exploration and settlement in the Californias, and opinions were sought from all who had any experience of the region, with Fr Antonio of course in the forefront. Most favoured an effort at northwards expansion, with the notable exceptions of two pilots, Enrico Martínez, who had been with Vizcaíno, and Esteban Carbonel; the former took his scepticism so far as to doubt even the value of the pearl fisheries. In the event the Viceroy reported in 1632 that 'nobody could be certain without seeing the said islands', and that he had licensed Francisco de Ortega to go and see. As Portillo remarks, this is a curious proof of the reiterated inconsequence of the authorities: in face of the 'mare magnum of contradictory opinions', all the experience of past voyages went for nothing.[27]

Ortega made two voyages in 1632 and 1633, with Carbonel as pilot; the first was a mere reconnaissance into the Gulf as far as 27°N, the second an ambitious but unsuccessful attempt at colonising La Paz near the tip of Baja California—it was just a hundred years since Cortés's attempt to plant an outpost there. On a third (and unlicensed) foray Ortega was wrecked near Cabo San Lucar and made his way to La Paz and the mainland with difficulty. The three voyages brought back only a few pearls, reports of more, and impossible demands for logistic support. Meanwhile the Cardonas of course were not backward in defending their rights; they were still protesting against interlopers in the 1650s.

In 1634 Nicolás de Cardona, then in Madrid, put up a grandiose project for planting three towns in California. His pretensions were not small: amongst other guarantees and privileges, he was to be 'Adelantado, Gobernador y Capitan General del Reyno de la California': a somewhat premature promotion of this semi-desert. In return, with God's help he would not only reduce the said Kingdom into the royal obedience and populate it, but would also discover the Strait of Anian, so that the navigation from Spain to China and the Philippines would be shorter, safer, and cheaper; moreover there was 'the fourth part of the Globe, which is the Tierra Austral ... which I desire to see and discover.'[28] Anian was still much in the air; it figured in the charges against Carbonel, who turned out to be French by birth and was accused, in 'hundreds' of memorials and depositions, of building— surreptitiously!—a ship of over 600 tons, in which he would load up with Californian pearls and sail directly to France by the northern passage: an index of the constant and extraordinary nervousness of the Spaniards on the South Sea. The affair seems to have been a gigantic mare's nest; a real threat was indeed to come, but not through Anian, and not until the advent of the buccaneers nearly fifty years later.

Nothing came of the Cardona project, and in 1636 the various conflicting authorisations were revoked; they included one to Pedro Porter y Casanate, who had had a fairly distinguished naval career and enjoyed good connections in Spain.[29] Like Nicolás de Cardona, he was a man of much pertinacity and extensive views: the Indians were convertible and would be useful, the country was fertile, there were gold and silver, coral and amber as well as pearls; way-stations could be found for the Galleons, and the discovery would facilitate trade with the kingdoms of Anian, Japan, Tartary and China. This was in complete disregard of the fact that the Viceroy had suspended his 1636 project on the grounds that such discoveries might open 'a port by which enemies might enter to infest those seas'. Perhaps because Porter asked of the Crown nothing material for himself (beyond of course the monopoly), he got his licence in 1640.

Porter was delayed by naval assignments, but by 1643 he was in New Spain, where he chartered a small ship and began building two more; but in December there was once again an alarm of Dutch pirates in the South Sea—Hendrik Brouwer's men in Chile—and in the first two months of 1644 Porter's fregata was employed in setting up watch-posts in Baja California to warn the Galleons. Meanwhile his ship-building on the Río Santiago, near San Blas, was impeded by

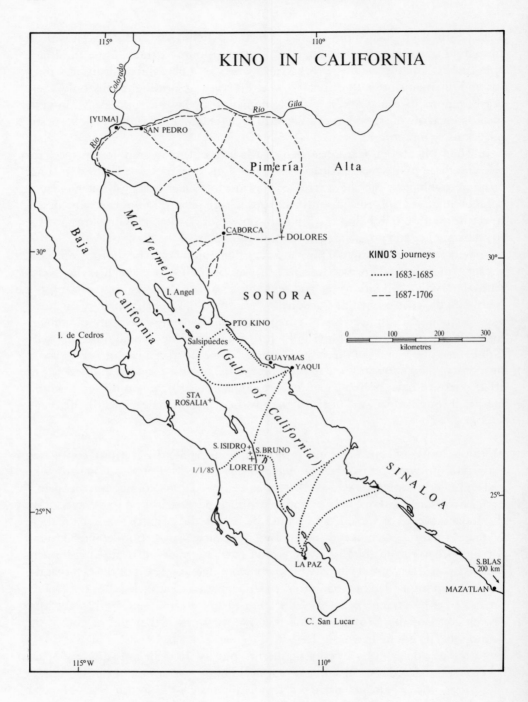

KINO IN CALIFORNIA

115°

110°

Colorado

[YUMA]

Rio   Gila

SAN PEDRO

Rio

Pimería   Alta

CABORCA

+DOLORES

30°   30°

Baja

Mar Vermejo

SONORA

California

I. Angel

KINO'S journeys

.... 1683-1685

--- 1687-1706

I. de Cedros

PTO KINO

Salsipuedes

0   100   200   300

kilometres

(Gulf

GUAYMAS

YAQUI

STA
ROSALIA+

of

California)

S. ISIDRO+ +S. BRUNO
+
1/1/85 ·LORETO

SINALOA

25°   25°

25°N

LA PAZ

S.BLAS
200 km

MAZATLAN

C. San Lucar

115°W   110°

mosquitoes and little worms which ate everything, and in April worse befell: his ships were burnt on the stocks. It was undoubtedly arson; illicit competitors and even, after a lapse of nine years, Carbonel's mysterious Frenchmen were blamed. Porter retained royal and viceregal favour, and after some rival chicanery got himself appointed Governor of Sinaloa so that he might use that province as a base, untrammelled by local officialdom.

At last he was able to sail for California, with two ships, in October 1648, and got as far as Santa Rosalia, half-way up the Gulf. Next year he tried again, and according to Portillo got further up the Mar Vermejo than had his predecessors; an untenable claim, overlooking Ulloa and Alarcon over a century before—Portillo seems never to check latitudes. In fact, he could not sail beyond Isla Angel de la Guarda, naming the shoals south of the island Salsipuedes—'Get out if you can'. These navigational difficulties made Porter think that this was the narrowest part of the putative strait, and in August 1651 he was able to write to the Viceroy Conde de Alba that 'what has hitherto been doubted is now assured, that there is a navigable strait to the Mar del Norte'.[30] This would be valuable not only as a shorter way to Europe, but with a few ports in California the long channel between the island and the mainland would offer perfect protection to the Galleons on this last leg of their course. One may question Portillo's tribute to the naval expertise of Porter, who should have known from his own experience that this was a dangerous navigation, especially for big ships—the winds are extremely variable in direction and force—and should have realised that from the strategic angle, on this route Cabo San Lucar would serve the pirates even better as an interception point, since the Galleons would not be able to fetch well out from the coast but be caught in a bottle-neck.

After 1650 Porter fades from the scene. There were further pearling voyages in the 1660s, but these are of no geographical and very little other interest. The Cardona and Porter voyages are significant, however, since they seemed to have confirmed Fr Antonio de la Ascensión's error, and the cartographers continued to show California as an island. There is, however, one slight hint that some Spaniards may have known more than they admitted. In 1686 William Dampier was off the coast of New Spain, and reported that the 'Lake' (i.e. Gulf) of California

is but little known to the *Spaniards*, by what I could ever learn, for their Drafts do not agree about it. Some of them do make *California* an Island, but give no manner of account of the [Lake]: Whereas on the West-side of the Island towards the *Asiatick* Coast, their Pilot-Book gives an account of the Coast from Cape St. *Lucas* to 40 d. North. *Some of their Drafts newly made do make California to join to the Main.*[31]

The first edition of Dampier's *New Voyage* was published in London in 1697, five years before the joining of Baja California to the Main had been conclusively

Figure 9. KINO IN CALIFORNIA. Only journeys relevant to the insularity problem are shown; routes as on map in H. E. Bolton, *Rim of Christendom* (New York 1960), 112.

demonstrated, and that not by a pearler coming up the Mar Vermejo but by a missionary coming overland from the northern marches of New Spain: Fr Eusebio Francisco Kino, SJ.

Kino: California no es Isla

Kino was born in 1645, of an Italian family in the Trentino, and educated in Austria and southern Germany, joining the Society of Jesus in 1665.[32] He was an accomplished mathematician and cartographer before he arrived in New Spain in 1681, and became a most indefatigable explorer of the northwestern borders, making over fifty journeys in the saddle, totalling thousands of miles (Fig. 9). These were mostly from the mission of Dolores which he founded in 1687, near the modern San Lorenzo in Sonora. Although this region—Pimería Alta—was his main theatre of work, his initiation, after a few months in Mexico City, was in Baja California.

By this time the authorities seem to have come round to Antonio de la Ascensión's view—that if any serious expansion was to be carried out, the Crown would have to subsidise it, and not leave it in the hands of the licensed pearlers; and a permanent settlement in the La Paz area might be of use as a strategic outpost, better than continued reliance on the chance of an odd pearler being available to warn the Galleons.[33] In 1681 Isidro de Atondo (or Otando) y Antillon, Governor of Sinaloa and 'Admiral of California', planned to colonise the peninsula: pearling and trade were to be secondary to a serious lodgement. Kino was attached to the little expedition—three small vessels—which sailed from Chacala in January 1683 and reached La Paz at the end of March. But the Indians, once friendly, had been antagonised by the depredations of the pearlers, the terrain was inhospitable, and once again the colony was abandoned, after less than four months. A second attempt, carefully planned and provisioned, was made later in the year at San Bruno, farther up the Gulf, and was more lucky: it lasted from October 1683 till May 1685, and here Kino had his induction into exploration.

This was by way of two expeditions from San Isidro, to which the colony had been moved from San Bruno, in late 1684 and early 1685. Atondo and Kino crossed the peninsula for the first time (some of their placenames still survive); on the Pacific shores the Indians presented them with fine blue abalone shells, a seemingly trivial detail which was to prove significant. But although San Isidro had better water and pasture than San Bruno, attempts at irrigation failed—their local 'Río Grande' dried out, and indeed in all of Baja California there is but one perennial stream.[34] Over Kino's protests it was decided to abandon the colony, temporarily; and immediately after the evacuation Atondo's ships were called upon—again!—to warn the Galleon, this time against Grogniet's French buccaneers. Atondo met the Galleon, which kept well clear of La Paz, and Kino returned to Acapulco on her. In 1686 it was decided to reoccupy Baja California when funds permitted, but Seville and Cadiz still cast their shadow over the Pacific: the finance had been arranged when a French demand for reparation for a ship lost at Cadiz imposed a sudden drain on the Mexican treasury.[35] Atondo's was, however, the most serious attempt at settlement to date, and the experience was valuable; though one can hardly go along with Bolton in holding that the records of the exploration of a thin wedge across the peninsula—here some 80 km wide—are comparable with those of Lewis and Clark.[36]

Kino's activities now shifted to the Sonoran frontier in Pimería Alta; the Pima Indians were on the whole docile and in any case were glad of Spanish aid against the raids of the Apaches to their northeast, and the mission of Dolores flowered remarkably. Such missions were of course agencies of Spanish conquest. In contrast to the Marianas, however, the military element was generally kept under control—in California Atondo was instructed to delete the word 'conquest' from his despatches and replace it by 'pacification and settlement' (*plus ça change . . .*); but except in purely local jurisdictional disputes, the Cross and the Crown were inseparable in the missionaries' minds. Nevertheless, it is not possible to doubt the loyalty and affection which Kino and his brethren gained from the Indians, and deserved; without them his constant journeyings, often with only one or two Spanish companions, would have been quite impossible.

By 1694 Kino's reconnaissances had taken him northwards as far as the 'Río Grande' (Gila) some 275 km north of Dolores, and westwards to the Mar Vermejo (Fig. 9). Meanwhile the activities of the buccaneers Swan and Townley in 1685–6 had renewed official interest in Baja California; an approach to the Jesuits, with the offer of a subsidy, was rejected, as their hierarchy saw no point in expansion into so sterile and thinly-populated a country. Kino and his friend Fr Juan Maria Salvatierra, however, maintained an enthusiastic propaganda, and a visit to Mexico by the General of the Order led to a change of heart. It was now the Crown's turn to withdraw, since Spain's involvement in the War of the League of Augsburg against Louis XIV made a subsidy impossible. When Salvatierra launched the definitive occupation of Baja California, the venture was supported by the 'Pious Fund of the Californias', voluntary contributions raised by the Society.[37]

Salvatierra sailed from Yaqui on 10 October 1697 and reached Baja California next day; it is an index of the navigational difficulties that his second boat, leaving at the same time, took over a month. He found San Bruno in ruins and the Indians converted by Kino were (naturally) backsliders. A week later he founded Loreto, the first Spanish settlement in the peninsula to survive. The first month was marked by a sharp little fight with the Indians, but Salvatierra held on, though progress was very slow; the initial population of Loreto was two Fathers, twelve soldiers and sailors, and four Christian Indians from the mainland. Despite the fact that legally the Jesuits were in absolute control, there were difficulties with the few soldiers and with illicit pearlers, and the little colony had to draw most of its needs from the Guaymas area across the Gulf, where Salvatierra set up an auxiliary mission as a provisioning base. But sea transport was so erratic and hazardous (there was about a wreck a year) that a land route was thought desirable; and by this time there were hints that one existed.

Though so deeply involved in Pimería Alta, Kino maintained a lively interest in his first love California, making several trips to the Gulf and planning to build boats near Caborca; he had indeed desired to go with Salvatierra, but his services in rallying the Pimas against the Apaches were thought too valuable.[38] Initially, he had accepted the insular view, and as late as 1698 he still thought that the Mar Vermejo extended indefinitely to the north, so that the Gila and Colorado (beginning to be recognised as the real 'Río Grande') entered it by separate mouths. However, in 1699 at a village on the Gila which he named San Pedro, he was given 'some curious and beautiful blue shells' like those he had seen on the Pacific side of Baja California, fourteen years earlier; but he had found none such on the shores of the Mar Vermejo: 'Afterwards it occurred to me that not very far distant there must be a passage by land to nearby California'. In the last year of the century he got to a point near the modern Yuma, and from a hill saw the Colorado-Gila confluence and 'above thirty leagues of level country, without any sea'; he now knew that he was above the head of the Gulf, and celebrated by adding some sweetmeats to his *al fresco* lunch. He recorded his findings in an excellent map of 1701, showing the 'Passo par Tierra a la California'.

The matter was not quite clinched: Salvatierra and Kino planned to finish by a pincher movement up both sides of the Gulf, but this did not come off. Kino however performed his share, going down to the mouth of the Colorado. More blue shells were gathered; they were not local, and the Indians gave 'very detailed information' that they came from the sea beyond the sea in front of them. And then on 11 March 1702 Kino watched as 'the sun rose over the head of the sea of California, proof most evident that we were now in California.'

It is to be feared that the success went to his head a little. There could be a great new kingdom, to be called perhaps New Philippines or New Navarre, and a new port for the Galleons. And of course Drake was a liar with his talk of a Strait of Anian hereabouts: the way lay open by land to Quivira and Alta California, even to Tartary, China, Japan, the Tierra de la Compañía (Compagnies Landt), crossing the narrow Strait of Anian far to the northwest—'it is patent that there is no other'. (The opening year of the War of the Spanish Succession was hardly the right time to sound this ancient roll-call.) There were still sceptics, even in New Spain, and even after Salvatierra's successor, Juan de Ugarte, sailed in 1721 to the head of the Gulf, accompanied by an Englishman, Guillermo Estrafort (= William Strafford).[39] Some were not convinced until Fr Fernando Consag sailed right round the Gulf in 1746 (Ulloa had done so in 1539!), and in the next year a Royal decree solemnly buried Drake's alleged heresy, proclaiming that 'California no es Isla.' But before Kino died in 1711, his cause was winning acceptance in Europe: his map had been pirated in France in 1705, and on 9 February 1708/9 at a meeting of the Royal Society in London 'a paper was read of ye discovery of California whereby it appears not to be an island.'[40] For Kino the Mar Vermejo, like an earlier Red Sea, had been made dry land: *Apparuit terra arida, et in Mari Rubro via sine impedimento.*[41]

Chapter 6

THE BUCCANEERS

There were forty craft in Avès that were both swift and stout,
All furnished well with small arms and cannons round about;
And a thousand men in Avès made laws so fair and free
To choose their valiant captains and obey them loyally.
Thence we sailed against the Spaniard with his hoards of plate and gold,
Which he won with cruel tortures from Indian folk of old ...
And the negro maids to Avès from bondage fast did flee ...
But Scripture saith, an ending to all fine things must be;
So the King's ships sailed on Avès, and quite put down were we.

While mutual civilities were passing between the
[Spanish] Governor and our Captain, our people
went out every day chasing the Indians, whom they
had full license to kill and destroy....

The first irruption of the buccaneers into the South Sea, in 1681, opened a more intensive phase of non-Iberian activity in the Pacific. From 1578 to 1643 there were eight hostile English and Dutch voyages into the Spanish Lake, and two explorations, those of Le Maire and Tasman; from 1644 to 1680, three or four attempts at peaceful trading, plus Henry Morgan's overland attack on Panama. But in the next sixty years there were eight buccaneer or privateer raids, one official attack (Anson), two ostensibly trading ventures (Narborough and Strong), one exploration (Roggeveen), and sixteen or more friendly French voyages to Peru and Chile, some of which went on to cross the Ocean: a minimum of twenty-eight.[1] There were also several attacks on Puerto Bello and Cartagena, not to mention the intrusion of the Scots colony of Caledonia in Darien.

The direct damage to the Spaniards in disruption of trade and of treasure shipments was compounded by enhanced defence expenditure; no less significant was the loosening of contacts between the metropolis and the Indies, which were increasingly forced to rely upon themselves or, in the War of the Spanish Succession, on direct but not disinterested French aid. There was also an intangible but potent by-product of buccaneering—a mass of publicity, in which solid strategic and commercial information was spicily garnished with tales of derring-do and atrocity: Exquemelin was the most lurid retailer of horror stories, Dampier the most weighty observer. The many books of *Voyages* and *Adventures* contributed powerfully to that obsession of British projectors, the subversion of the Spanish

---

The Revd Charles Kingsley, Canon of Westminster, 'The Last Buccaneer';
Ambrose Cowley, M.A. Cantab. [?] and buccaneer, at Guam, in [D. Henry],
Voyages Round the World (London 1774), I.447.

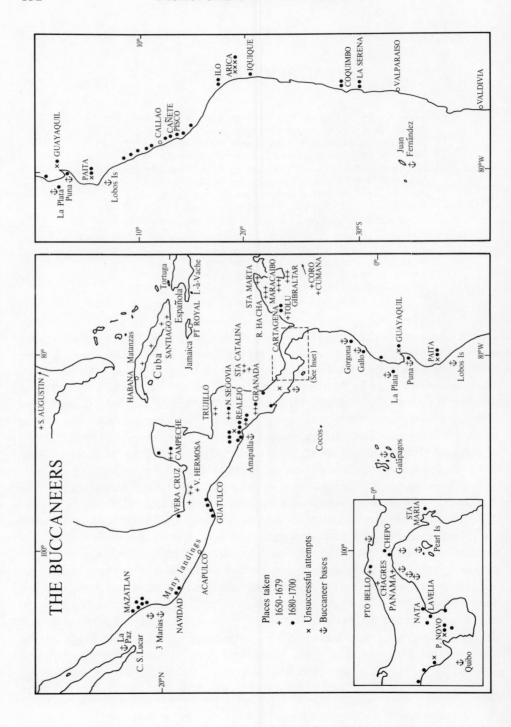

THE BUCCANEERS

Places taken
+ 1650-1679
• 1680-1700
× Unsuccessful attempts
⚓ Buccaneer bases

American empire, which persisted until the mooted descent on Venezuela by Arthur Wellesley and Francisco de Miranda was thrown into the discard by the outbreak of the Peninsular War.

Caribbean beginnings

The 1620s were ominous for the maintenance of Spanish security on the approaches to the Isthmian node. By 1624 Richelieu, wedded to his vision of French ascendancy, was firmly in power, and Buckingham and Prince Charles had trailed home from the comic-opera courtship in Madrid: King Jamie's long honeymoon with Spain was over. So also was the Twelve Years' Truce with the Netherlands, and their new West India Company had launched an offensive which would culminate in Piet Hein's devastating capture of the silver fleet at Matanzas in 1628. True, English, Dutch and French adventurers had followed Raleigh's footsteps in Guiana with no more success than his, and the strange Puritan colony of Old Providence (Santa Catalina) lasted only twelve years, 1629–41; it was located with provocative imprudence alongside the track of the galeones from Puerto Bello to Habana, and by 1635 'the history of Providence as a Puritan haven' was virtually ended, the colony being reorganised as a base whence privateers might prey upon coastal shipping, and the Company as an agency to sell commissions.[2] Once the Spaniards were roused, however, Providence was too small and isolated to be viable without Jamaica as a base, or even, as was to be proved, with it. But to the east the Spaniards had practically ignored the Lesser Antilles.

These islands had no gold and were too rugged and forested for cattle-ranching, while the Caribs were tough fighters and the Northeast Trades hindered communication with the Spanish bases to the west. Here, then, like tiny specks of decay, St Kitts, Barbados, Nevis and Guadeloupe were in English or French hands by 1635, and westwards the Dutch were strongly lodged in Curaçao. The decisive year was 1655, when Cromwell's commanders, to salve something from their wretched fiasco at Santo Domingo, passed on to seize Jamaica. What looked like a miserable remnant of his 'Western Design' (in the planning of which our unsavoury old acquaintance Thomas Gage, 'the English American', had a hand) turned out to be a solid base for the virtual domination of the western Caribbean: in Spanish eyes, a pistol pointed at Panama. Jamaica apart, Spanish losses in actual territory look negligible—only Jamaica and Curaçao had been in actual occupation, and that was thin; but there were now alien bases near at hand for smuggling, formal war, and the irregular hostilities of buccaneers and privateers.[3]

Figure 10. THE BUCCANEERS. Number of symbols corresponds to known raids; unsuccessful attempts include abortive approaches. Such a map can hardly be complete; e.g. Pope (258) says that between 1665 and 1671 Río Hacha was raided five times and Tolu eight. Only attacks for which there are definite references are included, but the map brings out the distinction between the earlier Caribbean-based phase and the irruptions into the South Sea after 1680.

Compiled from literary sources, mainly Burney, Vol. IV, and D. Pope, *Harry Morgan's Way* (London 1977).

Alongside these encroachments, which were at least sanctioned by respectable governments, there grew up the very unrespectable commonwealth of the buccaneers, in its origins anarchist and always terrorist. In Española much of the neglected west had long since lapsed from Spanish control; its woods and savannas were the domain of feral cattle and pigs and of cosmopolitan squatters from the sea—men deserting or wrecked or marooned, 'the misfits of all nations, the Jacks of no trade, broken courtiers', fugitive slaves, desperadoes of all sorts: 'the Caribbean was a cauldron where the bad blood of Europe boiled at will.'[4] These, the original buccaneers, lived very rough, bartering meat and hides to passing smugglers for their chief needs, arms and liquor; their name derived from their staple food, *boucan*, meat roasted or dried on a barbecue.[5] They provided ready recruits for any predatory venture; many of the French among them were (at least nominally) Huguenots, and at one time there was an association between their main base Tortuga (Ile de la Tortue) and Old Providence, whose Puritanism became diluted.[6] Religious motives and sympathy for the oppressed Indians were sometimes paraded, as by Montbars 'the Exterminator', one of the most savage cut-throats of the lot. The first sea-going buccaneers, after the Spaniards had bloodily (but briefly) crushed Tortuga, were undoubtedly no more than unspeakably murderous villains, and probably most who went to sea were pirates in the strictest sense, preying on all comers.

With the spread of non-Iberian settlements and the more open involvement of governments, the later buccaneers were as a rule more discriminating. They pre-ferred to have some sort of paper which could be passed off as a licence or com-mission as privateers. With frequent wars, such pieces of paper were not hard to come by (Portugal was a handy source, being at war with Spain from 1640 to 1668), and neither the authorities nor the buccaneers were too particular about their validity: they could be forged or falsely dated, and there was a black market in them. Even when home governments were meeting Spanish protests by proclama-tions against freebooting, local officials and Jamaican juries were very co-operative, and 'where the line was to be drawn between smuggler, pirate, privateer, buccaneer and man-of-war's man in Jamaica was indeed hard to say.'[7]

A buccaneer flotilla was an *ad hoc* commando; officers were elected—and sacked—by popular and often turbulent vote; despite clear-cut agreements, discipline sat loose on the captains. They sailed 'upon the old pleasing account of no purchase [i.e. plunder], no pay', and there were fixed rules as to the shares of the loot—not forgetting, if they did have a valid commission, those of the King and the Admiralty. There was also a fixed scale of compensation for injuries. Ships were usually small and fast; Morgan's 1670 fleet, a massive armament for the buccaneers, had thirty-six craft, ranging from 120 tons, 22 guns, to twelve tons with no guns. Important factors in the buccaneers' successes were their possession of long muskets and skill in using them, against the Spaniards' cumbrous old-fashioned arquebusses. They usually came off best in the land combats which were a principal part of their activities, and in which their tactics—especially Morgan's—were imaginative.

The later phases of buccaneering, especially in the South Sea, were less ferocious than the earlier; less wanton killing, less torture to gain knowledge of hidden treasure. It is true that our accounts of these phases are not from the sensationalist Exquemelin but from the more polished Dampier and Wafer; and Cowley can be nasty enough. The buccaneers remained essentially terrorists: the rules of François Grogniet's band barred rape, but 'with some reluctance' he sent the heads of twenty of his prisoners to Panama, to speed up the ransoming of the rest—'in truth, a little violent, but the only way to bring the Spaniards to reason.'[8]

Official attitudes to the buccaneers shifted with the shifting cross-currents of politics in Europe. In the West Indies themselves, there was a growing conflict of interest between those officials and traders (in effect fences) involved with the buccaneers, and those solid merchants who would have preferred to live and let live with the Spaniards, getting their profits from contraband; eventually *contrabandistas* and *filibusteros*, 'these two scourges' of Spain, 'were seen to be mutually inimical', until at last the home governments began to crack down in earnest.[9] In the interim, English official policy was highly fluctuant, depending not only on reasoned calculations of national interest (themselves often changing), but also on private ends and murky intrigues both in Charles II's court—the court of the Cabal—and in Jamaica.

The resultant was an alternation of attempts to maintain international comity by bridling the freebooters, thereby to achieve peaceful if illicit trade with Spanish colonists, and of covert encouragement of privateering to attain the same end by coercion of the Spanish government. As Madrid retained a strong desire, and some capacity, for a *revanche*, the privateers had to be kept sweet, since they were usually the only force locally available to meet a Spanish counter-attack—and after Drake, English seamen were seized of the correct view that attack is the best mode of defence. Sir Thomas Modyford, Governor of Jamaica, seems on the whole to have inclined to the softer approach, but perforce became adept at the balancing act necessitated by this devious policy; and his hand could be forced, as when in 1665 he licensed Edward Mansfield (or Mansvelt) to attack Curaçao. This of course was perfectly legitimate, the English and Dutch being at war; but Mansfield and his fellows, covering themselves with a Portuguese commission against Spain, pre-ferred to raid Cuba and then to retake Old Providence. This brought things to a head: the Spaniards were provoked to recapture Providence (treating their prison-ers with great cruelty), and by 1668 were preparing a serious attack on Jamaica itself. It was necessary to call upon the privateers: Mansfield was dead, but his mantle fell upon perhaps the most noted, surely the most notorious, of all Welsh seamen: Henry Morgan, a man of thirty-three who was only waiting on such an opening for his talents, or talons.[10]

Morgan at Panama

Morgan owed his start in life to his uncle Thomas Morgan, Monk's right-hand man in the Cromwellian subjugation of Scotland. He came out as an ensign in the force which took Jamaica, and by 1668 was a veteran of official and unofficial warfare in the Indies. Canny enough never to sail without a commission, he was a man of infinite resource and no scruples, even if not quite the monster that Exquemelin paints him; and indubitably a superb leader.

Morgan's first moves in 1668 were against Cuba, where he got little loot but much intelligence of the projected Spanish attack, and Puerto Bello, where the purchase made up for the Cuban disappointment. This successful spoiling operation seems to have convinced Modyford of the merit of the offensive-defensive, and the home government went so far as to send out the frigate *Oxford*, to be employed at Jamaican expense, in the defence of the colony and in 'suppressing the insolence of the privateers upon that coast'—which privateers not stated. She joined Morgan's rendezvous off Española on 1 January 1669, to become flagship for a descent upon Cartagena; on the 2nd she blew up while Morgan was dining his captains, only those on his side of the table surviving. Without her firepower Morgan decided against Cartagena and took his ships to Maracaibo. The Spaniards had sent out a refurbished Armada de Barlovento, and Morgan was trapped in the sack-like Lake of Maracaibo, forcing his way out by a magnificent combination of hard blows and sharp ruses.[11]

While these hostilities were going on, the diplomats were moving to a solution: the interests of peaceful trade, legal or illegal, were winning out. The great stumbling-block was the insistence of both sides on keeping Jamaica, but by the Treaty of Madrid (July 1670) Spain was at last brought to admit His Britannic Majesty's 'full right of sovereignty, ownership and possession' of all existing English holdings in the Americas.[12] The Treaty provided for mutual oblivion of all hostile acts; it was ratified by October, but eight months more were allowed to give time for its promulgation in the Indies: a loophole through which a fleet could be driven.

Morgan was planning a culminating exploit, to the shores of the South Sea itself; a Spanish counter-filibuster against Jamaica gave just enough 'provocation' for Modyford to commission reprisals. Around mid-1670 the Governor received warning of a probable treaty settlement, but this was not very specific, except that all hostilities by land were vetoed in advance: Morgan agreed to this, but with a rider in disfavour of places where warlike preparations were going on. By the time that Modyford received definite news—in December, from the Dutch—it was too late to recall Morgan; and in view of Jamaican feeling, he could hardly have reined in the buccaneers in any case.

By mid-December Morgan had assembled his biggest fleet, carrying 1850 men and 239 guns; nearly a third of the force was French. He began by taking Old Providence as an advanced base; thence he sent three ships to seize Chagres, which was done, against stout opposition, by the New Year.[13] The main body arrived a few days later, and on 8 January 1671 Morgan set out with 1200 men up the Río Chagres. Despite their ample warning, the Spaniards' delaying actions were petty; the buccaneers had a very hard time of it, but suffered far more from hunger and fatigue than from Spanish bullets or the arrows of hostile Indians. By the 17th they had emerged from jungle into savanna and were in sight of Panama, never before seen by an enemy.

The Governor, Juan Pérez de Guzmán, a Flanders veteran, had been poorly served, but he collected two or three thousand men, few of much quality, and made a stand in front of the unfortified city. His very mixed force included as a sort of panzer weapon two great herds of half-wild cattle, to be driven into the buccaneer ranks at the right moment to create confusion; the manoeuvre back-fired. In about two hours of fighting, some of it hard enough, the defenders were shattered, and in the afternoon of 19 January Morgan entered a Panama which was soon burning furiously.

We do not have to believe Exquemelin's story of Morgan's barbarous assaults on the virtue of 'a woman so steadfast her name deserves to live'; he does not give that name, and his tale looks like and probably was romantic fiction, progenitor of many trashy books and films.[14] Nevertheless it was a violent and cruel sack, and prisoners were vilely entreated to secure ransoms. Spectacular as the success was, in terms of plunder it fell short of expectations, and there was much grumbling at the smallness of each man's purchase. Morgan could have retorted that it was their own fault; the Spaniards had sent off a large ship laden with public and private treasure, and against the Governor's orders they had neglected to destroy all other shipping. Morgan sent out a captured vessel to search the neighbouring islands for fugitives, but her people got helplessly drunk on Tabago Island, and the treasure ship put in for water and departed under their noses.

There had been no other catastrophe like unto this in all the history of the Indies, not even in the days of Drake: as Morgan reported, 'Thus was consumed that famous and ancient city of Panama, which is the greatest mart for silver and gold in the whole world.' Panama was the first European city founded on Pacific shores; a Spaniard, writing almost on the spot, lamented with a Virgilian echo that 'one could say of her as of Troy, that Panama *was*.'[15] The city was rebuilt a few miles to the west, near the old outport of Perico, and today there remain only the ruined cathedral tower and a few low walls of Panama Viejo.

As for its destroyer, Modyford and the Jamaica Council publicly thanked him. Madrid of course protested violently, but although the spirit of the Treaty had been violated—the oblivion was meant for outrages before the signing—technically the aggression had taken place during the period of grace between ratification and promulgation.[16] Naturally something had to be done: Modyford was recalled and sent to the Tower, briefly; by 1675 he was back in Jamaica as Chief Justice. Morgan also was arrested and sent to England, but not to prison—instead to an interview with King Charles and a knighthood in 1674, rather indecently soon. Later, as acting Governor of Jamaica, poacher turned gamekeeper, he was to boast of his severity towards the pirates: 'nothing can be more fatal to the prosperity of this Colony than the temptingly alluring boldness and success of the privateers.'[17] The

Ironic Muse could say no more. He died in 1688, in worldly prosperity, but more in the odour of rum than of sanctity.

An incident during Morgan's stay in Panama was a portent of the future: some of his buccaneers planned to use captured shipping to go a-roving in the South Sea. Morgan put a stop to such a diversion of his force, but clearly he had shown the way to those who were soon to emulate and surpass John Oxenham's exploit of a century earlier: the main *locus* of English buccaneering was to shift from the Spanish Main to the South Sea.

Interlude: Narborough's bungle

The first Englishman to enter the Mar del Sur since Richard Hawkins in 1594 was, however, no buccaneer, but a naval officer, John Narborough, commissioned by Charles II to 'make a Discovery' as least as far as Valdivia, 'and if possible to lay the foundation of a Trade there.'[18] Perhaps this was in optimistic anticipation of a more forthcoming Spanish attitude to trade than was to accrue from the Treaty of Madrid; at any rate, stress was laid on a peaceable approach, though it is clear from Narborough's journal that the objective was commercial espionage, with strong undertones of conspiracy with the Indians. Narborough sailed in September 1669 with the King's Ship *Sweepstakes* (300 tons, 36 'great Ordnance') and a hired merchant storeship; he had a stock of goods worth £300, not much of a foundation, and a mysterious passenger, 'Don Carlos' or Carlos Henriquez, taken presumably as an expert but perhaps a supremely secret agent.

Narborough's consort deserted before he reached Port Desire in February 1670; here he found a lead plate left by Le Maire—which did not stop him taking possession—and in April he was at Port St Julian: true to past form for that port, the crew murmured at dangers to come, and Narborough had to appeal to the example of Drake a century earlier. Here, on Drake's 'Island of True Justice', they found trinkets and human bones, presumed to be relics of his visit; not impossibly the bones might have been Thomas Doughty's. Incidentally, Narborough found the Patagonians 'People of middle stature'; so much for the famous giants. He did not enter the Straits until 22 October, passing through in four weeks, and by 14 December he reached his destination, Valdivia. The ambiguous Don Carlos was put ashore just outside the harbour, in his best clothes, to contact the Indians; after an odd delay, he contacted the Spaniards.

Narborough was received with a wary politeness; the Spanish ladies were entranced to see a ship which had come all the way from Europe.[19] He gave out that he was bound for China and had merely called for wood and water; in fact, a shore party of 'Men of good Observation to inspect into matters of this Concern' was instructed to find out all it could about the harbour and its forts, and if possible to get in touch with the local Indians 'who are at Wars with the *Spaniards*, and have the Gold'; Indian gold runs like a refrain through the journal, as it did in Hendrik Brouwer's day. Lieutenant Thomas Armiger actually tried to take a boat to some

Indians on the shore who were waving a white flag, but the Spaniards stopped this. Narborough himself managed to have subversive speech with two Indians who came aboard, and carried naïvety to the point of showing the Spaniards a chart of the coast and questioning them on the ports, 'but they did not care to answer my desires, and frame[d] other Discourses to wa[i]ve mine.'

Plate XI. DARIEN AND PANAMA. Note 'The A[uthor']s Entrance into the South Seas' by the Río de Santa Maria, and his more westerly return. From W. Dampier, *A New Voyage Round the World.* Photo ANU.

It is not surprising that the day after the white flag incident Armiger and three others were most politely arrested. Narborough could think of nothing better than sending his lieutenant a letter telling him to get details of the defences, with a postscript 'Burn all the Letters you receive from me, and in case of Examination——':

most helpful to poor Armiger. The Governor of course refused a demand for the release of the four (he kindly sent a boat for their belongings), and after a stay of just one week the *Sweepstakes* simply sailed away. Narborough may have honestly thought himself not strong enough to force the issue—and yet on his own showing, 'any Ship may come in and beat them from their Guns. . . .'[20] Or at least he could have seized some local shipping for an exchange. The example of Drake was not working.

On his return to England in June 1671, Narborough learned that the Spanish Ambassador 'had resented our Voyage into the *South Sea*, but without any further notice being taken of it.'[21] His inept espionage had been detected and he had tamely abandoned his agents; no further notice was needed. Armiger and his companions were kept at Lima in 'not very strict confinement' (he himself seems to have died in 1673) until 1682, when the presence of real buccaneers led to the garrotting of Don Carlos, who had probably betrayed the object of the voyage, but too late; Narborough had denounced himself by his clumsiness.[22]

As exploration, Narborough's voyage was respectable: he brought back careful observations of Patagonia and a good chart of the Straits which was standard for many years; though he was not, as has been stated, the first to pass the Straits both ways—that had been done by Juan Ladrillero in 1557–8. He also brought commercial information—there was a good opening if the Spanish authorities would permit it; if, as was most likely, they would not permit it, trade could be forced by four ships of twenty to thirty guns, and there were always the restive Indians, who 'are Masters of the Golden part of the Country.' Apart from the petty social success with the Spanish ladies, 'It might ironically be said, that the business of Narborough's Voyage was to set four men on shore at *Baldivia*.'[23] The buccaneers were soon to find a more excellent way of tapping the South Sea's shores of silver: Drake's way.

To the South Sea: the first wave

The earlier buccaneer successes on the Spanish Main, against 'guns sans gunners, nominal companies sans soldiers, and citizens more inclined to comfortable accommodations than to arms', had been almost too easy.[24] In the 1670s the business faced more difficult days: Spanish trade had been preyed upon to the point of providing too little plunder for too many robbers. More positively, after the 'Treaty of America' the English government began to tighten its controls, and its local officers to demand too big a cut for evading them. On occasion English co-operation against the pirates was offered, in a bid to obtain the slaving *asiento* or monopoly to supply the Spanish colonies; this was refused, but the Spaniards began to take their own counter-measures.[25] There were many plans, but too few pesos to pay for them, and great schemes for the Armada de Barlovento foundered on this rock; something was done, but not nearly enough. But in 1674, 'after years of reluctance to allow this built-in incentive to take prizes', the Madrid authorities—or the Sevillean bureaucrats of monopoly—were brought to face facts and let the

Biscayans fit out the famous or infamous *guardacostas*—handy ships with tough men, effective counter-privateers.[26] The Caribbean had been over-ravished, but the South Sea, if not exactly virgin, had not been forcibly attempted since Brouwer's failure in 1643.

A campaign like Morgan's could not be mounted any day, but it was a heady stimulant. A direct attack on his Chagres line was now impracticable: new Panama was walled (rather poorly) and garrisons were set up or strengthened there and at Chagres, Puerto Bello, and Chepo. West of Panama, Veragua had a relatively dense population, Spaniards, Christian Indians, or wild *Indios bravos* who thought, not unreasonably, that the only good white was a dead white. The weakest Isthmian sector was in the east, Darien with its empty northern coast, mangrove-shrouded but with a fringe of handy islands, the Samballas (Plate XI), and its hinterland left to pagan Indians willing, often eager, to join in the cutting of Spanish throats. Darien was the entry for the first buccaneer assault on the South Sea, and remained a major route for reinforcements, and a major exit.[27]

The buccaneers tended to follow much the same routes and to sack the same unfortunate little towns (Fig. 10); places like Tolu and Río de la Hacha must have become as inured to attack as European towns in the last war were to air-raids, and they took their measures accordingly: when Tolu was captured in 1702, the townsfolk had 'not left so much as a Silver Candlestick in their Churches.'[28] The scratch task forces of the raiders were endemically fissiparous, a natural consequence of the buccaneers' innate anarchism, and hence to unravel their splits and rejoinings and respin them into a coherent narrative is a fiendish task, especially when one has probably not the leisure and certainly not the space enjoyed by the admirable Burney (Fig. 11).[29]

The first irruption began under John Coxon, whose company included three men of some literary note—Basil Ringrose, Lionel Wafer, and the incomparable William Dampier.[30] After a sacking of Puerto Bello, early in April 1680 some 330 men set out across the Isthmus in the weak Darien sector. The initial target was Santa Maria, east of the Gulf of San Miguel, where rich gold mines had recently been opened. The buccaneers had heard of them from the Cuna Indians, whose 'Emperor' Don Andreas, a former slave of the Spaniards, clearly manipulated the buccaneer movements—perhaps to get rid of them as well as to revenge himself on his old masters. Santa Maria, merely 'some wild houses made of cane', was easily taken, but the Spaniards had conveyed away the gold. It was resolved to make for Panama itself: 'having no Chymist to refine the Ore, we thought it best to go look for it where it was to be had with the King of Spain's Arms on it, for we like other children loved pictures strangely.'[31]

Having burnt Santa Maria, the buccaneers set out for·Panama in a flotilla of three dozen canoes and a couple of larger piraguas, accompanied by Don Andreas; by St George's Day, 23 April, they were in sight of the city—and of eight ships at Perico. Three of these bore down on them; the odds were against the buccaneers, and the

Biscayners, mestizos and blacks fought desperately, even after savage losses; but good shooting, and lucky explosions on the almiranta, decided the day. The ships left at Perico had been stripped of their crews to man the fighting 'Armadilla' and were easily mopped up; one, the *Santissima Trinidad* of 400 tons, became the buccaneers' flagship *Trinity*.

Ringrose thought that Panama might have been taken while the best of the Spaniards were aboard the Armadilla, an odd tactical notion, but their losses at Perico now left the buccaneers too weak for a direct attack. There were the usual disputes as to the next step, and in a huff Coxon took himself off to Darien with Don Andreas, who adjured his allies to carry on with the good work of spoiling the Spaniard; Richard Sawkins (a well-sounding piratical name!) took command. With some panache, he exchanged messages with the Governor of Panama, who asked his authority for these warlike acts in time of peace. Sawkins replied that he was acting for 'the King of Darien, who was the true Lord of Panama'; if the Spaniards would leave the Indians in peace and liberty, and pay a handsome Danegeld to the buccaneers for their trouble, they would go away; if not, they would come to Panama with their commissions on their guns, when 'he should read them as plain as the flames of gunpowder could make them.' Soon after this brave exchange Sawkins was killed in an attack on Pueblo Nuevo in Veragua, and Bartholomew Sharp was elected to command. His proposal to cruise into the South Sea and leave by the Straits led to another split; the malcontents departed across Darien, and it was with about 150 men, in the *Trinity* and a smaller prize, that Sharp sailed from Quibo early in June.

The rest of the year was spent on the Peruvian coast. Sharp stayed too long careening at Gorgona and lost any chance of surprising Guayaquil. He also called at La Plata, an island cherished by the buccaneers on account of a tale that Drake had shared out his silver there; it was also strategically placed off the bulge of Ecuador.[32] The design was now for Arica, but when they reached it at the end of October the surf was too high for landing, and the country was up in arms. They made up for this check by sacking the sugar-works at Ilo and the 'most excellent and delicate' city of La Serena, which is indeed a pleasant little town, very 'delicate' in design; its Arms bear a castle bursting out with flames, a charge more apposite to its history than to its name. They now bore away for Juan Fernández, where they anchored on Christmas Day—the beginning of the Island's career as a base for the rovers of the seas.

Christmas was not a season of good will. So far the loot of the South Sea had been most disappointing: Sharp had 'doubted not ... of purchase at least 2000 pounds every man' at Arica; they came away with $7\frac{1}{2}$ pounds—of Ilo sugar!—and had been bilked of the promised ransom of 95,000 pesos at La Serena. 'No purchase, no pay', and no loyalty either: Sharp now wished to leave by the Straits, and was supported by those who had not gambled away their pickings—a minority. He was deposed in favour of John Watling, who began his rule by remembering the Sabbath Day, to keep it holy, and throwing the dice overboard.

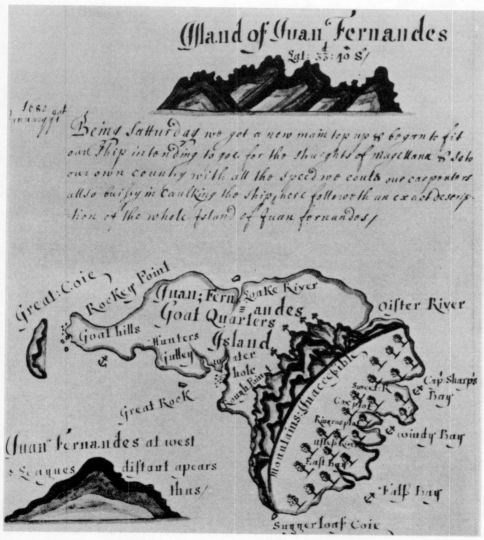

Plate XII. JUAN FERNÁNDEZ.   Mas-a-Tierra, from a journal by Bartholomew Sharp; Cox, Ringrose, and Sharp are represented in the names on the east coast. By courtesy of the Admiralty Library, London.

Three days after Watling took command, three Spanish warships arrived, on 12 January 1681; the buccaneers sailed in a great hurry, leaving behind them a Moskito Indian named William, prototype with Alexander Selkirk of Robinson Crusoe. Evading the Spaniards, they sailed for Arica, and on 30 January stormed most of the town. But Watling was killed, more Spaniards poured into the fight, and in great confusion only two-thirds of the landing party of ninety-two got away—once more under Sharp. It was only three days since he had literally washed his hands in protest against the wanton shooting of a prisoner—'I will warrant you a hot day for this piece of cruelty, whenever we come to fight at Arica'—and now he pulled the gang together.

Sobered by the fulfilment of his prophecy, the buccaneers sailed north, raiding Huasco and again Ilo, and in mid-April were at La Plata. Here over forty men seceded to make their way back to Darien; Dampier and Wafer went with them, and it is to Wafer's injury on the Isthmus that he owed his enforced stay with the Cuna and we owe his admirable *Isthmus of America*. With the seventy-odd remaining to him, Sharp cruised north as far as Nicoya and back to La Plata. His most important prize, taken in July, was the *Santo Rosario*, and this less for any metallic treasure than for a 'Spanish manuscript of a prodigious value'—a great atlas with detailed charts of the ports of the South Sea and their soundings. The Spaniards tried to throw it overboard, but too late, and 'cryed out when I gott the book (farewell South Seas now)'.[33] With the taking of this treasure Sharp's voyage was 'made': piracy could be forgiven to a man bringing back such copious if imprecise 'classified' cartography.

'All our hopes of doing further good upon the coasts of the South Sea being now frustrated', they resolved unanimously to bear away for the Straits. They left the coast on 29 August, sailing well to the west of Juan Fernández, and made a landfall on the mainland on 12 October, in about 51°S. The weather was generally murky and they missed the Straits entrance, being driven beyond 58°, meeting icebergs and sighting what may have been the Diego Ramirez Islands. No other landfall was made until they reached Barbados on 28 January 1682, a run of just five months from Paita.

This was a remarkable navigation: no Englishman had as yet rounded Cape Horn (whether or not Drake discovered it), and only one voyage, that of Brouwer's retreating fleet, had passed it from west to east. As a 'Roving on the Account', its direct gain to the buccaneers was probably much less than the damage to the Spaniards: the main attempt on Arica had failed, but there had been sackings of minor towns and some two dozen prizes, disrupting trade on the Pacific coast to such an extent that in 1684 the Treasury could not meet the payments due to the Huancavelica contractors for mercury supplies to Potosí.[34] More important in the long run was the information brought back and the lead given.

Sharp's adventures were not over when he arrived at Barbados; in May 1682 he was tried for piracy at Spanish behest, having made the mistake of bringing back a ship's boy from the *Rosario* to tell the tale. The charge was certainly not pressed very hard; after acquittal Sharp was able to present Charles II with a magnificently decorated copy of the Spanish atlas, entitled *The Waggoner of the Great South Sea*, and by November he was a Captain in the Royal Navy.[35] His later career was chequered, not to say piratical, and his end obscure; but his example was not lost on his compatriots.

The second wave

The example was very soon followed by John Cook, who had led the party which left Sharp at La Plata. They had been picked up by buccaneers on the north coast of Darien—Wafer, dressed and painted in the manner of his Cuna friends, sat amongst them for an hour before any of his old ship-mates recognised him. After various shady adventures in the Caribbean, Cook sailed from Virginia on 23 Arpil 1683 with some seventy men, including Dampier, Wafer, and a far less agreeable chronicler, Ambrose Cowley. They took the Atlantic route, and off Sierra Leone replaced their ship with a fine Dane, 36 or 40 guns, taken by a trick: pure piracy.[36] They rechristened her the *Batchelor's Delight*, and seem to have made her live up to her name by taking on a company of black girls, to perish in the cold of Cape Horn; if so, so much for Kingsley's negro maids. . . . According to Cowley they saw land in 47°40'S, which Hack, printing his journal, dubbed 'Pepys Island'. His latitude was wrong, and from Dampier it is clear that the landfall was on Sebald de Weert's Islands (the Falklands); but 'Hack's ingenious adulation of the Secretary of the Admiralty flourished a full century undetected; a Pepys Island being all the time admitted to the charts.'[37]

On 14 February 1684 'we chusing of Valentines, and discoursing of the Intrigues of Women, there arose a prodigious storm' which drove them past the Straits both of Magellan and Le Maire to 60°30'S, where it 'was so extream cold that we could bear drinking 3 quarts of Brandy in 24 hours each Man, and be not at all the worse for it, provided it was burnt'; but 'we concluded the discoursing of Women at Sea was very unlucky.'[38] Now however the prevalent Westerlies were replaced by easterly winds, and on 19 March, nearing Juan Fernández, they fell in with a ship, also bent on plunder, under John Eaton, who joined forces. At the island there was a pleasingly sentimental reunion: 'we stood with pleasure to behold the surprize, and tenderness, and solemnity' with which William, the Indian who had been left behind at Watling's hurried departure, was greeted by 'his Brother *Moskito* Man' Robin. William had seen the ships and prepared a dinner of goats, and all the company embraced him.[39]

After a couple of weeks at Juan Fernández (23 March–8 April) they moved over to the mainland coast, but luck was against them. Charles Swan, buccaneer turned trader, and Ringrose had attempted to open a genuine trade at Valdivia, and been smartly rebuffed: the alarm ran up the coast, and ships were held in port or set ashore their more valuable ladings. The *Batchelor's Delight* took three ships off Trujillo, but large cargoes of flour, eight tons of quince marmalade, and a fine but wooden image of the Virgin were not much compensation for missing the 800,000 pieces of eight offloaded when news came of Swan's activities. The buccaneers now decided to lie low in the Galápagos Islands until the Spaniards might think that they had left the South Sea. They reached the islands by latitude sailing, at the end of May; but they lacked both Drake's audacity and his patience, and stayed only twelve days, seduced by an Indian prisoner's offer of guidance to Realejo.

BUCCANEER MOVEMENTS - SECOND WAVE

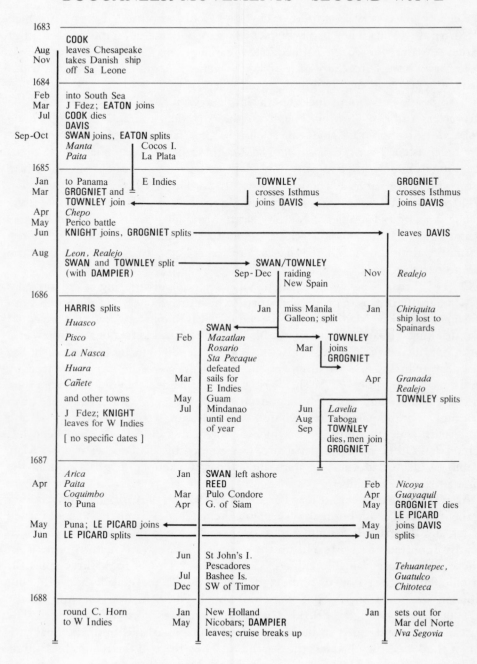

They cached 500 packs of flour as a reserve, intending to make a second dump on Cocos Island, which they missed. Cook died off Nicoya, in sight of New Spain, and the command fell by election on Edward Davis. Realejo had been warned and was judged too strong to attack; apart from careening and victualling, the two months spent on the coast were spent to no purpose. Davis's men, who had the bigger ship, refused to go equal shares with Eaton's, and it is not surprising that on 2 September they parted. Both captains sailed south, and met again three weeks later at La Plata; the quarrel was not resolved and Eaton, after some ineffectual cruising between Paita and Panama, took himself off to the East Indies in December 1684.[40]

Davis took Manta at the end of September but found 'no sort of Provision'; at La Plata a few days later they were joined by Swan, who had turned buccaneer again, throwing in his lot with a gang who had come from Darien under Peter Harris. Early in November their united forces took Paita, another blank—they found 'not so much as a Meal of Victuals left' and their demands, now reduced merely to provisions, were not met: the heroes of so many romances appear as vagrants. Burning Paita, they moved on for Guayaquil; but the approach was badly fumbled and not a shot was fired by either party. The silver of the Armada del Mar del Sur now seemed a more tangible prey, and there were reports that 'ten Sail of Frigots' were being equipped at Callao to drive the corsairs off. Davis and Swan therefore decided to sail north, and on 1 January 1685, near Gallo, they had the luck to take a packet-boat with despatches from Panama to the Viceroy in Lima: the galeones had reached Puerto Bello and it was urgent to send on the silver convoy.

By 14 February they had careened at the Pearl Islands (Islas del Rey) and were agreeably cruising on and off Panama. Reinforcements came across the Isthmus, French under François Grogniet and Le Picard, English under one Townley, and with prizes a little fleet of ten ships and nearly a thousand men was built up. This was the strongest buccaneer concentration ever seen in the South Sea, though only Davis's *Batchelor's Delight*, 36, and Swan's *Cygnet*, 16, carried cannon. A *coup-de-main* on Panama was thought of, but prisoners reported that 'all the Strength of the Country was there' and second thoughts prevailed: better to wait for the plate fleet, known from recently captured letters to be coming from Callao. These letters also indicated that the Armada might take an unusual course, well out to sea to avoid known pirate bases such as the Lobos Islands, and would close Panama from the west, by Veragua and Nata. The buccaneers preferred to believe local pilots who averred that the Armada always came in by the Pearl Islands; twice they left Tabago, well placed for interception on the more western track, and sailed east of Panama to fill in time by taking Chepo: as usual, the town was empty. Meanwhile the Armada landed its silver at Lavelia, in Veragua (Plate XI), and slipped into Panama from the west. On 28 May the buccaneers were off Pacheque, northern-

Figure 11. BUCCANEER MOVEMENTS—SECOND WAVE. Places underlined sacked by buccaneers. Compiled mainly from Burney, Vol. IV.

most of the Pearl Islands, when they sighted the Spanish fleet, by their reckoning fourteen ships, six of them mounting in all 174 guns, with nearly 3000 men.

The odds were not so great as might appear: many of the Spanish guns were served from platforms outside the bulwarks, so that the loaders could be picked off by musketry; and the crews were mainly Indians or slaves. But these defects were offset by buccaneer indiscipline: since the Spaniards were superior in big guns and the buccaneers in small arms, close fighting was in order, but neither Swan nor Grogniet, with the two heaviest units after Davis's, showed any disposition to come to grips—since the Spaniards were coming *from* Panama the silver had obviously been unloaded, and so there was no point in hard knocks. The first day's fighting was only 'the exchanging of a few Shot', and in the night the buccaneers were tricked into following a decoy light which they took to be on the Spanish flagship. Next morning the Spaniards were bearing down from windward; they could keep their distance for a gunnery fight, 'so we ran for it ... and having taken a turn almost all round the Bay of *Panama*, we came to an Anchor again ... in the very same place from which we set out.' On the morning of the 30th the Spaniards were to leeward and slipped back to Panama. Dampier reflected that this 'battle' (casualties were negligible) tamely ended the projects of five or six months, and 'instead of making overselves Masters of the *Spanish* Fleet and Treasure, we were glad to escape them', largely owing to the Spaniards' supine failure to press home their advantage.

Feeling ran high against Grogniet, who went off on his own account, according to Dampier cashiered for cowardice; he was replaced by William Knight, who after crossing the Isthmus had cruised far to north and south, getting nothing besides a good ship and ample provisions; off Peru he heard that the buccaneers were near Panama and hastened to join them, but was too late for the fight. The English went north, taking Pueblo Nuevo (empty again) and León, where the Spaniards stalled paying the ransom until the buccaneers gave up and left, after burning the town; here they lost 'a very merry hearty old Man' in his eighties, a stout Cromwellian veteran who had followed the wars since 1641 and now refused quarter. Realejo was much the same story: the only pickings were some flour and sugar, pitch and cordage, and 150 live cattle: and indeed in their own accounts, as opposed to the romances of later days, our buccaneers appear as often back-packing their groceries as revelling in the brave clink of pieces of eight.

Such lean success meant another split: late in August Swan and Townley left Davis, with amicable farewell salutes. Dampier went with them, Wafer stayed with Davis, who cruised off New Spain for a while, visited Cocos Island (where Harris left him for the East Indies), and towards the end of the year 1685 settled down in the Galápagos. Meanwhile Swan and Townley made their way northwards with an eye to the Acapulco Galleon; they landed and skirmished here and there, finding nothing left of once-famous Guatulco but a little chapel near the sea; Townley tried a nocturnal cutting-out of a rich Lima ship from Acapulco harbour itself, but she lay too snug under the fort. This diversion may have cost them the Galleon; early in

1686 'we did all conclude, that while we were necessitated to hunt here for Provisions, she was past by to the Eastward, as indeed she was'. This was enough for Townley, who parted company and sailed south.

Swan still had 'some expectations of mines', of which there were plenty of tantalising tales; the buccaneers were slow to realise that they were mostly well up-country. At Rosario indeed they were told that the mines were less than two leagues away, but to search for them meant risking the loss of 'Maiz ... to the quantity of 80 or 90 Bushels; and which to us ... was at that time more valuable than all the Gold in the World.' Still foraging for bare victuals, they learnt from an Indian in a corn-field that Santa Pecaque, five leagues inland, was an important supplier of food to Compostella and its silver-mines, and by now 'Captain *Swan's* only business ... was to get Provision.' They took the town on 17 February 1686, with no opposition; there was indeed plenty of corn, and horses to carry it off; but their undisciplined convoy became strung out and was ambushed. Over fifty buccaneers were killed—'among the rest, my ingenious Friend Mr *Ringrose*.'

This was a disaster ranking with Watling's at Arica. Swan thought that something might yet be done by making 'a discovery in the Lake of *California*' and trying to secure 'some of the Plate of *New Mexico*' in collaboration with rumoured Indian risings (Kino's pacification was not yet complete), but at the Tres Marias it was decided to make for the East Indies; Dampier seems to have had a major share in this choice. They had scraped together provisions for sixty days or less, and 'most of our Men were almost Daunted by the Thoughts' of a voyage which some feared might 'carry them out of the World.' Dampier was relying on the Trade Winds, and Swan argued that the distance was not the Spaniards' 2400 leagues but under 2000: it seems likely that there was some juggling with the length of a league.[41] What turned the scale was the promise of cruising for the Galleon on the other side of the Ocean.

They left Cape Corrientes on 31 March 1686 and reached Guam on 21 May, fifty-one days later and with three days' provisions in hand: Swan cracked a macabre joke on the likelihood of being eaten by the crew—'*Ah!* Dampier, *you would have made them but a poor Meal*, for I was as lean as the Captain was lusty and fleshy.' Passing themselves off as Spaniards, they lured a friar on board and used him as an intermediary in polite, and successful, negotiations for supplies, giving in exchange ammunition and (much against the crew's will) 'a delicate large *English* dog' to which the Governor took a fancy. While these courtesies were passing, however, the Spaniards sighted the Galleon from Acapulco and warned it off: another blank in the lottery. Leaving Guam on 2 June, the buccaneers passed over to Mindanao, where they slipped into an easy life—the Malays were exceedingly hospitable, at least until the money began to run out—and Swan was tired of roving; his 'Uneasiness and indiscreet Management' led to mutiny under one John Read. The captain and some others were left on Mindanao, where he was probably murdered; Read carried off the *Cygnet* and spent 1687 rather aimlessly cruising around the Indies; in January 1688 he careened in the Buccaneer Archipelago off northwestern Australia. The voyage now broke up, Read going a-pirating in the Indian Ocean, and the *Cygnet*, rotten with worms, sinking at anchor off Madagascar. Dampier left her in the Nicobars in May, but did not reach England until 1691; and here we must say farewell to a delightful guide. His adventures and observations after Mindanao are fascinating, but not to the present purpose except that the brief visit to New Holland gave him the concept of his own exploring voyage of 1699–1701.

After leaving Swan, Townley cruised off New Spain until in March 1686 he joined Grogniet. Together they took Granada, the French celebrating with a *Te Deum* in the Cathedral, but they were ill-assorted allies; de Lussan complains of the brutal religious intolerance of the English—and then the plunder was small.[42] Townley and some of the French took Lavelia in June, but fell into an ambush and lost their booty; they continued to terrorise the Veragua coast, reverting to the older more savage type; ransoms were enforced by sending in Spanish heads, and de Lussan establishes the true value of his piety by remarking quite casually 'We interrogated [the prisoner] with the usual ceremonies, that is to say, we gave him the torture.' Townley however died of wounds in September and his people rejoined Grogniet in January 1687; no very substantial gains had been made by either group in months of rapine, and many wished to throw in their hands and return to Europe across the Isthmus. Stouter counsels prevailed and they sailed for Guayaquil (Fig. 16) in two parties, reuniting at Santa Elena. Their luck now turned: the well-planned attack on Guayaquil (21–4 April) netted 700 prisoners, including the Governor, and a good deal of treasure—occasion for another *Te Deum*; with so many hostages, they demanded a ransom of a million pieces of eight. But Grogniet died of wounds on 2 May, and at this point Davis reappears as a leader: he had no part in the taking of Guayaquil, but the guns of the *Batchelor's Delight* ensured that his voice would carry weight.

We left Davis in the Galápagos at the end of 1685. He spent the next year raiding between Cañete and Coquimbo; the booty was considerable and was shared out at Juan Fernández, where Knight left him. Early in 1687 Davis returned to the attack, taking Arica and in April Paita, where he captured a despatch from the Deputy Governor of Guayaquil to the Viceroy. Unlike his Governor, the Deputy, not being in the buccaneers' clutches, was not disposed to trade dollars for heads, but was spinning out time until an armament could arrive from Callao. Taking the hint, Davis set off for the Gulf of Guayaquil, waiting at Puna for the expected Spanish succours: he had already driven ashore the privately fitted out *Catalina*, 8 guns, and might have captured it had his crew been sober. Reinforced by the buccaneers from Guayaquil, he engaged the ships of the Compañía de Nuestra Señora de Guia off Isla Santa Clara, a gunnery fight spread over several days with no close action and no decisive result.

The Spaniards however withdrew, the buccaneers settled down on Puna, to share out the plunder in a holiday atmosphere. The million pesos to which the Governor had agreed were not indeed forthcoming, and when it came to the point they baulked at carrying out their threat of beheading 500 prisoners; very possibly it was Davis's influence which secured a majority for moderation. Even so, for those who were abstinent from or lucky at the dice, the purchase was reasonably good: de Lussan, pluming himself on his amatory and gambling *bonnes fortunes*, gives the total at 400 pieces of eight per man. It was time to cut losses or to take profits and be gone. The French departed to the north in June, and in January 1688 took Nueva Segovia (in Nicaragua) on their way to the Mar del Norte; Davis retired first to the Galápagos, whence he sailed for Juan Fernández.

It is at this point, late in 1687, that the buccaneers make their solitary, and highly disputable, claim to a significant discovery. The two reports, one directly by Wafer, the other indirectly from Davis through Dampier (who thought it might probably be Terra Australis) are in complete agreement as to the sighting, in about 27°S and 500 leagues west of Copiapo, of a small low sandy island and, about twelve leagues west of it, 'a long Tract of pretty high land.'[43] There is no such combination anywhere near the position indicated. Near the given latitude, Easter Island is fairly high (520 m) but has no low island to the East; Sala y Gomez, 320 km to the east, might be called low but has no land visible to the west; SS Felix y Ambrosio are too high and too near to Chile. The discovery of Easter is of course officially credited to Jacob Roggeveen in 1722, and the suggestion that Davis really saw it from over a low island now disappeared is implausible, as there seems no hint of a sea-mount or submarine volcano. The probability is that Davis saw Sala y Gomez and beyond it high banks of cumulus, commonly enough mistaken for land. One must conclude with Andrew Sharp that 'Davis's Land is clearly not Easter Island.'[44] But it long remained on the maps, a shadowy outpost of a more shadowy Great South Land.

The return from Juan Fernández around Cape Horn was tempestuous, and Davis's navigation in the Atlantic went astray, but the *Batchelor's Delight* reached Philadelphia in May 1688. Wafer 'thought to settle' in Virginia, 'But meeting with some Troubles, after a three Years residence there, I came home for England in the Year 1690.' The residence was involuntary, in Jamestown jail under a charge of piracy; eventually he and Davis bluffed their way out, and Wafer, returned to respectability, was to play an important role in the planning of the Scots colony in Darien.[45]

The Spanish reaction

The buccaneer assaults initiated a significant shift in the balance of the Spanish Empire; the crisis compelled an unprecedented recourse to private enterprise, in both the North and the South Seas, and this was in itself a portent.

The buccaneers in the South Seas never numbered more than a thousand or so men; hardly any of their ships, other than the *Batchelor's Delight* and the *Cygnet*, carried cannon; they relied on captures of coastal traders and on seizing or building piraguas or large canoes. It may well be asked how such forces could terrorise the holdings of a great Empire, let alone have a geopolitical effect. From the more romantic retellings of their story, one might take the answer to be that the Spaniards were in the mass cowards and/or idiots, the buccaneers bonny and fearless fighters. This is far from the truth: there was a good deal of poltroonery, not confined to one side, but the individual human material was not so ill-matched, and blacks and mestizos as well as the Spaniards themselves often put up a very good showing. But there must often have been a disparity in morale, the difference between riding on the crests of the waves and wallowing in the breakers.[46] Nevertheless, the Spaniards were still able to launch damaging local counter-attacks, and the buccaneers had their disasters as well as their triumphs. But their enemy was at most times and places committed, through lack of naval resources, to the passive defence of a large number of isolated positions, and this in itself must have been depressing.

It was a classic instance of the advantages of command of the sea combined with guerrilla raiding: when the buccaneers really concentrated, in the fights off Panama, they were too much weakened in the first action to be able to follow up their success, while in the second, as Dampier confesses, they ran for it and were glad to get away. Again, for the defence, a draw may look as good as a win, in the local and short view. In the long run, however, local successes could do little or nothing for the safety of the coastal shipping on which so many places depended—Panama, the great node, most of all. The Spaniards could muster greater fire-power at specific points, but could never control the open sea; there the buccaneers roved at will, and by the end of 1686 they had taken seventy-two coastal traders—two-thirds of the merchant marine of the South Sea.[47] In a sense Peru was paying the penalty for its well-integrated littoral economy, itself a resultant of its geography.

In the Spanish bureaucratic tradition, the best defence of the American shores of the South Sea had been seen as residing in the difficulty of access from bases far away in Europe; a happy solution since it cost no money.[48] But now the barriers of ignorance had been breached, in the south by Le Maire and Brouwer, Narborough and Sharp, in the north by repeated thrusts into Nicaragua and across Darien. As for bases, the buccaneers made good use of outlying islands like the Galápagos and Juan Fernández, and, closer in, the Tres Marias, Quibo, Gorgona, Gallo, La Plata, the Lobos, and even Tabago and Puna, at the very gates of Panama and Guayaquil. It was now obvious that God and Nature would not help those who would not help themselves, and it was clear enough that the first prerequisite was adequate naval force—in the Caribbean above all, to seal off the approaches to Panama, 'escudo y defensa de los reinos del Peru.'

For this first prerequisite its own prerequisite—money—was lacking. In 1685 a special junta recommended increases in the Atlantic fleets which would have brought them up to something *under* their strength in 1600, but there was not enough cash even for so little. As for the South Sea, that had to be left very much to

Viceregal or local initiative; this was the more difficult in that of course Customs and other revenue fell sharply with the disruption of trade. The first official reaction was simply to close the ports, but despite the risks trade had to go on, under licences; fortunately the buccaneers, not wishing to kill the goose, often released unwanted ships as soon as they had robbed them. Ships of war were the obvious answer, but they were very difficult to find, though building went on at Guayaquil, and still more difficult to man and maintain. In order to economise, the Crown in 1682 ordered that the manning of the Armada del Mar del Sur should be reduced to a 'cuerpo de guardia' during the long spells at Callao between its own triennial convoys; with vast inconsistency, it also ordered that no merchant ship should put to sea without adequate and skilled crews, and sufficient guns: a manifest impossibility. Hardly any of them were even fit to carry ordnance.

'In truth, Sharp demonstrated that the Peruvian squadron was in practice a factor of little or no defensive value.'[49] The wretched Armada did make some sallies. In 1675, after the Narborough alarm, Antonio de Bea (Vea in English accounts) and Pascual de Iriarte were sent to reconnoitre Juan Fernández and southern Chile: Bea landed dogs on Mas-a-Tierra to kill the goats, a potential food-supply for intruders, and Iriarte found no trace of the feared English lodgements in the Straits.[50] Proposals to send out six frigates round the Horn, even for Peru to buy two permission ships at Buenos Aires, came to nothing; and then in 1682–5 the Armada, only two galleons and a patache, was immobilised by a chapter of accidents. When at last it was ready to sail, in May 1685, the Lima merchants refused to risk consigning by it. As we have seen, this Armada did take the Crown silver to the Isthmus and drive off the buccaneers; but this offensive stroke was dearly paid for when the flagship blew up at Paita.[51]

At this point the merchants of Lima and Callao, improving on a hint from the Crown that they might contribute directly to defence at sea, fitted out two ships and a patache and sent them to Panama. The cruise, July 1686–April 1687, was uneventful but for the loss of the *Catalina* in the fight with Edward Davis. Meanwhile a 'Compañía de Nuestra Señora de Guia' had been set up by a formal agreement with the Viceroy Duque de la Palata: arms were to be supplied by the Crown, ships by the merchants, and the Company would have complete administrative autonomy—a concession to private enterprise which shows how desperate things were. (As with the guardacostas in the Mar del Norte, Biscayners were prominent.) Two ships of twenty guns each were equipped by the Company and sailed in May 1687, engaging Davis's buccaneers in the Gulf of Guayaquil. One ship followed up the retreating French party to Amapalla Bay, according to Spanish sources inflicting severe damage on them: it is at any rate clear that, with or without fighting, the Company saw the buccaneers out of the South Sea.[52]

This was a marked success, although the buccaneers were leaving the South Sea anyway. The Company was dissolved in 1693: with the recession of the threat, enthusiasm also receded, and private enterprise could not be relied upon for routine work but could be for smuggling. Under Palata's successor, the Conde de

Monclava, the Armada was built up again—very largely by private if perhaps not always voluntary subscription—and by 1693 was stronger than it had ever been: three ships and two pataches, 144 guns, still not enough for its manifold duties. It was fortunate that there was little direct threat in the South Sea itself before the end of the century.

Such as there was came from France, since from 1688 to 1697 Spain was allied with two old enemies, the English and the Dutch, in the War of the League of Augsburg (or Nine Years' War) against Louis XIV. A powerful French expedition—six ships with 112 guns—sailed for the South Sea in June 1695; but the commander, J.-B. de Gennes, dawdled in the Atlantic, and after two months trying to pass the Straits (February–April 1696) dawdled back to France via the Caribbean. The abortive voyage was not, however, without significance; inspired by the glowing reports of the buccaneer Massertie, it in turn directly inspired the voyage of Beauchesne-Gouin (1698–1701), the first of the French trading ventures into—and later across—the Pacific, which were to be of great importance during the War of the Spanish Succession.[53]

The geopolitical shift was mediated by finance, or the lack of it; the military and the fiscal crises were inextricably intertwined. The net result of the buccaneer attacks was that an increasingly large proportion of the treasure of the Indies had to be spent in the Indies, while the inadequacies of the imperial bureaucratic machine had to be made good by private effort, the guardacostas in the Mar del Norte, the Compañía de Nuestra Señora de Guia in the Mar del Sur. These were small things in themselves but the first signs of a breach in the old system, a breach to be greatly widened in the next century with the Bourbon Reforms culminating in the 'Free Trade' measures of the 1770s.

Immediately, there were not lacking clear heads to see the priorities correctly. Palata put them as amphibious action in the Caribbean, the pacification and peopling of Darien, and a new Viceroyalty in New Granada to keep close watch on this vital area: only so could the Isthmian entry be blocked. In 1686 a three-pronged offensive against the Darien Indians, an ever-dangerous fifth column, was proposed: attacks from Panama, from Cartagena, and from Antioquia to cut off escape to the south. This was logical, but nothing was done: not only would it cost too much, but it would open a new route for contraband, that fearful obsession of the system. 'The line followed was therefore to try to close the road to the pirates but without opening it to the Spaniards', and so the way was left open for the Scots in Darien.[54] As for the new Viceroyalty, that had to wait until 1717 for its provisional proclamation, until 1739 for its definitive establishment.

As we have seen, Panama and its outposts were strengthened; in the far south Valdivia was 'a military complex worthy of some respect'; but it was impossible to fortify the long intervening string of ports at all adequately. Callao was the best-defended point, and both buccaneers and privateers always gave it a wide berth; but in 1673 its whole garrison, apart from the Viceroy's guard, was 354 men. Things improved somewhat in the 1680s, and of course in crises local levies could be called out; in 1684 Palata rapidly concentrated 4000 men, to demobilise them as rapidly, for financial reasons, once the danger had passed. In the late eighties Lima was strongly, or at least extensively, walled, but the great earthquake of 1687 was a disaster, the 'decrepit walls' of Callao serving as a refuge not from pirates but from flood.[55]

At every turn defence measures were hampered by the shortage of funds; it was still possible for funds already earmarked for frigates for the Indies to be diverted to Peninsular needs, to the great indignation of the President of the Council of the Indies; but an increasingly large share of Peruvian silver was being devoted to local defence. In 1686–90 no fewer than 6,500,000 pesos were so expended, only 750,000 being sent to Spain.[56] But there was never enough in the Treasury. All sorts of expedients were tried—monopolies, sales of titles and offices, loans forced or voluntary. The response was mixed; reluctance, even refusal, to contribute for distant or little-known ends, but often spontaneous offerings to meet clear local threats, especially if the contributors had some control over the funds. As with money, so with men: the militia was usually keen and brave enough on its own ground, ineffective elsewhere. It was not that the Spanish Americans were

> stingy or excessively selfish; they simply showed that they agreed
> with the President of the Council: they wanted for the Indies what
> was the Indies' . . . The Viceroyalty of Peru, with its own forces and
> resources, thus repelled all attacks and learnt how to keep itself secure,
> despite the losses incurred.

Céspedes del Castillo's statement may seem bold, yet it is true that the Mar del Sur had been left very much to its own resources, and had survived. This may not have been 'the first emancipation of Latin America', yet it may well be that the troublous times of the buccaneers saw the first glimmerings of those feelings of American identity which were to break into the blaze of the Liberation.[57]

The last buccaneers: Cartagena 1697

Before the century closed there were to be two more attempts on the Isthmian approaches to the South Sea. The more serious in its implications, the Scots colony in Darien, was a total failure; it will be discussed in the next chapter. The more successful, the French taking of Cartagena, was really only an episode, a by-blow of the 1688–97 war; but it marks the end of buccaneering.

With the armed support rather than the hostility of England and the Nether-lands, Spanish power in the Caribbean showed a distinct revival in the 1690s; in particular, Spanish and Anglo-Spanish attacks devastated the French settlements in Saint-Domingue, the western portion of Española, which they had taken over with no small assistance from the buccaneers, or rather (to use the French term) the flibustiers. These set-backs induced Louis XIV to support the private promotion of a large-scale attack on the Spanish Main; indeed the Sun King was not above invest-ing in this vulgar enterprise, which was the sequel to an abortive expedition aimed at Puerto Rico and the Armada de Barlovento, and if possible Jamaica. The armament was powerful: at least seven heavily-gunned ships, with frigates and bomb-vessels, and some 4000 sailors and regular troops. These were to be supplemented by local forces from Saint-Domingue, some 1200 men, mostly flibustiers, under the Governor Jean Ducasse. There was from the beginning bad feeling between Ducasse and the commander of the main force, the Baron de Pointis, between whom and the flibustiers there was an instant mutual distaste.[58]

The target was narrowed down to Cartagena; it was heavily fortified but, as Fernández Duro says, this was largely a theatrical façade: the guns were poor, on weak cedar carriages, and the forts were grossly under-manned. The French appeared off the town on 13 April 1697, and on 3 May it capitulated. Pointis, whose contempt for the flibustiers was bitter and perhaps warranted, seems to have been both arrogant and shifty. His promise to respect religious property was evaded or violated, and although Ducasse had a written agreement that the local forces should have equal shares with the King's men, Pointis concealed, or at least failed to make clear, the fact that the shares for the investors would be deducted before the booty was distributed: this reduced the locals' share from an expected 2,000,000 crowns to a miserable 40,000. Pointis sailed away on 2 June, leaving Ducasse to cope with the infuriated flibustiers; the result was a second and extremely brutal sack. However, at Versailles all was well for Pointis: Louis was charmed by the Baron's presents.[59]

The flibustiers decamped on the approach of an Anglo-Dutch fleet; in September the Treaty of Rijswijk ended the war. For His Catholic Majesty D. Carlos II, the Bewitched, the long agony of living was drawing unpeacefully to a close; in view of the uncertain succession, it behooved both France and the Maritime Powers to manage Spanish susceptibilities with extreme delicacy. The buccaneers had done their job as disavowable agents of empire, and every man's hand was now against them.

As a body then, they now disappear from history. Some, such as Dampier, turn up again in the less disreputable guise of privateers; some dissolved back into the littoral communities of the North Atlantic, as mariners, traders, planters, founders of colonial families or plain old soaks in Sailortown; some dispersed into sheer piracy in distant seas, a losing game in the long run. Their legend remained, and it was not without serious significance both in politics and, oddly enough, in literature.

The buccaneer legacy

'Only with the eighteenth century does the sea occupy a place in English literature at all comparable with its place in English life.'[60] Hakluyt indeed might be thought a host in himself; but the compilers of travel collections, while using his work as a quarry, thought him too old-fashioned to be admitted to the world of polite literature; there was no reprint of *The Principal Navigations* until 1809–12, and no major collection of voyages appeared in England between *Purchas His Pilgrimes* in 1625 and the end of the century. It is hardly too much to say that the success of

Dampier's *New Voyage* in 1697 changed all that: 'the vogue of travel literature, which was outrun in popularity among the reading public only by theology, became firmly established and was to be sustained throughout the [eighteenth] century.'[61] Exquemelin and Dampier became, and long remained, best-sellers. Dampier's *New Voyage* ran to five editions in six years, and his publisher, James Knapton, became a specialist in travel literature.

There was plenty of material: Dampier, Ringrose, Cowley, Sharpe, Funnell, Rogers, Betagh, Shelvocke, for the voyages up till 1719, and another crop of half a dozen writers around Anson's voyage alone. Defoe weighed in with an entirely fictitious *New Voyage round the World*, and William Chetwood, prompter at Drury Lane, introduced Dampier himself into his *Voyages and Adventures of Captain Robert Boyle* (London 1726), and married the buccaneer voyage with the picaresque novel; his hero meets Dampier (accompanied by an English eunuch!) in Brazil, has a fight with de Gennes's ships off the Straits, visits Juan Fernández, and takes the Galleon.

Both Wafer and Dampier are admirable writers, clear and lively; the former's account of his life with the Cuna is a precious document of ethnohistory. Dampier is more; at every point he is not just a narrator but a serious and acute scientific observer, while his *Discourse of Trade Winds* is at least a beginning of systematisation: 'The true distinction of Dampier is that he was a century ahead of his confreres in his intense devotion to the gathering, assessment, and recording of... natural and social phenomena ...'.[62] For all his protestations of being a rude unlettered seaman, and even if, in the manner of the times, he did accept some polishing from more practised hands, it cannot have amounted to much; there can be no manner of doubt that *A New Voyage Round the World* is at once a compendium of observations on natural phenomena and a splendidly personal narrative. And Dampier and his fellows inspired greater minds.

It is hardly necessary to stress Defoe's debt to Dampier and Wafer, and not only for the central idea of *Robinson Crusoe*; it is more interesting to note the divergences—the contrast between Crusoe's paternalistic usage of Man Friday and Wafer's acceptance of the Indians as simply human beings with a different mode of life, or that between Dampier's cool discounting of cannibal tales with Defoe's professional gusto in recounting man-eating orgies—he knew his market. No fewer than eight of Defoe's narratives are indebted to Dampier, on whom he apparently relies more than on any other travel writer.[63] Swift's genius took him into regions Dampier never knew, but the framework of *Gulliver's Travels* is no more than an inspired parody of the South Sea voyage genre—all the settings are in the North Pacific or off New Holland—and the very first sentence of the book has Captain Lemuel Gulliver referring to 'my cousin Dampier'.[64] The frame of *The Rime of the Ancient Mariner* is also precisely that of a buccaneer voyage into the South Sea, and the central symbol of the Albatross comes directly from the journal of the privateer Shelvocke.[65] Three of the greatest works in the English language thus owe much of their inspiration, and the germ of their particular form, to the buccaneers and privateers; not to mention such minor but in their kind admirable writings as *Treasure Island* and some of the earlier work of John Masefield, himself an editor of Dampier and chronicler of the Spanish Main. And nowadays, the rascal rubbish of the airport book-stalls.

The buccaneers engendered romance; they were anything but romanticists, and their writings had the utilitarian purposes of imparting information and inciting to patriotic action, while turning a more or less honest guinea. Wafer's part in the planning of the Scots' Caledonia in Darien was direct and decisive; Dampier, always good at spotting opportunities once they were lost, laments that after the failure at Guayaquil the buccaneers did not take the 1000 stout Negro-men captured at Puna and use them for working the gold mines of Santa Maria:

> the *Indian* Neighbourhood, who were mortal Enemies to the *Spaniards*, and had been flush'd by their Successes against them, through the Assistance of the Privateers, for several Years, were our fast Friends ... if all the strength that the *Spaniards* have in *Peru* had come against us, we could have kept them out. If they lay with Guard-ships of Strength to keep us in, we had a great Country to live in, and a great Nation of *Indians* that were our Friends. Besides, which was the principal Thing, we had the *North-Seas* to befriend us ... many thousands of Privateers from *Jamaica* and the *French* Islands especially would have flockt over to us; and long before this time we might have been Masters not only of those Mines, (the richest Gold-Mines ever yet found in *America*) but of all the Coast as high as *Quito*: And much more than I say might then probably have been done.
>
> But these may seem to the Reader but Golden Dreams. ... .[66]

Indeed they do; and Dampier himself was to find them so in 1704. But the vision or mirage of a great colony, an easy, godly, and profitable protectorate based on harnessing Indian resistance to the Spaniards, and tapping all the wealth of the Indies, begins with Hakluyt in the flush of enthusiasm kindled by Drake's South Seas exploit,[67] takes a more concrete if aborted form with Raleigh in Guiana, revives with Narborough and the buccaneers, and remains a constant in British projecting throughout the eighteenth century.

As well as Darien, Patagonia and that old favourite Chile were often envisaged as likely foci of subversion, as in Pullen's plan for a descent on the South Sea, which explicitly harks back to Hendrik Brouwer; and Defoe thought, or professed, that 'there is Room enough on the Western Coast of *America* ... for us to Fix, Plant, Settle, and Establish a flourishing Trade, without perhaps in the least Invading the Property or Commerce of the *Spaniards*'—an ironic *perhaps*? Ideas of supporting or fostering Creole revolt were also toyed with, as in the instructions for Anson's expedition, where they are incongruously mixed up with ideas of igniting Indian revolts.[68] This will-o'-the-wisp was at last dissipated not so much by recognition of its impracticability as by the changed situation presented by the Bonapartist usurpation in Spain itself. That great loosening of the bonds of the Spanish imperium gave openings for co-operation not with Indians but with anti-Peninsular Creoles, and in the turmoil of 'Liberation' the victims of Spanish—and Creole—oppression were forgotten.

Yet in 1790, the year of the Anglo-Spanish Nootka crisis, Dampier's golden dream of Darien found a new and lusty expression: the Isthmus once seized, 'the standard of Liberty should be errected', freeing the 'brave and oppressed [Indians] from the galing yoak' of Spain; and by this plan 'the King of Great Britain will become the Richest Monarch on the face of the Earth ... The Sun will never set in his Dominions.' A later version by the same hand proposed that the expedition should be carried out by sixty-odd privateers from the ports of the British Empire; and, by an engaging new touch, Botany Bay might send two ships via Juan Fernández and the Peruvian coast.[69] Buccaneer or privateer, the tradition died hard.

Chapter 7

BETWEEN WARS: DAMPIER AND DARIEN

Our men did not only daily to grow more weakly and sickly,
but more, without hopes of recovery; because ... we
found the several species of the little provisions
we had left in a manner utterly spoiled and rotten....

Thus, this door of the seas, and key of the universe,
with anything of a sort of reasonable management,
will of course enable its proprietors to give laws to
both oceans, and to become arbitrators of the commercial
world, without becoming liable to the fatigues, expenses,
and dangers, or contracting the guilt and blood, of
Alexander and Caesar.

The interval between the Peace of Rijswijk (September 1697) and the opening of the War of the Spanish Succession (May 1702) saw three ventures with a Pacific bearing, unrelated but grouped here for convenience. One of them, Dampier's voyage to New Holland and New Guinea, was the only true Pacific exploration, barring the Russians around Kamchatka, between Tasman and Roggeveen. The other two were of diverse political significance. The Scottish foundation of Caledonia had a far-reaching objective: nothing less than commercial colonisation on the Isthmus itself, designed to dominate the trade of both seas, North and South; its disastrous failure had the paradoxical consequence that the Union of Great Britain stemmed in part from a fever-ridden swamp in Darien. Beauchesne's expedition in its planning also had grandiose aims, ranging from Patagonia to Baja California; its more modest success laid the foundation for the massive French dominance of trade in the South Sea during the Succession War.

Dampier and Nova Britannia

William Dampier at twenty-three, a raw new hand on a Jamaica sugar plantation, was 'given to rambling and unlikely to settle himself to stay long in any place ... If he had been anything ingenious, he might have been a good boiler. Something, I think, he understands of sailing, after which I think he hankers still.'[1] As an employer's reference, this is hardly satisfactory, but it has its point: Dampier was not to settle down until he was sixty. In 1698 he was forty-seven and famous, and for half or more of his years he had indeed been 'given to rambling' in very mixed company, never seeking prominence, always rather detached: the sort of man who

---

William Paterson, 'Report of Matters relating to the Colony of Caledonia', 1699;
William Paterson, 'A Proposal to Plant a Colony in Darien', 1701; both in J. S.
Barbour, *William Paterson and the Darien Company* (Edinburgh 1907), 40, 114.

Plate XIII. WILLIAM DAMPIER. By T. Murray; by permission of the National Portrait Gallery, London.

is called 'the Prof'. His *Voyages* are really memoirs in which the more outrageous episodes and personalities are passed over with a smooth reticence or even complete silence, and in the midst of blood and rapine he seems less concerned with his proper business as a buccaneer than with the curious observation of the world: winds, clouds, the multitudinous forms of life. He can be perceptive about the human condition, and above all he 'surveys the lesser kingdoms with a calm,

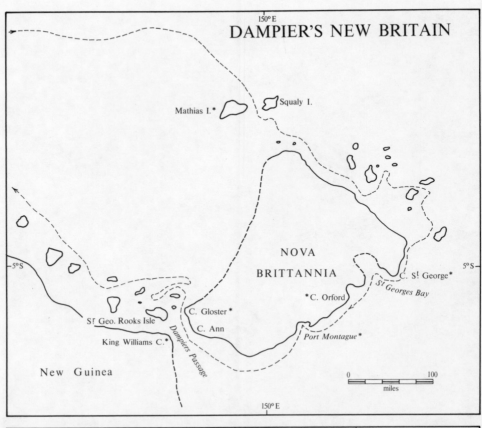

DAMPIER'S NEW BRITAIN

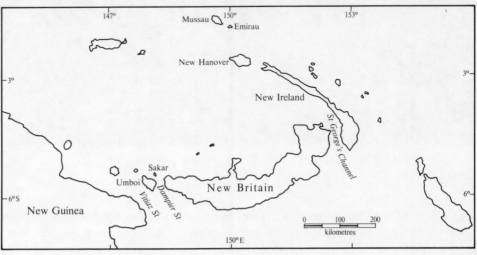

equable, untroubled and delighted vision.'[2] Buccaneering had been for him a means to that end, and now all those notes, lovingly carried through the streams and jungles of Darien in a sealed bamboo, had been moulded into the narrative, so vivid and so rarely ruffled, of *A New Voyage Round the World*. That book had indeed 'made his voyage', bringing him into contact with men of culture and influence— Pepys, Evelyn, Charles Montague the President of the Royal Society and Sir Hans Sloane its Secretary[3]—and he now thought to fulfil his passion for rambling scrutiny of the world as an end in itself, no longer as the mere by-product of a predatory raid. The sequel was to expose, cruelly, his limitations. As a sensible and resourceful subordinate, he was invaluable; as a commander, an almost pitiable failure.

Montague, to whom Dampier had dedicated *A New Voyage*, responded by becoming his patron and introducing him to Edward Russell, the newly created Earl of Orford and First Lord of the Admiralty. Despite the peace, which might and indeed did prove fragile, interest in 'The Spanish colonial empire, commercially regarded as a great and undeveloped estate with important frontages on the Pacific' and soon to come on to the market, was as lively as ever; and a scientific interest in geography was growing, as shown for instance by the Royal Society and the Admiralty sponsoring Edmund Halley's voyages to study magnetic variation in the Atlantic, the first of which sailed in November 1698.[4] Both interests had been enhanced by Dampier's own work, and it was logical that Orford should 'be pleased to order' a man apparently so well equipped for the task to propose 'some voyage wherein I might be serviceable to my Nation.'[5]

Thus given the freest of hands, Dampier conceded that there were several good options (unspecified), but for his part he 'would chuse ... the remoter part of the *East India Islands* and the neighbouring Coast of *Terra Australis*'. Since 'there is no larger Tract of Land hitherto undiscovered', whether 'a continued land or not', such a great area in warm latitudes must possess very valuable commodities; moreover it could be reached without trespassing on the preserves of any European neighbour. A compliant Admiralty allowed him virtually to write his own instructions; but the free hand did not extend to material things. He asked for two ships, but was granted only one, and the first offered was so unfit that he rejected it out of hand. The one in which he sailed can have been little better; the *Roebuck* was 290 tons with twelve guns and fifty men. Dampier wanted a larger crew, and provisioning for much longer than he was allowed.

The original plan was to go by the Cape of Good Hope to the northernmost part of New Holland, thence by New Guinea to Gilolo, perhaps picking up an unregarded spice island or so en route. From Gilolo 'I would range away to the Eastward of New Guinia and so direct my course southerly by the land'. The return

Figure 12. DAMPIER'S NEW BRITAIN.   Names marked * given by Dampier and retained on modern maps; spellings as on Dampier's map (those in text are as in his text). From map in his *Continuation of a Voyage to New-Holland* (London 1709); modern outlines below.

would be by Tierra del Fuego, or possibly (as he suspected when in the Dampier
Archipelago) there might be a passage through New Holland by which he could
double back towards Timor. There is here more than a hint of the old concept, in
the maps of the sixteenth century, of a Terra Australis reaching up from the
Antarctic to New Guinea, and perhaps his friend Captain Davis's strange sighting
was in Dampier's mind. Later he claimed that if he could have got away early
enough, in mid-September, he would have gone out by the Horn and coasted
north along the Terra Australis or New Holland coast to New Guinea, as Cook did
in 1770. But there were the inevitable short-falls and delays in fitting out the
Roebuck, and it was not until 14 January 1699 that she sailed from the Downs. Two
months earlier Dampier decided that it was too late to take the Magellanic route,
and reverted to his first plan. Either way, the Admiralty's laggardness and niggardli-
ness probably saved the lives of Dampier and his ship's company: one cannot rate
very high the prospects for a ship like the *Roebuck*, with her wretched crew, surviving the battling either around the Horn or through the hazards of the Great Barrier
Reefs.

Dampier in fact owed his commission not to any record of command—he had
none—but to patrons impressed by his undoubted literary and intellectual quality,
very likely enhanced by personal charm; the Admiralty had taken him on this
valuation,

> and sent the poor man out in command of a cheap expedition, with a
> rotten ship and an inferior crew, and without a single officer of any
> moral quality to supply his captain's deficiencies. The result was
> another classic and a quantity of dirty linen for public laundering.[6]

Right from the start Dampier had constant squabbles with his second in command
George Fisher, very much Royal Navy against 'temporary gentlemen', who lost no
chance of saying what he thought of an old buccaneer, almost a pirate, masquerad-
ing as a King's officer. Dampier retorted in kind, and the quarrels degenerated into
constant scrapping, verbal and even physical. In the upshot Fisher was simply
dumped at Bahia, where the Governor (a Lencastre, putatively descended from
John of Gaunt) obligingly locked him up in the local jail until he could be shipped
home. True to form, all that Dampier records of this imbroglio is that at Bahia he
took the 'Opportunity to compose the Disorders among my Crew . . . [and] to allay
in some Measure the Ferment that had been raised . . .'; and it would be tedious to
do other than follow his example.

From Bahia Dampier set a course to pass the Cape, making careful observations
on the variation, and on 1 August 1699 made his New Holland landfall near
Houtman Abrolhos. He turned north for various reasons: the ancient notion that
countries within the Tropics *ipso facto* abounded in riches, and (it was 'winter') a
nervousness about the cold in higher latitudes, his crew being 'heartless enough to
the Voyage at the best', though he thought that he might return around the south
of New Holland in the summer, or through it, since that land, like other parts of
Terra Australis, was probably not one single continent.[7] The great inlet of Shark

Bay was entered and named, and Dampier suspected that there might be a passage through New Holland to the east; but the coast was hazardous with shoals, and on land water was difficult to find, so he bore away from the present Dampier Archipelago for Timor and eventually Gilolo. Then he sailed eastwards well north of New Guinea, eventually turning southeast until on 25 February he came to islands which he named Matthias and Squally (Mussau and Emirau); they may have been already sighted by the Dutchman Martin Vries about 1645. Thence he stood over to what he took for the mainland of New Guinea: 'high and mountainous, adorn'd with tall flourishing Trees ... many large Plantations and Patches of clear'd Land'. It was in fact the northern coast of New Ireland.

By 9 March the *Roebuck* had passed beyond any Dutch discoveries (Fig. 12); the trend of the coast, never before seen by Europeans, changed from southeasterly to southwesterly. That evening they were off a deep bay which ran in for '20 Leagues or more'; Dampier named it for St George, and a cape beyond it for Lord Orford. 'Plantations' and 'Smoaks' showed that the land was well inhabited, and to this point some slight contacts had been made with natives in canoes: 'very black, strong, and well-limb'd People ... very dextrous active Fellows in their Proes'. Now, in a good harbour which he called Port Mountague, Dampier stayed for a week, trying to make friendly contact with its numerous inhabitants. There were tense moments: Dampier used warning shots with discretion, and there was a slight affray in which one native was wounded by a musket-shot, but no serious hostilities on either side. Now and then the entirely natural native shyness seemed wearing off, and coconuts were handed over; but serious trade was impossible. Eventually Dampier's men killed a few pigs and took from the otherwise empty huts some nets and 'Images', leaving in exchange a typical trade bargain: axes, knives, mirrors, bottles, beads, and few of any of them. This first encounter between Englishmen and Melanesians was inconsequential; but it might have been worse.

From Port Mountague Dampier coasted southwest, turning to northwest and then (25 March) north towards an active volcano (Sakar) detached from the mainland to the east: 'we look'd out very well to the North, but could see no Land that way; by which we were well assured that we were got through, and that this East-Land does not join to *New-Guinea*'. He had in fact passed through Dampier Strait, between 'Sir George Rook's Island' (Umboi) and the greater island which he named Nova Britannia. He indulged in a spate of patriotic nomenclature: Cape Anne and Cape Glocester (after Anne's little son) on the eastern side, King William's Cape for the bold northeastern promontory of New Guinea. As for Nova Britannia, 'it is very probable that this Island may provide as many rich Commodities as any in the World; and the Natives may be easily brought to Commerce, though I could not pretend to do it under my present Circumstances.'

These circumstances were that his pinnace needed repair and that he had only one carpenter fit for the job; and easterly winds had set in. He therefore decided (no

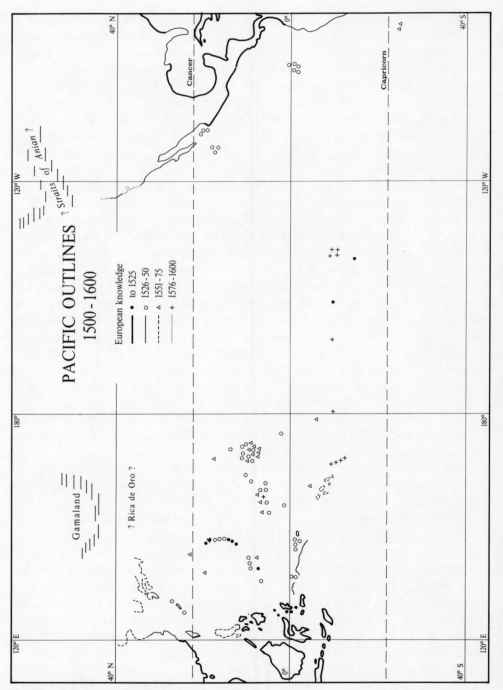

Figure 13. PACIFIC OUTLINES, 1500–1600.

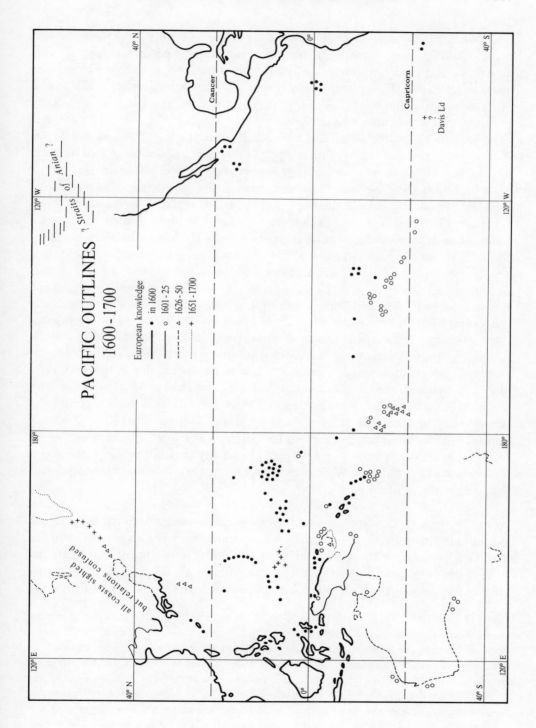

PACIFIC OUTLINES
1600 - 1700

European knowledge

●	in 1600
○	1601 - 25
△	1626 - 50
+	1651 - 1700

doubt with the strong encouragement of his crew) to return by the way he had come. As Williamson remarks, 'if he had resolutely pushed on southward' with such a ship and company, 'the odds are heavy that nothing would ever have been heard of him again. The answer to any charge of faintheartedness lies in the record of Cook's Australian passage.'[8] Yet Dampier's actual achievement, the lopping off of a sector of New Guinea, was meagre.

So back to Timor for water, and after a half-hearted attempt to look for Tryall Rocks, where the first English ship in Australian waters had been wrecked in 1622, to Batavia for repairs; the *Roebuck* proved more leaky after caulking than before, so he was obliged to empty the ship for careening. She sailed from Batavia on 17 October, and after calling at the Cape and St Helena reached Ascension on 21–2 February 1701, just in time, for within two days she sank at anchor. Dampier returned to England to face courts-martial not only for losing the *Roebuck* (there was no difficulty in acquittal for this) but also for cruelty to Fisher. All the dreary details of petty and violent squabbles were raked up before a court of four admirals and thirty captains—heavy metal to be faced by a mere buccaneer. The President was Sir George Rooke, and Dampier's complimentary island did not avail: the court was outraged at the throwing of a King's officer into a Brazilian jail. Dampier's counter-charges against Fisher were dismissed, he was fined the whole of his pay for the voyage, and declared unfit to command any of Her Majesty's Ships.[9]

Rough justice, undoubtedly. But it must be remembered that at this very time Halley, a civilian placed in command of a King's ship, had similar if less extreme troubles. From this the Admiralty deduced a general rule, that 'such appointment was totaly repugnant to the rules of the navy', and so eliminated the Royal Society's nominee, Alexander Dalrymple, from the command of what thus became Cook's first voyage. If the memory of Dampier played any part in the adoption of this uncompromising stance, as Williamson suggests, that was a result more important than the discovery of a distant strait.[10]

After Dampier, there was to be but one exploratory voyage of much significance, at least in the open Pacific, before the great opening which begins in the 1760s; this was Roggeveen's in 1722. The additions to European knowledge of the Ocean that were made in the seventeenth century were rather slight (Figs. 13 and 14). At the close of the century, the Russians on the northern margins knew the coast from the

Figure 14. PACIFIC OUTLINES, 1600–1700. Note the change in periodisation between the two maps; there was scarcely any European discovery between 1651 and 1700 except in the waters north of Japan (by the Russians), and here the confusions of contemporary maps are impossible to represent on a small scale, or probably on any scale without the use of colour (see text, Chs. 4 and 10). For the islands of Oceania, the maps are of necessity impressionistic to some extent, given the limitations of scale and the difficulty of establishing priorities, especially in Micronesia. It is highly probable that the Portuguese had some knowledge of northwestern Australia in the sixteenth century, and possibly of the east coast also; but as this did not enter into general European concepts, it is here omitted.

mouth of the Amur round to Kamchatka, and the true outlines of that peninsula were taking shape; but Dezhnev's rounding of his cape had been forgotten, while Fries (de Vries) in the Kurils had by no means cleared up the confusions of Yezo and Gamaland. On the eastern shores, Kino's work, also at the close of the century, amounted to the rehabilitation of a wrongly discredited earlier view.

Farther south, the biggest advances were also, in the main, marginal: the nearly complete filling in of the southern coast of New Guinea by Torres, knowledge of which, however, was restricted; Dampier's contribution in New Ireland; the Dutch charting of New Holland—but on coasts away from the Pacific; Tasman's discoveries of Van Diemen's Land, New Zealand, Tonga and Fiji, this last very minimal. Apart from this, there was very little activity in the open Pacific through the century: Quiros in the Tuamotus and the New Hebrides, including Tikopia; Schouten and Le Maire in the Tuamotus, Tonga, and the outliers on the north of New Guinea; some Spanish sightings in the Carolines, some Dutch in the Bonins; just possibly Davis's insubstantial land. And, except by Tasman, very little indeed was done between 1625 and the end of the century.

The Scots in Darien: dreams

Scotland in 1693 looked back on ninety unhappy years since her King had become the first monarch of a far from united Great Britain. He had never returned to his northern kingdom; his son had endeavoured to subvert the form of faith held by the majority of Scotsmen. After years of civil war, the toleration enforced by Cromwell was hardly more tolerable to good Covenanters than Charles I's attempted episcopalian revival, but the Restoration brought active persecution of the more godly. At the Glorious Revolution the kingdom had been 'casually re-assigned', and the bloody infamy of the Massacre of Glencoe was less than two years old.[11] Scotland had retained her ancient independence, though scarcely untrammelled, but also her ancient poverty; to all intent she was, like Ireland, an under-developed Third World country, with a proportionately fierce nationalism, and dangerously dependent on the English market. All this meant that 'Jacobite and Presbyterian were agreed upon but one thing, that this ignominious subordination of their common country to her great neighbour should cease.'[12] In such a climate of near-desperation, a man who had a confident vision of prosperity, even power, for his country was assured of a following. The Moses who should lead the people into a Promised Land was a Scot long resident in London, William Paterson, who had credentials: was he not the first proponent of the new but immensely successful Bank of England?

It was natural that the Scots should look to the methods by which their neighbour had become rich and powerful, and in 1693 the Scots Parliament passed an Act favouring the formation of chartered companies on the EIC model. On 26 June 1695, on a plan sent from London by Paterson, The Company of Scotland Trading to Africa and the Indies (usually called the Darien Company) was chartered—but perhaps not quite duly chartered, since William III's High Commissioner touched it with the Sceptre the same day, without taking the King's wishes as he should have done morally and perhaps in law.[13] The Company was given a widely privileged monopoly for thirty-one years; at least half of its capital was to be held by Scotsmen. Of the twenty original Directors, however, ten were Londoners, and while seven of these were Scots, the real interest of some of the London promoters was in interloping on the EIC's preserves. But the EIC's monopoly held against all the King's subjects, and hence what in Scotland was a government-backed patriotic enterprise, in England was an illicit operation to be carried on almost stealthily.[14]

The capital was fixed at £600,000, well beyond Scottish resources, and to be sure of a good initial subscription the books were first opened in England. Despite the need for privacy, London's half was fully subscribed in a few days of November, some of the applicants being EIC shareholders. Then the storm broke: the East India and Royal African Companies, themselves under pressure at home and abroad, could not tolerate a rival whose called-up capital was only 5 per cent of their own actual worth, but whose flotation had brought EIC stocks down by 46 per cent. Of course this uproar was largely factitious, the Scottish company being too feeble to be a real menace to such powerful corporations; but against their influence the upstart was powerless.[15] Lords and Commons examined the London Directors and presented a joint address to the King, who observed ominously that he had been ill-served in Scotland; the Commons resolved for impeachments. London subscribers withdrew more rapidly than they had joined. By New Year 1696 the English underpinning of the scheme had collapsed, and Paterson prudently withdrew to Scotland.

Rationally, that should have been the end of it; but the affront was too great for Scotsmen to stomach; and then, if the English were so frightened by the project, it must be worthwhile. It was decided to raise the Scots share of the capital to £400,000 (perhaps half the available investment capital of the Kingdom), and the rush to subscribe recalled the great days of the signing of the Covenant. Attempts to raise the remaining third of the £600,000 on the continent were wrecked by Dutch caution (William was Stadtholder as well as King) and by the intrigues of the English envoy in Hamburg.[16] England was in wealth the dominant but in Scots eyes by rights the junior, and coldly cruel, partner, and she should see what Scotland could do. The £400,000 was duly subscribed; but even the £170,000 of it actually called up was too much for the nation's capacity, and yet the full 100 per cent would have been too little to force a way into the East India trade, and that was the *raison d'être* of the project—so far.

Paterson, who was now an idolised oracle, was well aware that without an ample capital all that could result would be some petty interloping settlement, which its rivals would 'all agree to discourage and crush us to pieces'.[17] Yet that is precisely what he now proposed, in July 1696 (and precisely what happened), and in an entirely new direction. He fixed on Darien; he had lived in the West Indies and knew Dampier, from whom he borrowed the manuscript of Wafer's journal for the Company's use. Later (and indeed too late, as the first fleet was about to sail) Wafer himself was brought to Edinburgh, in great secrecy, to give oral information. He played fair: his liking for the place shone through, but he stressed the long and violent rains, the tormenting insects; the Directors had ears only for the stands of log-wood and the friendliness of the Indians.[18]

Ironically enough, a year earlier the English Committee for Trade and Plantations had examined Wafer and Dampier to find what they knew of Darien (much) and of the Scots plans (ostensibly, little). The Committee had reported in September 1697 that Darien had never been possessed by the Spaniards (an opinion they would change) and had recommended that the buccaneer rendezvous of Golden Island and 'the Port on the Main over against it' should be occupied.[19] Second thoughts prevailed, presumably because there was no point in risking the delicate balance of the Treaty of Rijswijk signed that same month.

Nevertheless, the Scots decision for Darien is rationally inexplicable. As the English Committee for Trade said later on, Spanish settlements had shifted, but their successors Panama, Puerto Bello and Cartagena so contained Darien that 'this changing of habitations is not judged a dereliction' of the Spanish claim; indeed, the Scots landed almost within sight of Acla where Balboa had been beheaded. Macaulay's parallel of Darien with Appin and Lochaber, where the clans scarcely heeded Edinburgh's writ'but whose seizure by Spain would be an outrage, is too highly-coloured, but has its point.[20] Even were Darien an empty *terra nullius*, it might well have been asked why the Spaniards had left it so. Insh has tried to show that the climate has been maligned and that the sickness was all the fault of the food; but his witnesses are buccaneers who were acclimatised, two of the colonists writing in general terms soon after arrival (he overlooks the evidence of Rose's journal), and a canal promoter succinctly described by Gerstle Mack as 'a liar of the first water'. The stubborn fact remains that since 1522–3, 'no white settlement has ever been able to maintain itself permanently in the Darien sector of the Isthmus'.[21] Of course the vile provisioning of the colony was a factor in its failure, and bad leadership perhaps a bigger one; but the climate played its part.

From a military point of view, the project at first sight may seem less unrealistic; the sack of Cartagena (by an armament much superior to anything Scotland could muster, however) showed up Spanish weakness, though the town was now again a Spanish base. However, Insh's appeal to buccaneer successes and Dampier's 'Golden Dream' is too simple. Dampier's notion was predicated on Black man-power, and remained a dream. As for the buccaneers, they were tough old hands, thoroughly at home in the milieu, backed by their fellows in the Caribbean, and supplying themselves when necessary by predation. None of this applied to a rooted colony of 2500 utterly inexperienced people, not self-sufficient and with no local support base. Success depended on more continuous succours than Scotland could provide, even had the political climate been benevolent or neutral; and it was neither. Webb and Lenman sum up: the Scots should have realised that

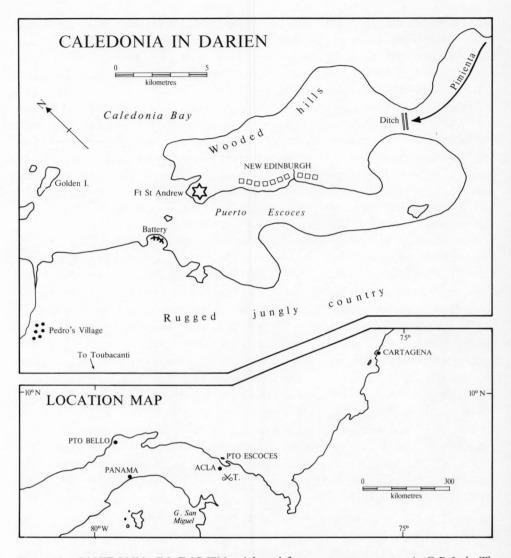

Figure 15. CALEDONIA IN DARIEN. Adapted from contemporary map in G. P. Insh, *The Company of Scotland* (London 1932) and map in J. Prebble, *The Darien Disaster* (Harmondsworth 1970). T = Toubacanti.

there was in 1695 no place where they could drive either a commercial or a plantation wedge without coming into contact with forces, physical and financial, much greater than they could command . . . that they were but a pygmy among giants . . . that their king was not really theirs, but England's. They knew all these things separately, but they did not put them together . . . As it turned out the rival companies . . . prepared the victim so thoroughly for the kill that the Spaniards had little need to make it. [Scotland was so poor and weak that] The only worthwhile objective for her in the colonial field was other nations' colonists ... A fraction of the capital thrown away in Darien, applied to honest smuggling to semi-independent American colonists, would have yielded solid dividends.[22]

But the die was cast: by November 1697 the Company's fleet was assembling in the Firth of Forth. The wars were over, and these were the 'seven ill years' of dearth and actual famine, so there was no lack of volunteers for a colony still, in public statements, non-committally 'in the Indies'.

The Scots in Darien: realities

Paterson's ideal was for a great free trade emporium with a footing on both oceans and attracting two-thirds of the trade between Europe and Asia; but he lost influence through the defalcations of a protégé and sailed as a mere volunteer. The Directors changed his plan into the less imaginative but seemingly more practicable form of a plantation colony to be called Caledonia, to be set up in 'some place or other' in America—a show of secrecy was kept up, but the destination had leaked. The Company had been energetic enough; it had two ships built for it in Lubeck, the *St Andrew* and the *Caledonia*, and bought the *Unicorn* in Amsterdam; they carried 46 to 70 guns each, and there were two tenders.

They were months in lading with heterogeneous merchandise: 1440 hats, 380 Bibles, 200 Confessions and 2806 Catechisms ('a bargain' at £50—remaindered?), bales of cloth and clothing, 25,000 pairs of shoes and slippers, twenty-nine barrels of clay pipes, campaign wigs and bob wigs and 'periwicks', 1000 locks, 3000 candlesticks, parchment for treaties.... Much fun has been made of this odd list, and apologists put forward two rationalisations: the cargo 'must needs be proper for a country where the Natives go naked for want of apparel, and fit to be exchanged' in European plantations, or that it was 'most for the use of our own people, and was suitable for the English Islands.'[23] In fact, while one may suspect some unloading of depressed stock with or without a patriotic discount, and some lines seem mistakes by merchants whose experience was in European markets, in total it was a good trade stock and a good magazine of stores for a colony—better than that provided ninety years later for Botany Bay, where nearly three years after his landing Governor Arthur Phillip had to write home that 'Two or three hundred iron frying-pans will be a saving of spades'.[24] For once an expedition was over-equipped—with one fatal exception: victuals consumed during the long waiting were not replaced, so that when they were inspected—*after* sailing—there was food not for nine months as planned, but for six.

The fleet sailed from Leith on 14 July 1698, carrying some 1200 settlers, each promised fifty acres of plantable land—in a country where not a soul, not even Paterson, had ever set foot. A quarter were 'Gentlemen Volunteers', probably too many touchy younger sons for good discipline, though there were enough with needed military experience. The colony was to be governed by seven nominated

Councillors, an ill-assorted squabbling lot; seamen and soldiers were immediately at loggerheads, and by a supererogation of idiocy they decided to hold the Presidency in rotation—week by week! With so little trust in each other, their trust could be only in God. Who helps those . . . .

The ships sailed with sealed orders and were separated in a very rough passage round the north of Scotland; only when reunited at Madeira did the expedition learn—officially—its destination: Golden Island and the main thereby, to be settled if not in possession of any friendly European power. There was much sickness and death on the voyage to the next rendezvous, Crab Island, which was also to be annexed—but the Danes of near-by St Thomas stepped in and hoisted their flag. An attempt to trade with a passing English ship failed: the Scots goods were unsuitable and their prices too high, and since the colony must initially depend upon trade, this was a bad start. More sickness and death on the Caribbean crossing, and then on 28 October they reached Golden Island. Beyond it, behind a small peninsula, they found a harbour wildly claimed to be 'capable of holding a thousand sail' and more soberly 'land-locked every way'—which meant that northerly winds could lock up ships for weeks. On 3 November eighty men were put ashore to build huts for the sick—and to dig graves, for the deaths continued, and Paterson soon lost his wife. But first impressions were favourable; one of the colonists, lulled by the 'pleasant melancholy Musick' of the trees which formed 'the Infinite beauty of a continued Natural Arbor, called them the *Shades of Love*.'[25] This fancy did not long endure; but on the maps the site is still Puerto Escoces.

There were Indian visitors. Very soon Captain Andreas turned up, delighted to boast of the old buccaneer days; the Spaniards had made him a headman, complete with silver-topped cane, and there was wariness on both sides, but after several drinking parties he accepted a Scots commission. Other chiefs, Ambrosio and Pedro, were eager to enlist the newcomers as allies against the Spaniard, and later a solemn 'TREATY OF FRIENDSHIP, UNION, AND PERPETUAL CON-FEDERATION [was] agreed and entered into between the Right Honourable the Council of Caledonia and the EXCELLENT DIEGO TUCUAPANTOS . . . Chief and Supreme Leader of the Indians. . . .' A much less welcome visitor was an English captain, Richard Long, an inquisitive fellow who spread malicious rumours amongst the Indians and aided them in provocations against the Spaniards; he was in fact an English spy.[26] A Frenchman brought the relevant news that the Barlovento fleet had arrived at Cartagena, and 'The Spaniards along the whole Coast are in a wonderful consternation'—and indeed, in Mexico the Viceroy was panicking. If twenty years earlier 200 pirates had ravaged the South Sea shores, what might 4000 stout Scots lodged so near Panama do? The threat did not end there—Callao, Acapulco, even the Philippines might be at risk.[27]

Meanwhile the colony was beset by faction and mismanagement, but at least the soldiers brought the seamen to see that the proper place for a fort was not in the morass where they had first put it, but near the tip of the peninsula, with a ditch across its neck (Fig. 15). Debilitated by their bad and scanty food and the constant rains, the settlers did little in November towards the building of New Edinburgh, and no clearance at all towards planting. On 29 November—St Andrew's Eve!—ten men deserted; they were soon rounded up, but already some of the leaders were just as anxious to escape. Some supplies were brought in by a Jamaica sloop, which on 29 December carried back Major William Cunningham, the first Councillor to be appointed and the first to desert, and the surgeon Walter Herries, whose malicious pamphlets set the tone for much of later comment, including Macaulay's. The accountant Alexander Hamilton, chosen as neutral between the factions, took with him despatches and the Council's sonorous Declaration: 'seated in the height of the World, between two vast Oceans ... more convenient than any other [place] for being the Common Storehouse of the unsearchable and immense treasures of the spacious South Seas', the country from henceforward was to be called CALEDONIA.[28]

In January 1699 the Armada de Barlovento reached Puerto Bello, in such bad shape that its commander would not risk a direct attack on Caledonia. He took 500 men to Panama and then to the Gulf of San Miguel and overland to Toubacanti, a militia post set up just across the cordillera from Puerto Escoces. For men weakened by the long voyage and with their morale depressed by Indian warnings, it was a frightful march; for once the rain was the Scots' ally. They had Indian allies too, and in a brisk little skirmish shot up a Spanish outpost; the numerically superior enemy withdrew, utterly demoralised.

Any euphoria was evanescent. The weather improved but the deaths continued. A tender sent out with trade goods was driven into Cartagena and her master, Robert Pincarton, and his men held as pirates; a naïve mission to demand their release nearly suffered the same fate. A few days' provisions reached the colonists, sent by New England Scots, and two Jamaican captains were willing to trade or hunt turtle for the colony, but very little came of this. Other Jamaicans wanted cash for food—the Scots had no coin, and their barter offers were refused. Another Jamaican sloop was seized under suspicion of being Spanish, which was hardly the way to attract more. Rations remained short and vile, apparently only brandy was in good supply; the rank-and-file were sick unto death, but for them the rule was no work, no food. Somehow the fort was finished, and the ditch; that, a few huts, and the ever-increasing graves were all that Caledonia, self-styled 'Emporium and Staple for the trade of both Indies', had to show. And there was no news from home.

It came in mid-May, and was devastating. There had been intense diplomatic activity; Spaniards bitterly resented the painfully negotiated Partition Treaty by which William had hoped to resolve their succession problem while avoiding the delivery of the whole empire of Spain and the Indies to either Bourbon France or Habsburg Austria; it needed only a touch to send the Spanish nation whole-heartedly into the French camp. Useless for William's Ambassador in Madrid to explain that his master's Crowns were as distinct as those of Castile or Aragon; only a positive deed could dispel Spanish suspicions. So in January 1699 a circular went out to all English governors in America, repudiating the Scottish venture and prohibiting any intercourse with it. The ensuing proclamation by the Governor of Jamaica was explicit: on no pretence were His Majesty's subjects to presume 'to hold any correspondence with the said Scots' nor to help them with arms, provisions, 'or any other Necessaries whatsoever.'[29]

It seems most likely that even without this blow the colony would have broken up. The over-worked, under-fed, fever-racked settlers were murmurous, openly saying that if rations could not be increased Caledonia should be abandoned. The Council gave them an evasive rebuff, and there was an abortive mutiny plot. The demand for departure was growing, and now the Proclamation legitimised it; Paterson, who had been brought on to the Council, alone stood out, indomitable, to the last. In mid-June 1699 they sailed, leaving behind six men too sick to care, and 400 in their graves. The voyage was frightful: a tender foundered in the Caribbean, the *St Andrew* had so many dead and dying that she was abandoned in Jamaica 'for want of men to carry her away'. The *Caledonia* and *Unicorn* reached New York, losing 275 men on the way. The sick on the *Caledonia* were treated with a brutality which horrified the Scots merchants who met her in New York; the callousness of the leadership surely played a part in the abjectness of the failure. She alone, with fewer than 300 survivors, reached Scotland.

Darien: the second expedition

Scotland had not been forgetful of her distant sons; in February 1699 some supplies had been sent, only to be lost by wreck in Scottish waters. Next month Alexander Hamilton arrived in Edinburgh, and was greeted with great enthusiasm. The Council's asseveration that Caledonia was unequalled for fruitfulness was accompanied by an appeal for food and a list of dead. These things were glossed over; the bereaved could take comfort that their loss was to Scotland's honour. In May two more relief ships were sent out, and in the Clyde a new fleet was gathering around its flagship the *Rising Sun*, which had been built in Amsterdam but held up (and frozen in) until the Company could meet its bills there; meanwhile Peter the Great was entertained on board.[30] (As Insh notes, this fitting-out on the west coast, in response to Paterson's protest from Madeira on the horrors of the northabout passage, was an important step in the commercial rise of Glasgow.) The four ships were to carry 1300 settlers, including technicians such as a goldsmith and a putative mint-master, and four clergymen. By mid-August they had dropped down to Rothesay, where they waited for a favourable wind.

In September three more Councillors arrived from Darien to present their versions of the quarrels to the Directors, who gave credence only to the 'official' one, Daniel Mackay. His despatches spoke of the desperate need for food and reinforcements; private letters were more despondent, and now there came from London rumours that the colony had been deserted or yielded to the Spaniards. Mackay scoffed at this, and the Directors wrote to the fleet dismissing such lying tales, a palpable English trick; but they were uneasy enough to instruct it to wait for Mackay and more stores. But a good wind was not to be thrown away, and the fleet sailed (with new Councillors) on 23 September 1699, a few hours before he should have joined. And then on 9 October came private letters from New York reporting the evacuation of Darien. The source was unimpeachable: the *Caledonia*'s supercargo.

So much national pride had been poured into the enterprise that at first blame was placed not so much on the auld enemy England (that was to come soon, and in plenty) as on the miserable Caledonians who had shamefully tarnished Scottish honour; a sentiment reflected in the letters of the Directors, who were always good at moral reprobation. To their credit, however, and apparently in defiance of the royal ban, they took some prompt and useful steps: one of the first was to open letters of account in New York and Jamaica, which if available a year earlier would have enabled food to be bought and so saved many lives. More calls were made on subscribers, the Kirk was asked for a day of Fast and Humiliation, and Parliament for an Address to the King appealing for his support. Mackay was sent out at once via New York and a new Councillor, Alexander Campbell of Fonab, via the West Indies, with orders for those on the *Rising Sun*—if they are not already at 'our shamefully deserted Colony', they are to repossess it, if need be by arms.

The two ships sent in May had reached Caledonia in August; from one of the six men left behind they learnt the story. The 300 settlers were landed, but after the accidental burning of one of the ships it was thought prudent to retire to Jamaica, leaving a little post of thirteen men. In November this handful was delighted to see two sloops under the Company's flag; Thomas Drummond, the only original Councillor to share Paterson's reluctance to leave, had returned from New York. Then on 30 November, just one week after the *Caledonia* had limped into the Clyde, the *Rising Sun* came in:

> Expecting to meet with our friends and countrymen, we found
> nothing but a howling wilderness . . . and we looked for Peace but no
> good came, and for a time of health and comfort, and beheld
> Trouble.[31]

Trouble began at once. They had come to strengthen an existing colony, but it was non-existent: were they obligated to start all over again? Drummond, a tough veteran (he had taken part in the Glencoe killing), protested against a new abandonment, and it was agreed to rebuild the fort. But provisions, even brandy, were short, and the old cycle of sickness and starvation began again, and the quarrels. Within a month Drummond was arrested. The new leaders were contemptuous of the Indians who warned them of Spanish designs; but in truth there was no leadership. The colony sank into a wretched inertia, through which the clergymen (who had no Gaelic, while many settlers had no Lallans) wandered like dark shades, proliferating unread tracts, unheeded godly advice, and uncharitable lamentation on the depravity of their flock: the ungodly deserved their miseries.[32] Caledonia was saved, or rather reprieved, by the arrival in February 1700 of Campbell of Fonab.

A soldier with the habit of command, he simply took over. It was time, for the Spaniards were well informed of the Scots' weakness, and had now a resolute leader in Juan Pimienta, Governor of Cartagena. From Panama orders went out for a double attack, by land through Toubacanti, by sea from Cartagena. But the good material in Caledonia, long kept down by Councillors who had lost all martial vigour except for bullying, now also had a real leader.

Campbell landed on a Sunday; on Tuesday he set out for Toubacanti with 200 Scots and thirty Indians, soon joined by forty more under Don Pedro. Campbell pushed them through a gruelling approach march; the Toubacanti stockade was stout enough but its men were careless, and it was over-run in one sharp rush. Exactly seven days after his landing, Campbell, himself wounded, was back at New Edinburgh. A brilliant little victory, but only a flash: for in another week Spanish ships appeared, and on 1 March Pimienta landed east of the peninsula.

He pushed on methodically, and by the 18th was across the ditch and could command New Edinburgh, with guns, from the heights along the coast. A request for terms was met with the reply that in law the Scots were mere adventurers with no valid status to treat. Pimienta received reinforcements from Toubacanti and his fleet landed guns close to the fort; the Company's ships seem to have done nothing. His demand for unconditional surrender was refused, and he relented—in fact, with the rains at hand and his own men sick, he was anxious to make an end. He was also nervous of strange ships, which might be succours; these were two sloops with which Drummond, who had gone to Jamaica, had returned to hover off the coast; he even slipped into the harbour by night, but it was too late. Pimienta allowed the Scots' plea that they should be allowed to keep all their ships, but the Revd Alexander Shiels, who made a feeble attempt to get assurances for the Indians, meekly accepted a sharp snub. The articles were signed on 31 March: the Scots could leave with the honours of war, which indeed they had belatedly earned. The golden dream had ended in nightmare.

Providence had not yet done with the Caledonians; not one of the fleet reached Scotland. Of the two smaller vessels, one was driven into Cartagena, one wrecked off Cuba. The *Rising Sun* and her consort reached Charleston in South Carolina, where they were overwhelmed by a hurricane. Of the 1300 souls who had left the Clyde, about 950 are known to have died, and very few of the remainder saw their old homes again.

There had been heroism at Darien amidst the squalor, but little common humanity and less commonsense; rotten leadership may have done more for the ruin of Caledonia than rotten food. Never, surely, was there a more bitterly ironic motto than that of the Company of Scotland: *Vis Unita Fortior*, Strength Stronger by Unity.

The aftermath of Darien

In hindsight, the Spanish reaction to Caledonia seems almost hysterical. In the summer of 1699 the Viceroy of Peru, Conde de la Monclova, was ordered to send 500 good men to Tierra Firme; Guatemala should also send a large force, and steps were to be taken to win over the 'negro stockades' and the Indians. This did not seem enough: in October a force of 2000 men from Spain was envisaged; the Viceroy of Peru, with enhanced authority, was to go himself to Panama or even nearer the front; and the President of Guatemala, though in New Spain, was to be put under his orders. Monclova could draw on all revenues 'without reservation of any fund whatever', and the Seville merchantry offered 300,000 pesos for the emergency. The Pope was induced to allot 1,000,000 ducats, chargeable on ecclesiastical estates in the Indies.[33] Such an unprecedented upheaval in the governance of the Indies is a measure of Spanish fears, and the suspicion, or even belief, that the power of England was behind it all.

Although in the event such terrors seem almost ludicrous, this 'new incursion, outwardly peaceable, [was] actually much more formidable in its implications than the violent raids of the buccaneers'.[34] The Spanish judgement of the potentiality of the threat was not at fault; Paterson's design was for a colony spanning the Isthmus, and that, if secured and maintained, would indeed have thrown open the *mare clausum* of the South Sea and thereby have upset the balance of the world. The error that was shared by Spaniard and Scot alike was in the over-estimation of the actual, not just potential, strength of the threat.

In the event, Darien did have far-reaching political effects, but not in the South Sea. Scots Addresses to the King produced more irritation on his part than satisfaction on theirs. The Spanish Succession had been plunged into renewed uncertainty by the death in February 1699 of the Electoral Prince of Bavaria,[35] the possible compromise between Bourbon and Habsburg candidatures, and Madrid was fishing for French aid against the Scots. The King was assailed by increasingly bitter reproaches from his Scottish subjects and from the Spaniards, whom he could not afford to offend. The English Committee for Trade supported the Spanish case, and the English Parliament once more denounced the Scottish threat to England's trade. Privately William now sympathised with the Scots, having a shrewd idea that the initiation of the whole affair lay in England, but there was little he could do publicly. In Scotland his administration tried with decreasing success to procrastinate.[36]

The news of Campbell's victory at Toubacanti reached Edinburgh in June 1700 and set off a violent anti-government riot. A week later came news of the surrender. It served only to harden the Scots assertion of their right to the colony; a swarm of addresses and petitions to the King brought a sympathetic reply, but a firm refusal to support the claim to Caledonia, which would mean war with Spain (and of course France). All that was gained from him was the release of Pincarton and his men from their Spanish prison, and the royal assent to the extension of the privileges of the Darien Company for another nine years. The Company had indeed sent out one venture to Africa which was profitable, bringing back enough gold-dust to mint the 'Darien pistoles', the last gold coins struck by the Scottish Mint; the ship returned just after news of the surrender and provided a much-needed lift to morale. But a venture in the *Speedwell* to Macao sped ill, and the *Speedy Return* never returned from the piratical Indian seas.[37]

King William's reply to the Scots Parliament had ended 'we doubt not but you will rest satisfied with these plain reasons'; a pious hope indeed. There was increasing provocation on both sides of the Border, and things were brought to a head by an English Aliens Act which would have meant economic ruin for Scotland, and by the hanging of three Englishmen on Leith Sands on a trumped-up charge of pirating a ship chartered by the Darien Company.[38] For years some Englishmen, and a few thoughtful Scots (including Paterson), had been coming to think that a real Union was the only feasible solution, and the Aliens Act was the trump card, or in Scottish eyes a fifth ace. In the enforced negotiations for Union the English side insisted on the dissolution of the Darien Company, against repayment, nominally from England, of its capital, with interest a sum of £232,884.5s.0⅔d. This was done through an 'Equivalent Company' whose books were not closed until 1850, when the Government paid off £248,550.0s.9½d.[39] History does not record who got the odd ha'penny.

Darien of course, though an important catalyst, was only one factor in the Union; others included the tricky question of the succession, after the death of Anne's little son the Duke of Gloucester. There had been a persistent Scots feeling for an economic nexus to gain wider markets, even if that meant an 'Incorporating Union'. In 1689 even Fletcher of Saltoun, the most inveterate enemy of Union when it did come, had accepted this logic.[40] The Darien Company's monument is therefore its unquantifiable but very definite share in the building of the Union; that, a few gold coins, a mass of papers, and the moat at Puerto Escoces, still used by Indian canoes. For of all who have come to Darien, the Cuna alone have remained, remarkably intact. In the nineteenth century they repelled canal prospectors by force, and while today visitors are welcome, it is on Cuna terms: day trips only, no over-night stops. 'They are indeed subjects of the Republic of Panama . . . But that does not mean much more than when Don Juan Pimienta told the Reverend Shiels that they were subjects of the King of Spain. They have never regarded themselves as anybody's subjects.'[41] Long may they so live, free men.

The entry of the French: Beauchesne

If Darien failed under the shadow of the Spanish Succession, the first commercial penetration of the South Sea by the French was a brilliant exploitation of the ensuing war; with more truth than the Scots, they might have sung

> It will be wonderful to see
> the *Sun rise in the West.*[42]

The original project was for an expedition on a large scale—seven ships and 700 men, not counting colonists and troops—to be commanded by J.-B. de Gennes, who, as we have seen, had made the first, and unsuccessful, French attempt to enter the South Sea. Much of the planning was probably by de Gennes himself, but the venture was taken up by two of the biggest contemporary French entrepreneurs, Jean Jourdain and the Malouin Noël Danycan. These men were involved in the tangled machinations of the successors to Colbert's East India Company; in September 1698 they formed a 'Compagnie Royale de la Mer Pacifique' with the powerful Minister Louis Phélypeaux, Comte de Pontchartrain, as President. Although France and Spain were once more at peace, after the Treaty of Rijswijk, the plans were not very pacific in spirit. Colonies could be founded in both Patagonia and Chile, bases for attacks on the Spaniards in the South Sea and for exploring the Terres Australes; a settlement in the Straits themselves could grow wheat and would need no wine from Europe, given the abundance of fermentable berries! This would be the task of four ships; three would press into the South Sea, where were islands with gold and silver mines, emeralds, and furs; and for perhaps the first time we have a reference to whaling in the South Sea. There would be peaceful trade reconnaissances up the South American coast—peaceful, but hopefully the local Spanish officials would insultingly refuse bribes, which would warrant the taking of prizes.

Jourdain's plans were too grandiose for Danycan, himself a bold operator, and after much confusion and chicanery the affair fell entirely into the former's hands, which, with his credit, were greatly strengthened by the timely return of the *Amphitrite* from her successful Chinese venture. The expedition was however cut down to four ships; de Gennes withdrew and was replaced as commander by Jacques de Beauchesne-Gouin. For pilot they had an old flibustier, who had been left on Juan Fernández by Massertie and returned by the Straits, and there was even an Abbe Noël Jouin, *soi-disant* Bishop-elect of any lands to be discovered. The instructions covered detailed exploration, colonisation and fortification, the search for amber, spices, silks, fine woods, and above all precious metals. These were scaled down in a revised version which called only for reconnaissance to see if settlement were possible; this was Danycan's original idea, but it was now given a needlessly extravagant force.

The *Phélypeaux* and *Maurepas* (named for the Minister's son—Jourdain was taking no chances!) sailed with two smaller ships from La Rochelle on 17 December 1698, but only the two larger reached the Straits, which they entered on 24 June 1699. They did not pass Cape Pilar until 21 January 1700, perhaps an inverse record for the passage. All they had to show so far were some good charts and the taking possession of Ile Louis le Grand (now Isla Carlos III). The first rendezvous in the South Sea was at Socorro in the Chonos Archipelago, but Beauchesne's second in command de Terville was not there. The two met off Valparaiso, where de Terville, after an initially suspicious reception, had been apparently well received once the authorities were assured that he was no flibustier; but then he was fired upon without warning and had to cut his cables.

Beauchesne sailed up the coast, meeting with a mixed welcome; trade was officially banned and he thought of using force, but at Arica the local merchants waved him on to Ilo, less under the eye of officialdom, and despite the poor condition of the French textiles, they sold well. The success was repeated at Pisco and even Callao. After a short stay in the Galápagos, where he found little wood and less water, Beauchesne crossed over to Guayaquil and Paita. Here he was firmly rebuffed, until at Ilo once more, with his crews suffering from scurvy, he threatened to use force, and very soon sold out; even rags, according to his account, found a market. He left Ilo on 5 December 1700, rounded the Horn in January, and reached La Rochelle on 7 August 1701.

Financially, despite those splendid sales, the expedition made a loss of some 110,000 livres; but it had done what Narborough had failed to do, opened a market. Despite their initially poor reception as suspected flibustiers, the French had found a ready sale for a wide range of goods, and this not in exchange for luxury imports or silver, as in Asian commerce, but for precious metal: an admirable result for a bullionist economy. The excellent charting supplemented the commercial intelligence brought back. De Gennes's failure had been wiped out, and the way opened for French merchants to take full advantage of the changed political situation which the impending war would bring. Its main impacts on the Pacific were to be the remarkable series of French voyages not only into but across the Ocean, from Peru to China; and renewed English (we may soon say British) assaults on Spanish ports and shipping, no longer by unauthorised buccaneers but in the more respectable form of privateering.

Chapter 8

THE SPANISH SUCCESSION AND THE SOUTH SEA

> *New Spain* is the Spouse of the *Old Spain*, and they will
> no more prostrate her to be debauch'd in Trade by us than
> they, *the most Jealous People in the World*, should allow
> us to come to Bed with their Wives.

> Hence (for in his peculiar reign were laid
> Schemes, that produc'd the sure increase of trade)
> Shall generations, yet unborn, be told
> Who gifted them with silver mines and gold;
> Who gave them all the commerce of the Main,
> And made South Seas send home the wealth of Spain.

The background

In 1600 the long sea-lanes between Europe and Asia, whether by the Indian or Pacific Oceans, were firmly in Iberian hands. By 1700 the Dutch and English had taken over most of the direct oceanic commerce between these continents; Asians still retained some share in the trade of the China Seas and that between India and the Levant, but it was a more marginal and a diminishing share. The informal division between the Dutch in Indonesia and the English in India was already chalked out, but the Dutch were alone in Japan; the China trade proper was yet in its infancy, with the English likely to make the running. From the Iberian commercial hegemony, Spain retained the perennial Manila-Acapulco line, but the Portuguese of Macao were reduced to ever-changing shifts to secure a bare survival, though always resilient to survive.

The Iberian claim to the whole New World, derived ultimately from Papal donations, had indeed been challenged long before 1600, but really only in theory. Canada, Newfoundland, Virginia, Florida, Drake's Nova Albion in California, had been taken into 'possession', but there was no effective or lasting occupation, unless we count a few seasonal fishing camps in Newfoundland; the first permanent French settlement in Quebec, Tadoussac, was founded in 1600 itself. Apart from these rudiments, only Spain and Portugal had any foothold whatever in either of the Americas. Before mid-century, however, French, English, and Dutch had installed themselves in lasting colonies from Quebec to Curaçao. Spain's actual territorial loss was very small, even by 1700, and her empire was to expand substantially in the next century; but the security of its great node, the Isthmus, was

---

D. Defoe, *A Review of the State of the British Nation*, 17 July 1711; Lawrence
Eusden, Poet Laureate, *Birthday Ode*, 1720, quoted in B. Pares, *War and Trade in
the West Indies* (Oxford 1936), 154.

compromised by the English seizure of Jamaica in 1655.[1] Her strategic position in the South Sea itself was weakened by the opening of the new entry around Cape Horn by Le Maire in 1616. This had to wait over sixty years for its exploitation, until the buccaneer forays of the 1680s; the resulting 'spate of books on the South Seas ... came at [the] critical moment' when with the Spanish Succession crisis 'the future of Spain's American empire became of acute concern to statesmen and merchants alike.'[2]

The world picture of 1700 was thus vastly different, and more complex, than that of 1600. Spain's Atlantic, defined by the Trade Wind belt, had been 'a new Mediterranean, five, six times greater than the old', but tightly locked into the regulated courses of the Carrera de Indias and its few fixed ports; the new Atlantic was 'open, ploughed in all directions by the men of the North', who had increasingly numerous and strong bases on the North American seaboard and in the Caribbean itself.[3] The 'urban thalassocracy' of Portuguese Asia was in ruins; Hollanders, Englishmen, Frenchmen, Scandinavians were disputing its inheritance. The Pacific, once a *mare clausum*, a Spanish lake, was now known to be readily penetrable, and had indeed been crossed by more than one Dutch armament. Necessarily, in these circumstances, European geopolitical ideas were taking a wider range, 'no longer understood in the narrow sense of continental possessions' but including the oceans themselves.[4] Thalassocracy, the dominion of the sea, was indeed nearly as old as navigation itself, as the histories of Athens and Carthage— later Sri Vijaya, Venice, the Hansa—show; but these were based on 'Narrow Seas'. Even the concept of *oceanic* control was not new: it must be credited to the fine geopolitical grasp of Afonso de Albuquerque. But the global range was now greater, colonies were more numerous and diversified, the financing of both commerce and war was more sophisticated, and merchants and mariners carried more weight in western European polities than they had in the sixteenth century. Colonial warfare was also nothing new, but in the eighteenth century it was to be 'distinguished by its scale, its formality, its close connection with declared wars in Europe', to the point at which the War of the Spanish Succession can be claimed as 'the first major European conflict in which control of colonial territory and trade figured prominently among the aims of the belligerents'. Louis XIV himself wrote that 'the principal object of the present war is that of the commerce of the Indies and the riches which they produce'[5]—in other words, the Spanish colonial empire.

There is much point in the revisionist case against an exaggerated picture of the depth and duration of the seventeenth-century crisis in Spain and against over-simple monetarist explanations for it; and it is most one-sided to ignore the fact that Spain's economic troubles were not altogether peculiar to herself but part of a general secular trend shared by the 'more advanced nations of western Europe. The undoubted recession in seventeenth century Spain was a reflection of Spain's links with those nations and with their economic crises.' On this view it is not so much a matter of a specially Spanish phenomenon but the reflection of her position as an undeveloped peripheral economy, dominated most thoroughly by France:

> In relegating 'decline' to the dust-heap of useless concepts we can
> begin to consider Spain in proper perspective as an underdeveloped
> country which never reaped the benefits of its imperial position.
> Through all the days of its greatness its weak economic potential
> remained a grim dead weight . . . The canker at the heart of Spain was
> something far deeper [than 'decline']: a pattern of dependence that
> sapped any possibility of alternative development, and frustrated
> hopes of escaping from the poverty cycle.[6]

Yet this hardly alters the over-riding geopolitical fact. It remains true that even if Spain at the death of Carlos II in 1700 were not absolutely weaker than she had been at the death of Philip II in 1598, she was certainly enormously weaker relative to her rivals England, the Netherlands, and France.

So long as Spain remained her old ineffective self, the 'Maritime Powers', England and the United Netherlands, had little reason to worry. In terms both of formal navies and informal privateering, they were incomparably stronger than Spain in time of war—in 1701 the 'Admiral-General of the Ocean Sea' had twenty warships to cover the Atlantic and the Caribbean; the Dutch and English between them had built 147 new ships in 1689–98.[7] In time of peace the system of Seville, so tight in theory but so leaky in practice, could be by-passed by a 'naturalistic sort of free trade', the contraband now so much facilitated by their colonial gains during the past century.[8] The guardacostas could harass and hamper smuggling, but Spanish resources could not put an end to it.

A Spain tightly harnessed to France by a Bourbon successor to Carlos II, however, offered a disconcerting prospect. Although France's great burst of navalism under Colbert was over, her sea forces were still formidable, and the 'alliance of Spanish rights with French efficiency' could menace the vast illicit trade of the Maritime Powers, which conducted their exports into Spanish markets and withdrew silver for their other trades: 'no energetic regime would connive at so much smuggling.' Mahan sums up this aspect of the succession crisis: 'The indifference [of the Maritime Powers, such as it was] could not last when there was a prospect of a stronger administration, backed possibly by alliance with one of the great powers of Europe.'[9] King Log was dying, better brand King Stork—in advance—as a usurper.

Concern for the American trade was of course but one strand in the tangle of ambitions and apprehensions which led to war, nor was it automatic that war would result from Louis XIV's acceptance, in November 1700, of Carlos II's Will which, in pathetic revulsion against the cool partitioning by outsiders of Spain's dominions, bequeathed his whole inheritance to the French King's grandson Philip of Anjou. Indeed, in Spring 1701 the Maritime Powers recognised Anjou as Philip V in order to negotiate guarantees or compensations, and it took time to rally their public opinions and to reach agreement with the Emperor Leopold I and the German princes. But French rearmament and diplomatic blunders, including the notorious recognition of the Old Pretender as King of England on James II's death, hardened belief in the Grand Monarque's intention of hegemony. Although the Treaty of the Grand Alliance (September 1701) stipulated a breathing-space for negotiations on partition and compensations, most statesmen on either side probably regarded this as no more than a decent formality. War formally began in May 1702.

By a significant clause in the Alliance Treaty, the Maritime Powers secured the right to keep any conquests in the Indies, and it has been said that 'The English and Dutch were committed to intervention principally because of their concern for the future of the Indies Trade.' This may be too strong, but in England there was a strong body of opinion, especially Tory, that the war effort should concentrate on the ocean and the Indies rather than on continental campaigns. It may also be significant that the first operations of the Maritime Powers were John Benbow's expedition to the West Indies and Sir George Rooke's attack on Cadiz (now rivalling Seville as base for the Carrera de Indias), both in 1702 and both failures. In October 1702, however, Rooke took or destroyed the American silver fleet in Vigo Bay—but without the silver. Paradoxically, the fleet had come to Vigo to evade the Anglo-Dutch squadron off Cadiz; in fact, it evaded the smuggling rings of Seville. Most of the bullion had been landed before the attack, and this 13,500,000 pesos (over half of which went straight into the royal treasury) was the largest amount of American silver accruing directly to the Spanish Crown in any one year in the whole history of the Carrera; much more than would have been gathered in had the fleet come to Seville, where much of it would have been taken care of by legal and illegal private interests. The real loss to Spain was not in treasure but in prestige and ships; henceforth the American silver was increasingly convoyed, and even carried, by French vessels.[10]

If Vigo was more a showy than a profitable success for the Allies, its geopolitical effect was to introduce a serious distortion into the aims and conduct of the War. Pedro II of Portugal was nominally in alliance with the Bourbons, but so spectacular a display of naval force a few kilometres from his own frontier induced second thoughts, the more so as his new gold shipments from Brazil would be very vulnerable. He therefore came to terms with the Alliance; and one of his terms was that the Archduke Karl, as the Habsburg candidate, should come to Lisbon and thence prosecute his claim to the Spanish throne. This was sensible from the point of view of Portuguese security, while to England it provided an excellent base for war in the Mediterranean and led to the Methuen Treaties, which gave assured markets for English cloth in Portugal and Brazil in exchange for two goodies, gold and port. But for the Alliance as a whole, or at least the Maritime Powers, it meant a turning away from the original objectives of the War. The Archduke, soon to become 'Carlos III', had to be supported in a Peninsular war with the slogan 'No Peace without Spain', and this by fleets and men which might have ravaged or occupied the Indies, now a mere side-show.[11]

The Caribbean and its treasure-ships could not of course be entirely neglected, and Sir Charles Wager destroyed some rich galleons off Cartagena in 1708, salvaging part of the treasure, but naval activity there was desultory, and there was no serious assault on the Isthmus. The South Sea was left to privateers, and the first of them was our old friend William Dampier.

Dampier tries again

Within a year of the Admiralty's ban on Dampier's employment in Her Majesty's ships the Lord High Admiral, Anne's consort George of Denmark, presented him to kiss Her Majesty's hands before he sailed on another voyage. The War offered good pickings in the South Sea, and private enterprise was willing to gamble on a man so experienced in those waters. A group of Bristol and London merchants appointed Dampier to command the *St George* (200 tons, 30 guns) on a voyage which, according to its chronicler William Funnell, was intended to take two or three galleons at Buenos Ayres, which should bring in £600,000. That failing they would attempt the Valdivia ships taking gold to Lima; that again failing, some rich Peruvian towns; that still failing, the Galleon off Acapulco. The result was another fumbled tragi-comedy, a bad replay of the buccaneer exploits twenty years earlier. The voyage started badly enough; an old shipmate from the *Cygnet*, Edward Morgan, whom Dampier wanted as owners' agent, had to be got out of gaol, where he should have been left; and a ship which was to have sailed in consort went off on her own account. However, at Kinsale, where he did his final fitting-out, Dampier was joined by the *Cinque Ports* galley, a small vessel (90 tons, 16 guns) but well adapted for commerce-raiding.[12] The two sailed from Ireland in September 1703; after losing or abandoning a couple of quarrelsome officers at ports *en route*, they rounded the Horn separately and rendezvoused at Juan Fernández in February 1704.

Here two-thirds of the *Cinque Port*'s people refused to serve under her Captain Thomas Stradling; Dampier patched things up, and at the end of the month they had a fight with a French 36-gun ship, the *St-Joseph*. The company thought that she could have been taken if attacked again and that her escape 'would discover us to the *Spaniards*, which would be of ill Consequence . . . But our Captain was against it', affirming that even if their merchantmen were kept in port 'he knew where to go and could not fail of taking to the value of 500,000 *l.* any Day in the Year'; Dampier's *Vindication* blames the cowardice of the crew. Returning to the island, they found two more Frenchmen, each stronger than the *St George*, and prudently sheered off for Peru.

On the approaches to Callao they again met the *St-Joseph*, and again Dampier 'thought it not advisable to venture upon her'. They took a couple of prizes, but Dampier let them go almost unsearched, 'alledging, that he would not cumber up his Ship, for that he intended to make a Voyage at one stroke upon some rich Town'. Whatever his reasons for this coyness, they were not shared by the shady Morgan, who hid a 1000-dollar silver dinner service in his linen. At least Dampier revealed his 'speedy Design': a direct attack on the Santa Maria of his old golden dream.

The attack was a bungle. Surprise was lost by mischance and mismanagement, and although the Spanish were beaten from their ambuscades, it was obvious that Santa Maria would have been emptied of anything of value. By sheer luck they took a large ship crammed with provisions, enough to keep them for four or five years; and once again Dampier was charged with missing 80,000 dollars by refusing to 'romage her to the bottom; because he thought loss of time would spoil his greater Designs', but Morgan got away with another service of plate.

Such shuffling could not last. In May Stradling parted company at the old buccaneer haunt Tabago, and made for Juan Fernández, where Alexander Selkirk voluntarily marooned himself.[13] Dampier cruised south to Ecuador, where he had a drawn fight with a Spanish cruiser, and north again to Nicoya; it was now the turn of his new lieutenant, John Clipperton, to desert in a prize more seaworthy than the *St George*. He sailed for China, probably discovering Clipperton Island on the way.[14] Dampier had now thought up a new design to mollify his remaining company: it was rather the old design of the Galleon. They sighted her off Colima on 6 December, obviously quite unprepared for action, and a brisk attack before she could clear her guns might well have taken her. But time was wasted in quarrelling over tactics and the chance was lost. According to John Welbe, Dampier behaved with equal incompetence and cowardice; Dampier wrote that 'The very man at the helm contradicted my orders'—a devastating comment on his loss of control—and that the crew were 'Drunk or Bewitch'd'. The Galleon ran out a tier of heavy guns and had no difficulty in beating off the *St George*.[15]

A month after this fiasco William Funnell, Morgan and Welbe took the lead in plain mutiny, sailing off in a prize with a final taunt: 'Poor *Dampier*, thy Case is like King James, every Body has left thee'.[16] Although all his officers but the surgeon deserted, twenty-seven men stood by Dampier, to cruise upon their own account. The *St George* was too rotten for them to risk a Pacific crossing, but after sacking Puna they took a seaworthy prize. There is no known account of Dampier's return, although it is known that he was imprisoned at Batavia on a charge of piracy, his commission having been lost at Puna or carried off by Clipperton. Somehow Dampier made his way back to England, arriving in late 1707 to find that Funnell was well ahead with the story.

Funnell's account has a studied moderation in its references to Dampier, but the flat recital of all those chances thrown away in favour of some greater but never-realised design amounted to an imputation of gross incompetence. Dampier was provoked to a hasty *Vindication*, almost stuttering in its indignation; much of Welbe's *Answer* may safely be discounted as mere scurrility, but there could be no disguising the fact of failure. Whether anybody but the light-fingered Morgan made anything out of the cruise of the *St George* is highly obscure; but for Dampier himself it was definitely no purchase, no pay.[17]

There was another way of tapping the wealth of the South Sea, one barred to the British by the state of war but noted by Funnell: 'the *French* at present make very great and profitable Voyages; and now that they find the sweet of it, will be sure to settle a firm and lasting Trade there.'[18]

The French in the South Sea

A sweet trade it was; even if Funnell's Spanish informants grossly inflated its profits to 5000 per cent or more, some voyages did fetch 350 or even 450 per cent. The seven ships convoyed to France by Michel Chabert in 1709 grossed Louis XIV over 16,255,000 livres (4,000,000 pesos); considering the desperate economic plight of France in that year, it is evident that such consignments of American silver, often in effect filched from Louis's grandson, alone enabled the War to be continued.[19] The scale of the trade, far exceeding any previous traffic in the Pacific, can be seen by the fact that between 1698 and 1725 no fewer than 168 French ships sailed to the South Sea; 117 returned, most making a good profit. The actual values cannot be ascertained, being lost in a chaos of sharp practices and false returns; but the *declared* treasure of fourteen ships was 29,000,000 livres, and Dahlgren reaches a total of over 200,000,000, or 50,000,000 pesos.[20]

There is no point in trying to follow Dahlgren through the maze of chicanery and peculation, the endless law-suits and political intrigues of the Compagnies de la Chine (of Paris and of St Malo), de la Mer du Sud, des Indes, and so on. His book indeed is almost a manual of shady finance, dominated by the Malouin Noël Danycan, a powerful and unscrupulous manipulator who seems to anticipate Balzac's bandits of the Bourse. All we can do is to concentrate on a few significant voyages, which must, however, be seen in their setting—the breakdown of the system of Seville and the first steps towards the Bourbon Reforms which were in time to bring new patterns of economic organisation to the Pacific as well as the Atlantic.

Before 1700, the interests of France in the South Sea were not essentially different from those of England or the Netherlands. French manufactures, mainly textiles, were estimated to be a quarter or more of the value of Sevillean exports about 1690;[21] but the Spanish system of 'controls and controls on controls' was a constant source of friction. The reports of buccaneers like Massertie and Raveneau de Lussan, and the reality of Beauchesne's success, whetted appetites. In 1699 we find François Froger, who had been with de Gennes, declaiming in the best heretic English manner: the Spaniards lived in beastly indolence amidst treasures cruelly wrung from the Indians, who cried out for vengeance on these enemies of God and nature.[22] The War seemingly changed this: France now needed not to break the Sevillean monopoly but to make it work for the joint war effort. But Philip V was not quite the French puppet that friends had hoped and enemies feared, Spanish habits died very hard, and beneath the surface of alliance there persisted a stubborn and often bitter conflict of interests.

The Carrera de Indias was in ruins: twenty-nine armadas sailed for the Isthmus in the fifty years prior to 1681; only three in the twenty years from 1681 to the outbreak of the War.[23] The efforts of the French economic and administrative advisers who came in with Philip V were frustrated by inertia and suspicion; the latter justified enough, since it might prove difficult to dislodge French interests from positions conceded in the stress of emergency. In 1704 it was proposed that the new Viceroy of Peru should go out under French escort, with Spanish ships taking merchandise; the fair might be held, this once, at Lima, which was safe, rather than Puerto Bello. The Council of the Indies put up all the old arguments: what would happen to the rich and famous fair, the finest in the world? (It had not been held for years!) And if Andalusian oil and wine were not sent to Cartagena, the sacrifice of Mass might lapse. ... Seven years later the very able and unusually upright Michel-Jean Amelot, until 1709 Ambassador at Madrid and virtually Prime Minister, remarked bitterly that many Spanish ministers were 'obsessed with the beauty and wisdom of the rules established by Philip II' and would not see that what might have been excellent under so powerful a prince just would not work in the decadence of a monarchy short of everything, especially of ships.[24]

Since the Spaniards were so slow to face facts, the French resorted to pressure and subterfuge. The first tiny official crack in the monopoly (there were gaping unofficial breaches) came in May 1702; in America, Spain depended on French warships for defence, and could hardly deny them her ports, so they were allowed to carry a limited amount of merchandise to exchange for supplies. The crack was readily widened: in 1706 the first galeones to reach Puerto Bello in ten years found the market glutted.

In the South Sea, the first venture was by Julien Bourdas's *St-Paul*, sent out in October 1701. This was a totally illicit voyage; she did not dare return to St Malo, but in April 1703 unloaded her silver in still (but only just) neutral Portugal. Danycan, who despatched the *Président Grénedan* and *Comte de la Bédoyère* later in October 1701, at least took the trouble to get Letters of Marque. His vessels passed themselves off as King's Ships, and were enthusiastically welcomed at Concepción, until the pretence was seen through. There was not enough trade for two ships at that little outpost, so the *Grénedan* went on to Arica and Ilo. Both reached St Malo in August 1703, with sufficiently handsome returns to set off another round of venturing.

This of course had not passed without Spanish notice and protest. Theoretically the total ban on non-Spanish merchant ships remained in force. but under the constant solicitation of the Malouins the French administration often granted authorisation for voyages under various thin disguises. Paris was prolific of assurances to Madrid, but stood to gain from the heavy duty on bullion imports, and after all the South Sea was a new and very promising field for French commerce. The Minister of Marine, Phélypeaux de Pontchartrain, shilly-shallied; he had close relations with Danycan. The Secretary for War was more forthright: 'If you were in my place, you would ignore all the great rules of policy, even of propriety, in order to make silver come into France, no matter by what means.'[25] Now and then there would be legal action against entrepreneurs who neglected to have the right friends, while official eyes were often too blind to see through the transparent pretences of Danycan and his like. A favourite ploy was a voyage to the Canaries, since these islands were by long-standing convention exempted from the normal restrictions, even in time of war. Other covers were voyages to China or, even more gloriously open to interpretation, 'for discoveries'.

Thus when Danycan sent out the *St-George* and *Murinet* in December 1703 they were licensed for China, but went straight to the South Sea, where their captains alleged that to avoid Anglo-Dutch cruisers in the Malacca and Sunda Straits they had taken this route to Canton; but they made no move to go there. The *Royal Jacques* joined them at Callao with letters from Pontchartrain prohibiting any trade, direct or indirect, with Spanish colonies on their return (!) from China; they obeyed—six months later. The captains also accepted a Viceregal commission to cruise against Dampier, but excused themselves from doing so because of the poor state of their ships, which, however, were capable of a trading cruise of some months. This abortive commission, however, came in handy on their return to France, when it was used to parry Spanish protests. The voyage was in flagrant violation of both French and Spanish prohibitions, but it made 357 per cent.

We may take this as typical, and need not follow the intricate deceptions and commercial fortunes of ensuing ventures; but a few specific points may be mentioned. The first French ships to enter the Pacific by Cape Horn, not the Straits, were the *St-Joseph*, *St-Esprit*, and *Baron de Breteuil* in 1703, and this then became the standard route. These ships had the brush with Dampier at Juan Fernández; they took away at least 6,000,000 livres.[26] The China cover was wearing thin by 1705, and was succeeded by 'discoveries'. The ingenious Danycan gave them a new twist; the east coast of New Holland—an interesting foreshadowing!—and Mindanao and near-by islands 'not possessed by European powers'. He probably banked too much on the government's geographical ignorance; this was not, as he claimed, the shortest way to China, Mindanao was not exactly *terra nullius*, and he failed to get a permit. A second project, for 'the island of California', was approved, but with the unfortunate proviso that his fitting-out must show it to be for a real colonisation and not just a pretext for South Sea trade; naturally it lapsed. For his venture of 1707–9 with four ships Danycan did manage to slip in 'China and other places', which of course meant Peru. No ship went to China, and although Danycan claimed a loss, the fleet brought back another 6,000,000 livres in treasure, as well as oriental luxuries abstracted from the Galleon trade by illicit New Spain-Peru traffic.

A voyage of real geographical significance was that of the *St-Louis*, which with the *Maurepas* and *Toison d'Or*, all belonging to the Compagnie des Indes Orientales, left Port-Louis (Penmarch in Brittany) in July 1706. The design was to send the ships on from Peru to the French factories in India; one need hardly stress the value of a direct input of silver to Asian trade. It was a well-found expedition—615 men and 124 guns—and finally established the superiority of the Strait Le Maire/Cape Horn route over the Straits of Magellan.[27] Financially the venture was a failure—there was too much Malouin competition on the coast, and the Compagnie could not even meet its wages bill; but the *St-Louis* sailed eastabout from Concepción to Pondicherry by the Horn and the Cape of Good Hope. This was the first known

voyage to take in both Capes, and moreover its track severely limited any hypothetical northern extension of Terra Australis Incognita in the Atlantic.[28]

Madrid fell to an Anglo-Portuguese force in June 1706; it was regained by
October, but the shock made the Spaniards less recalcitrant to French advice. There
was a reform of the Council of the Indies, and even talk of suppressing the Seville
Consulado. Amelot renewed a scheme for French escorts to the Caribbean fleets,
hoping to extend it later to Peru. Surprisingly, the Spaniards accepted; but apart
from Danycan and one other, who offered 150,000 livres between them, a score of
picked Malouin merchants refused to help with ships or money; as Pontchartrain's
agent remarked, money would not have been short for private contraband.[29] Little
came of this plan, but the Malouins did try, too late, to buy into the voyage of the
King's small frigate *l'Aurore*, which visited Peru in 1706–7 under de la Rigaudière
Froger. He sailed with a Spanish commission, since Madrid wished to counter
suspected intrigues in the Indies on behalf of the Archduke Karl, but most of the
silver he should have brought back was said to have been already shipped to
Panama. The voyage was a prelude to the more ambitious and successful exploit of
Michel Chabert, who sailed with two royal ships in August 1707.

Chabert's mission was to report on the political situation and to bring back as
much silver as possible, even by force and pillage should by any chance the
adherents of the Archduke have seized power. Once in the South Sea he was to fly
Spanish colours, but the natural demand for a Spanish commissioner on board was
evaded. There was the usual ban on trade, and the usual loophole that iron and cloth
might be exchanged for victuals. Only one of Chabert's ships, *l'Aimable*, reached the
South Sea; in Peru the Viceroy said he had no silver but eventually scraped together
300,000 pesos for his King. There was plenty of silver about, however—Chabert
escorted back to France seven or eight ships, including three of Danycan's carrying
at least 3,400,000 pesos. These were immediately seized by the French government
and minted to produce 10,255,000 livres. The 300,000 pesos were claimed by
France as part payment of Chabert's expenses, and altogether King Louis got over
4,000,000 pesos, King Philip perhaps 250,000.[30]

A brilliant success from the French point of view, but hardly likely to please the
Spaniards: the immediate reaction of Seville was to call for strict enforcement of the
total ban. However, rumours of seven English ships for the South Sea under
Dampier (really two under Woodes Rogers, with Dampier), perhaps to seize Juan
Fernández, gave point to renewed pressure for reform. An elaborate scheme was
accepted by all but a few ministers who thought that flotas and galeones had lasted
for two centuries and so could last two more; even the Andalusians professed satisfaction. But this proved an entirely nominal solution, the more so as under the
impact of his desperate crisis year, 1709, Louis XIV was trying to disengage himself
from too deep a commitment in Spain; in token, Amelot was recalled in September. On the other hand, Philip's position had been greatly strengthened by the
decisive victory of Almansa (April 1707) and other successes. Between 1709 and

1712 a series of decrees very seriously curtailed French commercial privileges.[31] But as usual, this was in theory.

In practice, the South Sea trade went merrily on, checked only by its own success in glutting Spanish colonial markets. Discoveries and China were still the cover stories, but the latter began to take on reality. The first French ship to cross the Pacific was the *St-Antoine* under Nicolas de Frondat, which left Pisco in March 1708 for Canton, returning by the north Pacific to reach Ilo in December 1710—an unwelcome infringement on the ancient preserve of the Manila Galleon. Frondat was followed by du Bocage de Bléville in *la Découverte* and Martin de Chassiron in *la Princesse*: both claimed to have discovered Clipperton Island. Altogether sixteen ships crossed to China on the Galleon track between 1707 and 1714, and ten went on by the Cape and so round the world.

A variant was introduced in 1714–16 by Forgeais de Langerie in *la Comtesse de Pontchartrain*, which sailed from Canton to the Tres Marias and home by the Horn—the first ship to sail eastwards around the globe, nearly sixty years before Cook.[32] Another variant was Duguay-Trouin's sending of three ships from Rio de Janeiro after his capture of the town in 1711; he had authority to send one ship into the South Sea, but sent two more on the specious pretext that his Portuguese loot was good enough only for Peru.

The Treaty of Utrecht (April 1713) should have meant the end of French voyages to the South Sea, but the Malouins were irrepressible—sixteen ships sailed in 1714, and attempts by a new Viceroy to check their activities were met by open attack at Pisco. In fact, the market was so glutted that the Malouins themselves proposed interdiction; but the commissioner sent out to recall French ships, Marchand de Chalmont, was to say the least very easy-going. Finally in December 1716 a Frenchman, J.-B. Martinet, sailed from Cadiz with three French ships and one Spaniard, and a Spanish commission to put down the trade by force. It seems likely that Martinet had originally intended a routinely illicit voyage with a Spanish cover—he had received easy credit from St Malo—and found himself compelled into a law enforcement role. Only two of his ships, both French, managed to round the Horn, but in 1717 he took six illegal traders, five of them in one swoop at Arica, and this stopped the traffic for a time. It is difficult to see Martinet's expedition as anything but a legalised hijack.

A new situation came about with Cardinal Alberoni's aggressive rebuilding of Spanish power in the Mediterranean, which led to the Quadruple Alliance (Britain, France, the Emperor, the Netherlands) against him, and John Law, who dominated French finance, seized the opportunity to break into the South Sea. He amalgamated the decrepit Compagnie des Indes Orientales with his grandiose Compagnie de Louisiane, and before his fall at the end of 1720 had sent out eleven ships. Two were taken by the Spaniards and the rest found no trade—for by this time British contraband was moving in, not directly to the South Sea but through La Plata and across the Andes. There was a final French ban in 1724, a final abortive attempt at illicit trading in 1725. Some French ships reached the Pacific in the 1740s, but under

Spanish charter, and with one exception—le Hen Brignon's *Condé* in 1745–9—under English captains.[33]

Geographically, the main significance of the French entry was to establish once and for all the route around Cape Horn as the standard passage between the Atlantic and the South Sea, while the mere number of voyages within a few years did much to dispel the terror of the passage and to change 'the silent Pacific of effective monopoly, a *mare clausum*' into a more peopled Pacific; the Spanish populations of what had been an almost hidden littoral were no longer lost to the world.[34] The turbulent seas first seen by Drake were to have a great future when the contrabandistas seeking silver were replaced by the whalers and the great wool and nitrate clippers.

Otherwise, all this activity had little strictly geographical significance, apart perhaps from the miniscule Clipperton and some minor discoveries in Magellanica: Davis's Land is highly dubious, and the Iles Danycan off California and the Falklands have long vanished from the map, although the strategic potential of the latter group was now first recognised, by Jean Doublet who recommended their colonisation. The voyages did, however, add substantially to the knowledge of what was half-known before.

The botanist and mathematician Père Louis Feuillée (or Feuillet) had been a pupil of J.–D. Cassini, founder of the family which directed the Paris Observatory for over 120 years. In 1707 he sailed to the South Sea with Doublet and spent nine months in Lima, botanising and making geophysical observations. His reports have been criticised for their prolixity by Dahlgren, of all people; but they provided a mass of geographical and scientific data, with more accurate longitudes and latitudes than had yet appeared.[35]

Although Feuillée's work was the more solid scientifically, it did not have the immediate impact (especially in England) of A.–F. Frézier's more concise *A Voyage to the South Sea*, which appeared in French in 1716 and was at once (1717) translated into English. Frézier, an engineer officer, was an admirable observer, and seems to have been commissioned to bring back as much topographical intelligence as possible while the South Sea was still accessible to the French. The report of his voyage of 1712–14 was illustrated by excellent plans of ports and towns, including Lima and Santiago, and described 'The Genius and Constitution of the Inhabitants, as well *Indians* as *Spaniards*: Their . . . Mines, Commodities, Traffick with *EUROPE*, &c.' It is worth noting that Feuillée and Frézier were the first trained observers, neither Spanish nor hostile, to publish connected accounts of these regions; previous writers, even Dampier, knew only the coasts—Funnell could think that 'the River of Chily' ran some hundreds of miles inland—and were too busy plundering to observe the lesser ports; 'and what idea can we form of a Turkey carpet if we look only at the border or, it may be, at the salvidge?'[36]

It is also highly significant that the English version of Frézier was dedicated to George Prince of Wales—in his capacity of Governor of the South Sea Company. The British had not been standing idly by while the French drove their sweet trade.

Privateers at play: Woodes Rogers

'Our Eyes are now all bent upon the New Undertaking of a Trade to the *South Sea*'—so Daniel Defoe opened a discussion which was to fill a dozen issues of his *Review* from June to August 1711.[37] In October of that year Woodes Rogers returned from a successful privateering circumnavigation; and the introduction to his narrative bears 'the imprint of Defoe's style and opinions', notably in the stress on Chile's potential as a base. The rival account by Edward Cooke devotes less than half of its 640 pages to the actual voyage: the rest is taken up by second-hand (or worse) history and geography; careful coastal directories, from captured Spanish pilot-books; and commercial information. It is in fact both propaganda and an intelligence handbook for commercial aggression.[38]

Rogers's two ships, the *Duke* and *Dutchess*, each around 300 tons and 30 guns, were fitted out with unusual care by a syndicate of Bristol merchants. Mindful of the internal hazards of the trade, they provided nearly twice as many officers as usual, including six medical men, chief of whom was Dr Thomas Dover, inventor of 'Dover's powder' (opium and ipecacuanha), a panacea popular almost to this century. As a heavy investor, he was appointed President, with a double vote, of the Council which was to agree on all important decisions. Dampier was 'Pilot for the South Seas', and found his niche at last.[39] Although the device of a formal Council by no means eliminated friction, not least with its highly opinionated President, it at least secured control, though Rogers was sometimes hampered by it.

The ships left the Bristol Avon on 1 August 1708, calling at Cork to fill up the crews, and at the Canaries. There was an agreeable interlude with the Portuguese at Ilha Grande, where the crews joined in the procession for the Conception of the Virgin and provided music for the service—'*Hey Boys up go we*! and all manner of noisy paltry Tunes'; a happy *festa* which ended in toasts to the Pope, the Archbishop of Canterbury, and William Penn (for the Dissenters!).[40] On Christmas Day they gave unsuccessful chase to a strange sail off the Falklands; then rounding the Horn they were driven down to 61°53'S, but on 31 January 1709 they sighted Juan Fernández. Dover insisted on taking a boat ashore, but returned hastily on seeing lights which were thought to indicate a French or Spanish presence; they had in fact been lit by 'A Man cloath'd in Goat-Skins, who look'd wilder than the first Owners of them'—Alexander Selkirk, 'the Absolute Monarch of the Island'. It was four years and four months since Stradling had left him there. Rogers's description of the ingenuity with which he had maintained himself forms the essential basis of *Robinson Crusoe*; and once he had been assured that a certain officer—Dampier?— was not in command, and had adjusted himself to a new-old life, he was appointed mate of the *Dutchess*, on Dampier's recommendation.[41]

In February they moved across to the Lobos Islands (Fig. 10), picking up a few prizes, and decided on 'the charming Undertaking' of an attempt on Guayaquil. After a sharp fight near Puna they took the French-built *Havre-de-Grace*; later renamed the *Marquis*, and fitted out with twenty guns, she was a useful unit although a slow sailer. Puna itself was taken by surprise; captured letters spoke of an

expected seven heavily-gunned ships under Dampier, although their actual arrival
was not yet known; but also of five French vessels on the coast, two as near as Callao
and each much stronger than the *Duke* or *Dutchess*. Rogers reckoned on a fortnight
for the attack on Guayaquil, which was to be made by small barks and pinnaces
carrying light guns, which would move up on the strong flood tides and lie low
under the mosquito-ridden mangroves during ebb (Fig. 16). By midnight on 22
April they came to the town, to find it blazing with lights and noisy with musketry
and cannon-shots. It was in fact the fiesta for the Eve of the Invention of the True
Cross, but the Indian pilots said that the town must have been alarmed.

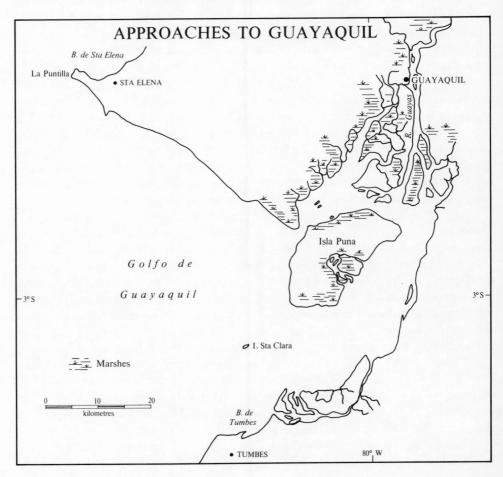

Figure 16. APPROACHES TO GUAYAQUIL.

The privateers withdrew to consult; Rogers was for a sharp assault in the confusion, but when he asked Dampier for buccaneer precendents on such occasions,
he was told that they never risked an attack on an alerted town. This was enough

for Dover and others, who proposed negotiations for the ransom of their prizes left at Puna. After much debate in the stifling boats, prudence prevailed; but by this time the corregidor had been informed by Indians that there were a thousand pirates in the river (they were in fact about 200). The corregidor was also an over-prudent man, and he in his turn thought fit to treat. He made little effective use of the time so gained, and when the haggling broke down on 24 April Guayaquil was taken in one rush, with scarcely any loss to the privateers and little to the Spaniards.

The next few days were spent in the search for plunder, which produced little but provisions and liquor; Dover's hesitation had given time for the valuables to be removed. Four guns which would be useful for the *Marquis* were carried off, and a raid up-river, under Selkirk, found a houseful of young ladies who were gently frisked and relieved of the gold chains and so on hidden under their light dresses—in such a manner that 'This I mention as a Proof of our Sailors Modesty', and the ladies, doubtless relieved in another sense, took it with good grace. Despite a little sniping from the bush, in the town an atmosphere of genteel bargaining prevailed. But on the whole the purchase was poor, and the ransom was beaten down from 50,000 to 30,000 pesos, of which under 27,000 were paid.

They had spent nearer three weeks than two on the Guayaquil affair, and most of the officers thought it time to get away. But the three ships of the Armada del Mar del Sur and the two French (one of which was the sail that had narrowly escaped Rogers off the Falklands) did not leave Callao until 6/16 July, visiting the Galápagos, Panama, and New Spain before returning in January 1710. As Dahlgren remarks, the Viceroy's report 'as usual, contains many details on the measures taken, but few on the results obtained', although he claimed to have driven the enemy from the seas.[42] If so, the privateers took their time in leaving. From Puna they sailed to the Galápagos, losing many men from infection by pest-corpses which had been buried hard by the church which was their Guayaquil headquarters. They found no water on these cindery islands, and lost Simon Hatley, the master of a small prize; he was given over for dead, but fell into Spanish hands, to reappear years later and gain a strange immortality as the original of the Ancient Mariner who shot the albatross.

They spent only nine days in the Galápagos before going over to Gorgona (Fig. 10) where at least they could water and careen, using some of 500 bales of captured Romish indulgences to burn off the ships' bottoms. They took a few prizes and engaged in very friendly trading on the remote coast between Buenaventura and Atacames. Relations with their victims were curiously easy-going; religious wares seemed a staple of the coasting trade, and a padre who had been very obliging in arranging for provisions was rewarded with '3 large Wooden *Spanish* Saints'; another cleric was made happy by the less spiritual present of 'the prettiest young female Negro we had'. There was obviously a gulf between buccaneer and privateer.

From their last prize they learnt that Panama had been warned and that the Franco-Spanish squadron was out at last. In September they briefly revisited the

Galápagos, to stock up with turtle before going north for the Acapulco Galleon. In October they rendezvoused at the Tres Marias and spent seven weeks cruising in an extended formation off Cape San Lucar. Provisions were now barely enough for an ocean crossing, and on 20 December they reluctantly decided to make for Guam; but a sail was sighted the next day. It was indeed from Manila; not the Galleon, but a frigate of 450 tons and 20 guns, the *Nuestra Señora de la Encarnación Disengaño*. With a crew reduced to 200 by the long voyage, she was no match for the two privateers (the *Marquis* was refitting) and on the 22nd, New Year's Day 1710 New Style, the *Duke*, practically single-handed, took her, suffering only two men wounded—but one was Rogers, with a shattered jaw. She had a rich cargo of China goods and was commanded by a Frenchman, Jean Pichberty, from whom they learnt that the even richer Galleon, the 900-ton *Nuestra Señora de Begoña*, was not far behind.

This was worth waiting for. Rogers in the *Duke* had had his turn, so over his protests he was to stay at their signal-station at Puerto Seguro, near the tip of Baja California, off which the *Dutchess* and the *Marquis* were to cruise for eight days. They had not to wait so long; on Christmas Day the signallers reported three sail in sight. Badly wounded as he was, Rogers could not keep out of the fight. With 450 crew and 150 passengers, the *Begoña* was a tougher proposition than the *Disengaño*; she mounted only twenty-four guns, but some threw twice the weight of the privateers' largest. After two days of fighting (in which Rogers was again wounded) they had had enough; there was clearly no hope of taking a ship so stout and so stoutly fought.

They had still on board the hostages for the balance of the Guayaquil ransom; through the good offices of Pichberty, brother-in-law of Ducasse and a man of standing, they were released against bills on Paris. The *Disengaño* was renamed the *Batchelor* (why did they step outside the peerage?) and there was a nasty row with the deplorable Dover, who insisted on commanding her: from his sick-bed Rogers protested in writing that the Doctor was incompetent to captain so valuable a ship. In the end there was a compromise, Dover being admitted to nominal command but with no say on the navigation.

The little fleet left Puerto Seguro on 10 January 1710 and reached Guam on 11 March, very short of provisions. A letter was sent in, promising payment for supplies but with the threat of 'Military Treatment' if they were refused: the Governor took the hint, and his response was most cordial. His parting present was a flying prau, which Rogers thought would be a great attraction on the canal in St James's Park. The way home was by Batavia where they sold the *Marquis*, and the Cape, which they left in a large Dutch convoy in 6 April 1711. By 23 July they reached Texel, but it was another two and a half months before they finally dropped anchor in the Thames. Much of this delay was due to legal threats by the EIC; although strict precautions had been taken against trading at Batavia, the Company held that its monopoly had been breached, and had to be bought off with £6000.

Rogers might have done better without his cumbersome Council, but the voyage stands out as exceptionally well conducted. It grossed nearly £150,000, of which a third went to the ships' companies as prize. Of the owners' two-thirds, half went on expenses, but the net profit was nearly 100 per cent. As well as this tangible return, the narratives of Rogers and Cooke provided not only the idea of *Robinson Crusoe* but grist to the mill of Defoe and other South Sea projectors.[43] Rogers arrived at Texel ten weeks after the Act for the establishment of a South Sea Company was passed, eight weeks before its Charter was signed. Its origins must be sought in the tangle of domestic and internal politics leading to the Treaty of Utrecht.

Towards Utrecht

1709, the year of Louis XIV's deepest distress, was also the year of Malplaquet, in Marlborough's words 'a very murdering battle'. Although the British share of the hideous Allied casualty list was light compared with that of the Dutch, there could have been no more forceful argument for the Tory view that the concentration on the continent, especially Flanders, was a basic flaw in the conduct of the War. The call was for a return to navalist principles, to break the power of France and Spain by cutting off the American silver at source—the doctrine put so succinctly by Francis Bacon in his *Considerations touching the War with Spain* of 1623: the greatness of Spain was 'ticklish and brittle' since it depended on the treasure of the Indies, and 'their Indies (if it be but well weighed) are indeed but an accession to those that are masters by sea.'[44] Between them, Rogers and the Malouins had greatly reinforced the argument. In 1711 there were at least five projects for forcing a South Sea trade by seizing bases in Chile and/or Patagonia; Juan Fernández was of course much favoured.[45]

The basically Whig ministry which ran the War after 1705 was indeed not unmindful of the Indies harvest, and sought to secure it by a secret clause in the Treaty of Barcelona (1707–8) with the Archduke 'Carlos III'. This provided for a joint Anglo-Spanish company to carry on the Indies trade, once Carlos (or Karl) should be in possession; until it could be formed the British should have the right to send up to 5000 tons of shipping, and they would escort both their own and Spanish vessels. With magnificent effrontery, French trade to the South Sea was branded as fraudulent and punished by an eternal ban.[46] The Allied disaster at Almansa sent such hopes into the discard.

The horror of Malplaquet, unjust accusations that England was receiving little Dutch support in fighting Holland's war, bad harvests and high prices, the serio-comic rivalry of Sarah Duchess of Marlborough and Mrs Abigail Masham for influence over Queen Anne, and the wave of High Church bigotry expressed in the Sacheverell affair combined to destroy the Whig Junto: Queen and voters together brought Robert Harley and Henry St John to full power in November 1710. Next month the surrender of an Allied army trapped at Brihuega demonstrated that 'No Peace without Spain' was an illusion, though the Whig majority in

the Lords reaffirmed it a year later. To begin with, however, the ministry had to
walk delicately; Harley, essentially opportunistic, was fearful of becoming a
prisoner of the extreme Tories, and the rivalry between him and the flamboyant St
John was intense, if concealed.

The French had been putting out peace feelers, to both British and Dutch, long
before the poet Matthew Prior's negotiations began in July 1711.[47] By this time the
French had surmounted the desperate crisis of early 1709, when Louis had been
reduced to accepting all demands except that he should himself expel his grandson
from Spain. The British government, Harley in particular, had to reckon with the
South Sea enthusiasm; they sought to get a grip on the trade by demanding four
fortified 'security ports', two on the Atlantic and two on the Pacific coasts of the
Indies. A French memorandum spoke of Juan Fernández as the least which could be
offered, but then baulked: in English hands it would soon become 'the greatest
entrepôt in the world for the manufactures of Europe and Asia'—an opinion
which, had they known of it, would have delighted Rogers and Defoe. Prior was
told that such a concession was out of the question; and St John suggested that as
compensation Britain should have the Asiento to supply slaves to the Indies for
thirty years. Since the French had held the contract and reaped nothing but losses,
they readily found this acceptable. The means for exploiting it lay to hand: the
newly formed South Sea Company.[48]

The later history of the SSC, culminating in the giant Bubble of 1720–1, and the
fact that it never sent a ship into the Pacific, have obscured its importance in the
bargaining for peace and its significance as the legitimate offspring of the long-
standing English concern to force an entry into 'the Spanish Lake'. Nearly everything else about it was illegitimate; but this was the sweetener for a grandiose plan
to restore the national finances, which were under severe strain, by funding the
'floating' or unsecured debt of about £9,000,000. Defoe, while defending the
scheme, lamented that the compounding of two distinct propositions—for the
funding and for the South Sea—had confused the public mind.[49] Yet the plan was 'a
marvellous synthesis of finance, commerce, and foreign policy. It pleased both the
[Tory] October Club and the City, which by itself was an achievement.'[50]

Its Act, passed in May 1711, gave the SSC a monopoly of British trade (except
with Dutch or Portuguese possessions) from the mouth of the Orinoco round the
Horn and right up the west coast of the Americas; but it said nothing as to how the
trade should be carried on. Characteristically for a Harleian project, it left or seemed
to leave options open: the SSC could be seen either as the agency of a tranquil trade,
perhaps based on the security ports, to be gained as part of a general peace settlement, or as a machine for forcing a trade by seizure of territory on the lines of
Defoe, Rogers, and other projectors. Certainly in January 1712 the Directors put up
a project for a stupendous expedition to the South Sea—a score of warships, two
score transports, 4000 soldiers—and with only vague encouragement from the
government gathered cargoes claimed to amount to £120,000. How much of this

was serious is open to sceptical conjecture; from the ministry's point of view, it may have been thought of as a blind for the public and a bluff *in terrorem* to influence the final negotiations which opened at Utrecht, also in January 1712.[51]

In April 1711, on the death of his father Leopold of Austria, the Archduke Karl succeeded as Holy Roman Emperor; despite the Whig diehards in the Lords, if a European balance was to mean anything at all 'No Peace without Spain' was now an utter nonsense. Riding over Dutch and Spanish suspicions and recalcitrances, Britain and France virtually arranged things to their own satisfaction; the Dutch for instance were told by Harley that he had obtained some concessions in North America which did not concern them, but he said not a word about the Asiento or about customs concessions for British goods shipped to the Indies via Cadiz. In the event these latter were not insisted upon—France and the Netherlands could have claimed most favoured nation treatment. The Asiento was enough for British appetites, with an important rider: seeing that other asientistas had made losses, and on the strict understanding that there should be no smuggling, the SSC might send one 'permission ship' a year, of not more than 500 tons, to trade in the Indies. The King of Spain was to have a cut of 28.75 per cent of the profits, but the goods were to be duty-free in the Indies. Alongside the Ambassador to Madrid, Lord Lexington, was sent as a negotiator one Manuel Manassas Gilligan, English by birth, Danish by naturalisation, one-time Portuguese asientista, smuggler by long practice: 'Choice of this sort of man shows that the English intended to make the most of the Asiento both legally and illegally.'[52]

At Utrecht Britain, the Netherlands, and Portugal concluded peace with France in April 1713, Britain with Spain in July, though the preliminary commercial agreement—the Asiento Treaty— had been signed in March at Madrid. From a Spanish point of view, it might seem that little had changed. The old system of Seville and Cadiz was still officially intact, 'on the same footing as in the reign of King Carlos II', except for the limited monopoly within a monopoly of the SSC's Asiento and its annual permission ship; this last was not included in the general treaty but ingeniously passed off as a favour to Spain, so that France and the Netherlands could not claim entry on most favoured nation grounds. France indeed was formally barred from the Indies trade. As for the Dutch Republic, it had been badly over-strained by the War; it could not meet its commitment to provide three-eighths of the naval forces to be employed, and even so 'It sacrificed its naval strength to a disproportionately great military effort in Flanders ... The strain broke the Dutch Republic as a great naval power.'[53]

The clear winner so far as world power was concerned was the newly-United Kingdom of Great Britain. With France banned from the Indies and the United Provinces increasingly lagging behind, it was now to Britain's advantage to prop up, in appearance at least, the old Spanish exclusivist polity, since with the Asiento she was better poised than any other power to erode it from within. She had extorted from her enemy Philip V what she had been promised by her ally 'Carlos III', and would share the Indies trade 'only with Spaniards, which was pretty much the same as not sharing it at all', since she could have a strong hold on the legal trade through Cadiz as well as the new facilities for contraband.[54] In practice things did not work out so smoothly; but after Utrecht Britannia, or *l'Albion perfide*, ruled the waves.

With the end of the Succession War, the South Sea might seem to have relapsed into the *status quo ante*. The French entry had been a brilliant episode, but it had no lasting effect and was soon half-forgotten. The Manila Galleon continued to plough its stately—and lonely—way; but despite some efforts at revival under the first Spanish Bourbon, the old system of flotas and galeones remained in decrepitude and in fact would soon be abandoned. While it lasted it was subject to erosion by contraband, in part under the auspices and behind the shield of the South Sea Company and that bastard offspring of Utrecht, its Asiento.

In the South Sea proper, things were more lively. One of the interesting features of the French South Sea trade was its extension to China, the first trans-Pacific trading apart from the Manila-Acapulco run; it was not followed up until the Yankee skippers of the young American Republic gave it a new dimension. By 1713 the Canton trade was not yet settled in its later very firm lines, but already China was well on the road to becoming the great magnet of European trade to eastern Asia: the era of tea would replace that of spices. Meanwhile, Chinese traders were nearly as essential to Batavia as to Manila.

The Philippines had, rather surprisingly, been left untouched during the War. British official effort had been largely diverted to continental campaigns, while private enterprise—which meant privateering—retained its old fixation on the South Sea in the narrower sense, from Juan Fernández to Cape San Lucar. In any case, the British had their more or less illicit 'country trade' between India and the Philippines, under cover of Armenian and other convenient fronts. As for the Dutch, they had lost the panache of Coen and had no longer the resources for more than local aggression against petty rajahs; they were intent on cultivating their gardens in Java and the Spice Islands (and uprooting other people's) and on nursing Deshima.

Far to the north, the Russians in 1713 had not yet pioneered the direct sea-route to Kamchatka. They were very soon to do so, and this in turn would lead them to their expansion into Alaska, the most positive and substantial development, from the point of view of both commerce and exploration, between Utrecht and the opening, in the 1760s, of the second great age of Pacific discovery. The interval was however a period of much diverse, if not always fruitful, maritime activity; and to it we must now turn.

Chapter 9

ALBERONI, THE ALBATROSS, AND JENKINS'S EAR

Ye mariners of England, chosen train
Of liberty and commerce, now no more
Secrete your generous valour; hear the call
Of injured Albion ... long in silence hush'd
Hath slept the British thunder; though the pride
Of weak Iberia hath forgot the roar;
Soon shall her ancient terrors be recall'd ...
Our angry fleets, when insolence and wrongs,
To arms awaken our vindictive power,
Shall bear the hideous waste of ruthless war ...

... between the pride of the one [commander], and the insolence
of another, the enterprise miscarried, according to the proverb,
'Between two stools, the backside falls to the ground.' ... Our
conductors, finding things in this situation, perceived it was
high time to relinquish our conquests; and this we did. ...

The title of this chapter reflects the inconsequentiality of events in, or bearing upon, the Pacific in the thirty years after Utrecht. Alberoni's forward policy for a revitalised Spain threw European politics into confusion, and both before and after his fall the South Sea Company, though it was never in the South Sea, was in the forefront of the commercial and diplomatic tangles, besides making its own contribution to history in the famous Bubble.

The Company was indeed ill named; nevertheless it was not without its influences on Pacific activities. The most long-lasting of these was admittedly a negative one—for the eastern Pacific, it was a monopoly sitting alongside that of the EIC in the western. Right through the eighteenth century British shipowners had to secure its licence to trade anywhere within 300 leagues of the American coasts, or alternatively, as John Meares did in 1788, arrange a faked Portuguese cover in Macao.[1] More important was its positive role in the penetration of the Indies by British contraband. All its legal factories, except Panama, were on the Atlantic shores, but Cartagena provided an avenue to Peru by the Río Magdalena: in 1737, forty-nine canoes and fifteen bigger boats stuffed with foreign merchandise were reported on that river. The entry by Buenos Aires was even more important, backed up as it was by the Portuguese Colonia do Sacramento across the La Plata estuary. This outlier of Brazil was the 'bastion of contraband'; the Spaniards made it a condition of its retrocession to Portugal in 1715 that no third nation—

R. Glover, *London, or the Progress of Commerce* (London 1739); T. Smollett on Cartagena 1741, *The Adventures of Roderick Random* (London 1748), Everyman ed. 189, 191.

which meant of course the British—should be allowed to trade there. But when they again took it in 1762, they also captured no fewer than twenty-seven fully-laden British ships.[2]

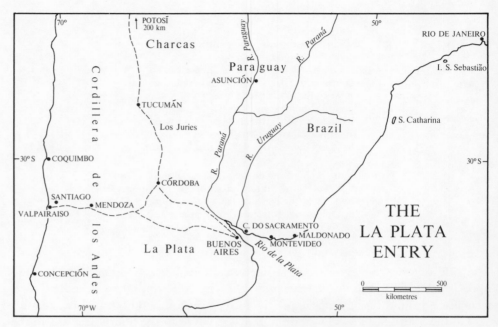

Figure 17. THE LA PLATA ENTRY.   Main routes after map in A. Jara, *Tres Ensayos*, 86.

A new way to the South Sea: La Plata

The basic *raison d'être* of the SSC, after Utrecht, was the Asiento contract to supply Spanish America with 4800 slaves annually for thirty years; to supervise reception and sales, half a dozen factors might reside at each major port—Buenos Aires, Caracas, Cartagena, Habana, Panama, Puerto Bello and Vera Cruz. The Company's 'monopoly' in the South Sea was not recognised by the Spaniards; here it was a nuisance to its compatriots only; the Asiento treaty gave it no right to trade into, though it might trade in, the Pacific. Such trade was to be narrowly confined to carrying slaves from Panama to Peru, and only in locally hired vessels; there were to be no direct voyages from or to Europe.[3] However, the replacing of the Indies trade 'on the same footing as in the reign of King Carlos II' implied the restoration of the fairs at Vera Cruz and Puerto Bello/Cartagena, and the SSC was to be allowed to send an 'Annual Ship' to one of them.

The quota of slaves was not fulfilled, and this trade was run at a loss; the first licensed ships—which were far beyond the agreed tonnage limits—were fairly profitable. But even discounting the stories of supply tenders hovering over the horizon and refilling the Annual Ship overnight as a matter of routine, there is no doubt that the permitted SSC trade was a cover for contraband, 'a shoe horn for a vast illicit commerce'[4]—so much so that the Jamaicans complained bitterly of this unfair competition. Smuggling was not of course carried on by the SSC corporately, but it is too much to believe that in such a hard-headed age, in which business motives were always (and often rightly) suspect of corruption, the Directors were not aware of what their officers were doing. Occasionally a too flagrant factor might be dismissed, 'for the record' or if he was too obviously feathering his nest to the Company's detriment. In 1731 one of the factors was so open in his illegal trading at Panama that the Spaniards transferred the whole factory to Puerto Bello. They remained suspicious, and with good reason; after all, they knew all about corruption themselves.[5]

Taken as a whole, there is little doubt that the contribution of the SSC to British trade with the Indies was, and still is, exaggerated. In fact, a shrewd pamphleteer who assigned initials—Q, Y, Z and so on—to the various sources of the Company's losses put against them 'the profits or advantages accrued to the Company by their trade, for several years past . . . I shall call it "O"'.[6] One need not be quite so cynical as this, although it has even been hinted, very tentatively, that the total sales of British goods fell off. But it is admitted that if this is so, it would be in the main the result of the diplomatic crises and actual hostilities with Spain, which cannot be laid at the Company's door alone. The Annual Ship, like its Spanish predecessors the flotas and galeones, was far from annual, and its declared profits were often small and sometimes nil; but then 'they might have very little to do with the private profits of the Directors.'[7]

The SSC's activities were disrupted by war, but even apart from this they appear disjointed and even at times almost incoherent, though there may have been method in this disorder—the accounts were never settled to anyone's satisfaction, least of all the King of Spain's. But its operations were not merely marginal, even in the Caribbean where the tradition of the 'free market' in smuggling and slaving, often joint activities, was so deeply rooted.[8] And in La Plata they were highly important, and this was the entry most immediate affecting the Pacific (Fig. 17).

Buenos Aires had been persistently neglected by the Spanish authorities; indeed, its use as an access and outlet for the silver heart-land in Andine Peru was legally banned, since fiscal control of a long land-route was so difficult and of course the interests of the big merchants of both Seville and Lima would be threatened by such a loophole in the closed system. Originally, the ban was not so irrational as it might seem: the Atlantic traverse would have been much longer, needing more shipping and lying more open to the corsairs, especially when the Portuguese (or the Dutch) in Brazil were hostile, which was most of the time. Hence 'instead of Buenos Aires becoming the centre of commerce for La Plata, Chile, and Alta Peru, which would have been appropriate to its favourable location, it became the bolt [*cerrojo*] for all the southern extremity of America.'[9] Ironically, the word *cerrojo* can also mean 'latch'.

A latch it was to prove; geography could not be totally denied, and 'if Spain did not appreciate the most natural route to South America, other European nations did.'[10] Already in 1623 it had been found necessary to set up a 'dry' customs post [*aduana seca*] at Córdoba, to try to kill the trade with a 50 per cent additional duty—but it was impossible to guard all entries into the 'Ocean of land' on the Atlantic slope of the Andes. From its foundation in 1680, Colonia do Sacramento had been a handy base for small Portuguese craft collecting hides and tallow (and silver) in exchange for tobacco, brandy, and European goods; it became 'the gigantic magazine which Buenos Aires needed to expand its trade.'[11] The numerous branches of the Paraná and its thickly wooded islands gave access and cover, the ranches along the river were so many warehouses; and it would be naïve to think that the sparse local population needed much storage space for its own needs. And behind Sacramento lay Brazil, where since Cromwell's day English ships had been allowed on remarkably easy conditions; so 'what Jamaica was for the Caribbean, Sacramento was for the Rio de la Plata.'[12]

Virtually the only economic activity of La Plata, certainly the only one needing external markets, was cattle-ranching. This is hardly a labour-intensive occupation, and the local demand for slaves was very slight. It was not much better across the Andes in Chile; in 1731, finding no sale in Buenos Aires for 244 Blacks, the SSC factor got permission to take them across to Santiago, only to find that the previous arrival of 127 had glutted the slave market. Nevertheless, the SSC stood by its rights to supply this unlikely market; one may suspect the hand of Gilligan. Then again it was necessary to feed the human cargoes stock-piled in its barracks, and there was also 'a great need to cover the nakedness of the negroes'; and what better cover than good British woollens?[13]

The solicitude of the Company's factors went further than the demands of decency. Of course the contrabandista was often in collusion with the customs officer and his superiors; but when the connivance broke down, as in times of war, the results were startling. Two ships seized in 1719 and 1727, the *Arbela* and the *Wootle* [*sic*], carried arms, beer, brandy, gunpowder, ivory, wax, China ware, rice, assorted cutlery, walking-sticks, snuff-boxes, silk stockings, candle reflectors, a wide variety of clothing and fine textiles, 'and a thousand other trinkets'. Few of these commodities strike one as necessities of slave, or even gaucho, life. Conversely, although of course the export of precious metals was prohibited, the *Sea Horse*, wrecked after clearing for Europe in 1728, was in ballast which happened to include 75,000 silver pesos.[14]

Lacking direct access to Chilean and Peruvian ports, this British trans-Andine penetration was less brilliant than the success the French had enjoyed during their *belle époque*. Nevertheless, it played a significant role in a shift of emphasis towards the south of the continent. There were of course other factors: the chaotic state of Anglo-Spanish relations under Alberoni and again in the 1730s hastened the further decay of the official trading system in the Caribbean and the Isthmus, and the economic activity of the traditional centres was dislocated by dearths or gluts of legal or illegal goods: for example, Quito's 400 shops and workshops, and its 2,000,000 pesos of circulating capital, were reduced to 60 and under 100,000 pesos in 1723; the ships which had brought indigo from Guatemala now by-passed Guayaquil. In the best of times the system of galeones and annual fairs meant the locking up of merchant capital for much of the year; merchants with money in hand but no merchandise naturally turned to the contrabandistas. The increasing use of permission or 'register' ships gave an impetus to smaller ports; already in 1706 the Consulado of Lima was complaining bitterly of the loss of its trade with Charcas and Chile to such ships coming to Buenos Aires—competition which would take a new turn when, in the 1740s, sailings around the Horn were officially permitted. Chilean wheat, wine, tin and copper were becoming more essential to Peru, which in return sent guano. Internal trade in the Chile-Charcas-Paraguay-La Plata region was also on the rise; the *yerba mate* (herbal tea) of Paraguay was widely diffused, and the cottons of Los Juries were distributed through Córdoba.[15]

Already the French had brought new 'felt needs' to Chile: 'the first European-style coaches and calashes began to roll, the first notes of the clavichord were heard, the first billiard-rooms set up', Versailles lace and Venice glass were in favour.[16] But the French had departed, and these new demands could no longer be adequately met by the old flow, now so precarious, across the Isthmus: hence those cargoes, so ill-suited to a slave barracks, on the *Arbela* and *Wootle*. Between them, the SSC's Asiento and Sacramento played their part in bringing a forgotten littoral into what was then 'the modern world'.

Alberoni

That the SSC as a trading corporation barely got off the ground is in large part attributable to the fact that Philip V was both uxorious and pious—'a man who could not do without a woman in his bed, but would allow into it no woman who was not his wife'[17]—and the opening this gave to Giulio Alberoni, an ecclesiastic of no birth, little devotion, much ability, more energy. Philip's first Queen died in February 1714, and the effect on His Catholic Majesty's mind and body made a new one a necessity. The lady chosen was Isabel (Elizabeth) Farnese, a Parmesan princess, an unknown quantity but soon to be notorious as a very strong-willed person indeed.[18] Alberoni, who was Parmesan envoy in Madrid, had dangled Isabel at the right moment; the marriage was consummated on Christmas Day 1714. A son, later to become Carlos III, the best of the Bourbon kings, was born in January 1716; Alberoni, already powerful, now became virtually the master of Spain. He was formally appointed first minister early in 1717, and a Cardinal's hat followed within six months. A fantastic ascension, especially in that age and that state, for the son of a poor gardener and a seamstress.

Between them, Isabel and Alberoni set about the reforging of Spanish strength. Conditions for doing so were more favourable than might seem likely after a long war which Spain had entered as a weakling. The successful outcome of the war in the Peninsula had done much for national morale, and Philip had not been a mere puppet. Even if in the last resort French power had enabled the war to be carried on for so long, and French diplomacy had ended it, Spaniards could justly feel that their stand had shown they were not pawns to be casually disposed of at conference tables. Although the grandees and the cumbersome Councils still ruled, winds of change had begun to blow through the dusty bureaus of administration—sharp northern winds from France. The loss of Flanders and the Italian holdings was a gain; they had immemorially been a drain on energy, manpower, and money. Conversely, Aragon, Catalonia, and Valencia had backed the losing side, and paid for it: many of their cherished traditional liberties had been surrendered, and the tighter control from Madrid enhanced the central revenue.[19] The demands of war had given at least some impetus to internal entrepreneurial and industrial activity. In short, as the British were to find at Cartagena, the Spain of Philip V, if far from the almost hegemonic power of Philip II, was far from the wreck of Carlos II.

There were foundations to build upon: already Philip's French adviser Jean Orry had weakened the stranglehold of the Councils and taken the first step towards a ministerial system of government. Tactless and overbearing, he did not long survive the advent of Alberoni, who carried on the work with more finesse and with relentless energy, itself shocking to the sinecurists and pensioners of the old régime. Pensions and perquisites were ruthlessly cut, currency reformed, the fiscal administration tidied up at least to some extent, manufacturing and agriculture fostered, with fair results; and a new army of 50,000 men was set up, decently armed, clothed, and disciplined. As regards the Indies, Martinet's expedition was sent to the South Sea in 1716, Alberoni experimented with register ships, and carried out the long overdue transfer of the Casa de Contratación from Seville to Cadiz, where the bulk of the Indies trade had long been centred.[20]

But the major thrust was towards the creation of a new and powerful navy. To this end neglected Spanish resources were exploited to the utmost: hemp, tar, and pitch, Asturian timber, Cuban copper for sheathing. The sailmaking industry of Biscay was revived, new dockyards were established in Galicia and Catalonia, and a naval college at Cadiz. In 1703–4 total military expenditure was 40,000,000 *reales de vellon*, and the navy's share was so minimal that it had no separate entry; in 1717–18 that share was 41,000,000 reales out of a total 183,500,000—over 22 per cent.[21]

Alberoni and Isabel Farnese had done much to put the country on her feet; unfortunately, the Queen's dynastic ambitions compelled Spain to run before she could walk. Philip, despite his renunciation of his claims in France, yearned after a regency on behalf of the child Louis XV; the actual Regent—and heir presumptive—Philippe, Duc d'Orléans, was thus made an enemy. Isabel was determined to secure some principality in Italy for her own sons, since there was already an heir to Spain by Philip's first marriage. A very confused diplomatic and territorial situation in Italy, where the one-time Spanish possessions had passed to Savoy-Sardinia and Austria, seemed to offer the Queen both excuse and opportunity for intrigues which passed into open aggression.

Alberoni, powerful as he was, was only powerful so long as he had the support of his royal master and mistress, who required the nicest management. Despite his fantastic fecundity of alliance projects, with any likely parties from Jacobites to Turks, he was forced, apparently against his better judgement, into an adventurism which isolated Spain. The resultant Quadruple Alliance crushed the renascent Spanish power at birth; Sardinia had been easily seized, but in an attempt to repeat this success in Sicily, the new fleet was destroyed by a superior British force off Cape Passaro in August 1718, long before any declaration of war.[22] Alberoni's audacity went so far as to send men and arms to aid the Scottish Jacobites, and 300 Spanish troops were rounded up at Glenshiels in June 1719; but by the end of that year, with a French army lodged in northern Spain and his ally Charles XII of Sweden killed in a petty siege, Philip was forced to secure peace by dismissing his dynamic Cardinal.[23] So spirited an effort as his perhaps deserved a better end.

Before the breach of 1718, however, the SSC was recovering from a poor start. It was cautious enough to refuse to have anything to do with the only proposal, apart from the grandiose but shadowy armament of 1712, for activity in the South Sea. This was John Welbe's 1713 project for a voyage to Juan Fernández and thence to the Solomons and New Guinea, the true Terra Australis abounding in gold; some of the inhabitants could be trepanned and brought back to be trained as interpreters for a future trade. Welbe was not a person to inspire confidence—at least one of his appeals was written from a debtor's prison—but the ostensible reason for rejection was fear of trespass on EIC preserves. However, in the Bubble year of 1720, anything went; Welbe's scheme was revived and its shares were actually bought at thirty-two times their par value.[24]

The Asiento provisions were in the best or worst tradition of Sevillean bureaucracy: so complex and cumbersome as to lead to friction even with the utmost good faith on both sides, and that was a commodity nearly as non-existent as Welbe's gold. If the Treaty was to work at all, it would have to be revised, and in 1715 formal negotiations were opened by George Bubb (later Dodington). The climate was propitious: the new Hanoverian government needed some diplomatic success and, in view of the strained relations between Philip of Spain and Philippe d'Orléans, Alberoni, just rising into power, was anxious to secure an Anglo-Spanish alliance, or at least a *rapprochement*. The result was a new Treaty of Madrid which gave the SSC much of what it wanted: more regular sailings to the Indies, more tonnage and more favourable regulations for the Annual Ships, and in particular the right to deposit excess cargo from its slave-ships at Buenos Aires.[25] All seemed set fair, when Isabel's Italian adventures threw all into disorder. By the end of 1718 the hostilities so informally opened at Cape Passaro had become a declared war between Britain and Spain.

For the time being the new door into the South Sea by La Plata was again bolted; there remained the old entry of the buccaneers and Woodes Rogers. Such an enterprise had already been taken in hand by a London group which had fitted out two ships in the Thames; the trifling difficulty that Britain was still officially at peace with Spain was met by procuring an Imperial commission at Ostend, signing on some Flemings as cover, and renaming the ships *Prince Eugene* and *Starhemberg*. So far as the Pacific was concerned, this last privateering voyage into the South Sea was the first, and only, result of the war; the formal declaration meant that a British commission could be taken out. The Flemings were sacked and the ships reverted to their more comfortable English names *Success* and *Speedwell*. It was also, perhaps, consoling to the conscience that the terms of the Emperor's commission, which put 'enemies of the Christian name', specifically Turks, first and Spaniards only in a postscript, could be dropped.[26]

The last privateers: Clipperton and Shelvocke

Success and *Speedwell* were misnomers.[27] At the start the designated commander, George Shelvocke, was displaced in favour of his original second in command John Clipperton, Dampier's old deserter and a rough tar with a great contempt for ex-Navy men like Shelvocke. The ships sailed from Plymouth on 13 February 1719, and on the 20th they lost company, not to meet again for two years, and then by accident. This seems to have been deliberate desertion by Shelvocke; Clipperton can be acquitted of any desire to separate, if only because all the wine and brandy (bought cheaply at Ostend) were on Shelvocke's *Speedwell*. By all accounts except his own, this must have suited Shelvocke, a mighty drinker even for his milieu.

The *Success* reached the rendezvous at Juan Fernández on 7 September 1719; the *Speedwell* dallied at Santa Catalina in Brazil, where a possibly collusive 'mutiny' adopted articles cutting down the owners' share. Nearly three weeks after Clipperton's arrival at Juan Fernández Shelvocke passed Strait Le Maire, and was driven far to the south. Now occurred the incident which alone immortalises a voyage otherwise notable only for drunkenness, dishonesty, and mutiny well beyond the ordinary run:

> In short, one would think it impossible that anything living could subsist in so rigid a climate; and, indeed, we all observed that we had not the sight . . . of one sea-bird, except a disconsolate black *Albitross*, who accompanied us for several days, hovering about us as if he had lost himself, till *Hatley*, (my second Captain) observing, in one of his melancholy fits, that this bird was always hovering near us, imagin'd, from his colour, that it might be some ill omen. That which, I suppose, induced him the more to encourage his superstition, was the continuous series of contrary tempestuous winds, which had oppress'd us ever since we got into that sea. But be that as it would, he, after some fruitless attempts, at length, shot the *Albitross*, not doubting (perhaps) that we should have a fair wind after it. I must own, that this navigation is truly melancholy . . .[28]

Simple, even halting, words to be transmuted into one of the most magical and most loved of English poems.

Shelvocke arrived at Juan Fernández on 11 January 1720, and after only four days stood across to the mainland, picking up some small prizes, including one laden with 'cormorants dung, which the *Spaniards* call *Guana*'—apparently the first English reference to this useful if odorous commodity.[29] At Ilo he had a brush with the *Sage Solomon*, presumably one of John Law's ships, but despite boasts of 'roasting this insolent *Frenchman*', his second thoughts prevailed: she had more men and more guns. Hatley, cruising ahead in a prize with William Betagh, the chronicler of the voyage, fell into Spanish hands. According to Betagh this was a deliberate plot to get himself and Hatley captured, so reducing the numbers sharing in the loot; to Shelvocke, the loss of two troublemakers was certainly a good riddance.[30] There was no honour amongst these thieves.

On 21 March the *Speedwell* was at Paita; Clipperton had been there, but had not laid hands on the 400,000 dollars which the people had carried into the hills. Shelvocke gibes at this failure, but did no better himself, and after the standard demand for ransom and procrastinatory response, he burned the town. He had to decamp when an armed merchantman came into the port; his account of a desperate fight against heavy odds must be measured against his casualty list—nil. However, the coast was getting too hot, and he made for Juan Fernández to refit.

There, on 25 May, the *Speedwell* was wrecked; according to Betagh, deliberately so that the crew could cruise on their own account, the owners' rights lapsing with the loss of the ship.[31] As might be expected with such a captain and such a gang, there was another 'mutiny' leading to new and yet more rigged articles, and spasmodic work on a new craft, so leaky when launched that a dozen men thought themselves 'not sufficiently prepared for the other world' to risk sailing in her. They, and a dozen Indians and Blacks for whom there was no room, were never heard of again.

After a horrible voyage, with forty-odd men lying on bales of smoked conger, they found ample supplies of food and liquor at Iquique, and at Pisco took a good ship of 200 tons, renamed the *Happy Return*. With a Spanish ship and Spanish colours, they were able to surprise Paita so completely that the children were playing on the beach as they landed; but there was no treasure, and not much else except five hundredweight of dried dogfish, and more liquor. They were turned out of Paita by a stratagem before they could burn it again; sailing north they fell in at last, on 25 January 1721, with a Europe-built ship off Quibo. A boat came towards them—the pinnace of the *Success*. The reunion was not cordial.

Clipperton's cruise had been almost too successful, since his prize crews left him under-manned, and prisoners had to be released prematurely. After careening in the Galápagos he took a vessel sailing from Panama to Callao which, if we can believe Betagh (which would be pleasing in this instance, but takes some effort), was the same ship which had taken Clipperton on a previous South Sea voyage.[32] She was carrying the President of Panama, the Marqués de Villa Roche, with his family, who were released on promise of a ransom befitting his rank; but he was to prove a man of higher title than honour. Clipperton spent the rest of 1720 ranging from Amapalla to Concepción, taking many but not very valuable prizes. In

November he had a narrow escape from capture off Coquimbo, losing twelve men not easily spared. There were discontents among the crew, and Clipperton took to the bottle.[33] Towards the end of the year he sailed for New Spain and the meeting with Shelvocke.

Clipperton had no desire to join forces with a man who had lost his ship, and sheered off. The two met again a few days later, and he suggested that if the money of which the owners stood to be defrauded by the 'New Article' of Santa Catalina and Juan Fernández were put into a joint stock (the legal thing to do), they could cruise on a sound footing, himself of course in command. Shelvocke says nothing of this reasonable proposal, preferring scurrilous abuse of the proposer; when he wrote he knew that his old enemy was safely dead, leaving no journal, but he did not know of the account of Clipperton's voyage in Betagh's hands.[34] Co-operation was obviously impossible, and although the two ships fell in with each other four times, they spoke only twice.

Clipperton was short-handed, his crew was sickly, and it was the wrong time to intercept the Galleon either going or coming. In March 1721, therefore, he bore away for Guam, reached on 13 May. The Governor was friendly and agreed to underwrite the ransom for Villa Roche, who was still aboard as a hostage for its payment. That slippery nobleman was foolishly allowed ashore, with a five-gun salute as he went, and Clipperton found that he had been tricked: the Governor turned hostile. An attempt to use force miscarried, the *Success* grounding in the harbour under fire; Clipperton was helplessly drunk in his cabin, his lieutenant was killed, and the next officer, one Cook, fought the ship out.

They reached Amoy in July, and here Cook led a mutiny, demanding the condemnation of the ship as unseaworthy, and an immediate share-out. When Clipperton correctly refused, a Mandarin's guard was called in to force him to comply. He got the *Success* to Macao, where she was sold for much less than her value; Clipperton sent off the owners' share in a Portuguese Indiaman, lost by fire in Rio harbour. In a last burst of spirit, he took passage to Batavia in his own old ship to show that she was in fact seaworthy. He and his companions made their way to Europe in various Indiamen, Clipperton reaching his Irish home in June 1722—a week before his death, doubtless of weariness of spirit aided by drink.

Left to himself, Shelvocke proceeded to Sonsonate, where he took the 300-ton *Sacra Familia*, a better ship than the *Happy Return*. There was now peace between Britain and Spain, but Shelvocke refused to believe this, and was promptly and properly declared a pirate. After a summer of marauding, he left San Lucar on 18 August 1721, and three days later sighted an island which 'my people called after my name': a touching modesty on Shelvocke's part which one may believe or not, probably not. It was most likely Roca Partida, first seen by Villalobos in 1542.

On 11 November he reached Macao and went up to Whampoa; by collusion with the Chinese he seems to have done very well for himself, at the expense of both his owners and his remaining crew.[35] The EIC's servants were naturally very cool, and it was with some difficulty that he secured a passage for England. Once there, charges of piracy by both the Portuguese and the Spanish ambassadors failed for want of eye-witnesses, but the owners had him arrested and charged with fraud; he broke gaol and fled the country. Later he managed to return, and Captain Shelvocke, who in part inspired *The Ancient Mariner*, was buried at Deptford with an epitaph which, even for the eighteenth century, achieved a remarkably high level of obituary untruth.

Clipperton seems to have been an honest man, and much of his misfortune seems due to bad luck and the bottle. As for Shelvocke, he was at best an embezzler: one of his prizes was returned with the usual list of petty provisions '&c'—the '&c' being a trifle of 106,638 pieces of eight, £25,000, not accounted for to the owners. One may discount Betagh's more atrocious charges—sponsorship of fake mutinies, wrecking of the *Speedwell*, deliberate abandonment of fifty-nine men to captivity or death—but even so, Shelvocke's morals seem lower than those of the more responsible buccaneers.

There could hardly be a greater contrast to the honourable dealing and cool professionalism of Woodes Rogers. However, a significant feature of Clipperton's luckless and Shelvocke's shady voyage was that the Spaniards showed unexpected spirit, organisation, and readiness to fight. Both men had very narrow escapes from capture, and Shelvocke complains naïvely that even under a brisk and well-directed cannonade 'the *Spaniards* were far from being such cowards as they were represented.' John Campbell lamented that 'the Issue of [Shelvocke's] Voyage gave the Public a bad Idea of all Expeditions to the South Sea, and induced many to suppose, that . . . they were calculated purely for the private Advantage' of their projectors, and that by taking the tale of mutinies and miscarriages too seriously, 'it is such Notions as these that keep us asleep.'[36]

At all events, until the rise of legitimate Pacific trading, three-quarters of a century later, this was the end (and no wonder) of British private enterprise in the South Sea.

The Isthmus again: Puerto Bello and Cartagena

Alberoni's fall marked the end of the war, but not a real peace. The Asiento was renewed, but the main counter-concession, a pledge by George I to return Gibraltar, was conditional on the highly unlikely consent of Parliament: naturally George's 'favourable opportunity' for bringing it forward never turned up. Even had the result of the Clipperton-Shelvocke voyage been less dampening, the aftermath of the great South Sea Bubble, which burst disastrously in September 1720, was not a propitious time for projectors. But the usual bickerings over the Asiento continued, smuggling both under SSC cover and by freelances was rampant, and a surprising *rapprochement* between Spain and Austria carried with it, in breach of the Utrecht settlements, a promise of most favoured nation treatment for Austrian shipping—in effect, support for the Imperial Ostend Company.[37] Nothing could be better calculated to infuriate the East India interest in England. Meanwhile, although in disfavour for some time after the disastrous Sicilian venture (which he disapproved of), Alberoni's very able lieutenant José Patiño was carrying on with restoration of the Spanish navy, which again began to look formidable.

With war apparently imminent, Admiral Francis Hosier was sent in April 1726 to the Isthmus to cut off the silver flow to Spain. There was no declared war and he was forbidden to take offensive action; he told the Governor of Puerto Bello that he had come simply to convoy the SSC's *Royal George*, then in the harbour—with a force of sixteen ships! The Spaniards obligingly sent the *Royal George* out, but Hosier continued to hover off the coast, to his own destruction. The action was successful in so far as the silver was cut off, which may well have prevented full-scale war in Europe, since Austrian support for a Spanish attack on Gibraltar was conditional on subsidies from the anticipated Indies treasure. But in the two years of the Jamaica-based blockade the fleet lost some 4000 men by disease, including Hosier himself.[38] This miserable affair was notable mainly as rehearsal for the real war which broke out in 1739, and as raw material for the propaganda leading up to it.

Such as it was, however, it witnesses to a continuing British fixation on the Isthmus, and marks a stage on the road to the formal entry of the Royal Navy into the Pacific under Anson. The South Sea business would no longer be left to privateers, and would have larger aims than treasure-hunting and commerce destroying: Anson's instructions envisaged the possibility of action in concert with Vernon's assault on the Isthmus, still regarded as the essential node linking the Spanish Mar del Sur with the Mar del Norte, and of subversion in Peru. In truth, this thin fillet of land was indivisible, the convergence of Atlantic and Pacific spheres of trade and war.

The events leading to the war of 1739 form a tedious catalogue of official but often half-hearted attempts by the authorities in Europe to attain a general settlement of Anglo-Spanish trade disputes, and their constant thwarting by whole-hearted bad faith and violence on the part of Caribbean local authorities condoning or backing the contrabandistas and their enemies the guardacostas. The SSC played its part: the reasonable convention between Britain and Spain reached at El Pardo in January 1739 was in effect wrecked by the Company's intransigence over its dubious and swollen financial claims against the Spanish Crown, and counter-claims whose prosecution it sabotaged.[39] But the root cause lay deeper.

So long as the Spaniards continued to claim that, notwithstanding all the inroads since the 1670 Treaty of Madrid, their system still stood and that basically they alone had the rights to the Indies trade (barring the SSC's limited access) there was bound to be friction: 'the pushing and expansive genius of English trade' and 'a colonial system like that of Spain could hardly coexist without conflict.'[40] With the new self-confidence of Bourbon Spain, there was a trend to toughening the defences of the system; *per contra*, the British addiction to smuggling was ineradicable and of course directly bound up with the rigidity of the closed system itself. To Spanish eyes an English trading captain and a contrabandista were one and the same thing, and the remedy was an increased use of guardacostas. Often enough the Spanish equation was correct; but there were very many exceptions, and the remedy was very rough and indiscriminate.

It is needless to try to straighten out the wearisome tangle of charges and counter-charges—'one's understanding ought to suffer as well as one's eyesight in reading such stuff... the sweepings of old escritoires and counting houses... never was there such a heap of tangled confusion'.[41] The Spanish government had not the resources to keep a regular patrol force except off Tierra Firme; elsewhere the task of surveillance was left to corrupt officials and their agents, the hard-bitten and usually completely unscrupulous guardacostas. There were sometimes retaliations in kind, with or without letters of reprisal, but the net result was a mounting list of depredations on honest as well as illicit British (and other) traders. In England the opposition to Robert Walpole assiduously orchestrated a campaign against his conciliatory stance, demanding redress for Spanish outrages. The celebrated case of Captain Jenkins's ear was only the most picturesque item in the catalogue, but it assumed a mythic symbolism, and indeed gave the ensuing war its popular name.

Robert Jenkins was engaged on his entirely lawful occasions when a guardacosta searched his ship for contraband, and finding none tried to extract information by violence. The captain cut off one of Jenkins's ears, or part thereof, and said that he would serve King George himself in like manner, were he available. This was in 1731; when the story surfaced in 1738, Jenkins told Parliament, apparently in response to a leading question, that in his dire position 'I commended my soul to God and my cause to my country.' There were of course other ways of losing one's ears—a tavern brawl, the pillory—and in seven years Jenkins had had ample time to evolve that rather too pat and dignified invocation; one suspects that his actual words were more earthy. But Jenkins was not, as is sometimes said, an unknown or disreputable person, but 'a capable and conscientious seaman' who had a meritorious career in EIC service, and the main thrust of his story need not be doubted. There were other outrages to choose from; as McLachlan remarks, it might easily (but less euphoniously) have been the War of Story King's Thumbs.[42]

Be that as it may, the ear, bottled in spirits, became a prime exhibit in the propaganda war which broke out in England. This was merely a continuation of the general anti-Walpole campaign, but such visible evidence of Spanish cruelty was a gift to the Opposition, whether 'Patriot' Whig or Tory. The Whig Richard Glover called for the chastisement of Spain in blank verse; the Tory Samuel Johnson denounced those who

> Explain their Country's dear-bought Rights away,
> And plead for Pirates in the Face of Day.[43]

They were backed by a horde of journalists and pamphleteers. Walpole was less supine than he was painted; in May 1738 a squadron was sent out to Minorca, a demonstration which only stiffened the Spaniards. He continued to struggle against what can only be described as a national hysteria—the first epigraph to this chapter is typical—but the final blow was the report of a projected Franco-Spanish royal marriage: a twist in European dynastic politics was to be a factor in sending Anson to the one splendour and many miseries of his trans-Pacific voyage. The war which officially began in October 1739 was to merge into the War of the Austrian Succession, a development which does not concern us; but in its beginnings a thoroughly navalist policy was pursued.

For all Walpole's desire for peace and seeming nonchalance, and the real (though perhaps somewhat exaggerated) incompetence of the Duke of Newcastle as the responsible Minister, the administration had decided on official reprisals and again ordered various preventive moves in June 1739, but for one reason or another these had been ineffective. The initial plans followed classic lines: a descent on Darien, to seize the gold mines; an attack from India on Manila, which when taken might become an EIC base for the China trade; an expedition to Chile—the last two might link up, or Panama might be attacked from both north and south. The seizure of Habana was considered, but would need too many troops; it was thought that Cartagena, although more unhealthy and with more difficult approaches than Habana, might be taken by 3000 men and some privateers, a proposal directly influenced by the success of Pointis in 1697 and disregarding the known fact that its fortifications were now much stronger. But to term such shifting notions 'plans' is perhaps an excess of courtesy; there were simply too many objectives, none of them clearly thought out.[44] There was in fact a conflict of interests between 'those who wanted to conquer new colonies for plantations and those who wanted only outposts for trade' with the Spanish Indies; North American colonists favoured conquest, the West Indian sugar interests wanted nothing less than for more sugar colonies to be included within 'the [fiscally] enclosed but expanding market of Great Britain'.... The actual conduct of the war was in keeping with the wishes of the West India interest.[45]

In the event, Admiral Edward Vernon was despatched for Jamaica in July 1739, with instructions to do as much damage as possible to Spanish shipping, royal and merchant, and to report on the best place and mode for an attack on Spanish holdings; very much the approach favoured by the Tories and navalists in the War of the Spanish Succession. A realist, Vernon gave short shrift to such way-out schemes as a descent on Darien, and if a territorial lodgement was to be made—on which he was wary—Habana would be the most useful, and the most damaging to Spain. But in any such operation, 'I should limit all expeditions to this country ... to be executed within six weeks, before their men would begin to fall sick.' Admiral Hosier's ghost must have been looking over Vernon's shoulder as he wrote: ironically, he was unable to act upon his own good advice.

He began well with the capture of Puerto Bello in November 1739, and even considered a dash across the Isthmus for Panama, where the arrival of the Peruvian silver was reported; but judged correctly that as there was no possibility of surprise, it was not likely to have been kept there. There was little loot at Puerto Bello, only 10,000 dollars, but the systematic destruction of the fortifications was a severe blow to Spain, morally and materially; indeed, it meant the end of the great fair and gave an impetus to the use of register ships as a replacement for the galeones, which as we have seen had for long been much less than annual; they now ceased entirely.[46] The total disruption of the Puerto Bello trade also gave even more openings for contraband. So striking a success so early in the war was greeted in England with altogether excessive rapture; although Vernon followed it up next year by taking Chagres, his laurels were to be sadly tarnished by the failure of the greater venture at Cartagena.

Little need be said about this unhappy affair. Vernon's advice against large-scale land operations was unheeded; it may not have got beyond that notorious ditherer the Duke of Newcastle.[47] Puerto Bello may have gone to his head; in any case the Duke had resolved, so far as he could ever resolve, on a great stroke, and as Habana seemed too strong and the last outward galeones were still at Cartagena, the latter was decided upon. Despite some incredible mismanagement, a force of some 12-15,000 men was collected, a third of them North Americans or Jamaica Blacks; most were either raw or undisciplined or both, poorly officered, and with inefficient ordnance services. The defence had only 1100 regulars, supplemented by militia, free Blacks, and 300 Indian archers; but it was stoutly commanded. The British attack was delayed owing to the necessity of ascertaining whether there were potentially hostile French ships to windward, but the armament which anchored off Cartagena on 4 March 1741 (OS) was imposing: twenty-nine ships of the line, a score of smaller naval units, eighty-five transports. Within a week the troops were ashore; and then the whole enterprise began to fall to pieces.

The original and competent military commander had died and was replaced by Brigadier-General Thomas Wentworth, 'a very sensible man' but with no experience of active service and no powers of leadership: everything had to be done by book. Vernon's advice was aggressive and generally sound, but he was not a man to advise tactfully, and his rough sarcasm seems to have broken down what little nerve Wentworth possessed. The forts around Boca Chica, the entrance to the outer harbour, were easily taken, and over-enthusiastic despatches were sent home; but the assault on Fort San Lazar, at the entrance to the town, was conducted with equal gallantry and muddle, and repulsed with heavy cost. Between battle casualties and disease, the effective force was now well under 4000 men, and the attempt was given over. The Boca Chica forts might have been held, to the practical paralysis of Tierra Firme and Isthmian trade, but the rains were at hand and the remaining troops were utterly demoralised; at the end of April they re-embarked. They did not sail until the captured forts had been thoroughly demolished, and by now yellow fever was rampant. In those few days of waiting to sail, scores of bodies were thrown overboard, 'many without ballast or winding-sheet; so that numbers of human carcasses floated in the water, until they were devoured by sharks or carrion crows …'.[48] A futile attempt on Santiago de Cuba merely repeated

Cartagena on a smaller scale. By late 1742 perhaps only a tenth of the original force was left.

Vernon was not prepared to give up the game; incredibly, the home government still allowed him and Wentworth, clearly two incompatibles, to run in harness. The fleet had suffered less than the army, and an assault on the Isthmus was always popular, especially in Jamaica. An old piratical hand, now a Lieutenant RN, advised that artillery could be taken up the Río Chagres to Cruces whence, he alleged, there was a good road through open country to Panama City itself.[49] There was even the possibility of co-operation with Anson's squadron on the Pacific side. The old dream of alliance with the Darien Indians was revived, although it was known that English slaving and Spanish conciliation had ensured that they would be at best neutral. But the enthusiasm of the Jamaicans did not run to making slaves available for transport, and there were the usual delays—and delays meant sickness. Vernon himself seems to have wasted time, and as soon as they arrived at Puerto Bello (28 March 1742), Wentworth and Governor Trelawny of Jamaica, hitherto a strong supporter of the scheme, called it off before any landing had been made. It was learned from captured letters that Anson had taken Paita and so might now be near the Gulf of Panama; Vernon consoled himself with the thought that his threat had provided a useful diversion by enforcing the recall to Panama of ships sent to cruise after Anson.[50]

With the recall of Vernon and Wentworth at the end of 1742, the formal war in the West Indies virtually lapsed. There were minor operations, but to no effect; indeed, in 1744 Admiral Rodrigo Torres was able to collect the treasure fleet at Habana and convoy it to Spain.

The successful defence of Cartagena owed a great deal to the gross ineptitude of the British military establishment, to the fierce dissensions between Army and Navy, and most of all perhaps to *Aedes aegypti*, the yellow fever mosquito. The British effort was a major one, and the failure of so great an armament more than offset the easy triumph of Puerto Bello. There can be little doubt that the town would have fallen to a more speedy and efficient attack; although in that case 'the soldiers would have had the satisfaction of dying of fever after victory, as they did at Havana in 1762, instead of dying frustrated outside the walls.'[51] But later West Indian wars showed that a determined leadership, at home and in the field, could take fearful losses from disease and yet maintain and secure its gains. Had the British secured Cartagena, the Isthmus would have been practically indefensible, and the great Empire of the Indies irreparably split. By this time the trans-Pacific sailing routes were well enough known for Panama in British hands to have given the Ocean a totally new orientation.

So high were the stakes; that even Newcastle, prodded by the Admiralty, had a glimmering of them is shown by the suggestions, vague as they were, for concert between Vernon and Anson. As it was, the failure meant that in British fantasy Panama remained what it had ever been, a golden dream—its seizure was projected over and over again in the rest of the century, and as late as 1804.[52] In Spanish reality, as the currents of trade into the South Sea increasingly followed new channels, by La Plata or the Horn, Panama became almost a ghost town, until in 1849 a new treasure, the gold of California, brought it new life.[53]

Anson failed to make the hoped-for connection with Vernon on the Isthmus, but his voyage was perhaps the most notable British naval exploit of the war, certainly the first by the Royal Navy in the Pacific. Before discussing it, however, it is convenient to deal with other developments during this rather confused period between Utrecht and 1739: Roggeveen in the South Pacific, the Russians in the North.

Chapter 10

ROGGEVEEN AND BERING

> ...nothing is to be found in our ships which in
> these lands can be charged for ... trifles which are
> not sought after by any peoples except the worst sort
> of blacks in Africa, whom we put equal with those
> whom we might have found in the South Sea if we had
> discovered any considerable land ...

> I could not help saying that we had come only for
> the purpose of bringing American water to Asia ...
> ten years the preparations for this great enterprise
> lasted, and ten hours were devoted to the work itself.

A lawyer at sea: Jacob Roggeveen

'Trade, which in the sixteenth century had been a prime stimulus to exploration, became its enemy in the seventeenth', since the great Companies which dominated the long-distance trades 'would not, as a rule, risk men, money, and ships in a profitless pursuit of knowledge.'[1] As we have seen, after Tasman exploration in the Pacific was literally marginal—in the Marianas, New Britain, California, and on the Russian coasts. Buccaneers and Malouins crossed the Ocean often enough, but on well-worn tracks. Between 1700 and Byron in 1764–5 there was only one voyage of Oceanic discovery, Jacob Roggeveen's; and it is significant that although he had spent nine years as a VOC judge in Batavia, his sponsor was the struggling West India Company, which was in recession and badly needed new openings.[2]

In 1673–5 Roggeveen's father Arend, inspired by Schouten's account, had put forward a proposal for trade in the South Sea; the States-General decided to grant him a charter, with provisions to protect WIC interests. These were years of war with France, and the scheme lapsed for lack of financial support. Arend died in 1679, by tradition adjuring his son to fulfil the grand design. Jacob waited forty years until, at the age of sixty-two, he acted upon the paternal request.[3] The objective of the voyage was the discovery and exploitation of the hypothetical Great Southland, following the leads given by the buccaneer Edward Davis and by

Figure 18. NORTHERN TUAMOTUS: SCHOUTEN AND ROGGEVEEN. Schouten/Le Maire's names above islands, Roggeveen's below, modern names in capitals. All islands are atolls or low coral reefs, except Makatea, which reaches 113 metres. Compiled from information in A. Sharp, *The Journal of Jacob Roggeveen* (Oxford 1970), 120–38.

Jacob Roggeveen, *Journal* (Oxford 1970), 143–4; Georg Steller on Kayak Island, Alaska, 20 July 1741 (OS), in F. A. Golder (ed.), *Bering's Voyages* (New York 1922–5), II.37, 54.

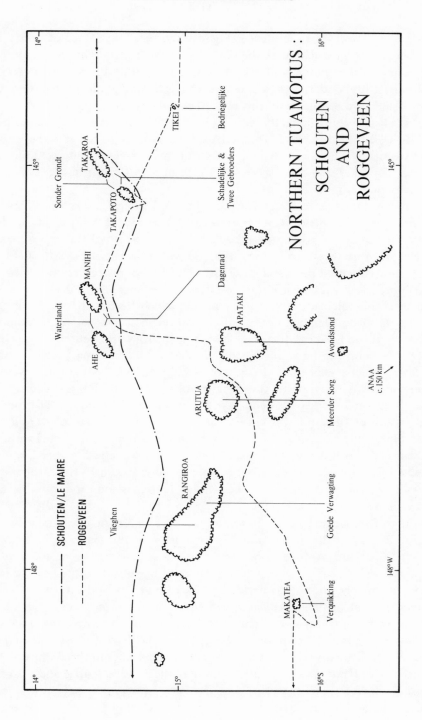

NORTHERN TUAMOTUS :
SCHOUTEN
AND
ROGGEVEEN

SCHOUTEN/LE MAIRE

ROGGEVEEN

Roggeveen's countryman Schouten. These were the 'long Tract of pretty high Land [which] might probably be the Coast of *Terra Australis Incognita*' reported by Dampier and Wafer, and Schouten's presumption that the absence of a swell from the south near his Sonder Grondt and Waterlandt Eylanden meant that there must be more land in that direction; this also Arend Roggeveen equated with Terra Australis.[4] His son approached the WIC, which backed the project (on rather better terms for itself than those of 1675), perhaps from a desire to forestall the Imperial Ostend Company.[5] Be that as it may, the Company provided and fitted out three ships, the 32-gun *Arend*, *Thienhoven* (24 guns), and *Afrikaansche Galei*. They sailed from Texel on 1 August 1721.

The plan had included a search for the 'Land of Auking' (i.e. Hawkins), but after victualling at São Sebastião in Brazil, Roggeveen decided it was too late to do so; however he did in fact come upon the Falklands at the end of the year, renaming them Belgia Australis. By 15 January 1722 he was at his farthest south, 60°44', and sensibly enough settled the disputed question of the boundary between the South and the North Sea by taking it as the meridian of Cape Horn; his legal habit of mind is seen in all his calculations and the councils which he called for all important decisions. He made a landfall near Valdivia and called at Mocha for provisions, to find that the island had been laid waste by the Spaniards to prevent its use as a pirate base. On 24 February he sighted Juan Fernández, and next day found that the *Thienhoven*, which had been lost to sight off Patagonia, had kept her rendezvous.

After three weeks refreshing the crews at Juan Fernández, Roggeveen sailed on 17 March in search of Davis's Land. By the 26th he was in the right latitude and turned west, but the land was elusive: perhaps Davis's estimate of distance was wrong? He decided to push on westwards for 100 German miles.[6] Late in the afternoon of 5 April, Easter Day, the *Afrikaansche Galei*, scouting ahead, signalled land; when the *Arend* came up Roggeveen named it Paasch Eylandt, for the day. Rapa Nui is still most generally known as Easter Island, and by this alone Roggeveen is generally remembered.

Although Easter rises to 600 metres, it has a low rolling profile, and at first was taken for Davis's small sandy island, 'the precursor of the extended coast of the unknown Southland.' As they closed with it, it was seen to be too big and hilly, and the sand was dried grassland, nor was any range of high land visible beyond it; but there were smokes, and it was decided to examine the island carefully. Cornelis Boumans, captain of the *Thienhoven*, had entertained and been entertained by a naked man who came out alone in his canoe; later, canoes crowded round the ships, and there was a good deal of pilfering. Roggeveen decided on a formal expedition, and on the 9th landed with a 'corps de bataille' of 134 men in three units of three ranks each with flankguards. Naturally enough, there was a scuffle and unauthorised firing, which left ten or twelve dead; Roggeveen seems to have restrained his nervous men, a chief initiated an exchange of fowls and bananas for linen, and amity was restored. Closer acquaintance with the Islanders was disappointing; what had been taken, from a distance, as rich cloths and silver ornaments turned out to be tapa and shell. They had religion, worshipping idols nine or ten metres high; Roggeveen wondered how people without heavy timber or ropes could erect such great images, but convinced himself that these were only clay or greasy earth stuck about with small smooth stones.[7] With legalistic objectivity he wrote that although it was clear that many people slept in a single hut, to conclude from this that the women were shared 'would, not being an inevitable deduction, be to make accusations too lightly and slanderously.'[8]

Plate XIV. EASTER ISLAND. Some of the famous statues were still standing, with their 'top-knots', sixty-four years after Roggeveen's discovery. From *The Voyage of La Pérouse round the World.* Photo ANU.

After a day of such observations, and the more practical deduction that 'fine metals could not possibly exist', Roggeveen summoned his council and decided to sail for a further 100 miles due west; Jan Koster, captain of the *Arend*, then suggested a short run eastwards to see if they could find the low sandy island: if they did so, Paasch Eylandt was after all Davis's Land, however disappointing in itself, and they could then sail northwest into Schouten's track, since the first part of the undertaking 'would come to a finish and stop.' This was agreed upon, but of course no island was found. After a week on an eastwards course from Paasch Eylandt, with still no sign of Terra Australis, they decided (21 April) to go up to 15°S and seek Schouten's Honden Eylandt by latitude sailing. Roggeveen relieved his feelings by an attack on Davis, Dampier, and Wafer for misleading him: 'these three (for they were English) were as much robbers of the truth as of the goods of the Spaniards.'[9]

By 2 May they were in the right latitude and turned westwards. On the 12th they saw a multitude of birds, but since there was a swell from the south Roggeveen deduced land to the north; a couple of days later he was in fact passing about 20 minutes (say 35 km) south of the little atoll of Pukapuka, Schouten's Honden Eylandt (and perhaps Magellan's first landfall), but did not sight it; and so naturally 'our thoughts [were] somewhat confused'.[10] But on the 18th they saw an island, which they thought must of course be Honden; but the confusion was enhanced when only thirteen hours later another island was seen—yet according to Schouten there were over 100 German miles between Honden and his next land-fall, Sonder Grondt.

In fact, they were in the northern Tuamotus and Roggeveen's first island was Tikei, not seen by Schouten; his second, the large atolls of Takaroa and Takapoto, was Sonder Grondt (Fig. 18). A few days later he came to the definite conclusion that his first was not Honden, and accordingly named it Bedriegelijke, 'Deceptive', because 'it deceived us and made us believe that we were sailing on the true route of Captain Schouten (which he never sailed).' The deception was of course put to the account of Schouten's journal-keeper, but at Takapoto his 'true route' and Roggeveen's came together.[11]

Here the expedition met trouble, the *Afrikaansche Galei* running aground on Takapoto; she had on board the bulk of such provisions as were still in good condition, and these were not saved. Only one life was lost, and the rest of her company hauled boats from the other ships over the reef and crossed the lagoon to the lee (western) side of the atoll, where they were picked up; on the lagoon they found an empty village whose people had probably fled on 'hearing something unheard-of', the *Galei*'s distress-guns.[12] Appropriately, Roggeveen gave Takapoto the name Schadelijke, 'Disastrous', and the two islets on Takaroa that of Twee Gebroeders, 'Two Brothers'. Before he left five 'brainless fellows' deserted, shouting an ironical *bon voyage* and greetings for their friends in Amsterdam; Roggeveen suspected that the spirit-casks of the *Afrikaansche Galei* kept them there, and that when drunkenness or lust drove them to intercourse with the island women they would all be killed. It seems likely, however, that they survived long enough to reach Anaa, and are perhaps responsible for the wooden cross seen on that island by Tomás Gayangos in 1744.[13]

Roggeveen left Schadelijke on the 24th, but his troubles were not yet over; at daybreak on the 25th another atoll was seen and named Dagenrad, 'Dawn'; this was Manihi or Ahe, Schouten's Waterlandt. Next day Roggeveen had difficulty with his crews: they had taken the cut in rations necessitated by the loss of the *Afrikaansche Galei* with good grace, but now the petty officers, speaking for all, politely requested that pay should be continued for the survivors from this or any future wrecks; contemporary practice was that the owners' liability for wages ceased with the loss of a ship.[14] Roggeveen replied that such losses were 'indeed a reason for lamentation, but not for the payment of wages'; one must submit patiently to the decree of Heaven. Act of God was not a good enough argument for the men, the polite request became a strike: 'we must have an assurance of our pay, or else homeward.' Roggeveen, after laying down the law on mutiny, had to submit.[15]

Matters thus settled, Roggeveen turned south, leaving Schouten's track, and on the 27th and 28th passed between two more atolls; Avondstond, 'Evening', and Meerder Sorg, 'More Trouble', so called because he feared that they might join together and he would be embayed; these were Apataki and Arutua. On the 30th he saw a large atoll to the northwest—Rangiroa, which Schouten had passed to the north. Here they hoped to obtain greens for the thirty-odd who were down with scurvy, and the island was accordingly called Goede Verwagting, 'Good Expectation'. In the event it was decided not to risk closing with a lee shore where, as they knew from other atolls, an anchorage was unlikely. On 2 June, however, a fairly high island was sighted, the uplifted atoll Makatea. Here an abundance of green stuffs was collected, but an attempt to reach the higher ground in search of coconuts and bananas ran into an ambush, although at the first landing some deliberately ill-aimed musketry had frightened the Islanders away. Several of them were killed, but Roggeveen called off the advance. Satisfied with what he had, he gave the island the name Verquikking, 'Refreshment'.

In a painstaking analysis of his track compared with Schouten's, Roggeveen concluded that Schouten's 'smooth water', on which so much stress had been laid as indicating a near-by landmass, was due simply to the reefs impeding the swell to the south. With this negative conclusion to his search, it was time to think of the return. Simply to turn in their tracks would be to attempt a course straight against the Trades; the alternatives were to sail southwards into the 'changeable winds'—the Westerlies—and so round the Horn, or to continue westwards, north of New Guinea to the East Indies. On the first of these, refreshment would be necessary, and the only known place was New Zealand. Its finding would be most uncertain, and even if it were found, there was no certainty of a safe anchorage; the impression of the steep-to reefs was strong. Then the sick would need fourteen days ashore, and Tasman's reports of the 'Indians' of Murderers' Bay were not encouraging. There remained the route by the East Indies. The WIC's instructions, made on the assumption that a fertile Terra Australis would be found considerably further east (near Davis's Land), implied a return by the Horn. To go west meant deliberate trespass into VOC preserves; but here the lawyer in Roggeveen came to the rescue, enabling him to rationalise a decision against his own strong doubts as to the wisdom of 'sin against the bidding of said their Most Mighty [the States-General]' in favour of the VOC. Finding that he could not carry the meeting with him, he turned to argue against himself that they could not be accused of undermining the

VOC's trade, since they carried only trivial items suitable for 'the worst sort of blacks in Africa', and moreover that by no law, short of tyranny, could anybody 'be committed to the impossible (so as to destroy himself).'[16]

On 4 June, therefore, they sailed westwards again, and on the 6th saw to the south two high islands, which Roggeveen took to be Schouten's Cocos and Verraders Eylandten—actually some 20° to the west of him. These were really Borabora and Maupiti, and this was the first European sighting of any of the Society Islands. For the next few days strong swells pushed them northwards, and when these ceased the course was altered to WNW. The next landfall, on the 13th, was a small reef, named for its foul ground Vuyle Eylandt. In the evening the *Thienhoven*, which was ahead, reported very high land to the west, which next day turned out to be three islands and an islet. That first seen on the 13th was Rose Atoll, easternmost outlier of Samoa, and the rest, collectively named Boumans Eylandten, were the Manua Group.[17] No anchorage was found and no landing made, but the people came out in canoes and were friendly, being anxious to obtain blue beads in exchange for coconuts. Roggeveen speculated on their origins: it was 'mockery rather than serious thought' to think that they arrived in ancient times when navigation was so primitive, and they could hardly be Chilean or Peruvian colonists; but still they were children of Adam, though human understanding could not comprehend how they reached these remote islands. There were more of these: on the 15th there was again very high land to the south and west, actually Tutuila and Upolo, which Roggeveen named Thienhoven and Groeningen.[18]

This again was a first European discovery, that of Samoa. They wished to visit such large and promising islands, which some officers thought must be close to Terra Australis, perhaps even part of that continent; but Roggeveen did not choose to lose time searching for an anchorage, since it was essential to get west of New Guinea before the onset of the westerly monsoon in a couple of months' time. The course was now northwest, presumably to avoid the risk of a New Guinea embayment, and then, when they were up to 4°S, west again. This took them between Kiribati and Tuvalu (the Gilberts and Ellices), but no more islands were seen until they came to what they thought was the north coast of New Guinea (and so within the VOC's claims) but was in fact New Ireland. A landing was made, probably on New Hanover, and at this point Roggeveen's *Journal* stops; he may well have thought it unwise to keep a record of his progress in VOC waters.[19] He was now back on Schouten's track to Batavia.

On 10 September the ships arrived at Japara, with only a handful of men not disabled by scurvy, and Roggeveen and his captains wrote to the Governor-General at Batavia, explaining their situation. The sequel was a replay of the Le Maire/Schouten affair; indeed, the Batavia Council took this as its precedent for seizing the ships and officers when they arrived, which they did on 4 October. Roggeveen protested against the seizure, after he had been allowed to come on from Japara, and refused to surrender his original papers; later, after the formal arrest of the ships, he handed over copies of some of them. He knew his law and he was not unknown in Batavia; although the ships were put into Company service, he continued his legal protests, and eventually the Council decided that a final judgement must be made in the Netherlands; Roggeveen and his men went home in East Indiamen.[20]

The Batavia Council had not looked up its precedent very carefully; indeed, while Roggeveen pointed out that Jan Pieterszoon Coen had acted in 1616 under orders from the Heeren XVII and had recognised that there might be a recon- sideration in the Netherlands, in his protest (basing himself solely on Schouten) he also seems to have been unaware of Isaac Le Maire's successful suit against the Company. In the Netherlands the WIC took over the case and did not neglect this useful precedent. The matter was settled by negotiation between the Companies; the VOC eventually paid up, including, one is glad to say, the full wages of the crews.

Apart from the discovery of Easter Island, Roggeveen's voyage has been neglected; in part this is due to the obviously poor quality of the accounts available to the earlier commentators. It was hastily planned and ill-provisioned, and was dogged by scurvy even before it reached Brazil. On the other hand, the conduct of the voyage in itself seems to have been judicious, and the decision to keep on west- wards from Makatea gave Europe at least the knowledge of the existence, and approximate location, of two substantial new island groups, the Societies and Samoa, as well as Easter Island. It is not just to say that Roggeveen followed the same track as many others and might almost be said to have 'joined the procession.' Of recorded voyages, only Magellan's and Le Maire's had come into the South Sea and struck across with the Trades, and it would be better to say that the mid- century voyages before Cook followed in Roggeveen's tracks.[21] Alexander Dalrymple called his voyage 'wonderfully ill conducted' because, being swayed by commercial views, he did not follow up 'seeing teal, &c, for 12° to the eastward of Easter Island', these being obviously signs of a continent; Roggeveen specifically comments on the *absence* of birds, apart from two pintails and a gull, for twenty degrees after leaving the island.[22]

Although what Roggeveen had really done was to establish a northern limit to the extension of any Terra Australis, the net result of his voyage was to confirm a belief in its existence; there were also optimistic readings of Behrens's inflated views on the potential of Juan Fernández as a seat of colonisation. More soberly, there were the glimpses of Borabora and Samoa, especially the latter:

>many of their officers were clearly of the opinion, that [Groeningen], was no island, but the great south continent they were sent to discover . . . As for the island of *Tienhoven*, it appeared to be a rich and beautiful country . . . They coasted along the shore for a whole day, without coming to an end of it. They observed, however, that it extended in the form of a semicircle towards the island of *Groninguen*; so that after all, it is very probable, that these two

countries, which were at first taken for islands, may, in reality, be
lands contiguous to each other, and both of them part of the *Terra
Australis incognita.*[23]

This is Behrens, not Roggeveen; but he was all the century had to build upon. This
became the tradition handed down by Campbell, Callander, Dalrymple: northern
offliers or promontories of the Great Southland, the spiritual dream of Quiros
reborn in a calculating age, with a Dutch lawyer for midwife.

The first voyage of Vitus Bering

If Terra Australis still beckoned illusively over tropic horizons, Terra Borealis was
still shrouded in fogs mental as well as physical. Behind them there loomed vague
landmasses, not only Swift's Brobdingnag but the more plausible Esso (Jesso, Yezo),
Compagnie Landt, Gamaland. At the hands of speculative geographers, the coasts
glimpsed by Russian explorers or ravaged by Siberian hunters twisted kaleido-
scopically over the maps. Old fantasies, Anian, Juan de Fuca's passage, were revived,
and a new one born—the voyage from the South Sea across North America of
Bartholomew de Fonte, Admiral of New Spain and Peru, 'Prince of Chili', and
totally fictitious. Their ghosts were finally exorcised not only by James Cook and
George Vancouver but also by the continental journeys westwards to the Pacific of
Alexander Mackenzie (1793) and of Thomas Jefferson's men Meriwether Lewis
and George Clark (1804–6), and by Spanish voyages north from New Spain; but
well before that the Russians had acquired much knowledge of the lands around
Bering Sea and the Gulf of Alaska; discrete data, very imperfectly reported, apart
from Bering's own voyages, and—not excepting these—often still more imperfectly interpreted in Europe.

We have seen that by 1713 the Russians knew that the Kurils led on to Japan,
and by 1720 the sea route from Okhotsk to Kamchatka was in use. After the Treaty
of Nystad (1721), which confirmed his grasp on the Baltic provinces wrenched
from Sweden, Peter the Great was free to turn to the remoter frontiers of his
realms. Maritime Europe still hankered after a Northwest or a Northeast Passage to
China and the eastern Indies; but although hints and even proposals for a Pacific
approach to a passage went back as far as the sixteenth century, to Gilbert and
Drake, and Dampier had argued cogently for it, in practice all attempts had been
made directly from the Atlantic. But clearly it would be futile to battle through the
ice-ridden Arctic Seas to find that there was no Anian, no way through. Asia and
America obviously approached each other in northern latitudes; their juncture or
their fissure must presumably lie within range of the recent Russian penetrations
into the farthest east of Siberia. Between 1697 and his death in 1719 Leibnitz wrote
at least five times to Tzar Peter urging him to settle the question. But proposals
came also from within Russia, and it is unlikely that outside hints were needed.[24]

The first serious step was taken in 1719–21, when Peter sent two trained
geodesists, Ivan Evreinov and Fedor Luzhin, to find whether Asia and America met
near Kamchatka. This instruction has been held to camouflage the real aims of

finding gold and silver in the Kurils (which they did visit) and a route to Japan, following up Ivan Kosyrevskii's report of 1713. If these were the true objectives, it is difficult to see why Evreinov and Luzhin began by journeying across the penin-sula, 600 km or more of wild and dangerous terrain from Bol'sheretsk to Nizhne-Kamchatsk, where they apparently found no information to suggest any near land to the east.[25] This may well have a bearing, in turn, on the problem of the objectives of Vitus Bering's first expedition, which Peter initiated in 1724.

The traditional view of this is straightforward: Bering's task was simply to find whether Asia and America joined.[26] This is not what Peter's orders, written about a month before his death, actually say. Golder, who finds them a model of brevity (true enough) and comprehensiveness (highly doubtful), translates that Bering is (I) to build boats in Kamchatka or elsewhere and (II) 'sail along the shore which runs to the north and seems to be a part of the American coast; (III) to determine where it joins with America. To sail to some settlements under European jurisdiction....'[27]

Where, not *whether*: a marked difference from the orders to Evreinov and Luzhin. It almost passes belief that Peter, who had mixed with mariners and maritime experts in England and Holland, should have believed that any European settle-ments lay on these Arctic or sub-Arctic shores, hard by a putative strait ('Anian') from the Pacific; but even without this, the wording, in Golder's own version, is almost meaningless unless the Tzar now believed that the continents did meet. Starting from this premiss, and with Russian precedents, Raymond Fisher develops elaborate arguments to show that the coast or land which Peter had in mind was 'Essonis' (Yezo), Gamaland, or some other of the old landmasses shown on the maps near Kamchatka; and that the real objective of the first voyage was to secure first-hand information about America.[28]

Vitus Bering, the Danish commander of the expedition, had as lieutenants another Dane, Martin Spanberg, and the Russian Alexei Chirikov, born in the year that Bering entered Russian naval service, 1703, and a man of keener mind than either of his superiors. The logistics of mounting even a modest expedition from eastern Siberia were daunting; Bering himself left St Petersburg in February 1725, and his whole party was not re-united at Okhotsk until January 1727. That summer Bering crossed to Bol'sheretsk and thence went overland to Nizhne-Kamchatsk, the passage round the tip of Kamchatka being thought too risky for the local craft.[29] By spring 1728 the whole expedition was concentrated at Nizhne-Kamchatsk (Lower Kamchatka or Kamchatka Post), and here the *Sviatoi Gavriil* (*St Gabriel*), under twenty metres long and with a complement of forty-four, was built and fitted out in three months. On 14 July 1728 he sailed north and northeast.

The voyage itself was not notable for incident (Fig. 20). Bering mapped the coast as far as the Chukotsk Peninsula, and from some Chukchi people he met on 8 August he learnt that farther on the Siberian coast turned west; there was sea, but with ice, to the Kolyma. He pushed on, discovering St Lawrence Island, until on 13 August he was out of sight of land, in about 65°30′N. Bering now asked his lieutenants for written opinions. According to the Chukchis they had passed the extreme east of the land: should they continue north, and if so how far, and where ought they to winter? (They had provisions for a year, but the Chukotsk coast seemed to offer no harbours or wood, and its people might be hostile.) Spanberg was for going on till 16 August, and if they had by then reached 66°, 'in God's name turn about and betimes seek shelter and harbor on the Kamchatka River'. Chirikov was for sailing to the Kolyma or as far towards it as the ice would permit; but if the land turned to the north again, by 25 August they must look for a wintering place—forests were reported from this region.

Spanberg's less resolute view prevailed. By 16 August they were in 67°18'; next day they found Great Diomede Island, but the fog was too thick for the American coast to be seen. By 2 September they were back at Nizhne-Kamchatsk. During the winter Bering picked up some reports suggesting that there was land nearby, to the east, and on his return journey to Okhotsk (June-July 1729) he sailed to the south and southeast of Nizhne-Kamchatsk in search of it; he must have narrowly missed seeing the island on which, twelve years later, he was to die.

Bering brought back a good map, but little else, although as a by-product of the overland journeys the positions of many places in Siberia had been accurately fixed. On the traditional view there is of course no problem about the voyage—this was the straightforward way to determine the Asia-America relation, and Chirikov's opinion would seem to support this: 'Obviously it was Chirikov, not Bering, who understood the nature of proof.'[30] It may not, however, be quite so simple as that. Fisher, following the lead of the Soviet scholar Boris Polevoi, thinks that the idea that the voyage was for the Asia-America determination was a politically-motivated blind to cover the American objectives. He goes further than Polevoi in maintaining that the search was really not for a strait but for an over-arching isthmus connecting the continents, and on a minute analysis there seems sufficient ambiguity in Chirikov's reply to allow of this hypothesis. There is some evidence that Bering may have misunderstood his instructions, and also have been misled by persistent local stories of 'impassable capes' between the Kolyma and the Anadyr, which led him to look northwards rather than eastwards for the passage, or the junction.[31]

Be that as it may, the result of the voyage was an anticlimax. If Bering's goal was the junction between Asia and America, he did not find it; if it was their separation, he did not show that either. He had indeed established the probability of a water passage between the continents, but the probability only. Not until Cook was the actual existence of a strait demonstrated, although as early as 1754 the name 'Bering Strait' was used.[32] As late as 1819 James Burney, who had himself sailed through the Strait with Cook, could argue that Asia and America might yet be found 'contiguous, or parts of one and the same continent'. So long as Dezhnev's voyage was not accepted as authentic, the non-existence of such a connection was not conclusively demonstrated until 1823, when Baron Ferdinand von Wrangel, travelling eastwards from the Kolyma, reached Cape Schmidta, which Cook had seen and named North Cape.[33]

Bering's was not the only Russian venture on these remotest confines of Siberia. Reports drifted in of islands east and north, potential sources of furs and tribute, and these helped in obtaining authorisation for Afanasii Shestakov, an illiterate but plausible Cossack, to muster a strong force for the subjugation of the Chukchi; it was to include geodesists and sailors. The main expedition was disastrously defeated by the Chukchi, but an offshoot brought Russians to America itself. In July 1732 Mikhail Gvosdev, in Bering's *Sv. Gavriil*, sailed from Nizhne-Kamchatsk in search of a rumoured 'Big Land' east of Anadyr. Gvosdev landed on Great Diomede and on 21 August anchored close to the tip of what is now Seward Peninsula; a Chukchi in a kayak came off to meet them, but divided counsels and an unfavourable wind prevented a landing. Reports of this voyage did not reach St Petersburg until 1738, and firm knowledge later still; it had no impact on the plans for Bering's second voyage. This was, however, the first assuredly known sighting by Europeans of western America north of Oregon. Gvosdev himself thought that his discovery was an island; but it was of rather more than episodic interest, since Müller and von Stählin placed it on their influential maps as part of the mainland.[34]

Bering's second voyage: plans and preparations

Bering returned to St Petersburg in 1730, to face criticism for an apparently ineffectual voyage, but also to receive a good deal of support for a new venture. Almost as soon as he arrived he submitted to the Admiralty College a program of research and development in eastern Siberia, and this was accepted, in principle, by the Senate. The conception of the Second Kamchatka or Great Northern Expedition was thus Bering's, although it was 'midwifed and nourished by others'.[35]

Bering's first plan was concerned largely with the infrastructure needed; Siberian resources—iron, pitch, salt—should be exploited to cut down on the fantastic transportation costs, administrative and working conditions improved, Okhotsk given proper port facilities. A second memorandum recommended that ships should be built in Kamchatka itself, to follow up various evidences that there was land (perhaps America itself) not far east of that peninsula, and to explore the seas south of Okhotsk in order to open trade with Japan. The Arctic coast of Siberia might also be explored, in sections. Expenses, except for salaries, provisions, and materials not available in Kamchatka, might amount to 10–13,000 roubles.

Nothing is said of determining the limits of Asia and America. The concern is for the extension of Russian trade and influence—if there were countries east of Kamchatka, 'it will be possible to establish trade ... to the advantage of the Russian Empire.' This comes out even more clearly in some of the modifications made or suggested by such influential men as Admiral Count Nikolai Golovin and Ivan Kirilov, secretary of the Administrative Senate, both strong backers of Bering. Golovin, worried lest Britain or France should forestall Russia in the North Pacific,

Plate XV. ASIA TO AMERICA, 1758. From the 'Müller' map; for comment see text. Published by Shorey Book Store, Seattle, Washington USA. Photo ANU.

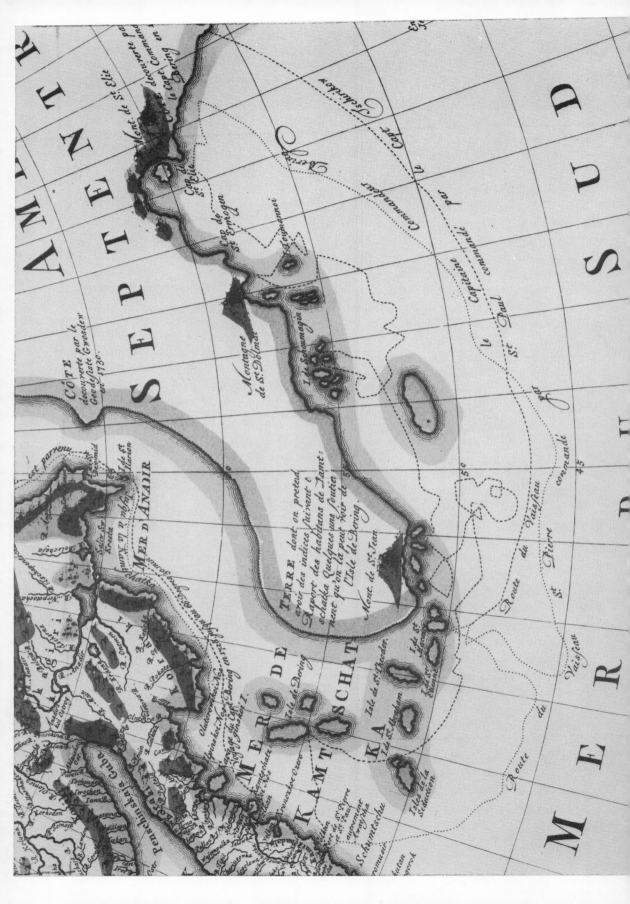

proposed sending two frigates and a supply ship to Kamchatka round the Horn: this would take one year each way, against six if everything had to be carried across Siberia for building in Kamchatka. He even anticipated Russian practice in the early nineteenth century by suggesting annual voyages for training, supplying the far eastern posts, and exploration. Golovin also drew attention to the gold and silver which might be found in the new lands.

Kirilov also mentioned the chance of mineral wealth in countries to be brought under subjection. Russia could expand as far as California (as in due course she did) and Mexico; the Spaniards will not be pleased but then the local people are embittered against them (it might be a British projector speaking) while 'on our side it is firmly established not to embitter such people'—a bitter irony in view of what happened to the Aleuts and Kamchadals and many others. 'To the south all the islands as far as Japan do not really belong to anyone', and they as well as Esso and Compagnie Landt must fall to Russia; the Japanese will not reject trade because they will be able to get goods more cheaply than from China. Okhotsk or some other port will flourish, and there will be bases in the event of war with China. Kirilov also hoped that it might be found for certain whether there was a passage from the Arctic to the Pacific, but the whole thrust of his paper is, in his own opening words, 'for the expansion of the empire and for inexhaustible wealth'.[36]

Eventually the idea of trespassing on Spanish preserves was to be prudently dropped; in the official statements the emphasis is on collecting tribute from hitherto unsubjugated peoples. There remains a sweeping program of imperialist expansion, much more than a mere second chance for Bering to discover the Asian/American limits. In this context Article 13 of the Senate's final instructions to Bering and his officers is highly significant. They are to keep secret their orders from the Admiralty College, but special open instructions will be issued. These will state that, at the request of the St Petersburg and Paris Academies, the eternally famous Peter 'out of curiosity' sent an expedition to determine whether Asia and America were united; the point was not settled. Now the Empress Anna, 'influenced by the same reasons', is sending a similar expedition; if Bering meets with European or Asian settlements or government ships, 'you may tell them what has just been said' and if requested show the public instructions: 'This will allay their suspicions'.[37]

Significant also is the provision of mineralogists and assayers, although owing to a bureaucratic bungle these were not sent on from the Ural mining district; in the event the rising young German naturalist Georg Wilhelm Steller sailed as geologist. The possibility of mineral finds was taken up by Chirikov, who urged that there was no point in looking for them in the far north, where if they existed they would be unexploitable; the search should begin in 65°N, where America was probably near at hand, and go down to 50°. Fifteen degrees of latitude would be enough to

Plate XVI. ASIA TO AMERICA, 1773. From the 'von Stählin' map for comment see text. Published by Shorey Book Store, Seattle, Washington USA. Photo ANU.

establish the location of America, and hence there would be no point in pressing on as far as Mexico, which in any case could not be reached and returned from in one season. The Mexican argument was readily accepted; it is pertinent that in 1732–3 Russian relations with France and Spain were under stress caused by the Polish Succession crisis. However, Chirikov's suggested route was not adopted; instead a final decision on the course to be taken was left to Bering, Chirikov, and the other officers, in consultation with a professor appointed by the Academy of Sciences, Louis Delisle de la Croyère. This was to prove of serious consequence.

The full program was extremely ambitious. It included (1) exploration of the Arctic coast between the Lena and Kamchatka Rivers; (2) a voyage to Japan, under Martin Spanberg; (3) the American voyage under Bering and Chirikov. The first of these hardly concerns us; it may be noted that the final stage, from the Kolyma to Anadyr, was covered by land in 1741, and resulted in the conclusion that a Northeast Passage was impracticable. A great deal of fundamental scientific work was done by Johann Georg Gmelin, Gerhard Friedrich Müller, and Steller, experts attached to the Academy, who accompanied the main party in Siberia.[38]

The crossing of Siberia was an immense logistic effort; at one time or another some 3000 people, from the astronomer Delisle to local carriers, were directly involved. With the best will in the world, this would have strained the administrative and material resources of eastern Siberia, especially in the wild mountainous region east of Iakutsk, the grimness of which is laconically summed up by Krasheninnikov: 'It seems almost beyond belief that a man can live ten or eleven days without eating, but this does not surprise anyone in this country ...'. But as bureaucratic incompetence, corruption, and factionalism were rife and extreme, even minimal good will was often lacking. Siberia could provide little in materials and less in skills; ironworks, ropewalks, tar distilleries had to be set up, and Okhotsk provided with shipyards, training facilities, and beacons. Orders for this work had been issued in 1731; when Spanberg reached the port in 1735 practically nothing had been done. Bering himself left St Petersburg in April 1733; four years later— by which time he should have sailed—he was still at Iakutsk, and 300,000 roubles had been spent or committed.[39] At length all difficulties were overcome or patched up, and on 29 June 1738 Martin Spanberg sailed on the first voyage of the Great Northern Expedition, the quest for Japan.

To Japan: Spanberg and Walton

As we have seen, in the aftermath of Atlasov's troubles in Kamchatka the rebel Cossacks, notably Ivan Kozyrevskii, had sought their pardons by seeking new territories for the Tzar. They did not get far into the Kurils, only to Paramushir; Japan was farther away than had been thought, but Kozyrevskii was able to produce a sketch map of the whole chain and from Japanese castaways learnt of 'Matmai' (Matsumae at the southern tip of Hokkaido) and the empire of 'Apon'. Evreinov and Luzhin in 1721 reached the fifth or sixth island from Kamchatka, probably Kharimkotan; thence they were driven southwards by a storm before being blown back and may have reached Kunashir at the extreme end of the chain. At any rate, Evreinov's map showed fourteen islands with reasonably correct latitudes, spanning over 1000 km.[40]

Beyond the Kurils, however, all was intolerably vague. Yezo, the modern Hokkaido, might be a small island or islands, according to Kozyrevskii, or, according to European cartographers, a big landmass adjacent to Compagnie Landt and reaching nearly to Kamchatka—indeed the island and the peninsula were sometimes conflated.[41] Spanberg had three ships, the *Arkhangel Mikhail, Nadezhda (Hope)*, and Bering's *Sv. Gavriil* reconditioned; the largest was under twenty-one metres long and they carried 151 men and eight officers.[42] His primary mission was to find Japan, but it also involved ascertaining which if any of the islands to the north belonged to the Emperor of Japan, and the most prominent part of the assumed no-man's-land was Yezo. The first attempt, in 1738, was utterly ineffective. Ice in the Sea of Okhotsk forced Spanberg across to Bol'sheretsk, which he did not leave until 26 July. Soon after reaching Paramushir he and his second, the Englishman William Walton in the *Nadezdha*, lost touch in a fog. Spanberg reached Urup, short of provisions, and turned back in 45°31′N; Walton went down to 43°, but neither landed in the Kurils and neither saw Yezo.

Next year Spanberg left Bol'sheretsk two months earlier, on 21 May. On 21 June he left Shumshu and sailed southeast, looking for Gamaland, and not finding it went south as far as 39° before turning west for Yezo. He had made too much southing, and when on 16 June he saw land it was in northeastern Honshu. He sailed south for two days along a green and populous coast, but did not risk landing. However, despite *sakoku*, the policy of seclusion, there was brisk trading from boats, and a Japanese official came aboard and obligingly pointed out Nippon on a globe. With excessive caution, Spanberg spent only two or three days on the coast before making his way back to Kamchatka.

Meanwhile Walton, now in the *Sv. Gavriil*, had been more enterprising. He had soon separated from Spanberg, probably by design, and made a landfall, also on 16 June, a degree farther south. He anchored in 35°10′N, off the Beso Peninsula east of Tokyo Bay (Fig. 19). A watering party was hospitably received and helped with the filling of the casks. Before finally turning back Walton reached Wakayama, the southernmost prefecture of Honshu. His reception was everywhere courteous; Japanese officialdom was taken by surprise, and had no notion of whence their strange visitors came until the Dutch at Deshima identified two coins as 'from the Muscovia country' and a card with a (doubtless suspect) cross as an ace of clubs.[43]

Figure 19. THE KURILS AND JAPAN 1739. Mercator projection, re-drawn from sketch-map (minus numbering of graticule!) in G. A. Lensen, *The Russian Push towards Japan* (Princeton 1959); Walton's landfalls added from his text. Kurilian place-names spelt as in J. J. Stephan, *The Kuril Islands* (Oxford 1974). On British Admiralty Chart 5215 (1960) Urup is named 'Kompaneyskiy', the last relic of the great 'Compagnie Land' of seventeenth century cartography.

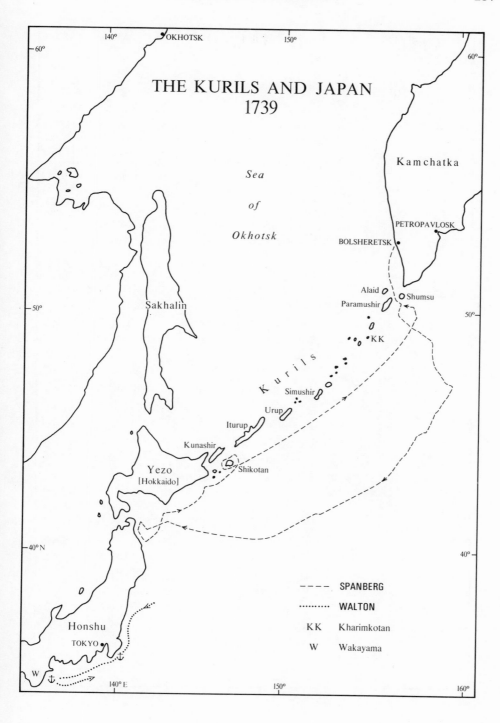

THE KURILS AND JAPAN
1739

Sea

of

Okhotsk

Kamchatka

OKHOTSK

PETROPAVLOSK

BOLSHERETSK

Alaid   Shumsu
Paramushir

KK

Sakhalin

K u r i l s

Simushir
Urup
Iturup
Kunashir
Yezo
[Hokkaido]   Shikotan

Honshu

TOKYO

W

- - - - - SPANBERG
. . . . . . WALTON
K K   Kharimkotan
W   Wakayama

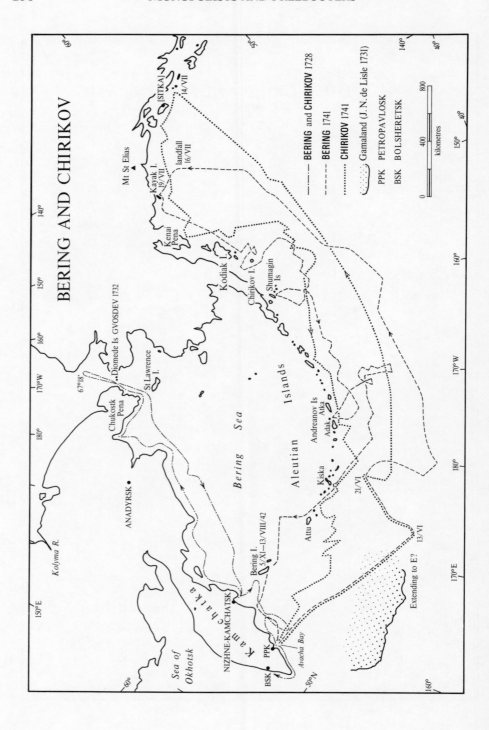

All the ships were back in Okhotsk early in September, the crews riddled with sickness and the officers with dissension. Spanberg's last voyage, in 1742 with four ships, was a fiasco; the only tangible result was the first European sighting, by the *Nadezdha*, of the east coast of Sakhalin, but her commander mistook it for Yezo and did not realise that he was in the strait—Soya or La Pérouse—between the two islands. The true relationship between Sakhalin and the mainland remained obscure, except to the Japanese, until the middle of the nineteenth century.[44]

In by-passing Yezo and reaching the main island of Japan, Spanberg had in a sense succeeded too well. There was still a blank, instead of the great land of Esso, between Japan and the Kurils. Moreover, even his achievement of visiting Japan was questioned. European maps placed Kamchatka and Japan on the same meridian, and as his longitudes for Japan were some 12° west of Kamchatka, it was even suggested that he and Walton had arrived in Korea; not until 1746 was it officially decided that Walton certainly and Spanberg probably had visited Japan.[45] It followed from this 'correction' of his course that some geographers ignored the fact that he had sailed over Gamaland.

The utter confusion as to Yezo persisted. Krasheninnikov remarks that 'Of the four islands which make up the land of Ezo, Spangberg has given proper names to only two: Matmai and Kunashir', and the Academy map of 1773 shows a vague 'I. Matsumai' and five islands northeast of it, two named Kunashir and Urup; their people were said to be called by the Japanese 'Ieso'. As late as 1784 so well-informed a man as J. R. Forster could write that Jesso contained a quantity of islands known to the Russians as the Kurils, and that 'It is also still uncertain whether *Matmai* is an island or not.'[46] So far as contact with Japan went, the visit of Spanberg and Walton was a mere runaway knock.

To America: Bering and Chirikov

Bering reached Okhotsk in 1737; in June 1740 he launched two armed brigs, each twenty-five metres long and with a complement of seventy-six—*Sviatoi Petr* and *Sviatoi Pavel* (*St Peter* and *St Paul*). In September he crossed to Kamchatka, reaching Avacha Bay, where Petropavlosk had just been founded, on 6 October. He had bad luck from the start; the unseaworthiness of his smaller tenders led to loss of supplies by wreck, and the alternative of transport overland from Bol'sheretsk meant loss of time. This points up the very poor quality of Russian shipping in these remote waters, and of many of the *ad hoc* 'seamen'; factors which, together with the high prevalence of fogs, must always be borne in mind when judging the hesitations of Bering and Spanberg.[47] Although he had intended to sail for America early in May, Bering did not get away until 4 June. His lieutenant in the *Sv. Petr* was the Dane

Figure 20. BERING AND CHIRIKOV. X, wreck of Bering's *Sv. Petr*; Y, loss of *Sv. Pavel*'s boats; 16/VII = day/month. Courses from Fig. 18 in D. M. Lebedev and V. L. Grekov, 'Geographical Exploration by the Russians', in H. Friis (ed.), *The Pacific Basin* (New York 1967); these differ in detail but not in substance from those in F. A. Golder (ed.), *Bering's Voyages* (New York 1925), Vol. II Plate I.

Sven Waxell, and Steller sailed with them, to their mutual displeasure; Chirikov commanded the *Sv. Pavel* and had with him Delisle de la Croyère, who seems to have compensated his discomforts with the bottle.[48]

A month before sailing Bering had held a council to fix on the course. The agenda papers were a map by Joseph-Nicolas Delisle, produced especially for Bering's guidance, and an accompanying memoir outlining three possible routes —east from Bering's farthest north in 1728; straight east from Kamchatka; or southeast in search of Gamaland.[49] Nicolas Delisle did not explicitly opt for any one of these, but his preference for the last was clearly implied, and probably lost nothing in the presentation by his half-brother Louis. It should be recognised, however, that although the council's decision for the third option was unfortunate, taking the voyage away from its primary objective and thus wasting time which was already running short, it was a genuine consensus, even if Chirikov may have been a little reluctant.

In the state of knowledge at the time, the choice was by no means illogical. Gamaland, in about 45°N, was generally accepted, if only because it had been on the maps for nearly a century; but after all, there was no reason to doubt that Juan da Gama had actually seen land, nor was there any way of knowing that it was probably Yezo or the Kurils; and nothing was easier, then and much later, than for a chain of islands (or even clouds) to be taken in good faith for a landmass, and so reported. Nicolas Delisle, son of the great Guillaume who was geographer to Louis XIV, was a high authority. No ridicule need attach to his map and memoir; his error was not in pointing the way to Gamaland, which should lead on to America, but in persisting in the belief that it was there after Bering and Spanberg had sailed over it. The decision, then, was to sail SE and E as far as 46°N; if no land was found, to bear E by N until America was met with, then to follow the coast up to 65°N and, time and weather permitting, to touch on Chukotka *en route* to Kamchatka. Apart from the first leg, this was Chirikov's recommendation in reverse.

By 14 June they were in 46°, with no land in sight, though Steller convinced himself that there were 'rather distinct signs' of it, and was bitterly contemptuous of the officers for not taking him seriously; a pattern he continued. Course was accordingly changed to northeast, but six days later Bering and Chirikov lost touch. They spent a few days looking for each other, but were never to meet again (Fig. 20).

Chirikov's voyage can be summarised briefly. He bore away E and then NE, without incident until early in the morning of 15 July a mountainous and forested land was seen in 55°21′N: Cape Addington, and behind it Prince of Wales Island. Coasting north, the *Sv. Pavel* passed the site where Novo-Arkhangel'sk (now Sitka) was to be founded, and on the 18th was in Lisianski Strait at the northern end of Chichagof Island. Here Chirikov sent out a landing party; it did not return, and a small boat sent to look for it also vanished. Two boats seen on the 25th were naturally taken for those missing, but when the smaller one, paddled not rowed, came near enough for figures to be distinguished, it was clearly not Russian. The reluctance of the Americans to come close to the ship convinced Chirikov that his men had been killed or taken; it is more likely that they had been swamped in the dangerous tide-rips of this intricate coast; near here, possibly in the same bay, La Pérouse was to lose two boats and twenty-one men in such an accident.[50] But as well as fifteen men the *Sv. Pavel* had lost both her boats, so that watering would be impossible; reluctantly Chirikov turned west.

On 1 August the Kenai Peninsula was sighted, next day Kodiak Island, and on 9 September the *Sv. Pavel* anchored off Adak, where seven men came out in kayaks. They were too shy to come aboard, and were not interested in any gifts but knives. A strong wind forced the ship offshore, with the loss of an anchor; her people were now stricken with scurvy, which increased after they sighted Agattu and Attu, the westernmost of the Aleutians. Chirikov himself was unable to keep the deck, and his lieutenants Chichagov and Plautin died. The *Sv. Pavel* was worked by the navigator Ivan Elagin, with Chirikov directing from his bed. Their Kamchatkan landfall was made on 8 October; two days later they entered Petropavlosk Harbour. Delisle de la Croyère died before he could be got ashore.

Chirikov's very businesslike report admitted that his longitudes were in error, correctly ascribing this to currents whose rate he was unable to determine. In May 1742 he again sailed eastwards, reaching Attu and Atka before being turned back by bad weather. In a milieu rife with inefficiency and irresolution, he stands out as an unusually competent and thoughtful seaman.

After failing to find Chirikov, Bering went south again as far as 45°40′N; there was still no Gamaland, and he accordingly bore E by N and then ENE. Steller had been against the first turn away from the southeasterly course—'a single day ... might have been decisive for the whole enterprise'—yet now convinced himself that land was very close to the *north*; but when on 14 July a more northerly course was set the reason was not his urgings but the fact that half the water had been consumed. On 17 July, in about 58°30′N, they saw mountains dominated by a towering volcano far to the north: Mount St Elias, which reaches nearly 5500 metres. Two days later they were at Kayak Island, about 100 km west of Mount St Elias, and here Bering decided to land.

This was the occasion for open quarrel between Bering and Steller, whose journal is one long diatribe against the naval men who were too stupid and conceited to accept his constantly proffered, and usually erroneous, advice. Sometimes he was right, as in a dispute over watering on Shumagin Island; but although a fine scientist on land, at sea he was a novice devastatingly unaware of his limitations.[51] On this occasion, however, one must sympathise with him, strongly. He was after all the scientific expert, and yet it took a heated protest before Bering grudgingly let him go ashore with the watering party, with only his own servant to help him: ten years to get to America, a miserable ten hours ashore. He made good use of this cramped allowance, but the disappointment was bitter.

Bering showed no enthusiasm over his discovery; the plain fact seems to be that at sixty-two he was worn out, after the gruelling Siberian years, and thought only of making his way back to Kamchatka in safety. The season was getting on, they had no provisions for wintering, and they had in fact discovered America—though singularly little information had been collected about it, except Steller's rushed observations on Kayak Island. Then there were the constant fogs: the *Sv. Petr's* log records fog on thirty-nine of the sixty-seven days between 12 June and 17 August. The later course of the voyage suggests that Bering's judgement may not have been at fault, except in his abrupt decision to depart before watering was completed.

On the 21st, therefore, they stood to the southwest. Early in August they sighted Tumannoi (Foggy) Island, later named after Chirikov by Vancouver, and on 10 August an officers' meeting formalised the decision to return along 53° without further coastal examination: there was not too much time to make Kamchatka by the end of September, twenty-one men had scurvy, and they feared the onset of westerly winds. The decision did not of course meet with Steller's approval, but it is difficult to see what he did want: at one point he thought that they were sailing between America and a land to the south, which he even convinced himself that he saw; it was indefensible not to investigate it.[52]

The feared Westerlies now set in strongly, almost constant for over a fortnight. Water was again running low, for which Bering's hurried departure from Kayak Island was responsible. They bore north to Shumagin Island (31 August), named for the first sailor to die, who was buried there. Here indeed there was water, and Steller was right to protest against taking it from the first brackish pool they met rather than from good springs farther on. Here too they met a few Aleuts, who were not unfriendly but did not understand the Russians' request for water, made with the help of a French vocabulary of Algonkian! Stormy weather delayed departure, but they got away on 6 September and on the 25th saw high land, probably Adak and Atka in the Andreanovs. Now however another fortnight of very heavy storms drove them backwards, until on 11 October they were down nearly to 48°N, and seven degrees of longitude east of the Andreanovs.[53]

The situation was becoming desperate: the rigging was breaking and thirty-two men were down with scurvy, including Bering; command was falling into the hands of Waxell and the sailing master Sofron Khitrov, both of whom seem to have been capable seamen. Towards the end of October they sighted Kiska, Buldir, and the Semichi Islands; some of the men, strongly backed by Steller, thought that they were in the Kurils. Finally on 4 November they came to Mednyy (Copper) Island, which was doubtfully taken for Kamchatka, and next day a larger island, ever since known by Bering's name. Food and water were now low, the rigging was rotten, twelve men had died, thirty-four were very ill with scurvy, and only ten, themselves weak, were really effective. It was decided to make for the land, although observations showed that it was two degrees north of Avacha Bay. The worst of their agony was about to begin.

Half an hour after the *Sv. Petr* anchored a heavy surf drove her over an offshore reef or bar, into calmer water; but two anchors were lost. Steller very soon decided that they were not in Kamchatka; Waxell at first thought that they were and hoped soon to make contact with Petropavlosk. But it was clear that for the time being they had no option but to commence wintering on the spot, in a little valley; the only vegetation was grasses, shrubs, dwarf alders and birch, but there was plenty of driftwood for fuel. There was also plenty of animal food: ptarmigans, sea-otters, blue foxes; later, when these became scarce through over-hunting, fur-seals (which were revolting), sea-lions, and manatees—Steller's famous sea-cows, extinct not many years after he described them, feeding on sea-grass and the best eating of all. There were also two stranded whales, one very rank, the other quite fresh. Nevertheless, the first weeks were dreadful.

The sick were brought ashore and made as comfortable as possible in little dug-outs, but

> Men were continually dying ... there was none able to drag the
> corpses away, nor were those who were still living able to move
> away from the dead. They had to remain all mixed up together in a
> ring with a little fire in the centre ... Sofron Khitrov, later Rear-
> Admiral, shared a hole with me. Between us lay our ship's commis-
> sary, Ivan Lagunov, dead ... Captain-Commander Bering died on
> 8th December. His corpse was tied fast to a plank and thrust down
> into the ground. None of the other dead were buried with a plank.[54]

As he lay dying, Bering was already half-buried in sand sliding down into his hollow, and begged to be left thus, for warmth. The foxes mutilated the dead and molested the almost helpless living, and for a time were not scared off by slaughter or horrible torturing of those caught and released.

Gradually they adjusted themselves. Steller, with Germanic efficiency, turned his dug-out into a hut roofed with fox-skins; although in his little mess the Russians did the household chores, there was a good deal of levelling, and with his good example and Waxell's alert but relaxed leadership, morale improved. There was no mutiny, probably because Waxell worked as much as possible by consensus. This was not complete; when the men began playing cards, he was told that he should stop it: it was against Her Imperial Majesty's regulations. It is not from Waxell but from Steller himself that we learn that he it was who took this unco' guid stance; it is only fair to say that his stated reason was the gambling in sea-otter skins. Waxell was sensibly glad that they had some pastime to overcome their melancholy, and replied that Her Majesty had not thought of this desert island.

A more serious dispute arose over the *Sv. Petr* herself. In November an attempt had been made to beach her, which failed—Khitrov had only four men in his working party, and they were too weak to raise the anchor. Two days later, on 28 November, the problem was resolved when a storm drove her ashore. After inspection, Waxell and Khitrov proposed that she should be broken up to build a smaller vessel. There'll always be an *apparatchik*: objection was made that nobody had ever heard of building a vessel from a wreck (!) and that 'it would be an unwarrantable action to break up one of Her Imperial Majesty's ships'; she should be moved back into the sea. This was manifestly impossible, but to get a formal agreement, so that if things went wrong he would not be blamed for not accepting one of forty or so propositions, Waxell had to call another meeting. There was still one dissentient, a demoted aide of Bering's, but he had to admit that it was uncertain that the ship could be refloated and repaired.

All save one of the carpenters were dead, but the Cossack Sava Starodubstov, who had been an ordinary labourer in the Okhotsk shipyard, volunteered to act as master shipwright, and all turned to willingly.[55] With spring, and some vegetable food (sought out by Steller), health improved, and exploring parties established that they were definitely on an island. On 6 May 1742 the stem and sternpost of the new *Sv. Petr* were fitted to her keel, the old mainmast; in default of other drinks, Waxell treated all hands to *saturman*, normally brewed with butter, wheat-flour, and tea, now with train-oil, musty rye-flour, and crakeberry. On 10 August the vessel was launched; in the euphoria, Steller found some kind words to say of Waxell.

They sailed on 13 August, their last act on the island being to erect a cross to Bering's memory. The foxes turned out in force to ransack the huts for meat and fat, 'to which ... they were heartily welcome.' The new *Sv. Petr* was fearfully cramped, but on the 17th they sighted a high volcano and were soon certain that this was Kamchatka; on the 27th they dropped their last anchor—only a grapnel— into Avacha Bay; Waxell can only babble of their inexpressible joy. They left their commander and many of his fellows on the island ever since known by Bering's name.

After Bering: the sea-otter trade

Steller was before his time in warning of the dangers of over-hunting; like his hints to navigators, and with far less reason, his advice fell on wilfully deaf ears. His sea-cow was extinct by 1768, and while a few of the beautiful and charming sea-otters still survive, carefully guarded, off California, the immediate result of the Bering/Chirikov voyages was a rush which took Russian hunters, the promyshlen-niki, farther and farther afield as the nearer grounds were depleted. In the 1780s the extraordinary profits made at Canton with pelts from northwest America set off a second rush, in which British and Americans were dominant, and which led to the Anglo-Spanish Nootka crisis of 1790.[56]

Between them, the crews of the *Sv. Petr* and *Sv. Pavel* brought 15–1800 sea-otter pelts to Kamchatka; at Kiakhta the Chinese would pay 80–100 roubles each for them.[57] The sea-otter pelt was even softer and finer than that of that 'merry little beast, and a beautiful', the sable, and soon dominated the Kiakhta market, where in the early 1750s skins fetched seven or eight times the Kamchatka price. Unluckily the fur of the female was more valuable than that of the male, and she bore but one pup a year.

This new phase of the fur trade owed nothing to official encouragement; it was a locally-based free-enterprise affair. Within ten years of Bering and Chirikov, 'more important discoveries were made [but not adequately reported] by these individuals, at their own private cost, than had hitherto been effected by all the expensive efforts of the crown.'[58] St Petersburg confined itself to levying its 10 per cent tax and issuing utterly futile instructions for the fair treatment of native peoples, 'warnings which were respected until the anchor was pulled.' The promyshlenniki who had pioneered Siberia now took to the sea, to begin with in wretched 'sewn-up ships', made from green timber put together without nails; they navigated by guess and by God. They were backed by merchants, but worked on a share system like the buccaneers, the sponsors providing the ships and taking half the profits, a sort of maritime *métayage* or share-cropping.

Profits could be very high indeed, but so were the risks—the crudely-built and ill-manned craft rarely survived more than a couple of voyages. Mortality from shipwreck, disease, and fighting with the Aleuts was heavy. Although the Russians carried trade goods such as tobacco and beads, they worked at least as much by atrocious terrorism, seizing women as hostages to force the Aleuts to hunt for them—in their light *baidarka* (kayaks), they were far more skilful at sea than were their exploiters—and attempts at resistance were crushed with sickening brutality. As the nearer islands were worked out and longer voyages became necessary, shipping, skills, and organisation gradually improved, and after the 1760s larger companies began to dominate the trade, a trend culminating in 1799 with the chartering of the monopolistic Russian-America Company, a mirror-image of the Hudson's Bay Company.[59]

There were forty or so voyages in the ten years after Bering, and despite their poor material resources, by 1770 the promyshlenniki had subjugated, in an anarchic fashion, the Aleutian chain from Attu to Unalaska. The first off the mark was Emelian Basov to the Kommandorskiyes (Bering and Mednyy) in 1743 and 1745; his second trip brought back 1000 sea-otter, 2999 fur seal, and 2000 blue fox pelts: 200,000 roubles, an enormous return.[60] In 1762–6 Stepan Glotov moved on beyond the Aleutians, to Kodiak. After 1762, under Catherine the Great, the government again took a hand in exploration, somewhat disjointedly. In 1764–8 Ivan Sind (or Sindt), who had been with Bering, sailed northeast from Kamchatka and landed on the Seward Peninsula near the present Nome; in the same years Petr Krenitsin sailed between Unimak and the tip of the Alaskan Peninsula, though it was not yet determined that the latter joined the mainland.[61] After this the Russian voyages and exploitations in Alaskan waters are better considered as part of the great geopolitical opening of the Pacific which began with Byron in 1764; by the time of Cook's third voyage, still more by 1790 and the Nootka crisis, the interests of four nations—Britain, Russia, Spain, the United States—were converging into a contest for control of the shores of the northeast Pacific—or, to adopt the American nomenclature, convenient from the continental viewpoint, the Pacific Northwest.[62]

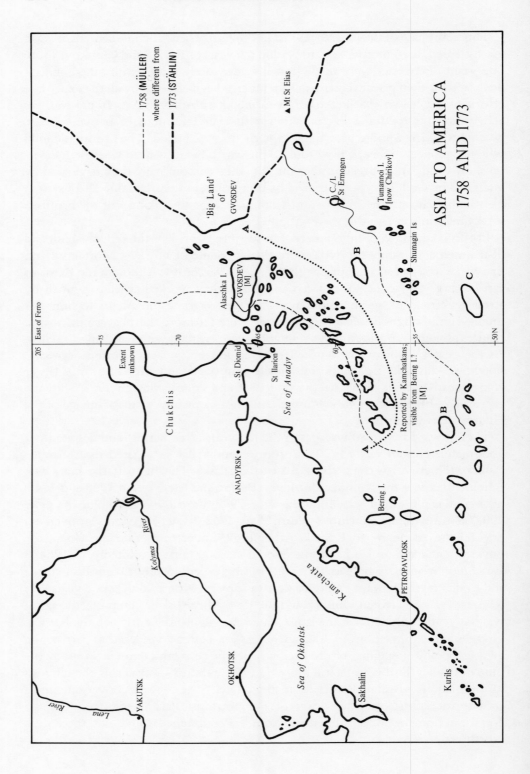

ASIA TO AMERICA
1758 AND 1773

The promyshlenniki were scarcely finished navigators or hydrographers. As James King put it,

> Every new adventurer falling in with Islands that did not coincide
> with those he found in his map ... directly concluded that he had
> discovered a new Group and as these people stay out 5 or 8 years it
> was a long time before these errors could be discovered.[63]

Moreover, 'Self-interest dictated that the reports of [their] discoveries be neither too precise nor too elaborate'; like other wealth-prospectors, they tended to be garrulous and boastful in generalities, habitually secretive as to the details—'many promyshlenniki would have risked disaster on a falsely charted reef rather than work under the eyes of a naval officer'. With less motivation to inaccuracy, Sind seems to have been little better, and hence—in Soviet words—'On generalised manuscript maps of the time we find an indiscriminate scattering of islands ... but no conjectural protrusion of Alaska'[64]; there is a general northwards shift of the Aleutians from their true position.

In any case, the maps of this time, such as they were, lay lost in Siberian archives or were held secret; as the British Ambassador wrote, if it were known that he was sending London reports of Bering's explorations in Kamchatka, 'some people may be sent to finish their days in that country'.[65] There was, however, enough straw for a lot of bricks to build into the speculative structures of western cartographers. A 'conjectural protrusion of Alaska' is the most striking feature on the Academy of Sciences map of 1754–8, on which Müller attempted to display the knowledge so far garnered; it is not so reckless as it looks at first glance. Sind and the promyshlen-niki dotted the Bering Sea with misplaced and duplicated islands, a confusion presented in the 1773 Academy map—von Stählin's—which so bewildered and exasperated Cook. By its very confusion, conflated with the old myth of Gamaland and the new hoax of de Fonte, the cartographical debate stemming from the Russian voyages produced a mirage which played an important part in directing, or misdirecting, the course of major exploration later in the century; in fact, an essential item in the prologomena to Cook's third voyage.

Cartographers in conflict

The obscurity surrounding the Bering voyages in western Europe is well displayed by one of the earliest English discussions, that by John Campbell in 1748. Campbell says that it was not possible to give a distinct account, but it would seem that there

Figure 21. ASIA TO AMERICA, 1758 AND 1773.   Outlines of the maps published by the St Petersburg Academy of Sciences in 1758 (G. F. Müller) and 1773 (referred to J. von Stählin); cf. Plates XV, XVI. Except for the (variously spelt) St Diomed and St Ilarion, all islands north and west of the line A ... A are absent, or merged into the hypothetical peninsula, in 1758; B, B, islands in 1773 shown as mountains on the peninsula in 1758; C, non-existent, presumably deriving from Steller's fancied indications of land to the south on 10 September 1741; [M] = according to Müller. The name Alaschka I. does not appear on the Academy maps but on von Stählin's own publication, reproduced in Beaglehole, III at lxiv.

was a great distance between Asia and America, filled up with broken lands. Since Siberia projected over 30° into the other hemisphere, to preserve the 'Balance of Sea' America in these latitudes must be quite narrow, and that this was indeed so was indicated by the absence of large rivers flowing into Hudson's Bay from the west: a Northwest Passage was therefore likely. Bering died on a desert island and may not have seen America at all; his landfall must have been on an island, since it was so close to Japan (a confusion with Spanberg?). The Russians probably brought the continents close together because they were convinced that there was indeed a Northwest Passage, but they wished to keep it secret, to the detriment of the rest of the world, particularly Britain; they were unlikely to succeed in this, for want of naval power. They might however find minerals or drugs, and there was a turn to commercial enterprise in Russia, so Britain should foster closer trade links. Campbell was using an account of the first voyage, into which he had to fit the known fact of Bering's death on a desert island.[66]

Campbell was in good company. J.-N. Delisle, suspected by the Russians (with good reason) of abusing his Academy position to send classified information to his Embassy, returned to Paris in 1747; in 1750 he read a paper to the French Academy of Sciences in which he stated that while Chirikov and Delisle de la Croyère had reached America, Bering had not. So long did full information take to reach St Petersburg, or so carefully was it guarded once there, that this statement was made in good faith; but Delisle at least seemed to be playing up his half-brother against Bering, perhaps against Chirikov as well, and it was becoming apparent that the policy of obscurantism, if not of positive secrecy, was leading to serious distortions of the Russian achievement.[67] Delisle's map of 1750 showed a long 'Coast seen by Tchirikow and Delisle' in about 52–53°N, which in his 1752 version has become a very large island—over 8° of latitude by 20° of longitude—which looks very much like a substitute, shifted north and east, for Gamaland, now reduced to a small island. On the American side these maps, and that of Philippe Buache (1752–3), indicate the Russian sightings of the American mainland, but interwoven with fantasies— the entries of Juan de Fuca and Martin Aguilar into a vast landlocked 'Mer de l'Ouest' covering a great deal of America west of the Rocky Mountains, and the weird waterways of Bartholomew de Fonte running to Hudson Bay or thereabouts.

This last had no better credentials than an anonymous article in the London *Monthly Miscellany or Memoirs for the Curious* of 1708; it was thoroughly demolished in 1757 in a Spanish work, *Noticia de la California*; the book was published in English in 1759, but the appendix dealing with de Fonte was silently omitted; British writers thereupon condemned its author for failing to mention the Admiral![68] As late as 1774, Robert de Vaugondy manages to combine Bering, Gvosdev, Anian, Aguilar, de Fonte, and even Fusang, the legendary Chinese discovery of America, which had also been shown by Buache. Despite several contemporary demolition jobs, such vain imaginings had a practical effect on the course of Pacific exploration: Byron for instance was instructed to explore the American coast from 38 to 54°N, and this stretch would have covered the entries of Aguilar, de Fuca, and de Fonte, as shown on most maps.

The task of setting the record straight and repudiating 'evil misrepresentations' was formally assigned by the St Petersburg Academy to G. F. Müller, who in 1753 published anonymously a *Lettre d'un Officier de la Marine Russienne*. This gave a 'readable, coherent, and generally accurate account of the Bering expeditions', and for good measure repudiated the speculative geography of Delisle and Buache on the American side.[69] Buache replied in 1753–5, reviving Gamaland; the debate was put on a new footing, though not silenced, by the St Petersburg Academy's publication in 1754 and 1758 of Müller's 'Nouvelle Carte des Découvertes faites par les Vaisseaux Russiens Aux côtes inconnues de l'Amerique Septentrionale' which, like von Stählin's similarly named and published map of 1773, is a fundamental document in the history of the North Pacific (Fig. 21, Plates XV, XVI).

On the American side, Müller leaves in the Aguilar and Juan de Fuca embouchures (which after all did reflect some reality) but marks de Fonte's Rio de los Reyes as 'Pretendue ... suivant Mr. Delisle'—pretended, after Mr Delisle. Marked as firm coasts are Gvosdev's Big Land, the American mainland discovered by Chirikov and the Mount St Elias region, and several islands—Tumannoi, Shumagin, Bering, and a few of the Aleutians. A fictitious island south of the Shumagins may represent one of Steller's deductions or fancied sightings of land. Islands corresponding to Adak and Atka are shown, and north of them a towering 'Mont. de St. Jean': this must be the high volcano seen from the *Sv. Petr* on 25 September 1741, probably on Great Sitkin Island. On Müller's map, this mountain forms the southern promontory of a great peninsula. Except for the firm coasts just noted, however, this huge extension from the American mainland is given as conjectural, with a dotted outline, and Müller says very fairly that 'My work herein has been no more than to connect together, according to probability, by points, the coasts that had been seen in various places.'[70]

This Müller peninsula looks absurd to modern eyes, but this is largely a function of the excessive width given to it. Actually the length of the mainland from Mount St Elias to the tip of the real Alaskan Peninsula is 22° out of the 34° of longitude between Mount St Elias and the Adak-Atka region where Müller's peninsula ends. At all events, even discounting the dotted lines, the map is less misleading as to the general relations of land and sea than is the 'improvement' which replaced it, von Stählin's; nor had Müller the passion for lost causes of Delisle and Buache. He later candidly admitted that he was wrong in believing America to be so close to Kamchatka, while continuing to hold, correctly, that farther north the continents approached closely.[71]

As Beaglehole says, von Stählin's map 'looks as if some large fist has come down on the fragile surface of Müller's north-western peninsula, shattered it into displaced fragments, and sent some of it into thin air.' The American mainland runs from the mysterious name 'Stachtan Nitada', Gvosdev's Big Land, almost straight southeast to Mount St Elias; west of this is nothing but sea and islands—over fifty in an area where there are in reality six! The most prominent of these, Alaschka, covers three-fifths of the exaggerated distance between the east point of Siberia and Gvosdev's landfall; Bering Strait is thus split in two, and is not named. With bland complacency von Stählin, having called his production 'a very accurate little Map' goes on inconsequentially 'As to the absolute accuracy of the first two articles, namely the true situation, as to geographical latitude and longitude, and their exact dimensions, I would not be answerable for them'.[72]

This unscholarly carelessness, to give it no worse name, was to have serious results. Although some of the well-informed were sceptical, the map after all came out under the imprimatur of the St Petersburg Academy, of which von Stählin was Secretary, and an English translation of his *Account of the New Northern Archipelago* (purportedly Sind's discoveries) came out in the year of its original publication, 1774, under the sponsorship of Dr Matthew Maty, Secretary of the Royal Society: what could be more authoritative?

The most significant difference between the maps of 1754 and 1773 was this: von Stählin showed a clear run northwest from California to a strait between Alaschka and America; but if Müller's peninsula existed, a ship coming from California would have to sail some 30° farther west to round it. If Müller were right, the approach to Bering Strait might more logically be made from the Asian side, from Kamchatka or even, as Maty and Daines Barrington suggested in 1774, using Canton as a final base for refitting and refreshing. (The experience of the Acapulco-bound Galleons, striking northeast to get into the Westerlies for the run to California, might have been taken into the reckoning.)[73]

A new factor was introduced by Samuel Hearne's great journey of 1770–2 from Hudson Bay to the Arctic mouth of the Coppermine River: this showed that there were no possible water passages from the Pacific into Hudson Bay; so much for de Fonte. Hence, in contradistinction to Byron, Cook could be directed on his third voyage not to waste time exploring possible inlets between 45° and 65°N, in which latter latitude he would find von Stählin's strait between Alaschka and the main-land. But Hearne also seemed to show that the Arctic in 72°N (correctly 68°) was not entirely frozen, and this fitted well with new geophysical theories of an open Polar Sea.[74]

In the event von Stählin's view prevailed, not Müller's: Cook was ordered to go north not from Kamchatka but from Nova Albion; this seemed the shortest and clearest way. Far from finding a clear run up to 65°N, Cook ran into the long south-easterly protrusion of Alaska, and perforce lost much time in searching up the various inlets which looked as if they might lead on to von Stählin's Alaschkan strait, or even by-pass it to the Arctic. As Bougainville was to write, from sad experience, 'Geography is a science of facts', and the scholar weaving systems in his study is liable to 'very great errors, which can often only be corrected at the expense of navigators.'[75]

The Russian achievement

It is true that 'Bering looks to have been a valuable rather than a great man, of little original force of mind, and entering on his last service when past his prime.'[76] One cannot but feel that his guiding star was simply his official duty and that he had little of the inward fire or devotion to the conquest of knowledge which inspired the greater navigators. Chirikov seems a better man in this respect, but he was far too junior to be chosen as leader. Nevertheless, Bering did his duty, and beyond that the Great Northern Expedition itself, however much such a thing may have been 'in the air' and however much it was fostered by others, takes shape in his memoranda. Steller's bitter gibe about ten years ending in ten hours is justified only in the strictly limited context of Kayak Island on 20 July 1741. The total achievements of the Expedition were far-reaching.

It had been clearly shown that Asia extended much farther to the east than had been supposed, and some key points were fixed with astonishing accuracy: the east point of Siberia on Bering's map of his first voyage, on Müller's the west point of America (from Gvosdev) and Mount St Elias, are only about one degree of longitude from their true positions. A Northeast Passage was shown to be impracticable; Terra de Jeso, Compagnielandt, Gamaland were demolished, if not, unfortunately, abolished in the minds of doctrinaire theorists; the northwesterly trend of the American coast was confirmed to far higher latitudes than had ever been reached by Europeans on the Pacific side of the continent.[77] A great deal of geographical and ethnographical information had been brought back, notably by Steller but not by him alone. If Spanberg had been ineffective and Yezo remained vague, the prevalent error as to the meridional relation of Japan and Kamchatka had been corrected.

As a bonus, though one of incalculable significance for the historiography of human origins, the demonstrated proximity of Asia and America pointed to the solution of a mystery which had agitated, even agonised, theologians and philosophers ever since it was realised that Columbus had found not Cathay but a New World. Gvosdev had met Chukchi on both sides of the strait: the Amerindians could now be seen as children of Adam after all.

These results were obtained with wretched ships, poorly manned and provisioned, and often with obstruction rather than support from a forward base itself at the end of a line of communications spanning Eurasia. Ignorance and a harsh environment combined to rack the crews with scurvy.[78] The seas traversed are some of the most hazardous in the world, alternately swept by tempest and shrouded in fog, and with a very short sailing season. In such very depressing circumstances the effort was heroic and the achievement recalls that of the Spaniards working from the bush ports of New Spain just two centuries earlier; instead of dwelling on the failings of the explorers, one might well wonder that so much was accomplished from so poor a base.[79]

The price in suffering is starkly displayed in the pages of Waxell and Steller. A yet higher price was to be paid by the Aleuts and other peoples of the new lands, so swiftly exposed to the brutalising assault of the promyshlenniki. There were a few exceptions, but at this far end of the Eurasian world, shielded from publicity by remoteness and dangers, greed was unchecked. Any elements of a 'civilising mission' are indeed hard to find until, in the next century, more formal administration brought some amelioration, though even then far too little. For in the realm not of academic geographers but of the market, the chief result of the voyages was to open up to practical and ruthless men new fields for a robber economy; for the devastation, on land and sea, of the fauna—including the human fauna—by the notoriously and recklessly exploitative fur trade. This was the economic and social result, an ecological and a human tragedy; politically, despite 'the miscalculations and setbacks of Bering and Chirikov on their memorable voyage in 1741', they in effect laid the foundations for the Russian America which endured until 1867.[80]

Chapter 11

BRITISH OFFENSIVES: ANSON, MANILA, AND SULU

Less shall proud Rome her ancient trophies boast;
The conquered country, and the captive host.
Her fierce Dominion, Asia, Afric, knew;
But round the Globe her eagle never flew,
Thro' every clime is Albion's thunder hurled,
And Anson's spoils are from a tribute world.

In this attempt, count o'er the numerous host
Of Albion's sons, unprofitably lost.
Then will your boastings into sorrow turn,
And injured Britons, Albion's fate shall mourn.

Anson's voyage: origin and preparations

By the mid-1750s, enough was known in Spain of the Bering-Chirikov voyages for Fr Miguel Venegas to urge the occupation of Alta California as a precaution, but nothing was done until the advent of José de Gálvez as the very energetic Visitor-General to New Spain in 1765; eleven years later the counter-move he inspired culminated in the founding of San Francisco, the northernmost Spanish establishment in the Pacific.[1] Until then, however, the menace, real as well as perceived, was the ancient one—British naval power in the South Sea. Six days after Bering sailed from Petropavlosk for America, Commodore George Anson anchored at Juan Fernández after a dreadful passage around Cape Horn. His voyage was a fully official act of war, with far-reaching military and political objectives; yet in the event it proved to be merely the last flare of the old privateering tradition.

Anson's venture was indeed conceived in a curious mating between Grand Strategy and the traditional 'Cruising Voyage to the South Sea'.[2] In 1739, a year filled to bursting by the heady gas of patriotism and hope of plunder, the Admiralty had no lack of advisers. James Naish, an old China hand who had left the EIC under a cloud, favoured the seizure of Manila; this would cut out the dangerous Franco-Spanish plan for direct trade from Cadiz round the Horn and on to China with American silver, and would also provide the opening for a mission by some 'gentleman, with a small, well-dressed retinue' to persuade the Celestial Emperor to adopt British woollens for his Court and army. Possession of Manila would give the EIC a monopoly of the China trade and much else, but initially the Company should be kept in the dark, since otherwise 'the Governor of Manila will be too soon acquainted' with the project.[3]

London *Daily Advertiser*, 5 July 1744; *Daily Post*, 6 July—in G. Williams (ed.), *Documents relating to Anson's Voyage* (London 1967), 237.

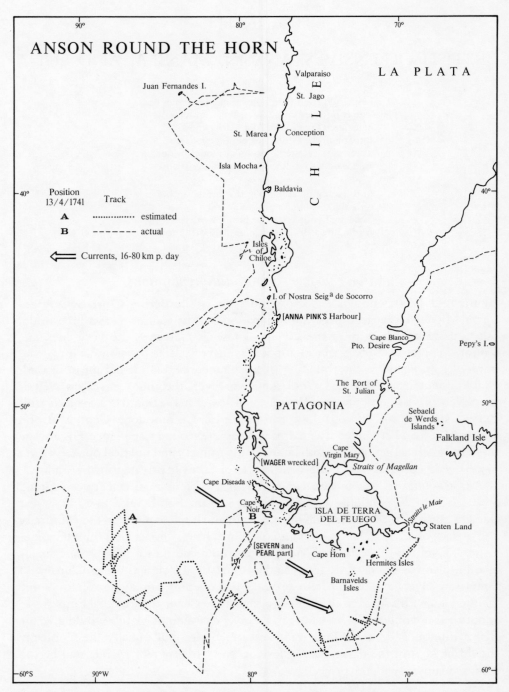

Figure 22. ANSON ROUND THE HORN. Based on map in R. Walter and B. Robbins, *A Voyage round the World ... by George Anson* (London 1748); place-names spelt as in original.

By December the Manila proposition was being shelved; the running was now made by two old SSC factors, Henry Tassell and Henry Hutchinson, the latter of whom had the scarcity value of having actually visited Lima. Under the influence of these experts, the old approach of a great raid up the American west coast was adopted; despite a disclaimer in one of Hutchinson's papers, it is probable that their main interest was in private trade. The Navy looked askance at this *mésalliance* between the Crown and contraband; nevertheless a small illegitimacy was allowed, some trade goods being carried despite Anson's disgust at the idea that his military operations might be 'regulated by the ridiculous views of their trading projects.' The trading result was a near-total loss.[4]

The factors had grander visions than mere smuggling. Juan Fernández could be fortified; with Indian help Chile could be conquered from Valdivia and a settlement could trade as far as California; Panama 'well deserves to be a principal part of this proposal', and after that the rich gold mines of Darien—Dampier's 'Golden Dream' once more. The expedition should carry printed manifestos for distribution after Lima was taken, offering the Creoles independence in alliance with a Britain 'only desirous of putting them on a footing with other nations . . . that in time they might be a glorious people'; the heirs of two former Viceroys were nominated as Quislings. At this point relative realism creeps in with the rider 'N.B. In case the inhabitants should not come to our terms a publication of freedom might be made to all mulatto and negro slaves . . .'.[5]

Anson's instructions of 31 January 1740 reflect this contrariety of ideas. On the one hand, he is to ravage the coasts and shipping of the South Sea and cultivate Indian alliances; on the other, he is to proclaim British benevolence and incite the Creoles to revolt. A manifesto drawn up before he sailed, after stressing the great goodness of George II and the pernicious counsel of Isabel Farnese (not to mention 'the artful insinuations of the Court of France'), follows Tassell and Hutchinson almost word for word. As regards operations, much is left to Anson's discretion. He may or may not attempt Callao, but should if possible take or burn Panama, and if the spring offensive in the West Indies comes to Puerto Bello he is to co-operate with it. (This was 'the one definite enterprise . . . which would have any bearing upon the general course of the war', and nothing came of it.) If he decides to go north for Acapulco and the Galleon, he may return by either China or Chile. There is a strange last provision: when Anson sails it may already be too late to pass the Horn or the Straits in safety, and if so he is to do as much damage as possible around Buenos Aires while waiting for the right season to press on into the South Sea. This of course would warn all of Pacific America, but that hardly mattered: secrecy had been lost long before the fleet sailed.[6]

The program was imposing, and compared with the scratch task forces of the buccaneers or even with Woodes Rogers's two ships, Anson's fleet also looked imposing. The flagship *Centurion* was of 1005 tons and 60 guns, and there were two 50-gun ships, the *Gloucester* and the *Severn*; with the *Pearl*, *Wager*, and *Tryal* sloop, the total was over 4000 tons with 236 guns, carrying altogether 1939 men; there were also two chartered tenders. No such force had sailed westwards for the Pacific since the unlucky Nassau Fleet of 1623–4. Unfortunately, Anson had a low priority compared with the pressing needs of the Caribbean and the Mediterranean. There were agonising delays in major repairs, and the process of manning his ships reached a nadir of inefficiency and inhumanity.

Even the complement of seamen was not fully made up. The land forces origin-ally assigned to the expedition were a whole regiment plus three companies of foot; these were replaced by 500 'invalids', out-pensioners of Chelsea Hospital, unfit for a marching regiment but cannon-fodder thought good enough to storm the walls of Callao. Very rightly 'all those who had limbs and strength enough to walk out of *Portsmouth* deserted, leaving behind them only such as were literally invalids', men in their sixties and seventies, who were forced to sail 'fully apprized of all the disasters they were afterwards exposed to'. Not one of them survived the voyage. Most of these poor old men probably had not many more years of natural life left to them; but simply through murderous administrative insouciance, they were sent to die in cold and filth and terror and the loathsome putridity of scurvy. The 241 who escaped were replaced by 210 marines, so raw that none had been 'so far trained, as to be permitted to fire'; but no matter, the Secretary at War thought that since 'a country fellow from the plough may be in three days taught' to load and fire a musket, on shipboard he was as good as a trained soldier.[7]

Anson and Pizarro: the race for the Horn

Anson sailed from St Helens in the Isle of Wight on 18 September 1740.[8] Despite an inept attempt at camouflage, the size and destination of the voyage were known to the French, and promptly passed to Madrid, as early as 30 January N.S.—actually before Anson received his instructions of 31 January O.S. With unwonted celerity the Spaniards were able to send out a strong force under Don José Pizarro in October; it carried at least 282 guns and 3200 men to Anson's 236 and 1939 men.[9] Pizarro was hovering off Madeira before Anson, delayed by heavy weather, arrived there, but luckily did not hover long enough; whatever the tactical result of an engagement, the British fleet would have been in no shape to proceed.

By 21 December Anson was at Santa Catalina, where he spent a month refresh-ing and refitting. The easygoing days of the privateers were no more, as the Portuguese Crown had strengthened its control of the island, and the Governor passed on news of the fleet to Pizarro, who was now at Maldonado on the La Plata estuary. In his haste to intercept Anson, or to anticipate him into the South Sea, Pizarro sailed without waiting to make up his provisions from Buenos Aires, leaving four days after Anson weighed from Santa Catalina. In February 1741 both fleets were moving down the Patagonian coast, and the *Pearl*, which had lost touch, actually fell in with Pizarro, who was flying a commodore's pennant like Anson's; she escaped only by sailing through water discoloured by fish spawn, which the Spaniards mistook for a shoal. On 17 February she rejoined the squadron, two days before Anson reluctantly put into Port St Julian to remast the *Tryal*. He sailed again on the 27th; at this time the Spaniards were running into disaster off Cape Horn.

Pizarro's reckless impatience in not waiting for his supplies was his ruin. It was as yet early in autumn, but there were over forty centimetres of snow on the decks, and with crews starving and crippled by scurvy, his fleet was scattered by tempests. The largest ship, the 74-gun *Guipuzcoa*, was totally dismasted and driven nearly to Santa Catalina before she was beached; the *Hermiona* foundered with 500 men; a thousand or more died of scurvy or lack of food. Only one ship struggled through to Chile, after being blown back to La Plata; and only one, the flagship *Asia*, ever returned to Spain—and that not until 1746.[10]

Anson and his people fared little better. The weather as they passed through Strait Le Maire was exhilarating, 'and hence we indulged our imaginations in those romantick schemes [of] the fancied possession of the *Chilian* gold and *Peruvian* silver'. These dreams were forthwith blown to shreds by six weeks of almost incessant savage gales, with snow and bitter sleet: 'this day of our passage was the last chearful day that the greatest part of us would ever live to enjoy.' (Amongst those lost was the seaman whose fate, though not his name, is so plangently commemorated in Cowper's 'The Castaway'.) Already scurvy had struck; in April forty-three died in the *Centurion* alone, and a plague of rats attacked the dead and the dying. All ships were seriously damaged in spars, sails, and rigging. Early in April the *Severn* and the *Pearl* lost touch with the squadron, and after a week of trying to work westwards turned back to the Atlantic. Pascoe Thomas wrote that 'they seemed to lag designedly' and termed the parting a defection, but the evidence is against him.[11]

By 13 April Anson was only 1° south of the latitude of Magellan's Cabo Deseado, now his own Desired Cape, and thought himself 10° west of it; his people expected to enjoy very soon 'the celebrated tranquillity of the *Pacifick* Ocean.' They were standing northward when, between one and two on the morning of the 14th, the haze cleared and the moon showed a rocky coast dead ahead: Cape Noir. Despite the fact that by their reckoning they had made double the westing from Strait Le Maire normally allowed to offset the eastwards current, they were actually nearly 9° (about 575 km) east of their estimated position (Fig. 22). A lucky shift of wind enabled them to stand off, but within ten days the remaining ships were scattered. The *Centurion* found no ships at the first rendezvous, Socorro, and was nearly driven ashore on Chiloé, and when she was only a few hours from Juan Fernández another over-estimate of her westing led her to sail eastwards, away from the island, until the Andes were sighted. Despite this delay, which cost seventy or eighty lives, she was the first to reach that refuge, on 9 June, with the crew so weak that she could not come to a proper anchorage until the 11th, closely followed by the *Tryal*, which had 'escaped more favourably than the rest'—with 52 per cent dead. The *Gloucester* was seen on the 21st; she had lost three-quarters of her crew from scurvy, and it was nearly a month before the enfeebled remnant could bring her to harbour. Last to arrive, in mid-August, was the victualler *Anna Pink*, which had wintered comfortably enough in a little harbour south of Socorro.

The *Wager* never appeared; she had been wrecked on the Chilean coast. The crew raised sharply the point made by Roggeveen's men: the end of Navy pay meant the end of Navy subordination. The captain, David Cheap, a hot-tempered man, wished to seize a Spanish vessel with the boats and rejoin Anson at Juan Fernández, but the majority had had enough. There were violent altercations, and after Cheap had shot a trouble-making midshipman, mortally, he was in effect deposed, and most of the crew fell under the ascendancy of the gunner James Bulkeley, a man of great ingenuity as a sea-lawyer and of considerable powers of leadership. There were mutinies and false reconciliations, and eventually, after effusive farewells to Cheap, Bulkeley with eighty men set out for the Straits of Magellan.

Some died of privation, some were quasi-marooned, some were captured by Patagonian Indians but ransomed and pressed into service on Pizarro's *Asia*. Bulkeley and his main group, some thirty men, were hospitably received by the Portuguese at Rio Grande; they and a few others eventually reached England after the strangest of Odysseys. Meanwhile Cheap and his handful of loyalists, who included John Byron, the future circumnavigator and grandfather of the poet, reached Santiago after many extraordinary hardships and adventures among the Indians; they were received with kindness, and also came home.

No official charge of mutiny was laid against Bulkeley's group; he had cannily dedicated his exciting narrative to Admiral Vernon, very much out of grace with Navy officialdom but with a great populist reputation, assiduously cultivated, as the seaman's friend. A court-martial correctly exonerated Cheap for the loss of his ship, but proceedings against the mutineers would have brought out, officially, some stories damaging to the Navy's prestige. There were some awkward moments, but eventually Bulkeley was actually appointed to command a naval cutter; with his usual flair, he declined the offer as 'she [was] too small to bear the Sea'—and she promptly sank with all hands. For wild drama, or melodrama, very few tales of the sea can match this of the *Wager*.[12]

Anson in the South Sea

At Juan Fernández, Anson was in a very bad way indeed. In the *Severn* and the *Pearl* he had lost two of his major fighting ships, while the *Wager* had carried the ordnance and stores needed to attack Valdivia, his first target, or any other fortified place. Worst of all was the appalling loss from scurvy, deadlier to Britons and Spaniards alike than any human foe. Excluding the *Anna Pink*, which was broken up, he had three ships remaining in September 1741; they had sailed from England with 950 or 1000 men, of whom 335 were still alive: fewer than the *Centurion*'s normal complement of seamen alone. Far from being capable of the ambitious offensive of his instructions, Anson owed his escape from an encounter 'that could

Plate XVII. THE BURNING OF PAITA.   From the painting by Samuel Scott, by permission of the National Maritime Museum, Greenwich.

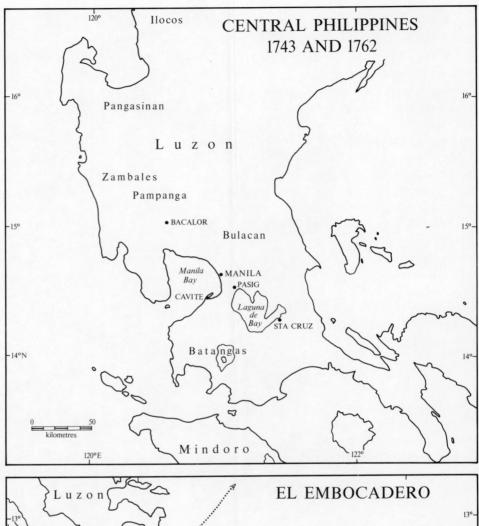

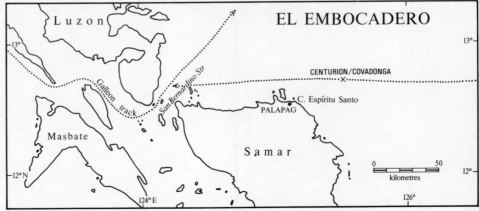

Figure 23.   CENTRAL PHILIPPINES 1743 AND 1762;   below, EL EMBOCADERO.

not but have been perplexing, and might perhaps have proved fatal' to mere chance. Peru had of course received early warning, following the failure of security before Anson sailed, and four well-armed ships (154 guns in all) were sent from Callao to look for him, three off Chile and one to Juan Fernández itself, where he found traces of its recent visit. When the enemy failed to appear, they left their stations in April; it was not so narrow an escape as Anson thought, but still he was lucky not to have run into a trap, with only thirty men capable of working and fighting his 60-gun ship.[13] As it turned out, he had over three months to recuperate and refit; if he could no longer conquer, he could at least despoil.

The powerful armament which had left England with lofty plans of conquest thus dwindled into a privateering venture of the old sort, although Anson made a more effective disposition of his force than had the old raiders. In September a couple of stray prizes were taken, one replacing the unseaworthy *Tryal*, and on the 19th Anson finally left Juan Fernández for Valparaiso and points north. Any attempt on Valdivia or Callao was out of the question, but there was always the old standby Paita. The *Gloucester* was sent to cruise off that unlucky little port, keeping out of sight of it, while the other ships swept up the coast. An Irishman from a prize taken near Lobos de la Mar told Anson that the *Gloucester* had been observed off Paita, where the corregidor was 'busily employed in removing the King's treasure and his own to *Piura*', but a rich Lima ship was about to sail for Sonsonate.

Although Paita was not completely surprised, there was scarcely any resistance, though next day (14 November) there was the usual show of force on the hill behind the town. The governor escaped (leaving his just-wed wife to follow in her shift) and disregarded attempts to treat for the ransom of the place, which was accordingly burned, on Anson's orders; in this desert climate, it was built mainly of cane, mud, and thatch (Plate XVII). He took care to spare the two churches and to treat his prisoners with great courtesy; the official account plumes itself with vast complacency on this novel form of psychological warfare. It had indeed the satisfactory result that those keen observers Jorge Juan and Antonio de Ulloa believed that the destruction of the town was unauthorised by, and unwelcome to, Anson, whose reputation as a chivalrous opponent still stood high at Paita eighty years later.[14] This final sacking of much-sacked Paita was in the classic tradition and a neat but, considering Anson's force, hardly a brilliant feat of arms against a practically open town.

Following the rules of the game, Anson sailed north and the Viceroy sent four ships after him, of course much too late. They were ordered to defend Panama, but Anson knew from captured letters of Vernon's ill-success at Cartagena and so went directly to Quibo to water and collect turtle. The next move was obviously for Acapulco and the Galleon. By early February 1742 Anson was cruising north of Acapulco; a boat sent into the harbour at night captured three Blacks from whom he learned that, as was suspected, the Galleon had arrived three weeks before he reached the coast, and was due to sail for Manila on March 3/14. Despite the well-spaced net thrown out for her, she did not appear—one of the squadron's smaller craft had been spotted, and she was held back—and Anson was considering an attack on Acapulco itself when he found that the régime of land and sea breezes would make a night surprise impossible. He had now been four months at sea since leaving Quibo, and was forced to put into Chequetan (Zihuantanejo) for water; he now wished only to get away from the Mexican coast, to avoid both its approaching storm season and an arrival on the Asian side after the onset of the westerly monsoon. The prizes were rifled and destroyed, the prisoners sent off in launches, and 'on the 6th of *May* we, for the last time, lost sight of the mountains of *Mexico*', in full expectation of meeting at Canton 'numbers of our countrymen ... [in] an amicable well frequented port, inhabited by a polished people', and that within a few weeks.

Anson's triumph

Anson had expected a crossing 'free ... of bad weather, fatigue, or sickness' and lasting some eight weeks; it was nearly sixteen before he saw land. He sailed nearly two months after the normal departure date of the Galleon from Acapulco, and it took seven weeks to get into the Northeast Trades, which proved unexpectedly weak and irregular. Early in the traverse the *Gloucester* sprung her mainmast so badly that it had to be cut down to a stump for a jury-mast; the *Centurion* had to run under topsails only, and even so lie-to at intervals to enable her laggard consort to keep touch; and scurvy struck again. Eventually the *Gloucester* was virtually dismasted; of her original company of 396, only ninety-seven remained alive, less than a third of them fit for duty, and on 15 August she was burned. The *Centurion*, herself in bad shape, was forced well north of Guam, and when on 23 August the Marianas were at last sighted it was at Anatahan (Fig. 8), where an anchorage was impossible; the ship was blown south and was unable even to send a boat to get coconuts for the sick. Her situation seemed desperate; she had been burying eight to twelve men a day, and even with the *Gloucester*'s remnant was so short-handed that the Commodore himself had to help with the hauling—'an occurrence of some novelty in the navy of the period.'[15]

Three days later, however, they were off Tinian, and from the Spanish sergeant in charge of a score of Chamorros jerking beef for Guam they learned that it was uninhabited, well-watered, and abounding in feral cattle, pigs, and poultry, as well as coconuts, citrus, and breadfruit. Even the official account takes on a romantic glow as it describes 'this delightful island' which 'had the air of a magnificent plantation', and which would have been missed had the *Centurion* not been driven north of her intended course for Guam. It was matter of wonder that so delectable a place should be uninhabited, though the tall foundation pillars of old Chamorro buildings showed that it had not always been so; but the Indians explained the Spanish policy of forced transfer to Guam—so that 'their remote situation could not prevent them from sharing in the common destruction of the western world, all the advantage they received from their distance being only to perish an age or two later.'[16] But Tinian's depopulation was Anson's salvation—his sick could recover in peace.

Their troubles were not over. The anchorage was poor, and when the *Centurion* with its skeleton crew was driven out of sight 'all, both on sea and on shore, [were] reduced to the utmost despair.' Anson, concealing his own fears, maintained that she would return, or if not make for Macao; to be prepared for the latter event, the small bark belonging to the Spanish party should be enlarged so that those on the island could rendezvous with the *Centurion* in China. Work began, the Commodore wielding axe and saw with the rest; but after nearly three hazardous and harrowing weeks the ship struggled back to Tinian. Three days later she went absent again, but briefly, and by 21 October all was ready for departure.

Many a commander, reduced to one leaking ship with a shaky mainmast and a depleted crew, would have made for Batavia and home. The voyage so far was a failure: the modest loot of the South Sea, the burning of Paita, were morally and materially damaging to the Spaniards, but a poor offset for the loss of at least three of His Britannic Majesty's ships—and hundreds of his too lightly expendable seamen. Anson was not willing to cut his losses; having missed the Galleon in the classic hunting ground between Acapulco and San Lucar, he determined to take it off the Philippines. First, however, it was necessary to refit in Canton River.

Anson reached Macao on 12 November, and naturally sought the advice of the EIC factors. Equally naturally, they advised the time-honoured, and time-devouring, approach through the Chinese 'Security Merchants' of the Hong. Anson held that as a King's ship the *Centurion* was not liable to harbour dues; there was no precedent, and his distinction was lost on the Chinese. The factors for their part were anxious to avoid any risk of disruption to their trade by forcing the issue on behalf of a warship, in a neutral port run by officials so jealously suspicious of affronts and indeed of any novelty in procedure. By parading his armament to local officials, threatening to go upriver in armed boats, and by dining (and especially wining) an important Mandarin, Anson at last got a licence to refit at Taipa, near Macao, where the port charges did not apply. Nevertheless, it was late in February 1743 before work started, and 19 April before the *Centurion* could clear from Macao.[17]

Although of course Anson gave out that he was bound for Batavia, the Governor of Manila had letters from Canton giving a good account of his proceedings, and indicating that he was likely to cruise for the Galleon.[18] A galleon and two galliots were despatched to Cape Espíritu Santo to escort the incoming *Nuestra Señora de Covadonga*, but these were so Spanishly dilatory that they were still well within the San Bernardino Strait nearly a month after her capture. While the *Covadonga* was still east of the Marianas her captain, Geronimo Montero, a Portuguese and 'the most approved officer for skill and courage of any employed in that service', had proposed to avoid those islands, where Anson might be waiting, and to mount the heavy lower-deck guns; his council of war rejected both these commonsense measures. On arrival at Guam (16 June 1743, N.S.) they had news of Anson's departure from Tinian with a wretched skeleton crew; the officers saw no possible danger, and Montero's renewed proposal to mount the guns was again rejected. Anson meanwhile had been cruising off Cape Espíritu Santo since 20/31 May (Fig. 23). He had only 227 men, including a couple of dozen lascars and Dutchmen picked up at Macao (the EIC captains of course 'could not spare' the able seamen he requested of them), while the *Covadonga* carried about 530 souls. Of these, however, only 266 were crew, half of them Filipinos, and the rest— passengers, servants, convicts—cannot have been worth much in a fight, while Anson had put his men through a crash course in both great guns and small arms. Despite patriotic British rhetoric, in everything but mere numbers the odds were heavily on the *Centurion*: she was the larger ship and much the more heavily armed, and morale was pitched in proportion to the rich booty in prospect.[19]

So superior was the *Centurion* that her officers were astonished that when the ships met on 20 June/1 July, the *Covadonga* made no attempt to avoid battle; Pascoe Thomas even hints that if Montero was not out of his senses he must have been in confederacy with Anson![20] It is most likely that he mistook the *Centurion* for a friendly ship from Manila until it was too late for evasion. The Spanish resistance was spirited enough for well over an hour, until Montero, by British testimony 'the life of the action', was badly wounded; then it collapsed. Besides weight of metal, the *Centurion* had technical gunnery advantages, and her superiority is shown by the casualty lists; British, under twenty, only two dead; Spanish, about 160, of whom sixty or seventy were killed.[21] After the *Covadonga* struck there was an affecting reunion; among her passengers was the Governor of Guam, who in 1707, at the battle of Almansa, had taken prisoner another veteran, Captain Crowden of the Marines, 'who after this long Revolution of Time, had turned the Tables on his then Conqueror.' How one would have loved to see these two old boys as they 'renewed their ancient Acquaintance'![22]

This was the first capture of a Manila-bound—hence silver-laden—Galleon, and the prize was rich indeed: nearly 1,315,000 dollars and 35,862 ounces of uncoined silver, some not on the manifests but in lumps disguised as cheeses. The total value, excluding cochineal and some other commodities, was about £313,000. With this booty, and an embarrassing number of prisoners (who had a dreadful journey in the holds, on a pint of water a day), Anson returned to Macao, which he reached on 11 July.

By threatening to hang the reluctant Chinese pilot, Anson took the *Centurion* above the Bocca Tigris forts, which were about 45 km from Canton and proved to be negligible.[23] His request for provisions was met with unusual promptness, so far as daily needs were concerned, but promises and contracts for victualling the homewards voyage were evaded, and he was told that the *Centurion* would have to pay port dues, despite her status as a King's ship. This was unacceptable, and the Commodore demanded an interview with the Viceroy himself. This was granted, after consultation with Peking, and in October Anson went upriver in his barge with as much splendour as he could manage: his men were fitted out with silver-trimmed uniforms—a naval innovation—and he was accompanied by the supercargoes of the English, Danish, and Swedish East Indiamen. There was of course more evasion and obstruction when he reached Canton, but luckily his men were able to give the Chinese much assistance in coping with a disastrous fire. This, and the impression made by probably the most heavily-armed ship yet seen in Canton River, 'an overmatch for all the naval power of that Empire', opened all doors. The interview with the Viceroy, an unprecedented event, was highly successful. Anson's main point—the exemption from dues—was granted; but it did not become the 'authentic precedent' on which he flattered himself.[24] However, he had broken down the barriers of Chinese protocol and enforced his views on the Viceroy, and British prestige stood triumphant, in European as well as Chinese eyes.

Fully refreshed and recruited—nineteen nations were represented in his final crew—Anson sailed from Macao on 13 December 1743: three months later, by which time he was nearing the Cape of Good Hope, four ships sailed from Manila to seek him off Canton River—as Fernández Duro remarks, 'A buena hora!'[25] The voyage home was uneventful until near the very end, when the *Centurion*, protected by a timely fog, sailed unknowingly through a strong French force in the English Channel. On 15 June 1744 she dropped anchors at Spithead, after a voyage of three years and nine months, the only ship of the original six to complete the circumnavigation. Anson had lost four men by enemy action, over 1300 by privation and disease.

The significance of the voyage

As the operation of formal war for which it was designed, Anson's voyage was a failure; nor was it, as has been absurdly claimed, 'the first naval expedition which ever crossed the Pacific Ocean.'[26] But in a war so far marked mainly by inefficiency and irresolution, the industrious valour with which Anson outfaced every difficulty was an inestimable stimulant to national morale. As a mere privateer-type raid, the cruise was a success: the total prize may have been nearly £500,000. Against this must be set the dreadful death-roll and the loss of three ships; but Pizarro lost nearly as heavily in men and more so in ships. The losses and the poor old invalids were forgotten as the treasure was carried to the Tower of London in a triumphal procession of thirty-two wagons, and Anson himself was exalted above Homer's Ulysses—

> Our second Drake, arrived on British ground,
> Requires no Pope his honours to resound.

The euphoria was marred by the inevitable bitter quarrels over promotions and prize-money; 'we had more terrible engagements in the courts of law than ever we had in the South Seas'.[27]

John Campbell saw the voyage as a glorious exemplar of what could and should be done if Britain were not to decline; a later judgement, more sober and more professional, is that this militarily inconsequential operation 'illustrates the conservative tendency of naval thought ... But it was the last of its kind ... the dissipation of naval strength in predatory voyages was to be relegated to the past.'[28]

Nevertheless, it played its part in modifying naval conservatism. Anson became an energetic and reforming First Lord of the Admiralty, and many of his reforms stemmed from the sad experience of his circumnavigation. They ranged from the introduction of copper sheathing, lightning-rods, and uniforms (but only officers, senior, for the use of) to a more systematic rating of ships, separating ships of the line from cruisers, and to the remodelling of the Marines, hitherto temporary *ad hoc* units, into a regular and permanent corps. The problem raised by the *Wager* mutineers was resolved: half-pay from the date of the wreck, but full discipline.[29] The greatly enhanced power and efficiency of the Royal Navy from the Seven Years' War onwards owed much to Anson's cool firmness in administration as in battle and tempest; ironically, there was not to be a deployment in force in the Pacific proper until the bungled fiasco of the attack on Petropavlosk in the Crimean War.

Strategically, there was a significant result for the Pacific. Anson stressed the need for a South Atlantic way-station other than some Brazilian port, and suggested Cowley's Pepys's Island or, more seriously, the Falklands:

it is scarcely to be conceived, of what prodigious import a convenient
station might prove, situated so far to the south-ward, and so near
Cape *Horn* . . . a voyage might be made from *Falkland*'s Isles to *Juan
Fernandez* and back again, in little more than two months. This, even
in time of peace, might be of great consequence to this Nation; and,
in time of war, would make us master of those seas.

So began the 'contention for a few spots of earth, which, in the deserts of the ocean, had almost escaped human notice, and which, if they had not happened to make a sea-mark, had perhaps never had a name.'[30]

The value of the Falklands as commanding the entry to, or exit from, the South Sea had been recognised by Jean Doublet in 1698; but we have now the germ of a persistent British interest. Anson himself in 1749 projected a British base in the Falklands, but this foundered in the face of Spanish protests; in 1764, however, the islands figure prominently in Byron's instructions for his circumnavigation, and his planting of a 'pritty little Garden' at Port Egmont (nine months after Bougainville had taken possession for France) was the first step towards the dangerous Anglo-Spanish crisis of 1770.[31] In the event, and after a long interval, the Falklands fell into British hands, although there was no strategic pay-off until the destruction of von Spee's squadron in 1914: a long time to wait for the vindication of Anson's insight, but a vindication nonetheless.

In the South Sea itself the immediate effect was to awaken the Spaniards to a sense of the urgency of securing the Falklands' opposite number in the Pacific, Juan Fernández. Jorge Juan and Antonio de Ulloa, two able young naval officers engaged on a geodetic survey in Quito, were recalled to Lima and sent to report on the Pacific coast and Juan Fernández, which they visited in 1743. Their reports were very thorough indeed, and left no doubt as to the parlous state of the defences from Guayaquil to Concepción; even Callao was vulnerable, and only Valdivia was reasonably safe. In particular, they stressed the strategic importance of Juan Fernández as a place of recuperation and a base for corsairs, strongly recommending its fortification. The disastrous Lima earthquake of 1746 made immediate action impossible, but the appearance of Anson's narrative in 1748 drove the lesson home. The island was occupied and fortified in 1750, and in the 1760s strengthened by the energetic and indeed expansionist Viceroy Manuel de Amat, who was also responsible for the Spanish expeditions to Tahiti and Easter Island. Nothing was known of this development in Europe; indeed, in 1756 Charles de Brosses recommended its colonisation by France. But eleven years later Philip Cartaret, calling for water in HMS *Swallow*, was astonished to find the Spanish colours flying over a fort with a score of embrasures. Rather late in the day, a dangerous gap in the Spanish defensive system had been plugged, as a direct result of Anson's voyage.[32]

The Commodore has even a place, rather a negative one, in the history of ideas. He provided the peg for an anti-Utopia, Coyer's *Supplement* to his voyage, deservedly less well-known than that of Diderot to Bougainville's; a mildly entertaining satire on the artificiality of French society, set in 'Frivola', an island discovered but concealed by Anson.[33] More to the point, the official account of the expedition gave a hint to Montesqieu, who called to witness 'le grand homme mylord Anson', amongst others, to support his scepticism as to the perfection of the Chinese polity. But it gave pain to Voltaire, who was shocked that 'the oldest and most polished nation of the world' should be judged by the rascalities of 'the populace in a corner of a province' (and yet, if one wishes to see how a house is really run, surely one goes in by the back door?).[34]

'From the China of the missionaries to the China of the traders, by way of that of the *philosophes*, such was the traverse made by the eighteenth century which, after having idealised beyond all limits, took to denigrating with an equal passion'; and in this reversal of opinion the record of Anson's transactions in the river of Canton played its part—it had a wider circulation than the business letters, in the same tone, of China factors. The polity of the Celestial Empire, as depicted by Jesuits and *philosophes* alike, was almost Utopia. Voltaire's 'the first nation of the world in ethics and the science of government' was now seen, in the actual working of one of its greatest cities, as a governmentally cumbersome and ethically corrupt despotism, and the Chinese themselves as industrious and ingenious, but over-subtle and yet at bottom stupid, 'polished but false, superstitious and ridiculous, as radically backward as fundamentally hostile to foreigners'.[35]

If Anson contributed to this long-enduring stereotype, he also—in European eyes—showed how to deal with its manifestations. Gunboat diplomacy was nothing new in Asian seas, but the Celestial Empire itself had always been treated with great caution and respect, except by occasional flyaway freebooters; never before had it been as one may say formally and officially affronted by an officer of His Britannic Majesty, or of any other European ruler. This of course cut both ways: if Anson, in Dermigny's phrase, 'made Sinophobia fashionable', what he prided himself on as firm but polite insistence on civilised procedures was to the Chinese the most uncivilised and vulgar insolence, and so contributed to their own equally denigratory stereotype of Europeans. The contempt, the reliance on a tough line with Orientals, set the tone for the habitual European approach in the next century, and beyond.

For all that, Anson's voyage itself was a great saga of human endeavour and endurance.

Dalrymple in Sulu

Anson's way had been the conventional one by the South Sea, in the old tradition of Westward Ho!; but it will be recalled that among the options considered in 1739 was an attack on Manila. This was discarded, but with the entry of Spain into the Seven Years' War (January 1762) the project came into its own. Although there was no direct connection between the taking of Manila and Alexander Dalrymple's immediately preceding activities in the Sulu Archipelago, the two together may be taken as opening the British 'Swing to the East'.[36]

The young Dalrymple, well-connected, able, ambitious, and enterprising, was marked for immediate advancement in the EIC service at Madras, but declined it in favour of an exploration of the commercial possibilities of the eastern seas beyond the sphere of tight Dutch control, to which he had been led by intensive study of the Company's archives and Spanish records. He was also inspired by William Wilson's round voyage to Canton in 1758–9. Wilson, captain of the East Indiaman *Pitt* and a close friend of Dalrymple's, found himself too late to reach the South China Sea before October, when the northeast monsoon sets in. South of the Equator, however, this winter monsoon swerves to blow from west or northwest, and Wilson took advantage of this to sail through the Java Sea and between Gilolo and New Guinea until he had reached out sufficiently east and north to make for Canton, passing east of the Philippines, sailing not into but athwart the northeast monsoon: a new route, with the sole disadvantage that it lay through little-known waters, studded with islands and reefs and in the Dutch sphere of influence.

The impression of Anson's spirited conduct at Canton seems to have worn off, and trade was subject to all the old frustrations; in particular, so long as Canton was the sole port of entry the potential market for woollens in northern China was virtually inaccessible, and at this very time efforts to gain entry into other ports were being firmly rebuffed. Yet Chinese traders swarmed in Manila, Batavia, and many other ports, and if their junks could be attracted to some entrepôt in British hands, Canton might be bypassed by a lively indirect trade. Dalrymple grasped the locational advantages of the Sulu region for such an emporium: 'A British settlement in the Sulu archipelago would overcome the human barrier to Anglo-Chinese trade, exemplified by Chinese officialdom in Canton, in the same way that Wilson's new route circumvented the physical barrier of the monsoons.' He had the ear of George Pigot, Governor of Madras, who authorised him to take the *Cuddalore* ostensibly to find a new route to China 'through the Molucca Islands and

New Guinea, that the China ships may avoid the danger in time of war of going through the Straits of Malacca'.[37] Dalrymple's sights were set on Sulu, which he regarded as a grey or neutral area, an independent state beyond any but sporadic Dutch interest, and clearly not under Spanish control (Fig. 24). But it is hard to understand how he could have failed to realise that to the Spaniards it was a most sensitive zone. The intermittent war with the Moros, nearly as old as the Spanish presence in the Philippines and to last nearly as long, was in full swing.

Zamboanga had been refounded in 1718 as a bar against the Moros and a base for Spanish raids; it was not as a rule very effective, Le Gentil remarking that 'the King's galleys are kept there when there are any . . .'.[38] In 1737 a formal, and equal, treaty was concluded with Sultan A'zim-ud-Din of Sulu, who pursued a pacific and pro-Spanish policy so far as to admit Jesuit missionaries; like some Islamic rulers of our own day, he went too far and too fast. His brother Bantilan led the reaction; A'zim-ud-Din fled to Manila and in time was baptised as 'Don Fernando', while Bantilan proclaimed himself Sultan with the most politic title of Muiz-ud-Din, 'Defender of the Faith'. The Spanish brought A'zim-ud-Din to Zamboanga in an effort to reinstate him, but arrested him for suspicious communications with the Sultan of Mindanao, and proclaimed an all-out war in which the Moros were to be extirpated or enslaved *en bloc*. This led them only to a disastrous defeat at Jolo itself in 1752, and the next year was terrible: Muiz-ud-Din's raiders ravaged all the Visayan coasts and even Zambales and Batangas on either side of Manila Bay; thousands were carried into slavery. In the last years of the decade, however, a more conciliatory Spanish policy restored a semblance of good relations.

Troubled waters indeed, and it is not surprising that Dalrymple hooked a prize. He sailed from Madras in April 1759, and after a voyage which took him to Cochin China and twice to Macao, reached Jolo in January 1761. Since on his return journey the *Cuddalore* was guiding four much larger East Indiamen through these hazardous seas, his stay was brief—only five days—but fruitful.[39] He was able to secure a provisional treaty of commerce and friendship, permitting not only a factory but also the right to buy land for plantations; and the British, but no other Europeans, might trade freely within the vague but extensive bounds of Sulu's dominion. The snag was in the provision, disapproved by the EIC Directors, that 'The English shall be assistant to the Sulus if attacked . . .'.[40]

Leaving his convoyed East Indiamen at Sumbawa, Dalrymple sailed north to Makassar, where the Dutch were unfriendly, and then to Zamboanga and a more surprising cordial reception: the Governor, a fellow hydrographer, gave him an introduction to his brother in Manila. Dalrymple, so notoriously prickly in later life, must have been capable of much charm; in Manila he managed to see A'zim-ud-Din and get him to countersign the treaty, while the Governor, Archbishop Rojo, was so forthcoming as to raise, later on, strong suspicions of his loyalty. Other Spaniards thought that Dalrymple's surveying of the harbour was 'sinister', being 'unused to such hydrographical zeal'; the line between hydrography and espionage is still sometimes blurred.[41] The *Cuddalore* was back in Madras by the end of January

1762, and Pigot lost no time in following up this striking initial success: by June Dalrymple was again on his way to Sulu, in the *London*.

News of war with Spain had not yet reached Madras, and Pigot relied on the doctrine of effective occupation, by which neither Spaniards nor Dutchmen could validly object to a British settlement. Dalrymple was however instructed to tread warily—enquiries from other Europeans were to be parried with the assurance that the Suluans had declared themselves free of all engagements to other states. The design was to secure the 'absolute cession' of some island, and Dalrymple's vision was of a free port drawing to itself not only the Chinese junk traders but the enterprising Buginese from Celebes (Sulawesi). This would gather together the exotic products from the eastern islands—birds' nests, drugs, dyes, trepang (sea-slug or *bêche-de-mer*), sandalwood, spices, all in great demand in China—while the junks, having entry into all Chinese ports, could carry British woollens to the cold north, and the sub-standard Indian cottons which the EIC often found on its hands could be unloaded in the islands, not to mention opium.[42] There would be a great saving in silver. The industrious Chinese would furnish the infrastructure of middlemen, artisans, and perhaps plantation labour. Sulu, accessible in either monsoon, lay central to Japan (through the Ryukyus), Korea, littoral China, Bengal, and New Holland (Fig. 24 inset)—as Fry points out, this was a dazzling prevision of Singapore.

On this second voyage Dalrymple reached Jolo in August 1762, to find a confused situation. Muiz-ud-Din had sent a peace mission to Manila, and plans were afoot to bring A'zim-ud-Din back, on a basis very favourable to the Spaniards.[43] Some of Dalrymple's chief Suluan backers had died in a smallpox epidemic, and matters were not helped by the non-arrival of a promised East Indiaman. These difficulties were smoothed over, and Dalrymple turned to his main objective, the 'absolute cession' of a base. On his way to Sulu he had secured from local chiefs Usukan Island and adjacent parts of Borneo, but his eye was fixed on Balambangan. This island had a fine strategic position—within the Suluese realm but far enough from Jolo itself and the main area of Moro or pirate raiding to avoid complications, and commanding the passage between Palawan and Borneo connecting the South China and Sulu Seas. In September the cession was negotiated and on 23 January 1763, on his way back to Madras, Dalrymple took formal possession.

In November 1762 Dalrymple learned from a Spanish ship off Zamboanga that Britain and Spain were at war, and on his return to Jolo in December that the situation had been transformed by the fall of Manila to a British force.

Manila taken

A week before the British declaration of war on 4 January 1762, Anson as First Lord put to the Directors of the EIC a proposal for an attack on Manila. By mid-January the Company's Secret Committee had acquiesced, grudgingly. The Directors feared disruption to trade, risk to their Indian holdings by the dispersion of forces, and vast expense, while Manila was 'of such infinite importance to the Spanish nation' that it could hardly be retained at the peace; but if HMG was bent on the expedition, the Company must have its share of the loot. 'Apprehending it will be His Majesty's pleasure' that any conquest would be put into their own hands, the Directors would co-operate. Accordingly Brigadier William Draper was ordered to proceed to Madras and organise the expedition, and George III's 'will and pleasure' coincided with the Company's demand.[44]

Draper, a scholar turned soldier, had spent a sick leave at Canton informing himself of the state of the Philippines, and had himself produced a plan for the reduction of Manila.[45] He reached Madras in June; the military men on the Madras Council were reluctant to spare troops, but Rear-Admiral Samuel Cornish 'scented prize before he worried much about the scent of blood', and Pigot, his appetite whetted by Dalrymple's success, was strong in support.[46] There were unpleasant wrangles over the sharing of prize, and the Council was inordinately jealous in asserting its claim to any conquests, though it did condescend to direct its agents to call Draper to their aid 'in all affairs of a military nature', when he would be allowed third place on the local council. Draper had only one King's regiment of 450 men —his own, the 79th, 'my tenth and indeed my only legion'—and 50 Royal Artillery, but the balance of his force was truly an infamous army—550 sepoys, against 2000 promised, and the rest included 200 French deserters, many of whom of course redeserted to their more natural allies: 'such banditti were never assembled since the time of Spartacus'.[47] Fortunately he was able to draw 820 seamen from the strong squadron (ten ships, 558 guns, 4120 men) under the tough but co-operative Cornish. The total landing force was only 2000 men, but it was enough.

Draper and Cornish were fortunate in their opponents, and especially in the interim Governor, Archbishop Manuel Antonio de Rojo y Vieyra, a man 'not fitted by age, or status, or personal qualities' to face any sort of crisis.[48] Their main body left Madras on 1 August—ten days before Habana surrendered to the British after a tough resistance. That city had received two years' warning of what might happen, but no news of the war had reached Manila; nonetheless, there had been rumours from Armenian merchants and warnings from friars in China, but these were as little heeded as Dalrymple's recent actions. On 22 September the whole fleet entered Manila Bay 'with great serenity'; Rojo expressed pained surprise and offered humanitarian help if needed. He was presented with a demand, made in accordance with 'the principles of moderation and humanity so peculiar to the British nation', for the surrender of Manila and its dependencies.

The defences were in the usual wretched state; there were only about 500 poor troops, of the 131 guns over half were defective, and there were only eighty Indio gunners. Rojo tried to play for time to enlist a few militia and call in more Indios, but on the 24th Draper, bypassing his original target of Cavite, landed two miles from Manila itself. The high surf offered a fine opening for a counter-attack, but none came, and the British seized an abandoned advanced fort which made an excellent base. The only resolute action on the Spanish side was a wild assault by a thousand ill-armed Pampangans, whose courage gained them nothing but a tribute from Draper. On 6 October the walls of Manila were stormed with little loss, and the demoralised Rojo surrendered the citadel at once. In twelve days, at the price of about fifty dead, the British had become masters not only of the capital of the Philippines but of their thoroughly subservient Governor. But on the 3rd, much against the wishes of Rojo, the Audiencia had sent out of the city one of their number, Simón de Anda y Salazar, with a commission as Lieutenant-Governor and a provident supply of blank but sealed official paper. The game was just beginning.

Anda was a man of ability and vigour, and when at the end of October Rojo was forced to announce the surrender of the islands as well as Manila, he lost no time in repudiating the Governor's authority as well as his actions, proclaiming himself Governor and Captain-General. Indeed, while Rojo did try to parry some British measures with legalistic demurrers, he was so much their puppet that he denounced a protest by the Cabildo and the religious against the general surrender, as a matter improper to be discussed on the birthday not of Carlos III but of George III![49] The natural result was a rallying to Anda, and the British soon found that 'they were not the masters they thought they were'.

The Sangleys were naturally enough on the British side (though some were willing to smuggle deserters out of Manila in sedan-chairs), and attempts to win over the Indios by relieving them of taxes and labour burdens had some success, notably in Ilocos where an anti-Spanish rising had broken out before the fall of Manila, and its leader, Diego Silang, before his assassination, had formally accepted George III as his king.[50] Nevertheless, Anda had Bulacan and Pampanga (Fig. 23) solidly behind him, and was able to set up a foundry and arsenal at his headquarters, Bacalor. He gained Indio support by dismissing some Spanish alcaldes and remitting tributes and services—a point not lost on Rojo, who denounced Anda's backers as 'common, stupid, and ignorant rustic people'. Disgust at Rojo's pusillanimity brought some influential and competent Spanish officials into Anda's camp; and he had the sinews of war. On the very day that he surrendered the citadel, Rojo signed orders to the officers of the Galleon *Filipino*, just arrived at Samar from Acapulco, to hand over her silver to British commissioners as part of the Manila ransom. Alleging that they did not know, officially, of the fall of the city, the officers resolved that the silver should be lodged in a hastily constructed fort at Palapag—for safety. By the time the British reached the *Filipino* her treasure, over 2,300,000 pesos registered, was indeed safe—in Anda's hands.[51]

With these material resources, and the zealous support of the Augustinian and Franciscan friars in the villages, Anda launched a very effective guerrilla war; places as near Manila as Pasig were kept in constant alarm by hit-and-run raids, and in December Indio archers inflicted a sharp little defeat on a small British column near Santa Cruz. On 2 December 1762 Draper, who was returning to India, formally handed over to Dawsonne Drake as Deputy-Governor for the EIC. Drake faced, inadequately, a formidable combination of problems: the struggle against Anda, the restoration of trade, the gathering of the ransom, and not least the keeping of the peace between the Company's servants and the King's military men, and within both groups.[52]

Drake cannot be said to have succeeded in any one of these tasks. According to Draper, he reimposed the taxes on Indios and Sangleys 'with additions, so that the whole island is now against us'. With much effort and intimidation, 508,000 dollars were collected towards the ransom, the balance being met by bills against the Madrid Treasury; this figure, or even the nominal ransom of 4,000,000, contrasts nicely with James Naish's 1740 estimate that at least 10,000,000 could be extracted from Manila.[53] As for Anda, Drake's offer of 5000 pesos for his capture alive was naturally countered by Anda's of 10,000 for Drake alive or dead, and Rojo's proclamation of him as a rebel was met by a virulent paper war. The honours were with Anda, who has a fine polemical turn of phrase—'very great was the effort of your archbishop to efface the image of your Majesty'—though one wishes he had not made an issue of the festival when the ladies were allowed to use the Archepiscopal privy.[54]

More serious was Anda's real war. Even after news of the cessation of arms reached Manila in July 1763, he refused to desist from hostilities, since Drake refused him recognition as the legitimate Governor, which would mean that Rojo's concessions, including the ransom, had no validity. In February 1764 Anda's bands were infiltrating the suburbs of Manila, and not until confirmation of the definitive peace and the arrival of a new Governor in March did he lay down his arms. Almost simultaneously, Drake was forced to resign by the dissidents on his Council. The permanent retention of Luzon had never been seriously contemplated, and in any case was barred by the provision of the Treaty of Paris for the restitution of conquests unknown in Europe at the time of its signing. It fell to Alexander Dalrymple, on his way to Sulu, to take the responsibility for the formal handing over of Manila. The new Governor being ill, perhaps tactfully, early in May 1764 Anda entered the city, to receive a hero's welcome from the Spaniards and a banquet from his British foes.

Materially, the Galleon *Santissima Trinidad* (taken by accident) and her 2,000,000 pesos formed the main item in the rewards of conquest; the balance of the ransom was never paid, and ten years later the EIC was still trying to collect £140,000 from the Crown for its expenses. Morally, the prestige gained by the easy capture of Manila was largely squandered by ineptitude, corruption, and outrageous factionalism in its administration. As so often, the Spanish loss was greater than the British gain; despite Anda, the Indians of the Philippines now 'judge[d] that the Spaniards are now more than the Indians, but much less than the other nations.'[55] Nevertheless, the British were transients, and Draper's exploit ended in Drake's fiasco. In Sulu, however, there was unfinished business, to which Dalrymple and the Company now turned.

Balambangan and 'Felicia'

In all the confusion of the conquest, the old Sultan A'zim-ud-Din, 'Don Fernando' in Manila, had not been entirely forgotten by either party. If the British were not to retain Mindanao, Sulu might well be a good alternative, and accordingly Drake

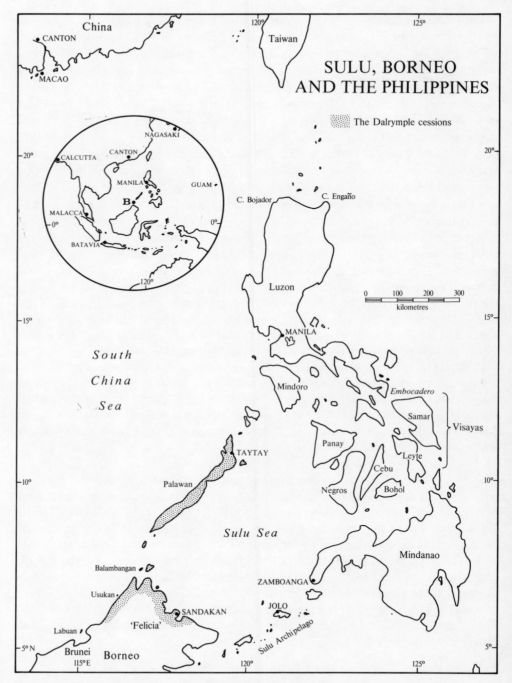

Figure 24. SULU, BORNEO, AND THE PHILIPPINES.   Areas of cessions approximate, status of Palawan north of 10°N doubtful. Inset: 1000 miles (3220 km) around Balambangan (B).

secured from the Sultan a treaty providing for exclusive trade privileges and sites for forts or factories. Rojo protested: he had a prior treaty to much the same effect. When Dalrymple arrived in Manila, he thought Drake had gone too far; better to back Sulu not so much as a British protectorate, with its risks of ulterior involvement in Suluese quarrels, but as a buffer, and to concentrate on more solid cessions in Balambangan and parts adjacent.[56]

In the summer of 1764 Dalrymple took A'zim-ud-Din to Jolo, where he was reinstated and a new treaty negotiated; Muiz-ud-Din had opportunely died and his son A'zim-ud-Din II was compliant. Dalrymple had brought with him as the nucleus of his colony many Manila Chinese, anxious to escape Spanish wrath, and (without authority) some EIC sepoys. The Dutch had been showing an inconvenient interest in the area, and he decided that more than Balambangan and his earlier rather slight acquisitions from Bornean chiefs was needed; he obtained from Sulu the island of Palawan, or at least its southern half, and over against it almost the same territories as those taken over by the British North Borneo Company in 1877–8 (Fig. 24). Nominally this was a sale rather than an outright cession, and, doubtless to respect Suluese and perhaps European susceptibilities, government was vested in A'zim-ud-Din I's son Sharaf-ud-Din, Dalrymple's 'Dato Sarapodin'.

On the map this was a fine acquisition: a flank-guard to the traditional route to Canton through the South China Sea, a way-station on the *Pitt*'s new route, a barrier against piratical incursions from Mindanao, a spoiling thrust between possible Spanish and Dutch pretensions. Balambangan might become 'the Capital of Oriental Polynesia', backed by 'Felicia' in northern Borneo.[57] Moreover, while the spice trade was no longer the dominant it had been in preceding centuries, it was still worth entering; with the help of the Buginese from Celebes, the unexploited islands east of the Moluccas and beyond Dutch control might be tapped, and plantations might be established in Balambangan itself and in Felicia.

It was in pursuit of this objective that, when the Balambangan settlement was actually formed, Thomas Forrest was sent to search for cloves and nutmegs in places where the Dutch 'are, or affect to be strangers'. Forrest sailed in the *Tartar*, a Suluese prau of ten tons, both the craft and the crew (only the mate and the gunner were Europeans) being chosen to attract as little notice as possible. He owed much to the expert adviser who sailed with him, Tuan Hadji, a man 'of rank, education, and good behaviour', and old servant of the VOC who had travelled widely in the eastern islands. In a very remarkable voyage (1774–6), which found a few nutmegs and of course raised Dutch suspicions, Forrest circumnavigated Gilolo (Halmahera) and reached Dorei Bay, on the east of the Vogelkopf in New Guinea.[58]

In 1765 Dalrymple returned to England to press his case with the EIC Directors. There had been much backing and filling in the six years since Pigot had given Dalrymple his clearance, and the Company was inclined, though not decided, to cut its losses in Sulu. It was in a somewhat critical position, since exaggerated reports of great revenue surpluses from Bengal had led to a bull market in its shares; dividends were forced up from 6 to 10 per cent and there were demands for 16. To meet such increases there would have to be a crippling withdrawal of specie from Bengal, which in fact was short of coin. A plausible solution lay in an extension of the China trade, but based not as heretofore dominantly on silver, but rather on the export of Indian commodities—cottons and so on, and opium—to the eastern islands, where they could be exhanged for the exotic products in demand on the Chinese market—excluding birds' nests, which the Suluese providently reserved to themselves. This aspect of the Company's affairs brought Dalrymple's scheme back into favour, and in July-August 1768 it was formally adopted by the Directors.

In their new enthusiasm, they neglected to inform the Government—that of Grafton and North—until October. The dispute with Spain over the Falklands was sharpening; the administration was anxious to resolve it pacifically but was under heavy pressure to take a harder line, and an intrusion so near the Philippines was a most unwelcome complication; it expressed its extreme surprise that the EIC had taken an island 'without the least information of any other right ... than that of Utility'.[59] The Directors apologised for their presumption, but in view of the striking commercial prospects they held forth, the ministry accorded them a cold acquiescence: the Company could go ahead, but the Government intended to keep its distance from any adventurism.

The continuing international tension however meant further delay, and the next move was merely another reconnaissance, by Captain Savage Trotter of the *Tiger*, who visited Sulu in 1769. He warmly commended Dalrymple's choice of Balambangan, but his further advice, received in London in June 1770, was that 'If ever the Honourable Company should adopt any views of sharing the Moluccas with their present Possessors' [!], then Bachian, only recently subdued by the Dutch and still restive, was the proper place. This was too adventurous for the Company, and his proffer to protect the Sultan of Sulu against all other Europeans was too adventurous for the Government. By this time Spain and Britain were very close to war over the Falklands, and George III and North, both basically pacifist in this crisis, wanted nothing that might look like a provocation to the Spaniards. There is in fact a constant interplay of governmental concern with developments at the south Atlantic gateway to the South Sea and with those at the other end of the 'Magellanic diagonal', the classic Trade Wind route which amounted to a geopolitical spanning of the Pacific.[60]

With the settlement of the Falklands crisis early in 1771 the way to Sulu seemed clearer, but the Government was still wary; it refused the EIC's request for a recommendatory letter from King George to the Sultan of Sulu, and warned strongly against aggression on any Spaniards who might be found on Palawan.[61] The Directors nevertheless decided to proceed, cautiously; but the enterprise was not to be conducted by the man best fitted to do so, Dalrymple, nor was the brief history of Felicia to be felicitous.

Dalrymple indeed was not only the obvious choice but the Company's actual choice for the command; but he would not 'act in a mode not entirely agreeable to myself'—precisely the stance which prevented him from sailing with Cook. In the Balambangan case he had much reason for his stand. He wanted no hampering Council, with its open invitation to faction, and if his financial terms were too stiff for the Company to accept, at bottom they were more sensible than its offer to him, which was based on 'the vicious system of remuneration which was the bane of India—a low salary with wide opportunities for indulging in private trade'. Dalrymple even offered to 'devote my whole life' to Balambangan and 'look upon it as my home' (there was no Mrs Dalrymple to consider), which would have made him an intriguing link between Francisco Vieira de Figueiredo and Rajah James Brooke.[62] The final break came in 1771, with his dismissal from EIC service; the actual leader of the expedition to establish Balambangan, John Herbert, promptly proceeded to vindicate Dalrymple's judgement.

Herbert arrived at Balambangan in December 1773. His sole positive achievement was the despatch of Forrest on his voyage, and even this may have been a device to get an honest man out of the way while Herbert and his Council used the EIC's ships, men, and money to promote their private ends,[63] which went so far beyond the norms of illicit private trade as to become sheer swindling: as the Directors wrote, 'Your proceedings . . . exhibit a scene of irregularity, duplicity, and presumption not to be equalled upon the records of the Company': a large testimonial indeed! In Sulu itself Herbert seems to have concentrated on the traffic in arms, gunpowder, and opium, with predictably calamitous results for the Visayans. However, he fell foul of the Suluese, and in 1775 they overran the settlement: 'Within a few hours the results of fifteen years' planning had been destroyed.' Herbert escaped with his personal belongings but minus the accounts, and tried to start again amongst the friendly Bruneis, traditional rivals of Sulu, but was soon dismissed from EIC service. An attempt to secure reparation for the Company's losses was adroitly rebuffed by the Suluese, and apart from a reoccupation of Balambangan in 1803–5, when neither Spanish nor Dutch susceptibilities needed consideration, British expansion in northern Borneo was checked until the cession of Labuan by Brunei in 1848.[64]

Dalrymple's great vision had foundered in incompetence and corruption; but the basic idea survived. This was the replacement, or at least the large-scale supplementation, of the traditional basis of the China trade—the exchange of silver against tea, porcelain, and silk—by a system of multilateral exchanges, 'a multiple trading association, within which British woollen and metal manufactures, Indian piece goods and opium, and China tea and ceramic wares could be given unrestricted circulation, [and] enormous profits would accrue to the British as the dominant partner.'[65] An essential component of such a system was a free port as entrepôt somewhere between India and China, and well placed to attract the local traffic of the eastern isles (Fig. 24 inset). Raffles was the heir of Dalrymple, Singapore the splendid reincarnation of squalid Balambangan.

This was for the future; in the interim, the EIC found the solution to its problem in the China trade in one word—opium. And in the Philippines, the shock of the fall of Manila led to a search for new solutions breaking away from total dependence on the Galleon; the islands became a field for experimentation under the aegis of the Bourbon Reforms.

Chapter 12

MANILA: THE LAST GALLEON

... striking is the correspondence of the feet of
this symbolic figure of the Hispanic World, which are
these Philippine Islands (whence, Señor, we offer it),
with the feet of the chaste Judith. For as that which
most ravished the soul of Holofernes, to his total
perdition, were Judith's sandals, so Lucifer is most
terrified by these Islands, as the sandals of the
Hispanic World ... this Colossus as beautiful as superb,
as lovely as firm-based, although in Regions so distant
from the Court, and the Presence of their King ... these
Islands maintained with as much security, and governed
with as much good judgement as vigilance ....

A dream of Empire

In 1759, the year of Carlos III's accession, Manila, with only a few hundred
Spaniards, could boast of two Universities, Jesuit San José and Dominican Santo
Tomás.[1] San José's celebration of that auspicious event included the public defence
of nine theses and ninety propositions by the theology student Don Vicente de
Memije; he had been a naval purser and a captain of marines, and his theses had an
appropriate nautical bearing. Longitudes should be reckoned westwardly—
cosmographical, geographical, and hydrographical evidences favoured this, and also
the westwards course of empire, from the Chaldeans to the Spaniards;[2] and, it goes
without saying, Holy Writ. All this argues for the opening of navigation between
Spain and the Philippines by Cape Horn, which in turn will open up the unknown
austral regions for the Faith. The theses are accompanied by a most magniloquent
dedication to D. Carlos, the Magnanimous, and a charming and instructive icono-
graphic map (Plate XVIII).[3]

The Catholic Religion, the soul of the Hispanic World, is shown as a queenly
figure surrounded by symbols of the Crown and the Faith; her crowned head rests
on Castile, her feet are firmly planted in the Philippines. The jewel on her breast is a
compass rose hanging from a chain of galleons, and the staff of her banner also does
duty as a prime meridian, graduated in degrees of latitude. The Americas form her
royal mantle, and her flowing skirts cover the Pacific. Their folds represent the
routes of the South Sea, and by a refinement of conceit these are hatched to indicate

---

Vicente de Memije, Dedication to Carlos III of his *Theses Mathematicas ... en qve el
Globo Terraqveo se contempla por respecto al Mundo Hispanico* (1761).

Plate XVIII. AN ICON OF EMPIRE. Vicente de Memije's 'Aspecto Symbolico del Mundo
Hispanico'. For comment see text; by permission of the British Library, London.

the directions of the prevalent winds. As D. Vicente complacently remarks, all this is done without shifting anything from its proper geographical position; he reinforces his point by a more sober map of the geographical aspect of the Hispanic world.

He has done his homework: Chirikov's discoveries are shown and named, and the New Guinea-Solomons area is in accordance with informed cartography of the day, such as Robert de Vaugondy's maps in de Brosses's *Histoire de Navigations aux Terres Australes* of 1756. Memije links New Zealand with Van Diemen's Land rather than Le Maire's Staten Landt, and gives plausible outlines for the Reyno del Austro or Terra Australis. More significant, however, is the 'Route which one can follow by Cape Horn for the Austral Kingdom and the Philippines'. The text, a lyrical paean to the virtues of D. Carlos and the glories of his Empire, looks for the extending of the royal mantle to 'the unknown Kingdom of the South: so that you should take under your sovereign protection its unhappy inhabitants and make them happy with your most just Laws, and more, the celestial light of the Gospel.' The Spanish Pillars must be placed *Plus Ultra*, farther into the South Sea, and to this end we of the Philippines 'are adding to these Theses the new course, by which these Islands [may] communicate with Spain in one single voyage.'

A single navigation between Spain and the Philippines, cutting out the breaks of bulk at Vera Cruz and Acapulco and the laborious portage between them (and the middlemen's interests in Mexico) was indeed much talked of as a desideratum; even as a supplement, let alone as a replacement, it would break the Galleon's stranglehold on the Philippine economy. But it would also be a gross breach with tradition; this lapse apart, nothing could better typify Old Spain, the ghost of Carlos II still walking under Carlos III, and nothing could be less in touch with reality, than Memije's vision of the Hispanic World as one of great well-armed fleets, strong fortified places, wise and incorrupt tribunals, universities with chairs in all sciences, spread round the globe. Those feet so firm-planted in the Philippines were soon to crumble as feet of clay. Memije's public examination was in April 1761; his audience included Archbishop Rojo, who within eighteen months would become the puppet of the heretic conquerors of Manila.

Magnificently backward-looking as Memije's temper and motivations may seem, the Cape Horn proposal, made in the interests of the Faith, carried a hint of menace for the Galleon trade. More realistic commentators were in the field. Memije hardly appears a modern man; but his auditors almost certainly included one who was, the Fiscal (Attorney-General) of the Audiencia, Francisco Leandro de Viana, whose office gave him an inside view of Filipino problems. Although he had signed the surrender, he rallied to Anda, and after the retrocession in 1764 was prominent in the rethinking of 'post-war reconstruction'. The Bourbon Reforms were at their take-off point, and a comfortable remoteness 'from the Court, and the Presence of their King' could not shield the Philippines from their impact. The probably unconscious threat in Memije's project was to be replaced by open hostility to the conservatism of the City and Commerce of Manila; within twenty-five years the immemorial total dependence on the Galleon was being greatly modified, and the mere raft for barter, silver against silk, was becoming an economy.

Cadiz versus the Galleon

Between 1705 and 1714, the Galleon trade suffered two major wrecks and two poor fairs at Acapulco; nevertheless, the economic revival from the seventeenth century trough, which began about 1660–80, did not peak until 1716–20; in the first quarter of the new century the Philippines ceased to be a drain on the Royal Treasury. This happy state did not last long; there followed a recession which lasted until mid-century.[4] The very basis of the trade, the export of Chinese silks to New Spain, was challenged by Peninsular interests.

Reading Alvarez de Abreu's massive *Extracto Historial* of the proceedings in the Council of the Indies on 'the manner in which the Commerce and Trade of Chinese Textiles in New Spain' should be carried on, one has a feeling of *déjà vu*: the City and Commerce of Manila, still a single entity, is ranged against Seville and Cadiz (the latter from 1717 the seat of the Casa de Contratación), and all the arguments of a hundred years before are endlessly refurbished. In 1712, investigations into the Customs accounts at Acapulco, 'a confusion the depth of which cannot be ascertained', showed at least that the permissible return of 600,000 pesos on the annual cargo from Manila was sometimes exceeded by as much as 2,000,000 and that the fraud was so extensive that little could be done about it. Across the Ocean, Governor Fernando de Bustamante attempted to suppress graft and to collect the Crown's due by somewhat arbitrary methods, which involved imprisoning the Archbishop of Manila; the Governor and his son were murdered by a mob, and the efforts of his successor to find those responsible failed. Once more nothing could be done because 'in fact almost all the powerful elements in the colony' were implicated.[5]

Given such openings, the Andalusian ports attacked, alleging that despite the ban on the heretically woven silks of China, illicit imports, 'so dexterously packed by those infidels', were pouring into New Spain, to the ruin of Spanish silk-workers and traders to the Indies. In 1718 a decree, repeated in 1720 over Mexican protests, banned even raw silk imports; the Galleon was to be confined to porcelain and to local products such as sugar, inferior textiles, and spices. To the Manileños, this was a mockery; on their own, the islands (still undeveloped after 150 years!) could not produce 300,000 pesos' worth of saleable goods annually, and with a rising population (882 citizens in 1722, against 400 in 1702), their *permiso* should really be increased to 500,000, to bring back a million. They would obey the decree, but must ask permission to leave the Philippines.[6]

In 1724 the ban was lifted, and then for a dozen years the Council considered alternative plans while Andalusia and Manila exchanged rebuttals and demurrers. Manila claimed that she really needed a return of at least 1,200,000 pesos—that is, doubling the permiso—and loudly trumpeted that the proposed restrictions could extinguish the Catholic Religion in these distant provinces, a catch-cry in which the Clergy joined with City and Commerce. Cadiz retorted that this argument 'has always been the Achilles to oppose the just representations of the commerce of España', that the Manileños were given over to sloth, and that if they were really so anxious to preserve the Faith, they would not be so familiar with the heathen Chinese.[7] Neither side seems aware of a main factor in Manila's difficulties—the rise in Chinese prices due to the increasing demand from the European companies at Canton; this was the take-off period of the great China trade.[8]

However, the example of the European chartered companies doubtless suggested the idea of using such an organisation for direct trade between Spain and the Philippines, which was first seriously projected in 1732. José Patiño was behind the plan, but it was seized upon by Manila to show that Spain could not supply the American market; the company would have to obtain Chinese silks, and in doing so hand over more silver to heretics than ever the Galleon did. European powers trading to Canton were not anxious to see any change which might increase competition in that port, and in face of their hostility the project was dropped.[9]

In a final bid to cut the knot, Cadiz offered Manila the entire spice trade to New Spain, in return for a complete ban on Chinese silks; it protested that the new company was already inactive and that 'in any case Cadiz would feel responsible for not allowing that company to injure Manila's spice trade'. Manileños might be forgiven for raucous laughter at this generous offer, which was doubly worthless: the trade had never been forbidden to Manila anyhow, and was scarcely existent —of the eight flotas to New Spain between 1733 and 1776, only two carried spices—one cargo of cinnamon and one of cloves—fifty quintals, 2300 kg, of them![10] In the end the Manileños had their way; in 1734–6 it was ordained that the Galleon trade should carry on as before, with the important gain that the permiso was lifted to 500,000 pesos, to bring in 1,000,000 on the return.

The Galleon now seemed safe, and the Philippines could remain 'nothing more to the Spaniards than a kind of floating dock upon which to trans-ship bales of Chinese silk from junk to galleon.'[11] All the old abuses persisted, and in 1737 the City and Commerce secured the dismissal of the two officials appointed by the Governor to keep a watch on the lading of the Galleons. The formation in 1769 of a Consulado was the recognition of the fact that the old identity of City and Commerce had broken down, since the actual consignors on the Galleon were now a small ring of moneyed men, buying up the *boletas* or permits of the smaller fry. Although the rights of non-mercantile groups (officials, widows, the *obras pias* such as the Misericordia) were safeguarded, the management of the trade was now formally in the hands of a few consuls. This put it on a more businesslike footing, but provided the conservatives with a very stout bastion for 'a long and stubborn defense of the monopoly'.[12] Thus the Consulado resisted, in the long run successfully, the adoption of proposed new routes for the Galleon. One of these was southwards between Mindanao and New Guinea, a harking back to the early attempts to find a return route; the more practicable of the two was up the west coast of Luzon and northabout into the Pacific past Cabos Bojador and Engaño (Fig. 24). In the opinion of expert pilots the latter was 'undoubtedly safer and easier than that by the San Bernardino Strait', providing sailings were made before the typhoon season opened in July—but as it avoided passing by a host of islands, it was obviously 'less convenient for adding to a ship's unregistered cargo.'[13] That was enough for the Consulado.

Projects and trial runs

The fixation on the Acapulco trade 'nipped in the bud the economic development of the Philippines . . . It is difficult to conceive of a type of trade more restful to the trader, and more useless for the country'.[14] Le Gentil makes the same point, two hundred years earlier: the Philippines have better resources for export production than has Java, Manila is as well located as Batavia, the Indios make superb fabrics with abaca fibre, why not with cottons? Because they are instructed in sloth by the Manileños, whose 'ambition lags from galleon to galleon and goes no further.' Indeed, the accused gloried in their indictment. After fifty years of 'Bourbon Enlightenment' the Manileños, irritated or frightened by the innovations forced upon them by reforming governors, could protest magnificently:

> The Spanish conquerors of these islands did not leave Spain to take up
> the plough in the Philippines; much less did they undertake so long
> and unknown a navigation to set up looms and transplant new fruits.
> At the first insinuation of this, they would have left the islands . . .
> That which led those great men to abandon home and country and to
> face so many dangers was their interest in gold and spices . . . The
> natural inclination of men to seek their fortune by the shortest road
> led them to migrate with the sole aim of freighting the Philippine
> galleon . . . the only base and foundation of the subsistence of this
> commonwealth.[15]

Plans for developing the islands invariably proposed using a route by the Cape of Good Hope and/or Cape Horn, and with one exception the agent of development was to be a chartered company. The exception was that put forward in 1759 by Nicolas Norton Nicols, English by birth but a naturalised convert and a fine specimen of the eighteenth-century projector at his most meticulously absurd. He put his faith in plantation cinnamon and secondarily in pepper. 'España might with as good reason send to Olanda [Holland] to buy her wine as her cinnamon' (which was virtually a Dutch monopoly, from Ceylon), and since there must be 4,000,000 Spanish subjects who drank chocolate sixty-four times a year, they would need 400,000 pounds of cinnamon to flavour it. Production in the Philippines could undercut Dutch prices by up to 50 per cent, and if the Maritime Powers resented Spain profiting from her own resources, she could 'limit the commerce of Francia, Inglaterra, and Olanda whenever she desires, without cannon-ball or gunpowder, by the prohibition of silver alone.'[16]

Don Nicolas need not be taken too seriously; Viana, writing after the catastrophe of 1762–4, gives a much more thorough analysis of Philippine perils and potentialities. It could be argued that it would be better to cut losses and abandon these costly islands; but then the English, already 'arrogantly establishing their factory in Sulu', would seize them and could then 'without difficulty make themselves masters of the Californias', which in turn could be connected, by land if not by a Northwest Passage, with their Mississippi frontier, recently gained by the Treaty of Paris (1763)—a remarkable prefiguration of American Manifest Destiny in the next century.[17] Such are the perils, but a determined policy could reduce all Indian villages (in one year!) and then subjugate Mindanao and Sulu; the costs would eventually be met by increased numbers paying tribute and by enhanced taxes.[18]

Beyond this, a properly organised company could not only achieve a great saving in transport costs by using the Cape route but could develop Philippine resources. These are particularly good for ship-building: worm-resistant timber; canvas, hemp, coir for sails and cordage; pitch. Anchors and arms could be produced from the very rich iron deposits and mines of lead (exploited by Anda at Bacalor) and copper; there is also gold. Agricultural possibilities include cacao, coffee, wheat, rice, tobacco, silk mulberry, sugar, indigo; there is much sulphur as well as semi-precious stones and herbal drugs. All these could find good markets in China and India, and the Indios provide an abundance of cheap labour, easily trained to form excellent artisans and seamen.[19]

The agency for this great work is to be a government-backed company which might even take over much of the administration of the Philippines. Opposition is to be expected from the bureaucracy, but this can be overcome by good regulations well enforced—the old will-o'-the-wisp of the Spanish reformer!—and the taking up of shares by the highest nobility. As a final grace-note, should the Cape route prove impracticable, the company could use the Isthmus, with factories at Panama and Puerto Bello; if it prospered sufficiently, it might seek 'the easiest mode of joining the two seas . . . by water'.[20]

The first attempt at direct trade between Cadiz and Manila, virtually simultaneous with Viana's memorial, was made by the warship *Buen Consejo* in 1765–7. She had a French captain and pilot, and according to Le Gentil (who was aboard) they were very nervous when passing the Sunda Straits, which they did under French colours and cleared for action—so much for Norton Nicols's naïve idea that the Spaniards could use an island in those Straits as a way-station. For obvious reasons, the ship was very grudgingly received in Manila—she was promptly nicknamed *Mal Consejo*, 'Ill Counsel', and her victualling was impeded. Whatever its trading success, the voyage aroused British jealousies, on the ground that the exclusion of British trade from Spanish America was by way of being an equivalent for the restriction of Spanish trade in the Orient to the Galleon; and once more we find the Falklands, as the entry into the Pacific, linked with Manila as the goal. Despite persistent Manileño hostility, there were some fourteen similar voyages up to 1783. Some of these were financed by the 'Cinco Gremios Mayores de Madrid', a consortium of five guilds, which in 1780 opened trade with Canton; but they were seduced into the easy profits of the Galleon, and in 1783 loaded at least a fifth of its cargo.[21] All this activity, as well as a trade mission to southern India in 1777, prepared the way for the long-heralded Real Compañía de Filipinas (RCF).

An important restraint on economic activity was the paucity of the Spanish population, in large part transient, and its overwhelming concentration in Manila. Even this problem was linked with the Galleon monopoly: so long as 'A dozen merchants in charge of the *obras pias* control[led] the mechanics of this system',[22] there could be no inducement for many Spaniards to come to this hot and humid end of the earth; yet without such an influx little improvement was likely. The Sangleys of course provided artisans and dominated internal trade, but official Sinophobia led to restriction on their entry even before the shock of the British attack: Governor Pedro Manuel de Arandía (1754–9) carried out notable military reforms (their effect was lost in the confusion of Rojo's disputed succession) but refused admission even to Chinese iron-founders, and tried to supplant Chinese retailers by organising a joint-stock company to supply Manila. Anda, Governor in 1770–7, was preoccupied with both aspects of the demographic problem; he sought a solution in expelling the Sangleys and bringing in new settlers, who were to be encouraged to go into the provinces to take over domestic trade. Some useful miscegenation resulted, but although by 1788 there were only 1500 Chinese left around Manila, most of them at least nominal Christians, the basically Spanish population grew very slowly.[23]

However, there were several efforts to promote a development along the lines suggested by Viana, notably under the aegis of the enlightened Governor José de Basco y Vargas (1778–87), who on his arrival announced an ambitious development plan and in 1781 founded the first 'Sociedade Económica de Amigos del País' outside Spain herself.[24] Apart from some Indio production of gold, the only serious mineral exploitation was that of the Santa Inés iron mine, not far from Manila, which had a chequered career. Initial development in the 1750s foundered on Arandía's refusal to let in Chinese technicians, the works were razed by Indios during the British occupation, and although Governor Anda relaxed his anti-Chinese stance, not much was done until Basco arrived. A limited output of ordnance material and farming implements was then achieved, using Chinese techniques.[25]

More success attended agricultural experiments. The high hopes from cinnamon were never realised; thousands of trees were raised, but no way was found to get rid of a bitter gum in the local bark. Pepper and nutmegs had no more success. Indigo, started by Norton Nicols and Francisco Xavier Salgado in the 1760s, was quite successful in the long run. It had to cope with the competition of an inferior local variety produced by Indios under missionary guidance, and with the hostility of the Consulado, which refused to give it cargo space on the Galleon; however, the RCF took it up and attained an export of about 16,000 kg in 1790, and indigo remained an important commodity well into the next century.

As for fibres, around 1760 Salgado was producing cotton cloth for sails and uniforms, and some of his cloth was even exported to Batavia; but the British broke up his looms for firewood. A new start was made in the 1780s by the Sociedad Económica and the Compañía, and although Basco's attempts to introduce

European hemp and flax were total failures, there was soon a brisk internal trade in fabrics made from abaca (*Musa textilis*); this 'Manila hemp', used mainly for ropes and cables, was to be the leading Filipino export for much of the nineteenth century.[26] The Philippines were well placed to supply the big Chinese market for cottons, but there was also a large local demand for the raw fibre; although the export of cotton pieces became a principal base of the RCF's prosperity, nothing like the objective of cutting British India out of the Canton market was ever attained. The RCF also tried its hand at disseminating the silk mulberry, distributing some 600,000 saplings in 1793; but most of them failed and production was never on a large scale.[27] It had much better success with sugar, but the rise in exports probably owed more to the opening of the port of Manila than to the RCF's experts from Cuba.

Tobacco was an old-established crop—in 1641 Governor Corcuera sent two boxes of cigars to the Viceroy in Mexico—and was very widely grown by the Indios, especially in Cagayan and Pampanga, sometimes to the neglect of other cropping. Basco introduced a state monopoly: except in the Visayas, tobacco could be grown only in specified areas, and everywhere the leaf could be sold only to the government, which manufactured the famous Manila cigars and sold them for export as well as locally. The fiscal results were very showy, and despite its cumbersome and costly administration and its vulnerability to corruption, the monopoly soon enabled the Philippines to make a direct contribution to the Madrid Treasury and in time came to cover half the colony's budget; 'this costly and wastful, but absolutely certain source of revenue' was not abolished until 1882.[28]

Viana had been vindicated: hapless or halting as these beginnings mostly were, they laid the foundations for an economic diversification which was to stand the Philippines in good stead when the Galleon trade came to an end.

Galleon versus Company

The Real Compañía de Filipinas, chartered in March 1785, was the direct heir of the Caracas Company, then facing liquidation as a consequence of the opening of 'free trade' to the Americas—that is, trade open to most Spaniards, not just the Andalusian cliques, but not free trade in the modern sense. A large proportion of the new company's initial stock was represented by transfer from the older venture. Despite opening applications for nearly five times the nominal issue, eventually only about 6,600,000 of the authorised 8,000,000 pesos were subscribed. Of the 32,000 shares, 3000 were reserved for Filipino investors; it is significant, though not in the least surprising, that not one was taken up. In contrast, the Indian communities of New Spain were induced to invest nearly 100,000 pesos.[29]

The RCF was to have an initial monopoly of trade between Spain and the Philippines for twenty-five years, whether by the Cape of Good Hope or by Cape Horn; but to protect Spanish markets in the Indies against direct Asian imports, South

American ports could be visited on the outward voyage only. Trade with China was to be open to all, and Manila was to be an open port for ships of strictly Asian nations, carrying their own produce only. Local interests were to be protected: one-fifth of cargo space on RCF ships was to be reserved for Filipinos sending island products to Spain, one-third of the crews were to be locally recruited, and 4 per cent of profits were to be applied to Philippine economic development. The Acapulco trade was to continue, and neither the RCF nor its employees were to share in it.

Despite these soothing provisions, the shock to Manila was terrible. The RCF was to be allowed to ship 800 tons a year of Asian goods into New Spain through Vera Cruz; the continuation of the Galleon trade was perhaps ominously *por ahora*—'for the present'.[30] The announcement of the formation of the Compañía was therefore received 'with enormous hostility', and the Consulado took only five days to send off the first of many lamenting protests. They fell on deaf ears; Governor Rafael Maria de Aguilar was blandly instructed 'to extinguish rivalries' between the rivals in such a way that neither should suffer injury or prejudice. Since Aguilar thought that the RCF had 'immensely improved the lot of the islands, dragging them from the oblivion in which they lay submerged', the Manileños had little chance.[31]

The RCF began reasonably well with ten round voyages in 1785–9, though the obligation to call at Manila added 25 to 40 per cent to the cost of voyages by the Cape to Indian or Chinese ports and so kept profits down to 14 per cent. In 1790, however, it was sensibly decided that Cavite was on the way to Canton but not to Calcutta, and the direct trade between Spain and India became the RCF's most profitable line. From a Pacific point of view the most significant aspects of its operations are its already noted contributions, quite in the modern manner, to Philippine internal development; its trading to Peru, a reprise on a limited scale of the French activities in the Spanish Succession War; and its role in opening the port of Manila and furthering the decline of the Galleon. These indirect results transcend any formal success in its operations, which had to face many vicissitudes arising from shifts in government policy and from the almost incessant wars after 1793.[32] The Company could also play a negative role itself; it had been granted the privilege of importing Chinese mercury, and sabotaged an elaborate scheme for bartering California sea-otter skins for quicksilver (and extending Spanish colonisation beyond California to Nootka on Vancouver Island), by first insisting on taking over the project, and then reneging before the uncertainties and risks.[33]

The competition between Galleon and Compañía was direct from the start. In 1786 the Consulado for the first time made effective use of an augmentation of the permiso to 750,000 pesos, allowed in 1779; in the next year the first RCF Asian cargo reached Vera Cruz. The Mexican market was glutted; the Galleon was suspended in 1788, but the Acapulco fairs of the preceding and the succeeding year were failures.[34] By 1804, three Galleons had been lying idle at Acapulco for up to three years, and complaints to the Crown were useless. The RCF did not propose the abolition of the Galleon, but it got permission, as a wartime emergency measure, to trade directly from Asia to America, and some of its ships used the new port of San Blas, opposite the Tres Marias, as a way-station. By the end of the century Lima could be called 'the market of Peking'.[35]

There were of course more general factors in the dwindling of the Manila-Acapulco trade, but Cheong seems beside the point in saying that the Real Compañía was not among 'the real enemies of the galleon interests' but rather the 'revolution of Western ideas of trade and political events'. The RCF was the most active agent in this revolution, so far as the Philippines were concerned, and the three specific factors Cheong mentions—diversification of the economy, opening of Manila, direct Spanish-Asian trade—were all in large part the work of the Compañía.[36]

Consulado and Compañía were indeed able to agree on one measure—the opening of the port of Manila. The free access of Asian vessels granted by the charter proved ineffective, because the 'nations properly Asiatic' had insufficient shipping. Despite fears that the privilege might be used for the dumping of goods not saleable elsewhere, the port was opened to European shipping in 1790. Of course only Asian goods were to be admitted, but it is unlikely that this restriction was taken very seriously on the spot; certainly Nathaniel Bowditch in 1796 seems to have found no impediment to the sale of Madeira wine and Salem-made compasses, and had offered his cargo to Governor Aguilar and the RCF. The greatly increased movement of the port, and the boost in exports of sugar and indigo, led to a prolongation of the concession, and Aguilar thought that in three or four years the islands would be 'el imperio del universo'.[37]

The last Galleon

It was not to be. This 'conquest of the Philippines' by Cadiz was caught up in the great fission of the Napoleonic wars and the revolution of the Americas which also 'smash[ed] the venerable trans-Pacific link of the Galleon'.[38] In 1796 Godoy's Spain joined forces with revolutionary France; by 1810 the RCF had given over its operations in the Philippines, where agriculture and industry had been 'reduced almost to a nullity'. But in 1814 the Manila authorities opened the port to all nations without restriction, and 'soon the deserted bay was crowded with shipping from all parts.' There was a strong revival of export production, which enabled the Philippines to stand on their own feet after the breaking of the link with New Spain, soon to become the United States of Mexico. The Consulado's archaic reliance on the Galleon had been refuted by events which also swept away its thrusting rival. The RCF did indeed drag on a shadowy existence for two decades after the end of the wars; about 1820 it claimed to have made over fifty voyages to Asia and more to America, but the temper of the times was against commercial privilege. Fernando VII's famous annulment of all the acts of the liberal Cortes was held not to apply to matters of trade and navigation, and in 1834 the Real Compañía de Filipinas was formally dissolved.[39]

The Galleon trade had predeceased it. Acapulco was under attack by Mexican insurgents in 1810–11 and 1813; it is reported that an incoming Galleon expecting a fair found instead a siege, and put back to San Blas.[40] The town was burned by the rebels in August 1813; two months later, at the instance of the Cortes, Fernando VII abolished the Manila–Acapulco line.

By this time the Galleon's track in the North Pacific, solitary for so long, was but one among many; since the Nootka crisis of 1790, Spain was being squeezed out of the once-Spanish Lake, and her cumbrous monopoly had yielded to the freest of free enterprise—that of the fur-traders across to China and the Yankee skippers who scoured the oceans and islands for cargoes of occasion, changing ships as land-travellers might change horses. Honolulu was already on its way to becoming a cross-roads of the Ocean, Sydney an entrepôt for the south. In this new Pacific there was no place for the hidebound conservatism and bumbling inefficiency of the Galleon. Yet, with all its corruption and its cost in human lives, this was the end of one of the greatest sagas of commerce under sail.

By one of history's touches of sombre poetry, when the last Galleon cleared from Acapulco in 1815 she bore the name of *Magallanes*.[41]

Chapter 13

CALIFORNIA: THE LAST ENTRADA

The whole matter consists in restoring our commerce with the
same courage and perseverance which the foreigners display . . .
it cannot be denied that our nation has devoted very little
attention to that most useful study, the science of commerce . . .
the elevated and magnanimous royal soul of our beloved King and
sovereign Don Carlos III (whom may God preserve) and his zealous
ministers . . . will hasten with suitable remedies to check the
ruin of our dominions, which had its origin in the great amount
of illicit commerce of the foreign nations. Perhaps they will
form an entirely opposite idea from that of other times,
regarding the conduct of our commerce. . . .

On the other side of the Ocean from Viana's Philippines, and long before the
accession of Carlos III, Jorge Juan and Antonio de Ulloa had carried out their
thorough and incisive survey of the administration, resources, and defences of the
Spanish holdings from Panama to Chile (1735–44); and in the year of Viana's
memorial, José de Gálvez began his tempestuous visitation of New Spain. These
were evidences of a new temper in Old Spain itself, and one which was to have a
critical impact on the Spanish Pacific. Carlos III and his 'zealous ministers' undertook measures of economic and administrative reform which achieved a good deal
of success: 'the ruin of our dominions' was more than checked, until the tidal waves
unloosed by the French Revolution and Napoleon's usurpation washed away all
bulwarks. If Don Carlos and his ministers did not, in Viana's words, recast 'the
conduct of our commerce' on lines 'entirely opposite' to those of Carlos II's day, at
least the system of Seville—or rather, after 1717, of Cadiz—was subverted in
favour of a loosening of the old commercial regulations, a relaxation which, if very
far from the classic Manchester meaning of 'Free Trade', was also very far from the
constrictions, as entangling as concertina wire, of the ancient Andalusian monopoly.

This chapter and the next will endeavour to outline changes in the Spanish
Pacific polity in this period of the Bourbon Reforms, reserving for later discussion
the more narrowly politically motivated expeditions of the 1770s from Peru to
Tahiti, of the 1770s and later from New Spain to Alaska. These more properly
belong to that great opening of Oceania which begins with Byron and culminates
in Cook, and its aftermath, which are intended to be main themes in the next
volume of this work. But something must be said of the Reforms in Spain itself, by
way of providing a setting for the changes which they produced in 'the Indies'—a
term which Spaniards, Creole and Peninsular, were rapidly dropping in favour of

Francisco Leandro de Viana, 'Memorial of 1765', in Blair & Robertson
XLVIII.206, 336–7.

'America'; and this conforming to general European usage was itself a change of intangible but psychologically profound significance, a symbol of a new entity.

The Bourbon Reforms

The advent of the Bourbons meant that 'a European concept of life now attempted to modify and even supplant the Spanish mentality which had been molded by the Counter-Reformation',[1] to break down the separatisms of the historic kingdoms surrounding Castile, to promote a more pragmatic and forward-looking approach to national problems—an emphasis on what might rationally be expected to work, not on what might be in accord with the workings of an idealised Golden Age under Philip II.

Although in later life both Philip V and his successor Fernando VI lapsed into melancholia almost as hapless as Carlos II's, and at times into outright madness, both were well-intentioned monarchs, and the impetus given by the French advisers of the Succession time and by Alberoni was never quite lost.[2] A new breed of administrators was growing up; the cumbersome Councils, efficient engines of procrastination, fell more and more into suspended animation while the real work was increasingly done by 'specialised persons held directly responsible to the king', that is through a ministerial rather than a conciliar system. At a lower level, the supervision and co-ordination of provincial administrations were improved, at least in theory, by the introduction of the French system of multi-competent intendants.[3]

'The reign of Philip V was the golden age for the foundation of privileged companies', which began to erode the Andalusian monopoly; it is significant that the most successful had no connection with Andalusia—the Caracas Company, based on San Sebastián, which rehabilitated Venezuela, and the Royal Trading Company of Barcelona (1756), which rehabilitated the Antilles. So far as there was a Spanish bourgeoisie (as distinct from a middle class of officials, professional men, and retailers), it was peripheral, practically confined to a handful of ports.[4] Some initiative came directly from the Crown, which set up factories for Court luxuries (porcelain, tapestries) and armaments, and to exploit the tobacco monopoly; but it also gave support, on the whole discriminating, to entrepreneurs. From the 1730s Catalonia began to build up a cotton piece-goods industry which by the end of the century would be second only to England's. Internal customs barriers were lowered, and a start was made on the desperately needed improvement of roads and communications.[5] All this took place against a background of demographic recovery, the population rising from somewhere around 6,000,000 in 1700 (much less than that of the sixteenth century) to about 10,500,000 in 1800, with the increase more marked in the littoral regions.[6]

Much had already been done, and more had been foreshadowed, when Carlos III left the throne of Naples for that of Madrid in 1759. The new king was a much stronger personality than his predecessors, shrewder and more hard-working, and despite early mistakes such as bringing in Neapolitan advisers and moving too quickly, he became a good judge of men.[7] Although many of his agents, at all levels, were impressed by Enlightenment ideas and ideals, so that Spain became far more open to external influences, there was little of an over-riding ideological program: rather an intelligent pragmatism. Very little was done, for example, towards agrarian reform—that would have been a far too dangerous tampering with the foundation of society. The Church was kept in its place, but then that had ever been the concern of the most pious absolutists, and a sincere Catholicism was found quite compatible with a judiciously selective use of infidel knowledge, though the great *Encyclopédie* itself was normally banned.[8] Absolutism remained absolute, and the objective was neither welfare nor, for its own sake, progress, but a more powerful Spain. 'In effect, Spain drained the Enlightenment of its ideology and reduced it to a program of empirical reform within the existing social and political order.'[9]

In the 1750s, under Fernando VI, there had been a distinct *rapprochement* with Great Britain, but two years after the accession of Don Carlos he agreed to join France in the Seven Years' War. Like Alberoni and Isabel Farnese forty years earlier, Carlos impetuously misjudged both his own strength and his enemy's; yet, apart from Choiseul's seductive and Pitt's provocative diplomacy, there were some objective grounds for Spanish participation. British dominance in the trade from Cadiz, which in Spanish eyes stemmed from unequal treaties, was a constant irritation; to the old British encroachments in Honduras were added new ones in Georgia; and the existing naval war led to outrages on Spanish shipping. The fall of Canada destroyed the balance of power in North America—Carlos III said it made his blood run cold—and Britain's conquests in the Antilles bade fair to give her an overwhelmingly strong position on the approaches to New Spain and Tierra Firme.[10] And this position might well be used not only for a vast increase in contraband but for active aggression. Moreover, at no time during the century did British promoters and publicists show much restraint in discussing the ways and means of aggression upon Spanish America.[11]

Intervention, however, was immediately disastrous: Habana, Manila, Florida fell to the enemy, and this last was not returned at the Peace of Paris (1763). If the Empire was to be protected, clearly much more in the way of administrative and military efficiency was needed, and that meant economic development: 'Defence demanded revenue; revenue demanded reform.'[12] The work of reconstruction was carried on with more vigour, foresight, and stamina than in the preceding reigns. It is significant that the first of the 'Economic Societies of the Friends of the Country', the Sociedad Bascongada, was founded in 1764–5.

The stirring of the Indies into more vigorous life in Carlos III's reign was unquestionably in response to perceived and in fact genuine geopolitical threats:

> Spanish authorities spent almost fifty years after Utrecht fiddling
> with changes in the obviously inadequate trading and administrative
> system. It took only three years, once the British had seized Havana
> and Manila simultaneously in 1762 . . . to begin a series of changes

> long contemplated and tenaciously resisted by entrenched groups
> among the Spanish elite at home and in the colonies.[13]

At the extremities, the Russians from the north were to be forestalled by advance into California; in the south, the elevation of Buenos Aires from a disfavoured outlier into the capital of the new Virreinato del Río de la Plata was designed to counter the menace of British activities in the Falklands and those of their Portuguese clients across the estuary in Colonia do Sacramento, and was followed by a major and (at last) a permanently successful offensive against that outlier.[14] What began as a provisional military arrangement succeeded so well that it became a permanency. Both San Francisco and the Viceroyalty date from 1776, a year of destiny also for Britain's Thirteen Colonies; but while Spanish California never amounted to anything much economically, the rise of Buenos Aires and the associated policy of *comercio libre* ('free trade') had profound effects on the economic orientation of the Pacific littoral.

Despite a new and only modestly successful military intervention in the American War (1779–83), Spain at the death of Don Carlos in 1788 was far stronger and more prosperous than she had been for at least a century and a half. A striking index of this recovery is that in 1784–9 Spain herself produced 45 to 50 per cent of the goods exported through her ports to America, against a trifling percentage around 1700; and the historian William Robertson, alarmed at her inroads into her own trade, called for 'the most vigorous efforts, of the nations now in possession of the lucrative trade which the Spaniards aim at wresting from them.'[15] *Cet animal est très méchant, quand on l'attaque, il se défend. . . .*

This achievement was greatly facilitated by a striking revival of silver mining in New Spain, if indeed such a revival were not a *sine qua non*. A new phase of territorial expansion, in Chile and beyond the northern borders of New Spain, extended effective Spanish occupation of the Pacific shores over 82 degrees of latitude, from San Francisco to Chiloé. The new Viceroyalty in La Plata brought serious loss to Peruvian economy and prestige, but strengthened Spain's economic and strategic hold on the southern marches of the empire. Finally, and perhaps most significant of all, the introduction of 'free trade' spelled the final end of the system of Seville and Cadiz.

This did not mean the end of economic domination by the Peninsula, rather a new beginning. As in Spain itself, the objective of the reforms was simply to increase the strength of the Spanish Crown; the great inspectorial visitations of José de Gálvez in New Spain and José Antonio de Areche in Peru had as their main task the improvement of the revenue, and the tobacco monopoly, hardly a progressive measure, was a most useful tool to this end. It is even plausible to see 'comercio libre' as 'one of the great misnomers of history', giving the Americans 'neither commerce nor freedom', but containing 'built-in safeguards for peninsular monopolists' and forming one wing of a conscious tightening of metropolitan control, a new imperialism more efficient than the old. The other wing was the new administrative organisation of *Intendencias* under officials directly paid by the

Crown, a system much more modern than that of the old locally-based *corregidores* and *alcaldes mayores*, local district officers dependent on what they could screw out of their Indian charges. In theory, and to some extent in practice, the *intendentes* would be much less likely to slide into easy-going corruption and savage exploitation of the Indians, and many of them did a good deal for the better governance and development of their areas; but the criterion was nearly always that of the centre, not the localities.

Comercio libre did get rid of that old reproach that Spain could not furnish the Indies with their needs, and would not let other nations do so; trade increased mightily, contraband fell off. But in many areas this meant the glutting of markets and the ruin of local consumption industries. To the ruling circle, this was as it should be: as a Viceroy remarked, 'The day [the Americas] can supply all their needs themselves, their dependence will be voluntary.'[16]

New Spain: the mining revival

Mexican mining fared badly during the long depression of the seventeenth century; in New Spain 'this crisis lasted from 1653 to 1689; in Peru its sharpest phase began only in 1680.' That this was truly a 'century of depression' may be arguable, given for instance the active cultural life of the capital; but there is no doubt as to the decline in silver output, whether this be ascribed to a catastrophic fall in available Indian labour or to the 'absurdly simple' reason that the Crown diverted Almadén mercury to Peru, where it still took a 'Royal Fifth' against only a tenth in New Spain.[17] In the next century the tables were turned; the Bourbon reforms were underpinned by the great recovery in American silver output, basically from New Spain. Tea sold by the EIC increased nearly tenfold between 1760 and 1800, and until Pitt slashed the duty in 1784, even more was brought from China by other national companies—Swedish, Danish, French—which contrabanded it into England on a giant scale; and tea still needed silver.[18] For Britain, the cheap textiles of the Industrial Revolution and the opium of India were overtaking silver in the Chinese market; other nations, and notably the rapidly rising Yankees, had not these resources. The Americans soon supplied their lack with furs and ginseng from the Pacific Northwest, but 'Western Europe was experiencing a silver famine in order to fill the Chinese vacuum ... this could only be satisfied by American silver coming in through Spain.'[19]

> During the eighteenth century, silver production in New Spain
> showed a continuous [upwards] trend ... each decade, with the single
> exception of the 1760s, registered an increase over its predecessor.
> Moreover, this expansion was internally engineered; unlike its
> nineteenth century counterpart, it did not depend either on foreign
> technique or foreign capital. Nor was it, as in the sixteenth century, a
> spontaneous boom consequent upon new discoveries. Many of the
> old minefields, such as Zacatecas, Real del Monte, and Guanajuato,

continued to number among the leading producers until the end of the colony.[20]

By 1725 Mexican remittances to the Madrid Treasury far outstripped those from Lima, and (part cause, part consequence) mercury shipments from Almadén were almost uninterrupted for half a century after Utrecht, save in the war years of the early 1740s. By 1759, however, there was some faltering, only 70 out of 112 mining camps being in production.[21] After the Seven Years' War, British power north of the Caribbean and the Gulf of Mexico was no longer offset by French Canada, the safety of the Spanish empire depended more than ever on the health of Mexican mining, and Carlos III's government took the problem firmly in hand.

But official action would have been of little help had there not been already a strong tradition of enterprise in the great camps of the north, the domain of a frontier society much more vigorous than that of Peru. Its magnates were not particularly welcoming to innovation, but they thought big, and the technical achievements of their engineers were remarkable: amongst others, a shaft of 530 metres, the deepest pit in the world, and a drainage adit 2405 metres long. Great horse-drawn whims gradually took over, in the larger mines, from the murderous long ladders up which the ore had to be carried on men's backs. The mineworkers, largely mulattos and mestizos, formed a labour aristocracy, mobile and paid well, in part by shares of the ore, though this privilege was gradually lost after the Gálvez *visita* of 1765–71.[22]

This visitation or inspection of the realm by José de Gálvez was intended to improve the revenue yield of New Spain in all fields, and as we shall see Gálvez was a prime promoter of northern expansion. His activities included devastating attacks on the corruption in the Customs at Vera Cruz and Acapulco, and the firm establishment of the tobacco monopoly, which produced excellent fiscal results at the price of severe restriction of the area under the crop and some consequent depopulation of the Pacific littoral on either side of Cabo Corrientes.[23] He also organised, with great secrecy and efficiency, the highly unpopular expulsion of the Jesuits in 1767, and repressed the resulting disorders.

Although the 1760s did see some decline in mining, this was soon checked. The Visitor's first step was to reduce the cost of mercury, now in better supply owing to thorough reconstruction at Almadén; in 1767 the price was cut from 82 pesos per quintal to 62, and then in 1778 to 41; consumption rose by 40 per cent and there was a marked fall in the proportion of silver produced by the less efficient smelting method. Tax concessions were also granted, and tax exemptions or even direct subsidies for high cost or high risk but promising ventures.[24] Later, as Minister for the Indies, Gálvez introduced a more rational and streamlined mining code which seems to have reduced litigation, always a menace to the brisker entrepreneurs; but the credit bank set up by his new mining tribunal was a disaster, so recklessly and corruptly managed that 'Possibly ... the court's net effect was to divert capital from mining and instead to lay the foundation of the Mexican national debt.'[25]

Another Gálvez initiative had mixed results. Huancavelica mercury mining was in full decline, Almadén shipments could be interrupted by war, plans to get mercury from China in exchange for sea-otter pelts failed, and European opinion was in favour of smelting as against mercury amalgamation, although the latter was much less demanding of fuel. Anxious to bring the best of European expertise and technology to bear upon Mexican mining, and very strangely oblivious of the utter lack of forests in most of New Spain's mining regions, Gálvez tried to foster a turn to smelting until, luckily, the Viennese Baron Ignaz von Born discovered a long wished-for amalgam process which would use much less mercury (it had in fact been discovered, and forgotten, nearly two centuries earlier, in Peru!). In 1785 Gálvez commissioned Fausto de Elhuyar to investigate the 'new' method, and, in the next year, to introduce it into New Spain.[26] However, after prolonged trials even one of its German sponsors admitted that the Born process was not so good as the old patio, at least under Mexican conditions, and other attempts at technical improvements had little success. The most notable achievement of the Elhuyar mission was the founding in 1792 of the Royal College of Mining in Mexico City. This well-planned institution was praised by the great Humboldt, who had begun his career as a trained Inspector of Mines; but while it did produce some admirable experts, it was perhaps of more significance as a general modernising influence, a symbol and a centre of the Enlightenment approach.[27]

The government's economic incentives, rather than its institutional or technical innovations, seem to have been the main factors in the mining revival. Its success was striking: 'Mintage quadrupled from 6 million [pesos] in 1702 to 24 million in 1798 ... The one mining camp of Guanajuato equalled the mintage of the entire Viceroyalty of Peru, or of La Plata.'[28] Alongside this mining resurgence was a steady growth of population, white and Indian and mixed, and a general expansion of economic activity. Cotton, leather, tobacco, and ceramic workshops flourished, and the export of raw cotton and sugar through Vera Cruz was increasing. The second export, after silver, remained cochineal, and this came mainly from Oaxaca on the Pacific side.[29] Mexico City itself contained much squalor but was by far the largest and finest capital of the New World; the somewhat bizarre Baroquery of the seventeenth century was fading before the rays of Enlightenment. This was the 'apogee of New Spain', when Mexico meant 'much more than that name evokes today', since her frontiers were in Asia (economically), in Alta California, and on the Mississippi.[30] Backed up by the upwelling of so much new treasure, Spain was able to regain in 1783 the strategically almost vital Florida on the Atlantic flank of North America, and on the other side of the continent to occupy, for the first time, the littoral of Alta California from San Diego to San Francisco.[31] This, the most important strictly Pacific activity by Spain in the century, involved the building of a naval presence, perhaps one can hardly call it a naval power, in the North Pacific, based on the new port of San Blas.

Gálvez and the Californias

Kino had established that a land link between Sonora and Baja California existed, and this seemed important in view of the delays and hazards of crossing the Mar

Vermejo in the wretched little local schooners—even much later, the first seven months of 1771 saw the loss of five craft on the voyage from San Blas to Loreto, some 750 km, and a sixth was blown nearly to Panama and took 201 days on the passage. This was an extreme case, but the loss of a ship a year was normal, and even the short run from Guaymas, as a rule only a day or two, might take a month or more.[32] Kino's explorations never met up with Salvatierra's in Baja California, and no use was made of the land route. There was hardly anything to use it for: the Jesuits maintained their fourteen missions in the barren peninsula and looked askance at the few prospectors for mines or pearls; their aim was a little Paraguay, with their charges safely cocooned against the corruption of the world. Kino himself had expansionist ideas, which may have influenced Alberoni in the issue of a remarkable directive of 1716, looking to settlement beyond the Gila and the Colorado and to a colony on the Pacific, linked with the Philippines; but it was opposed by his brethren of the Society, and nothing happened. Over against Baja California, in northern Sonora, Indian troubles even led to some recession from Kino's mission frontier.[33]

Nevertheless, there was always the fear that the long empty littoral might attract undesirable neighbours for New Spain: the traditional rivals, heretic Englishmen coming by the South Sea or the Northwest Passage, or Frenchmen overland from the Mississippi-Missouri to the Colorado headwaters; in the early 1750s, before the fall of French Canada, the latter seemed the most pressing threat. The next decade saw a new and perhaps more dangerous menace—Russian expansion down the coast from Alaska. In 1757 the Venegas/Burriel *Noticia de la California* sounded a general warning; its demonstration of the strategic value of the region was much appreciated in Britain. There was even an alarmist work *I Muscoviti nella California* (Rome 1759), but they were as yet nowhere near, and the Spanish ambassador in St Petersburg discounted the peril. A few years later there were more specific reports from a more credulous ambassador: a Russian force from Anadyr had landed somewhere in America and lost 300 men in battle with the Indians; and Krenitsin had been joined in Arctic waters by two ships under 'Ctschacow' or 'Estehacowy' (Chichakov) and 'Pandwafen' or 'Panowbafew' (?)—from Archangel! José de Gálvez and the Viceroy Francisco de Croix were seriously considering the occupation of Monterey before they received this 'information'; such an advance had been in the air for years.[34] But fear of the Russians was the prime factor in the move into Alta California; the dynamic and authoritarian Visitor-General provided a catalyst and a driving force.

His plans included a sweeping administrative reorganisation of the frontiers through a Commandancy-General embracing Nueva Vizcaya (Durango and Chihuahua), Sinaloa, Sonora, and California, with a forward capital in Northern Sonora or even at the Gila-Colorado confluence, the apparent node of Sonora and both Californias, and as yet well beyond the limits of Spanish control.[35] This new order, a Viceroyalty in all but name, did not come about until 1776, when Gálvez became Minister for the Indies, but he began laying its foundations forthwith.

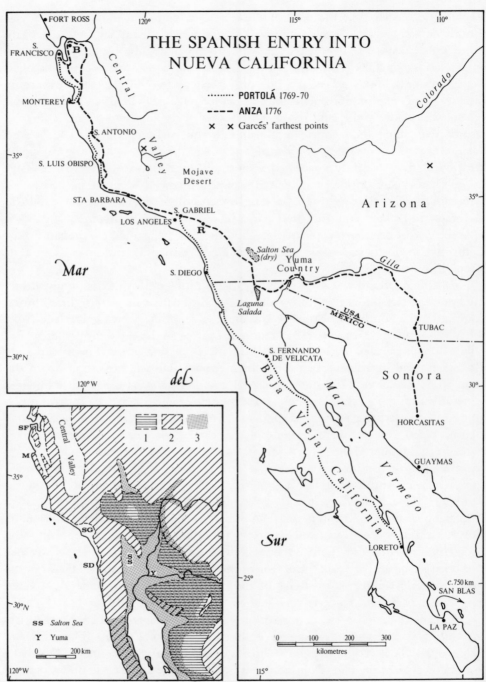

Figure 25. THE SPANISH ENTRY INTO NUEVA CALIFORNIA.   Portolá's route shown only where different from Anza's; B, Berkeley; R, Riverside. Mainly based on maps in H. E. Bolton, *Outpost of Empire* (New York 1931). Inset: 1, plateaus; 2, hilly to mountainous; 3, creosote scrub desert—data from *Fiziko-Geograficheskiy Atlas Mira* (Moscow 1964), Plates 150–1.

Before any advance to the Gila could be made, control of northern Sonora, shaken by Indian risings, had to be restored by arms, and this took until May 1771. Meanwhile, in 1767–8, Gálvez established the 'Naval Department of San Blas' to serve as a maritime base.

In broad locational terms San Blas, some 110 km north of Cabo Corrientes, was well placed: with much easier access than Acapulco to the heart of New Spain, the course thence to both Baja and Alta California was more direct than that from any other port, although of course this was far from guaranteeing a quick passage, given the southeast-setting California current and Drake's 'often calmes and contrary windes' along the coast. But the particular site was execrable, and execrated. There was an extensive roadstead, but the inner harbour had a tricky entrance, was shallow and liable to silting, and could hold only four ships of any size. The little town was set in swamps and subject to severe floods, while the climate was so unpleasant and unhealthy that senior officers were allowed to live for much of the time at Tepic, in the hills 68 km away; in fact, the port was practically unusable except between November and May, which of course were not the best months for navigation in northern waters. Provisions, cordage, canvas soon deteriorated in the humidity. In the thirty-odd years during which San Blas was an active naval base, there were several moves to transfer its functions to Acapulco (too far away) or to near-by Matanchel, merely an open roadstead but with fewer mosquitoes. But Gálvez was not the man to admit a mistake, and when the question was raised acutely by the grounding of a laden supply ship in the harbour itself, too much capital had been invested for a shift to be generally acceptable.[36]

San Blas had two solid resources: salt and timber. Apart from its use in the home and by fishermen, salt in great quantity was essential in silver refining, and San Blas was central to the main producing region; Gálvez earmarked the profits of the Crown salt monopoly for the development of his port. The valley of the Río Santiago had good stands of cedar and pine, and some resinous trees. Other marine stores had to be imported, and all iron work and special tools came from Mexico City itself; guns and anchors were brought from as far as Callao and Manila. As for manning, always an intensely difficult problem, local pilots had a good rule of thumb knowledge of the coastal waters but little or no professional training, and although some admirable officers were later drafted from Old Spain, it need hardly be said that service on this unhealthy edge of the Spanish world was most unpopular. A general air of inefficiency and almost amateurishness hangs over New Spain's Pacific marine. Nevertheless, there were some very notable exploring voyages, preceding Cook on the coasts north from Juan de Fuca Strait, and in emergency some remarkable building feats. Thus in its first year the little yard set up on the Río Santiago launched two 'packets', *San Carlos* and *San Antonio* (or *Principe*), of 193 tons each, and two 30-ton schooners.[37] The emergency was the impending arrival of Gálvez.

The Visitor-General was on his way to Baja California, which he reached, after a six weeks' crossing, in May 1768; on the way he formally took possession, rather belatedly, of the Tres Marias, only 110 km from San Blas. This journey was in part motivated by his belief that the just-expelled Jesuits had concealed the peninsula's wealth in gold, silver and pearls; he was soon undeceived. In a country the size of England there were 7149 mission Indians, now in Franciscan care, and a few thousand others, whom Humboldt thought were the nearest of all savages to 'that which is called the state of nature.'[38] Gálvez promulgated nineteen decrees to regulate the affairs of what he intended to be a self-supporting colony; it has been said that he wished to create an impression of progress for the celebrated French astronomer Chappe d'Auteroche, who came to Baja California to observe the Transit of Venus, and died there; but one suspects that this activity was the automatic reaction of a born commissar. The colony so meticulously provided for lacked most things, but most of all colonists, and the more so since the best spots in this desert peninsula had been pre-empted by the missions: by 1793 there had been only fourteen land-grants under Gálvez's legislation, to under 100 settlers. The Visitor-General's grandiose economic planning simply collapsed, for lack of any resource base.

It is perhaps not surprising that after his return to the mainland, Gálvez suffered two attacks of complete lunacy, thinking himself to be (amongst others) Charles XII of Sweden, Frederick the Great, St Joseph, 'and, what is more than all, the Eternal Father'; in which last capacity, doubtless, he projected a deep-draught canal from Mexico City to Guaymas.[39] But he was a man of great gifts and will, and recovered to leave an enduring monument: the colonisation of Alta California, where some relics of the Spanish cultural landscape yet survive, the quiet cloisters and silent bell-towers of Presidios and Misiones, fossils now tenderly insulated from the noise, the colour, the turbulent vorticism of Californian life.

The authorisation for Gálvez to occupy Alta California was vague enough— merely to observe and if possible frustrate the Russians—but it was sufficient warrant, for a man of his temper, to despatch the *San Carlos* and *San Antonio* for Vizcaíno's port of San Diego, where they were to meet a land expedition from Baja California.[40] Gálvez personally helped in the relading of the ships at La Paz, whence they sailed respectively in January and February 1769, arriving, in reverse order, in April, too stricken with scurvy to do anything beyond making a camp for the sick and dying. On 14 May the first of the two land parties came in; the second, led by the Governor of Baja California, Gaspar de Portolá, left Loreto on 9 March and arrived on 1 June; with him came the famous Father Junipero Serra, founder and until his death in 1784 President of the Franciscan mission in Alta California.

San Diego was only an advanced base; the immediate intent was to occupy Monterey, known from the glowing reports of Vizcaíno. The *San Antonio*, with only eight of her twenty-eight crew fit for duty, was sent back to San Blas for supplies; the *San Carlos*, with only two able men left, had to be laid up. On 14 July Portolá set off for Monterey with sixty-three men. Vizcaíno had reported a safe protected harbour, but at the right latitude they found only a broad open bay, and

Portolá decided to push on. This was on 30 September; by 1–2 November they had come to the entry to San Francisco Bay, at the tip of the peninsula between the Bay and the open Pacific (Fig. 25). To a land party, this was a cul-de-sac, and they had to retrace their steps. Once beyond Monterey, which they still could not recognise as Vizcaíno's fine harbour, they had to subsist by killing a mule a day and eating it with their eyes shut, 'like hungry lions'; when at last (24 January 1770) they reached the little stockade that was the new mission of San Diego, they were 'smelling frightfully of mules'. They were still on very short rations, and by some accounts Portolá had decided to abandon the colony if relief had not come by 20 March; the *San Antonio* arrived back on the 19th. This sounds, and probably is, too good to be true,[41] but without the succour abandonment might well have been forced upon him; with it he was able to take up the search for Monterey once more. Towards the end of May Portolá and the *San Antonio* rendezvoused at what was now agreed to be Vizcaíno's port, and there on 3 June 1770 the mission of San Carlos Borromeo was formally established. Portolá, in his own words, 'proceeded to erect a fort to occupy and defend the port from the atrocities of the Russians, who were about to invade us'; as yet they had only just reached the tip of the Alaskan Peninsula.[42]

At most some three score soldiers and rather fewer Indians were involved, with a staff, clerical and lay, of eight or ten: such were the tiny beginnings of California. Despite the resolution of Portolá and Serra, the precarious little colony had only the most tenuous links with 'civilisation'. There were 360 km of rough country between San Diego and the next mission south, San Fernando de Velicatá, itself only just founded by Serra on the march north; and beyond this latter post stretched another 580 km of desert to Loreto, the capital (such as it was) of the province. Serra reckoned that it would take 1500 mules to supply Alta California by this route, there were simply not enough beasts in both Californias put together, and if there had been, there was not enough fodder and water *en route* for mule trains of the requisite size. As for supply by sea, the *San Carlos* on her maiden voyage took 110 days from La Paz to San Diego and lost all but two of her twenty-six crewmen from scurvy, while the *San Antonio* was five months on the San Blas-San Diego round trip in 1769–70; in 1772 the supply ships for Monterey got no farther than San Diego, again doubtless owing to scurvy. And there were other calls on these little ships, notably the long-distance voyages to northern waters, to check on the Russians, beginning in 1774 with that of Juan Pérez, which anticipated James Cook at Nootka and beyond.[43]

Only with the greatest difficulty, therefore, was it possible to keep up a skeletal and dubiously reliable maintenance service for the few dozen priests and soldiers in Alta California; yet if these were not to be mere hostages to fortune, some more substantial colonisation was needed, and in particular the effective occupation of the most tempting port of San Francisco. But to implant a colony of any numbers, and given the paucity and unreliability of shipping, a new way, and that by land, must be found. A direct approach westwards from New Mexico (where Santa Fe had been founded as early as 1609) was considered, but the distances were too great and the unknowns too many. A new way was indeed found, from Sonora; it was to be used only twice before it was closed by the Yuma Indian rising in 1781, but that was enough.

Anza's anabasis

By 1773 three new missions had been founded between San Diego and Monterey—San Gabriel, forerunner of the vast Los Angeles conurbation; San Luís Obispo, which survived as an agreeably modest town until snatched from obscurity by the anti-nuclear affrays at Diablo Canyon; and San Antonio, now a ruin hidden away in the Coast Ranges, a charming picnic spot.[44] But in February of that year Antonio Bucareli, one of the ablest Viceroys, was considering the early abandonment of the infant colony. At this point, however, the distant ambassador in St Petersburg, Conde de Lacy, took a hand in the game, with a stream of most alarmist reports on Russian designs: the ships from Archangel had explored the American coast from 40 to 75°N; the Russians were preparing a force of 25,000 men to storm the Great Wall of China and planning an invasion of Japan under an Englishman, General Lloyd; despite their rivalry with the Hudson's Bay Company, which had posts from Baffin Bay to the Sea of Kamchatka, they might expect help from the British—indeed, Okhotsk officials had been ordered to welcome any English ships which might arrive there, and even 'to obey the English commanders as if they were their own'. Most of this nonsense was sensibly discounted in Madrid and Mexico, but there was a residue of doubt, a feeling that there might be some fire behind Lacy's inordinate clouds of smoke. (Indeed, there had been some thought in Russia of an approach to the British, abandoned when it was learnt that Portolá had advanced only to 48°N; actually he had reached only 38°.) It is not surprising that both Arriaga, the Minister for the Indies, and Bucareli recognised the need to ascertain whether there really was a Russian presence on the coast, and if so how far south it extended.[45] In any case, some forward move was desirable, either to block or to pre-empt a Russian advance.

Although Bucareli took very calmly these rumours of Russian activity in the north, and of British probes from Hudson Bay or across the polar sea, he began to prepare for an occupation 'to avoid the consequences of having other neighbours than the Indians.' In September 1773 he authorised the opening of a land route from Sonora to Alta California, and in December Pérez was ordered on his northern voyage; he sailed in January 1774 and he found none but Indian settlements for 20° north from Monterey. His reconnaissance was not altogether conclusive, however, and on his return, eleven months later, Bucareli decided to send him north again, under Bruno de Hezeta and accompanied by Juan de Ayala, who became the first European definitely known to have taken his ship, the *San Carlos*, into San Francisco Bay, on 5 August 1775. Far from giving over the colonisation, Bucareli had now resolved that the occupation of San Francisco was 'indispensable'.[46]

The conduct of this great move forward was entrusted to Juan Bautista de Anza, like his father and grandfather an experienced warden of the Sonoran marches; some thirty years earlier the second Anza had proposed the reduction of the Gila-Colorado region. Now, in 1774, his son took the reconnaissance party to the confluence of those rivers, and thence through the hazardous desert between the Salton Sea (then dry) and the Mar Vermejo to San Gabriel; he was accompanied by Fr Francisco Garcés, a mighty traveller in his own right, who had already been in the Gila country. Between them they made a very good job of winning over the Yuma Indians, who occupied the strategically vital country around the river-junction.[47]

The first real colonists, fifty-one persons from Sinaloa, including a few women, had reached San Diego via Baja California in 1774; Anza's entrada was to make straight for San Francisco (Fig. 25). He was to prove a humane, resourceful, and inspiring leader; Bucareli placed equipment and recruitment in his hands, and these tasks were carried out with thoroughness and intelligence. Anza warned that the emigrants would have to be fitted out 'from shoes to hair ribbons'—each woman's kit included six yards of ribbon, three chemises, three Puebla-made cotton petticoats, two pairs of workaday stockings and two of 'fine Brussels'. . . .[48] Assembly began at Horcasitas in Sinaloa and was completed at Tubac, whence the long march began on 23 October 1775. Anza had a staff of six (Fathers Garcés, Font, and Eixarch, with a commissary, a lieutenant, and a sergeant); twenty-nine soldiers with an equality of wives; 136 members of families, mostly children. With muleteers and so on, they were altogether 240 souls, not counting the unborn. They had with them 695 horses and mules and drove 355 head of cattle, for food on the march and as stock for the colony. At the very first camp out of Tubac, one of the women died in childbirth—in Anza's best tent—but the baby boy survived. There were four more births on the rough journey of some 1500 km from Tubac to Monterey, but despite snow and bitter cold in both the desert and the mountains, no other death. The camp discipline must have been excellent.

Arrived at San Gabriel on 3 January 1776, Anza was distracted from his objective by bad news from San Diego, where the Indians had risen, sacked the mission, and attacked the *presidio* or military post some little distance away. The latter's garrison of eleven (of whom four were sick and two in the stocks) beat them off, but Anza and some of his troopers were called to San Diego to restore order, and he was not able to leave San Gabriel for the north until 21 February. Despite a brief but severe illness at Monterey, he pushed on with an advance party, and by the end of March was camped in what was to be the heart of today's San Francisco, selecting sites for the presidio and mission. With characteristic devotion to duty, he did not return to Monterey by the direct route, but went right round the southern lobe of San Francisco Bay and then fetched a compass well to the west of the Berkeley Hills.

It was not given to Anza himself to inaugurate the new settlement, as he wished; the commandant in Alta California, Fernando de Rivera, was a nervously erratic obstructionist. Anza returned to Sonora, parting at Monterey from his colonists with much sorrow on both sides. Rivera's hands were forced by new Viceregal orders, and Anza's lieutenant Joaquín Morga took twenty-one families to establish the farthest outpost of Spanish dominion.[49] On 28 June 1776 a rude chapel of boughs became the cradle of the city of San Francisco; across the continent, just one week later, the bells of Philadelphia rang in the Independence of the nation which was to supplant or exclude Spaniard, Russian, and Briton alike.

The last colony: Nueva California

A century and three-quarters after Vizcaíno's propaganda for Monterey, Alta or Nueva California, that is its littoral south from San Francisco, was at last occupied —very thinly. By 1800 there were twenty-eight settlements (some so close together as to be virtually one), none farther than 40 km or so from the coast (Fig. 26). Of these four were *presidios*, administrative and military posts with garrisons of three or four score men apiece, and six were pueblos, townlets intended to be the nuclei of true colonisation, each close to a mission or presidio. Each had a nominal four square leagues of land, allotted to settlers on very easy terms, with the standard Spanish central plaza and rectangular layout. Their progress was slow: the pueblo with the most spectacular future, Nuestra Señora la Reina de los Angeles de Porciuncula, was founded in 1781 but by 1800 had only about 315 Spaniards, or rather *gente de razón*—that is poor whites, mestizos, and mulattos, as distinct from hopelessly irrational Indios.[50] Away from the sea, there was even a notable failure —the settlements founded near the Gila-Colorado confluence in autumn 1780 were wiped out in the Yuma rising of July 1781; punitive expeditions were ineffective, and Anza's route was never reopened.[51] Nevertheless, as early as 1776 Monterey was ordained the capital for both Californias, the peninsula, under a lieutenant-governor at Loreto, being definitely subordinate: 'In six years the child had outgrown its parent' Baja California. At the century's end, there were 1800 or more Spaniards and gente de razón in all the settlements.[52]

Although the Crown's primary motive for the occupation was strategic, the core of the colony lay in the Franciscan missions, carefully sited in the most fertile and populous pockets (Fig. 26). La Pérouse, the first outsider to visit the colony (1786), was pained by the highly paternalistic discipline, including the lash, by which two to four fathers and half a dozen soldiers in each mission controlled hundreds of Indians—in 1800, 13,500 of the 50–70,000 all told who lived in the littoral belt. But he was enchanted with the 'fertility of the soil, [which] exceeds conception . . . a fertility of which the European husbandman can form no adequate idea.' And yet, 'California, notwithstanding its fertility, cannot be said to have a single inhabitant' —the merest handful of friars and soldiers 'constitute as yet the whole of the Spanish nation in this part of America.' What was needed was private property, an open commerce, religious toleration, less celibacy, and 'a certain degree of liberty'—all very proper Enlightenment sentiments.[53]

Seeing only Monterey, La Pérouse was a little less than fair; economic development was not entirely neglected in favour of the cure of souls. In the missions,

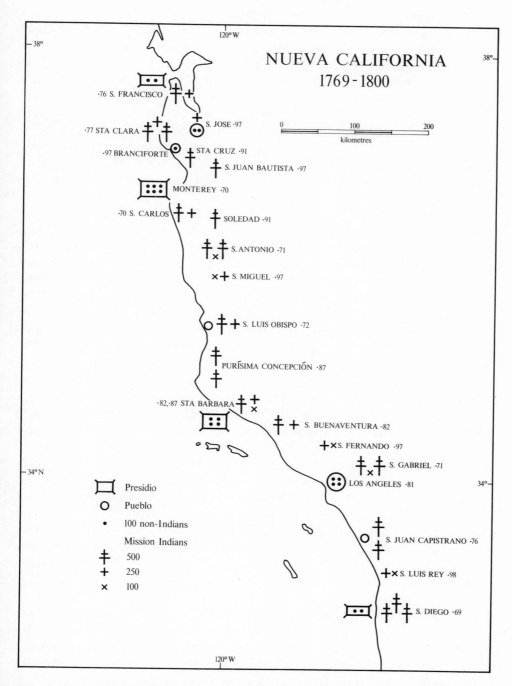

·76 S. FRANCISCO

NUEVA CALIFORNIA
1769-1800

·77 STA CLARA   S. JOSE ·97

·97 BRANCIFORTE   STA CRUZ ·91

S. JUAN BAUTISTA ·97

0   100   200
kilometres

MONTEREY ·70

·70 S. CARLOS   SOLEDAD ·91

S. ANTONIO ·71

S. MIGUEL ·97

S. LUIS OBISPO ·72

PURÍSIMA CONCEPCIÓN ·87

·82,·87 STA BARBARA

S. BUENAVENTURA ·82

S. FERNANDO ·97

S. GABRIEL ·71

LOS ANGELES ·81

S. JUAN CAPISTRANO ·76

S. LUIS REY ·98

S. DIEGO ·69

Presidio
Pueblo
100 non-Indians
Mission Indians
500
250
100

Figure 26. NUEVA CALIFORNIA 1769–1800. Numerals shown thus .97 indicate foundation in [17]97. Population figures for *c.* 1800 extracted from H. H. Bancroft, *History of California*, Vols. I and II; separate figures for non-Indian population in pueblos of San Luís Obispo and San Juan Capistrano not available, but probably very small.

indeed, the two went together; the colony, or one might say the Franciscan colonies, fairly soon became self-supporting in the staples, and even a little more. Substantial amounts of grain and vegetables were raised—La Pérouse brought in the first seed potatoes, from Chile—and the Indian converts were taught to weave blankets and rough clothing. By the end of the century hemp was grown, and samples were sent to New Spain; most temperate and sub-tropical fruits were well established; wine-making began in 1797–8. Except for the abortive venture in sea-otter skins, and a little salt to San Blas, one can hardly speak of external trade until the next century, but the few foreign ships to visit California were supplied, however illicitly, with fresh provisions, against desperately-needed European-style consumption goods.[54]

Vizcaíno's original argument for Monterey as a place of refreshment for the Acapulco Galleons was not forgotten, and they were ordered to stop there, though trading was still forbidden; but the old pressures of the Mexican merchants still prevailed, and most captains preferred to pay a fine rather than delay on this last lap of their voyage.[55] In 1783, two years before James Hanna became the first British captain to cash in on the reports of the huge profits made by Cook's men at Canton on sea-otter skins from Nootka, the Manila-bound Galleon carried over 700 pelts sent from the missions to Acapulco. As we have seen, Vicente Vasadre's ingenious follow-up scheme for exchanging pelts for Chinese mercury was wrecked by the obstructionism of the Real Compañía de Filipinas.[56]

However, stock-raising soon became the backbone of the Californian economy, and this industry almost monopolised exports, in the form of hides and tallow, until the American annexation and the gold finds of 1849. Alongside the missions there grew up great private estates given over to extensive pastoralism. The first land grant was made in 1775, and by 1790 there were nineteen private *ranchos*. At the end of the century, however, the missions still had over 83 per cent of the stock, which numbered about 74,000 cattle, and 88,000 sheep.[57]

The first tiny foreshadowings of trans-Pacific contracts athwart the Magellanic diagonal, so lively in the wake of the forty-niners, date from as early as 1790, when the British government planned to send two ships via recently-founded Sydney to steal a march on the Spaniards by securing a base at Nootka, and 1792, when Vancouver was presented with six bulls, twelve cows, and fourteen sheep for New South Wales; only four sheep survived the voyage to Port Jackson.[58]

The occupation was virtually complete by 1800. Humboldt exclaimed on the shocking contrast between the Spanish principles of colonisation and those used by the British 'to found in a few years the towns on the east coast of New Holland.' The contrast is perhaps not so much in California's disfavour as Humboldt thought (at his base date, 1802, there were exactly three towns in New South Wales),[59] but the Spanish hold was undeniably very light. The total military force at La Pérouse's visit was 282, spread along a littoral of over 750 km, and even in 1820 it consisted of only 700 ill-equipped men, with a few exceedingly ill-kept batteries. Any competent force could have taken any of the presidios, as indeed was shown in 1818, when two Argentine privateers, with the most motley crews, had no difficulty in taking and sacking Monterey itself.[60] Nor were the Spaniards able to prevent the Russians building Fort Ross in 1812, and hunting sea-otter on the Farallons, within sight of San Francisco. But the purpose of the occupation was pre-emptive, and that purpose was served.

The Spanish presence was sufficiently tangible to ensure that no European power would venture to attack California except as part of a formal war originating elsewhere. All the same, it was perhaps lucky that the Canadian and American advance westwards interposed a buffer, in the Oregon country, between Russian America and Spanish (or Mexican) California. But by the same token, Bucareli's dread of 'the consequences ... from having other neighbours than the Indians' was prescient: in June 1846, even before the outbreak of war between the United States and Mexico was known on the Pacific coast, Yankee infiltrators had subverted Mexican rule and declared a short-lived independence, the stepping-stone to annexation.

Decadence of the Isthmus

The vitality of the mines and the northern marches of New Spain was not matched in the southern provinces of the Viceroyalty, nor on the Isthmus. On the Atlantic slope of central America, both climate and Indians were tough and hostile, so that Guatemala and its dependencies continued to live 'folded back on the Pacific coast' while economic life, paradoxically, was largely bound up with the British intruders on the Caribbean shores, and their smuggling. The Anglo-Spanish quarrels over the logwood-cutters of Belize and over British 'protection' of the Moskito Indians dragged wearily on from stalemate to stalemate. Despite the preponderance of population on the Pacific side, maritime activity on this coast was restricted to a couple of ships a year taking marine stores and dyestuffs to Peru; the once-valuable export of cacao to Mexico was ruined, or forced into illicit channels, by the reservation of this trade to Caracas, in the interests of the Real Compañía Guipuzcoana.

In 1774, however, all the Pacific colonies were allowed to trade freely with each other—in their own products only, not in Asian or European goods. There was some revival in mining and in Realejo ship-building; but as late as the 1790s, the oligopolistic obstruction of the new Consulado of Guatemala, tightly linked with the old Cadiz vested interests, could frustrate efforts to enter the new market for indigo in the United States, and this in despite of the Captain-General, the Economic Society, the indigo growers, and even the Consulado's own local branches. The old economic Adam was still stronger than Adam Smith.[61]

If the story of Guatemala is one of virtual stagnation, in the Isthmus itself it is one of mere decay. After the Succession War, the convoys to Cartagena and Puerto Bello were re-established, but they were irregular and poorly stocked, and Vernon's capture of the latter (1739) was the final blow. To provide a more autonomous and on-the-spot administration, New Granada (modern Colombia) was detached from Peru and made a Viceroyalty in 1739; to it was added Venezuela, hitherto a dependency of New Spain, and although this province became the virtually independent Captain-Generalcy of Caracas in 1742, the new structure was more logical for defence than the old one in which Panama was subordinate to distant Lima.

Nevertheless, although in 1735 Juan and Ulloa could still describe the fading Isthmian fairs in the present tense, after 1740 there were no convoys, only occasional register ships, and the legalisation of the Cape Horn route for Spanish shipping to some extent 'meridionalized the current of commerce in the Pacific.'[62] If legal trade languished, contraband remained lively enough; according to Dionisio de Alsedo, President of the Audiencia of Panama, there were highly organised and British-backed societies of smugglers in Veragua who went so far as to build their own fort, from which, after the peace of 1748, Don Dionisio in person expelled them. But in 1751 official recognition was given to the reality of decline in Panama, by the abolition of the Audiencia.[63].

Yet in British eyes, at least, the Isthmus retained the glamour given to it by Dampier and Wafer, its magnetism for projectors strangely surviving Paterson's failure at Darien. Every Anglo-Spanish crisis, and there was at least one in every decade of the century, brought forth its plans for a descent on Nicaragua or Darien; but after Vernon's repulse from Cartagena, the only official project to get much beyond the paper stage was that of 1780, a thrust up the Río San Juan to Lake Nicaragua—abortive, but in it the young Horatio Nelson made his name.[64] On the other hand, the end of the American War saw a tightening of Spanish control: in 1783–7 troops from Panama and ships from Cartagena sealed off the Cuna country, including 'Calidonia', renamed Carolina del Darién. These trifling operations drew attention to the possibility of water communication from Atlantic to Pacific, by the Río Atrato on the Darien side and the (Colombian) Río San Juan.[65] Paradoxically, it was at this very time when Panama was most deeply sunk in neglect and decay, that an interoceanic waterway began to be not only canvassed in a vague academic way, but at least tentatively surveyed.

The Abbé Raynal, whose immense work was as influential as it was superficial, lamented that 'Oriental despotism and Spanish indolence had for too long a time deprived the globe of so considerable a benefit' as navigation through the Isthmuses of Suez and Panama; but Spanish interest concentrated at first on Tehuantepec and Nicaragua. When, in 1771, some Manila-cast cannon were found in the Vera Cruz defences, enquiries showed that they had reached the Atlantic shores by Cortés's old route via the Río Coatzacoalcos, and the Viceroy Bucareli ordered a proper survey of the portage, which also figured in Gálvez's plans for access to California. The surveyors reported that a canal, only 30 km long with one tunnel, might be feasible in Tehuantepec, and in 1779–81 surveys were also made of various Nicaraguan routes. At this time also Juan Bautista Muñoz put the case for a canal at Panama itself, arguing that since 'the Atlantic and Pacific seas are the same

Ocean, united in the south', there could not be a significant difference in their levels.[66] Early in the new century Francisco de Miranda was trying to get Pitt to support Spanish American revolution by dangling the bait of special rights in a hypothetical canal. More to the point, perhaps, as an inducement to British sympathy was the continued need for silver—not only for the China trade, now less demanding than it had been, but to subsidise Britain's continental allies.[67] The old dream of subversion in the Indies might have been given material substance but for the twist given to events by Napoleon's subversion of Spain herself.

Chapter 14

PERU: THE LAST OF EMPIRE

I made it plain that we wanted our old master
or none; that we were far from possessing the
means required for the achievement of independence;
that even if it were won under the protection
of England, she would abandon us if she saw some
advantage in Europe, and then we would fall under
the Spanish sword ... He agreed with me ... and was
of the opinion that it would take a century to
achieve.

Such are the calculations of men! A year passed,
and behold, without any effort on our part to
become independent, God himself gave us our
opportunity with the events of 1808 in Spain. ...

While New Spain was reaching a degree of material and cultural progress which evoked the admiration of Alexander von Humboldt, Peru was falling behind: it is perhaps an indication of down-grading that while the viceregal seat at Lima had traditionally been filled by promotion from Mexico, three of the century's most able rulers of Peru—Manso de Velasco, Manuel de Amat y Jumient, and Ambrosio O'Higgins—came from the humble province of Chile, which became a Captaincy-General only in 1778.[1] Natural, economic, and political calamities befell the Vice-royalty: thousands died in the great earthquake of 1746, which devastated Lima and Callao and ruined the agriculture of the coastal Valles; in 1776 Potosí, the silver mountain, passed with Charcas to the control of Buenos Aires; and the 1780s saw more devastation, this time in the Andean Sierra, through the last and greatest Indian revolt, that of Túpac Amaru II.[2]

Nevertheless, Peru did to some extent recover from the deplorable state depicted by Juan and Ulloa—they were themselves among the agents of recovery—and it was in the 1770s, under Amat, that Callao once more took up the mission of Mendaña and Quiros (albeit in a more secular spirit) and sent ships far into the South Sea, to Tahiti and to Easter Island. If in 1970 John Fisher headed a chapter 'The Decadent Viceroyalty', in 1975 he could say that 'the late eighteenth century, at least, was not a period of decline', and that 'if an economic crisis was experienced' it was mitigated rather than accentuated by the state of silver mining.[3]

The Argentine patriot Manuel Belgrano, reporting his talk with the British
General Craufurd at Buenos Aires, 1807; in R. A. Humphreys and J. Lynch (eds.),
The Origins of the Latin American Revolutions, 1808–1826 (New York 1965), 280.

'Comercio Libre'

Jorge Juan and Antonio de Ulloa were early exemplars of a new breed of Spanish official: trained naval men, they were only twenty-two and nineteen respectively when they were sent out, in 1735, to assist in La Condamine's measurement of a degree of longitude on the Equator. That a foreign scientific mission, even if that of the French ally, should be admitted into the Indies is itself a striking index of change in Spanish official thinking.[4] In nine years the couple took part in geodetic survey in the Andes, helped in the defensive measures against Anson, and carefully inspected nearly all the littoral from Cartagena to Valdivia; after their return to Spain they produced not only the published *Relación Histórica* of their travels but also a highly confidential report, the *Noticias Secretas*. The two works together form a survey which for wide scope joined with fine detail might be envied by any modern intelligence agency, which however might probably brainwash itself not to envy the spirit and freshness of their style.[5]

Much of the *Noticias* is a sort of sociopolitical report, a long litany of abuses, stressing the oppression of the Indians, the feuds between peninsular Spaniards and American-born Criollos (Creoles), the uselessness of many civic posts, the scandalous conduct of the clergy, the neglect of natural resources: Juan and Ulloa were bright young men, writing in patriotic good faith but not too averse to using shock tactics on their hierarchical superiors. The first part of the book includes an extremely detailed gazetteer of the ports, defences, shipyards, and arsenals; an account of all aspects of shipping both naval and mercantile; and an analysis of the illicit trading network. Credit is given where due, and there are some bright spots—the ship-building resources of Guayaquil and its splendid timbers, the readiness of the fort at Valparaiso and the good morale of its garrison, some of the dockyard staff and artisans at Callao, including the mestizo silversmith who did such a fine job of bushing the gaping touch-holes of the cannon that 'his name should not be forgotten'.[6] But for the most part the picture is one of slackness and confusion amounting to utter unreadiness to meet any threat; Valdivia for instance was strongly fortified but in much corruption and disorder; it was responsible directly to distant Lima, not to Santiago, and its Governor issued furloughs to all and sundry of the militia as soon as they arrived....

The morass of obsolescence, incompetence, and corruption was perhaps worst in the merchant marine. Its ships were clumsily designed and badly built, heavily overloaded, with wretched crews and untrained pilots who had no instruments beyond the compass and the ancient cross-staff;[7] it was indeed passing strange that it was left to the Bishops to regulate shipping, which they did by banning winter sailing to Chile, but masters sailed anyhow and got absolution.

As for contraband,

> this way of tolerating or even patronising the smugglers is called 'eat and let eat', and magistrates who go along with it for the sake of their bribes are called 'good fellows' [*hombres de buena indole*] who do no harm to anybody

except, through his Treasury, to the King.[8]

Louisiana 1768
N. ORLEANS
New Spain 1789
VERA CRUZ
ACAPULCO
Guatemala 1770
S. TOMAS
OMOA
HABANA
Cuba
BATABANO
TRINIDAD
SANTIAGO
MONTECRISTI
S. D'GO
Sto Domingo
S. JUAN
Pto Rico
1765
CAMPECHE
R. HACHA
STA MARTA
PTO BELLO
PANAMA
CARTAGENA 1776
New Granada
MARGARITA
TRINIDAD
1789
Venezuela
1774
1768
GUAYAQUIL
CALLAO
Peru 1778
ARICA
Charcas
Chile
Brazil
La Plata
VALPARAISO
CONCEPCIÓN
1778
BUENOS AIRES
1778
MONTEVIDEO
1776
C. Horn

CORUNA
GIJON
SANTANDER
BARCELONA
TORTOSA
Spain
PALMA
SEVILLE
ALICANTE
CARTAGENA
CADIZ
MALAGA
0   200 km
× STA CRUZ DE TENERIFE (Canaries) 0°

'COMERCIO LIBRE' 1765-89

×   1
•   2
←--→ 3
⟺   4

The only way to counter this contraband would be to ensure that Peru and Chile were sufficiently provided with consumption goods, by Puerto Bello or better by register ships around Cape Horn—admittedly a difficult passage for Spaniards, there could be storms with snow and hail even in summer, but they could get used to it, especially the Biscayners, and in a few years there would be no need to hire foreign pilots or masters. In principle, this was the solution eventually adopted; in practice, although some ships came round the Horn, in the absence of marine insurance on so hazardous a route most trade came across the Andes from Buenos Aires.[9]

As early as 1740 licensed register ships had been allowed to enter the Pacific by the Straits of Magellan or the Horn, but the first major step towards a general liberalisation was taken in 1765, when trade with the Spanish islands in the Caribbean was opened to a number of peninsular ports besides Cadiz and Seville (Fig. 27); there was no need to get licences, and customs dues were much simplified. It is perhaps significant that this followed hard on 'the bustling, riotous trade fair conducted [at Habana] for the best part of a year' when it was in British hands in 1762–3.[10] The results of even this limited relaxation of the old system were most striking: the number of ships in the Cuban trade is said to have increased over thirty-fold in thirteen years, although of course a larger number of ships probably implies small individual tonnages.[11]

The policy was gradually extended until, with Britain locked up in her own colonial troubles and anxious not to offend Spain, it was safe to make a decisive move against her protégé Portugal. In 1776 the Viceroyalty of La Plata was set up, initially rather in the nature of an *ad hoc* regional military command, although there may have been from the beginning some intention to make it permanent. Colonia do Sacramento, the 'gigantic warehouse' for the illicit trade of La Plata, was taken, at last to be held permanently, in 1777; with the elimination of this nest of smugglers, the main reason for the old ban on importation through Buenos Aires went by the board.[12] In the next year, 1778, was promulgated the famous *Reglamento* which set up a 'free and protected commerce' for all subjects of the Spanish Crown, between any part of Spain and any non-excepted part of the Indies,[13] and within the Indies in colonial produce; the exceptions, still under restriction, were Venezuela (to safeguard the interests of the Caracas Company) and New Spain.

Of course this was not 'Free Trade' in the Manchester sense; but in the eighteenth century restriction of colonial trade to co-nationals was still orthodox standard practice, as witness the British Navigation Acts. Once more, and despite the American War, the results were spectacular.[14] In five years the export of hides

Figure 27. 'COMERCIO LIBRE' 1765–89. 1, traditional ports of the Seville-Cadiz monopoly, and Acapulco; 2, ports open to trade, without licence, by 1778; 3, intercolonial trade permitted, with date of permission; 4, packet services opened 1764. Dates underlined are those when 'free trade' between Spain and the Indies was permitted to Spanish shipping; note that Acapulco was closed to all but Philippine trade until 1789. Compiled from literary sources.

from La Plata rose from 150,000 to 1,400,000 per annum, and from 1776 immigrants from Spain built up a valuable export trade in salted beef, dried or in pickle,
precursor of the Argentine presence on British working-class tables of the earlier
twentieth century.

The economies of aggregation provided by her long-established facilities
(finance, insurance, warehousing, links with European suppliers) and her intimate
liaisons with the old merchant rings in the Indies enabled Cadiz to retain the great
bulk of the colonial trade; but when Caracas, Vera Cruz, and Acapulco were
thrown open in 1788, the functions of the once-mighty Casa de Contratación had
been eroded away: with its formal abolition in 1790, the last vestige of the ancient
ocean-spanning system of Seville had ceased to be.

The Pacific littoral under 'free trade'

To meet the menace implied by British activity in the Falklands and the Portuguese
presence at Sacramento called for a military effort impossible to mount from
distant Lima; it was made by a large expedition direct from Spain, and it would have
been idiotic to bring 19,000 men by sea to Buenos Aires only to place them under
the control of a Viceroy nearly a thousand miles away across the Andes. Hence the
new Viceroyalty of La Plata; but to give this entity an economic base beyond the
hides, tallow, and salt beef of the Pampas, it received the Presidency of Charcas—
Upper Peru, essentially the modern Bolivia—which brought with it Potosí, no
longer so hegemonic in the world of silver as it had been, but still a giant. This
drastic amputation from Peru was followed within two years by a ban on the
export of bullion from Charcas to Lower Peru and by the fulfilment of comercio
libre, which subverted or at least weakened the Limeño hold on trade along the
Pacific littoral. Cuyo, the wine-rich trans-Andine extension of Chile around
Mendoza, also went to La Plata.

Charcas in 1776 had over three-fifths of undivided Peru's silver production;
however, by 1792 output in the remnant Lower Peru had more than doubled, in
large part owing to new finds and to expansion at Cerro de Pasco, and in fact had
outstripped that of Charcas. The problem at both Pasco and Potosí remained, as
ever, the supply of mercury for amalgamation, since the Huancavelica quicksilver
mine had been failing badly since the mid-1750s. Antonio de Ulloa was put in
charge of the mine, which he compared to 'an old woman slowly losing her
teeth'—after all it was nearly two centuries since the Viceroy Francisco de Toledo
had made that shining match between the mountain of Potosí and that of Huancavelica. Ulloa was unable to improve matters in the face of the combined obstruction of the Viceroy Amat, the Audiencia, Treasury officials, and even the clergy,
groups of whom many were doing only too well out of alliance with the corrupt
gremio or guild of mining entrepreneurs. He resigned, the mine continued to
decline. Any mercury ores found elsewhere were tested by Huancavelican experts,
who of course pronounced them worthless, and attempts to build up a stockpile
from Almadén failed before the keen demand of the silver boom in New Spain.

The Visitor-General José de Areche tried to restore output by contracting with a single entrepreneur, who robbed the mine, and direct government operation in 1782–95 coincided with its ruin, ending with physical collapse from reckless cutting away of pillars and buttresses.[15]

However, Indian fossickers and prospectors found small new deposits, and there was a temporary revival of output in the 1790s; but although after 1776 Potosí came to rely on European mercury, rendered more readily available by comercio libre, it was difficult to meet the local demand in Lower Peru. Here the recovery in silver output, though sustained rather fitfully into the next century, was precarious and, relative to new Spain, technology remained backward until the introduction of steam pumping (in which Richard Trevithick in person played a part) in 1815–19. In contrast to that of Gálvez in New Spain, Areche's visitation (1777–81) was largely a failure, and although the tobacco monopoly and the new system of local government through intendants brought a marked increase of revenue, nearly all of it went on the administration of Peru itself, on defence, and on measures to prop up the mining industry.[16]

Potosí, then, slipped as it were from the Pacific into the Atlantic zone; bureaucratic tradition had at last yielded to locational factors—it took seventy-two days for goods to cover the 450 leagues, all but 100 of them in the plains, between Buenos Aires and Potosí; the 500 leagues of mountains (and what mountains!) between Lima and Potosí took four months,[17] and of course the landed price of European goods was very much greater at Callao than at Buenos Aires. In the end, 'The predominance of Peru had passed for ever' in face of 'the indisputable geographical reality' which underpinned the rise of Buenos Aires.[18] But such a shift in the linkages of a great economic node, perhaps the biggest centre of consumption in either America (for such Potosí was), could not but bring with it great changes in the commercial orientation of the Pacific littoral (Fig. 28). While Buenos Aires gained a new grip on Charcas, no longer merely by contraband but official and organisational, her enhanced activity enabled her to strengthen her old economic reach into Chile, and again this reach was now officially legitimated by the application of comercio libre.

All this of course did not take place without much resistance and more lamentation from the vested interests so injured, and especially from the old guard of merchants entrenched in the Consulado of Lima. The Limeños had to concede the geographical diseconomies of trade through Puerto Bello or Cartagena, 'the hazards of the Seas, the Mountains, the Rivers, especially on the long and horrible Magdalena'; but they ingeniously turned this enforced admission into an argument for compensation or protection. As early as 1706 the Consulado was complaining of the intolerable losses caused by the supplying of Chile and Charcas by permission ships coming to La Plata, and not until as late as 1795 did it abandon the struggle against the establishment of a Consulado at Santiago.[19]

The old Viceroyalty was indeed over-extended territorially, and the fiercely

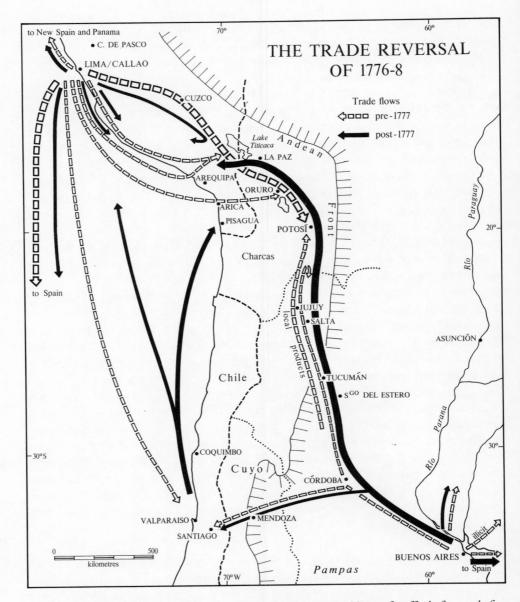

to New Spain and Panama
• C. DE PASCO
LIMA/CALLAO

THE TRADE REVERSAL
OF 1776-8

CUZCO

Trade flows

◁□□□ pre-1777

◀━━ post-1777

Lake
Titicaca
• LA PAZ

A n d e a n

AREQUIPA

ORURO

ARICA

F r o n t

• PISAGUA

POTOSÍ •

to Spain

Charcas

20°

l o c a l

JUJUY
SALTA

ASUNCIÓN •

p r o d u c t s

Chile

TUCUMÁN
• S^{GO} DEL ESTERO

Río

Paraná

30°

• COQUIMBO

C u y o

CÓRDOBA

30°S

Paraguay

Río

VALPARAISO
SANTIAGO

MENDOZA

0   500

kilometres

Pampas

70°W

BUENOS AIRES

illicit

60°

to Spain

Figure 28. THE TRADE REVERSAL OF 1776–8. Principal lines of traffic before and after 1777, adapted from Figs. 4 and 5, 'Reversión de corrientes commerciales, originarse al crearse el Virreinato de Buenos Aires', in G. Céspedes del Castillo, 'Lima y Buenos Aires'.

monopolistic Consulado fought hard to keep its markets in otherwise neglected peripheral regions, markets bequeathed to it by accident of history rather than for any geographical or economic reason; and Lima's commercial hegemony was far too narrowly based on the export of bullion and on her legal monopoly of the distribution of European goods. Very naturally the Limeños blamed all their woes on comercio libre and the loss of Upper Peru, but actually that only 'aggravated rather than caused a trend already under way', while at the heart of the problem lay the over-concentration on mining and the failure to diversify.[20] Other factors were at work, quite apart from the decay of Huancavelica. There, and at Potosí, the *mita* system of forced Indian labour still applied, if on a reduced scale; but elsewhere it had been abandoned, and the plantations of the irrigated coastal Valles were traditionally worked by black slaves. Indians were very reluctant to leave the Sierra for the Valles, and slaves were in short supply; a few were brought in by the RCF, at very high rates. Indian risings were endemic—there were four in 1770–4— culminating in Túpac Amaru's, which ravaged all the country from Cuzco to La Paz and beyond. Nevertheless, though of course Limeños put the blackest possible face on the new order of things, it was yet true that comercio libre of itself did obviously shatter their comfortable monopoly, already eaten into by contraband, and 'Peru rapidly emerged as a casualty of imperial rationalisation and reform . . .'.[21]

Elsewhere, while comercio libre was a great success on its own terms—that is, for the increase of *Spanish* trade—the sustained growth of importation into the Indies outstripped their demand and so produced 'profound maladjustments in a colonial economy based on semi-isolation.'[22] No longer were American markets starved of European consumables; rather, they were glutted, and imports made severe and even disastrous inroads on colonial artisan and *obraje* (=workshop) trades; the annual value of Quito's textile output, for instance, is said to have fallen from 1,500,000 to 600,000 pesos. (Such trades did not disappear entirely, of course; as in remoter parts of the modern Third World, there was a level of poverty where labour forced to accept a starvation wage combined with a mass demand for tiny units of sale to enable local crafts to survive, barely.) The general effect of the new régime was to foster mercantile activity on the littoral, which reacted against the interests of local producers in the interior, as when the wines and brandy of Cuyo had to meet the competition of imports through Buenos Aires. But coastally located industries of course fared as badly; in 1789 'the abundance of European goods' was seen as the main factor in the extreme depression of Chilean domestic industries.[23]

Although the freedom to sail around the Horn has been said to have given Chile the 'inestimable advantage' that her harbours were now the first ports of call in the South Sea,[24] in practice the effects of comercio libre on the local coasting trade were ambivalent. Peru was still largely dependent on Chilean wheat (which in turn needed Peruvian guano), and also imported Chilean copper; this trade of course was not affected either way by the legal changes. Apart from such inelastic exchanges, however, after 1778 Chile's ancient wholly maritime trade with Peru was largely supplanted by a great increase in trans-Andine traffic by mule-train; by the 1790s only about a third of Santiago's imports came by sea from Peru. But Chilean merchants had little capital and often could not hold out against the price-falls due to the influx from Europe; the better-found Limeños were able to reconsolidate their hold on much of the market.

The Chilean reaction was to attempt, at least to desire and project, a breakaway from the Lima middlemen and the initiation of direct trade with other provinces, bypassing Callao. There could be no better illustration of the tendency of comercio libre, in practice, to foster an incipient feeling of economic nationalism—precisely the opposite of the metropolitan intent. Thus there were plans to export Chilean wine, wheat and flour to Guayaquil (at this time included in New Granada, beyond Lima's control), Panama, and Acapulco, against sugar, cloth, and special timbers; it was even proposed to export Guayaquil cacao to San Blas. There was also the notion of attaining self-sufficiency by growing sugar, rice, and cotton in Chile itself, despite the not very favourable climate and the absence of a large servile labour force. Unrealistic as they were, such projects were viewed favourably by the energetic Governor Ambrosio O'Higgins, whose bastard Bernardo was to become Chile's George Washington; they came to nothing, and indeed could remain only dreams so long as Chilean producers remained heavily indebted to the Limeños.[25]

In 1798 Chile became administratively independent of Lima, though it remained an economic dependency, and Lima revenues met the expenses of Juan Fernández, Valdivia and Chiloé, as main bulwarks of the Viceroyalty against attack by sea. Despite its economic troubles, Chile grew in stature during this period, an advance strikingly symbolised by the refounding in 1796 of Osorno, destroyed by the Araucanians in 1600; by O'Higgins's orders, the original 1558 plans of the city were used for the rebuilding. Osorno, from which O'Higgins took the title of his marquisate, was strategically important as a staging-post between the two advanced bastions of Valdivia and Chiloé, and a granary for them. Other new towns—all characterised by 'a marked accent of the camp [acento castrense]', defence being still the first priority—pushed forward agrarian settlement into what had been for two centuries a debatable ground with the Araucanians: a mini-Reconquista.[26] Retaining the virility of a marcher-state, Chile was already beginning to have some sense of a national identity.

On the inland sector of the old Viceroyalty, a detailed statement of the trade of Potosí supplements Céspedes del Castillo's map (Fig. 28) and shows how by the end of the century the old direct links with Lima had been broken—not, however, all those with Lower Peru, for sugar and textiles came to the silver city from Cuzco, whose merchants however thought of themselves as under Lima's thumb. Excluding mercury and meat, Charcas itself supplied about one-fifth of Potosí's needs (coca, cottons, shoe-leather, sugar from Santa Cruz), and another fifth was made up of European goods, mainly from Buenos Aires but some through Arica. About two-fifths came from Chile and the far south of Peru, through Arica and Pisagua or direct from the fertile intermont oasis of Arequipa: copper, wine, brandy, vegetable oils, pulses, dried fruits and nuts, cottons. From Santiago del Estero, Tucumán, Jujuy, Salta came meat (dried or on the hoof), leather, wax, tallow, ponchos, mules. Through Lima itself came Guatemalan indigo, Quiteño cloth, Guayaquil cacao—but only a trickle, nearly matched by the *yerba mate* (herbal tea) from Paraguay.[27]

It is evident that Potosí maintained, in a different setting and with largely different linkages, its old role as a magnet for consumption and luxury goods. But the Chilean experience points to a new turn in comercio libre, an undesigned and unexpected side-effect. The policy had as a main objective the fostering of metropolitan exports, explicitly (in the counsels of Madrid) as a means of maintaining dependence on Spain; and so far as impeding colonial industry went, it seems to have been largely successful. But of its nature, comercio libre gave openings to competition all round; and hence desires such as those favoured by O'Higgins, looking at once towards autarky and towards distant commercial enterprise.

Liberalisation therefore tended in the long run to favour particularism rather than unity, a tendency greatly enhanced when, in 1797, Godoy's French alliance and the resulting war with Great Britain enforced the opening of Spanish American ports to neutral flags; not, it is true, to neutral trade, since—in theory—the ships, overwhelmingly Yankee, could carry only goods consigned between Spanish subjects. In theory again, ports on the Pacific were still closed to foreigners; in fact the years 1797–1809 saw no fewer than 226 North American ships in Chilean ports: only twenty-two were arrested on suspicion of smuggling, and of these only twelve were condemned.[28] Godoy's policy was a signal for a new wave of contraband, and, at least at its distributing end, smuggling is inherently decentralising, seeking out the areas where, for reasons of remoteness or terrain or local attitudes, central control is least well enforced. The net result was a climate of ideas favourable to incipient nationalism or, as Ramos puts it, the laying of foundations for an economic 'provincialisation', in one aspect extractive and linked to overseas trade, in another tending to form more or less autonomous and competitive units. 'Independence would soon come to complete this process . . .'.[29]

Corregidores and intendentes

Comercio libre was but one thrust of Bourbon reform in America; another was the ambitious recasting of territorial administration into the new mould of *intendencias*, multi-purpose governmental units on the French pattern first tried in Spain itself in the Succession War.[30] In the Indies the new set-up was first used in Cuba in 1764, to facilitate reconstruction after the British occupation, and four years later José de Gálvez experimented with it in Sonora and Sinaloa; but his projected expansion of the system had to wait until after he became Minister for the Indies in 1776. The enormous area of La Plata, a congeries of jurisdictions only recently brought together in the new Viceroyalty, offered a clear field for comprehensive rationalisation: Tucumán and Córdoba became intendencias in 1778, and by 1782 the whole vast area from Lake Titicaca to the Pampas had been parcelled out under the

new dispensation. In old Peru the proximate (and potent) impulsion to the change was the great Indian rising of 1780–3, which was duly followed by the installation of intendencias in 1784.

This revolt was only one of many, but by far the greatest and most dangerous. Basically it was a giant protest against the manifold and unbearable tyrannies of the old system of local government which put the Indians into the hands of the *corregidores de indios*. The district officials, together with the local Indian chiefs or *caciques*, were supposed to be the guides, guardians, and protectors of the Indians; in actuality, corregidores and caciques in collusion were often their worst and, but for the priests, their most immediate exploiters. Their cruelties had been naïvely but graphically illustrated nearly two hundred years earlier in Pomo de Ayala's *Nueva Corónica y Buen Governo* (Plate XIX);[31] costumes had changed more than customs, and their exactions and oppressions form a main theme of the bitter analysis of the Indians' plight by Juan and Ulloa in the *Noticias Secretas*.

The corregidor was on the lowest rung of the bureaucratic ladder, and yet, like the District Officer of the British Raj in India, he had a wide range of administrative and judicial functions which struck deep into the lives of the people; and while the laws supposedly governing his actions were admirably humane in intent, they were lamentably unenforceable, so that he had even more, and less checked, power over his charges than had his British Indian counterpart. Unlike the latter, however, he was completely untrained, miserably paid, and had no definite ladder of promotion before him; yet the posts were in demand. Very often the corregidor secured his post by purchase or bribery, and if, as many did, he came from Spain itself, he had very heavy travel and outfit expenses, so that he was normally deep in debt when he entered on his term of one to five years, during which he expected to discharge his obligations to his financial backers and hoped to secure a competence, or more.[32]

Corruption was thus a necessity of life, and the openings for extortion were many and wide, for instance by demanding bribes to manipulate the draft for the mita or the Indian tribute lists, which were sometimes kept in two sets, double but not duplicate. But the most reliable source of the corregidor's income was normally the *repartimiento* of merchandise, which made him, in Viceroy Amat's words, 'a hybrid of Merchant and Judge'. By way of improving the Indian way of life, corregidores (and they alone) were authorised to sell to their charges various items of consumption goods, at a fair price and up to a fixed total value per annum; this was the repartimiento. The stock in trade was bought on credit, at high rates, from Lima merchants, who provided goods, often rejects, at a high mark-up. The results were

Plate XIX. EMPIRE AT WORK. A Spanish priest and layman taking up the White Man's Burden; seventeenth century, but Jorge Juan and Antonio de Ulloa, amongst others, witness that 150 years later 'costumes had changed more than customs'. From MS Gl. kgl. Saml. 2232, 4° belonging to the Royal Library, Copenhagen, and reproduced from *Letter to a King* by Huamán Poma, translated by Christopher Dilke. Copyright © 1978 by Christopher Dilke. Reprinted by permission of the publishers, E. P. Dutton, Inc., and George Allen & Unwin, London. Photo ANU.

startling: not only was there no question of a reasonable price or of adherence to the legal annual limit, but often unsaleable items, utterly useless to the Indians, were forcibly dumped on them—in once case eleven volumes of a work on the Christian Year, plus fourteen by Fr Benito Feijóo OSB (the pioneer of modern learning in Spain), and two of a dictionary of economics![33] The conclusion of a most detailed and dispassionate study is that these 'operations could not be carried out without violence'.[34]

José Gabriel Condorcanqui Inca, a direct descendant of the Túpac Amaru executed, or judicially murdered, by the Viceroy Francisco de Toledo in 1572, and as Marqués de Oropesa holder of the only hereditary fief in Peru, had for long tried to secure some official action against the mita and the oppressions of corregidores and Spanish landowners. Losing patience at the lack of response to official legal representations, in November 1780 he seized the corregidor of his home district, Antonio de Arriaga, at a dinner-party, and forced him to hand over the local reserves of cash and armaments—seventy-five muskets, demanded ostensibly for defence against English pirates—a somewhat hypothetical menace on the plateau southeast of Cuzco.[35] He then had Arriaga publicly executed.

Condorcanqui may well have been inspired by the proud story of El Inca Garcilaso de la Vega's *Royal Commentaries of the Incas* (1609). Styling himself Túpac Amaru II, he followed the standard practice of traditional rebels in so many ages and countries—proclaim loyalty to the Good King Don Carlos, denounce to the death his evil counsellors and governors; later, as the ethnic lines became more tightly drawn, he may have assumed more grandiloquent regal and even imperial titles, but it seems likely that these rest on forgeries.[36] His Indian support was massive, only a few caciques holding aloof, and he had much appeal for the lower ranks of mestizos; but his attempts to induce Criollos to make common cause against the peninsular oppressors foundered on the irreconcilable clash of interests between exploiters and exploited, and the practically inevitable escalation of atrocities on either side. Few of the thousands who flocked to the Inca's standard could be given firearms; nevertheless, he defeated one force levied against him and might well have taken Cuzco had he pressed his early advantage, but he went over to the defensive and was soon betrayed. In May 1781 he and his family were executed at Cuzco with a savagery exceeding that which Toledo had used two centuries earlier; like Damiens, who in 1757 attempted the life of Louis XV, he was condemned to mutilation and to be torn to pieces by horses. The revolt did not die with the Inca; others took up the title and the struggle. La Paz had to undergo two severe sieges, and fighting went on into 1783.

Thousands had died in fight or massacre or of privation. The immediate result was of course ruthless repression; the name of Inca was to be blotted out, Indian music and dress forbidden—as in the Scottish Highlands after the '45. But the great rising was a signal, unmistakable, for the sweeping away of corregidores and repartimientos; much more than a separatist or a precursor of independence, Túpac

Amaru was a 'catalyst for the abolition' of these parasites.[37] The old system had proved both inefficient and inhumane; the new was to do more for efficiency than for humanity.

This new order sought to centralise administration, but in manageable units—twelve intendencias in New Spain, eight each in Peru and La Plata. To this end, a single carefully chosen and well-paid official, the *intendente*, would be given a very wide range of powers, covering (*inter alia!*) revenue collection, the oversight of justice, public works, the quartermaster side of military affairs, economic planning and ecclesiastical patronage.[38] Not all these multifarious tasks needed to be carried out all at once and all the time, but such a concentration of duties demanded able and devoted men, very different from the rabble of corregidores, who for the most part give the impression of being failed lawyers or the younger sons of the seedier gentry. The duties of the intendentes were most demanding, but the career possibilities for a good man were obvious, and fit men were found—in Spain, and largely in the army.

There was clearly a built-in likelihood of friction with other authorities, from Viceroys and Archbishops down to town councillors and rural priests, but from a strictly administrative point of view the change began well enough; there was a new vigorous tone in governmental style, much improvement in public works, and initially at least a marked rise in public revenue, though here gains were dissipated by the three decades of war, external and internal, which began in 1793. As a matter of course the instructions to intendentes called upon them to foster agriculture, industry, and trade; simultaneously comercio libre was breaking down the 'protection no less effective because it was involuntary' which had been given by isolation; and it was inconsequential to call for the promotion of local industry while unloosing against it an often crushing competition.[39]

Not much, therefore, was achieved by the intendentes as regards manufacturing industry, but of course mining was in a different category, and so also was agriculture so far as it was oriented towards self-sufficiency in food and not towards producing raw materials for local industries or anything which might compete with Spanish interests.[40] In Peru, the great rebellion had disrupted economic life on the Andean plateau, depleted both food supplies and labour resources, and enforced the abolition of the repartimiento—a combination of factors which 'tended to remove the Indian sector from the market economy.' The intendentes did strongly support the mining upturn of the 1790s, especially at Cerro de Pasco, and this in turn increased demand for agricultural products. Comparing 1785–9 with 1790–4, Peru's non-bullion exports (mainly re-exported Guayaquil cacao and Chilean copper, and vicuña wool) rose from 3,635,657 pesos to 4,127,250, or from 12 to 15 per cent of a somewhat diminished total. Callao clearly retained some entrepôt role, but this increase was no basic change, and the economy was still far too little diversified. Once again, the constraint was paradoxically imposed by 'free trade', since

there was little that either the crown or the intendants could
do without upsetting the very foundations of the reformed
commercial and economic structure of the empire.[41]

The success of the new system was thus limited and uneven, and as regards Indian
policy it was a failure. The hated corregidores were indeed swept away, but not
even the most energetic and zealous intendente could be omnipresent as well as
omnicompetent. The duties of the corregidores were taken over by the intendente's *subdelegados*, unsalaried but entitled to 3 per cent of the tribute intake. The
natural consequence was that new subdelegado soon became old corregidor, writ a
little less large. The repartimiento was abolished, for the time being, or attenuated;
but the other burdens and exactions on the Indians remained, and their protection
against excessive exploitation depended on the conscience and capacity of the
individual intendentes, who had many other tasks. In the end, 'The fact is that the
names have changed but the substance remains the same ... it is certain that the lot
of the Indians has not improved with the new code ...'.[42]

Among the most marked successes of the intendentes was their 'roads and bridges'
work in the provincial towns, where they not only added a great deal to material
amenities but in many cases managed to instil a more active temper into the sleepy
cabildos or town councils. This was to prove an ironic success: the new bureaucracy
was staffed, overwhelmingly, from the Peninsula, the cabildos in the nature of
things were Criollo strongholds. Either in co-operation with the prodding intendentes or in reaction against their interference, cabildo members gained a new
measure of their own capacities for affairs; but there was very little room for
exercising Criollo ability in responsible positions in the bureaucracy. Hence

> By giving Americans a vision of better government and denying
> them a share in its operations, the reforms of Charles III, both
> in their administrative and their commercial aspects, helped to
> precipitate the collapse of the imperial régime they were intended
> to prolong.[43]

When violent external shocks were superimposed upon internal tensions and discontents, the 'open' cabildo (*cabildo abierto*)—an extraordinary session, in which the
normal oligarchic membership was extended, sometimes very widely, by invitation—was to prove an extremely useful and flexible instrument for taking over
authority; so much so that in some regions liberation from the Spanish yoke was
indeed 'the revolution of the cabildos'.[44]

Towards Independence

Whether we regard the Bourbon Reforms as a new imperialism, a second and
bureaucratic Conquista, or as shoring up a 'gothic edifice', they were certainly
designed to tighten Madrid's administrative control and 'to increase revenue, but in
fact [they were] more effective in alienating the Crown's American subjects.'[45] On

the other hand, we have seen how the 'free trade' side of the reforms stimulated nascent economic separatisms, a tendency reinforced by the creation of new and geographically more logical territorial units and by the reactivation of the Criollo-dominated cabildos. This is not the place for any comprehensive or in-depth treatment of the liberation of Spanish America, but we may note some factors in this great upheaval. It is often overlooked that one of its most crucial campaigns, perhaps the decisive one bringing together the northern and southern theatres of revolution, Bolívar and San Martín, took place on the eastern shores of the Pacific. There also the geopolitical result was perhaps most striking: the replacement, by 1838, of one single and economically exclusionist empire by eleven separate succession states, all avid to attract foreign trade and capital.

Colonial Spanish America was by no means universally a culturally stagnant backwater, enlivened only by ecclesiastical architecture and bizarre displays of baroque literary conceits: the many costly scientific and technical missions saw to that, from Feuillée in 1707 to the Elhuyars and Malaspina in the 1790s. As regards the acceptance, or at least the discussion as hypotheses, of Cartesian and Newtonian views in physics and cosmology, some of the universities of the Indies seem to have been ahead of Salamanca. There was indeed an 'Enlightened' intelligentsia, however small a minority of a minority. But the Enlightenment was not a solid bloc of doctrine; it had its merely reformist and simply technological aspects, and these could appeal at one and the same time both to the absolutist Ministers in Spain and to such tiny but significant élites as that associated with the periodical *Mercurio Peruano*, published at Lima from 1791 to 1795. The Liberator himself, Simón Bolívar, tells us that he had read Condillac, Helvétius, Montesquieu, Rousseau, and Voltaire, all on the Church's list of forbidden books; but the direct role of such subversive thinkers can easily be exaggerated.[46]

After all, the Criollos who made the revolutions were mostly men of standing, with a great deal to lose if the Rights of Man were extended too generously down the line to the lower ranks of mestizos and mulattos, let alone mere Indios and Blacks. Moreover ideas, even ideas as liberating and intoxicating as Rousseau's, do not work without something tangible to work upon. The Enlightenment, as murkily refracted through the French Revolution and reinterpreted with Spanish panache, provided heady slogans for the liberators; but ideas, however serious, may be a necessary but can hardly be a sufficient factor in the complex of instabilities and acute tension which come to a head in those drastic breaches of continuity called revolutions. Also needed are the 'objective conditions', in some ways as pointedly displayed by Carlyle as by any Marxist; among them gross and increasing discrepancies between the prestigious but largely ornamental status of the traditional rulers and the unshowy real power of money or of massive discontents. 'Revolutions are not made without ideas, but they are not made by intellectuals. Steam is essential to driving a railway engine; but neither a locomotive nor a permanent way can be built out of steam.'[47]

Probably more to the point than the ideological values expressed in the writings of the philosophers were those more tangible attitudes expressed in the deeds of the American and French Revolutions, and there can be little doubt that the former was the more potent: in fact the precursor of emancipation, Francisco de Miranda, affirmed that the idea of liberation first came to him while fighting in the American cause at the taking of British-held Pensacola (Florida) in 1781.[48]

The distinction between the two Revolutions was sharp. As Parry says, the American was led by colonial-born 'patricians, land-owners, slave-owners, prosperous merchants'; and they did not lose control. The French revolutionaries decreed the abolition of black slavery and made war upon the Holy Catholic Church; the Americans did not—points which could hardly fail to be taken by the Criollos. It is true that before things came to a head in Spanish America, Napoleon had reversed both policies; but then it was Napoleon himself who brought things to a head by the usurpation of 1808.[49] The great majority of the foreign ships which flocked to the Spanish American ports opened to neutral flags in 1797 (and to Chilean ports not so opened) flew the Stars and Stripes, and according to their own accounts some of their captains thought it a moral duty to spread the evangel of republican independence and consequent prosperity.[50] Such germs of subversion found a very rich culture-bath in the internal contradictions of the Spanish American policy, above all in the basic and growing antipathy between Criollos and Peninsulares. As the level of political *nous* and the firmness of grasp at the centre declined under the feeble Carlos IV and his (and/or the Queen's) favourite Manuel de Godoy, so on the periphery a new consciousness of separate selfhood was growing: 'Since the peace of Versailles [1783], and, more especially, since the year 1789, we frequently hear proudly declared: "Yo no soy *español*, soy *americano!*" '[51]

The expulsion of the Jesuits in 1767 exiled to Europe several hundred educated Criollos, some of them talented men who devoted themselves to writings in honour of their native lands, such as refutations of the then-popular theories of Cornelis de Pauw on the automatic degeneration of all created things exposed to an American environment. One of the exiles, Juan Pablo Viscardo, vainly attempted to secure British military support for Túpac Amaru II; he also wrote what Salvador de Madariaga called 'the first clear statement advocating independence', a powerful and eloquent 'Letter addressed to the American Spaniards', not however published until Francisco de Miranda had it printed in Philadelphia and London in 1799.[52]

Although many Criollo families must have been shocked and deeply grieved at the banishment—without even a day's notice—of those dear to them, many others undoubtedly cashed in at the disposal sales of the Society's far-flung, well-ordered, and very wealthy estates, now expropriated. In any case, by the crucial date of 1808 this tragedy was forty years in the past—in 1791 Miranda, the fiery John the Baptist of Emancipation, gave William Pitt a list of 300 Jesuit exiles but had to admit that 'very few' of them would be of the slightest use in any movement. One cannot then credit the Jesuits with much of a direct role; nevertheless, their 'literature of nostalgia' played some part in evoking that self-consciousness [*conciencia de sí*]— which the Peruvian historian Jorge Basadre saw as the very root of the liberation.[53]

The sharpening of the immemorial tension between Criollos and Peninsulares (also called *Godos*—'Goths'—and other hard names) owed a great deal to changes in the volume and nature of Spanish immigration into the Indies. Arrivals in 1780–90 are said to have been at four or five times the rate in 1710–30, and a much higher proportion now came not from Andalusia but from the north—tough, frugal, and enterprising men, clannish and very much on the make, who 'were not content, as the old monopolists had been, to dump their goods on the beaches and await purchasers', but instead brought new and aggressive trading practices to upset the complacency of the old-established stick-in-the-mud middlemen. To be sure, in seeking their own fortunes they were also adding substantially to the productive capacities of their adopted countries, but equally of course it never looks like that to those long set in comfortable traditional ways. Basques, Catalans, and Montañés from Asturias played a big part in the economic revival of New Spain, Catalans organised large-scale fishing for export in Chiloé;[54] but such successes attract the envy and resentment of the less pushful, as Jews and overseas Indians and Chinese know too well. Easy-going Criollos, fond of conspicuous consumption and fiestas, 'saw the Catalan as a miser and the Basque as a bird of prey … parvenus and climbers who wanted to monopolize wealth, jobs, and the richest heiresses.' Such sentiments were naturally met with contempt for Criollo fecklessness.[55]

During the entire colonial régime, 754 men held governmental positions from President of an Audiencia upwards; of these eighteen were Criollos. At the top, of course, it was only commonsense that Viceroys and Captains-General should be without local ties or family interests; the tiny handful at this level who were born in America were not bred there. However, it is all very well for Madariaga to remark that 'No Canadian has ever been Governor-General of Canada, no Australian of Australia'; but the Indies were big enough to provide high appointments for Criollos far from their native hearths. (Incidentally his remark had been untrue for Australia for some fifteen years when he wrote, and soon would be so for Canada.)[56] There were in fact many Criollo judges in the rank-and-file of the Audiencias, and local magistracies—*alcaldias mayores* in the towns, *corregimientos* in the country—provided a 'comfortable, slipshod system of outdoor relief' for impoverished Criollo gentry.[57] But the imbalance at really responsible levels was extreme. As early as 1773 the Cabildo of Mexico City reacted by demanding 'the selection of [American] natives for every kind of office in their country—not only in preference to but to the exclusion of foreigners'; this seems hardly likely to have been meant as a realistic demand, but is a sure index of incipient nationalism.[58]

The Reforms did nothing to improve things, from the American point of view; quite the contrary. In Peru, the confusion and incoherence at all levels of administration displayed during Túpac Amaru's rebellion 'accentuated a pattern of discrimination against creoles which had begun to appear even before 1780', and was far from discouraged by José de Gálvez. The new temper of administration under Carlos III, with its emphasis on hard work and efficiency, had little use for Criollos; of the twenty-five intendentes in La Plata whose birthplace is known, just one was American-born.[59]

The Church of course offered careers, and about a seventh of all archbishops and bishops in New Spain had been born there; but there seems to have been an intense communal feeling at lower levels, so much so that in those Orders which elected their Provincials, these posts had to be rotated between Peninsulares and Criollos triennially. Remained the army. After 1764 the militias were greatly enlarged and put on a more permanent footing, especially in New Spain. In part at least this expansion was designed to provide places and honours for the Criollo gentry, who naturally filled a majority of the officer cadres, although the key ranks were dominated by Spanish-born veterans. Many militia officers were parade soldiers, and the parades were often enough far from models of military precision. The new organisation seems to have been most successful in New Spain; the Peruvian forces seem to have been of poor quality, and after Túpac Amaru their Americanisation was checked.[60] But in some times and places the militias could give a good account of themselves, as the British learnt, at heavy cost, at Buenos Aires in 1806–7.

There were thus plenty of long-accumulating discontents even before the shock of the new system of intendentes and comercio libre came to tighten central control, screw up tax levels, and disrupt the old settled courses of trade and the markets of local industries. More positively, in an American if not an imperial sense, the new territorial arrangements sharpened the sense of regional identities. Madrid was uneasily suspicious of the stability of its own structures in America, and disconcerted by the dangerously attractive example of the successful revolt of the Thirteen Colonies: if Great Britain could not put down a rebellion so much nearer the metropolis, how could Spain keep under subjugation her more distant and more extensive domains?[61]

No sooner had the Conde de Aranda, the most overtly enlightened of all Carlos III's Ministers, signed for Spain the peace treaty of 1783 than he wrote to his King: 'The American colonies are independent: this is my sorrow and fear.' After a perceptive review of the difficulties the Spanish Crown would face in controlling and defending distant America, and of the grievances of its American subjects, including the compounding of the law's delays by appeal to courts in Spain, he expressed his alarm at the prospect of living with

> this federative republic which has been born, let us say,
> as a pigmy, because two such powers as Spain and France
> have formed it and given it being [by] aiding its independence
> with their forces. Tomorrow it will be a giant . . . and later
> a colossus irresistible in those regions . . . it will forget
> the benefits it has received from both powers and will think
> only of its own aggrandisement.[62]

The Americans will begin with Florida (as they did), then Mexico, impossible to defend from Europe against so formidable a neighbour. His solution: a devolution into a confederacy of kingdoms (New Spain, Peru, the rest of the continent) ruled by Bourbon princes, at their head the King of Spain as a true emperor, the four nations bound in a reciprocal commercial union. So bold a restructuring had little chance of adoption even under Carlos III, let alone under his nerveless successor.

Nevertheless, despite these tensions and despite the slackening of the springs when Carlos IV and Godoy took over, at this stage very few Criollos indeed would have wished for more than a considerable degree of autonomy under the Spanish Crown. The ancient monarchy was not so decrepit as its British foes wishfully assumed, though its position was obviously weakened, and the system might have carried on indefinitely but for Napoleon's sudden dispossession of both Carlos IV and his heir Fernando in 1808, in favour of his own brother Joseph. 'José I' was never recognised by the Americans, but this totally unforeseen catastrophe left no clear authority in the Indies.

In Spain itself the resistance of *ad hoc* regional juntas to the usurper in Madrid was more or less co-ordinated by a more or less self-appointed Regency sitting, ominously for Americans, in Cadiz, 'a captive if not a creature of the Junta de Cadiz dominated by merchant guild members'[63] or, if this is rather too extreme a description, at least (flowery words on liberty and equality put aside) no more sympathetic to American grievances than the old Casa and Consulado had been. But the time for petitioning was passing. The bloody repulse of the British army from Buenos Aires in 1807 (powerfully assisted by inept British generalship) had been the work not of the Viceregal authorities, which collapsed, but of the Criollo militia guided by the Cabildo; after such a taste of power Americans were not likely to submit too easily to the doctrinaire edicts of so distant and so dubious an authority as that of Cadiz. What authority they *were* to accept was precisely the problem, and it was to take years of intrigue and atrocious civil war before republican institutions prevailed from Texas to Chiloé.

There was thus a great deal of contingency in the arrival of independence; even if it seems too perfunctory to dismiss so great an upheaval as Chaunu does, as merely 'a chronological error', yet Simón Bolívar, *the* Liberator, confessed that 'America was not prepared for secession' and that the Americans 'were left orphans':[64] and the long history of *coups* and *caudillismo* would seem to bear him out. But in the turbulence of the Napoleonic usurpation and the vicious reaction under the restored Fernando VII, many Criollo leaders came to feel themselves left with no option but to declare for independence. For one thing, in the travail of the old order there was the risk that the exploited masses of Indios and Blacks might rise on their own account, and not distinguish overmuch between native-born and peninsular oppressors. Such fears were given point not only by Túpac Amaru but by the racial violence which marked Hidalgo's rising in New Spain (1810–11), the first armed struggle avowedly proclaiming independence; and this despite Criollo initiation and leadership. The men-on-the-spot, as ever in the history of imperialism, had always thought the home government too indulgent to the indigenes. That government had never been strong enough to give real protection to the oppressed masses; now it might prove not strong enough to give protection against them. For the Criollo leaders, then, better to make sure of the revolution—from above.[65]

Decision on the Pacific: 'la Expedición Libertadora'

Only one phase of the tragic and savage warfare which swept Spanish America from end to end need concern a Pacific history, but it was central to the outcome: the 'Liberating Expedition' to Peru under José de San Martín. To the very end, Peru remained the heart of royalist power; as we have noted, this stronghold was breached by a naval campaign on the Pacific.[66]

In January 1814 San Martín, a splendidly professional soldier, took command of the forces with which the (nominally United) Provinces of La Plata were trying to regain control over Upper Peru, now firmly in royalist hands. He realised that it was useless to keep battering away on the direct approach to the plateaus, via Tucumán; both the physical and the social terrain could be considered counter-revolutionary. He therefore determined on a vast outflanking attack by sea; but for this of course he needed a base in Chile. That neglected corner of the empire had almost glided into a position of autonomy, until in 1813 the able and vigorous Viceroy of Peru, José Fernando de Abascal, decided to put an end to this incipient independence. The ending of the Peninsular War, releasing thousands of experienced soldiers, and the restoration of Fernando VII, a legitimate and (briefly) a constitutional King, obviously strengthened the royalist cause.

Chiloé, as we have seen, was an outpost directly dependent on Lima, and Abascal's first move was to send a force which secured the island as a base, a royalist enclave which was not to be liquidated by the patriots until 1826. Despite a clear warning of the danger—Chiloé was to windward of all other Chilean ports—the junta in Santiago did nothing effective to meet it, and one small royalist ship was able to foment counter-insurrection everywhere south of the Biobío.[67] From Chiloé the royalists moved on by sea to take Valdivia, Talcahuano, and Concepción; in October 1814 they inflicted a crushing defeat on Bernardo O'Higgins at Rancagua, south of Santiago. The patriot leaders fled across the Andes to join San Martín in Mendoza, while in Chile a ferocious repression thoroughly alienated the hearts and minds of the people; for which, as usual, read the educated classes. Juan Fernández found a new use, as a place of harsh penal exile.

San Martín had been systematically building up his forces and supplies in Cuyo, until on 9 January 1817 he was able to launch a campaign, as meticulously planned as it was daring, which in five weeks took his little army of some 5000 men across the Andes and into Santiago; a model of military art. The royalists still held the south, and from Talcahuano staged a counter-offensive which by April 1818 brought them to Maipú, on the southern outskirts of modern Santiago. There they were decisively defeated; the independence of Chile was now secure under O'Higgins, with whose close support San Martín was able to prepare his next move—by sea to Peru.

Abascal's neat little lesson on sea power had not been lost on the Chilean leaders. They enthusiastically commissioned privateers—there were plenty of discharged British naval men looking for something better than half-pay—and by purchase and capture got together a little fleet whose flagship, the *O'Higgins*, 1220 tons 50 guns, was originally one of the Russian ships given by the Tsar to Fernando to assist in the reconquest; fir-built and 'as rickety as an old basket', she had been captured by the Chilean Admiral Blanco Encalada. Chile also secured the services of Thomas Cochrane, later Earl of Dundonald but now recently expelled from the British Navy and Parliament for a Stock Exchange fraud and professionally, if not morally, close kin to Horatio Hornblower, some of whose exploits seem modelled on Cochrane's. His style may be judged from his remark that in order to be sure of taking a stronger Spaniard he had only to lay the eternally leaking *O'Higgins* alongside—and tell his crew that there were no pumps on the enemy.

While San Martín was organising a striking force in Chile, Cochrane was insulting or blockading Callao, ranging as far north as Guayaquil—he did not forget to raid Paita!—and almost casually taking Valdivia, the strongest fortified place anywhere on the Pacific, by an astonishing *coup de main*. This effectively bottled up the royalists on Chiloé, and the way was clear for the *Expedición Libertadora* to sail from Valparaiso on 20 August 1820: seven warships with 220 guns, eighteen transports carrying 4500 men. Three weeks later Pisco, only about 200 km from Lima, was occupied; another neat demonstration of the decisive advantage of commanding the sea.

The rest was in a way anticlimax; San Martín, a most conservative revolutionary, was anxious to be truly a liberator, not a conqueror, and hence to give the Peruvians time to free themselves; he was feeling his way towards a political solution, and when he did move it was to place his army north of Lima, cutting it off from the populous agricultural northern Valles. Such political subtlety was of course lost on Cochrane, who was all for a direct drive on Lima and Callao. While San Martín was finessing, Cochrane cut out the *Esmeralda* from the heart of the Spanish squadron in Callao harbour and sailed to Acapulco in search of Spanish ships, before departing after a final quarrel with the too-politic soldier.

Not until July 1821 did San Martín enter Lima; a year later he withdrew from the wars after a mysterious interview at Guayaquil with Bolívar, who had come down from the north and took over the revolution. The royalists still held the Andean plateaus, and in February 1824 mutiny and treason delivered both Callao and Lima into their hands. In December Lima was retaken, and the last Viceroy, José de la Serna, was defeated and captured at Ayacucho, west of Cuzco. Even then the waterfront fortress of Real Felipe at Callao held out until 23 January 1826; Chiloé had surrendered five days earlier. These posts on the Pacific shores were the last points on or adjacent to the mainland of either America to own allegiance to the Spanish Crown.

San Martín seems to have made some political miscalculations and hence his campaign was less immediately decisive than it might have been had he sought a quick military solution; it was none the less decisive, in the context of the practical veto by Britain and the United States on aid to Fernando VII by the Holy Alliance of Russia, Austria, and Prussia. The old British dream of subversion in the Indies was now reality. But Andean Peru had been the strongroom of Spanish power, the taking of Callao and Lima burst in its door, and it was San Martín's strategy and Cochrane's command of the sea which made that possible. This naval operation was indeed the *ne plus ultra* of the Platine outreach to Potosí and Chile, the final act in the contest between Buenos Aires and Lima.

Coda: a prospective epilogue

With the surrender of Real Felipe, the saga of Spain in the eastern Pacific ends, except for a seriocomic postscript: the scientific (really flag-showing and debt-collecting) expedition of 1866, which held for a time Peru's guano-rich Islas Chinchas but otherwise achieved nothing but the bombardment of an undefended town, Valparaiso, and a repulse from a fortified one, Callao; it is chiefly notable for the first circumnavigation by an armoured warship. Across the Ocean, the curtain did not fall in the Philippines until May-day 1898, when a Spanish squadron, wretchedly weak in all respects but courage, was annihilated by the Americans under the batteries of Cavite.

But the Pacific played an even greater part than before in the life of the successor-states south of Panama; it was the one great highway on the immensely long littoral where land transport was made so difficult, by desert, mountain, or jungle, that most of the pockets of population were in effect so many islands or oases. The Chilean naval tradition, so briskly initiated by Blanco Encalada and Cochrane, was maintained in two wars against Peru and Bolivia, in 1837–8 and the more serious nitrate-generated War of the Pacific in 1879–81, not to mention the civil war of 1891, all models of the application of sea power. Chilean traders reached out to Tahiti and Sydney, Peruvian slavers devastated Easter Island amongst others. The California gold rush resurrected the Panama crossing (with a railway) and brought a burst of intense activity to the littoral: in 1849 over 6000 fortune-hunters crossed the Isthmus, 15,000 rounded Cape Horn.

After 1860 Californian and Australian gold production levelled off, but world silver output rose steeply: the great Comstock Lode in Nevada was at its peak after 1873. Despite the bimetallist agitation, the resultant depreciation of silver could not be warded off, and seriously affected the Andean economy; but after the gleaming metal, more earthy treasures came into their own. There was a vast change in the *mise-en-valeur* of the Andean littoral, from an almost total reliance on silver and copper to such bulky products as guano and nitrates.

Guano exports began in the 1840s; Peruvian politicians soon learned how to raise money in a big way, by selling concessions to French, British, or American entre-preneurs—Dreyfus, Gibbs, Grace—and indulging in an orgy of beautifying Lima (in parts) and, with the enthusiastic aid of the Yankee Henry Meiggs, of building railways into the Andes, magnificent engineering but fiscal folly. In time, however, these railways were to cut into the vertebral linkage of Oruro and Potosí to La Plata; Buenos Aires could not retain its old grasp on the trade of Charcas. With steam navigation and the clipper ships, Chile also fell outside of the sphere of influence of La Plata: the east Pacific trading zone was now independent of such local influences, although tightly locked into the wider world of metropolitan investment.

By the 1870s the Chincha guano deposits were nearly exhausted and overall production was declining; nitrates were in the ascendant. To the fiscal devastation of Peru's reckless boom exploitation of her guano was now added that of the disastrous War of the Pacific, which was fought on balance of power principles to help Bolivia retain the nitrate fields in her desert coastal strip, fields which, in default of decent management skills of her own and the political stability to attract investors, she had allowed Chile, or Chilean-based overseas interests, to exploit. The clash of United States and British interests played its part in the political history of the War of the Pacific and the 1891 Chilean counter-revolution against José Manuel Balmaceda, in some respects an earlier Allende; the 'Constitutional' reaction was able to build up its forces in the nitrate fields of the north, protected by the navy and backed by British interests. The stakes were nitrates and copper.

Unlike gold and silver, high value but low bulk commodities, guano and nitrates demanded cheap bulk loaders: the sweltering dusty little ports from Pisagua to Antofagasta, the prizes of the Pacific War, became crowded with the great steel clippers, barque-rigged with four or five masts, the ultimate triumphs of sail; tall Cape Horners also carried Australian wool and wheat to Europe. In the days of sail South America and Australia were relatively close, as for instance the Tichborne Case so casually indicates.

All this was to dwindle to vanishing point with the supersession of sail by steam, the decline of nitrates before synthetic fertilisers, and the great reversal of traffic flow along the Pacific shores brought about by the opening of the Panama Canal: the fulfilment of a vision first glimpsed under Don Carlos I, Rey de Castilla, Aragon y otros Reinos; but made reality only under Woodrow Wilson, President of the United States of America, in the fateful month of August 1914.

APPENDIX

Modern Chinese Names

Amoy	Xiamen
Anping	Anping
Canton	Guangszhou
Chekiang	Zhejiang
Cheng Ch'eng-kung	Zheng Chenggong
Cheng Chih-lung	Zheng Zhilong
Cheng Ching	Zheng Jing
Chenkiang	Zhenjioung
Ch'ing	Qing
Ch'uan-chou	Quanzhou
Chusan	Zhusan
Foochow	Fuzhou
Fukien	Fujian
Han	Han
hopou ('Hoppo')	Hu Bu
Kang-hsi	Kangxi
Keelung	Jilong
Kiakhta	Qiaketu
Kiangsu	Jiangsu
Kien-lung	Qianlong
Kwangtung	Guangdong
Lung-wu	Longwu
Macao	Aomen
Maimatschin	Maimaicheng
Manchu	Manzhou
Ming	Ming
Nanking	Nanjing
Ningpo	Ningbo
Peking	Beijing

Penghu	Penghu
Quemoy	Jinmen
Shanghai	Shanghai
Shih Lang	Shi Lang
Si-kiang	Xijiong
Taipa	Taibai
Taipan	Daban
Taipei	Taibei
Taiwan	Taiwan
Tanshui	Danshui
Tsing-tao	Qingdao
Whampoa	Huangpu
Yang-tse	Yangzi
Yunnan	Yunnan

NOTES

Notes for Chapter 1

[1] J. H. Parry, in *NCMH* III.542.

[2] Blair & Robertson, IV.313. For a vivid account of Dasmariñas's end, see A. de Morga, *Sucesos de las Islas Filipinas*, HS 2nd Ser. 140 (Cambridge 1971), 73–7 [*Sucesos*]. There are further details in the abridged translation of B. L. de Argensola, *Conqvista de las Islas Malvcas* (Madrid 1609), in Blair & Robertson, XVI.211–317 at 256–61 [Argensola, *Conqvista*].

[3] This fantastic story may be found in Morga, *Sucesos*, 80–8; Argensola, *Conqvista*, 264–9; Blair & Robertson, IX.161–80, 197–203. Its relevance to general history, such as it is, is brought out in D. Lach, *Asia in the Making of Europe* (Chicago 1965), I.309–12.

[4] A. C. Burnell and P. A. Tiele, *The Voyage of Jan Huyghen van Linschoten to the East Indies*, HS 1st Ser. 70–1 (London 1885), I.xxxvi–xxxvii and 112—this is the 1598 translation of the First Book, with footnote corrections. On Linschoten, see G. Masselman, *The Cradle of Colonialism* (New Haven 1963), 70–6 [*Colonialism*] and D. W. Davies, *A Primer of Dutch Seventeenth Century Overseas Trade* (The Hague 1961), 46–9. Although the *Itinerario* was not published in full until 1596, relevant parts were available in print earlier.

[5] George Canning, cipher despatch to HBM's Minister at The Hague, 31 Jan. 1826.

[6] For these early voyages, see Masselman, *Colonialism*, 86–97, 109–17; E. S. de Klerck, *History of the Dutch East Indies* (Rotterdam 1938), I.196–9—factually useful but very old-style colonialist [*East Indies*]. I greatly regret my inability to read the naturally very numerous sources in Dutch. For the founding and structure of the VOC, see Masselman, 133–50; Klerck, I.202–6; C. R. Boxer, *The Dutch Seaborne Empire 1600–1800* (Harmondsworth 1973), 25–7, 49–52 [*Dutch Empire*]; also D. Hannay, *The Great Chartered Companies* (London 1926), 38–9 [*Companies*]; F. Mauro, *L'Expansion Européenne (1600–1870)* (Paris 1967), 131–4; B. H. M. Vlekke, *Nusantara: A History of the East Indian Archipelago* (rev. ed. The Hague 1959), 118–19 [*Nusantara*]. There is an admirably succinct and lucid section on the VOC and EIC in C. G. F. Simkin, *The Traditional Trade of Asia* (London 1968), 191–202. The functioning of the VOC 'in the field' is discussed in detail by K. Glamman, M. A. P. Meilink-Roelofsz, A. Steensgard, and J. C. van Leur, in works which will be cited in Ch. 4 below. For political narrative, see D. G. E. Hall, *A History of South-East Asia* (3rd ed. London 1968), Chs. 15–18 [*History*].

[7] Masselman, *Colonialism*, 153; cf. Klerck, *East Indies*, I.205–6.

[8] Masselman, *Colonialism*, 280—not eighteen times, as given in A. Hyma, *The Dutch in the Far East* (Ann Arbor 1953), 83 and cf. 15–26 [*Far East*]; A. D. Innes, *The Maritime and Colonial Expansion of England under the Stuarts* (London 1931), 65 [*Expansion*].

[9] Innes, *Expansion*, 78 (cf. Hyma, *Far East*, 87–8); J. S. Furnivall, *Netherlands India* (Cambridge 1944), 26–7—but cf. Hall, *History*, 295.

[10] For the Bantamese-Jacatran-English siege of the Dutch fort which became Batavia, see Masselman, *Colonialism*, 377–89. Much of Batavia's success was due to its location, very favourable for taking advantage of the alternating monsoons—F. B. Eldridge, *The Background of Eastern Sea Power* (Melbourne 1948), 239.

[11] R. Picard *et al.*, *Les Compagnies des Indes: Route de la Porcelaine* (Paris 1966), 114–15; Masselman, *Colonialism*, 338–9, 350–2, and cf. Furnivall, *Netherlands India*, 27. For Danes and 'Danes', see Vlekke, *Nusantara*, 127, 177, 415; but cf. M. A. P. Meilink-Roelofsz, *Asian Trade and European Influence* ... (The Hague 1962), 205. Makassar, Danes, and local bottomry are discussed in B. Schrieke, *Indonesian Sociological Studies* (The Hague 1955), I.70–5. There is an excellent introduction to the Dutch-Iberian conflict, not neglecting the 'country powers', in C. R. Boxer, 'War and Trade in the Indian Ocean and South China Sea, 1600–1650', *Great Circle* (Nedlands, W. Australia) 1/2, 1979, 3–17 ['War and Trade']. Further discussion of assorted companies in Chs. 4 and 8.

[12] E. Sluiter, The Voyage of Jacques Mahu and Simon de Cordes into the Pacific Ocean, 1598–1600 (Berkeley MA thesis 1933), 26–8. Sluiter's work, the source of all details given here, appears to be based mainly on F. C. Wider (ed.), *De Reis van Mahu en de Cordes ... naar Zuid-Amerika en Japan* (Linschoten Vereeniging Werken 21, 22, 24, The Hague 1923–5) [not seen].

[13] For the *Liefde*'s voyage and Will Adams, see his letters 'to my unknowne Friends and Country-men' and to his 'Loving Wife', 22 Oct. 1611, in S. Purchas (ed.), *Hakluytus Posthumus or Purchas His Pilgrimes* (1625; Glasgow ed. 1905–7), II.326–46 [*Pilgrimes*]. Adams 'received a living, like unto a Lordship in England', and when he died in 1620 divided his estate equally between his long-unseen English and his Japanese families; his memory and his tomb are still respected in Japan, his memorials being graced with lines by a Japanese poet and by Edmund Blunden—P. G. Rogers, *The First Englishman in Japan* (London 1956), 113–20, 134–8—and he is the hero of a good historical novel by R. Blaker, *The Needle-Watcher* (London 1932, paperback ed. Tokyo 1973). J. Murdoch thought it likely that the *Liefde*'s guns and munitions 'proved very serviceable' at Sekigahara (*A History of Japan* (London 1949), III.400, 467); but G. Sansom, *A History of Japan 1334–1615* (London 1961), 403, thinks this improbable, though they (presumably the guns, not by this time the ammo) 'were certainly used in the siege of Osaka castle in 1615.'

[14] The standard work is J. W. IJzerman (ed.), *De Reis om de wereld door Olivier van Noort* (Linschoten Vereegniging Werken 27–8, The Hague 1926 [not seen]). Accounts in English may be found in Purchas, *Pilgrimes*, II.187–218, source of my direct quotations, and J. O. M. Broek, *A Letter from Olivier van Noort* (Minneapolis 1957) [*Letter*]. For the battle off Corregidor, see Morga, *Sucesos*, and as an offset to his provoking self-esteem the criticism of him by the Manila town council in Blair & Robertson, XI.235–51; there are several other documents on the affair in this volume. On the Peruvian side, G. Lohmann Villena, *Historia Marítima del Perú, T. IV: Siglos XVII y XVIII* (Lima 1975), 377–84, is useful on Spanish movements, although he says that van Noort was sent out by the VOC (before it was founded) and that the *Hendrick Frederick* was lost near Cape Horn (before it was found) [*Hist. Marítima*].

[15] J. O. M. Broek, 'Geographical Exploration by the Dutch', in H. Friis (ed.), *The Pacific Basin: A History of Its Geographical Exploration* (New York 1967), 151–69 at 154 [*Pacific Basin*]. One ship had been burnt in the Atlantic as unseaworthy, so after losing the *Hendrick Frederick* van Noort was left with two only.

[16] P. Gerhard, *Pirates on the West Coast of New Spain 1575–1742* (Glendale 1960), 104–7 [*Pirates*].

[17] But the cloves received at Ternate in exchange for the *Hendrick Frederick* may have covered most of the investment, though the accounts were not settled until 1630!—Broek, *Letter*, 9.

[18] Morga, *Sucesos*, 225; his account, vivid as usual, is on 206–9, 217–30 (and cf. 243–4). See also Blair & Robertson, X.173, 259 (Tello), XII.83–97 (the Mandarins), 142–68 (reports by the Audiencia and Acuña); XIV.38–52 (relations with China), XVI.290–5 (from Argensola, *Conqvista*); and R. Bernal, 'The Chinese Colony in Manila, 1570–1770' in A. Felix (ed.), *The Chinese in the Philippines: I.1570–1770* (Manila 1966), 40–66 at 51–3 [*Chinese*]. This volume includes much detail on the Parian; the Chinese version of the three Mandarins story is at 248–9.

[19] Blair & Robertson, XII.155, 158–9. For the Imperial reactions, or lack of them, Bernal in Felix, *Chinese*, 53–5; for Chinese numbers and Spanish attempts to limit them, L. Diaz-Trechuelo, 'The Role of the Chinese in the Philippine Domestic Economy', ibid. 175–210 at 184–8.

[20] This *ad hoc* promotion of the Stadtholder was necessary to overcome the little difficulty that the Ambonese naturally wanted to know with whom they were ultimately dealing, and equally naturally could hardly be expected to understand the complicated federative government of the United Provinces—Vlekke, *Nusantara*, 115; cf. below, note 8 to Ch. 4.

[21] Vlekke, *Nusantara*, 110–11, 117–19; Blair & Robertson, XII.29–41 (Viceroy at Goa and Acuña); Argensola, *Conqvista*, 282–5; Morga, *Sucesos*, 204–6, 212–16; Fernández Duro, III.279–80, 286–7.

[22] J. C. van Leur, *Indonesian Trade and Society* (The Hague 1955), 181–2. There is a Dutch account of Matelief's attack on Malacca in B. Penrose (ed.), *Sea Fights in the East Indies* (Cambridge, Mass., 1931), 55–85; despite its title, only three of the ten pamphlets reprinted in this book deal with actions in the East Indies proper. As the Sultan of Johore was a descendant of Sultan Mahmud, ruler of Malacca when the Portuguese took it in 1511, he may well have reflected on the fable of the monkey, the cat, and the fire.

[23] See notes by José Rizal in Blair & Robertson, XVI.60, 64.

[24] Morga, *Sucesos*, 232–42; Argensola, *Conqvista*, 301–17; Masselman, *Colonialism*, 169–71; Klerck, *East Indies*, I.209; Fernández Duro, III.293–5.

[25] Hannay, *Companies*, 102; Hyma, *Far East*, 76; for a concrete example of evasion, see J. A. J. Villiers (ed.), *The East and West Indian Mirror*, HS 2nd Ser. 18 (London 1906), 146 [*Mirror*].

[26] B. Hilder, *The Voyage of Torres* (St Lucia, Queensland, 1980), 127. Details of the curious mosaic of petty forts are in Blair & Robertson, XV.324–5, and a Dutch list in Villiers, *Mirror*, 154–60.

[27] Gregorio Lopez SJ in Blair & Robertson, XVII.102–26; Masselman, *Colonialism*, 263–4; but the best account I have seen is still in Fernández Duro, III.383–90. Alas, that we no longer have Morga.

[28] Ibid., III.391–3, a clear narrative; see also the Jesuit accounts in Blair & Robertson, XVII.249–79, and for the five caravels, XVIII.91–2, 164 (Boxer, 'War and Trade', 3, says that there were seven caravels and 300 soldiers). For Silva in Gilolo, see Villiers, *Mirror*, 143–4.

[29] The Jesuit Provincial de Ledesma, in Blair & Robertson, XVII.253–4.

30 But not only heretic and infidel could combine effectively upon occasion: in 1629 the rise of Atjeh brought together Catholic Malacca, Muslim Johore, and Siamese Patani, and 'the allied fleets crushed the power of Atjeh in a great naval battle … a turning point in Atjeh's history'—Vlekke, *Nusantara*, 122.

31 Broek, in *Pacific Basin*, 154–5. Van Spilbergen's name is also given as Speilbergen (as in Villiers, *Mirror*), Spielbergen, Spelbergen, Spitzberg, and doubtless other variants.

32 The instructions—battle orders, not an order of battle as Broek terms them—are in Villiers, *Mirror*, 56–61; this volume contains both van Spilbergen's journal and that of the Le Maire-Schouten voyage. Apart from the *Mirror*, my main source is P. Rodríguez Crespo, 'El peligro holandés en las costas peruanas a principios del Siglo XVII: La Expedición de Spilbergen y la Defensa del Virreynato', *Rev. Histórica* (Lima) 26, 1962–3, 259–310 ['El peligro']; Fernández Duro, III.395–408, is as usual much to the point.

33 Gerhard, *Pirates*, 109–10—Spanish accounts give the ships more guns, 48 for the *Groote Sonne* and 38 for the *Groote Manne*.

34 Broek, in *Pacific Basin*, 154–5; the rutter had been published about 1600.

35 F. T. Bradley, 'The Defence of Peru (1600–1688)', *Ibero-Amerikanisches Archiv* (Berlin) Neue Folge Jg 2 H.2 [*sic*] 1976, 79–111 at 80 ['Defence']; Fernández Duro, III.395; Rodríguez Crespo, 'El peligro', 270–80.

36 Lohmann Villena, *Hist. Marítima*, 45, and 45–93 for the general history of the Armada at this time; see also P. T. Bradley, 'Some Considerations on Defence at Sea in the Viceroyalty of Peru during the Seventeenth Century', *Rev. de Historia de América* (Mexico) 79, 1975, 77–97 at 80 ['Considerations'], and 'Maritime Defence … of Peru (1600–1700)', *The Americas* 36, 1979, 155–75; also G. Lohmann Villena, *Las Defensas Militares de Lima y Callao* (Lima 1964), 14–15 [*Defensas*].

37 Historians of technology ascribe the invention of the telescope to the Dutch, between 1600 and 1608, and it was at once taken up by Galileo—L. Hogben, *Science for the Citizen* (2nd ed. London 1940), 132–3; T. K. Derry and T. I. Williams, *A Short History of Technology* (Oxford Paperback ed. 1970), 112. It is then surprising that a minor local official in Peru should have had one so soon, but the fact is vouched for by Fernández Duro (III.397) and Lohmann Villena. Already in 1613 Saris's presents to Ieyasu included '1 prospective Glasse cast in silver Gilte'—E. M. Satow (ed.), *The Voyage of John Saris to Japan, 1613*, HS 2nd Ser. 5 (London 1900), 113. For capitana and almirante, see note 59 below.

38 J. S. Cummins, in Morga, *Sucesos*, 10; Lohmann Villena, *Hist. Marítima*, 398. Esquilache's escape is referred to in a very alarmist 'Discurso sobre los combenienzias' of sending Lorenzo de Zuazola's 1619 succours for the Philippines by 'el estrecho do Magellanes o el de S^n Vizente'—Mitchell Library, Sydney, Prado MSS. VI.

39 Bradley, 'Considerations', 82–9, and 'Defence', 88–95; Lohmann Villena, *Defensas*, 39–45.

40 Gerhard, *Pirates*, 107.

41 T. Oteiza Iriarte, *Acapulco: La Ciudad de las Naos de Oriente y de las Sirenas Modernas* (n.p. 1963), 105–9 (but he is quite wrong about the Nassau Fleet, 119); Gerhard, *Pirates*, 42–5; E. Sluiter, 'The Fortification of Acapulco, 1615–1616', *HAHR* 29, 1949, 69–76, who notes that the engineer was a Dutchman, Adrian Boot, better known for his work on the drainage of the Lake of Mexico—H. H. Bancroft, *History of Mexico* (San Francisco 1883–6), III.85–91.

42 A. del Portillo y Diez Sollano, *Descubrimientos y Exploraciones en las Costas de California*

(Madrid 1947), 221–2; he calls the pirate 'Jorge Spitzberg' and takes Vizcaíno's account at face value, a rash compliment to his veracity. We shall see, in Ch. 5, that Portillo's authority is not impeccable.

43 Blair & Robertson, XVII.276–7.

44 See the tribute of a practised seaman in Burney, II.352. The fleet was split up in the Moluccas, and Villiers (*Mirror*, xxxii, 8, 153) is wrong in saying that van Spilbergen returned to Holland with the *Groote Sonne* and *Groot Manne*, though there is some uncertainty as to the ships that he did have—personal information from Mr C. F. L. Paul, Nederlands Scheepvaart Museum, Amsterdam.

45 Masselman, *Colonialism*, 142, 172–5, 338–9.

46 R. Hough, *The Blind Horn's Hate* (London 1971), 156–64 at 156. Hough's account, like that by F. Riesenberg in *Cape Horn* (London 1941), 146–68, has some errors of detail but is clear and vivid.

47 Spate, 57 (Magellan), 250 (Hondius).

48 Broek in *Pacific Basin*, 377–8 at note 10, and G. Schilder, *Australia Unveiled: the share of Dutch navigators in the discovery of Australia* (Amsterdam/Canberra 1976), 33–4 and Figs. 12 and 13 for the title-pages [*Australia*]. The standard modern edition of the Dutch accounts is in W. A. Engelbrecht and P. J. van Herwerden (eds.), *De ontdekkingreis van Jacob le Maire en Willem Cornelis Schouten* (Linschoten Vereeniging Werken 49, The Hague 1945 [not seen]). Le Maire's voyage has received more attention from English writers than have earlier Dutch ventures into the South Sea: apart from Villiers, Hough, and Riesenberg, see i.a. G. A. Wood, *The Discovery of Australia* (revised ed. Melbourne 1969, original Sydney 1922), 152–4, and J. C. Beaglehole, *The Exploration of the Pacific* (3rd ed. London 1966), 127–37.

49 C. Kelly OFM, *La Austrialia del Espíritu Santo*, HS 2nd Ser. 126–7 (Cambridge 1966), I.5.

50 Riesenberg, *Cape Horn*, 156.

51 Ibid., 72–4. J. Goebel, in *The Struggle for the Falklands* (New Haven 1927), 17–24, convincingly demolishes the claim put forward by the Chilean Admiralty and Sir Clements Markham for Camargo's ship; in view of the inconsistencies in the record, his further inference that the wintering was in the Falklands is perhaps another matter. For good measure Goebel (34–43) goes on to discount the sighting by John Davis and Richard Hawkins, though with rather less assurance. This is an instance of unserendipity: had I read Goebel before writing *The Spanish Lake* (96), these points would have been put differently; but if one reads everything, one writes nothing.

52 Villiers, *Mirror*, 188; source of all direct quotations in the remainder of this section.

53 Island identifications and dates from A. Sharp, *The Discovery of the Pacific Islands* (Oxford 1960), 71–8 [*Pacific Islands*]. For the influence of this voyage on Roggeveen's, see Sharp's edition of *The Journal of Jacob Roggeveen* (Oxford 1970), 7, 133–41 *passim*.

54 They did not know what they were missing: kava or yaqona is a most delectable drink, mildly stimulating, and as the seventeenth century might have put it, of exceeding vertue for the hangover; but admittedly I have not seen it prepared, as Le Maire did, in the classical style—chewed by the village girls before the infusion.

55 Schilder, *Australia*, 36. They may also have seen, as Tasman certainly did, the outliers north of New Ireland—the Tanga, Lihir, and Tabar groups—Sharp, *Pacific Islands*, 77, 84–5.

56 Schilder, *Australia*, 51–2.

57 Wording of the title-page of the first edition (Madrid 1621) of the *Relación* of the voyage; this was translated by Sir Clements Markham in *Early Spanish Voyages to Magellan*

Strait, HS 2nd Ser. 27 (London 1911), 169–272, from which my account is drawn. Those of Hough, *The Blind Horn's Hate*, 163–73, and Riesenberg, *Cape Horn*, 169–79, have some good points but are rather over-written. There is a *Derrotero* dated Madrid, 30 Sept. 1619, in the Prado MSS., Mitchell Library, Sydney.

[58] See the opening of the dedication of the Nodals' account, referring to 'the new discovery of the strait of St Vincent' and of 'another new way',. which are due to the efforts of the dedicatee, the President of the Council of the Indies. Fernández Duro (*Armada*, III.371–2) says that Spanish seamen had for long presumed there was a seaway south of Tierra del Fuego and in 1549 offered to find it, but the authorities paid no attention.

[59] *Nuestra Señora de Atoche*, under Bartolomé, the elder brother, capitana; *NS del Buen Suceso*, under Gonzalo, almiranta. Somewhat confusingly for modern readers, the flagship of a Spanish squadron was the capitana, our 'Admiral' was the 'General', and the second-in-command or almirante sailed in the almiranta.

[60] Burney, II.461–2.

Notes for Chapter 2

[1] Spate, 80.

[2] There is black comedy in Coen's 'rage at this "hideous monopoly" [of the Chinese at Bantam] when compared to his own policy of monopoly, violence, and destruction'—J. C. van Leur, *Indonesian Trade and Society* (The Hague 1955), 377–8 at note 88 [*Indo. Trade*]. Double-talk was not invented by George Orwell.

[3] Oddly enough, Coen did not like this name, perhaps because the christening was in his absence, by subordinates after a drunken debauch; he would have preferred Nieuw Hoorn, after his birthplace—G. Masselman, *The Cradle of Colonialism* (New Haven 1963), 387–9, 393–4 [*Colonialism*].

[4] B. M. Vlekke, *Nusantara: A History of the East Indian Archipelago* (rev. ed. The Hague 1959), 132–8 [*Nusantara*]; this is on the whole the clearest concise account of Coen's plans that I have seen, though they are of course discussed in all the standard works cited in these chapters.

[5] Dermigny, I.114–15; see also D. G. E. Hall, *A History of South-East Asia* (3rd ed. London 1968), 312–13 [*History*], and cf. M. A. P. Meilink-Roelofsz, 'Aspects of Dutch Colonial Development', in J. S. Bromley and E. H. Kossmann (eds.), *Britain and the Netherlands in Europe and Asia* (London 1968), 56–82 at 71 [*Britain/Netherlands*].

[6] Details in Blair & Robertson, XVIII.31–41, XIX.225–34.

[7] C. R. Boxer, *Fidalgos in the Far East 1550–1770* (The Hague 1948), 72–92 [*Fidalgos*]; but there was a British battalion with the Japanese when they took Tsing-tao from the Germans in 1914—R. P. Porter, *Japan: The Rise of a Modern Power* (Oxford 1918), 257–61. Boxer notes that the Dutch fleet finally sailed from Camranh Bay in Annam, the last rendezvous of Rozhestvensky's ships before Tsushima, and of the main Japanese convoy to Malaya in December 1941. Dermigny (I.90) rather grandly calls the 1622 affair 'one of the decisive combats of modern times'; why?

[8] D. W. Davies, *A Primer of Dutch Seventeenth Century Overseas Trade* (The Hague 1961), 61.

[9] W. Foster, *England's Quest of Eastern Trade* (London 1933), 127–35 [*Quest*]; Hall, *History*, 286–8, is more concise. See also W. Foster (ed.), *The Voyage of Sir James Lancaster . . . 1591–1603*, HS 2nd Ser. 85 (London 1940); for Fenton and Wood, Spate, 278–9, 289.

[10] The principle of a fixed capital with dividend payments was not adopted until 1658. For the survival of old concepts and methods in the EIC, and comparisons with the VOC, see E. F. Heckscher, *Mercantilism* (2nd ed. London 1955), I.356–67, 400–5. K. N. Chaudhuri, *The English East India Company . . . 1600–1640* (London 1965) is a careful study of the workings and trade of the early Company [*English EIC*].

[11] M. A. P. Meilink-Roelofsz, *Asian Trade and European Influence in the Indonesian Archipelago between 1500 and about 1630* (The Hague 1952), 191–5 and notes at 377–8 [*Asian Trade*]. For factionalism amongst EIC agents, see W. Foster (ed.), *The Journal of John Jourdain 1608–1617*, HS 2nd Ser. 16 (London 1905), xliii–xlv, lviii–lx, 304–8 [*Jourdain*], or even better the squabbles between Saris and Middleton in E. M. Satow (ed.), *The Voyage of John Saris to Japan, 1613*, HS 2nd Ser. 5 (London 1900), xx–xxiv. On the demand for silver and cottons, J. B. Harrison, 'Europe and Asia', in *NCMH* IV.644–71, especially 649, 660–1 ['Europe and Asia']; C. F. G. Simkin, *The Traditional Trade of Asia* (London 1968), 192, 201. For the Dutch use of silver specie, initially Spanish but later on often their own *negotiepenningen*, K. Glamman, *Dutch Asiatic Trade 1620–1740* (Copenhagen/The Hague 1958), 50–3 [*Dutch Trade*]. The EIC's exertions to secure an adequate supply of silver are detailed in Chaudhuri, *English EIC*, 126–36.

[12] W. Foster (ed.), *The Voyage of Sir Henry Middleton to the Moluccas, 1604–1606*, HS 2nd Ser. 88 (London 1943), xx, xxv–xxix, 28–59—a wonderful maze of intrigue. There is a highly colourful account of conditions at Bantam at this time in the same volume, 81–167— E. Scott, 'An Exact Discourse of the *Subtilties, Fashishions* [*sic*], *Pollicies . . . of the* East Indians *as well* Chyneses *as* Javans . . .'.

[13] Foster, *Quest*, 154–72, 200–5.

[14] C. R. Boxer, *The Dutch Seaborne Empire 1600–1800* (Harmondsworth 1973), 225 [*Dutch Empire*].

[15] Foster, *Quest*, 155–78, and Masselman, *Colonialism*, 395–9; on Jourdain and Coen, Masselman, 301–3, 366, and Foster, *Jourdain*, 259–63. For Coen's savagery in Banda, P. Geyl, *The Netherlands in the Seventeenth Century, 1609–48* (London 1961), 178–9 [*Netherlands*]. He has found defenders—see Masselman, 418–22, but *contra* Meilink-Roelofsz, *Asian Trade*, 197–9. There was undoubtedly much sadism in Coen; he had Sara Specx, the young Eurasian daughter of a future Governor-General, publicly whipped and her betrothed executed for anticipating their marriage—Geyl, 181, and Boxer, *Dutch Empire*, 261.

[16] For the Dutch side, Geyl, *Netherlands*, 38–95 *passim*, and E. H. Kossmann, 'The Low Countries', in *NCMH* IV.359–84 at 371–84; for the Spanish, H. R. Trevor-Roper, 'Spain and Europe 1598–1621', ibid. 260–82 at 280–1, and J. H. Elliott, *Imperial Spain 1469–1716* (London 1963), 316–21.

[17] They may be followed in G. N. Clark and W. J. M. van Eysinga, *The Colonial Conferences between England and the Netherlands in 1613 and 1615* (Leiden 1940, 1951), I (texts) and II (Clark's discussion) [*Conferences*]. Of general histories in English, A. Hyma, *The Dutch in the Far East* (Ann Arbor 1953), 87–107, 123–6, gives the fullest account, though otherwise this is a rather poor book [*Far East*]. Hyma has at least one howler: he ascribes the final agreement of 1619 to 'terrific pressure' from King James (true in part) and Jan van Oldenbarneveldt; but the Dutch commissioners sailed for London in December 1618, while in

August Oldenbarneveldt had been arrested by Prince Maurice, and he was executed in May 1619, two months before the signing of the treaty.

[18] This 'represented a private success of the Dutch company against its opponents at home, since its charter was due to expire in three years' time'—Clark, *Conferences*, II.132.

[19] John Morre to Winwood, Ambassador at The Hague, in Clark, *Conferences*, II.40; Masselman (*Colonialism*, 405) ascribes this to Winwood himself, which hardly squares with his attitude in the talks.

[20] Blair & Robertson, XVIII.116–65 (Governor Fajardo to Philip III on shipbuilding and manpower difficulties (cf. ibid., 169–88) and relations with the English); XIX.36 (Zuazola's Cape fleet), 235–46 (Rios Coronel against abandonment); XX.29–33, 46–51 (Anglo-Dutch blockade).

[21] Ibid., XXII.89.

[22] Harrison, 'Europe and Asia', 660. Chaudhuri is a good corrective to extreme views of the EIC's inferiority.

[23] For an excellent example of the non-working of the accord, see B. Schrieke, *Indonesian Sociological Studies* (The Hague 1955), I.49–50 [*Indo. Studies*].

[24] Details in Masselman, *Colonialism*, 429–32. Ten Englishmen and nine Japanese were executed after confessing—under torture—to a plot to seize the Dutch fort. In what seems a very fair analysis, D. K. Bassett rejects the reality of a plot but concedes that the responsible Dutch official may well have genuinely believed in one—'The "Amboyna Massacre" of 1623', *Jnl SE Asian History* 1 (2), 1960, 1–19 ['Amboyna'].

[25] Hyma, *Far East*, 282 note 19; Boxer, *Fidalgos*, 113.

[26] Bassett, 'Amboyna', 8–18, and 'Early English Trade and Settlement in Asia, 1602–1690', in Bromley and Kossmann, *Britain/Netherlands*, 83–109 at 90–4—most English capital went to the more attractive Indian markets, but 'the actual English investment in Indonesia was greater in the 1660s and 1670s than it had ever been'; and cf. Harrison, 'Europe and Asia', 653–6, 660–1. For Bantam pepper, Glamman, *Dutch Trade*, 74–5—Chinese interests were strong here. For the EIC's Makassar links, and its continuing share in the pepper trade, see Chaudhuri, *English EIC*, 71, 140–61, 168–9.

[27] Burney, III.1.

[28] The fullest account of the whole voyage I have seen is that of Adolph Decker, one of the fleet's officers, in J. Callander, *Terra Australis Cognita or Voyages to the Terra Australis* (London 1768, reprint Amsterdam 1967), II.286–331 [Decker]; for the operations in South American waters G. Lohmann Villena, *Las Defensas Militares de Lima y Callao* (Lima 1964), 47–58 [*Defensas*], is better than his later version in *Historia Marítima del Perú, Tomo IV: Siglos XVII y XVIII* (Lima 1975), though this adds some picturesque detail [*Hist. Marítima*]. P. Gerhard, *Pirates on the West Coast of New Spain 1575–1742* (Glendale 1960), 123–30, deals with the Acapulco visit. Burney (III.1–36) summarises Decker, commenting that his Journal, though intelligent, 'is not to be esteemed a candid narrative; it throws a veil over the conduct of the expedition . . .'.

[29] Decker, 304; Lohmann Villena, *Defensas*, 48–50, implies that this pilot merely relied on the published account of the Nodals' voyage, and mentions undercover agents of the Dutch in Peru. It must be remembered that at this stage Dutch-'Belgian' lines and loyalties were not so rigidly drawn as they were later; there were many Catholic Flemings in Spanish service, and conversely emigré Protestant Walloons (such as the Le Maires and l'Hermite) were a distinctive and active group in the United Provinces, while the early

years of the 1609 Truce saw much two-way movement across the political boundary—Geyl, *Netherlands*, 18. Hence there were ample opportunities for agents and double-agents.

³⁰ From scattered references in seamen's journals—Richard Hawkins and James Lancaster, amongst others, could be cited—it is clear that many empirical captains were well aware of the anti-scorbutic value of citrus fruit long before its academic acceptance in the days of Dr Lind and Captain Cook.

³¹ J. van Walbeck's chart in Burney, at III.9.

³² P. T. Bradley, 'The Defence of Peru (1600–1648)', *Ibero-Amerikanisches Archiv* Neue Folge Jg2 H.2 1976, 79–111 at 90–1 ['Defence']; his 'Lessons of the Dutch Blockade of Callao (1624)', *Rev. Hist. Amer.* 83, 1977, 53–68, are rather obvious.

³³ A. Sharp, *The Discovery of the Pacific Islands* (Oxford 1960), 79–80; the island may have been seen by the Portuguese in the 1530s and Villalobos in 1543.

³⁴ Burney, III.32.

³⁵ Bradley, 'Defence', 96–106; Lohmann Villena, *Defensas*, 122–31, 148–50; J. M. Zapatero, 'El Castillo Real Felipe del Callao', *AEA* 37, 1977, 707–33.

³⁶ For the Spanish attack of 1866, see W. C. Davies, *The Last Conquistadores* (Athens, Ga., 1950).

³⁷ Masselman, *Colonialism*, 447–53; Hall, *History*, 313–14, 318.

³⁸ Ibid., 316–17.

³⁹ Blair & Robertson, XXVII, 312–14.

⁴⁰ Schrieke, *Indo. Studies*, I.68–70, citing the Batavia Daghregister and other contemporary documents. For a full account of a Makassar-based Portuguese shipowner and entrepreneur, see C. R. Boxer, *Francisco Vieira de Figueiredo: A Portuguese Merchant-Adventurer in South East Asia, 1624–1667* (The Hague 1967).

⁴¹ J. J. Stephan, *The Kuril Islands* (Oxford 1974), 34–5. Stephan is rather too hard on Fries; J. A. Harrison, *Japan's Northern Frontier* (Gainesville 1953), 145–9, is fairer. There is a wealth of documentation, in Dutch and German, in P. Teleki, *Atlas zur Geschichte der Kartographie der Japanesischen Inseln* (Budapest 1909, reprint Nendeln, Liechtenstein, 1966), and the journal of the *Castricum*'s first mate, Cornelis Janszoon Coen, may be found in Dutch and English in W. C. H. Robert (ed.), *Voyage to Cathay, Tartary, and the Gold- and Silver-Rich Islands East of Japan, 1643* (Supplement 4 to *Contributions to a Bibliography of Australia and the Pacific*, Amsterdam, 1975) [*Contributions*]; Coen gives much interesting detail on the Ainu. The adventures of the *Breskens*'s people in Japanese custody are in Burney, III.167–77. The gradual clarification of the geography of the Sea of Okhotsk region is further discussed in Chs. 4 and 10 below. For a refutation of Japanese claims to priority in the Bonins—their first validated visit was apparently in 1670—see H. Kublin, 'The Discovery of the Bonin Islands: A Reexamination', *Annals Asstn American Geographers* 43, 1953, 27–46.

⁴² J. O. M. Broek, 'Geographical Exploration by the Dutch', in H. R. Friis (ed.), *The Pacific Basin: A History of Its Geographical Exploration* (New York 1967), 151–69 at 168–9; much of Hamel's account is reproduced or summarised, with comment, in Burney, III.197–237.

⁴³ Perhaps the fullest discussion in English of the *Duyfken*'s voyage is in T. D. Mutch, 'The First Discovery of Australia', *Jnl Royal Australian Histl Soc.* 28, 1942, 303–52. For the Dutch on Australian coasts before Tasman, see J. E. Heeres, *The Part borne by the Dutch in the Discovery of Australia* (Leiden/London 1898), largely documents in Dutch and English [*Australia*]; G. A. Wood, *The Discovery of Australia* (Sydney 1922, Beaglehole/Spate revised ed. Melbourne 1969), 152–75—brilliantly written, but perhaps, to borrow from *1066 and*

All That, overstressing the contrast between Iberians as Wrong but Romantic, Hollanders as Right but Repulsive [*Discovery*]; A. Sharp, *The Discovery of Australia* (Oxford 1963), 32–69 [*Australia*]; G. Schilder, *Australia Unveiled: the share of Dutch navigators in the discovery of Australia* (Amsterdam/Canberra 1976), *passim*—a magnificently illustrated book—and the maps and place-name indexes in E. and G. Feeken, *The Discovery and Exploration of Australia* (Melbourne 1970). The excerpts given in Dutch and English by W. C. H. Robert, *The Dutch Explorations, 1605–1656 of the . . . Coast of Australia* (Amsterdam 1973, Supplement 2 to his *Contributions*) are not very relevant to our purpose. For the claim of Portuguese priority, see K. G. McIntyre, *The Secret Discovery of Australia* (rev. ed., Sydney 1982).

44 Sharp, *Australia*, 30–1, 47; Spate, 140–1.

45 Schilder, *Australia*, 54–8; the key paragraphs of the *Seynbrief*, laying down the course, are reproduced in his Plate VII.

46 This depends on the 'mile' used. Until 1617 the value of the Dutch or German mile would be in modern terms 5338 metres, but in that year a new determination of a meridian was published by W. Snellius, by which the mile would come to 7158 metres, and this was in general use by Dutch navigators in 1617–20. As the *Seynbrief* was issued in August 1617, it is not clear whether the old or the new 'Snellius mile' was meant—ibid., 60, 69.

47 The plate survives in the Amsterdam Rijksmuseum. Plain Dirck Hartog is delightfully transformed into Theodoric Hertoge by Burney, II.456.

48 The story has often been told, never better than in H. Drake-Brockman, *Voyage to Disaster* (Sydney 1963), with translation by E. Drok of Pelsaert's journal. Two of the mutineers, Wouter Loos and Jan Pelgrom de Rye, became the first European inhabitants of mainland Australia, receiving 'grace in place of rigour'—they were marooned on the very slim chance that, if picked up later, they might still serve the Company with information on the country. The wreck itself, discovered in 1963, is an archaeological treasure of the first order.

49 Heeres, *Australia*, 18–21, 65; A. Sharp, *The Voyages of Abel Janszoon Tasman* (Oxford 1968), 37 [*Tasman*].

50. J. E. Heeres, 'The Life and Labours of Tasman', in his splendid facsimile (with English translation) of *Abel Janszoon Tasman's Journal* (Amsterdam 1898, reprinted Los Angeles 1965), 48 [*Tasman*]. G. H. Kenihan's 'edition' of the journal (Adelaide ?1964) is a mere reprint of Heeres's text, without his notes and without any acknowledgement, and its promised 'Documents' on the 1644 voyage number exactly one, the Instructions. Sharp, *Tasman*, also translates the journal, signed but probably not entirely written by Tasman, and direct quotations are from this version. He also gives (40–53) the first published account (1671), apparently by the barber-surgeon Haalbos, who is very lively—much better than Tasman on manners and customs, especially the 'frightful' but aggressively amorous giantesses of Tonga (45); and a 'Sailor's Journal' (263–310) which adds little except to note (naturally) the occasions of extra liquor issues, and why the steward jumped ship before they reached Batavia ('He had had to do with the Skipper's Boy'). There are good discussions in Schilder, *Australia*, 139–205; Wood, *Discovery*, 175–98; J. C. Beaglehole, I.lvii–lxviii and *The Exploration of the Pacific* (3rd ed. London 1966), 138–64, as well as his sketch in *The Discovery of New Zealand* (2nd ed. Oxford 1961), 10–23.

51 Beaglehole, I.lvii. Visscher's remarkable 'Memorandum concerning the discovery of the Southland' actually sketches out voyages from the Netherlands into the South Sea both by

the Cape and by Strait Le Maire (Schilder, *Australia*, 59–60), but only the latter concerns us here; it is printed in R. MacNab (ed.), *Historical Records of New Zealand* (Wellington 1908, 1914), II.14–17.

[52] Letter of 12 Dec. 1642, in Heeres, *Tasman*, 137–9; the Council also asked for advice as to whether such activity would infringe the charter of the West India Company. Cf. J. A. Williamson's introduction to W. Dampier, *A Voyage to New Holland* (London 1939), xxi–xxii.

[53] The laconic, almost telegraphic, account of Haalbos is shorter but much more tense and vivid than that of Tasman's journal. For topographic details, see Sharp, *Tasman*, 118–38. R. A. Langdon, *The Lost Caravel* (Sydney 1975) has interesting speculations on the possibility of earlier European contacts, suggestive but not to my mind convincing; see also the negative conclusions of E. Stokes, 'European Discovery of New Zealand before 1642; a review of the evidence', *NZ Jnl of History* 4, 1970, 3–19 (which however misunderstands my views on Australian discovery).

[54] Schilder (*Australia*, 146) points out that Tasman seems to have had a penchant for closing off embayments he had entered but not followed through—perhaps an index of a tidy but unenterprising mind, which seems in keeping. On the relations of the various charts, ibid., 143–9, and Sharp, *Tasman*, 57–9, 132–3.

[55] Details ibid., 172–8, and in G. C. Henderson, *The Discoverers of the Fiji Islands* (London 1933), 50–61 [*Fiji*]. Henderson stresses the high navigational hazards of Fijian waters (7–17), pointing out that Tasman was in his 'Prins Willems Eylanden' in one of the worst months of year, and that this particular area of Fiji was given a wide berth by later navigators.

[56] H. Wallis, The Exploration of the South Sea, 1510–1644 (Oxford D. Phil. thesis 1953–4), 423–4 [Exploration].

[57] Heeres, *Tasman*, 143–9; Sharp, *Tasman*, 311–22; Schilder, *Australia*, 180–3, and succeeding pages of all three for the 1644 voyage. See also Wood, *Discovery*, 199–208, and for Caron in Ceylon, C. R. Boxer (ed.), *A True Description of the Mighty Kingdoms of Japan and Siam* (by Caron and F. Schouten; London 1935), lxxv–lxxxv.

[58] Wallis, Exploration, 439–43; Beaglehole, I.clvii–clxiv, 380, 410–11; H. C. Fry, *Alexander Dalrymple and the Expansion of British Trade* (London 1970), 121–2. This seems the place to acknowledge that, following a correspondence with Lt-Cdr Geoffrey C. Ingleton, I am no longer convinced that Brett Hilder was correct in claiming that Torres sighted Australia —see Spate, 139.

[59] Henderson, *Fiji*, 52; A. Villiers, *The Coral Sea* (New York 1949), 123, giving the credit to Visscher; but cf. Sharp, *Tasman*, 65 note 2. Villiers calls Tasman 'perhaps the greatest of the Dutch navigators' and then writes him down very thoroughly; but his account has several errors.

[60] To Heeren XVII, 23 Dec. 1644, in Sharp, *Tasman*, 316–17.

[61] Heeren XVII to Batavia, 9 Sept. 1645, in Heeres, *Australia*, xvi.

[62] Boxer, *Dutch Empire*, 54; cf. 27, 97–9, and in general his *The Dutch in Brazil 1624–1654* (Oxford 1957).

[63] The only full account that I know in English is in Burney, III.113–15; I have followed mainly J. T. Medina, *Los Holandeses en Chile* (Santiago 1923, Collección Historiadores de Chile, Tomo XLV), source of all direct quotations. This gives a Spanish translation of the expedition's journal, probably by its secretary Johan van Loon, published Amsterdam 1646.

[64] Hence either the VOC itself or its official cartographer Joan Blaeu, on his 1648 globe,

renamed Tasman's Staten Landt Zeelandia Nova, at the same time applying Hollandia Nova to the Australian mainland—Sharp, *Tasman*, 341–3; cf. E. H. McCormick, *Tasman and New Zealand: A Bibliographical Study*, Alexander Turnbull Library Bull. 14 (Wellington 1959), 10–11.

[65] Burney (III.118, 130–1) states that for some strange reason—I can think of no English voyage to account for it—this was previously known as Puerto Inglés or English Haven.

[66] Cf. the instructions to Tasman: if the locals have gold or silver, '[you] must conduct yourself as if [you] did not value this specie, showing copper, spelter or lead, as if those minerals were with us of greater value'—Sharp, *Tasman*, 36–7.

[67] At this point Burney (III.137–9) has an interesting digression on the local drink '*Schitie* otherwise called *Cawau*', which was made in much the same way as Polynesian kava, by women chewing a root; since 'by the conformity of language a line of communication has been traced from the Indian Sea to Easter Island', this points to contact across the Pacific. Thor Heyerdahl and Bob Langdon please note.

[68] Lohmann Villena, *Hist. Marítima*, 417; see 414–19 for these Spanish moves. Mancera built two 1000-ton galleons at Guayaquil, one of which promptly ran aground—see P. T. Bradley, 'Some Considerations on Defence at sea in the Viceroyalty of Peru during the Seventeenth Century', *Rev. de Historia de América* (Mexico) 79, 1975, 77–97 at 88–9, and M. Moreyra y Paz-Soldán, *Estudios sobre el Tráfico Marítima en la Epoca Colonial* (Lima 1944), 91–106.

[69] Blair & Robertson, XXII.137–41.

[70] Ibid., XXIV.197–228 at 218–20, Tavora to the King, 8 July 1632; 'Brief relation of the loss of the island Hermosa', XXXV.128–62 at 155–7.

[71] A. Santamaria OP, 'The Chinese Parian', in A. Felix (ed.), *The Chinese in the Philippines: I. 1570–1770* (Manila 1966), 67–118 at 103–5.

[72] N. M. Saleeby, *The History of Sulu* (Manila 1908, reprinted 1963), 49–68 [*Sulu*]; see also G. F. Zaide, *Philippine Political and Cultural History* (rev. ed. Manila 1957), 306–13 [*Philippines*].

[73] Blair & Robertson, XXVII.215–26 (Tagal's raid), 253–305 (Corcuera), 333.

[74] Saleeby, *Sulu*, 67; Vlekke, *Nusantara*, 159.

[75] Fr José Fayol, 'Relations of the events . . . in the Filipinas Islands', Blair & Robertson, XXXV.212–75 at 214, 216; main source for the 1646–7 actions. Even an English ship was welcomed at Cavite for its merchandise, though advances from the EIC looking to a more permanent trade were politely rebuffed—apparently not so much on ideological grounds as from doubts of a stable performance by that Company—ibid., 184, 209–11. This may have been one of the rare temporary relaxations of exclusionist policy implied by H. Furber, *Rival Empires of Trade in the Orient, 1600–1800* (Minnesota 1976), 271.

[76] Zaide, *Philippines*, 265.

[77] R. van Goens to the Heeren XVII, Amsterdam 8 Sept. 1655, cited in van Leur, *Indo. Trade*, 244.

Notes for Chapter 3

[1] An allusion to the triad summing up the characters of Nobunaga, Hideyoshi, and Ieyasu—only the last would have the self-control to wait for a caged bird to sing. This

chapter is largely based on the relevant sections in J. Murdoch, *A History of Japan II. During the Century of Early Foreign Intercourse (1542–1651)* (London 3rd imp. 1949) [*Japan 1542–1651*]; the volumes of G. B. Sansom's *A History of Japan* for 1334–1615 and 1615–1867 (London 1961, 1964) [*Japan 1334–1615* and *1615–1867*] and his *The Western World and Japan* (Vintage paperback ed., New York 1973) [*Western World*]; J. W. Hall, *Japan from Prehistory to Modern Times* (New York 1970) [*Japan*]. See also C. Totman, 'Tokugawa Japan' in A. E. Tiedemann (ed.), *An Introduction to Japanese Civilisation* (New York 1974), 98–138 [*Introduction*]; A. L. Sadler, *The Maker of Modern Japan . . . Tokugawa Ieyasu* (London 1973) *passim* [*The Maker*]; and the works of C. R. Boxer cited below.

² Fiefs were valued in so many *koku* (5 bushels, 1.8 hectolitres) of rice; even before Sekigahara, Ieyasu's estate was over twice the value of the next two domains put together —details in Sansom, *Japan 1334–1615*, 413–16, and Murdoch, *Japan 1542–1651*, 387–91, 437–43. Of the 214 holders of over 10,000 koku in 1598, 87 were in the Western army at Sekigahara, and of these 81 lost their lives or their fiefs—Sadler, *The Maker*, 270.

³ Sansom, *Japan 1615–1867*, 17; the ordinance was issued after the fall of Osaka. Cf. Murdoch, *Japan 1542–1651*, 697–701.

⁴ Sansom, *Japan 1615–1867*, 6, 35; Blair & Robertson, XVIII.230. Other details from C. R. Boxer, *The Great Ship from Amacon* (Lisbon 1959), 75–6 [*Great Ship*] and *The Christian Century in Japan 1549–1650* (Berkeley 1951), 261–7, 296 [*Christian Century*]. The chapter (XXXIV) on Japanese abroad in Yosoburo Takekoshi, *The Economic Aspects of the History of the Civilisation of Japan* (London 1930), I.480–503, which sounds promising, is very disappointing—it has more on freebooters and derring-do than on trade [*Economic Aspects*]. But as Boxer says (*Christian Century*, 462), the work as a whole 'is full of misprints, mistranslations, and misapprehensions'.

⁵ H. Kublin, 'The Discovery of the Bonin Islands: A Reexamination', *Annals Asstn Amer. Geographers* 43, 1953, 27–46 at 29–30. They may of course have been seen by Wako pirates, but the first recorded Japanese visit was an accidental one, by a coastal junk blown out to sea in 1670.

⁶ L. Knauth, *Confrontación Transpacifico: El Japon y el Nuevo Mundo Hispanico* (Mexico 1972), 161–4, 185 [*Confrontación*].

⁷ G. H. Kerr, *Okinawa: The History of an Island People* (Rutland Vt/Tokyo 1958), 151–64 [*Okinawa*]; R. K. Sakai, 'The Ryukyu (Liu-Ch'iu) Islands as a Fief of Satsuma', in J. K. Fairbank (ed.), *The Chinese World Order* (Cambridge Mass. 1968), 112–34 [*World Order*]; Sakai, 'The Satsuma-Ryukyu Trade and the Tokugawa Seclusion Policy', *Jnl Asian Studies* 23, 1963–4, 405–16.

⁸ Ta-tuan Ch'en, 'Investiture of Liu-Ch'iu Kings in the Ch'ing Period', in Fairbank, *World Order*, 134–64 at 152.

⁹ Kerr, *Okinawa*, 179, 183–4. The Daimyo of Tsushima was allowed to trade with Korea, but as that country was itself secluded, this did not amount to much—Hall, *Japan*, 188; Totman, in Tiedemann, *Introduction*, 123.

¹⁰ A. de Morga, *Sucesos de las Islas Filipinas*, HS 2nd Ser. 140 (Cambridge 1971), 161–4, 194–7 [*Sucesos*]. As Knauth remarks (*Confrontación*, 181), Fray Jerónimo was 'optimistic to the level of innocence'—surely not inappropriate to a Franciscan? In general this section is based on Knauth, 181–6, 196; R. H. Drummond, *A History of Christianity in Japan* (Grand Rapids 1971), 82–92 [*Christianity*]; D. Pacheco SJ, 'The Europeans in Japan', in M. Cooper SJ

(ed.), *The Southern Barbarians* (Tokyo 1971), 35–96 ['Europeans']. Boxer's *Christian Century* is a richly detailed and classic treatment of the whole era.

11 The hero of the fight was a black slave who went down over the bows and hacked through a rattan cable stretched across the channel. See Morga, *Sucesos*, 198–201, 240; Knauth, *Confrontación*, 182–6; W. L. Schurz, *The Manila Galleon* (Dutton paperback ed., New York 1959), 122–5 [*Galleon*]. For ito wappu and pancada, Knauth 159–60, Schurz 74–8.

12 Murdoch, *Japan 1542–1651*, 474.

13 Strictly, the ex-daimyo, since in the Japanese manner he had *de jure* passed on the daimyoship to his heir; but, in the same manner, he continued to exercise the *de facto* power.

14 Murdoch, *Japan 1542–1651*, 463–71, 484; A. Hyma, *The Dutch in the Far East* (Ann Arbor 1953), 147–53 [*Far East*]; P. G. Rogers, *The First Englishman in Japan* (London 1956), 24–53 [*First Englishman*].

15 R. Hakluyt, *The Principal Navigations . . . of the English Nation* (1589; Everyman ed., London 1907), II.203–44 at 213–14; W. Foster, *England's Quest of Eastern Trade* (London 1933), 45–6, 170–1.

16 The basic sources for the EIC venture in Japan are E. W. Satow (ed.), *The Voyage of John Saris to Japan, 1613*, HS 2nd Ser. 5 (London 1900) [*Voyage*] and E. M. Thompson (ed.), *Diary of Richard Cocks . . . 1615–1622*, HS 1st Ser. 66–7 (London 1883) [*Diary*]. See also M. Paske-Smith, *Western Barbarians in Japan and Formosa in Tokugawa Days, 1603–1868* (Kobe 1930), 1–64 [*Western Barbarians*]; Murdoch, *Japan 1542–1651*, 580–92.

17 Saris, *Voyage*, 204, 208 for the shop-list (I have run together the almost identical remarks of 1608 from Bantam and 1614 from Japan). For his doubtful financial dealings and the burning by the EIC of his lewd books and pictures, ibid., lviii–lxxiv; he was buried at least in the odour of respectability.

18 Saris, *Voyage*, 112.

19 On this point, Saris, *Voyage*, liii–liv, lxxiii–lxxv, 136, 138, 183; Murdoch, *Japan 1542–1651*, 587–9; Paske-Smith, *Western Barbarians*, 17; Rogers, *First Englishman*, 68–70.

20 Murdoch, *Japan 1542–1651*, 589; Rogers, *First Englishman*, 68–78; Cocks, *Diary*, II.263, 269, 321–2; and the judicious remarks of T. Rundall in *Memorials of the Empire of Japon*, HS 1st Ser. 8 (London 1850), 77–81.

21 Cocks, *Diary*, II.259; Saris, *Voyage*, 103, 117.

22 Paske-Smith, *Western Barbarians*, 24–34, 53.

23 D. W. Bassett, 'The Trade of the English East India Company in the Far East, 1623–84', *Jnl Royal Asiatic Soc.* 37, 1960, 32–47, 145–57, at 34–35; Cocks, *Diary*, II.259–63—the naivety shown in these instructions to his agent is in itself an index of poor management. However, according to K. N. Chaudhuri, *The English East India Company . . . 1600–1640* (London 1965), 47, 55, 62–3, by 1614–15 'there was already emerging in the minds of the Directors the idea of an interegional and integrated trading system in Asia'; but in southeast Asia in the 1620s both ground and interest were being lost.

24 Cocks, *Diary*, I.11, II.59.

25 The local tradition of the event was still alive when HMS *Phaeton* visited Nagasaki in 1808. The story is vividly told in Boxer, *Fidalgos in the Far East 1500–1770* (The Hague 1948), 53–63, and *Christian Century* 269–85, and at 428–33 for the Japanese version and the smoothing-over of the affair by Nuno Soutomaior. For political implications, Pacheco,

'Europeans', 78–9. The wreck of the *Madre de Deus* was discovered in October 1980, and the Portuguese government has agreed that any treasure salved may revert to the City of Nagasaki—*Canberra Times*, 28 Dec. 1980.

[26] Morga, *Sucesos*, 196–7; Schurz, *Galleon*, 120.

[27] Z. Nuttall, 'The Earliest Historical Relations between Mexico and Japan', *Univ. of California Pubtns in Amer. Archaeology* 4, 1906–7, 1–47 at 5–11 ['Mexico and Japan']; Murdoch, *Japan 1542–1651*, 42–51, 478–80. There is a good account of the whole episode, from Fr Jerónimo to Vizcaíno, by Naojiro Murakami, 'Japan's Early Attempts to Establish Commercial Relations with Mexico', in H. M. Stephens and H. E. Bolton (eds.), *The Pacific Ocean in History* (New York 1917), 467–80.

[28] Blair & Robertson, XIV.182–8, 231, 270–7. For fuller discussion of Rica de Oro/Plata, and Monterey, see Spate, 106–8.

[29] Knauth, *Confrontación*, 197–206, and Nuttall, 'Mexico and Japan', *passim*, give accounts based on Vizcaíno's own relation and are sources for unreferenced statements in this section. According to Rogers (*First Englishman*, 45), Sadler (*The Maker*, 242), and Schurz (*Galleon*, 125–6) Nuno de Sotomayor was the diplomatic head of the mission, or a cover for Vizcaíno's activities, and Murdoch (*Japan 1542–1651*, 485–9) refers contemptuously to 'skipper Sebastian ... in the train of Sotomayor'. But Vizcaíno in official documents styles himself Captain-General and Ambassador, incredible folly if he were not in command. Neither Knauth nor Nuttall mentions a Spanish Sotomayor; there may be confusion with the Portuguese Dom Nuno Soutomaior (see note 25 above); Nuttall mentions the latter but states (wrongly) that he was rebuffed.

[30] Knauth, *Confrontación*, 201.

[31] Quoted in Boxer, *Christian Century*, 314. See in general Knauth, *Confrontación*, 206–16; Nuttall, 'Mexico and Japan', *passim*; Sadler, *The Maker*, 265–9.

[32] Japan in general was within the ecclesiastical patronage of the Portuguese Crown, but Edo was held to be on the Spanish side of the demarcation line by the Treaty of Zaragoza, 1529—Knauth, *Confrontación*, 209, 304–5.

[33] Cocks, *Diary*, 191; Knauth, *Confrontación*, 212.

[34] Boxer, *Great Ship*, 83–5; Drummond, *Christianity*, 96–7.

[35] *Diary*, I.35, 106.

[36] Knauth, *Confrontación*, 287–90; Murdoch, *Japan 1542–1651*, 320–2; Cocks, *Diary*, II.216–23.

[37] Knauth, *Confrontación*, 308. Murdoch (*Japan 1542–1651*, 626) puts the end of the trade in 1626, but Tavora was still trying in 1632—Blair & Robertson, XXI.86, XXIII.54–5, 62–9, 93–4; XXIV.171–2, 205, 214.

[38] F. Caron and J. Schouten, *A True Description of the Mighty Kingdoms of Japan & Siam*, ed. C. R. Boxer (London 1935; original Dutch ed. 1645), xix–xxvi [*Kingdoms*]. Boxer's introduction to this work and his *Great Ship*, 117–63, are my main sources for the commercial side of events leading to seclusion; there are many more details in *Christian Century* and *Fidalgos*.

[39] Text of final decree in Boxer, *Christian Century*, 439–40, and Takekoshi, *Economic Aspects*, II.128–9.

[40] See Boxer, *Great Ship*, 130–2, and *Fidalgos*, 116–21.

[41] Boxer, in Caron, *Kingdoms*, xl, l–li, and *Fidalgos*, 115.

⁴² Authorities generally concur in such estimates; see e.g. Boxer, *Christian Century*, 334, 448, and Drummond, *Christianity*, 90–104. Tortures included hanging head-downwards in a pit, with artful incisions to let blood from the temples, so that the victim might take days in dying, and pouring water from boiling sulphur springs into open wounds.

⁴³ Boxer, *Great Ship*, 148.

⁴⁴ My account is based on Boxer, *Christian Century*, 375–83; Knauth, *Confrontación*, 339–44; Murdoch, *Japan 1542–1651*, 642–62.

⁴⁵ For the odium which befell the Hollanders, see e.g. E. Kaempfer, *The History of Japan* (Glasgow 1906; original ed. 1727), II.172–4 [*Japan*]. There is an apologia in the article by Dr Geerts, 'The Arima Rebellion and the conduct of Koeckebacker', *Trans. Asiatic Soc. Japan* 11, 1883, 51–116, and Koeckebacker did send away one of the two available ships. But this seems to have been for commercial reasons, and there is no trace of the honourable reluctance usually allowed him: he may have had no option but to assist, but he sent 'the largest and most uniform guns' (75), offered to stay at Hara after he had been told he might go (95), and 'wished often, for the sake of the reputation of the Dutch nation [!], that our vessel had been a larger and more warlike yacht' (105). If he was forced, this was a very co-operative rape.

⁴⁶ For the oath, Sansom, *Western World*, 176; for the moving story of the 'Hidden Christians', Drummond, *Christianity*, 109–17, 302–4.

⁴⁷ Blair & Robertson, XXXVI.257; this was written in reference to Coxinga's menace.

⁴⁸ Cocks, *Diary*, I.178; Boxer, *Christian Century*, 373–4, 382; Murdoch, *Japan 1542–1651*, 631, 687–8. There had been talks on the project in 1634, and in 1637 François Caron had to parry awkward questions on the failure at Macao in 1622, and as to why the Dutch did not use their command of the sea to root out the Iberian bases themselves (*Kingdoms*, xliii–xliv).

⁴⁹ For the final expulsion, Boxer, *Great Ship*, 155–67, and *Christian Century*, 383–8; Murdoch, *Japan 1542–1651*, 663–70; Pacheco, 'Europeans', 94–5; Sansom, *Japan 1615–1867*, 39–44.

⁵⁰ For an abortive Danish-Portuguese project of 1644, by a renegade Hollander who ended murdered as a Dutch spy in Manila, see Boxer, *Great Ship*, 166–7. Some indirect trade was possible, using Chinese or Coxingan intermediaries—ibid., 168–9.

⁵¹ Boxer in Caron, *Kingdoms*, cli–lxiv at lvi; Murdoch, *Japan 1542–1651*, 673–82.

⁵² One of these presents, a magnificent candelabrum, still survives—C. R. Boxer, *Jan Compagnie in Japan 1600–1817* (Tokyo/Oxford 1968), 30–7 [*Jan Compagnie*]. Cf. the frontispiece to D. Keene, *The Japanese Discovery of Europe* (London 1952) [*Discovery*].

⁵³ Kaempfer, *Japan*, II.174; for details on Deshima and the life of its internees, 174–98, 264–7, and G. K. Goodman, *The Dutch Impact on Japan (1640–1853)* (Leiden 1972), 19–36 [*Impact*].

⁵⁴ Goodman, *Impact*, 24. In the eighteenth century visits to brothels were allowed, and Goodman gives the curiously nice statistic that in 1722 there were 270 Dutch and 20,738 Chinese visits (a well-policed state!). But this is from Takekoshi (*Economic Aspects*, II.148), who claims that this shows more friendly feelings towards fellow-Asians! As Boxer acidly points out (*Jan Compagnie*, 129–30), Takekoshi fails to mention that in that year there were thirty-two Chinese junks in the port, against one Dutch ship.

⁵⁵ C. R. Boxer, *The Dutch Seaborne Empire 1600–1800* (Harmondsworth 1973), 223–4 [*Dutch Empire*]. D. W. Davies, *A Primer of Dutch Seventeenth Century Overseas Trade* (The

Hague 1961), 75–7 [*Primer*]; Goodman, *Impact*, 75–7. For restrictions on metal exports, Sansom, *Japan 1615–1867*, 144–6.

⁵⁶ For this odd incident—there was much to-do about the St George's Cross in the English flag, and embarrassing questions about Charles II's children by Catharine of Braganza—see C. R. Boxer, 'Jan Compagnie in Japan 1672–1674: Anglo-Dutch Rivalry in Japan and Formosa', *Trans. Asiatic Soc. Japan* 2nd Ser. 7, 1930, 138–202; Paske-Smith, *Western Barbarians*, 65–81; and the contemporary account in Kaempfer, *Japan*, III.339–60, which is also in Burney, III.384–93. In 1635 Courteen's Association, a rival to the EIC, had included Japan in its objectives, but its ships under John Weddell got no further than Macao and the Canton estuary—H. B. Morse, *The Chronicles of the East India Company trading to China 1635–1834* (Oxford 1926–29), I.14–30, and below Ch. 4.

⁵⁷ Sansom, *Western World*, 167–80; Dermigny, I.118–20. Murdoch (*Japan 1542–1651*, 682–8) and Knauth (*Confrontación*, 356–60) draw interesting comparisons between Japanese and Spanish polity. For the highly-organised Osaka-Edo trade, see Sansom, *Japan 1615–1867*, 122–3, and Totman, in Tiedemann, *Introduction*, 116.

⁵⁸ 'An Enquiry, whether it be conducive for the good of the Japanese Empire, to keep it shut up, as it now is. . . .', *Japan*, III.301–36 at 335; my italics. Kaempfer, who was in Japan 1690–2, gives both sides and answers his questions with a resounding Yes. The application of the passage quoted to our own century is obvious.

⁵⁹ Sansom, *Western World*, 178.

⁶⁰ The limited contacts through Tsushima and the Ryukyus hardly affect the issue.

⁶¹ Sansom, *Japan 1615–1867*, 183–7; Hall, *Japan*, 192–210; H. Borton, 'Peasant Uprisings in Japan of the Tokugawa Period', *Trans. Asiatic Soc. Japan* 2nd Ser. 16, 1938, 1–219 at 23, 39. For the growing pains of a market economy, see E. S. Crawcour, 'The Premodern Economy', in Tiedemann, *Introduction*, 461–84 at 471–7.

⁶² Hall, *Japan*, 226–32; R. A. Crighton, *The Floating World* (London 1973).

⁶³ Sansom, *Western World*, 207.

⁶⁴ For details of this fascinating chapter in the history of ideas, see Sansom, *Western World*, especially 199–205; Boxer, *Jan Compagnie*; Goodman, *Impact*; and Keene, *Discovery, passim*. For Titsingh, Boxer, *The Mandarin at Chinsura* (Amsterdam 1949).

⁶⁵ Honda Toshiaki, in Keene, *Discovery*, 109; Honda vastly admired Catharine the Great! For Western Sinophilia, Dermigny, 22–41.

⁶⁶ Ting-yee Kuo, 'The Internal Development and Modernisation of Taiwan, 1683–1891', in P. K. T. Sih, *Taiwan in Modern Times* (New York 1973), 171–240 at 173 [*Taiwan*].

⁶⁷ For earlier history, Ting-yee Kuo, 'Early Stages of the Sinicization of Taiwan, 230–1683', in Sih, *Taiwan*, 21–9; Wen-hsiung Hsu, 'From Aboriginal Island to Chinese Frontier: The Development of Taiwan before 1683', in R. G. Knapp (ed.), *China's Island Frontier* (Honolulu 1980), 31–54; W. G. Goddard, *Formosa: A Study in Chinese History* (London 1965), 3–40 [*Formosa*], a rather rhetorical book with an obvious bias.

⁶⁸ In general, see W. Campbell, *Formosa under the Dutch* (London 1903, reprint Taipei 1967), a badly organised book which includes at 1–86 an account from F. Valentyne's *Oud en Niew Oost-Indien* (1724–26) and much else [*Formosa*]. There is a clear narrative of the Dutch and Coxinga periods in C. Imbault-Huart, *L'Île Formose* (Paris 1893, reprint Taipei 1968); but 'it was only under Cromwell . . . that the English drove the Dutch from Malacca (1641)'! See also G. M. Beckmann, 'Brief Episodes—Dutch and Spanish Rule' in Sih,

Taiwan, 31–57; Davies, *Primer*, 60–9; Goddard, *Formosa*, 49–78. Interesting trade details in Campbell, 57–9, 341.

69 Blair & Robertson, IX.304–5 (los Rios), XXII.74–5, 97–101, 142–7, 168–77; XXVI.269–90 at 278–9 (Corcuera); XXXV.128–62 (loss of Hermosa). For Nuyts, Campbell, *Formosa*, 53–6.

70 Details, including Nuyts's own account, in Campbell, *Formosa*, 37–50, 60–1; for the lengthy negotiations, which included demands for the surrender of Zeelandia, Boxer in Caron, *Kingdoms*, xvii–xxvii, xxix, xxxiv. Nuyts was unscrupulous and venal—as he said himself, 'he had not come out to Asia to eat hay'—Boxer, *Dutch Empire*, 58.

71 Contrast the very hostile remarks in Goddard, *Formosa*, 54–6, 61, with the view of C. P. FitzGerald—no Sinophobe!—that 'their rule seems to have been quite acceptable to the immigrant Chinese' and that had Coxinga's challenge not come so soon, they would probably have retained Taiwan until modern times—*The Southern Expansion of the Chinese People* (Canberra 1972), 110 [*Expansion*].

72 Boxer in Caron, *Kingdoms*, lxxxviii–xc.

73 There were also Dutch missions in Amboyna and Ceylon, but these were directed to making Calvinists of the Portuguese Catholic converts—Boxer, *Dutch Empire*, 161–6. There is a vast and damnably dull documentation in Campbell, *Formosa*, 89–379, and also de Mailla's extremely interesting report of 1715 (ibid., 504–18).

74 There are at least fifteen variants of the name; the clearest account of these, and one of the best sketches of Coxinga's life, is in D. Keene, *The Battles of Coxinga: Chikamatsu's Puppet Play* (London 1951), 44–75 [*Battles*]. Keene also brings out Coxinga's significance as a symbol of Sino-Japanese cultural *rapprochement* (1–5, 85). Other accounts in Goddard, *Formosa*, 63–85; P. H. Chang, 'Cheng Cheng-kung (Coxinga) and Chinese Nationalism in Taiwan, 1662–1683' in Sih, *Taiwan*, 59–86; J. E. Wills, *Pepper, Guns, and Parleys: The Dutch East India Company and China 1622–1681* (Cambridge Mass. 1974), 15–27 [*Guns and Parleys*]. The significance of Coxinga's achievement is brought out in FitzGerald, *Expansion*, 111–12; R. Grousset, *A History of the Chinese Empire* (London 1952), 276–8.

75 Campbell, *Formosa*, 401. Keene, *Battles*, 47–53 gives a very good account of this phase; see Chang, in Sih, *Taiwan*, 66–8 for the Taiwan decision.

76 Campbell, *Formosa*, 383–492, gives a detailed and bitterly *ex parte* account by a supporter of Coyett, wittily summarised by Davies in *Primer*, 67–9. Coyett, who had pleaded for further resistance and been granted the honours of war by Coxinga, was condemned to death but instead banished to Pulo Wai, whence he was not released until 1675.

77 Jesuit 'Relation of events in the city of Manila (1662–63)' in Blair & Robertson, XXXVI.218–60; the direct quotations are at 259, 247. See also Keene, *Battles*, 66–8.

78 Ibid., 69–75.

79 For details of the twisted Sino-Dutch negotiations and operations, Wills, *Guns and Parleys*, 30–99 *passim*. Bort had been sent on a reprisal raid against Cheng shipping in 1662.

80 Wills, ibid., 136–52; Dermigny, I.288–306 *passim*: 'where official China thought only of the moral significance of tribute, the Barbarians were interested only in the material value of trade' (297).

81 Paske-Smith, *Western Barbarians*, 83–110; Wills, *Guns and Parleys*, 152–75; D. K. Bassett, 'The Trade of the English East India Company in the Far East, 1624–84', *Jnl. Roy. Asiatic Soc.* 37, 1960, 32–47, 145–57 *ad fin*.

[82] Cf. the remarks in G. F. Hudson, *Europe and China* (London 1931), 22–4, and Dermigny, I.130–6.

[83] Chan Lien, 'Taiwan in China's External Relations, 1683–1874', in Sih, *Taiwan*, 87–170 at 87–101. Benyowsky was escaping from the Russians in Kamchatka; his narrative is given in Campbell, *Formosa*, 518–36. For Psalmanazaar, see R. Aldington, *Frauds* (London 1957), 33–52.

Notes for Chapter 4

[1] C. P. FitzGerald, *The Southern Expansion of the Chinese People* (Canberra 1972), 5–7 [*Southern Expansion*].

[2] To the references (Braudel, Lach, Lane, Magalhães–Godinho, Steensgaard) cited in Spate, 297 note 60, add M. A. P. Meilink-Roelofsz, *Asian Trade and European Influence in the Indonesian Archipelago between 1500 and about 1630* (The Hague 1962), 133–5 [*Asian Trade*].

[3] N. Steensgaard, *The Asian Revolution of the Seventeenth Century* (Chicago 1974), 89–92, 111–13 [*Trade Revolution*]; V. Magalhães–Godinho, *L'Économie de l'Empire Portugais aux XVe et XVIe Siècles* (Paris 1969), 774–80; Meilink-Roelofsz, *Asian Trade*, 133.

[4] J. C. van Leur, *Indonesian Trade and Society* (The Hague 1955), 188–9 [*Indonesian Trade*].

[5] Steensgaard, *Trade Revolution*, 84, 93; A. R. Disney, *Twilight of the Pepper Empire* (Cambridge Mass. 1978), 27. Readers of C. R. Boxer's *Fidalgos in the Far East 1550–1770* (The Hague 1948) will see how thin the line was; in fact, even the Dutch Admiral Matelief complained that having to be 'a soldier and a merchant in one person was a lost labour'—H. Furber, *Rival Empires of Trade in the Orient 1600–1800* (Minneapolis 1976), 343 note 10 [*Rival Empires*]. But the difference between the Lusian and the Anglo-Dutch styles was first borne in on me by the armorial bearings on the tombs in the ruins of Old Bassein, the Portuguese fortress north of Bombay.

[6] There is a splendid and sombre irony in the fact that at Goa in 1961 the only real resistance was put up by the sloop *Afonso de Albuquerque*. See also Meilink-Roelofsz's tribute to Lusian (and Luso-Asian) vitality, *Asian Trade*, 126. I would add my own tribute to the excellent 'black' Sergeant de Mello under whom I served as a private in the Burma Volunteer (by this time conscript) Force in 1941.

[7] Ironically enough, in 1718 Batavia was compelled to fall back on Macao for supplies of tea—K. Glamman, *Dutch-Asiatic Trade 1620–1740* (Copenhagen/The Hague 1958), 217 [*Dutch Trade*]; in fact, Macaonese competition was one factor in the Dutch abandonment of their efforts at direct trade with China—J. E. Wills, *Pepper, Guns and Parleys: The Dutch East India Company and China 1622–1681* (Cambridge Mass. 1974), 196 [*Pepper and Parleys*].

[8] C. H. Alexandrowicz, *An Introduction to the Law of Nations in the East Indies* (Oxford 1967), 41 [*Law of Nations*]; he elsewhere (29, 32, 100) points out that Asian Princes shrewdly sought to contact real Sovereigns, e.g. finding it easier or more fitting to deal with Portuguese Viceroys than with the mere Presidents of factories; hence some of the VOC's difficulties. However, Taiwan was treated (before Coxinga!) as *terra nullius*, and the Spanish acted on this basis in the Marianas and in the Philippines, except in the Muslim South.

[9] Furber, *Rival Empires*, 314; cf. M. A. P. Meilink-Roelofsz, 'Aspects of Dutch Colonial Development in Asia in the Seventeenth Century', in J. S. Bromley and E. H. Kossman

(eds.), *Britain and the Netherlands in Europe and Asia* (London 1968), 58–82 at 68–70. An amusing 'equal' treaty is that of 1631 between the States-General and Persia, Iranian merchants (who had no sea-going ships) being given like privileges to those of the English at Delft—C. R. Boxer, *The Dutch Seaborne Empire 1600–1800* (Harmondsworth 1973), 116 [*Dutch Empire*]. Indian shipowners under the Raj complained of such 'equality' with British shipping lines.

10 Alexandrowicz, *Law of Nations*, 98, 169, 180; Furber, *Rival Empires*, 311–14; van Leur, *Indonesian Trade*, 226–7. For a good specific discussion of the differing concepts of 'treaty', see L. Y. Andaya, *The Heritage of Arung Palakka: A History of South Sulawesi in the Seventeenth Century* (The Hague 1981), 107–16 [*Arung Palakka*].

11 A. Toussaint, *History of the Indian Ocean* (London 1966), 128–9 [*Indian Ocean*]; cf. F. Mauro, *L'Expansion Européenne (1600–1870)* (Paris 1967), 347–9 [*Expansion*].

12 In Java itself, the Dutch sent present-embassies to the Susuhunan of Mataram, in much the same way as the British long recognised the shadowy overlordship of the Great Mogul at Delhi; but in 1677 intervention in a succession war reduced Mataram to a virtual vassal—Boxer, *Dutch Empire*, 212–17. For the political events generally, see D. G. E. Hall, *A History of South-East Asia* (3rd ed. London 1968), Chs. 16–18 [*History*].

13 See A. J. Reid, 'Trade and the Problem of Royal Power in Aceh', in *Pre-Colonial State Systems in Southeast Asia* (Royal Asiatic Soc., Kuala Lumpur 1975), 45–55 ['Trade in Aceh']; L. Andaya, 'De VOC en de Maleise Wereld in de 17de en 18de eeuw', in M. A. P. Meilink-Roelofsz (ed.), *De VOC en Azië* (Bussum 1976), 107–56—I am indebted to Dr Andaya for an English version of this most interesting paper—and his *Arung Palakka*, 163–72, 208–18, for the diaspora. Admittedly in 1783 the Dutch were weakened by the 1780–4 war with Britain, and they had their revenge the next year, though Atjeh itself was not subjugated until a bloody war of more than thirty years, 1873–1908—R. O. Winstedt in J. Bastin and J. W. Winks (eds.), *Malaysia: Selected Historical Readings* (Nendeln, Liechtenstein 1979), 112–17, and A. J. Reid, *The Contest for North Sumatra 1858–1898* (Kuala Lumpur 1969). J. E. Hoffman, 'Early Policies in the Malacca Jurisdiction [of the VOC]', *Jnl SE Asian Studies* 3, 1982, 1–38, seems to me rather to confirm than to weaken the van Leur position.

14 Meilink-Roelofsz, *Asian Trade*, 104; cf. her article 'Trade and Islam in the Indo-Malaysian Archipelago . . .', in D. S. Richards (ed.), *Islam and the Trade of Asia* (Oxford 1970), 137–58 at 147–53—the bigger ships came from Pegu (Burma)—and van Leur, *Indonesian Trade*, 127–9. There is an admirable introductory sketch by R. Brissenden, 'Patterns of Trade and Maritime Society Before the Coming of the Europeans', in E. McKay (ed.), *Studies in Indonesian History* (Carlton, Vic. 1976), 65–97.

15 Dermigny, I.117–18; there were eight reals to the peso or 'piece of eight'. Glamman, *Dutch Trade*, 177, mentions 'a veritable copper adventure' by a South Indian operator, in which the VOC burnt its fingers to the tune of nearly a million florins. As for borrowing, in 1633 the VOC and EIC lodges at Surat raised £92,000 from local merchants (some at 24 per cent!); it will be recalled that the EIC's initial investment in London was £68,000, about the same as its Surat loan. Of course this shows how much the EIC had grown in thirty years, but also how much that growth depended on Asian aid—van Leur, *Indonesian Trade*, 194–208, 214–15, 223–6.

16 Furber, *Rival Empires*, 331; but cf. van Leur, *Indonesian Trade*, 133–4, and Reid, 'Trade in Aceh', 47.

[17] B. Schrieke, *Indonesian Sociological Studies* (The Hague 1955), I.69–72 [*Studies*]; Meilink-Roelofsz, *Asian Trade*, 262; Glamman, *Dutch Trade*, 215–19.

[18] Schrieke, *Studies*, 78–9; C. F. G. Simkin, *The Traditional Trade of Asia* (London 1968), 228–9 [*Traditional Trade*].

[19] C. R. Boxer, *Francisco Vieira de Figueiredo: A Portuguese Merchant-Adventurer in South-East Asia, 1624–1667* (The Hague 1967), 3–4 and *passim*.

[20] The fascinating details are in Andaya, *Arung Palakka*, *passim*; see also Glamman, *Dutch Trade*, 83–5; Furber, *Rival Empires*, 85–7. On the general significance of piracy, see the illuminating pages of Dermigny, I.92–9.

[21] Furber, *Rival Empires*, 265–70; it lasted longer in the Indian Ocean, where there were stronger rulers and stateless but economically well-knit groups such as the Armenians— ibid., 272, 283, and S. D. Quiason, *English "Country Trade" With The Philippines, 1644–1765* (Quezon City 1966), 37–41, 88–9. The house-flags of such merchants could pass for the 'Moorish' colours which the Spanish still insisted upon.

[22] M. Ly-tio-fane, *Mauritius and the Spice Trade: The Odyssey of Pierre Poivre* (Mauritius Archives Pubtn 4, Port Louis 1958), 10–11 [*Mauritius*]; M. Flinders, *A Voyage to Terra Australis* (London 1814, reprint Adelaide 1966), II.228–33. For a full account of the trepang fishery, which lasted into this century, see C. C. Macknight, *The Voyage to Marege': Macassan Trepangers in northern Australia* (Melbourne 1976).

[23] Furber, *Rival Empires*, 178–81 and Ch. 6 *passim*; many references in Dermigny.

[24] M. Townsend, *Asia and Europe* (London 1901), ix.

[25] J. T. Pratt, *The Expansion of Europe into the Far East* (London 1947), 70–2 [*Expansion*]; Meilink-Roelofsz, *Asian Trade*, 132; Simkins, *Traditional Trade*, 252. Cf. J. Dyer, *The Fleece* (London 1757), Book IV, 376–9:

> for affluent life
> The flavoured tea and glossy painted vase;
> Things elegant, ill-titled luxuries . . .

[26] Mauro, *Expansion*, 326; for the reaction of European textile interests, Dermigny, I.396–403. The penetration of European markets by 'indiennes' is ably discussed by P. Leuilliot, 'Influence du commerce oriental sur l'économie occidentale', in M. Mollat (ed.), *Sociétés et Compagnies de Commerce en l'Orient et l'Océan Indien* (Paris 1970), 611–30 [*Sociétés*].

[27] D. Hannay, *The Great Chartered Companies* (London 1926), 170 [*Companies*]; van Leur, *Indonesian Trade*, 234–6.

[28] Boxer, *Dutch Empire*, 48, 77.

[29] R. Davis, *The Rise of the English Shipping Industry in the Seventeenth and Eighteenth Centuries* (Newton Abbot 1962), tables at 17, 184–6, 200, text 257–8 [*English Shipping*]. By 1771–3, however, while import values were 16.7 per cent of the total, exports were 6.6 per cent: the Industrial Revolution was on the way.

[30] Glamman, *Dutch Trade*, 13, 14, 143; the actual values of spices and pepper rose from 2,178,000 to 3,546,000 florins, but total values had more than quintupled. See also Boxer, *Dutch Empire*, 222–5.

[31] Dermigny, I.388–92.

[32] Bouvet in 1742, quoted in full in O. H. K. Spate, 'De Lozier Bouvet and Mercantilist Expansion in the Pacific in 1740', in J. Parker (ed.), *Merchants and Scholars* (Minneapolis 1965), 221–37 at 230–1; Furber, *Rival Empires*, 248–9.

[33] Furber, ibid., 230–4; Dermigny, II.703. Book IV of Dyer's *The Fleece* surveys world trade from the viewpoint of English wool, and is a magnificent contemporary gloss on Dermigny's 'uniformisation européocentrique du monde'.

[34] According to Albert Hyma, in 1649 the VOC's profit from Japan was nearly 710,000 guilders, against 467,000 for the next most paying branch (Taiwan) and 623,000 from all other areas—*The Dutch in the Far East* (Ann Arbor 1953), 159. Hyma is not always meticulously accurate, and gives no specific source for these figures, which are however precise to the last guilder.

[35] Dermigny, I.90–1, 104, and 137–8 for the revival of the junk trade; for the Manila crisis years, P. Chaunu, *Les Philippines et le Pacifique des Ibériques* (Paris 1960), 240–52—contractions, on various indices, of 70 to 90 and even 95 per cent at Manila and Acapulco until recovery begins in the 1680s [*Philippines*]. English uncertainties are well brought out in D. K. Bassett, 'The Trade of the English East India Company in the Far East, 1623–84', *Jnl Roy. Asiatic Soc.* 37, 1960, 32–47 and 145–57.

[36] Figures in Dermigny, II.536–9; for the Dutch retreat, Wills, *Pepper and Parleys*, 194–8, and cf. Glamman, *Dutch Trade*, 213, 215–20, 264.

[37] Furber, *Rival Empires*, 232; Glamman, *Dutch Trade*, 181, 264; F. Spooner, *The International Economy and Monetary Movements in France, 1493–1725* (Cambridge Mass. 1972), 33–5, 40–5.

[38] Glamman, *Dutch Trade*, 113–22; Furber, *Rival Empires*, 245–6; Dermigny, I.392–5.

[39] Glamman, *Dutch Trade*, 58, 63; Dermigny, I.417–22.

[40] Dermigny, I.410–11; Glamman, *Dutch Trade*, 167—unreferenced statements about Japanese copper are from Glamman's Ch. IX. He would appear to have exaggerated the competitive effect of Japanese copper in Europe—see R. Carr, 'Two Swedish Financiers . . .', in H. E. Bell and R. L. Ollard (eds.), *Historical Essays 1600–1750 presented to David Ogg* (London 1963), 18–34 at 24 note 2.

[41] Dermigny, I.140–1; Glamman, *Dutch Trade*, 177–8 for the attempted corner; J. Hall, 'Notes on the Early Ch'ing Copper Trade with Japan', *Harvard Jnl Asiatic Studies* 12, 1949, 444–61.

[42] Furber, *Rival Empires*, 251, 368 note 23; Glamman, *Dutch Trade*, 181–2; B. H. M. Vlekke, *Nusantara: A History of the Indonesian Archipelago* (The Hague 1959), 217–18 [*Nusantara*]. Originally van Imhoff had intended to take advantage of Anson's interruption of the Galleon sailings; his expedition, initially welcomed by the isolated Jesuits of Baja California, was eventually repelled by force, taking refuge at that old haunt of the buccaneers, the Tres Marias—P. Gerhard, 'A Dutch Trade Mission to New Spain, 1746–1747', *Pac. Histl Rev.* 23, 1954, 221–6.

[43] van Leur, *Indonesian Trade*, 186–7, 239–45; Boxer, *Dutch Empire*, 105; Glamman, *Dutch Trade*, 108–9. For the earlier debate, Meilink-Roelofsz, *Asian Trade*, 207–22.

[44] D. W. Davies, *A Primer of Dutch Seventeenth Century Overseas Trade* (The Hague 1961), 55–8. Some Dutchmen had the grace to see the parallel with the Black Legend of Spain in the Indies, and even the stoutly colonialist E. S. de Klerck found the initial genocide of the Bandanese and the extirpation policy, if not quite too hard to stomach, at least very hard to explain away—*History of the Netherlands East Indies* (Rotterdam 1938), I.229–30, 238, 255–7. See also van Leur, *Indonesian Trade*, 240; Vlekke, *Nusantara*, 203–4.

[45] João de Barros, *Décadas da Asia*, Dec. I Liv. 5 Cap. v (1552–63; Lisbon ed. 1945–6, III.261–2).

[46] Glamman, *Dutch Trade*, 100–1, 105, 257; Boxer, *Dutch Empire*, 222.

[47] Furber, *Rival Empires*, 239; for the inextricable accounting complexities, Glamman, *Dutch Trade*, 246–61. So immense was the mass of paper work that Furber remarks (191) that hundreds of pages sent to Amsterdam cannot have been read, the student of to-day opening a volume being likely still to find between the folios the fine sand used for blotting the ink.

[48] Toussaint, *Indian Ocean*, 179–80; for the full story, Ly-tio-fane, *Mauritius*. The decline of the VOC is discussed in Boxer, *Dutch Empire*, 312–20; he points out (xxii) that 'perhaps more of the gross national product of the Netherlands was consumed by war than in any other European state' in the seventeenth century.

[49] Dermigny, I.364–5, II.508–9; as he says, 'an involuntary monasticism, it goes without saying excluding any spirituality, and also any urbanity'. The off-season was about April-September, the ships arriving with the end of the SW Monsoon and leaving at the onset of the NE. Macao retained some trade of its own; in 1739–40 there were twelve Company ships (EIC, VOC, French, Danish, Swedish) at Canton, totalling 6815 tons, but at Macao ten Portuguese and two Spanish (all for Asian ports) with 4400 tons—H. B. Morse, *The Chronicles of the East India Company trading to China 1635–1834* (Oxford 1926–9), I.274–5 [*Chronicles*]. This was exceptional; cf. Dermigny, I.281–4.

[50] E. M. Thompson (ed.), *Diary of Richard Cocks*, HS 1st Ser. 66–7 (London 1883), I.xix–xx, 119, II.21–2, 125–6; Dermigny, I.108–9. The famous, and failed, Macartney Embassy to Peking in 1793 was instructed to ask for 'a small detached piece of land . . . as a depot for commerce. It was to be so far north that the English might find a ready sale for their woollens'—E. H. Pritchard, *Anglo-Chinese Relations during the Seventeenth and Eighteenth Centuries* (Urbana, Ill. 1929), 179—a useful work, intermediate between Morse and Dermigny in density and sophistication [*Relations*].

[51] FitzGerald, *Southern Expansion*, 112; Dermigny, I.33, 275–8, 285–6, II.447. Dimensions of the factories from map in Morse, *Chronicles* III.1; that in Dermigny's Album has no scale. On the attitudes of the Ch'ing and especially Kang-hsi to Foreign trade, M. Mancall, 'The Ch'ing Tribute System', in J. K. Fairbank (ed.), *The Chinese World Order* (Cambridge Mass. 1968), 68–89 at 80–2, 87–9.

[52] *The Principal Navigations and Discoveries of the English Nation* (2nd ed. 1598–1600), Everyman ed., VIII.312–14; W. Foster, *England's Quest of Eastern Trade* (London 1933), 138–41 [*Quest*]. For Fenton, Spate, 278–9 and references there.

[53] Documents in R. C. Temple (ed.), *The Travels of Peter Mundy*, Vol. III, HS 2nd Ser. 45–6 (London 1919), Part II 429–45, and the conflicting Portuguese and English accounts, 473–531. Mundy's own narrative, artless and vivid, is in Part I, 158–289 [*Travels*]. It is interesting to note that in a sort of indemnity to Weddell (who did not receive it, being lost on the return voyage), Charles refers to his instructions not to prejudice the EIC's trade; the instructions themselves say nothing of this and indeed warn off the EIC (III.437–40, 445), which seems typical of Charles. For other accounts, Morse, *Chronicles*, I.12–30; Pritchard, *Relations*, 54–8; and Foster, *Quest*, 170–1 (Michelborne), 327–9; Charles's backing for Weddell, and the EIC's reaction, are documented in W. Foster and E. B. Sainsbury (eds.), *Court Minutes of the East India Company 1635–1639* (Oxford 1907), 142–64 *passim*, 241, 295.

[54] See the plaintive exculpatory letter from the City of Macau to the King of England, Mundy, *Travels*, Vol. III Part II, 502–28.

55 Even Morse (*Chronicles*, I.30) speculates on what might have happened to 'a Chinese *Dragon* [Weddell's ship] . . . ordered to wait below Tilbury Fort' and taking soundings; for a livelier version, J. Bell, 'Arms and the Man', in M. Roberts (ed.), *New Signatures* (London 1932), 36–47.

56 J. H. Parry, *Trade and Dominion: The European Overseas Empires in the Eighteenth Century* (London 1971), 82–3 [*Trade and Dominion*] for other contacts, at Amoy and Taiwan; see also Pritchard, *Relations*, 66–9.

57 Bassett, 'Trade of EIC', 153–6; Dermigny, I.142–7.

58 Morse, *Chronicles*, I.84–98; the Old Company continued to trade at Amoy and Chusan, the two Companies agreed to act in harmony in 1702 and were fully united in 1709 (122, 146). For the *Amphitrite*, E. W. Dahlgren, *Les Relations Commerciales et Maritimes entre La France et les Côtes de l'Océan Pacifique* (Paris 1909, with a subtitle as long again!), I.130 [*Relations*]. For the two Companies, W. R. Scott, *The Constitution and Finance of English, Scottish and Irish Joint-Stock Companies to 1720* (Cambridge 1912, reprint New York 1951), II.150–90.

59 Morse, *Chronicles*, I.99; Pritchard, *Relations*, 77–80.

60 Dermigny, I.203-46. Apart from one ship each in 1735–6, Amoy and Chusan dropped out in 1704 and 1710 respectively, but in 1700–9 they totalled more EIC ships and tonnage than Canton. The ships of other companies tended to be larger than the English, at least nominally. In 1744–7, eighteen EIC ships in a row were rated (officially) at 498 tons, and 499 was a common figure; in fact, they might be of 600–650 tons—Morse, *Chronicles*, I.307–13; Davis, *English Shipping*, 362; see also Pritchard, *Relations*, Appendix XXVI.

61 Morse, *Chronicles*, true to his title gives a year-by-year blow-by-blow narrative; Dermigny, *passim* but especially I.274-369, presents a broader but still very detailed account. See also Pritchard, *Relations*, Chs. VII and VIII, and for later developments, including the Macartney Embassy, his *The Crucial Years of Early Anglo-Chinese Relations 1750–1800* (1936, reprint New York 1970). Short, clear, and balanced accounts may be found in J. H. Parry, *Trade and Dominion*, 82–7, and Pratt, *Expansion*, 47–60. The background of misunderstanding stemming, inevitably, from conflicting Chinese and European *Weltanschauungen* is well brought out in Wills, *Pepper and Parleys*, especially the last chapter, 'The Broken Dialogue'.

62 Dermigny, II.496, III.1423.

63 Morse, *Chronicles*, I.99–100; Baddeley, *Russia*, II.363 note (see note 70 below).

64 Pratt, *Expansion*, 49, 53; by 1800 there may have been nearly 8500 Europeans and Americans in Canton River during the season—Pritchard, *Relations*, 152–3, 224–5.

65 Council at Chusan to Directors of EIC, *c.* 1700—Morse, *Chronicles*, I.114. Other details in this paragraph from Morse, *passim*.

66 Pritchard, *Relations*, 159–61.

67 Ibid., 70; Dermigny, I.379–82; Morse, *Chronicles*, I.125.

68 Furber, *Rival Empires*, 114–16, 218–26; Morse, *Chronicles*, I.199. For the Danes, K. Glamman, 'The Danish East India Company', in Mollat, *Sociétés*, 471–9.

69 Furber, *Rival Empires*, 201–11; Hannay, *Companies*, 13 ('cut flowers'). Even the great talents of François Caron, recruited into French service by Colbert, and of François Martin had much difficulty in making any head against intrigue and incompetence—Furber, 103–24. For the interweaving of the China companies to *c.* 1715 read (if you have patience) Dahlgren, *Relations, passim*, and for Danycan especially 151–76, 183–95, 210–19. There is a

pungent survey, from which most of my details are drawn, by L. Dermigny, 'East India Company et Compagnie des Indes', in Mollat, *Sociétés*, 452–69; his remark on the style of the oligarchies is the same volume, 451.

[70] J. F. Baddeley, *Russia Mongolia China* (London 1919), I.lvii [*Russia*]. Baddeley gives a vivid account of Yermak (lxix–lxxiii), ending by comparing him with John Nicholson, the Hero of Delhi; this passage is more readily available in G. A. Lensen (ed.), *Russia's Eastward Expansion* (Englewood Cliffs 1964), 17–22. For Novgorod, G. V. Lantzeff and R. A. Pierce, *Eastward to Empire: Exploration and Conquest on the Russian Open Frontier, to 1750* (Montreal 1973), 38, 48–9 [*Eastward*]; this book is especially useful for military and political details.

[71] T. Armstrong, *Russian Settlement in the North* (Cambridge 1965), 9 [*Settlement*]; for detail on Yermak, see Armstrong's introduction to *Yermak's Campaign in Siberia*, HS 2nd Ser. 146 (London 1975), which reproduces the interesting strip-cartoon illustrations of the Remezov Chronicle, and Lantzeff and Pierce, *Eastward*, 94–107.

[72] Spathary, Russian Ambassador to Peking in 1675–7, quoted in Baddeley, *Russia*, II.271.

[73] Armstrong, *Settlement*, 19; Lantzeff and Pierce, *Eastward*, 109–54 *passim*.

[74] R. J. Kerner, *The Urge to the Sea* (Berkeley 1946), 84–8 [*The Urge*]. The standard work in English is R. H. Fisher, *The Russian Fur Trade 1550–1700* (Berkeley 1943)—for the expansion, 20–45, and 106–8 for the depletion of furs as a factor in the speed of advance [*Fur Trade*]. See also J. R. Gibson, *Feeding the Russian Fur Trade … 1639–1856* (Madison 1969), which concentrates on Okhotsk and Kamchatka [*Feeding the Fur Trade*].

[75] Gibson, *Feeding the Fur Trade*, 5–8.

[76] Armstrong, *Settlement*, 36–7; some craft on the Lena could carry over 200 tons, downstream—Gibson, *Feeding the Fur Trade*, 74–5. Full details of portages and ostrogi in Kerner, *The Urge*; see his Map 1 for the 'grand trunk' lines.

[77] Kerner, *The Urge*, 69–81. It is of interest to note that early Russian activity on the lower Ob may have been inspired, at least in part, by fears of Dutch and English commercial penetration across the Barents and Kara Seas—Baddeley, *Russia*, II.66–7; Armstrong, *Settlement*, 17–18 (and 21 for Mys Chelyushkin); Lantzeff and Pierce, *Eastward*, 128–9, 184.

[78] Baddeley, *Russia*, II.34, 68, 229. There was a profitable caravan from Tobolsk to Peking in 1670—ibid., II.194. The weird reference to Alexander the Great may refer to the tale that he walled up Gog and Magog somewhere in the distant North, a tale found in some versions of the Prester John Legend—see i.a. S. Baring-Gould, *Curious Myths of the Middle Ages* (1866, reprint London 1977), 29, or R. Silverberg, *The Realm of Prester John* (New York 1972), 65–6. For 'The Seizure and Loss of the Amur' in general, see Lantzeff and Pierce, *Eastward*, 155–82.

[79] Baddeley, *Russia*, II.64–86; oddly enough, the first published account of their mission was in English—S. Purchas, *Purchas His Pilgrimes* (London 1626, XIV.272–6 in the Glasgow ed., 1906). A mission sent by the Governor of Nerchinsk in 1670 actually dared to demand, in the standard form used to summon local chiefs, that Kang-hsi should accept Russian sovereignty; luckily the Chinese could not read the barbarous missive, and the Russian envoy bearing it was quick to reverse its gist—J. Sebes SJ, *The Jesuits and the Sino–Russian Treaty of Nerchinsk (1689)* (Rome 1961), 62–5 [*Jesuits*]. For Russian missions before Spathary, Baddeley, *Russia*, II.46–203 *passim*.

[80] One Ch'ing rebel and Muscovite client, Gantimur, was for years a bone of contention in Manchu-Russian relations; a directly descended Prince Gantimur rode with despatches through the Japanese lines around Port Arthur in 1904—Baddeley, *Russia*, II.428.

81 Gibson, *Feeding the Fur Trade*, 159; Sebes, *Jesuits*, 21. F. A. Golder, *Russian Expansion on the Pacific 1641–1850* (Glendale 1914, reprint New York 1971), 36–65 [*Expansion*] gives details on the wars, with an apparent anti-Russian bias and a treatment *in vacuo* making no reference to either the Russian or the Manchu political background—see Baddeley's review in *Geogl Jnl* 47, 1916, 468–70. Sebes, *Jesuits*, Chs. I–III, is far superior to Golder. A detailed if outdated treatment in English will be found in E. G. Ravenstein, *The Russians on the Amur* (London 1861), 9–64; he states (45) that there were 1100 hectares in cultivation around Albazin.

82 Also Spathar, Spatharia, Spatharios. Golder (*Expansion*, 56) gives him a cursory footnote, but his mission is the climax of Baddeley's *Russia* (II.204–422; Macartney reference at 423): when the Great Autocrat's envoy met the Celestial Emperor, the problems of protocol were intricate and bizarre. Sebes (*Jesuits*, 65–7) is briefer by far, but adequate.

83 For the negotiations, Sebes, *Jesuits*, 65–75; the Fathers of the Society were themselves most delightfully at cross-purposes (78–95). The Russian sleight-of-hand is explained in V. S. Frank, 'The Territorial Terms of the Treaty of Nerchinsk, 1689', *Pac. Histl Rev.* 16, 1947, 265–70.

84 Armstrong, *Settlement*, 62; Sebes, *Jesuits*, 123–8. For the Kiakhta trade, Fisher, *Fur Trade*, 213–14, 222–7, and W. Coxe, *An Account of the Russian Discoveries between Asia and America* (3rd ed. London 1787, reprint Ann Arbor 1972), 308–53. The English share is patriotically noted in Dyer, *The Fleece*, Book IV, lines 395–452.

85 Quoted in Gibson, *Feeding the Fur Trade*, 115–24 at 122; for Okhotsk itself, 12, 126–9, 147–9.

86 Müller's account is in *Voyages from Asia to America* (London 1761), Summary iii–iv [*Asia to America*], S. P. Krasheninnikov's in his *Observations on Kamchatka* (St Petersburg 1755, trans. and ed. E. A. P. Crownhart-Vaughan, Portland, Oregon, 1972), 199–300 [*Kamchatka*]; both better in R. H. Fisher, *The Voyage of Semen Dezhnev in 1648*, HS 2nd Ser. 159 (London 1981), 31–8 and 87–8, which can be regarded as the definitive work in English [*Dezhnev*]. Golder devoted a whole chapter (67–96) of *Expansion* to 'A Critical Examination of Dezhnev's Voyage'; he was effectively answered by Fisher in *Pac. Histl Rev.* 25, 1956, 281–92, and *Terrae Incognitae* 5, 1973, 7–26, but these are now superseded by *Dezhnev*, which is the basic source for statements in this and the preceding paragraph. The statement sometimes made that Russian Arctic sailors did not even have a compass is incorrect; they had primitive 'lodestones in bone' (*Dezhnev*, 166–8, q.v. also for the koch). Despite the acceptance of Golder's doubts by many non-Russian writers (he was after all the doyen in the field in America), L. Breitfuss, in 'Early Maps of North-eastern Asia', *Imago Mundi* 3, 1939, 87–99, and all the British and American writers cited in this section appear to accept the reality of the voyage, except Baddeley in a review of Golder (note 81 above).

87 D. M. Lebedev and V. I. Grekov, 'Geographical Exploration by the Russians', in H. R. Friis (ed.), *The Pacific Basin* (New York 1967), 170–200 at 171–5; they present the outlines of the Godunov and one of the Remezov maps, also given by Golder—but, perhaps typically, he has no general map! The best reproductions are in Vol. I of Baddeley, *Russia*.

88 Gibson, *Feeding the Fur Trade*, 23–4; this of course was not available to Golder. In this connection mention may be made of two articles by T. S. Farelly, 'A Reported Sixteenth Century [European] Settlement in Alaska', *Jnl Amer. Hist.* 25, 1931, 156–61, and 'The Russians and Pre-Bering Alaska', *Pac. Histl Rev.* 3, 1934, 444–8; the alleged settlers were

refugees from the troubles of Ivan the Terrible's reign, and the whole story is much more speculative than substantial.

89 Krasheninnikov, *Kamchatka*, 299–300; J. J. Stephan, *The Kuril Islands* (Oxford 1974), 38–9; but cf. Fisher, *Bering*, 4, 25 note 9. Krasheninnikov was an admirable reporter. On early contacts with Kamchatka, see Fisher, *Dezhnev*, 192, 262; however, at 190–1, he gives plausible reasons for thinking that Alekseev ended up not far south of Anadyr.

90 Müller, *Voyages*, Summary ix; Golder, *Expansion*, 97–9; Armstrong, *Settlement*, 15 and Plate IV; Baddeley, *Russia*, I.cxliii–cxlvii. The first appearance of the name Kamchatka on a map was apparently in 1673 (Fisher, *Bering*, 28 note 13) or 1667 (Lantzeff and Pierce, *Eastward*, 195).

91 Stephan, *Kurils*, 40; G. A. Lensen, *The Russian Push to Japan ... 1687–1875* (Princeton 1959), 26–30 [*Russian Push*].

92 Krasheninnikov, *Kamchatka*, 301–21 at 307–8; Lantzeff and Pierce, *Eastward*, 196–204, and 212–18 for later savageries.

93 Lensen, *Russian Push*, 32–4.

94 Krasheninnikov, *Kamchatka*, 309; G. Barratt, *Russia in Pacific Waters, 1715–1825: A Survey of the Origins of Russia's Naval Presence* (Vancouver 1981), 3–4.

95 Ibid., 4–7; Lensen, *Russian Push*, 38–9; Golder, *Expansion*, 107–9; Gibson, *Feeding the Fur Trade*, 131–3.

96 J. V. Polišenský, *The Thirty Years War* (London 1971), 89–90. The ensuing discussion is based mainly on Chaunu, *Philippines*, 243–67; F. Braudel, 'European Expansion and Capitalism: 1450–1650', in J. Blau (ed.), *Chapters in Western Civilization* (3rd ed. New York 1964), I.245–89 at 280–5 ['European Expansion']; Mauro, *Expansion*, 301–4; J. H. Elliott, *The Old World and the New 1492–1650* (Cambridge 1970), Ch. 3 [*Old and New*].

97 Chaunu, *Philippines*, 250.

98 J. H. Elliott, 'America y el Problema de la Decadencia Española', *AEA* 28, 1971, 1–23 at 17–19.

99 Dermigny, I.109–23.

1 J. V. Polišenský, 'La Plata Americana y los Comienzos de la Guerra de los 30 Anos', *AEA* 28, 1971, 209–18 at 217; Elliott, *Old and New*, 70–2.

2 Chaunu, *Philippines*, 250.

3 Braudel, 'European Expansion', 285; Dermigny, I.137–9.

4 Mauro, *Expansion*, 140–1, 326; on the fiscal role, L. Dermigny, 'L'organisation et la rôle des Compagnies', in Mollat, *Sociétés*, 443–51 at 449.

5 van Leur, *Indonesian Trade*, 234.

6 Furber, *Rival Empires*, 263.

7 *Dutch Trade*, Ch. XII ('Profit and Loss'), 244–65 at 261, 258. Cf. van Leur, *Indonesian Trade*, 231–3; Furber, *Rival Empires*, 191; Parry, *Trade and Dominion*, 78–80.

8 A. Arnould (1790), quoted in Dermigny, II.684; for Pliny, R. C. Majumdar et al., *An Advanced History of India* (London 1946), 137 or E. H. Warmington, *The Commerce between the Roman Empire and India* (2nd ed. London 1974), 174–6; there is a rather more sophisticated treatment in J. Innes Miller, *The Spice Trade of the Roman Empire 29 B.C. to A.D. 641* (Oxford 1969), 220–30, and a sceptical comment in W. C. Bark, *Origins of the Medieval World* (Stanford 1958), 125.

9 *Rival Empires*, 238.

10 In Mollat, *Sociétés*, 450.

[11] See the review of Jonas Hanway's *A Journal of Eight Days Journey from Portsmouth to Kingston upon Thames* (London 1756) in M. Wilson (ed.), *Johnson: Prose and Poetry* (London 1950), 333–47.

Notes for Chapter 5

[1] A. Sharp, *The Discovery of the Pacific Islands* (Oxford 1960), 86–7 [*Discovery*]; Blair & Robertson, X.162.

[2] A. Spoehr, *Saipan: The Ethnology of a War-Devastated Island* (Chicago 1954), 40 [*Saipan*]. Six survivors of the 1638 wreck reached the Philippines; two stayed on to meet Sanvitores thirty years later.

[3] My account in general follows P. Carano and P. C. Sanchez, *A Complete History of Guam* (Rutland, Vt/Tokyo 1964), 61–88 [*History*], with some points from Spoehr, *Saipan*, and E. K. Reed, *Archaeology and History of Guam* (Washington 1952) [*Guam*]. A Jesuit relation of the early days of the Mission is given in W. Barrett (ed.), *Mission in the Marianas: An Account of Father Diego Luis de Sanvitores and His Companions, 1669–1670* (Minneapolis 1975) [*Mission*]. There is little in Blair & Robertson, since the islands were run from New Spain, though Saravia had a temporary independent status (Carano, 79), and contacts were almost confined to those of the Manila-bound Galleons; the wind-roses on Fig. 8 provide a sufficient reason for this. The primary sources are F. García, *Vida y Martirio de el Venerable Padre Diego de Sanvitores* ... (Madrid 1683; trans. in *Guam Recorder*, 1937–9), and C. le Gobien, *Histoire des Isles Marianes nouvellement converties* ... (Paris 1700). I have seen neither of these edifying works, but Burney (III.271–315) summarises and part-translates le Gobien, with the proper Enlightenment embellishments on priest-craft and 'unfortunate Barbarians!'; he obviously enjoys himself as a rather heavy-handed Gibbon. All direct quotations are from Burney unless otherwise stated.

[4] Ambrose Cowley in [D. Henry (ed.)], *An Historical Account of all the Voyages Round the World Performed by English Navigators* (London 1774), I.446–9.

[5] Barrett, *Mission*, 55.

[6] Reed, *Guam*, 44–5, 51–2; he discounts large-scale killings and tales of mass suicide. As Burney says (III.311), when disease strikes a people sunk in hopeless depression, 'life is thought not worth care, and is abandoned without a struggle.'

[7] It is not quite certain that Magellan landed on Guam itself, though this is enshrined in the historical tradition and there is a marker to him there; he may have first sighted Saipan and Tinian, as Anson thought, and landed on the latter—Reed, *Guam*, 39, 64–6.

[8] Spoehr, *Saipan*, 55–61.

[9] Lucretius, *De rerum natura*, I.101.

[10] For Europeans in the Carolines up to 1710, see Sharp, *Discovery*, 10–95 *passim*; Villalobos, Spate, 97. Clain's letter is in Blair & Robertson, XVI.39–56 (with contemporary maps of 'las Nuevas Philipinas') and, with other early notices of the islands, in Burney, V.1–29.

[11] J. H. Parry, 'Colonial Development ... outside Europe', in *NCMH* III (1968), 507–58 at 515; P. James, *Latin America* (New York [1942]), 617–20. For a classic statement of the political aspect of the missions, see H. E. Bolton, 'The Mission as a Frontier Institution in the Spanish-American Colonies', *Amer. Histl Rev.* 23, 1917–18, 42–51 ['The Mission'].

[12] Spate, 65–7; Alarcon had been sent by Cortés's rival, the Viceroy Antonio de Mendoza, to make contact with Coronado's great northern expedition by land, and probably reached the vicinity of Yuma—though hardly 36°N (about the Hoover Dam) as seems implied by M. G. Holmes, *From New Spain by Sea to the Californias 1519–1668* (Glendale 1963), 91–9 at 97 [*New Spain*]. The 1541 map is reproduced in S. E. Morison, *The European Discovery of America: The Southern Voyages 1492–1616* (New York 1974), 626–7. 'Mar Vermejo'='Red Sea'; the name was apparently given for the colour of its waters in places, but I have been unable to find the reason for this.

[13] The world maps in G. Schilder, *Australia Unveiled* (Amsterdam/Canberra 1976) show nineteen peninsular against eleven insular versions, none of the latter being before 1622.

[14] A. del Portillo y Diez Sollano, *Descubrimientos y Exploraciones en las Costas de California* (Madrid 1947), 188–9 [*Descubrimientos*]; cf. J. B. Leighley, *California as an Island* (San Francisco 1972), 27 [*California*]. The instructions are in H. R. Wagner, *Spanish Voyages to the Northwest Coast of America in the Sixteenth Century* (San Francisco 1929, reprint Amsterdam 1966), 376–7 and his discussion is at 176–8 [*Voyages to NW*]. There is nothing on Anian in the instructions, though *if* Vizcaíno could enter the Gulf, he might go up to 37–38°N.

[15] Leighley, *California*, 24–5, 30–3, 39; H. Aschmann, 'A Late Recounting of the Vizcaíno Expedition', *Jnl Califn Anthropology* 1, 1974, 174–85—as Aschmann puts it, such impressions of Baja California 'could be developed only after long absence.' Morena's tale first appeared in the *Relaciones* of Fr Gerónimo de Zarate Salmeron (*c*. 1529)—Wagner, *Voyages to NW*, 389, who notes that when Drake visited Guatulco, one of his company seems to have been recognised as a pilot named Morera; in *Sir Francis Drake's Voyage around the World* (San Francisco 1926, reprint Amsterdam 1969) 148–9, Wagner thinks that there may be something in the story.

[16] Cristobal de Oñate's expedition from New Mexico in 1604–5 came down the Colorado to its mouth and was not responsible, as had been thought, for the insular concept—contrast H. E. Bolton, *The Spanish Borderlands* (New Haven 1921), 175–6, and C. E. Chapman, *A History of California: The Spanish Period* (New York 1921), 162 [*California*].

[17] J. B. Brebner, *The Explorers of North America 1492–1806* (Meridian ed., Cleveland 1964), 337–8. Lok's map appeared in Hakluyt's *Divers voyages . . .* (London 1582) and is reproduced in D. B. Quinn (ed.), *The Hakluyt Handbook*, HS 2nd Ser. 144–5 (London 1974), I.56–7; Gilbert's is in 'The Gilbert Map of c. 1582–3', *Geogl Jnl* 72, 1928, 235–7. Lok was of course responsible, later on, for the Juan de Fuca story which played so large a part in later Anianism; see i.a. H. R. Wagner, 'Apocryphal Voyages to the Northwest Coast of America', *Proc. Amer. Antiquarian Soc.* N.S. 41, 1931, 179–234.

[18] For Briggs's scientific standing, see C. Hill, *Intellectual Origins of the English Revolution* (Oxford 1965), 37–48, 53–5. A very similar map by Abraham Goos appeared in John Speed's atlas of 1626 and is ascribed by R. H. Power to 1624; he credits Goos with altering the name—*Early Discoveries of San Francisco Bay* (Nut Tree, Calif., 1968), 3; but H. R. Wagner thinks that Goos copied Briggs—*The Cartography of the Northwest Coast of America to the Year 1800* (Berkeley 1937), I.114 [*Cartography of NW*]. The point of priority is not of great moment. Leighley (*California*, 31) says that the Briggs map was probably not directly from Ascensión's; R. V. Tooley seems to imply that it was—*California as an Island* (London 1964), 3 [*California*]. Wagner, thorough as ever, comes down 'It is certainly a copy of one of [Ascensión's] with a few errors and some changes', and adds that 'The Briggs map was copied, one might say, hundreds of times'—*Voyages to NW*, 387–91. In view of this wide

diffusion, it seems to me that the myth of Drake's responsibility for the island idea is more likely to stem from Briggs than from the dubious Morena story.

[19] Leighley, *California*, 29.

[20] T. Jefferys, map facing title of his translation of S. [*sic*: G. F.] Müller, *Voyages from Asia to America* (London 1761); Tooley, *California*, 3–4.

[21] W. L. Cook, *Flood Tide of Empire: Spain and the Pacific Northwest 1543–1819* (New Haven 1973), 14–19; Spate, 112–15 and references there.

[22] Portillo, *Descubrimientos*, 212; for Vizcaíno 1596, H. R. Wagner, 'Pearl Fishing Enterprises in the Gulf of California', *HAHR* 10, 1930, 188–210. Portillo corrects Chapman (*California*, 159–67) on some points; for instance, there can be no doubt that Nicolás de Cardona, if not Tomás as well, did come to New Spain, though perhaps not to the Gulf. He must however be used with caution; he is often uncritical, and so careless as to contradict himself on two consecutive pages. Better treatments are S. A. Mosk, 'The Cardona Company and the Pearl Fisheries of Baja California', *Pac. Histl Rev.* 3, 1934, 50–61 ['Cardona Company'] and P. Hernández Aparicio, 'La Compañía de los Cardona . . .', *AEA* 33, 1976, 405–30, with drawings of some of the diving gear the Cardonas claimed to have invented or introduced.

[23] Mosk, 'Cardona Company', 50–1.

[24] Above, Ch. 2. In all this Portillo insists that Cardona was in direct command, not Iturbe. See Mosk, 'Cardona Company', 59–61, for the value of the pearls obtained.

[25] Portillo absurdly speaks of Panama City as under blockade 'by sea *and land*' [bloqueo maritimo *y terrestre*; my italics]—*Descubrimientos*, 224.

[26] Leighley, *California*, 27: Portillo, *Descubrimientos*, 220.

[27] Chapman, *California*, 162–5; Portillo, *Descubrimientos*, 229–35, and 235–42 for Ortega and Carbonel—he is here sensible and to the point.

[28] Portillo, *Descubrimientos*, 239.

[29] My discussion of Porter is based on Portillo, 245–90. It is amusing to compare Portillo, for whom Porter is not only a selfless patriot but almost a genius, with the very cool treatment in Chapman, *California*, 165–7, and Holmes, *New Spain*, 221–5. The 'y' is often dropped from his name, but appears on the title page of his *Reparo a Errores de la Navegacion Española* (Madrid 1634), in Portillo, 254.

[30] At this point Portillo ties himself into knots: 'Porter quit [*dejaba*] without exploring the last section' of the Gulf and did not 'come to suspect the debouchment of the Colorado in the depth of the Gulf', yet 'after his expedition, these countries remained completely demarcated'!—*Descubrimientos*, 283–4.

[31] *A New Voyage Round the World* (3rd ed. London 1698), I.272 (Dover ed., New York 1968, 189); I have italicised the last sentence. Dampier's own map is firmly insular.

[32] My account is based mainly on H. E. Bolton, *Rim of Christendom: A Biography of Eusebio Francisco Kino* . . . (New York 1960), which runs to nearly 600 pages and contains practically all that one might reasonably wish to know about Kino; it is both full and fulsome, in places verging on hagiography [*Kino*]. It is corrected on a few points by E. J. Burrus SJ, *Kino and the Cartography of Northwestern New Spain* (Tucson 1965). Details of Kino's journeys, and all direct quotations from him, are from Bolton.

[33] Chapman, *California*, 168–71.

[34] James, *Latin America*, 622. There is a contemporary account in H. R. Wagner, 'The Descent on California in 1683', *Calif. Histl Soc. Qly* 26, 1947, 309–19.

[35] Bolton, *Kino*, 224–6.

[36] Ibid., 227–8.

[37] Chapman (*California*, 172–9) is rather better on the background than Bolton (*Kino*, 343–9, 445–9), though the latter adds some detail.

[38] Bolton, 'The Mission', 51.

[39] Chapman, *California*, 179.

[40] Tooley, *California*, 4; Bolton, *Kino*, 569. Guillaume Delisle 'was the principal factor in spreading Kino's discoveries'—Wagner, *Cartography of NW*, I.146–7.

[41] From Kino's *Favores Celestiales*, cited in Bolton, *Kino*, 485: 'The dry land appeared, and they entered the Red Sea without hindrance.' This looks like the Vulgate, but though there are several similar phrases in Exodus 14 and Psalms 77, 106, and 136, I have found nothing quite so definite and appropriate, even with the kind help of Fr John Eddy SJ.

Notes for Chapter 6

[1] Owing to the shifting composition of some expeditions, both English and French, it is difficult to disengage the exact number of distinct voyages; allowing for this, perhaps half a dozen might be added. For 1578–1680, voyages averaged 0.10 per year, for 1681–1741, 0.47; the figures include those of Antonio de la Roche and of Thomas Peche (said to have attempted Anian) in 1674–5, and an even more obscure Anglo-Dutch trade venture to New Spain in 1671–2, all doubtful—Burney, III.363–4, 392–403; P. Gerhard, *Pirates on the West Coast of New Spain 1575–1742* (Glendale 1960), 141–4 [*Pirates*].

[2] A. P. Newton, *The Colonising Activities of the English Puritans* (New Haven 1914), 171, 194, 208–36 *passim* [*Puritans*]. For the WIC and Piet Heyn, C. Ch. Goslinga, *The Dutch in the Caribbean . . . 1580–1680* (Assen, Nethlds, 1971).

[3] For these beginnings see A. P. Newton, *The European Nations in the West Indies 1493–1688* (London 1933), 29–67 [*European Nations*]; A. Burns, *History of the British West Indies* (London 1954), 176–231 [*West Indies*]; S. A. G. Taylor, *The Western Design* (London 1969); D. Pope, *Harry Morgan's Way: The Biography of Sir Henry Morgan 1635–1684* [*sic: recte* 1688] (London 1977), 35–41 [*Harry Morgan*]. C. and R. Bridenbaugh, *No Peace Beyond the Line* (New York 1972) is misleadingly titled, being concerned not with public or private violence but with the socioeconomic history of the English in the Caribbean 1624–90, and as such excellent. N. M. Crouse, *French Enterprise in the West Indies 1624–1664* (New York 1940) and P. A. Means, *The Spanish Main: Focus of Envy* (New York 1965, original ed. 1931) offset the usual English viewpoint; the latter is refreshingly different, if too sentimental, in its pro-Spanish bias [*Spanish Main*]. Finally E. Williams, *From Columbus to Castro* (London 1970) presents the view of a Trinidadian Black nationalist, in a book better and less bitter than its academic reputation suggests.

[4] A. P. Thornton, 'Agents of Empire: the Buccaneers', in *For the File on Empire* (London 1968), 79–89 at 81–2 [*For the File*]; C. H. Haring, *The Buccaneers in the West Indies in the XVII Century* (London 1910), provides an unusually sober account of the Carribbean phase of buccaneering.

[5] Both words are of Caribbean origin. The French reserved *boucanier* for the Española cattle-hunters, using *flibustier* (from Dutch *vrijbuiter*=freebooter) for the marine sub-

species—Burns, *West Indies*, 193. *The Oxford English Dictionary* gives 1690 for the first English use of 'buccaneer' in the latter sense, but the title of the 1684 translation of A. O. Exquemelin's *De Amerikaensche Zee-Roovers* was *The Bucaniers of America*. In the seventeenth century buccaneers like Dampier, and officials and traders who in a double sense did well by them, promoted them to privateer status, whether they had valid papers or not; when they went too far, pillaging neutrals or compatriots, they became pirates, which they all were to the Spaniards. See P. K. Kemp and C. Lloyd, *Brethren of the Coast: Buccaneers of the South Sea* (New York 1961), 2–3 [*Brethren*], and for Exquemelin and his book ibid., 10–13; C. Steele, *English Interpreters of the Iberian New World ... 1603–1726* (Oxford 1975), 84–8 [*Interpreters*]; and J. Beeching's introduction to *The Buccaneers of America* (Harmondsworth 1969), 17–20—after three centuries of reprintings, this vivid and sadistic narrative has reached the pinnacle of 'now available in paperback' [*Buccaneers*]. This edition does not include Sharp's voyage, added in the English translations of 1684 and 1685 (see note 29 below).

6   Newton, *Puritans*, 101–11, 201, 211–16.

7   C. E. Carrington, *The British Overseas* (Cambridge 1950), 47; see also A. Winston, *No Purchase, No Pay* (London 1970), 17–21 [*No Purchase*], and for blank commissions and traffic in them, Burney, IV.171. Coxon's people had a three months' commission bought for ten pieces of eight and 'contrived to make it last for three years'—Stallybrass, *Buccaneers*, 257–8 (full reference in note 29). True privateers were commerce-raiders ancillary to formal declared war, and were supposed to bring their captures into prize courts, an impossibility for South Sea buccaneers; they often cruised not on their own account but for owners in home ports. Strictly speaking, their commissions differed from Letters of Marque, which empowered merchantmen to make captures by way of reprisal while on normal voyages, not to seek out their prey (R. G. Albion and J. B. Pope, *Sea Lanes in Wartime* (New York 1943), 24–5), but the lines in the continuum Letter of Marque-privateer-buccaneer-pirate were blurred.

8   Burney, IV.275–7; M. E. Wilbur, *Raveneau de Lussan: Buccaneer of the Spanish Main* [*sic: recte* South Sea] (Cleveland 1930), 121, 164, and cf. 214, 219 [*de Lussan*]. This is a translation of his *Journal du Voyage fait à la Mer du Sud ... en 1684* (Paris 1689); her introduction is a mistresspiece of sentimental special pleading to gloss over atrocities, only matched by R. Carse's reference to the buccaneers' 'amazing' humanity in *The Age of Piracy: a history* (New York 1957), 10, a very careless book (Guayaquil is in Chile and Santiago de Chile is a port—57, 85). De Lussan preens himself (87–9) on the French Catholic respect for religion; Burney (IV.174) speaks accurately of his—and Ambrose Cowley's—'disposition delighting in cruelty.'

9   R. D. Hussey and J. Bromley, 'The Spanish Empire under Foreign Pressures, 1688–1715', in *NCMH* VI.343–80 at 349 ['Spanish Empire'].

10   The criss-cross of events was far more complicated than can be indicated here: see i.a. Newton, *European Nations*, 232–3, 256–62; Pope, *Harry Morgan*, 106–10, 133–7; Means, *Spanish Main*, 206–12—this last a very different view of Modyford and Morgan from Pope's. For an excellent example of Jamaican attitudes, see the 'astonishing' Council resolution of 22 February 1666 in E. A. Cruikshank, *The Life of Sir Henry Morgan* (Toronto 1935), 61–2 [*Henry Morgan*].

11   All the too-numerous secondary buccaneer books describe the Maracaibo and Panama exploits, usually after Exquemelin, *Buccaneers*, 167–208—splendidly picturesque, but when

most picturesque least plausible. P. Lindsay, *The Great Buccaneer* (London 1950) is full-blooded but undocumented; he tends to favour Exquemelin, except in the tale of Morgan and the virtuous lady of Panama, which is too much for him. Cruikshank and Pope naturally tend to give their hero the benefit of many doubts, but both are solid, detailed, and well-documented—Pope rather better on political intrigues both in England and Jamaica, while Cruikshank gives more documents *in extenso*.

[12] Newton, *European Nations*, 268–73; Burns, *West Indies*, 323–4. This was the 'Treaty of America'; there had been a Treaty of Madrid in 1667, less decisive. Modyford did not receive formal official notification of the 1670 Treaty until May 1671—Newton, 271.

[13] Pope, *Harry Morgan*, 212–47, and Cruikshank, *Henry Morgan*, 158–98 for details, not all from Exquemelin! Winston, *No Purchase*, 68–82, is succinct but good. Indian hostility, almost unnoticed by Pope, is clear from Exquemelin (*Buccaneers*, 189–92), and he had here no reason to lie.

[14] This was amongst the lurid stories which the publishers of the 1684 English translations had to withdraw after Morgan's successful libel action; for this intriguing imbroglio, see Pope, *Harry Morgan*, 333–5; Steele, *Interpreters*, 84–7; Winston, *No Purchase*, 99–102; fuller accounts in Lindsay, *The Great Buccaneer*, 254–60, 281–8, and Cruikshank, *Henry Morgan*, 373–92, though the latter is in error as to Exquemelin's identity. By 1684 Harry Morgan was Sir Henry and could pull rank, but it is clear that Exquemelin was all out for sensationalism regardless.

[15] Winston, *No Purchase*, 79; 'Relacion del subceso, y ymbasion del Castillo de Chagre, y Ciudad de Panama por Henrique Morgan', No. X in *Papeles Varios de Indias y Portugal*, Mitchell Library, Sydney, A 2508; the echo is from *Aeneid* II.325, 'fuit Ilium', and a reluctant admiration for Morgan seeps through the rhetoric. Exquemelin directly accuses Morgan of having ordered the fires to be secretly set, which is idiotic; buccaneers often burned towns, but *after* the looting. Pérez's own report (Pope, *Harry Morgan*, 241–2) makes it clear that the fires were started by the Spaniards and their slaves, 'at which they say the enemy fretted very much, being disappointed of their plunder'. This makes sense, and is decisive.

[16] Newton, *European Nations*, 271, 276.

[17] Winston, *No Purchase*, 93–5; Cruikshank, *Henry Morgan*, 303, 314–15, 325–8. Pope (*Harry Morgan*, 309–12) rather glides over this aspect of his hero's career.

[18] Narborough's own journal is in *An Account of Several Late Voyages and Discoveries to the South and North* (London 1694, reprint Amsterdam 1969), 1–129 [*Account*]; Burney, III.316–76, as ever does a fine job in summarising this and bringing in points from other journals; all direct quotations are from *Account* unless otherwise stated. See also P. T. Bradley, 'Una expedición . . . a las costa de Chile', *Historiografia y Bibliografia Americanistas* (Seville) 7, 1974, 1–17 ['Una expedición']. Bradley stresses ulterior motives, concentrating on the misadventurer Don Carlos, who claimed to have served Queen Henrietta Maria and may have been, of all things, a Jewish agent. The statement that the voyage was 'promoted by the Admiralty with the double purpose of breaking the Spanish monopoly . . . and opening a North-West Passage from the Pacific' rests on a passage in Burney (III.317–20) which seems to me rather thin evidence, at least of any official objective—see G. R. Crone and R. A. Skelton, 'English Collections of Voyages and Travels, 1625–1846', in E. Lynam (ed.), *Richard Hakluyt and His Successors*, HS 2nd Ser. 113 (London 1946), 63–140 at 72 ['English Collections'].

[19] 'Four of the Spaniards Wives must needs go into the *English* boat and sit down on the Benches, to say they had been in a Boat which had come from *Europe*. These were very proper white Women . . .'—*Account*, 98.

[20] *Account*, 109; this seems to refer to the outworks, but even 'After you are in, Saint *Peter*'s Fort can do very little or no hurt at all to your Ship, except it be accidental dropping shot'. In face of this and the '36 great Ordnance', it is difficult to accept F. E. Dyer's kindly apologia in *The Life of Sir John Narbrough* (London 1931), 84–9 [*Narbrough*]. It is only fair to add that Narborough became an Admiral and was successful against the Algerine corsairs; but he was obviously no Hornblower.

[21] Lt Pecket's journal, in Burney, III.373.

[22] Bradley, 'Una expedición', 12–13. Dyer (*Narbrough*, 89) says that Armiger lived at Valdivia for sixteen years and then was executed for high treason, but this seems unlikely.

[23] Burney, III.375; see IV.329–37 for the private attempt at peaceful trade by John Strong in 1689–91; repulsed from Valdivia and La Serena, he sold some goods at Tumbes and visited Juan Fernández. The venture was a loss—'A Traverse of near 40,000 miles . . . we for a long time, and to little purpose, conversed with Beasts and Men'—F. E. Dyer, 'Captain John Strong', *MM* 13, 1927, 145–59 at 157 ['John Strong'].

[24] Fernández Duro, V.161.

[25] E. W. Dahlgren, *Les Relations Commerciales et Maritimes entre la France et les Côtes de l'Océan Pacifique (commencement du XVIIIe siecle)* (Paris 1909), I.63 [*Relations*]; G. Céspedes del Castillo, 'La Defensa Militar del Istmo de Panamá a fines del siglo XVII y comienzos del XVIII', *AEA* 19, 1952, 235–75 at 239 ['Defensa']; but cf. A. P. Thornton, 'English and Spanish Slavers in the Caribbean', in *For the File*, 90–112. For an example of local Anglo-Spanish co-operation in 1685, see L. E. Elliott-Joyce in L. Wafer, *A New Voyage and Description of the Isthmus of America* (1699), HS 2nd Ser. 73 (Oxford 1934), note at xxxix [Wafer, *Isthmus*].

[26] Céspedes del Castillo, 'Defensa', 243–4; Hussey and Bromley, 'Spanish Empire', 249; Fernández Duro, V.180, 269.

[27] Céspedes del Castillo, 'Defensa', 237–40; Gerhard, *Pirates*, 145–6; M. Luengo Muñoz, 'El Darién en la política internacional del siglo XVIII', *Estudios Americanos* 18, 1959, 139–56 at 147. Dampier lays particular stress on Indian aid—*New Voyage*, 26, 37 (wild Indians), 128–9 (full reference in note 29).

[28] N. Davis, 'Expedition to the Gold Mines', in Wafer, *Isthmus*, 152–65 at 155 (from his 2nd ed., 1704). Davis goes on 'which was very mortifying to us, since we reckon'd upon the sharing near two hundred Pounds a Man'—an often-sung tune.

[29] The bibliography of the buccaneers is almost as murky as their deeds. For a general picture, Burney's volume IV is still good, and so also, on the whole, are those by Kemp and Lloyd and by Gerhard already cited; but G. Wycherley, *Buccaneers of the Pacific* (London 1929) is very poor stuff. Of original accounts, Exquemelin himself is very cursory on the South Sea; the two English translations of his book published by W. Cooke and by T. Malthus in 1684 were not from the original Dutch of 1678 but from a Spanish version significantly entitled *Piratas de la América*, very anti-Morgan (see Steele, *Interpreters*, 84–8). Morgan appears to have sponsored the version which appeared in P. Ayres, *The Voyages and Adventures of Capt. Barth Sharp* (London 1684—rare and not seen by me). In 1685 Crooke published Basil Ringrose's narrative, the basic account of Sharp's voyage, in a new edition of Exquemelin—this has been edited by W. S. Stallybrass in the Broadway Translations

(London, n.d.), 289–475 [Stallybrass, *Buccaneers*]; but Ringrose's MS. was doctored by adding complimentary references to Sharp, either by Sharp himself or his friend William Hack(e)—see A. Gray's introduction to W. Dampier, *A New Voyage Round the World* (1697) in either the Argonaut edition (London 1927) or the Dover (New York 1968); both also contain N. M. Penzer's valuable bibliographical note. Dampier is basic for the earlier part of Davis's voyage and for Swan's; my references are to the excellent Dover edition [*New Voyage*]. The Hakluyt Society edition of Wafer (note 25) is much better than G. P. Winship's (1903, reprint New York 1970). Since all these accounts are chronological, there seems as a rule no point in giving precise references to specific dated events.

30 Ringrose covers the 'first wave'. Wafer is very brief until his return across the Isthmus, and avowedly leaves the 'second wave' to Dampier, who carries on with it until he parts from Davis (Wafer, *Isthmus*, 28–9, 112). The best of Wafer's book is the excellent account, still ethnohistorically valuable, of the Isthmus itself and the Cuna Indians with whom he lived, happily. Dampier is very brief on the first wave and the Isthmian crossing (Introduction and Chs. I–III); the bulk of the *New Voyage* deals with the second wave and his East Indies adventures. Direct quotations in this section, unless otherwise indicated, are from Ringrose in Stallybrass, *Buccaneers*.

31 P. Ayres, cited by Elliott Joyce in Wafer, *Isthmus*, 44.

32 Ringrose has another tale ('scarce deserving any credit') that in Cromwell's time a ship was wrecked hereabouts, carrying 30,000,000 pesos (!) as a free gift (!!) from the Lima merchants for King Charles (of England: !!!) in his distress. This would be the treasure that John Strong sought at Santa Elena in 1690—Dyer, 'John Strong', 146, 152.

33 One of Sharp's MS. journals, cited in Kemp and Lloyd, *Brethren*, 52. Ringrose says not a word of this incident, but there is an account of it in the same volume of Crooke's—Stallybrass, *Buccaneers*, 277–8.

34 G. Lohmann Villena, *Las Minas de Huancavelica* (Seville 1949), 400; Gerhard quotes a Spanish estimate of 4,000,000 pesos total damage—*Pirates*, 153.

35 'Waggoner', a rutter or nautical atlas, from Lucas Waghenaer, whose *Spieghel der Zeevaerdt* was translated in 1588 as *The Mariners Mirror*. For Sharp's later career, C. Lloyd, 'Bartholomew Sharp, Buccaneer', *MM* 42, 1956, 291–301; oddly enough, Lloyd states that the decision to return was made at Juan Fernández and that Sharp saw 'no land at all' between that island and Barbados.

36 Kemp and Lloyd, *Brethren*, 87–8. Dampier, ever respectable, simply omits this incident; Cowley's printed *Voyage Round the Globe*, in W. Hack(e), *An Original Collection of Voyages* (London 1699), 3–4, is casual about it [*Voyage*].

37 Burney, IV.137–9; Dampier, *New Voyage*, 63—de Weert was with the Mahu-Cordes fleet of 1598 and the islands were generally called by his name in the seventeenth century, but in all probability had been seen by John Davis in 1592 and Richard Hawkins in 1594, if not by Camargo's ship in 1540 (see above, Ch. 1, note 51). Cowley's MS. journal agrees with Dampier's identification—Beaglehole, I.lxxi. The name Falklands seems to have originated with John Strong—Burney, IV.331. B. M. Chambers, 'Where was Pepys Island?', *MM* 19, 1933, 446–54, makes out a good case that Cowley's harbour which could take 500 sail was really Port Desire in Patagonia; he also argues that Hawkins's 'Maidenland', usually taken to be the Falklands, was also on the mainland.

38 Cowley, *Voyage*, 6–7.

[39] Dampier, *New Voyage*, 67; all direct quotations in this section from Dampier unless otherwise indicated.

[40] This return voyage is narrated by Cowley, whose account is of interest mainly for the light it throws upon his unpleasant character, as shown by his almost jocular story of the atrocities against the Chamorros and his strange lament that the crew, 'being under no government', refused to attack thirteen 'Tartar' ships near Canton. This throws some doubt on his protestations that he had been tricked into buccaneering—[D. Henry], *An Historical Account of All the Voyages Round the World performed by English Navigators* (London 1774), I.437, 445–50.

[41] One suspects some sleight-of-hand. In his MS. journal Dampier says that 'it was ever a design between Captain Swan and myself . . . to persuade the unthinking rabble' (Kemp and Lloyd, *Brethren*, 116), but in print he says that 'The *Spaniards*, who have the greatest Reason to know best' reckoned the crossing at 2300–2400 leagues, English books at under 2000, and that Swan argued for the latter—'his Reasons were many, although but weak'—*New Voyage*, 193.

[42] Details in this section from Burney, IV.263–94, and Wilbur, *de Lussan*, 80–213 *passim*.

[43] Dampier, *New Voyage*, 240; Wafer, *Isthmus*, 125 and note. One can hardly count Clipperton Island as significant, nor Dampier in New Britain as a buccaneer.

[44] A. Sharp, *The Discovery of the Pacific Islands* (Oxford 1960), 88–90; Sharp tends to follow H. Carrington (in G. Robertson, *The Discovery of Tahiti*, HS 2nd Ser. 98 (London 1948), 274–7) in opting for SS Felix y Ambrosio: but as these small islands reach 479 m they do *not* 'agree reasonably well' with Wafer's and Dampier's accounts of low sandy islands backed at a distance by a large tract of highland; and the plate in P. Vidal de la Blache and L. Gallois, *Géographie Universelle* XV (Paris 1927), to which Carrington refers, seems not at all to the point. Burney (IV.205–10) leaves the question open but leans to the belief that Davis did see Easter Island, and F. W. Beechey argues unconvincingly for this—*Narrative of a Voyage to the Pacific . . .* (London, new ed. 1831), I.36–41. Temoe atoll in the Tuamotus has also been suggested, in which case the high land would be Mangareva, 40 km to the northwest—B. G. Corney (ed.), *The Voyage of Captain Don Felipe Gonzalez . . . to Easter Island in 1770–1*, HS 2nd Ser. 13 (Cambridge 1908), xviii; but this seems impossibly distant from Chile, as well as 4° out in latitude, and these islands are usually credited to James Wilson of the *Duff* in 1797.

Heights of islands from Naval Division Handbook *Pacific Islands* (London 1943–5), II.54–5, 65, 78.

[45] Wafer, *Isthmus*, 130–1; Kemp and Lloyd, *Brethren*, 127–33. Davis may well have been involved with a more famous pirate, Captain Kidd, against whom one Edward Davis gave evidence.

[46] Anyone who was on the losing side in such campaigns as those of France in 1940 or Burma and Malaya in 1942 will know this feeling only too well; *experto credite*.

[47] Céspedes del Castillo, 'Defensa', 242–3, 250. Details and direct quotations in this section are from this paper unless otherwise indicated.

[48] G. Lohmann Villena, *Historia Marítima del Perú, T. IV: Siglos XVII y XVIII*, (Lima 1972) 137 [*Hist. Marítima*]. As J. H. Parry puts it, 'the Spanish government rel[ied] on the facts of geography rather than on military or naval strength'—*Trade and Dominion* (London 1971), 20.

[49] Lohmann Villena, *Hist. Marítima*, 133.

[50] Fernández Duro, V.85; R. L. Woodward, *Robinson Crusoe's Island* (Chapel Hill 1969), 21–2; Lohmann Villena, *Hist. Marítima*, 422–4—where Narborough's visit to Valdivia is strangely described as an intended 'golpe de mano' by two ships out of an original eight.

[51] P. T. Bradley, 'Some Considerations on Defence at Sea in the Viceroyalty of Peru during the Seventeenth Century', *Rev. Hist. de América* (Mexico) No. 79, 1975, 77–97 at 89–91.

[52] Ibid., 92–6; Céspedes del Castillo, 'Defensas', 251–2; Lohmann Villena, *Hist. Marítima*, 144–50, 438–42; cf. Burney, IV.287.

[53] Dahlgren, *Relations*, I.98–103; Massertie claimed to have passed the Straits twice and to have been as far north as the Tres Marias. For Beauchesne-Gouin, see below, Ch. 7.

[54] Céspedes del Castillo, 'Defensa', 242, 257–8.

[55] Ibid., 254, 259–62; G. Lohmann Villena, *Las Defensas Militares de Lima y Callao* (Lima 1964), 131.

[56] J. Lynch, *Spain under the Habsburgs* (Oxford 1964–9), II.223.

[57] Ibid., II.193; Céspedes del Castillo, 'Defensa', 266, 274.

[58] Fernández Duro, V.285–97; Burney, IV.303–20, is lively as usual. Means (*Spanish Main*, 217–19) is almost comic in his insistence that it was all 'good clean warfare'; he says nothing of the abominable second sack. Much the best account I have seen is in N. M. Crouse, *The French Struggle for the West Indies 1665–1713* (New York 1943), 197–244.

[59] C. de la Roncière and G. Clerc-Rampol, *Histoire de la Marine Française* (Paris 1934), 127.

[60] W. H. Bonner, *Captain William Dampier: Buccaneer-Author* (Palo Alto 1934), 3. Bonner introduces Dampier neatly as 'a Baedeker, a Holinshed, and a very definite leaven in the loaf' [*Dampier*].

[61] Crone and Skelton, 'English Collections', 67, 83, 133; but perhaps the novel was out-stripping travel, if not theology, by the end of the century. See this essay *passim* for the great outbursts of travel publication, and also Steele, *Interpreters*, Chs. IV and V.

[62] R. I. Ruggles, 'Geographical Exploration by the English', in H. Friis (ed.), *The Pacific Basin: A History of Its Geographical Exploration* (New York 1967), 221–55 at 233–4.

[63] C. Wilkinson, *William Dampier* (London 1929), 148–9, is convincing on this point. Such polishing is not unknown today, if less frankly admitted. Swift faithfully follows this convention of self-depreciation in the prefatory letter to *Gulliver's Travels* (1726). It will be recalled that Cook's own journal of his first voyage was reworked, or rehashed, by John Hawkesworth, a fact which makes nonsense of the critique of Cook in *The Cambridge History of English Literature*, XIV.245. For Dampier's *Discourse*, see J. C. Shipman, *William Dampier: Seaman-Scientist* (Lawrence, Kansas, 1962), 8–23.

[64] *New Voyage*, 325–6; *Life and Strange Surprizing Adventures of Robinson Crusoe* (1719; ed. J. D. Crowley, London 1972), 164–5, 182–4, 201, 230–7; Bonner, *Dampier*, 72, 153.

[65] Bonner's Ch. IX discusses Dampier's influence on Swift; he points out (176) that the only contemporaries named in *Gulliver's Travels* are 'my cousin Dampier' and the carto-grapher Hermann Moll. Dampier influenced Defoe and Swift; Dampier, Defoe and Swift influenced Robert Paltock's delightful *Life and Adventures of Peter Wilkins* (1751); at least the last three of these (plus Lucian, Cyrano de Bergerac, Rousseau, and Lord knows who else) influenced Rétif de la Bretonne in his ideologically interesting *La Découverte australe Par un Homme-volant, ou le Dédale français* (Leipsick [*sic*] 1781), and so the great game of Lit. Crit., like the Great Chain of Being, goes on.

[66] J. L. Lowes, *The Road to Xanadu* (Cambridge, Mass., 1927), 223–8; Coleridge also had a high opinion of Dampier—'a rough sailor, but a man of exquisite mind', ibid., 49.

67 *New Voyage*, 114.

68 Hakluyt's proposal relied on Cimmarons rather than Indians, but the principle is the same—see 'A Discourse of the Commodity of the Taking of the Straight of Magellanus', in E. G. R. Taylor (ed.), *The Original Writings . . . of the Two Richard Hakluyts*, HS 2nd Ser. 76–7 (London 1935), I.139–46; cf. Spate, 353 note 36.

69 J. Pullen, *Memoirs of the Maritime Affairs of Great Britain* (London 1732, but apparently written *c.* 1711 for Harley), 36–43; D. Defoe, *A Review of the State of Great Britain*, VIII No. 49, 17 July 1711; G. Williams (ed.), *Documents relating to Anson's Voyage round the World, 1740–1744*, Navy Records Soc. 109 (London 1967), 34–41, and Book II Ch. XIV of R. Walter and B. Robins, *A Voyage round the World . . . by George Anson* (1748; 255–64 in Williams's ed., London 1974)—a chapter devoted to what might have been. For Thomas Bowrey's 'Proposal for Taking Baldivia in the South Seas', also of 1711 and inspired by Woodes Rogers's voyage, see R. Bourne, *Queen Anne's Navy in the West Indies* (New Haven 1939), 144, 178–9. In evaluating Defoe's opinion, it should be recalled that the War of the Spanish Succession was still on, and victory over the Bourbons would have meant a Habsburg ruler of the Indies under heavy obligations to the British.

70 L. B. Kinnaird (ed.), 'Creassy's Plan for Seizing Panama', *HAHR* 13, 1933, 46–78, and for his revamping of it in 1804, M. E. Thomas under the same title in *HAHR* 22, 1942, 82–103. This amazing project, which resurrected William Paterson's Caledonian colony (below Ch. 7), included a partly subterranean canal across the Isthmus. The phrase about the never-setting sun is ascribed to Christopher North, in 1829, by *The Oxford Dictionary of Quotations*; alas, Christopher Hill points out that actually it was applied to the *Spanish* Empire by Francis Bacon in 1622—*Intellectual Origins of the English Revolution* (Oxford 1965), 155, citing Bacon's *Advertisement touching on a Holy Warre* (1622), in *Works* (London 1858–74), VII.11–36 at 21.

Notes for Chapter 7

1 Quoted in C. Lloyd, *William Dampier* (London 1966), 20.

2 J. Masefield (ed.), *The Voyages of Captain William Dampier* (London 1906), I.11; this is the most comprehensive collecion of Dampier's writings [*Dampier's Voyages*].

3 C. Wilkinson, *William Dampier* (London 1929), 149–55; Montague became Earl of Halifax in 1714 and is not to be confused with George Saville, Marquess of Halifax, the Trimmer.

4 J. A. Williamson, introduction to Dampier's *A Voyage to New Holland* (London 1939), xxvi; J. B. Hewson, *A History of the Practice of Navigation* (Glasgow 1963), 146–9. Dampier's book was originally published in two parts, 1703 and 1709; direct quotations in this section, unless otherwise stated, are from Williamson's edition [*New Holland*]. On Halley, see N. J. W. Thrower, 'Edmond Halley and Thematic Geo-cartography', in Thrower (ed.), *The Compleat Plattmaker* (Berkeley 1978), 195–228 at 208–16.

5 Dampier's proposals, with abstracts of other papers on the *Roebuck* expedition, in *Dampier's Voyages*, II.325–35, source of quotations in the next two paragraphs.

6 Williamson, in *New Holland*, xxxi.

[7] *New Holland*, 121–4. He seems curiously inconsistent in his references to Terra Australis, and should have been less confused about New Holland's insularity from Tasman, whose results appeared in Blau's *Nova et Accuratissima Totius Terrarum Orbis Tabula* (1662) and many other maps before 1699—see G. Schilder, *Australia Unveiled* (Amsterdam/Canberra 1976) for reproductions.

[8] In *New Holland*, xliii.

[9] Records of the courts-martial in *Dampier's Voyages*, II.594–605. William III was still alive when Fisher was jailed, but the trials were held under Queen Anne.

[10] Beaglehole, I.cv, 513, IV.125; J. A. Williamson, *The Ocean in English History* (Oxford 1941), 163. Hawke, First Lord at the time, is said to have exclaimed that he would suffer his right hand to be cut off rather than sign such a commission, but H. C. Fry has shown that Hawke supported Dalrymple—'Alexander Dalrymple and Captain Cook', in R. Fisher and H. Johnson, (eds.), *Captain James Cook and His Times* (Vancouver/Canberra 1979), 41–58 at 47.

[11] J. Prebble, *The Lion in the North* (Harmondsworth 1973), 261–76; on toleration, D. Daiches, *Scotland and the Union* (London 1977), 29.

[12] G. M. Trevelyan, *Ramillies and the Union with Scotland* (Fontana ed., London 1965), 198.

[13] J. S. Barbour, *A History of William Paterson and the Darien Company* (Edinburgh 1907), 7–9 [*Paterson*]; J. Prebble, *The Darien Disaster* (Harmondsworth 1970), 24, 35–6, 58—a detailed and very fine account [*Darien*].

[14] W. R. Scott, *The Constitution and Finance of English, Scottish and Irish Joint-Stock Companies to 1720* (Cambridge 1911–12, reprint New York 1951), II.209 [*Companies*].

[15] Ibid., II.213–14. For the cross-currents in the English over-reaction, see P. W. J. Riley, *The Union of England and Scotland* (Manchester 1978), 207–9, and indeed the whole chapter on 'Trade and propaganda' [*Union*].

[16] G. P. Insh, *The Company of Scotland Trading to Africa and the Indies* (London 1932), 65, 86–96 [*The Company*]. Insh's *Historian's Odyssey* (Edinburgh 1938) is a charming account of his quest for Darien records [*Odyssey*]. All moneys are in sterling, not the Scots pound which = 0. 1s. 8d. sterling—as Sir Patrick Spens hath it (in Q's version), 'The poun' I most admire is not/In Scottish currencie'.

[17] Quoted in Scott, *Companies*, II.214. According to Riley (*Union*, 209–11) this was the original target, 'Africa and the Indies' being only a cover device which misfired. Yet the Company did send ships to these places, and Riley's otherwise excellent discussion oddly ignores the international aspect almost completely.

[18] Insh, *The Company*, 109–14; Prebble, *Darien*, 75–88, 118–21.

[19] Scott, *Companies*, 221; Insh, *The Company*, 97–100.

[20] F. R. Hart, *The Disaster of Darien* (London ?1929), 148–56—valuable for Spanish documents [*Disaster*]; D. Howarth, *The Golden Isthmus* (London 1967), 114—perhaps the best brief telling of the story [*Isthmus*]; T. B. Macaulay, *History of England* (London 1872 ed.), IV.301–2—marred by prejudice and a horrid superciliousness, but so readable!

[21] Insh, *Odyssey*, 235–9; G. Mack, *The Land Divided: A History of . . . Isthmian Canal Projects* (New York 1944), 31—a superb book by an art historian [*Land Divided*]. Hugh Rose, secretary to the colony's Council, records rain, unusually heavy and once 'prodigious', on day after day of the first month—Barbour, *Paterson*, 69–77. Insh, following his 'authority' the canal projector Cullen, seems almost to think heavy rain beneficial; anyone who has lived in a monsoon climate knows how depressing it is even when one is well housed and

well fed. On Cullen, see Mack, 249–59—Insh did not know of his shady background, but might have been warned by his style.

[22] Insh, *The Company*, 77–8, and *Odyssey*, 233–4; W. P. Webb, *The Great Frontier* (Cambridge Mass. 1952), 204–5; B. Lenman, *An Economic History of Modern Scotland 1660–1976* (London 1977), 51. I cannot see that Wafer's 1704 preface supports Insh's claim that 'he emphasized the fact that the failure was due not primarily to military reasons but to lack of provisions'. He does not mention the Scots at all in this context; he did think that a military expedition could be successful but this was based on a command of the sea which the Scots did not have.

[23] Fletcher of Saltoun, in Prebble, *Darien*, 109–10; Robert Pincarton (perhaps bluffing his Spanish interrogators), in Insh, *Odyssey*, 230.

[24] F. W. Watson (ed.), *Historical Records of Australia* Series I (Sydney 1914–25), I.308.

[25] Quoted in Howarth, *Isthmus*, 113.

[26] Prebble, *Darien*, 107, 161–3, 169; the suggestion (not Prebble's) that he was sent to forestall the Scots in taking Darien makes no political sense. In general, details of events in the colony are drawn from Prebble's excellent book.

[27] Barbour, *Paterson*, 76–7; Hart, *Disaster*, 212, 258–9.

[28] Barbour, *Paterson*, 211–14.

[29] Insh, *The Company*, 146–53.

[30] Insh, *The Company*, 169–71.

[31] The Revd Francis Borland, in Prebble, *Darien*, 247.

[32] Prebble, *Darien*, 243–4, 258–9, 269–70, 330.

[33] Royal Memorandum of 30 October 1699, in Hart, *Disaster*, 323–7.

[34] Mack, *Land Divided*, 84.

[35] The Partition Treaty of October 1698 allotted this neutral prince, then six years old, Spain, the Indies, the Spanish Netherlands, and Sardinia; the Italian possessions of the Spanish Crown going to the Dauphin or to the Archduke Charles of Austria.

[36] Insh, *The Company*, 180–2, 203–20.

[37] Ibid., 245–77.

[38] The mysterious affair involving the *Speedy Return*, *Annandale*, and *Worcester* is too complex to be related here; see Prebble, *Darien*, 9–18, 335–7, and Insh, *The Company*, 278–312. It is generally agreed that this was a judicial murder under mob pressure; for a dissenting view, see A. Lang, *Historical Mysteries* (London ?1904), 240–64, who thought that Green and his men had not taken the *Speedy Return* but had pirated some ship somewhere and so, in classic Scots phrase, would be no' the waur o' a hangin'. R. C. Temple, in a full discussion (*New Light on the Mysterious Tragedy of the 'Worcester'*, London 1930), bases himself on the papers of Green's English backer, Thomas Bowrey, and concludes that 'Green was guiltless of any piracy whatsoever'.

[39] Barbour, *Paterson*, 178–81, 194–5, 226; Paterson had to wait until 1715, four years before his death, for his share. The arrangement was not quite so generous as it may seem, since the repayment would come from 'the equivalent' to be allotted to Scotland in compensation for additional fiscal burdens arising from Union—Riley, *Union*, 184–8. Riley emphasises the importance of purely (and often impure) political factors in the Union. Darien of course was both an economic and a political factor.

[40] T. C. Smout, 'The Road to Union', in G. Holmes (ed.), *Britain after the Glorious Revolution 1689–1714* (London 1969), 176–96 at 185–8.

[41] Howarth, *Isthmus*, 113, 259–62; Mack, *Land Divided*, 247. The only threat lies in a proposed nuclear-dug canal, which would certainly disrupt them whatever the guarantees —Howarth, 262–8.

[42] 'A Lady of Honour', *The Golden Island or the Darien Song*, in Insh, *The Company*, 178–9. Beauchesne's voyage is briefly described in J. Dunmore, *French Explorers in the Pacific* (Oxford 1965–9), I.11–13; but my details are from E. W. Dahlgren, *Les Relations Commerciales et Maritimes entre La France et les Côtes de L'Océan Pacifique* (Paris 1909), 112–44. The first published account of the voyage, from Beauchesne's journal, is in Woodes Rogers, *A Cruising Voyage round the World* (London 1712, reprint Amsterdam 1969), 117–21, which adds a few touches to Dahlgren.

Notes for Chapter 8

[1] H. and P. Chaunu, *Séville et l'Atlantique (1504–1650)* (Paris 1955–60), VIII(I).922–3 [*Séville*].

[2] G. Williams, '"The Inexhaustible Fountain of Gold": English Projects and Ventures in the South Seas, 1670–1770', in J. E. Flint and G. Williams (eds.), *Perspective of Empire* (London 1973), 27–53 at 32 ['The Fountain'].

[3] Chaunu, *Séville*, VIII(I).6–7, 29.

[4] A. T. Mahan, *The Influence of Sea Power upon History, 1660–1783* (Boston 1890; American Century ed., New York 1957), 179 [*Influence*].

[5] J. Parry, *Trade and Dominion: The European Overseas Empires in the Eighteenth Century* (London 1971), 91, 96 [*Trade and Dominion*]; Louis XIV is cited from Dahlgren, *Relations*, 561 (full reference in note 19 below).

[6] H. Kamen, 'The Decline of Spain: A Historical Myth?', *Past and Present* No.81, 1978, 24–50 at 48–9.

[7] H. Kamen, *The War of Succession in Spain 1700–1715* (London 1969), 59 [*Succession*]; J. S. Bromley and A. N. Ryan, 'Navies', in *NCMH* VI.790–833 at 792 ['Navies'].

[8] M. Savelle, *Empires to Nations: Expansion in America, 1713–1824* (Minneapolis 1974), 80–3.

[9] J. O. McLachlan, *Trade and Peace with Old Spain 1667–1750* (Cambridge 1940), 30 [*Trade and Peace*]; G. Clark, 'From the Nine Years War to the War of the Spanish Succession', *NCMH* VI.380–409 at 384, 391; Mahan, *Influence*, 180. According to P. Vilar, some of Louis XIV's advisers fervently pressed him to accept the Spanish succession for his grandson, 'Many of them imagin[ing] that this would result in a joint Franco-Spanish rule of America'—*A History of Gold and Money 1450–1920* (London 1976), 246.

[10] Kamen, *Succession*, 9–11, 179–81.

[11] A. J. Veenendal, 'The War of the Spanish Succession in Europe', *NCMH* VI.410–45 at 418–19; V. Magalhães Godinho, 'Portugal and her Empire, 1680–1720', ibid., 509–40 at 523–6; Mahan, *Influence*, 185; C. R. Boxer, *The Dutch Seaborne Empire 1600–1800* (Harmondsworth 1973), 118 [*Dutch Empire*]. For naval activity in the Caribbean, see R. Bourne, *Queen Anne's Navy in the West Indies* (New Haven 1939), and cf. H. W. Richmond, *Statesmen and Sea Power* (Oxford 1946), 78–86, 94–9, which perhaps takes a too 'Mediterranean' point of view.

[12] The original account of the voyage, up to the separation in January 1705, is in W. Funnell, *A Voyage Round the World* (London 1707, reprint Amsterdam 1969); although not on a par with Dampier's *New Voyage*, this is a better narrative than is generally allowed, even if it has some bizarre errors—e.g. that Lima is on an island, which does however point up the wide berth given to Callao by raiders after Drake and the Dutch [*Voyage*]. Funnell's bias is evident though muted; he avoids direct attacks on Dampier, as may be seen from the three accounts of the fight with the Galleon, by these two and Welbe, conveniently juxtaposed in P. K. Kemp and C. Lloyd, *Brethren of the Coast* (New York 1961), 153–6 [*Brethren*]. Recent accounts may be found in C. Wilkinson, *William Dampier* (London 1929), 187–202 [*Dampier*]; *Brethren*, 139–59; and C. Lloyd, *William Dampier* (London 1966), which has some odd slips such as the ascription to Dampier of the 'palpable nonsense' of Spanish galleons at Rio de Janeiro (97) when Funnell (2) says 'the River of *Plate*' which is palpable sense [*Dampier*]. Direct quotations in this section are from Funnell, unless otherwise indicated.

'Galley' in this context would be a flush-decked sailing ship with oars for use in calms, heavily armed and manned for its size by cutting down on cargo space—Lloyd, *Dampier*, 102.

[13] Stradling was wrecked in Peru, taken to France as a prisoner of war, and got away by spinning an ingenious yarn about hidden pirate gold—Kemp and Lloyd, *Brethren*, 148–50.

[14] It may well of course have been found earlier by the Spaniards, though hardly by Magellan as is claimed in G. E. Nunn, 'Magellan's Route in the Pacific', *Geogl Rev.* 24, 1934, 625–33.

[15] Dampier's *Vindication of his Voyage to the South Seas* (London 1707), in J. Masefield (ed.), *The Voyages of Captain William Dampier* (London 1906), II.579–85 at 584; J. Welbe, *Answer to Captain Dampier's Vindication* (London 1707), ibid., II.585–92 at 590.

[16] Funnell's gang eventually reached Amboyna, where the suspicious Dutch gaoled them. Funnell had visions of another Massacre of Amboyna, and ascribes their release (without restitution of ship or goods) to the Dutch reading of their journals, which showed that they were 'Part of Captain Dampier's Company . . . and so they knew, if we fared otherwise than well, we should be enquired after'—a nice irony (*Voyage*, 251, 269).

[17] Lloyd, *Dampier*, 120–2; Wilkinson, *Dampier*, 200–1; for the legal tangle after the voyage, B. M. H. Rogers, 'Dampier's Voyage of 1703', *MM* 10, 1924, 366–81.

[18] Funnell, *Voyage*, 147.

[19] Kamen, *Succession*, 151, 185–94. For details, E. W. Dahlgren, *Les Relations commerciales et maritimes entre la France et les Côtes de l'Océan Pacifique (commencement du XVIIIe siècle) I. Le Commerce de la Mer du Sud jusqu'à la Paix d'Utrecht* (Paris 1909), 408–77 *passim*. The long-windedness of the title is more than maintained in the text, which Dahlgren elsewhere refers to as an attempted sketch—an outline running to 729 pages! These are crammed with valuable detail, but there is much repetition and no index; one hardly knows whether to be glad or sorry that the promised second volume never forthcame, but exists only in manuscript at the University of Rennes (Kamen, 144). The book is doubtless exhaustive, if also exhausting—and indispensable. Direct quotations and factual detail not otherwise attributed are from Dahlgren [*Relations*].

[20] J. Dunmore, *French Explorers in the Pacific: I. The Eighteenth Century* (Oxford 1965), 25— an excellent short survey of the trade [*Explorers*]; E. W. Dahlgren, in 'Voyages français à destination de la Mer du Sud avant Bougainville (1695–1749)', *Nouvelles Archives des*

Missions Scientifiques (Paris) 14, 1907, 423–568, gives precise summaries for each voyage. His financial estimate is at 431–4 (8–11 in separate pagination).

[21] J. Vicens Vives, *An Economic History of Spain* (Princeton 1969), 433.

[22] Dahlgren, *Relations*, 103.

[23] M. Moreyra y Paz-Soldán, *El Tráfico Marítimo en la Epoca Colonial* (Lima 1944), 75–82 [*Tráfico*].

[24] Dahlgren, *Relations*, 263–6, 672–3; cf. Kamen, *Succession*, 87–90, on the obstructionism of the ruling cliques: the Duque de Medina Sidonia was 'seven times grandee of Spain, and consequently seven times more corrupt . . .'.

[25] Kamen, *Succession*, 144–58.

[26] Dahlgren, *Relations*, 293–306; Paz-Soldán, *Tráfico*, 10–13.

[27] With unaccustomed but welcome humour Dahlgren notes that at Ilha Grande in Brazil (now hostile), their journal 'gave future voyagers the precious hint' that to ensure supplies 'it was enough to threaten to burn the two convents'—*Relations*, 379.

[28] Ibid., 378–94; Dunmore, *Explorers*, 17.

[29] Dahlgren's account is amusing: the merchants were told that the King would take a refusal very ill, and there would be no licences for the South Sea or the North; but there were limits to the Grand Monarque's absolute power when it came up against money power—*Relations*, 350–8.

[30] Nine ships seem to have left Callao, seven to have arrived at Port-Louis (near Lorient) —ibid., 418–19; Kamen, *Succession*, 185–6. Dahlgren gives a lengthy account (420–80) of the financial tangle.

[31] Dahlgren, *Relations*, 486–96; Kamen, *Succession*, 152–63.

[32] Dermigny, I.152–4; Dunmore, *Explorers*, 19–20. The voyage of *la Comtesse*, after the Treaty of Utrecht, was strictly speaking illegal, and her consort *le Brillant* was taken by Martinet.

[33] For the grotesque chicanery and the paralegal twistings and turnings in the Marchand and Martinet affairs, see E. W. Dahlgren, 'L'Expédition de Martinet . . .', *Rev. de l'Hist. des Colonies Françaises* 1, 1913, 5–80—even Dahlgren cannot make these shady dealings dull; for Brignon, J. Callander, *Terra Australis Cognita* (London 1767, reprint Amsterdam 1967), III.669–72. The end of French and the rise of British contraband are discussed in S. Villalobos R., *Comercio y Contrabando en el Río de la Plata y Chile 1700–1811* (Buenos Aires 1965), 28–37—at Mendoza, on the trans-Andine route, officials trying to stop the trade were run out of town by a meeting headed by the local Fiscal or District Attorney!

[34] Chaunu, *Séville*, VIII(I).1177–8.

[35] Dahlgren, *Relations*, 552–7; Feuillée's *Journal des Observations . . . sur les Côtes Occidentales de L'Amérique Méridionale* was published in three volumes (Paris 1714–25), not seen. In 1727 Frézier published a severe *Réponse à la Preface Critique . . . du R. P. Feuillée*, which attacked his own *Voyage de la Mer du Sud*: the most interesting passage (31) defends reckoning longitude to 180° East and West, which Feuillée thought an innovation of Frézier's; as the latter points out, citing Halley and others, the English, 'who give us the best charts', reckon this way. It had in fact been used and explained by Père du Chasles (or Challes) SJ, Professor of Hydrography at Marseilles, fifty years earlier, presumably in his *Principes Généraux de la Géographie Mathématique* (Paris 1676), which I have not seen.

[36] Funnell, *Voyage*, 204; English preface to J. Juan and A. de Ulloa, *A Voyage to South America*

(London 1758), cited in C. Steele, *English Interpreters of the Iberian New World* (Oxford 1975), 166.

[37] *A Review of the State of the British Nation*, VIII No.41, 28 June 1711 [*Review*]; this 'fullest and most perceptive discussion' is itself perceptively discussed in Williams, 'The Fountain', 36–45, a passage which led me to Defoe himself. W. L. Payne, *Mr Review: Daniel Defoe as Author of 'The Review'* (Morningside Heights 1972) manages to avoid all reference to Defoe and the South Sea, and seems to imply acceptance at face value of his remark that he had nothing to say on the Union: tunnel-vision with a vengeance!

[38] W. Rogers, *A Cruising Voyage round the World*; E. Cooke, *A Voyage to the South Sea and round the World*; both London 1712, reprinted Amsterdam 1969 [respectively *Cruising Voyage* and *Voyage*]. Cooke is far inferior to Rogers as a writer, but gives additional detail and many coastal profiles and plans of ports, both very crude and in sharp contrast to Frézier's elegant work. For Defoe's possible or probable hand in Rogers's 'highly political' introduction, see Williams, 'The Fountain', 43, and B. Little, *Crusoe's Captain: Being the Life of Woodes Rogers* (London 1960), 155–8—an admirable short biography using Spanish as well as English sources [*Crusoe's Captain*]. There is an extraordinarily 'literary' recounting of the voyage in F. MacLeish and M. L. Krieger, *The Privateers* (New York 1962), which cites W. H. Auden, Catullus, and the Bhagavad Gita: the present author does not mind divagation, but this exceeds! The book however has some useful notes on the voyage as influencing the South Sea projecting vogue. Direct quotation is from *Cruising Voyage*, unless otherwise indicated.

[39] One of the owners' agents, Carleton Vanbrugh (brother of the architect and playwright?) was to cause much trouble, beginning at the Canaries where real or pretended ignorance of the relaxed local rules for shipping (which applied to all peaceably behaved comers, even in wartime) led to disputes with the largely Catholic British colony as well as the Spaniards—Rogers, *Cruising Voyage*, 16–20; Little, *Crusoe's Captain*, 57–8. For Dover, see the *Dictionary of National Biography* and the entertaining note in A. Winston, *No Purchase, No Pay* (London 1970), 214.

[40] Rogers is pleasantly relaxed on religious differences; he 'allow'd Liberty of Conscience on board our floating Commonwealth to our Prisoners', who had Mass in the great cabin while the Anglican service was being held on deck, 'so that the Papists were here the Low Church-men'—*Cruising Voyage*, 42–5, 224.

[41] Rogers's phrase is the direct source of Cowper's 'I am monarch of all I survey'. In 1966 the Chilean Government formally adopted the name 'Robinson Crusoe's Island' for Mas-a-Tierra; with less reason the other main island of the group, Mas Afuera, was named for Selkirk.

[42] *Relations*, 528–34; G. Lohmann Villena, *Historia Marítima del Perú: Tomo IV. Siglos XVII y XVIII* (Lima 1975), 469–70, is not only cursory but also vague.

[43] Little, *Crusoe's Captain*, 142–65; B. M. H. Rogers, 'Woodes Rogers's Privateering Voyage of 1708–11', *MM* 19, 1933, 196–211. Woodes Rogers ended his days as Governor of the Bahamas.

[44] *The Works of Francis Bacon* (London 1858–74), XIV.469–505 at 499–500; G. Holmes (ed.), *Britain after the Glorious Revolution 1689–1714* (London 1969), 20–2 [*Revolution*]; J. Sperling, *The South Sea Company* (Boston 1962), 9–10 [*Company*].

[45] Williams, 'The Fountain', 38; he does not include John Pullen's project of this date published as *Memoirs of the Maritime Affairs of Great Britain* (London 1732).

[46] Dahlgren, *Relations*, 568–71; D. Francis, *The First Peninsular War 1702–1713* (London 1975), 269.

[47] Ibid., 619–60. Dahlgren gives the fullest account I have seen of the negotiations so far as the South Sea entered into them; for more general accounts see H. G. Pitt, 'The Pacification of Utrecht', in *NCMH* VI.446–79 and A. D. MacLachlan, 'The Road to Peace', in Holmes, *Revolution*, 197–215.

[48] Dahlgren, *Relations*, 634–5, 647–55. A French counter to the demand for security ports put up the curious idea of an international consular commission at Cadiz, under the protection of a Catholic Swiss garrison—perhaps the first hint of such an arrangement, later taken up at such places as Tangier—ibid., 632. See also Williams, 'The Fountain', 42–3.

[49] *An Essay on the South-Sea Trade* (London 1712), 30–3, 42–4; see also his anonymous *A True Account of the Design, and Advantages of the South-Sea Trade* (London 1711). For the financial history of the SSC, far too complex to go into here, see Sperling, *Company*, *passim*, and W. R. Scott, *The Constitution and Finance of English, Scottish, and Irish Joint-Stock Companies to 1720* (Cambridge 1912, reprint New York 1951), I.388–438, III.288–362. For the credit crisis, Scott, I.385–7, and MacLachlan, in Holmes, *Revolution*, 202–4—an important factor in making the new ministry move slowly.

[50] J. Carswell, *The South Sea Bubble* (London 1960), 53—an entertaining as well as solid study of the political and social, as well as financial, aspects of this Grand Skulduggery.

[51] Williams, 'The Fountain', 44–5; Sperling, *Company*, 9–10, 14–16.

[52] Sperling, *Company*, 13–14 (with summary of agreement); Dahlgren, *Relations*, 703–29; McLachlan, *Trade and Peace*, 49–52. For Gilligan, who was to receive 7.5 per cent on SSC profits, perhaps as a cover (Sperling, 19), and died a Spanish pensioner, see also R. Pares, *War and Trade in the West Indies 1739–1763* (Oxford 1936), 11, 424.

[53] Boxer, *Dutch Empire*, 118; Bromley and Ryan, 'Navies', in *NCMH* VI.798–9.

[54] Mahan, *Influence*, 196.

Notes for Chapter 9

[1] W. L. Cook, *Flood Tide of Empire: Spain and the Pacific Northwest, 1543–1819* (New Haven 1973), 101, 137–42. Meares flew Portuguese colours, but took care that the engravings in his *Voyages in the Years 1788 and 1789* (London 1790) displayed enormous Union Jacks.

[2] Olga Pantaleão, *A Penetração Commercial da Inglaterra na America Espanhola de 1713 a 1783* (Sao Paulo 1946), 154–6, 159 [*Penetração*]; S. Villalobos R., *Comercia y Contrabando en el Río de la Plata y Chile 1700–1811* (Buenos Aires 1965), 17–21 [*Contrabando*]—both excellent studies; M. Savelle, *Empires to Nations: Expansion in America 1715–1824* (Minneapolis 1974), 122–3 [*Empires*]. It should be noted that 1737 was after the SSC's annual ship had lapsed.

[3] Pantaleão, *Penetração*, 49; J. O. McLachlan, *Trade and Peace with Old Spain 1667–1750* (Cambridge 1940), 60 [*Old Spain*].

[4] W. L. Dorn, *Competition for Empire 1740–63* (Torchbook ed., New York 1963), 123 [*Competition*].

[5] J. G. Sperling, *The South Sea Company: An Historical Essay . . .* (Boston 1952), 20–4 [*Company*]; McLachlan, *Old Spain*, 78–85; specific examples of corruption at Puerto Bello and Buenos Aires in Pantaleão, *Penetração*, 148.

6 Cited in J. Carswell, *The South Sea Bubble* (London 1960), 179 [*Bubble*]. But in 1723–4 the *Royal Prince* sold over 1000 tons of merchandise at Vera Cruz and made several hundred per cent—J. H. Parry, *The Spanish Seaborne Empire* (Harmondsworth 1973), 295–8 [*Seaborne Empire*].

7 R. Pares, *War and Trade in the West Indies 1739–1763* (Oxford 1936), 18 [*War and Trade*]; J. H. Parry, *Trade and Dominion: The European Overseas Empires in the Eighteenth Century* (London 1971), 102–3, 107 [*Trade and Dominion*]; Sperling, *Company*, 20, 24, 42–3, plays down the SSC's contraband role, but admits the Directors' share after 1723. The ramifications of both the legal and the illegal trade were intolerably complex; I have deliberately avoided citing Pantaleão or Villalobos on the general issue, in favour of British sources.

8 On this see A. P. Thornton, 'English and Spanish Slavers in the Caribbean', in *For the File on Empire* (London 1968), 90–112.

9 Villalobos, *Contrabando*, 17; D. Ramos, *Minería y Comercio Interprovincial en Hispanoamerica (siglos XVI, XVII, y XVIII)* (Vallodolid n.d.), 197–201—Buenos Aires was 'una economía-islote' [*Minería*]. See also A. Jara, *Tres Ensayos sobre Economía Minera Hispanoamericana* (Santiago 1966), 82–6, on the rise of Córdoba [*Tres Ensayos*]; these essays are also to be found in M. Mollat (ed.), *Les Grandes Voies Maritimes dans le Monde XVᵉ-XIXᵉ Siècles* (Paris 1955) at 247–55. For the *earlier* validity of the Lima monopoly as against the Platine entry, see G. Céspedes del Castillo, 'Lima y Buenos Aires: repercusiones económicas y políticas de la creación del virreinato del Plata', *AEA* 15, 1947, 667–874, at 38–45 in the separate pagination provided. This is a most important article which will be much referred to in the last chapter of this volume ['Lima y Buenos Aires'].

10 J. Lynch, *Spanish Colonial Administration, 1782–1810* (London 1958), 32 [*Administration*].

11 Céspedes del Castillo, 'Lima y Buenos Aires', 15–16, 27–34.

12 Lynch, *Administration*, 32; Ramos, *Minería*, 202; Villalobos, *Contrabando*, 21; V. Magalhães-Godinho, 'Portugal and her Empire, 1680–1720', in *NCMH* VI.509–40 at 528–30. For the 1654 Treaty, see L. and E. Hertslet, *A Complete Collection of Treaties ...* (London 1840–1925), II.8–20 at 13: By Article XI, English ships are to sail with the Portuguese convoy, but once dues have been paid in Brazil they 'shall freely proceed to any other harbour or place whatsoever ...'.

13 Villalobos, *Contrabando*, 33. It is pertinent that Chile claims to have been the second country, after Denmark, to abolish slavery, partially in 1811, fully in 1823—L. Galdames, *A History of Chile* (Chapel Hill 1941), 169, 224. The SSC's slave barracks in Buenos Aires were in a quarter still known as Retiro de los Ingleses—Parry, *Seaborne Empire*, 297–8.

14 Villalobos, *Contrabando*, 33–4.

15 Pantaleão, *Penetração*, 204–7; Ramos, *Minería*, 256–65; Jara, *Tres Ensayos*, 85.

16 C. Alcázar y Molina, *Los Virreinatos en el Siglo XVIII* (Barcelona 1945), 392.

17 S. Harcourt-Smith, *Alberoni or The Spanish Conspiracy* (London 1943), 93—baroque, almost rococo, in style, but soundly based as well as entertaining [*Alberoni*].

18 In 1744 she tried hard to make a Franco-Spanish army invade Piedmont along the Riviera coast—she *knew* the road, having travelled it (in a sedan chair, without a train of artillery) on her way to marry Philip, thirty years earlier!—S. Wilkinson, *The Defence of Piedmont 1742–48* (Oxford 1927), 128–31.

19 J. O. Lindsay, 'The Western Mediterranean and Italy', in *NCMH* VII.269–91 at 277—expenditure down by a half, revenue up by a third.

[20] The reforms are summarised in Harcourt-Smith, *Alberoni*, 128–44; for the move to Cadiz, see Parry, *Seaborne Empire*, 286.

[21] H. Kamen, *The War of Succession in Spain, 1700–15* (London 1969), 229; I have rounded the figures (1 real = 15 pesos).

[22] J. O. Lindsay, 'International Relations', in *NCMH* VII.191–213.

[23] Alberoni had sent 5000 men and 30,000 stand of arms from Corunna, but the winds were Protestant and Hanoverian and only 300 Spaniards reached Scotland—J. Prebble, *The Lion in the North* (Harmondsworth 1971), 296; Harcourt-Smith, *Alberoni*, 196–7. The last 'international' exploit of the man who had defied and dazzled Europe was the reduction of the turbulent Republic of San Marino to Papal obedience, in 1739 when he was seventy-five; he lived until 1752—Harcourt-Smith, 211–12.

[24] Burney, IV.517–18; Carswell, *Bubble*, 60, 166; W. R. Scott, *The Constitution and Finance of English, Scottish and Irish Joint-Stock Companies to 1720* (Cambridge 1912, reprint New York 1951), I.418, 421, III.457. Welbe's plan is printed in J. A. Williamson's ed. of Dampier's *A Voyage to New Holland* (London 1939), lx–lxii, and in G. Mackaness (ed.), *Some Proposals for Establishing Colonies in the South Seas*, Australian Histl Monographs 11 (Dubbo, NSW, 1981), 8–11.

[25] Sperling, *Company*, 24; McLachlan, *Old Spain*, 66–73; Harcourt-Smith, *Alberoni*, 114–18, 120–2. Bubb, later the very archetype of the place-hunter, is best known for his verses 'Love thy country, wish it well/Not with too intense a care . . .'.

[26] See the commission in J. Callander, *Terra Australis Cognita or Voyages to the Terra Australis* (Edinburgh 1768, reprint Amsterdam 1967), III.447–50 [*Terra Australis*].

[27] Shelvocke's *A Voyage round the World by the Way of the Great South Sea* (London 1726, reprint Amsterdam 1971) is a mendacious apologia devoted to showing that all his miscarriages were due to treacherous officers, a mutinous crew, and Clipperton's villainy [*South Sea*]. Clipperton had died a few days after his homecoming in June 1722 and left no journal, but the mate of the *Success*, George Taylor, kept one which he gave to William Betagh, Shelvocke's captain of marines, for his *A Voyage round the World* (London 1728), a vicious work [*Voyage*]. What Welbe was to Dampier, Betagh was to Shelvocke, and more; the latter pair were obviously hard liars both, though it would be as difficult as unprofitable to try to decide which was the more atrocious traducer. Taylor as presented by Betagh and an account by an unknown officer of the *Success* form the basis of the narrative, very favourable to Clipperton (who at least acted honestly by his owners), by John Campbell in his edition of John Harris, *Navigantium atque Intinerantium Bibliotheca* (London 1744–8), I.184–98 [*Navigantium*]. Callander in *Terra Australis* (III.444–583) impartially pirates his fellow-Scot Campbell as well as the (unnamed) 'French writer' Charles de Brosses; his impudence extends to pages of editorial comment in the first person *singular* lifted word for word from Campbell. For these relationships, see G. R. Crone, 'English Collections of Voyages and Travels, 1625–1846' in E. Lynam (ed.), *Richard Hakluyt and his Successors*, HS 2nd Ser. 103 (London 1946), 93–7, 119–21, and Beaglehole, I.lxxiv–lxxxiii. In addition to all these, the lively and coherent narrative in P. K. Kemp and C. Lloyd, *Brethren of the Coast* (New York 1961), 196–237, uses an unpublished report by Shelvocke to the Admiralty [*Brethren*]. Direct quotations in this section are from Shelvocke, *South Sea*, unless otherwise indicated.

[28] Shelvocke, *South Sea*, 72–3; For Coleridge's use of the incident see J. L. Lowes, *The Road to Xanadu* (London 2nd ed. 1951), 222–8, 529–32. It is rather odd that Lowes, so vastly read

in the relevant literature, should not have noted that already in 1816 Burney devotes over two pages (IV.526–9) to the link between Hatley and *The Ancient Mariner*.

29 *The Oxford English Dictionary* gives two earlier occurrences (1604, 1669), but both are in translations. Shelvocke has a graphic account of the horrible diggings—*South Sea*, 270–2.

30 Ibid., 178–9; omitted in the Campbell/Callander version. Shelvocke goes on to accuse Betagh of being a Papist and of asking his Spanish captors to let him lead the prospective attack on Shelvocke's ship.

31 Since the 'new Bottom' was largely built from the *Speedwell*'s timbers, it would have been less dubious in law, as well as simpler and safer, to condemn her and transfer to a prize.

32 Betagh, *Voyage*, 127; as Burney remarks (IV.546), there is no other evidence. Fernández Duro (VI.186) confirms Villa Roche's shady character: 'a personage with a history in contraband [who] fooled Clipperton like so many others'.

33 Campbell, followed by Callander, has a diverting apology: 'drunkenness is doubtless an aggravation rather than an excuse', but then Clipperton 'was a mere sailor, and had not the benefit of a liberal education'—*Navigantium*, I.192; cf. *Terra Australis*, III.474.

34 See note 27 above. According to Kemp and Lloyd (*Brethren*, 225), Shelvocke refused to accept Clipperton's command on the ground that as the original orders named the *Speedwell* as second ship and she no longer existed, they were no longer binding on him. The relevant passages are Shelvocke, *South Sea*, 307–13, and Betagh, *Voyage*, 147–51, 190–3.

35 For details of Shelvocke's financial villainies, see Kemp and Lloyd, *Brethren*, 233–5; for the epitaph, 236.

36 *Navigantium*, I.239, plagiarised in Callander, *Terra Australis*, III.581–3.

37 B. Williams, *The Whig Supremacy 1714–1760* (Oxford 1945), 186–91; the Emperor for his part was to support Spanish moves to regain Gibraltar and Minorca. This odd alliance was the work of an engaging rogue, Baron Jan Willem Ripperda, who played (briefly) Alberoni's role, with as much energy but less ability, and then turned renegade in Morocco. He was by turns Catholic, Protestant, Catholic, Protestant, orthodox Muslim, and head of his own Islamic sect, and at his death was meditating a reconciliation with the Pope in order to become King of Corsica—A. Ballesteros y Beretta, *Historia de España* (Barcelona 1929–53), V.68–74.

38 W. Laird Clowes, *The Royal Navy: A History* (London 1897–1903), III.43–6 [*Royal Navy*]; for the strategic consequences, H. W. Richmond, *Statesmen and Sea Power* (2nd ed. Oxford 1947), 108–10.

39 For this complicated story, see Sperling, *Company*, 46–8; McLachlan, *Old Spain*, 114–21; Pares, *War and Trade*, 48–56. The SSC's actual trading, licit or illicit, was hardly an issue—Sperling, 46. There is a lucid account of the pre-war manoeuvring in R. Browning, *The Duke of Newcastle* (New Haven 1975), 88–96, including the doddery Duke's splendid *faux pas* of basing a memorial to the Spanish Court on the wrong treaty—Madrid 1667 instead of 1670!

40 Pares, *War and Trade*, 59; cf. A. T. Mahan, *The Influence of Sea Power upon History 1660–1783* (Boston 1890, reprint New York 1920), 216–18. Pares's remark is strikingly anticipated in a letter to Newcastle, 2 October 1738, from Benjamin Keene, British Minister in Madrid, quoted in H. W. V. Temperley, 'The Causes of the War of Jenkins' Ear, 1739', *Trans. Roy. Histl Soc.* 3rd Ser. 3, 1905, 197–236 at 205.

41 Keene to Delahaye (Newcastle's undersecretary), 11 April 1732, quoted in McLachlan, *Old Spain*, 91; see 89–96, 102–8, for vivid details of the guardacostas. As she remarks, only

'sailors of fortune' or desperadoes would take on this job; cf. Parry, *Seaborne Empire*, 299–300.

[42] McLachlan, *Old Spain*, 106–7; for Jenkins in the EIC, Parry, *Trade and Dominion*, 154–5. The loss of this most famous ear, which must rank with Cyrano's nose, is documented in J. K. Laughton, 'Jenkins' Ear', *English Histl Rev.* 4, 1889, 741–9.

[43] Glover, *London, or the Progress of Commerce* (London 1739); Johnson, *London: A Poem* (London 1738); for another prime example of the British Lion *rampant et rugissant*, see Mark Akenside, *A British Philipick* (London 1738). After Vernon took Puerto Bello, Glover summoned Hosier and 3000 more ghosts from their 'oozy tombs' to demand vengeance and a more vigorous war; this ballad, 'Admiral Hosier's Ghost', has a plangency lacking in the rest of Glover's dull verse, but thousands more were to find oozy tombs at Cartagena. 'Rule, Britannia' is also a by-product of the war, first sung in *Alfred: A Masque* (1741) by James Thomson and David Mallet. By 1770 Johnson was on the side of moderation—and the Government—in the Falklands crisis.

[44] H. W. Richmond, *The Navy in the War of 1739–48* (Cambridge 1920), I.24–35 [*Navy*]; Pares, *War and Trade*, 43–52, 85–9; G. Williams (ed.), *Documents relating to Anson's Voyage round the World 1742–1744*, Navy Records Soc. 109 (London 1967), 3–4, 14, 37–8. Nevertheless, Fernández Duro thought (VI.247) that when Anson was in the Pacific, 'the presumption of an attack on the Isthmus by the waters of the South and the North was logical'.

[45] Dorn, *Competition*, 127–8.

[46] Pares, *War and Trade*, 110–14.

[47] Richmond, *Navy*, I.101–2; for general accounts, ibid., I.101–24; Clowes, *Royal Navy*, III.67–79; J. W. Fortescue, *A History of the British Army* (London 1910–30), II.58–79 [*Army*]. See also J. A. Robertson, 'The English attack on Cartagena 1741', *HAHR* 2, 1919, 63–71, and C. E. Nowell, 'The Defence of Cartagena', *HAHR* 42, 1962, 477–501; for the Spanish side, Fernández Duro, VI.247–53, who makes much justified play with the premature rash of British victory medals. Pares, *War and Trade*, 89–92, gives a variant from the usual view of the Cartagena imbroglio, stressing personal motivations and to some extent defending Wentworth. There is a vivid if nauseating account by a cynical participant observer in Chs. XXXI–XXXIV of T. Smollett, *The Adventures of Roderick Random* (London 1748).

[48] Smollett, *Roderick Random* (Everyman ed., London 1927), 190–1. This horrible detail is not vouched for by Smollett alone but also by Vernon himself—Fortescue, *Army*, II.73.

[49] Richmond, *Navy*, 130–2; but see Pares, *War and Trade*, 93–6, for a criticism of Vernon.

[50] Vernon to Newcastle, 31 March, 27 April 1742, in 'Original Papers Relating to the Expedition to Panama', *Vernon Pamphlets* Vol.I, Admiralty Library (London) Ca.376. Nevertheless, competent Spanish observers thought that Vernon could have taken Panama before succours could have reached it from Peru—J. Juan and A. de Ulloa, *Noticias Secretas de América* (London 1826), 130–7.

[51] Pares, *War and Trade*, 92.

[52] For Creassey's plans of 1790 and 1804, see above, note 73 to Ch. 6.

[53] Parry, *Trade and Dominion*, 111.

Notes for Chapter 10

[1] J. H. Parry, *Trade and Dominion: The European Overseas Empires in the Eighteenth Century* (London 1971), 236 [*Trade and Dominion*]; cf. the remarks on 'phase B' and the lapse in exploration in Chs. 4 and 7.

[2] The second WIC; the first had little *raison d'être* after the loss of Brazil and was liquidated in 1674, when a new WIC was formed. It was never much of a success: average annual dividends were 2.5 per cent until 1720, then 1 per cent until 1772, thereafter nil—D. K. Fieldhouse, *The Colonial Empires* (New York 1966), 51–2.

[3] A. Sharp (trans. and ed.), *The Journal of Jacob Roggeveen* (Oxford 1974), 1–4 [*Journal*]. This is the base for this section and the source of all direct quotations unless otherwise indicated. The MS. was lost until 1836 and first published in 1838; the standard edition is F. E. Mulert (ed.), *De Reis van Mr. Jacob Roggeveen*, Linschoten-Vereeniging Werken 4 (The Hague 1911). Eighteenth-century accounts are 'T. D. H.', *Kort en Naukeurig Verhall van de Reize der Drie Schepen* (Amsterdam 1727); *Tweejarige Reyze random de Wereld* (anon., Dordrecht 1728), and C. F. Behrens, *Histoire de l'Expédition de Trois Vaisseaux* (The Hague 1739, from a German edition of the same year); Behrens claimed to be Captain of Marines, but was probably an NCO. I have seen none of these, except as presented in summary or paraphrase in Burney (IV.558–80); J. Campbell's ed. of J. Harris, *Navigantium atque Itinerantium Bibliotheca* (London 1744–8), I.256–320 [*Navigantium*]; J. Callander, *Terra Australis Cognita* (Edinburgh 1767, reprint Amsterdam 1967), III.584–641 [*Terra Australis*]; and A. Dalrymple, *An Historical Collection of the several Voyages and Discoveries in the South Pacific Ocean* (London 1770–1, reprint Amsterdam 1967), II.85–120—two volumes in one with separate pagination [*Collection*]. They are often inaccurate, sometimes wild—*Tweejarige Reyzen* has twelve-foot high giants on Easter Island (Dalrymple, II.113), Behrens has elephants in Brazil. The originals are detailed and evaluated in Sharp's introduction to the *Journal*, 13–18; the eighteenth-century summaries are of more interest for editorial comment that for factual content; Campbell for instance loses sight of Roggeveen in a long dissertation (277–312) on Dutch policy in the Indies.

Attention should be drawn to the view of my colleague Robert Langdon, that Roggeveen was long anticipated at Easter Island, if not by Europeans at least by part-Europeans—specifically, descendants of the crew of the *San Lesmes*, lost from Loaysa's voyage (1526). A main strand in the complex argument is the possession by Easter Islanders of reputedly pure descent of HLA blood genes peculiar to Caucasians, especially Basques. Publication from Langdon's research since *The Lost Caravel* (Sydney 1975) is awaited with interest.

[4] W. Dampier, *A New Voyage round the World* (London 1697; Dover ed. New York 1968), 240 [*New Voyage*]; J. A. J. de Villiers (trans. and ed.), *The East and West Indian Mirror*, HS 2nd Ser. 18 (London 1906), 195.

[5] Sharp, *Journal*, 5, following Roggeveen's Dutch editor Mulert.

[6] One German mile = 4 nautical miles = 4.6 statute miles = 7.4 km; all Roggeveen's miles are of course German.

[7] They are actually of a volcanic tuff, which might give a pebble-dash appearance to a superficial observer, and were transported and erected by sleds and bipods—see i.a. P. Bellwood, *The Polynesians: Prehistory of an island people* (London 1978), 118–21.

[8] Bolton Corney's translation is engagingly different: 'if one should therefore conclude that the women are held in common among them, one must naturally expect bickering and depravity to ensue'—*Voyage of Captain Don Felipe González to Easter Island, 1770–1*, HS 2nd Ser. 13 (Cambridge 1908), 19. *Traduttore e traditore!* I am assured by my colleague Dr A. J. Reid that Sharp's is the correct version. Corney gives the delightfully serendipitous touch that Roggeveen's Journal turned up in a search for papers on Surinam!

[9] It is typical of Roggeveen's legalism that Davis, being a mere buccaneer, is always 'the so-called' Captain.

[10] *Journal*, 116–20, and Sharp's note at 116. Considering the eternal difficulty of the longitude, Roggeveen's (or more likely his captain's) usual error of 5°, more or less, is venial.

[11] *Journal*, 116–19, 133–5, 145–7.

[12] In 1765 Byron found on Takaroa 'the carved Head of a Dutch Long boats Rudder' and some iron tools, which he ascribed to the 'cutting off of one of those Dutch Ships, who attempted to make Discoveries this way many Years ago, & who were never afterwards heard of', a muddled reference to Roggeveen—R. E. Gallagher (ed.), *Byron's Journal of his Circumnavigation 1764–1766*, HS 2nd Ser. 122 (Cambridge 1964), 100–1.

[13] For the Anaa cross, see R. A. Langdon, *The Lost Caravel* (Sydney 1975), 128–9; but his colleague and mine H. Driessen makes a case for connecting the cross with these deserters (personal communication). There is a confused echo of the incident in Tahitian tradition —Beaglehole, I.557.

[14] The question was raised acutely on the loss of HMS *Wager* from Anson's squadron; see Ch. 11.

[15] Although at first he took the line that he had no authority to incur such expenditure, he was in fact covered by a 'verbal mandate' from the WIC to make such a promise, the case arising—*Journal*, 129–33. Roggeveen's legal training seems to come out in his account of a mutiny unusual only in its politeness.

[16] *Journal*, 6, 141–4; again we must be grateful to Roggeveen's legalistic preciseness for an illuminating example of the debates which accompanied most voyages. According to Behrens, there was a party for seeking 'the countries mentioned by *Ferdinand de Quiros*'— Callander, *Terra Australis*, III.609–10, followed by his long argument for a southern continent.

[17] Ta'u, Olosenga, Ofu, Nuu. The NID Handbook *Pacific Islands* (?London, 1943–5), II.675, says that Rose Atoll was discovered by Louis de Freycinet in 1819 and named for his wife, who was on board; I follow Sharp.

[18] He explains 'Groeningen' by saying that the other main Chambers of the WIC were already on the charts: Tasman's Amsterdam and Rotterdam in Tonga, and his [Nieuw] Zeeland.

[19] Sharp, in *Journal*, 163–4.

[20] For all this, see Sharp, in *Journal*, 166–77. As he points out, it was probably lucky for Roggeveen's people that the ships were seized. The *Arend* alone had lost 68 out of 129 men, mostly from scurvy, the VOC would have been most unlikely to let them take on any hands, and the voyage home might have been disastrous.

[21] Parry, *Trade and Dominion*, 240. The French westwards crossings, so far as their courses are known, Van Noort's, and all those of the buccaneers followed the Manila Galleon

route. The *Hoop* and *Liefde* of the Mahu-Cordes expedition presumably crossed by the Trades, but their courses were, and are, unknown.

²² Dalrymple, 'Conduct of the Discoverers', 11 (in *Collection*, II, with separate pagination); cf. *Journal*, 107, 112. Had these birds 'inflamed his pursuit', Roggeveen might just possibly have discovered the minute atoll of Ducie. However, at 'Conduct', 10, Dalrymple says that at the Bauman Islands 'there is great probability that the continent approaches nearest the equator'; but he misses the significance of Thienhoven and Groeningen by confusing them with the Solomons.

²³ Callander, *Terra Australis*, III.614–15, from Behrens; similar versions in Dalrymple, *Collection*, II.107; Harris/Campbell, *Navigantium*, I.270–2.

²⁴ Dampier, *New Voyage*, 190; R. H. Fisher, *Bering's Voyages: Whither and Why* (Seattle 1977), 8–9 [*Bering*]. Leibnitz's letters may not have reached Peter, and Fisher discounts statements that the Paris Academy of Sciences proposed its own expedition. Cf. G. Barratt, *Russia in Pacific Waters, 1715–1825: A Survey of the Origins of Russia's Naval Presence . . .* (Vancouver 1981), 2–3, and 7–9 for Saltykov's 1714 Northeast Passage project [*Russia*].

²⁵ Fisher, *Bering*, 57–61; F. A. Golder, *Russian Expansion on the Pacific, 1641–1850* (Glendale 1914, reprint New York 1971), 113–15 [*Expansion*]. Golder, long the American doyen in this field, is still to some extent useful, and often quoted; but of course he could know nothing of the intensive Soviet research presented by Fisher. The '1850' in the title may be a misprint for '1750', since only about a dozen of 340 text pages are allotted to 1743–1850.

²⁶ S. [*sic*: G. F.] Müller, *Voyages from Asia to America* (London 1761), 1 [*Asia to America*]; later statements to this effect are too numerous to cite.

²⁷ Golder, *Expansion*, 134; yet on the preceding page he says flatly 'to determine *whether* [my italics] Asia and America are united'. Cf. the translation in Fisher, *Bering*, 23–5 and his gloss at 67–70. He reads the vital clause II as 'along the land which goes to the north, and according to expectations . . . that land, it appears, is part of America'.

²⁸ Fisher, *Bering*, Chs. 3–4 *passim*. The book is immensely detailed and very subtly argued. It is impossible to summarise the complex reasoning here, and it is obviously not for one who knows no Russian to arbitrate the question. I can only say that I find Fisher's case impressive (and very tough reading!) and think that any interpretation must reckon with it very seriously; though oddly enough (since Seattle and Vancouver are not so very far apart) G. Barratt does not refer to it in his otherwise admirable work; his translation of the orders in substance bears out Fisher—*Russia*, 14. R. Murphy, *The Haunted Journey* (London 1962) is undocumented, but a good account simply as a story—and what a story it is!

²⁹ Golder, *Expansion*, 133–49 at 139; G. V. Lantzeff and R. A. Pierce point out that the labour demand meant that 'This decision was ruinous for the Kamchadals'—*Eastward to Empire: Exploration and Conquest on the Russian Open Frontier, to 1750* (Montreal 1973), 210–11 [*Eastward*]. One of Bering's reports, brief and unsatisfactory, is in Golder (ed.), *Bering's Voyages: An Account of the Efforts of the Russians to Determine the Relation of Asia and America* (New York 1922–5), I.6–20—a most valuable compilation, including original logs *verbatim* and Steller's narrative [*Voyages*]. The reader is reminded that all dates relating to Russian voyages are in Old Style.

³⁰ Beaglehole, III.lvii; cf. Barratt, *Russia*, 18.

³¹ Fisher, *Bering*, 73–80, 90–4; this microscopic analysis is but a small part of his data. One significant point is that in December 1732 the Admiralty stated that Peter told Bering to

'search for where the Kamchatka land joined America, nevertheless ... [Bering] sailed between north and east ...'.

[32] J. R. Forster spoke of the straits 'which I have named *Beering's* [*sic*], and others *Cook's*, and others again *Deschneff's Straits*, [but] might likewise just as well be called the *Straits of Anian*'—*History of the Voyages and Discoveries made in the North* (London 1786, original German ed. 1784), 463 [*Discoveries*]; he also says (481) that the Aleutians were justly called the Catherina Archipelago, no great compliment to the hot-blooded Semiramis of the North. According to L. Breitfuss, the name was first placed on the maps by Comte de Redern in 1754—'Early Maps', 87 (full reference in note 67 below), but it appears in the maps and text of 'John Green' (i.e. Bradock Mead) in 1753—L. A. Wroth, 'The Early Cartography of the Pacific', *Papers of the Biblio. Soc. of America 38* No. 2 (New York 1944), 87–268 at 225–6 ['Cartography'].

[33] J. Burney, *A Chronological History of North-Eastern Voyages of Discovery* (London 1819, reprint Amsterdam 1969), 297–310 at 300–2 [*NE Voyages*]; P. H. Neatby, *Discovery in Russian and Siberian Waters* (Athens, Ohio, 1973), 95–6.

[34] Golder, *Expansion*, 151–64; Fisher, *Bering*, 164–9; Barratt, *Russia*, 34. Gvosdev's map, not published until this century, is reproduced in G. Williams, 'Myth and Reality', 61 (full reference in note 61 below).

[35] Fisher, *Bering*, 109, and see his Chs. 5–7 *passim*; Golder, *Expansion*, 165–71, and *Voyages*, I.25–32; Barratt, *Russia*, 23–5.

[36] Golder, *Voyages*, I.28; Fisher, *Bering*, 120–3, 130–2—the text of Kirilov's memorandum is given at 184–7. Cf. Barratt, *Russia*, 27–8.

[37] The instructions, of 28 December 1732, are given in Golder, *Voyages*, I.29–32.

[38] Golder, *Expansion*, 235–49. Stepan Petrovich Krasheninnikov was also involved, producing his admirable *Explorations of Kamchatka* (St Petersburg 1755, trans. and ed. E. A. P. Crownhart-Vaughan, Portland 1972) [*Kamchatka*].

[39] Barratt, *Russia*, 18–19, 33; S. Waxell, *The American Expedition* (Edinburgh 1952), 21–31 (M. A. Michael's introduction), 64–6, 92–7 [*Expedition*]; Golder, *Expansion*, 170–3, and *Voyages*, I.33; Krasheninnikov, *Kamchatka*, 339–52; J. R. Gibson, *Feeding the Russian Fur Trade 1639–1856* (Madison 1969), 11–16, 78–87—he estimates that by 1750 there were only 1500–2000 Russians on the Okhotsk seaboard and Kamchatka [*Fur Trade*].

[40] G. A. Lensen, *The Russian Push towards Japan* (Princeton 1959), 48–9 [*Russian Push*]; J. J. Stephan, *The Kuril Islands* (Oxford 1974), 40–6; D. M. Lebedev and V. I. Grekov, 'Geographical Exploration by the Russians', in H. Friis (ed.), *The Pacific Basin: A History of Its Geographical Exploration* (New York 1967), 170–200 at 175 ['Exploration']. I follow Stephan for the spelling of Kurilian names.

[41] The cartographical confusions of the region are well displayed in the plates of P. Teleki, *Atlas zur Geschichte der Kartographie der Japanischen Inseln* ... (Budapest 1909, reprint Nendeln, Liechtenstein, 1966) [*Atlas*].

[42] Lensen, *Russian Push*, 48–9; see 46–60 for a general account, which is my main source for this section. There is a good comment in Barratt, *Russia*, 35–7.

[43] Lensen, *Russian Push*, 52–5, for interesting details of this first Englishman to visit Japan since the *Return* in 1673.

[44] Both La Pérouse in 1787 and Broughton in 1797 penetrated most of the way up Tatar Strait, between the island and the main, but thought that there was no through passage. The Japanese Mamiya Rinzo established the facts (by land) in 1809 and the Russian

Gennadii Nevelskoi (by sea, from the north) in 1849. As late as the Crimean War a British squadron thought it had trapped an inferior Russian force by blockading the southern entrance; the Russians slipped out northwards—J. J. Stephan, *Sakhalin: A History* (Oxford 1871), 24–7, 34–40 and map at 30.

[45] Golder, *Expansion*, 227 note 448; cf. Homann's influential map of 1725 in Fisher, *Bering*, 65.

[46] Krasheninnikov, *Kamchatka*, 64; Forster, *Discoveries*, 425. The earlier phases of this bewildering story may be followed in Teleki, *Atlas, passim*; Wroth, 'Cartography', 201–15; and Appendix, 'The Discovery of Yezo', in J. A. Harrison, *Japan's Northern Frontier* (Gainesville 1953), 145–64; as he says, J.-N. Delisle's repudiation of the insularity of Yezo 'is a masterpiece in the rejection of evidence' which he himself cites. Later developments in Russo-Japanese contacts are in Lensen, *Russian Push, passim*.

[47] See e.g. Krasheninnikov's sea-sick-making account of his 1737 voyage from Okhotsk in the mis-named *Fortuna*, whose 'planks were so rotten that one could easily break them by hand' and whose sailors did not understand the tides—*Kamchatka*, 352–3.

[48] My account is based on the logs and reports in Golder, *Voyages*, I, and on Steller's journal, ibid., II.9–188—very vivid, and an unintentionally unfavourable self-portrait. Equally vivid, and essential as a corrective to Steller, is Waxell, *Expedition*.

[49] The memoir is in Golder, *Expansion*, 304–13, the map in *Voyages*, at II.72; for comment see Fisher, *Bering*, 135–42—for once in agreement with Golder. Delisle is severely criticised by Barratt, *Russia*, 24.

[50] Golder, *Voyages*, I.311; *Expansion*, 186–7.

[51] Much of Steller's journal is paranoid, and humbler and more patient men than the officers might have been infuriated by his self-righteousness, vanity, and pedantry. His nautical opinions are mostly nonsense; almost his only good point, also made by Chirikov, is on the currents. A tiny example of his style: he complains of the naming of Cape St Elias 'notwithstanding the fact that it was plainly represented to [the officers] that an island cannot be called a cape, but that only a noticeable projection of land into the sea . . . can be so designated'. Pedantry could go no further; but in fact both the island and its southern cape were given the name St Elias—Golder, *Voyages*, II.36 and Khitrov's map at 42.

[52] They were at about 52°N and 158°W: the nearest land to the south was about 22°N, in Hawaii, some 3330 km away. Steller strongly hints that the officers conspired to hush up this 'landfall'; in fact, they brushed him aside with the obviously ironic remark that it was Gamaland—ibid., II.68.

[53] During September, Chirikov, much closer to the Aleutians (i.e. well above 50°N), was making good the westerly course which brought him to Petropavlosk on 10 October; an ironic comment on Steller's insistence that favourable winds would be found in 49–50°—ibid., II.68.

[54] Waxell, *Expedition*, 134. Both Waxell (127–56) and Steller (*Voyages*, II.137–83, 208–14) give very vivid accounts of living and dying on Bering Island; Waxell's official report [*Voyages*, I.270–82) is far more discreet. Steller's description of the island (II.189–241) is excellent; he describes the torture of the foxes with disturbing gusto. See also the photograph of the camp-site, ibid. at 158.

[55] It is pleasing to note that on Waxell's recommendation Starodubstov was made a *syn boyarski*, a minor Siberian nobleman.

[56] A. Ogden, *The California Sea Otter Trade 1784–1848* (Berkeley 1941), *passim*; W. L. Cook, *Flood Tide of Empire: Spain and the Pacific Northwest, 1543–1819* (New Haven 1973), 41–2, 88, 100–17.

[57] Gibson, *Fur Trade*, 16–18, 27–33, for the economics; Steller, in *Voyages*, II.214–24, for the animal and its hunting.

[58] W. Coxe, *Account of the Russian Discoveries between Asia and America* (London 3rd ed. 1787, reprinted Ann Arbor/New York 1966), 21 [*Account*].

[59] In addition to Gibson, see on this phase W. R. Hunt, *Arctic Passage: The Turbulent History . . . of the Bering Sea 1697–1975* (New York 1975), 37–48.

[60] H. Chevigny, *Russian America* (New York 1965), 33–42; for Glotov, A. I. Andreyev (ed.), *Russian Discoveries in the Pacific and in North America* (Ann Arbor 1952), 19–25. In the 1760s the cost of building and outfitting a ship in Kamchatka was 10–30,000 roubles— Gibson, *Fur Trade*, 31.

[61] Barratt, *Russia*, 50–1, 56–66; C. C. Hulley, *Alaska 1741–1953* (Portland 1953), 62–3; Coxe, *Account*, 205–25; Lebedev and Grekov, 'Exploration', 181–3. See also Krenitsin's map in G. Williams, 'Myth and Reality: James Cook and the Theoretical Geography of Northwest America', in R. Fisher and H. Johnston (eds.), *Captain James Cook and His Times* (Canberra/Vancouver 1979), 59–80 at 65 ['Myth and Reality'].

[62] American usage for Oregon, Washington, and (often) British Columbia; 'Pacific Northeast' from an oceanic point of view, but a convenient shorthand term.

[63] King in Beaglehole, III.1447.

[64] Barratt, *Russia*, 46, 59; Lebedev and Grekov, 'Exploration', 183.

[65] Hyndford to Chesterfield, 21 November 1747, in Fisher, *Bering*, 181.

[66] Harris/Campbell, *Navigantium*, II.1018–40; cf. Fisher, *Bering*, 12–13, 181–2. This was not the first account of Bering in English, which is in the translation (1736) of J.-B. du Halde SJ, *Description . . . de la Chine*, a good narrative of the first voyage which appears at IV.561 of the revised edition (The Hague 1736). I was led to du Halde by Professor Glyndwr Williams.

[67] L. Breitfuss, 'Early Maps of North-Eastern Asia and of the Lands around the North Pacific', *Imago Mundi* 3, 1939, 87–100 at 90–3; Golder, *Expansion*, 212; Wroth, 'Cartography', 223–4. There are good discussions of this cartographical war in Williams, 'Myth and Reality', *passim*, and *NW Passage*, 138–56. Breitfuss's paper is particularly useful for the easy comparison of the outlines of nineteen maps, on three pages only. The *Gentleman's Magazine* (London) 24, 1754, discusses Delisle's map (and notes Delisle de la Croyère's daily 'great quantity of brandy'); in the May issue it reproduced the map itself.

[68] The *Noticia*, by M. Venegas and/or A. M. Burriel, is discussed in G. Williams, 'An Eighteenth-Century Spanish Investigation into the Apocryphal Voyage of Admiral de Fonte', *Pac. Histl Rev.* 30, 1961, 319–28; the *Monthly Miscellany* article is reprinted in his *NW Passage*, 277–82—the tale of the 'Prince of Chili' is entertaining, but a fake if ever there was one. See Figs. 9–11, 15–16, 18 in Breitfuss, 'Early Maps', the last showing de Fontean channels in 1821! The *locus classicus* for all this is H. R. Wagner, 'Apocryphal Voyages to the Northwest Coast of America', reprint from *Proc. of the American Antiquarian Soc.* (Worcester, Mass., 1931); he points out (7, 14–28) that the real vogue of Juan de Fuca and de Fonte began after Bering, and that the de Fontean place-names stem from Dampier and Hack. Müller's denunciation of de Fonte as a forgery is noted in the *Gentleman's Magazine*

24, 1754, 166. For Fusang, see Müller, *Asia to America*, 74–5, and C. E. Chapman, *A History of California: The Spanish Period* (New York 1921), 24–30.

[69] Williams, *NW Passage*, 144–6. The letter has been ascribed to Waxell (e.g. by Golder, *Voyages*, II.6, 25) but there is no warrant for this.

[70] Müller, *Asia to America*, 73.

[71] Williams, 'Myth and Reality', 86–7; cf. Coxe's defence of Müller, *Account*, 431–3.

[72] Beaglehole, III.lxiv; see lviii–lxv, cxxiv–cxxvii, for illuminating comment on both maps. 'Alaschka' is shown but not named on the Academy map of 1773, but appears with its name on the map, otherwise identical in the area covered by both, in von Stählin's 1774 *Account*, reproduced in Beaglehole at lxiv. Note that the coast from Gvosdev's 'Big Land' to southern California is shown in 1773 but not in the 1774 map given in Beaglehole.

[73] Williams, *NW Passage*, 165–7, 172–3; Beaglehole, III.liii–lv, lxi–lxv.

[74] Williams, 'Myth and Reality', 66–9. For Hearne, see E. E. Rich, *Hudson's Bay Company 1670–1870* (London 1959), II.44–65, which is however very short on his geographical significance.

[75] L. A. de Bougainville, *Voyage autour du Monde* (Paris 1771), 183–4.

[76] Beaglehole, III.lx; cf. Barratt, *Russia*, 16, 40. Recent Soviet research indicates that Bering got up to 67°24′ (not that 4.36 km matter!)—R. H. Fisher, *The Voyage of Semen Dezhnev in 1648*, HS 2nd Ser. 159 (London 1981), 211 note 1.

[77] Breitfuss, 'Early Maps', 991; Golder, *Expansion*, 248–50.

[78] See the comments of Major Magnus von Behm, Governor of Kamchatka, recorded by David Samwell in 1779—Beaglehole, III.1247.

[79] Even Golder, often rather Russophobe, in the end pays tribute to the heroic rather than the squalid side of the venture, and sketches the later careers of the leaders.

[80] Fisher, *Bering*, 178–9, see also Lantzeff and Pierce, *Eastward*, 227–30, for interesting comment on the expansion *vis-à-vis* the American frontier experience as interpreted by F. J. Turner and on the ecological consequences.

Notes for Chapter 11

[1] Unless the short-lived San Lorenzo de Nutka and Neah Bay are counted. For the Venegas/Burriel *Noticia de la California* (Madrid 1757) see C. E. Chapman, *The Founding of Spanish California* (New York 1916), 56–60.

[2] The intriguing details are given in G. Williams (ed.), *Documents relating to Anson's Voyage round the World 1740–1744*, Navy Records Soc. 109 (London 1967), 3–44 [*Documents*], and conveniently summarised in his ' "The Inexhaustible Fountain of Gold": English Projects and Ventures in the South Seas, 1670–1750', in J. E. Flint and G. Williams (eds.), *Perspective of Empire* (London 1973), 27–53 at 47–9. See also H. W. Richmond, *The Navy in the War of 1739–48* (Cambridge 1920), I.97–9 [*Navy*].

[3] Williams, *Documents*, 9–12, 27–33, 42–4; the gentleman (who but Naish?) 'would be conducted in a pompous manner, at the Emperor's expense' to Peking. Naish claims to have planned both the expedition to Manila and that actually carried out by Anson.

[4] On this point see G. Williams (ed.), *A Voyage round the World . . . by George Anson* (London 1974, original ed. 1748), 24–7. This account, long attributed to Richard Walter, is now

considered to be basically by Benjamin Robbins; it 'reflects the views and in places the private thoughts' of Anson himself (xxi-xxv) [*Anson's Voyage*].

5 Williams, *Documents*, 12–26.

6 Ibid., 35–42; R. Pares, *War and Trade in the West Indies 1739–1763* (Oxford 1936), 75–7, 104–6.

7 *Anson's Voyage*, 22–4, 26; Williams, *Documents*, 47–8.

8 Most details of the voyage, and all direct quotations unless otherwise indicted, are from *Anson's Voyage*. Other accounts consulted are Pascoe Thomas, *A True and Impartial Journal of a Voyage to the South-Seas* ... (London 1745, reprint Amsterdam 1971) [*Journal*]; 'John Philips', [pseud.], *An Authentic Journal of the Late Expedition* ... (London 1744) [*Authentic Journal*]; L. Heaps (ed.), *Log of the Centurion* (London 1973), from the journals of Philip Saumarez; and the journal of Lawrence Millechamp, in Williams, *Documents*, 65–82, 111–38, 186–94. Of these, Thomas was 'Teacher of the Mathematicks' on the *Centurion*, and on some points is useful as a corrective to the official suavity of *Anson's Voyage*; Saumarez ended the voyage as Anson's second in command; and Millechamp was a purser, critical of Anson over the case of the officers of the *Gloucester* and the *Tryal Prize*, who thought they were robbed of their due. There is an edition of *Anson's Voyage round the World* by G. S. Laird Clowes (London 1928) with useful notes on nautical terms [*Voyage*], and a study by Vice-Admiral Boyle Somerville, *Commodore Anson's Voyage* (London 1934), marred by some rather odd dicta [*Commodore Anson*].

9 Fernández Duro, VI.286. For the security failure, see Williams, *Documents*, 48, 62–4.

10 Fernández Duro, *Armada*, VI.288.

11 Thomas, *Journal*, 24, 26. His opinion was enlarged upon by Somerville (*Commodore Anson*, 43–5) and this produced a spirited riposte from Lt-Col. The Hon. Arthur Murray (Viscount Elibank), a descendant of Captain George Murray of the *Pearl*. The correspondence given in his *An Episode in the Spanish War 1739–44* (London 1952), 41–81, is highly entertaining; the Vice-Admiral apparently preferred to abandon ship rather than strike his flag to the Lt-Colonel. At Rio de Janeiro Murray wished to return to the South Sea, but was over-ruled by his senior Edward Legge; Murray's letter to the Admiralty makes it clear that Somerville's charge of concerted desertion fails completely—Williams, *Documents*, 64–5, 88–103. For the rats, 'Philips', *Authentic Journal*, 49–50.

12 The account in *Anson's Voyage* (141–9) is cursory on Bulkeley's enterprise and officially *ex parte* on the mutinies. Just as *ex parte* and far more lively is that in J. Bulkeley and J. Cummins, *A Voyage to the South-Seas by His Majesty's Ship Wager* (London 1743, reprint New York 1927); J. Byron, *The Narrative ... of the Honourable John Byron* (London 1768) is remarkably fair and balanced [*Narrative*]—it is interesting that Bulkeley got the conception for his own adventure from Cheap's copy of Narborough's voyage, which he found Byron reading. A. Campbell, in *The Sequel to Bulkeley's and Cummins's Voyage to the South-Seas* (London 1747), defends himself against the charge of having entered Spanish service; the account in 'Philips', *Authentic Journal*, 325–480, purports to give a good deal of direct speech but is admittedly hearsay. I. Morris, *A Narrative of the Dangers and Distresses which befell Isaac Morris* ... (London n.d.) is an artless but touching story, much more affecting than J. Young's anonymous *An Affecting Narrative of the Unfortunate Voyage and Catastrophe of His Majesty's Ship Wager* (London 1751)—an affected mixture of artful demagogy and sententious moralising, 'Intermix'd with several entertaining *Passages* and *Remarks*', a few of which do entertain.

Two modern accounts are reliable and readable: P. Shankland, *Byron of the Wager* (New York 1965) and S. W. C. Pack, *The Wager Mutiny* (London 1964).

[13] *Anson's Voyage*, 129–30, 158–60, 380; J. Juan and A. de Ulloa, *Relación Historica del Viage a la América Méridional* (Madrid 1748, reprint 1978), II.270–93, 363–4 (their visits to Juan Fernández were well *after* Anson's in 1743) [*Relación*]—also in Williams, *Documents*, 138–44. G. Lohmann Villena, *Historia Marítima del Perú, Tomo IV: Siglos XVII y XVIII* (Lima 1975) adds nothing and leaves out Pizarro; a fine historian on land, his work at sea is disappointing.

[14] Juan and Ulloa, *Relación*, II.262–3; B. Hall, *Extracts from a Journal . . . on the Coasts of Chili, Peru, and Mexico* (London 1824), II.99. The Corregidor of Puna rallied 150 men, only twenty-five of whom had firearms, and made such a nocturnal row with drums and trumpets that in his own opinion he alone saved Piura—Juan and Ulloa, *Noticias Secretas de América* (London 1826), I.180–1 [*Noticias*]. 'Philips' gives a less chivalrous cast to the sack of Paita: 'We likewise took about a dozen *Indian* women; to these we gave no Quarter, tho' they begged hard for it, but sacrificed all'—*Authentic Journal*, 81–4.

[15] Williams, in *Anson's Voyage*, 387.

[16] Ibid., 282–3—*of* not *by* the western world—here the phrase, oddly enough for an Asian isle, refers to the Americas in general; a common usage of the time, as in Charles Churchill's *Gotham* (London 1764): 'Bar this pretence, and into air is hurl'd/The claim of Europe to the *western world*.'

[17] For the local EIC point of view, and Anson's reactions, see Williams, *Documents*, 144–54, and his judicious comments at 109–11; also Heaps, *Centurion*, 189–213.

[18] Williams, *Documents*, 183–5, 205–9.

[19] *Centurion*, 1005 tons, 60 guns 24 of them 24-pounders; *Covadonga*, 700 tons, 32 or 36 guns mounted, the heaviest being five 12-pounders—see G. Williams, 'Commodore Anson and the Acapulco Galleon', *History Today* 17, 1967, 525–32; W. L. Schurz, *The Manila Galleon* (Dutton ed., New York ?1959), 334–8 [*Galleon*]; and the sardonic comments of G. J. H. J.-B. Le Gentil de la Galaisière (*nom d'un nom d'un nom!*) in *A Voyage to the Indian Seas* (Manila 1964), 160–3—this is a translation of the Philippine section of his *Voyage dans les Mers de l'Inde* (Paris 1779–81) [*Indian Seas*]. As for morale, Williams (*Documents*, 185) most appositely cites Admiral Wager, one of the originators of Anson's voyage: 'A man who would not fight for a galleon would fight for nothing.'

[20] *Journal*, 290–1.

[21] The *Centurion*'s gun-ports had a wider arc of fire than those of the *Covadonga*, which after all was basically a cargo carrier; and shortage of hands forced Anson to organise his gun-teams for independent firing, a few guns at a time. This meant less intense but more continuous firing, which confused those Spaniards with any combat experience, who expected the normal simultaneous firing of the whole broadside, with safe intervals.

[22] Thomas, *Journal*, 285.

[23] The pilot was duly flogged by his superiors, but compensated by Anson with 'such a sum of money, as would at any time have enticed a Chinese to have undergone a dozen bastinadings'—*Anson's Voyage*, 347. One hopes so.

[24] The next British warship to refit, in 1764, was measured for duty like any merchant-man—ibid., 365 and Williams's note at 394; E. H. Pritchard, *Anglo-Chinese Relations during the Seventeenth and Eighteenth Centuries* (Urbana 1929), 145.

[25] *Armada*, VI.292. The *Covadonga* was sold at Macao for a mere 6000 dollars.

26 And, also absurdly, to be 'properly looked upon as a voyage of discovery'!—W. Laird Clowes, *The Royal Navy: A History* (London 1897–1902), III.20.

27 Williams, *Documents*, 234–8; Millechamp, ibid., 194.

28 Campbell in his edition of J. Harris, *Navigantium atque Intinerantium Bibliotheca* (London 1744–8), I.164–5; Richmond, *Navy*, I.100. Single-ship predatory voyages in the Pacific continued—the CSS *Shenandoah* in 1864–5, German raiders in 1914–18—but the strategic circumstances differed.

29 S. W. C. Pack, *Admiral Lord Anson* (London 1960), 140–4, 162–4, 184; Clowes, *Voyage*, xxi–xxii. For the previous history of the Marines, see Richmond, *Navy*, I.167–75. Byron (*Narrative*, vii) makes the connection between the *Wager* mutiny and the act for continuing pay.

30 *Anson's Voyage*, 97, and Williams's note at 379; Samuel Johnson, *Thoughts on the late Transactions respecting Falkland's Island* (1771), in Vol. X of the Yale Edition of his *Works* (New Haven 1977), 349–86 at 350.

31 R. E. Gallagher (ed.), *Byron's Journal of his Circumnavigation 1764–1766*, HS 2nd Ser. 122 (Cambridge 1964), xxxvi–xliii, lxv–lxvii, 4–6, 60—the Instructions speak of 'His Majesty's Islands called Falkland's Islands', somewhat prematurely as there had been no Act of Possession; J. Goebel, *The Struggle for the Falkland Islands* (New Haven 1927), 195–202, 225–34 [*Falkland*]. The 'Malvinas' (from Malouins) are of course still claimed by Argentina.

32 Juan and Ulloa, *Relación*, II.284–7, and *Noticias*, I.71–7; de Brosses, *Histoire des Navigations aux Terres Australes* (Paris 1756), II.364–6 [*Histoire*]. There is a good account of the colonisation in R. L. Woodward, *Robinson Crusoe's Island* (Chapel Hill, NC, 1969), 80–92; Cartaret's surprise is recorded in H. Wallis (ed.), *Cartaret's Voyage Round the World 1766–1769*, HS 2nd Ser. 124–5 (Cambridge 1965), 128–30.

33 Abbé [G. F.] Coyer, *A Supplement to Lord Anson's Voyage* (London 1752; original French ed. The Hague 1749); a well-executed but rather milk-and-watery following of Swift and, in its plea for a simple life, a mild anticipation of Rousseau's *Discours sur les Sciences et les Arts* (Paris, November 1750).

34 C. de Secondat de Montesquieu, *De l'Esprit des Lois* (Paris 1748), Liv. VIII Ch. 21 (Pléiade ed. Paris 1951, 365–8); the phrase does not occur in the earlier editions, and one rather suspects that the casual reference was added to give an air of up-to-dateness, a practice not unknown today. Voltaire's comment is in *Le Siècle de Louis XIV* (Paris 1755–69), Ch. XXVII (*Oeuvres Complètes*, Paris 1825–8, XXVII.294–5); for similar reservations by James Naish, see *Anson's Voyage*, 393–4. Williams led me to Voltaire, Dermigny to Montesquieu.

35 Dermigny, I.21–43, 52. The Jesuit J.-B. du Halde does allow himself some mild criticism of the 'bad faith of the Chinese towards foreigners', but adds that it is said that some Europeans have not refrained from learning OR teaching such tricks—*Description . . . de la Chine* (The Hague, rev. ed. 1736), II.91.

36 H. T. Fry, *Alexander Dalrymple and the Expansion of British Trade* (London 1970). Chs. II–IV, gives a full and admirable account of the Sulu enterprise [*Dalrymple*]. See also V. T. Harlow, *The Founding of the Second British Empire 1763–1793* (London 1952–64), I.70–97 [*Second Empire*] and N. Tarling, *Sulu and Sabah* (Kuala Lumpur/Oxford 1978), 1–35 [*Sulu*]. N. M. Saleeby, *The History of Sulu* (Manila 1908, reprint 1963), 69–83, is cursory but has some points; see also the documents at 195–203. J. F. Warren, *The Sulu Zone, 1768–1898: The Dynamics of External Trade, Slavery, and Ethnicity in the Transformation of a Southeast Asian Maritime State* (Singapore 1981), 17–37 is a valuable discussion [*Sulu Zone*].

³⁷ Fry, *Dalrymple*, 21, 25.

³⁸ Blair & Robertson, XLVIII.37–51, 149-91; for Zamboanga and its Governor, an old Africa hand whose response to reports of Muslim attacks was to 'tell you a long story about the Moros in Africa', see Le Gentil, *Indian Seas*, 61–3.

³⁹ These ships, originally five but one was lost, were taking this new route, entering the Indian ocean by Sumbawa, to avoid a French squadron in the Sunda Straits—Fry, *Dalrymple*, 29–31.

⁴⁰ Tarling, *Sulu*, 13–14. Dalrymple appears to have had a cavalier attitude in matters of diplomatic import. In a row over a handful of deserters, he told the Chinese that it would be his 'Glory and Happiness' to assist in an attack on Macao—this irrespective of our Oldest Alliance and of Chinese sovereignty. My mind boggles at the repercussions in Peking, London, and Lisbon.

⁴¹ Simón de Anda, in Blair & Robertson, XLIX.284–7; Fry, *Dalrymple*, 33. Fry does not think that the survey was 'primarily motivated by military considerations', but what could have been thought of a Spanish ship surveying, without permission, Madras Roads or the Hooghly?

⁴² Tarling, *Sulu*, 21–3; Fry, *Dalrymple*, 45–52. However, Dalrymple did think that 'the hazard of corrupting the Sooloos', who were not opium addicts, was 'a Sufficient Reason to forego any Pecuniary Consideration'—ibid., 45. On the trade potential, Francisco de Viana a few years later was to argue on much the same lines as Dalrymple, in favour of his projected Real Compañía de Filipinas—Blair & Robertson, XLVIII.197–338 at 278–9, 306. For the importance of the Buginese, see Warren, *Sulu Zone*, 11–15, 85.

⁴³ Tarling, *Sulu*, 15–16.

⁴⁴ Although the Crown's ultimate right of disposal was reserved—N. P. Cushner (ed.), *Documents illustrating the British Conquest of Manila 1762–1763*, Camden Soc. 4th Ser. 8 (London 1971), 11–26 [*Conquest*]. Further documents, British and Spanish, including the violent recriminations between Archbishop Rojo and Simón de Anda, are in Blair & Robertson, XLIX, a volume entirely devoted to the Luzon campaign. These two collections are my basic sources. J. W. Fortescue, *A History of the British Army* (London 1910–30), II.553–4 is useless, but the military events are sketched from the Spanish point of view in Fernández Duro, VII.92–9, and C. Alcázar y Molina, *Los Virreinatos en el Siglo XVIII* (Barcelona 1945), 461–4. Le Gentil's version (*Indian Seas*, 177–208), is drawn either from Rojo himself or someone very close to him; as might be expected, the military judgements are bizarre. The account in S. D. Quiason, *English 'Country Trade' With The Philippines, 1644–1765* (Quezon City 1966), is good on the economic aspects of the British occupation [*'Country Trade'*], and there is an excellent essay by A. P. Thornton, 'The British in Manila 1762–4' in *History Today* 7, 1957, 44–53, reprinted in his *For the File on Empire* (London 1968), 113–24 ['Manila'].

⁴⁵ The plan given in Blair & Robertson, XLIX.27–43, is not by Draper, as they suggest, but by Dalrymple, as can be seen from the opening quoted in Fry, *Dalrymple*, 64; Draper's plan is apparently that in Cushner, *Conquest*, 12–15.

⁴⁶ Thornton, 'Manila', 117. Draper's orders envisaged holding Mindanao at the peace, and the Directors in London had 'directed the Presidency of Fort St. George [Madras] to improve that incident in the most beneficial manner as subservient to [i.e. supporting] the present prospect'—Cushner, *Conquest*, 18, 21.

⁴⁷ Pigot and Draper, ibid., 32–6, 40–2. Draper's Augustan sense of style doubtless stemmed

from King's College, Cambridge, of which he had been a Fellow, and is well displayed in the grandiloquent monument he erected on Clifton Downs, overlooking Bristol, to the glory of the 79th and himself.

48 Fernández Duro, VII.68. He had become Governor, against opposition, in 1759.

49 Blair & Robertson, XLIX.233; see also Cushner, *Conquest*, 140, 180–2, and the fulsome Latin letter to Draper at 151–3. 'More imbecile than traitor', Rojo was released from the contempt of his countrymen by his death on 30 January 1764, his funeral receiving British military honours.

50 Thornton, 'Manila', 122; for Silang and his activities, H. de la Costa SJ, *Readings in Philippine History* (Manila 1965), 102–4, and D. Routledge, *Diego Silang and the Origins of Philippine Nationalism* (Quezon City 1979), 15–40.

51 Cushner, *Conquest*, 131–4; Quiason, 'Country Trade', 175–7; Schurz, *Galleon*, 338–9. The British had better luck with the *Santissima Trinidad*, which had sailed for Acapulco early in September 1762 but been driven back by tempest, to be captured in mistake for the *Filipino*. The Manila merchants protested that the seizure of her cargo—worth some 2,000,000 pesos—was illegal, being after the capitulation which assured them of their private property, but she was judged good prize and not reckoned in the ransom calculations. When she reached England her huge size, over 2000 tons, created a sensation—Schurz, 339–51; Cushner, 156–67.

52 For Anda's activities see the extremely interesting 'Diario de la invasión Ynglesa', Cushner, *Conquest*, 88–120, and the letter of Thomas Backhouse, who took over the British forces after their commander had attempted a coup against Drake—ibid., 196–9. There is an amusing account of the imbroglio by K. C. Leebrick, 'Troubles of an English Governor in the Philippine Islands', in H. M. Stephens and H. E. Bolton (eds.), *The Pacific Ocean in History* (New York 1917), 192–213.

53 Cushner, *Conquest*, 203–4 (Draper); Williams, *Documents*, 44 (Naish). The breakdown of ransom contributions is interesting: 38.6 per cent from the Misericordia; 24.2 from the Orders, excluding the Jesuits' 9.7; 9.6 from two dozen wealthy families, about 2000 pesos each; and a miserable 2.4 from the Royal Treasury—Quiason, 'Country Trade', 173–4 (there seems an error of 20,000 pesos in his total).

54 Blair & Robertson, XLIX.156, 269. Rojo's attempt at exculpating himself is pathetic as well as disingenuous—ibid., 176–261.

55 Francisco de Viana's 'Memorial of 1765', ibid., XLVIII.197–238 at 199; cf. G. F. Zaide, *The Philippines since Spanish Times* (Manila, revised ed. 1957), 357–61, and U. Mahajani, *Philippine Nationalism* (Brisbane 1971), 26–33.

56 On all this complex story, here much foreshortened, see Harlow, *Second Empire*, I.77–97; Tarling, *Sulu*, 14–30; Fry, *Dalrymple*, 65–93; Warren, *Sulu Zone*, 18–34. They have different emphases: Harlow, broad imperial policy: Tarling, Suluan politics; Fry, Dalrymple's relations with the EIC; Warren, the Suluese point of view.

57 'Polynesia' was a recent coinage by de Brosses (*Histoire*, I.ii, 80).

58 T. Forrest, *A Voyage to New Guinea and the Moluccas* (London 1780, reprint Kuala Lumpur/London 1969), 2–11, 106–8, 144–8, 215–16 [*New Guinea*]. Forrest obtained the cession to the EIC of Bunwoot Island, Mindanao, but this naturally lapsed with the collapse of Balambangan. His narrative shows a lively curiosity, a remarkable rapport with the diverse peoples he met, and an unexpected *penchant* for Latin verse.

59 Harlow, *Second Empire*, I.86–8; Fry, *Dalrymple*, 82–6.

⁶⁰ For a history of the dispute, see Goebel, *Falkland*, Chs. VI–VIII *passim*; the Falklands and Manila ransom disputes are linked by V. Rodríguez Castro, 'El Pacífico en la política internacional Española hasta la emancipación de América', *Estudios Americanos* (Seville) 2, 1950, 5–30 at 15–17. There are also French intrigues; see the proposal of 1771 for the occupation of Mindoro in Serv. Hydro. de la Marine, 109³, Carton 117 No. 13 (Mitchell Library French Marine Transcripts, B1190)—this would help the Spaniards by blocking Moro raids, but would open up an immense trade for France via her Indian Ocean holdings and cut out the British Country Traders. The 'Magellanic diagonal' figures in the map 'De la voie magellanique à la découverte totale' in M. R. de Brossard, *Histoire Maritime du Monde* (Paris 1974), 287.

⁶¹ Where 'for anything which appears, [they] may have been established at the time of the Treaty of Munster', the base-line (1648) in British discussion of Spanish claims—Harlow, *Second Empire*, I.91; cf. Tarling, *Sulu*, 26–9. Dalrymple, in his 'Plan of Conquest' of November 1762 (note 45 above) was aware of the Spanish fort of Taytay in the north of the island.

⁶² Harlow, *Second Empire*, I.89; Fry, *Dalrymple*, 77–85, 89–90. Dalrymple's precedent for a settlement without a Council—Negrais in Burma—was not very happy; it ended in massacre. Nor, *pace* Fry (at 270), were his precedents for civilian command of a naval vessel—Halley and Dampier.

⁶³ Cf. D. K. Bassett in his introduction to Forrest, *New Guinea*, 7. For the Balambangan fiasco in general and the direct quotations in this paragraph, Harlow, *Second Empire*, I.92–7.

⁶⁴ Warren, *Sulu Zone*, 14, 41–9 is revealing on the opium and munitions, and gives a graphic account (34–6) of the fall of Balambangan. For later British activities in the general area, see Harlow, *Second Empire*, I.103–6, 140–2; Fry, *Dalrymple*, 136–65; Tarling, *Sulu*, 34–6, and *Anglo-Dutch Rivalry in the Malay World 1750–1824* (Cambridge 1962), 62–6 and *passim*.

⁶⁵ Harlow, *Second Empire*, I.102.

Notes for Chapter 12

¹ This superfluity is the first of nineteen clerical abuses listed by Simón de Anda; there had also been a 'secular university', but the two Orders, rivals in all else, combined to strangle it—'Anda's Memorial, 1768', in Blair & Robertson, L.137–90 at 137–41.

² This was a potent concept long before Bishop Berkeley's famous poem, being associated with Nebuchadnezzar's dream of the Four Monarchies (Daniel 2.31–45), and presumably reached its apogee in American Manifest Destiny—see A. Gerbi, *The Dispute of the New World* (Pittsburgh 1973), 129–45, and M. Góngora, *Studies in the Colonial History of Spanish America* (Cambridge 1975), 213, 220, 224.

³ V. de Memije, *Theses Mathematicas ... en qve el Globo Terraqveo se contempla por respecto al Mundo Hispanico ...* (?Madrid 1761) and the map *Aspecto Symbolico del Mundo Hispanico*, British Library, K. Top CXVIII. 19. Continuing his foot-obsession, Memije goes on to infer that if the Hispanic World lacked these Filipino feet, it might be no more exempt from ruin than was Nebuchadnezzar's statue with feet of iron and clay.... I owe my

introduction to the truly and delightfully quixotic D. Vicente to the kindness of Dr Helen Wallis.

[4] N. P. Cushner SJ, *Spain in the Philippines* (Quezon City 1971), 130–1 [*Spain*]; P. Chaunu, *Les Philippines et le Pacifique des Ibériques* (Paris 1960), 135, 255–61.

[5] [J. A. Alvarez de Abreu], *Extracto Historial del Expediente que pende en el Consejo Real, y Supremo de las Indias, a Instancia de la Ciudad de Manila . . .* (Madrid 1736); 648 folio pages [*Extracto Historial*]. I have gone through the original but have drawn my citations mainly from the condensed translation in Blair & Robertson, XXX.23–109, XLIV.227–312, XLV.29–88. For the Bustamante affair, ibid., XLIV.148–95; H. de la Costa SJ, *Readings in Philippine History* (Manila 1965), 70–1 [*Readings*]; C. Alcázar y Molina, *Los Virreinatos en el Siglo XVIII* (Barcelona 1945), 455–6, source of the direct quotation.

[6] *Extracto Historial*, in Blair & Robertson, XLIV. 243–73 (fol. 35–47 of original).

[7] Commerce with whom should be prohibited, being 'even of less estimation than that of those expelled Moriscoes' (not a happy precedent)—*Extracto Historial*, ibid., XLV.77–9. The Andalusian view was supported by G. J. H. J.-B. Le Gentil de la Galaisière: the Indios learnt sloth from the Spaniards, and although it is a fine idea to let Asians come to Manila that they may be converted, in over 150 years no Moor or Armenian has been won for the Faith—*A Voyage in the Indian Seas* (Manila 1964, original ed. Paris 1779–81), 148–50 [*Indian Seas*]. This was not in fact true—see C. F. Nunn, *Foreign Immigrants in Early Bourbon Mexico 1700–1760* (Cambridge 1979), 183 note 17.

[8] W. L. Schurz, *The Manila Galleon* (Dutton ed., New York ?1959), 78–9 [*Galleon*]; Blair & Robertson, note at XLV.38; Cushner, *Spain*, 138.

[9] M. L. Diaz-Trechuelo Spínola, *La Real Compañía de Filipinas* (Seville 1965), 5–6—a full and admirable study [*Compañía*]; Blair & Robertson, XLV.46–7. Cushner (*Spain*, 188–9) suggests that the project was inspired by the success of the Real Compañía Guipuscoana de Caracas (1728), which however seems unlikely. That company, though in time successful, made a slow start; while its first dividend was 20 per cent, this was largely anticipatory, and even so was not declared until December 1733 and not paid until 1735—R. D. Hussey, *The Caracas Company* (Cambridge, Mass. 1934), 69–72, 86–9. Cf. A. Christelow, 'Great Britain and the Trades from Cadiz and Lisbon to Spanish America and Brazil, 1759–1783', *HAHR* 27, 1947, 1–29 at 22–3 ['Trades from Cadiz'].

[10] *Extracto Historial*, in Blair & Robertson, XLV.63–88, especially note at 70 (fol. 265–324 of original).

[11] de la Costa, *Readings*, 96.

[12] Diaz-Trechuelo, 'Commerce', 263–5, 270 (see next note); Schurz, *Galleon*, 57, 156–64; W. E. Cheong, 'Canton and Manila in the Eighteenth Century', in J. Ch'en and N. Tarling, *Studies in the Social History of China and Southeast Asia* (Cambridge 1970), 227–46 at 238–42 ['Canton and Manila']. For the system of permiso and boletas see Spate, 160.

[13] Spínola, *Compañía*, 256, and her 'Mining', 773 (see next note); Schurz, *Galleon*, 224–6.

[14] M. L. Diaz-Trechuelo, 'The Economic Development of the Philippines in the Second Half of the Eighteenth Century', *Philippine Studies* (Manila) 11, 1963, 195–231 at 213 ['Development']. This is the general introduction to a series of five articles in the same journal; the others are 'Philippine Development Plans, 1746–1779', in 12, 1964, 203–31 ['Plans']; 'Eighteenth Century Philippine Economy: Mining', 13, 1965, 763–800 ['Mining']; 'Eighteenth Century Philippine Economy: Agriculture', 14, 1966, 65–126 ['Agriculture']; 'Eighteenth Century Philippine Commerce', 14, 1966, 253–79 ['Commerce'].

¹⁵ Le Gentil, *Indian Seas*, 147–9; Memorial of 1788, cited in Schurz, *Galleon*, 40–1. To be fair, such contempt for honest work still persisted in Spain; this Memorial comes only five years after Carlos III's decree which endeavoured to get rid of the social stigma attaching to labour, and permitted artisans to hold public office (in their proper and implicitly lowly sphere)—W. N. Hargreaves-Mawdsley, *Spain under the Bourbons, 1700–1833* (London 1973), 166–7.

¹⁶ N. N. Nicols, 'Commerce of the Philippine Islands', in Blair & Robertson, XLVII.251–84 at 261, 279. Perhaps because of his fine Dickensian name, Nicols seems to have attracted more attention than he deserves.

¹⁷ Viana's 'Memorial of 1765', in Blair & Robertson, XLVIII.197–338 at 200–12.

¹⁸ Ibid., 217–41, 251–6.

¹⁹ Ibid., 296–312.

²⁰ Ibid., 330–5.

²¹ Le Gentil, *Indian Seas*, 171–5; Schurz, *Galleon*, 409–11; Diaz-Trechuelo, 'Development', 22–4, 'Plans', 212, 'Commerce', 257, 271–5. For the diplomatic point, Christelow, 'Trades from Cadiz', 22–3; he also says that the first ship from Manila to Cadiz (apparently the *Buen Consejo*) sold cinnamon there at 65 per cent of Dutch and British prices, which is puzzling in view of the failure of attempts to produce saleable cinnamon in the Philippines. For the first and abortive attempt at direct sailing from Cadiz to Manila—in 1619, and a context not of trade but of war—see above, Ch. 2.

²² Basco y Vargas, 10 May 1780, cited in Diaz-Trechuelo, 'Commerce', 270–1.

²³ Alcázar, *Virreinatos*, 459–61; Cushner, *Spain*, 187; Diaz-Trechuelo, 'Development', 207–12, and her 'The Role of the Chinese in the Philippine Domestic Economy', in A. Felix (ed.), *The Chinese in the Philippines 1570–1770* (Manila 1966), I.175–210.

²⁴ For these 'Economic Societies of Friends of the Country', which played an important role in Carlos III's time, see J. Vicens Vives, *An Economic History of Spain* (Princeton 1958), 154–63.

²⁵ Diaz-Trechuelo, 'Mining', 764–87.

²⁶ Diaz-Trechuelo, 'Agriculture' *passim*; Cushner, *Spain*, 192–4. Salgado was a remarkably active entrepreneur, involved in schemes in iron- and copper-mining, iron-founding, cinnamon, indigo, and textiles, most of them in the long run abortive. Even in Guam there was some development under the versatile and energetic Governor Mariano Tobias (1770–4), a one-man Sociedad Económica—P. Carano and P. C. Sanchez, *A Complete History of Guam* (Rutland, Vt/Tokyo 1964), 106–9, 113.

²⁷ Spínola, *Compañía*, 269–74.

²⁸ de la Costa, *Readings*, 115–18, 169–73; for Corcuera, Spate, 340–1.

²⁹ Unless otherwise indicated, factual statements and direct quotations in this section are from Spínola, *Compañía*, a work of fascinating detail. There are brief accounts of the RCF in Cushner, *Spain*, 190–5; Schurz, *Galleon*, 409–18; and E. Arcila Farías, *Reformas Económicas del siglo XVIII en Nueva España* (Mexico 1974), 43–50, which has details of the Indian investment.

³⁰ Schurz, *Galleon*, 60, 413–15.

³¹ Spínola, *Compañía*, 243–7.

³² As late as 1817 an RCF ship was taken off Cadiz by privateers flying the colours of the rebel United Provinces of La Plata—ibid., 208–9, and for the RCF's activities in Peru, 228–34.

³³ For this very complicated story, see W. L. Cook, *Flood Tide of Empire* (New Haven 1973), 107–11.

³⁴ Ibid., 254–5. The first ship to attempt to use the new permiso was lost at sea in 1782—Diaz-Trechuelo, 'Commerce', 266–70, q.v. for the increase in the permiso.

³⁵ Schurz, *Galleon*, 60; Spínola, *Compañía*, 196–200; S. Villalobos R., *Comercio y Contrabando en el Río de la Plata y Chile 1700–1811* (Buenos Aires 1965), 62–5.

³⁶ Cheong, 'Canton and Manila', 245–6.

³⁷ R. R. and M. C. McHale (eds.), *Early American Philippine Trade: The Journal of Nathaniel Bowditch in Manila, 1796* (New Haven 1962), 15, 30. As the McHales remark, with a degree of understatement, 'We cannot completely discount the possibility that the *Astrea*'s sale of non-Asiatic goods was extra-legal'; in fact, the decree opening the port specifically banned all European goods—Spínola, *Compañía*, 276–7.

³⁸ Chaunu, *Philippines*, 20.

³⁹ Spínola, *Compañía*, 119–53, 278–9—but the final liquidation was held up until 1840 by a law suit.

⁴⁰ T. Oteiza Iriarte, *Acapulco: La Ciudad de las Naos de Oriente y de las Sirenas Modernas* (?Mexico 1965), 175–7—vivid but one suspects somewhat romanticised [*Acapulco*]. The irrepressible James Creassy was projecting an attempt upon the Galleon as late as 1804—R. H. Dillon, 'The Last Plan to Seize the Manila Galleon', *Pac. Histl Rev.* 20, 1951, 123–5.

⁴¹ Schurz, *Galleon*, 60. But Oteiza Iriarte (*Acapulco*, 280) and M. Carrera Stampa, 'Las Ferias Novohispanos', *Hist. Mexicana* 2, 1952–3, 319–42 at 333–4, speak of a galleon in 1820–1. Perhaps this was really an RCF ship?—a guess I find confirmed in S. Zavala, *El Mundo Americano en la Epoca Colonial* (Mexico 1967), II.184 note 53.

Notes for Chapter 13

¹ J. Vicens Vives, *An Economic History of Spain* (Princeton 1969). 471 [*Spain*]; cf. the similar statement by J. H. Parry, in 'Latin America', *NCMH* VII.487–500 at 492 ['Latin America'].

² For narratives of the earlier Bourbon period, see J. D. Bergamini, *The Spanish Bourbons: The History of a Tenacious Dynasty* (New York 1974) or W. N. Hargreaves-Mawdsley, *Eighteenth Century Spain 1700–1788* (London 1979), which is however marred by a deliberate refusal to consider any economic factors at all, as irrelevant to the art of history ... not only the Bourbons themselves learnt nothing from history.

³ Vicens Vives, *Spain*, 476–7; J. Lynch, 'The Iberian States', in *NCMH* VIII.360–78 at 365–6.

⁴ Vicens Vives, *Spain*, 496–8, 572–4. M. Góngora points out that the enterprising Basque and Cantabrian traders who at this time were entrenching themselves in New Spain did not form a bourgeoisie—*Studies in the Colonial History of Spanish America* (Cambridge 1975), 159, 163–4 [*Studies*]; but his main reference on this point, while admitting their addiction to hidalgoismo, also notes some pretty bourgeois traits—D. A. Brading, *Miners and Merchants in Bourbon Mexico 1763–1810* (Cambridge 1971), 104–14 [*Miners*]. But then again R. Herr, in *The Eighteenth Century Revolution in Spain* (Princeton 1958), 148–50, speaks of the rise of a strong middle class [*Revolution*]. Had there really been a *strong* middle class, the history of Spain in the nineteenth century might have been happier.

[5] Vicens Vives, *Spain*, 524–39, 561–4; Herr, *Revolution*, 120–53 and his maps. Herr's seems the standard account in English of Enlightenment Spain, but see also J. Sarrailh, *L'Espagne éclairée de la seconde moitié du XVIIIe siècle* (Paris 1954), which has much curious detail—e.g. at 90–2 the view of the University of Salamana in 1772 that 'Jean Lochio' [John Locke] was not only dangerous, which is understandable, but also obscure, which isn't [*Espagne*].

[6] Vicens Vives, *Spain*, 483–5.

[7] He had had a successful reforming career in Parma and later as King of the Two Sicilies (Naples), the most positive result of his mother Isabel Farnese's dynastic determination. There is no doubt at all that Carlos III was far the best of the Bourbons and one of the best of all Spanish monarchs, but for his limitations see J. Lynch, *Spanish Colonial Administration 1782–1810* . . . (London 1958), 2–4 [*Administration*].

[8] However, the pioneer Sociedad Bascongada de los Amigos del País received papal permission to use it, and the Barcelona Junta de Comercio had a copy obtained from Lyons by one Diego Lambert, perhaps a significant surname—Herr, *Revolution*, 43, 161; Sarrailh, *Espagne*, 269.

[9] R. A. Humphreys and J. Lynch (eds.), in *The Origins of the Latin American Revolutions, 1808–1826* (Borzoi ed., New York 1965), 10; cf. J. Basadre, ibid., 295.

[10] Lynch, *Administration*, 13–16; W. L. Dorn, *Competition for Empire 1740–1763* (Torchbook ed., New York 1963), 372–6; and especially A. F. Christelow, 'Economic Background of the Anglo-Spanish War of 1762', *Jnl Modern Hist.* 17, 1946, 22–36 ['Background'].

[11] Lynch, *Administration*, 19–21; examples are scattered through Vol. I of V. T. Harlow, *The Founding of the Second British Empire* (London 1952–64) [*Second Empire*]. For Spanish reactions, see W. N. Hargreaves-Mawdsley, *Spain under the Bourbons, 1700–1833: A Collection of Documents* (London 1973), 122, 125–6.

[12] R. A. Humphreys, 'The Development of the American Communities outside British Rule', in *NCMH* VIII.397–420 at 400.

[13] S. J. and B. H. Stein, *The Colonial Heritage of Latin America* (New York 1970), 95–6 [*Heritage*].

[14] Góngora, *Studies*, 70–1; more details in Lynch, *Administration*, 34–45, and B. Moses, *Spain's Declining Power in South America 1730–1806* (Berkeley 1919, reprint New York 1965), 153–65 [*Declining Power*]—the timing is significant in that Portugal's ally Britain was involved with the American rebellion. For Céspedes del Castillo's important study 'Lima y Buenos Aires' see Ch. 14 note 2.

[15] Quoted in Herr, *Revolution*, 147; Herr gives 12 per cent as the Spanish share about 1700, but a generally accepted estimate for 1691 is only 3.8 per cent—Vicens Vives, *Spain*, 433.

[16] J. Lynch, *The Spanish American Revolutions 1808–1826* (New York 1973), 5, 126. Lynch's first chapter presents an unfavourable view of the reforms from an American standpoint; this is of course linked with his idea of an earlier economic 'emancipation' of Spanish America—see his *Spain under the Habsburgs* (Oxford 1964–9), II.193, 222–4. Similar opinions are expressed in J. H. Parry, *The Spanish Seaborne Empire* (Harmondsworth 1973), 288–9.

[17] D. A. Brading and H. E. Cross, 'Colonial Silver Mining: Mexico and Peru', *HAHR* 52, 1972, 545–79 at 561–2, 574 ['Mining']. W. Borah, *New Spain's Century of Depression* (Berkeley 1951), 20–6, presents the labour thesis; Brading argues that the mining decline began after the population had stabilised—*Miners*, 7–12. See also M. F. Lang, 'New Spain's Mining Depression and the Supply of Quicksilver from Peru', *HAHR* 48, 1968, 632–41,

and P. J. Bakewell, *Silver Mines and Society in Colonial Mexico: Zacatecas 1546–1700* (Cambridge 1971), 162–4. For cultural life, see I. A. Leonard's entertaining *Baroque Times in Old Mexico* (Ann Arbor 1966).

[18] Pitt's Act cutting the tea duty from 119 to 12.5 per cent was aimed at smuggling but led to tea becoming a necessary comfort for the masses; the EIC's London sales tripled in two years—E. H. Pritchard, *The Crucial Years of Early Anglo-Chinese Relations 1750–1800* (New York 1936, reprint 1970), 146–51 [*Crucial Years*], and Harlow, *Second Empire*, 529–33.

[19] Vicens Vives, *Spain*, 547, 557–8; cf. K. A. Ballhatchet 'Relations with Asia', *NCMH* VIII (1965), 218–36 at 230–1. For the changing terms of Anglo-Chinese trade, Pritchard, *Crucial Years*, 142–98 *passim* and Appendices; Dermigny, II.688–93, III.1210–14 and Tables 5, 15.

[20] Brading, *Miners*, 129–30, 132–7; for an excellent short account, see his 'Mexican Silver Mining . . . The Revival of Zacatecas', *HAHR* 50, 1970, 665–81.

[21] L. Navarro García, *Hispanoamerica en el Siglo XVIII* (Seville 1975), 73–4 [*Hispanoamerica*]; W. Howe, *The Mining Guild of New Spain . . . 1770–1826* (1949, reprint New York 1968), 15–17 [*Guild*].

[22] Brading, *Miners*, 132–7, 146–9; Howe, *Guild*, 24–6.

[23] H. I. Priestley, *José de Gálvez: Visitor-General of New Spain (1765–1771)* (Berkeley 1916), 142–55, 172–209 [*Gálvez*]; C. E. Chapman, *A History of California: The Spanish Period* (New York 1921), 207–10 [*California*].

[24] A. von Humboldt, *Ensayo Politico sobre el Reino de la Nueva España* (Mexico 1973), 372, 383–4 (III.251, 285–6 in the translation, *Political Essay on the Kingdom of New Spain*, London 1811–14) [*Ensayo*]. This great work, which might be regarded as the first modern geography, was first published as *Essai Politique sur le Royaume de la Nouvelle Espagne* (Paris 1811); Ch. XI is a very full analysis of the mining industry. See also Brading and Cross, 'Mining', 564, 577, and Graph I; Brading, *Miners*, 139–42. Blasting powder, another Crown monopoly, was also cut in price.

[25] Ibid., 164–8; Howe, *Guild*, 149–54.

[26] The process had been discovered about 1609 by Fr Alvaro Alonso Barba, but over-shadowed by the easier patio method. The Gálvez program included missions to New Granada by Juan José de Elhuyar and to Peru by Thaddeus von Nordenflicht, and began with espionage at the Carron ironworks in Scotland, an interesting mating of scientific and military research—A. P. Whitaker, 'The Elhuyar Mining Missions and the Enlightenment', *HAHR* 31, 1951, 551–85. For Barba's *El Arte de los Metales* (Madrid 1640), see C. Prieto, *Mining in the New World* (New York 1973), 80, 85, 185—the first edition was suppressed by the Inquisition (only three copies are known), but despite at least three translations in each of English, German, French, and Dutch, the work seems to have suffered from the general scorn for things American.

[27] C. G. Motten, *Mexican Silver and the Enlightenment* (Philadelphia 1950), 46–54, 59–63, a book which does not quite live up to its attractive title. For a somewhat less favourable view of the College, see Brading, *Miners*, 165–6; but Howe's chapter on 'Mining Education' (*Guild*, 300–69) is more sympathetic; it gives details of the College's working and confirms the point about German methods. Humboldt's praise is in *Ensayo*, 80–1 (I.216–18).

[28] Brading and Cross, 'Mining', 576–7; the new Viceroyalty of La Plata included Potosí. Cf. P. Vilar, *A History of Gold and Money* (London 1976), 288.

[29] Brading, *Miners*, 14–19; M. C. Meyer and W. L. Sherman, *The Course of Mexican History* (New York 1969), 255–6; for cochineal, Humboldt, *Ensayo*, 304–10 (III.62–79).

[30] Navarro García, *Hispanoamerica*, 173.

[31] I use the terms Baja (Lower) and Alta (Upper) California for convenience, although of course they meant little until the Spanish settlement in the latter, which is now comprised in the State of California USA, while the peninsula remains in Mexico. The first use of Baja California was apparently by Fr Junipero Serra in 1781—H. H. Bancroft, *History of California* (San Francisco 1884–90, reprint Santa Barbara 1963), I.325 [*History*]. In Humboldt's *Ensayo*, Alta and Baja California are referred to as Nueva and Vieja respectively.

[32] Chapman, *California*, 178, 251; I have generally followed this source and Chapman's *The Founding of Spanish California . . . 1687–1783* (New York 1916) [*Founding*], both old but still very useful. Shorter accounts of the advance may be found e.g. in J. W. Caughey, *California* (New York 1953), 72–134, and A. F. Rolle, *California: A History* (2nd ed. New York 1969), 59–91—both [*California*].

[33] Chapman, *California*, 192–3, 201–6; Caughey, *California*, 98–9.

[34] E. Vila Vilar, 'Los Rusos en América', *AEA* XXII, 1965, 569–672 at 597–9 ['Los Rusos']; G. Barratt, *Russia in Pacific Waters, 1715–1825* (Vancouver 1981), 51–3 [*Russia*].

For the *Noticia*, see Chapman, *Founding*, 56–60; on the timing, Chapman, *California*, 199–201, 209–18; Priestley, *Gálvez*, 246–7; Cook, *Flood Tide of Empire: Spain and the Pacific Northwest, 1543–1819* (New Haven 1973), 44–50 [*Flood Tide*]. The reports were forwarded from Madrid to Mexico on 23 January 1768; on that day Gálvez and Croix were already discussing a plan which included the pre-emptive occupation of Monterey—ibid., 49.

[35] For 'forward capitals' (Monterey as headquarters for both Californias was to be an example), see V. Cornish, *The Great Capitals* (London 1923), vii and *passim*. Gálvez's proposed Intendancies were not set up until 1786—Lynch, *Administration*, 51–6, 61. The general discussion of his work is based on Chapman, *California*, 207–20, 230–9, 319–22, and *Founding*, 68–92; Priestley, *Gálvez*, 234–94; see also the brief but incisive comment in Góngora, *Studies*, 171.

[36] M. E. Thurman, *The Naval Department of San Blas . . .* (Glendale 1967), 32–9, 223–8—a very detailed work, 382 pages for 31 years [*San Blas*]. E. L. Inskeep, 'San Blas, Nayarit', *Jnl of the West* 2, 1963, 133–4, gives photographs of the ruined buildings and an aerial view of the site; the place has regained a modest prosperity.

[37] Thurman, *San Blas*, 52–9, 68–9; on their first voyage both ships took nearly three months to reach La Paz, and arrived in very bad shape. Thurman's use of the term 'frigate' for the larger ships built at San Blas, though in accordance with his contemporary Spanish sources, is misleading unless explained, and he does not explain. The largest of them was the *Santiago*, 225 tons, 6 guns, 84 men; by the 1760s 'frigates' in European navies carried 24 to 40 or 44 guns and ran from 500 to 750 tons or more—W. Laird Clowes, *The Royal Navy* (London 1897–1902), III.8–12, 154). The San Blas ships seem in fact to have been more like armed brigs or barks, probably of much the same strength as Cook's *Endeavour* or rather less. Hence it is perhaps better to speak of a naval 'presence' rather than a naval 'power'. See *San Blas*, 97, and Cook, *Flood Tide*, 56–7, 94, 550.

[38] Priestley, *Gálvez*, 251; Humboldt, *Ensayo*, 201–2 (II.331–3)—by his day the settled population had fallen to 4000–5000.

[39] Priestley, *Gálvez*, 251–66 ('The one accomplishment of his visit [was] the permanent occupation of upper California'); Chapman, *California*, 234–7—in *Founding*, 88, he refers to Gálvez insanity simply as 'a serious illness'. Chappe d'Auteroche (1722–69) was stricken mortally while actually observing—see his *A Voyage to California* (London 1778, facsimile

Richmond 1973), 63–70; the little book has some interesting glimpses of New Spain and Baja California.

⁴⁰ Bancroft, *History*, I.113–15, and Gálvez's very interesting instructions for the *San Carlos* at 129, note 7. Out-dated as it is, Bancroft's work is still good background reading; it was produced largely by a paid staff on factory lines, and his magnificent collections formed the basis for the Bancroft Library at Berkeley—see his *Retrospection Political and Personal* (3rd ed. New York 1915), 301–44, and Chapman, *California*, 498–500.

⁴¹ The story is accepted by Caughey (*California*, 110–11), Rolle (*California*, 68–9), and H. E. Bolton, *Outpost of Empire: The Story of the Founding of San Francisco* (New York 1931), 23 [*Outpost*]. However, Bancroft (*History*, I.164–8) seems not too clear on the point, and Chapman gives what seem to me sound reasons for regarding this story as a monkish fable—*California*, 230 note 2, and *Founding*, 98–101. On why Monterey was not at first recognised, see Bancroft, I.150–5.

⁴² Chapman, *California*, 227–31.

⁴³ Ibid., 251–2, 284–6.

⁴⁴ T. D. Murphy, *On Sunset Highways* (Boston 1915), 354–8, confirmed by personal information from Ms Dorothy C. Ronald, Colton Hall Museum, Monterey.

⁴⁵ Vila Vilar, 'Los Rusos', 609–13; Barratt, *Russia*, 66–9; Chapman, *Founding*, 219–35. There was a very level-headed appreciation of the situation by Vicente Doz, who had been one of d'Auteroche's astronomical assistants in Baja California—ibid., 240–1.

⁴⁶ Chapman, *California*, 271.–8; the northern voyages will be treated in the next volume of this work, the view that Drake may have preceded Ayala has been discussed in Spate, 256–8, 261. The name 'Golden Gate' was bestowed on the entrance by J. C. Frémont in the 1840s—Rolle, *California*, 67.

⁴⁷ Garcés, who was killed by the Yumas in the 1781 massacre which closed the new route, was the first European to cross the Mojave Desert and penetrate the great Central Valley of California; later, with only two or three Indians, he journeyed to the Grand Canyon and northeastern Arizona—J. B. Brebner, *The Explorers of North America 1492–1806* (Meridian ed. Cleveland 1964), 351–5. Brebner also gives a good short account of Portolá's journey and Anza's reconnaissance, but for the latter's main expedition Bolton's *Outpost of Empire* is meticulously detailed, though marred by a cloying sentimentality verging on hagiography. It is not always too easy to follow the sequence of his narrative, however, and his maps, though accurate and based on first-hand coverage of the ground, are in places confusing.

⁴⁸ For the extremely interesting detailed costing of the expedition see Chapman, *Founding*, Appendix IV (461–6).

⁴⁹ Much later two missions were established north of the Bay, San Rafael (1817) and San Francisco Solano (1823); these were the last such foundations.

⁵⁰ Bancroft, *History*, I.659 and note 21 at 610; for the settlement pattern in general, ibid., 600–23 and the succinct outline in Rolle, *California*, 72–3; the Porciuncula is or was a little stream. For *gente de razón*, see Brading, *Miners*, 23–4. As late as the 1840s Lt Charles Wilkes USN thought that 'under the recent changes' (the American takeover) Los Angeles would lose its importance, and doubted that a town of any size could arise on San Francisco Bay—*Western America* (New York 1849), 39–40, 45.

⁵¹ Chapman, *California*, 330–42 (with an odd and amusing moral *ad fin.*); Bancroft, *History*, I.353–71, 449.

[52] Ibid., I.307, II.158. Chapman (*California*, 348) gives 1200 as the white population in 1800, and scattered notices in Bancroft suggest a figure nearer 2000. It makes little odds.

[53] M. L. A. Milet Mureau (ed.), *The Voyage of La Pérouse round the World* (London 1798), I.201–20 [*Voyage*]; at this time even J. R. Forster was aware only, and rather vaguely, of the existence of Monterey—*History of the Voyages and Discovereies made in the North* (London 1786), 453. Cf. with La Pérouse's views the criticism by J. Espinosa y Tello (?) in *A Spanish Voyage to Vancouver . . . in the year 1792* (London 1930), 124–6.

[54] Rolle, *California*, 99, 102–3; Bancroft, *History*, I.619–21.

[55] Ibid., I.330, 438, 442.

[56] A. Ogden, *The California Sea Otter Trade, 1784–1848* (Berkeley 1941), 2–13, and 'The Californias in Spain's Pacific Otter Trade, 1775–1795', *Pac. Histl Rev.* 1, 1932, 444–69; see also La Pérouse, *Voyage*, I.217–19, and Cook, *Flood Tide*, 107–11. One cannot however see how the Spaniards can have learnt of these windfall profits from 'deserters during Britain's attack on Manila in 1779' (*Flood Tide*, 107), since this attack is otherwise unrecorded.

[57] Bancroft, *History*, I.621.

[58] A. Frost, *Convicts and Empire* (Melbourne 1980), 155; B. Anderson, *The Life . . . of George Vancouver, Surveyor of the Sea* (Washington ed., Seattle 1966), 124–5. Chapman is of course quite wrong in saying (*California*, 405) that 'these were to be the first animals of that type in the great island continent'; see D. Collins, *An Account of the English Colony in New South Wales* (London 1798, reprint Sydney 1975), I.237, 248.

[59] Humboldt was premature, but not by much. In 1802, his base date, there were 1800–2000 Spaniards (including mestizos) in Alta California, with 14–16,000 mission Indians, and over 107,000 sheep; in September 1800 New South Wales had 4936 whites, no converted Aborigines, and, by 1803, 10,157 sheep. But of the whites, 2051 were transportees and their children: how balance convicts against converts? At a comparable *age*, New South Wales was far ahead: over 35,000 Europeans in 1828, against under 4000, and 338,000 sheep against 200,000 plus—Humboldt, *Ensayo*, 205, 209 (II.347–8, 353–5). Bancroft, *History*, II.158, 181, 393–5; T. A. Coghlan, *The Wealth and Progress of New South Wales 1889–90* (Sydney 1890), 314; E. O'Brien, *The Foundation of Australia* (London 1937), 337; G. J. R. Linge, *Industrial Awakening* (Canberra 1979), 55.

[60] Accounts of this rather *opéra bouffe* affair—three of the 'pirates' were captured by lasso—in Bancroft, *History*, II.220–49; Chapman, *California*, 441–50; and P. Corney, *Early Voyages in the North Pacific 1813–18* (Fairfield, Wash., 1965), 215–23. Corney commanded one of the ships; his account appeared in the London *Literary Gazette* of 1821 but was not reprinted in English until 1896, at Honolulu; but significantly enough a Russian version appeared in 1822–3—ibid., 12–13.

[61] Navarro García, *Hispanoamerica*, 90–2, 160, 196–7; J. Lang, *Conquest and Commerce: Spain and England in the Americas* (New York 1975), 78–9. For the earlier vicissitudes of the cacao trade and the way in which Costa Rica was virtually enforced to smuggle to Jamaica and Curaçao, see M. J. MacLeod, *Spanish Central America: A Socioeconomic History 1520–1720* (Berkeley 1973), 235–52, 330–40. T. S. Floyd clarifies the muddled story of *The Anglo-Spanish Struggle for Mosquitia* (Albuquerque 1967) [*Mosquitia*] and provides a detailed and scathing analysis of the Guatemalan economic situation in 'The Guatemalan Merchants, the Government, and the *Provincianos*, 1750–1800' *HAHR* 41, 1961, 90–110.

[62] D. Ramos, *Minería y Comercio Interprovincial en Hispanoamerica (siglos XVI, XVII, y XVIII)* (Valladolid n.d.), 255–63. The territorial changes are outlined in Parry, 'Latin America',

495–6. The first three books of J. Juan and A. de Ulloa, *Relación Histórica del Viaje a la América Méridional* (Madrid 1748, reprint 1978) are devoted to Tierra Firma and the Isthmus, which they visited in 1735–6; see especially I.139–51.

⁶³ O. Pantaleão, *A Penetração Comercial da Inglaterra na America Espanhola de 1713 a 1783* (Sao Paulo 1946), 125–8, but citing J. Zaragoza, *Piraterias y Agresiones de los Ingleses ... deducidas de las obras de D. Dionisio de Alsedo y Herrera* (Madrid 1883), a source just possibly not totally objective; C. H. Haring, *The Spanish Empire in America* (Harbinger ed., New York 1963), 315–16.

⁶⁴ One would like to say 'won his spurs', but that is not right for a naval hero; his story, with that of his comrade-in-arms 'the unfortunate Colonel Despard', is well told in T. Pocock, *The Young Nelson in the Americas* (London 1980) and in Floyd, *Mosquitia*, 141–52; from the Spanish side, in R. Trigueros, 'Las Defensas Estratégicas del Río de San Juan de Nicaragua', *AEA* 11, 1954, 413–513 at 491–3.

⁶⁵ M. Luengo Muñoz, 'Genesis de las Expediciones Militares al Darién en 1785–6', *AEA* 18, 1961, 335–416 (with excellent maps); Navarro García, *Hispanoamerica*, 207–8; Moses, *Declining Power*, 270–2; and for the impracticability of the Atrato routes, G. Mack, *The Land Divided: A History of Isthmian Canal Projects* (New York 1944), 236–45—by far the best, and best-mapped, account of proposals and attempts to pierce the Isthmus, from 1534 to 1913 [*Land Divided*].

⁶⁶ G. T. C. Raynal, *A Philosophical and Political History ... of the Europeans in the East and West Indies* (London 1788, original French ed. 1770), III.352; Mack, *Land Divided*, 97–102; Chapman, *Founding*, 230–1; J. B. Muñoz, 'Discurso sobre la navegacion al Oceano Pacifico ...' (1779), 69–72—Archivo General de Indias, Sevilla, Filipinas 687; a reference I owe to Mr R. J. King, Canberra.

⁶⁷ J. H. Parry, *Trade and Dominion: The European Overseas Empires in the Eighteenth Century* (London 1971), 190–3.

Notes for Chapter 14

¹ J. E. Fagg, *Latin America: A General History* (New York 1963), 347; J. Lynch, *The Spanish American Revolutions 1808–1826* (New York 1973), 130 [*Revolutions*].

² B. Moses, *Spain's Declining Power in South America 1730–1806* (Berkeley 1919, reprint New York 1965), 293–6 [*Declining Power*]; J. M. Zapatero, 'El Castillo Real Felipe del Callao', *AEA* 34, 1977, 707–33 at 716; G. Céspedes del Castillo, *Lima y Buenos Aires, repercusiones económicas y politicas de la creación del Virreinato del Plata* (Seville 1947), 149–54—a separate from *AEA* 15, 1947, 667–874, which carries both serial and separate pagination. I have treated this admirable work, the *locus classicus*, as a monograph, for brevity's sake referring to it as C. del C., *Lima y BA*.

³ J. R. Fisher, *Government and Society in Colonial Peru: The Intendant System 1784–1814* (London 1970), 1, 4–6 [*Colonial Peru*], and 'Silver Production in the Viceroyalty of Peru, 1776–1824', *HAHR* 55, 1975, 23–43 at 39–41 ['Silver']. The voyages of Felipe González to Easter Island (1770) and of Domingo de Boenachea to Tahiti (1772–3, 1774–5) will be treated in the next volume of this work.

⁴ E. J. Goodman, *The Explorers of South America* (London 1972), 184–94.

[5] *Noticias Secretas de América*, mainly by Ulloa, was first published in London in 1826, as propaganda for the revolutionary cause, but the authenticity of the book is not in doubt. It is however pertinent that while the text itself was not materially tampered with, the Prologue, which made clear that the report concentrated on abuses, was suppressed—A. P. Whitaker, 'Jorge Juan and Antonio de Ulloa's Prologue to their Secret Report of 1749 on Peru', *HAHR* 18, 1938, 1939, 507–13. There is a translation, from MSS. and with the original title, in J. J. Te Paske (ed.), *Discourse and Political Reflections on the Kingdom of Peru* (Norman, Okla. 1978), with a judicious introduction. My references are to the London 1826 edition [*Noticias*]. For the extremely interesting careers of the authors, see Whitaker, 'Antonio de Ulloa', *HAHR* 15, 1935, 155–94, and J. P. Merino Navarro and M. M. Rodríguez San Vicente in their introduction to the facsimile of the *Relación Histórica del Viaje a la América Méridional* (Madrid 1978) [*Relación*].

[6] It was Francisco de Villachica—*Noticias*, 57–67, 82–3, 142–4.

[7] Ibid., 114, 119–28; for English seamen, the cross-staff (*ballestilla*) would have been a century or more out-of-date—P. Kemp (ed.), *The Oxford Companion to Ships and the Sea* (London 1976), 274. Ironically, in 1750 Jorge Juan was in London, incognito, seducing British shipwrights to come, illegally, to Spain, at the same time as British experts were gleefully copying the captured Spanish *Princesa*—'history sometimes plays these jokes'—*Relación*, lxxxii.

[8] *Noticias*, 202–24; one of the pleasures of the book is its range in denunciation, from sombre eloquence to breezy colloquialism.

[9] Moses, *Declining Power*, 400.

[10] J. H. Parry, *The Spanish Seaborne Empire* (Harmondsworth 1973), 310 [*Seaborne Empire*]; it seems unlikely, however, that over 700 merchantmen entered Habana in eleven months, as stated in S. J. and B. H. Stein, *The Colonial Heritage of Latin America* (New York 1970), 97 [*Heritage*]. Unless most of these were very small local craft, C. H. Haring's 'nearly a hundred' looks more realistic—*The Spanish Empire in America* (Harbinger ed., New York 1963), 318–19 [*Spanish Empire*].

[11] Ibid., 320–1.

[12] C. del C., *Lima y BA*, 33–4, 107–18, 197–8; D. Alden, 'The Undeclared War of 1773–1777; Climax of Luso-Spanish Platine Rivalry', *HAHR* 41, 1961, 55–74. For the British refusal to support Portugal, see M. Rodríguez, *Revolución de 1776*, 20–1, 84 (full reference in note 48 below).

[13] This is the usual interpretation, and is accepted by J. Lynch in *Spanish Colonial Administration, 1782–1810: The Intendant System in the Viceroyalty of the Rio de la Plata* (London 1958), 19 [*Administration*]. Fifteen years later, however, he wrote that 'Americans were confined to intercolonial trade', citing a letter from José de Gálvez, as Minister for the Indies, 22 Oct. 1778—ten days after the issue of the *Reglamento*: 'The Americans can practice commerce between themselves, in their own ports, leaving the trade from Spain to America in the hands of Spaniards of this peninsula'—*Revolutions*, 13. There is an interesting discussion in I. Dias Avelino, 'Institução do "Comercio Livre" no Mundança Estructural do Sistema Colonial Espanhol', *Rev. Hist. América* 85, 1968, 59–83.

[14] Haring, *Spanish Empire*, 320–1; S. Villalobos R., *Comercio y Contrabando en el Río de la Plata y Chile 1700–1811* (Buenos Aires 1965), 54–6, 97 [*Contrabando*]; Parry, *Seaborne Empire*, 311–12, 320–1. Despite their precision, the figures given in Lynch (*Revolutions*, 12) showing an increase in returns from America 1778–84 of 1528 per cent seem difficult to

accept, especially as during four of these six years Spain was at war with Great Britain; one cannot but suspect that their source, an *Examen imparcial de las disensiones de la América con la España*, may be more polemical than reliable, given place and date of publication—Cadiz 1812. The more modest and oft-repeated statement that trade between Spain and America increased by 700 per cent in 1778–88 rests on an estimate of 1816 by the Abbé du Pradt; J. Vicens Vives seems doubtful (*An Economic History of Spain* (Princeton 1969), 577–9), while Parry says that a four-fold growth was a conservative estimate (*Seaborne Empire*, 321). But cf. P. Chaunu, 'Interpretación de la Independencia de América Latina', in J. M. Mar (ed.), *La Independencia en el Perú* (Lima 1972), 123–53 at 141–2 ['Interpretación'].

[15] D. A. Brading and H. E. Cross, 'Colonial Silver Mining: Mexico and Peru', *HAHR* 52, 1972, 549–79 at 551–2, 564–7, 577–8; Fisher, 'Silver', 52–6, and *Colonial Peru*, 140–6; A. P. Whitaker, *The Huancavelica Mercury Mine* (Cambridge, Mass., 1941, reprint Westwood, Conn., 1971), 27–80 *passim* [*Huancavelica*].

[16] L. Navarro García, *Hispanoamerica en el siglo XVIII* (Seville 1975), 220–7 [*Hispanoamerica*]; Fisher, *Colonial Peru*, 18–19, 113, 122–3, and 'Silver', 36–9; Whitaker, *Huancavelica*, 90–1.

[17] C. Furtado, *Economic Development of Latin America* (Cambridge 2nd ed. 1976), 25, citing R. Puiggros.

[18] Villalobos, *Contrabando*, 53. For the sound rationale (given the Spanish system) of the earlier restraints on Platine trade, see Spate, 218, 340, and C. del C., *Lima y BA*, 38–43.

[19] E. Romero, *Historia Económica del Perú* (Buenos Aires 1959), 188 [*Perú*]; Fisher, *Colonial Peru*, 131–6; D. Ramos, *Minería y Comercio Interprovincial en Hispanoamerica (siglos XVI, XVII, y XVIII)* (Valladolid n.d.), 260, 275 [*Minería*]; Villalobos, *Contrabando*, 59–60, 116. During the Succession War, of course, Lima herself was served by French ships round the Horn.

[20] Fisher, *Colonial Peru*, 129–33; Romero, *Perú*, 174–5, 182–8, 255.

[21] Fisher, *Colonial Peru*, 148–9, 155; Navarro García, *Hispanoamerica*, 220; C. del C., *Lima y BA*, 177–82, 186–8.

[22] Villalobos, *Contrabando*, 97.

[23] Lynch, *Revolutions*, 230; Ramos, *Minería*, 280–2. Villalobos, *Contrabando*, 103–9, gives a balanced view, pointing out for example that the building and repair of small craft for riverine and coastal traffic was stimulated—not without a hint of contraband.

[24] C. Alcázar y Molina, *Los Virreinatos en el Siglo XVIII* (Barcelona 1945), 397–8 [*Virreinatos*]; for Peruvian-Chilean economic relations in general, C. del C., *Lima y BA*, 53–62, and for the background of ports and local cabotage, albeit at an earlier date, Juan and Ulloa, *Relación*, II.348–53, 365–70, and *Noticias*, 29–49.

[25] Ramos, *Minería*, 292–8.

[26] Navarro García, *Hispanoamerica*, 230–2; G. Guarda, *La Ciudad Chilena del siglo XVIII* (Buenos Aires 1968), 12, 17, 41–54, 71; J. Eyzaguirre, *O'Higgins* (3rd ed. Santiago 1950), 30–2.

[27] Ramos, *Minería*, 287–9; his percentages add up to only 97.66.

[28] A. P. Whitaker, *The United States and Latin American Independence, 1800–1830* (Norton ed., New York 1954), 4–16 [*Independence*]. The standard work on this first Norteamericano penetration into the South Sea must now be E. Pereira Salas, *Los Primeros Contactos entre Chile y los Estados Unidos 1778–1809* (Santiago 1971); he gives a detailed list of 291 visits in 1778–1809, most of them sealers and whalers but with some outright smugglers [*Contactos*].

[29] Villalobos, *Contrabando*, 80–90; Romero, *Perú*, 255; Ramos, *Minería*, 313.

30 For the evolution and complex workings of the new system in Peru and La Plata, I have relied mainly on Fisher, *Colonial Peru*, and Lynch, *Administration*, both *passim*; shorter accounts of both the old and new arrangements are in Haring, *Spanish Empire*, 128–38, and Parry, *Seaborne Empire*, 327–9. That given here is of course greatly simplified.

31 See C. Dilke (ed.), *Letter to a King: A Picture-History of the Inca Civilisation*, by Don Felipe Huamán Poma de Ayala (London 1978). Huamán Poma says that his father, a Viceroy under the last legitimate Inca ruler Huascar, had welcomed Pizarro at Tumbes. Despite the editor's subtitle, two-thirds of the book deals with life under Spanish rule.

32 Stein and Stein, *Heritage*, 76–7.

33 Doubtless remaindered!—Fisher, *Colonial Peru*, 13–17, 21; Antonio de Arriaga, Condorcanqui's victim, had distributed goods to a 'value' of 300,000 pesos, against his legal limit of 112,000. See also Lynch, *Revolutions*, 7–9, and Fisher's 'La Rebelión de Túpac Amaru y el Programa de la Reforma Imperial de Carlos III', *AEA* 28, 1971, 405–21, especially the quotation from Amat at 408.

34 A. Moreno Cebrian, *El Corregidor de Indios y la Economía Peruana del Siglo XVIII (Los Repartos de Mercancías)* (Madrid 1977), 739—a definitive treatment of the subject, at once austere and damnatory [*Corregidor*].

35 L. E. Fisher, *The Last Inca Revolt 1780–1783* (Norman, Okla., 1966), 44–5, 50, 115–17— 'lampoons' spoke of English help for the rebels, and the authorities took this sufficiently seriously to close ports on both the Atlantic and Pacific coasts. Spain was at war with Great Britain from May 1779, and the Viceroy Manuel Guirior fitted out a squadron of seven ships to guard the Chilean coasts—Alcázar, *Virreinatos*, 368. There were indeed plans for descents on both American coasts—V. T. Harlow, *The Founding of the Second British Empire 1763–1793* (London 1952–64), I.103–21; B. Lewin, *La Rebelión de Túpac Amaru y los Orígenes de la Emancipación Americana* (Buenos Aires 1957), 279 [*Túpac Amaru*]. But at this time, with the American War in full swing, the Royal Navy was greatly extended, and Lewin has to admit that the 'prophecies' and placards which he cites as pointing to a British connection (287–93) amount to very little.

36 Much of Túpac Amaru's success must be ascribed to inefficiency, irresolution, and factionalism among the loyalists—see the detailed account in L. G. Campbell, *The Military and Society in Colonial Peru 1750–1810* (Philadelphia 1978), 99–153 *passim* [*The Military*]. For a very idiosyncratic commentary on Túpac Amaru himself, see S. de Madariaga, *The Fall of the Spanish American Empire* (Collier ed., New York 1963), 198–204 [*The Fall*].

37 Moreno Cebrian, *Corregidor*, 586–96.

38 See the awesome list of responsibilities in Haring, *Spanish Empire*, 135–6. The actual ordinance governing the new structure is translated in L. E. Fisher, *The Intendant System in Spanish America* (Berkeley 1929); G. Morazzani de Pérez Enciso, *La Intendencia en España y en América* (Caracas 1960) is very thorough but legalistic.

39 Lynch, *Administration*, 169–71.

40 It is significant that one of the few final restrictions to comercio libre was that Peru and Chile should not send wine, raisins, olives or almonds to the northern provinces—Haring, *Spanish Empire*, 320.

41 Fisher, *Colonial Peru*, 131–6, 155.

42 Victorián de Villalva, Fiscal of the Audiencia of Charcas, 2 January 1795, cited in Lynch, *Administration*, 182—see ibid., 179–85, 195–200; Parry, *Seaborne Empire*, 343; Moreno Cebrian, *Corregidor*, 697–702, a section headed 'the subdelegados on the road of the

corregidores'. Cf. C. I. Archer, *The Army in Bourbon Mexico, 1760–1810* (Albuquerque 1977), 124–35 [*The Army*].

43 Lynch, *Administration*, 287–9.

44 See V. A. Belaúnde, *Peruanidad* (3rd ed. Lima 1965), *194–223*. F. X. Tapia, *El Cabildo Abierto Colonial* (Madrid 1966) gives a pleasing picture of the institution, but oddly enough says little or nothing of its political use in the liberation.

45 Lynch, *Revolutions*, 2–7; Stein and Stein, *Heritage*, 96–7; the quotation is from S. Villalobos R., *Tradición y Reforma en 1810* (Santiago 1960), 89 [*1810*].

46 See A. P. Whitaker (ed.), *Latin America and the Enlightenment* (Great Seal ed., Ithaca 1961), 35, 72–84, and especially C. C. Griffin's essay on the Enlightenment and Independence, 119–41; also Haring, *Spanish Empire*, 219–32; Góngora, *Studies*, 180–4; and Madariaga, *The Fall*, 205–25, though it seems more in rhetoric than fact that 'The leader of Creole America was Rousseau' (205). For Rousseau in Spanish America see R. Levene, *El Mundo de las Ideas y la Revolución Hispanoamericana de 1810* (Santiago 1956), 189–206, a strangely dry and legalistic work considering its theme [*Ideas*]. Perhaps more to the point than any of these is the closer look by F. Barreda Laos, *Vida Intellectual del Virreinato del Perú* (3rd ed. Lima 1964), 186–230. The Biblioteca Nacional has issued a facsimile of the *Mercurio Peruano* (12 vols, Lima 1964–6).

47 C. Hill, *Intellectual Origins of the English Revolution* (Oxford 1965), 3; cf. C. Brinton, *The Anatomy of Revolution* (Vintage ed., New York 1960), 52: 'No ideas, no revolutions. This does not mean that ideas *cause* revolutions.'

48 M. Rodríguez, *La Revolución Americana de 1776 y el Mundo Hispanico: Ensayos y Documentos* (Madrid 1976), 22 [*Revolución de 1776*]. Specific examples in Archer, *The Army*, 81–5.

49 Lynch, *Revolutions*, 28–30; Parry, *Seaborne Empire*, 349; and the essays from diverse points of view in R. A. Humphreys and J. Lynch (eds.), *The Origins of the Latin American Revolutions, 1808–1826* (Borzoi ed., New York 1965), 75–110 [*Origins*].

50 For Yankee skippers as 'travelling salesmen of rational liberty' (which did not exclude slaving), see Whitaker, *Independence*, 13–15, and Pereira Salas, *Contactos*, 308–12; and for the activities of the American agent Joel Poinsett in Chile, Whitaker, 65–8, 71–3. French republican propaganda also filtered in but was naturally more suspect to the respectable classes, even when Godoy's Spain was allied to France; approaches were made to Blacks in Buenos Aires in 1794–5—R. Caillet-Bois, in *Origins*, 100–3; Levene, *Ideas*, 180–5.

51 'I am not a *Spaniard*, I am an *American!*'—A. von Humboldt, *Ensayo Político sobre el Reino de la Nueva España* (Mexico 1973), 76 (I.205 in the English version, London 1811; reprint New York 1966). The significance of the style 'United States of *America*' had been noted by the Conde de Aranda as early as 1776—R. Ezquerra Abadía, 'En Torno de la Memoria de Aranda', *AEA* 33, 1976, 273–307 at 284–5 ['Aranda'], Levene, *Ideas*, 157–78, has a good deal on the diffusion of Thomas Paine's views in South America, despite their 'atheism'.

52 R. Donoso and M. Batllori SJ in Humphreys and Lynch, *Origins*, 55–72; Madariaga, *The Fall*, 260–1. Most of Viscardo's *Carta dirijida a los Españoles Americanos* is reprinted in Rodríguez, *Revolución de 1776*, 66–74; see also Lewin, *Túpac Amaru*, 221–5; this enormous work (1023 pages) is devoted to supporting the thesis of Túpac as a progenitor of independence. For a balanced view, see Villalobos, *1810*, 74–6. The de Pauw controversy, with Jesuit and other retorts to his idiocies, is reviewed in A. Gerbi, *The Dispute of the New World* (Pittsburgh 1973), Chs. 3–6—a work of vast erudition and delightful wit.

[53] Lynch, *Revolutions*, 30–2; Basadre, 'Conciencia de síí', in Humphreys and Lynch, *Origins*, 193–300.

[54] P. Chaunu, *L'Amérique et les Amériques* (Paris 1964), 199 [*L'Amérique*], and 'Interpretación', 136–8; Parry, *Seaborne Empire*, 312, 345–6; D. A. Brading, *Miners and Merchants in Bourbon Mexico 1763–1810* (Cambridge 1971), 106–9, 252–6.

[55] F. A. Encina, in Humphreys and Lynch, *Origins*, 243–9; somewhat at variance with his remarks in *Resumen de la Historia de Chile* (4th ed. Santiago 1964), I.375–85, qualified at 477–8.

[56] *The Fall*, 40. On Criollos and office in general, see D. M. Dozer, *Latin America: An Interpretive History* (New York 1962), 168–73, and the opposing views of S. Villalobos R. and J. Eyzaguirre in Humphreys and Lynch, *Origins*, 250–60. It is difficult to accept Chaunu's view ('Interpretación', 134–5) that Peninsular domination of administration was no more than compensation for their exclusion from key positions in economic life.

[57] Parry, *Seaborne Empire*, 342–4.

[58] Eyzaguirre, in Humphreys and Lynch, *Origins*, 260.

[59] Campbell, *The Military*, 155–9; Lynch, *Administration*, 292–301; but even before the Reforms, and at the low level of corregidor, Moreno Cebrian speaks of a definite preference for Peninsulares—*Corregidor*, 738.

[60] Madariaga, *The Fall*, 43–4, 47–9; Lynch, *Revolutions*, 10–11; Campbell, *The Military*, 174–7 and *passim*. Archer, *The Army*, gives a graphic account of the vicissitudes of military affairs in New Spain.

[61] José de Abalos, an intendente in Venezuela, to the King, 24 September 1781, in Rodríguez, *Revolución de 1776*, 54–63 at 58; like Aranda, Abalos proposed three or four kingdoms in the Indies (and the Philippines).

[62] *Ibid.*, 63–6. The plan has also been attributed to Godoy, a lightweight but not a fool, as a forgery designed to discredit Aranda, but in any case such ideas were in the air—Ezquerra Abadía, 'Aranda', *passim*. For debate on its authenticity, see papers by A. P. Whitaker and A. R. Wright, *HAHR* 17, 1917, 287–313, and 18, 1938, 445–60. It seems to be generally accepted by students of the period as Aranda's; three years later he proposed a complicated scheme giving Peru and perhaps Chile to the Braganzas in exchange for Spanish annexation of Portugal itself—Rodríguez, 27.

[63] Stein and Stein, *Heritage*, 109–13. The outline of events given here is of course vastly foreshortened.

[64] *L'Amérique*, 203; Chaunu's argument is presented with more sophistication in 'Interpretación', which makes some good points but sometimes seems to be flogging a dead horse; revisionism *in excelsis*—see Góngora's comment, *Studies*, 242–5. Bolívar is quoted from Humphreys and Lynch, *Origins*, 261–2.

[65] Lynch, *Revolutions*, 23, 305–12, (Hidalgo), 325–6.

[66] Apart from general national histories, see L. Langlois, *Influencia del Poder Naval en la Historia de Chile* (Valparaiso 1911), 61–105, and D. E. Worcester, *Sea Power and Chilean Independence* (Gainesville 1962), *passim*. There are short accounts in Lynch, *Revolutions*, 137–40, and R. A. Humphreys, *Liberation in South America 1806–1827: The Career of James Paroissien* (London 1952), 82–99.

[67] I. Gajardo Reyes, 'Ensayo histórico sobre las operaciones maritimas en la primera campaña de la Independencia . . .', *Rev. Chilena de Hist. y Geografia* 12, 1914, 371–406 at 373, 386–8, 395–6.

INDEX

Merely 'marker' and *en passant* references omitted. References to authors, and to the notes, are given only when there is comment or additional information. Abbreviations: *pm*, *passim*; GP, Governor of the Philippines; VP, VNS, Viceroy of Peru/New Spain.

Text computer photocomposed in 10 point Bembo two point leaded
and printed on 95 gsm Glopaque at
Griffin Press Limited, Netley, South Australia

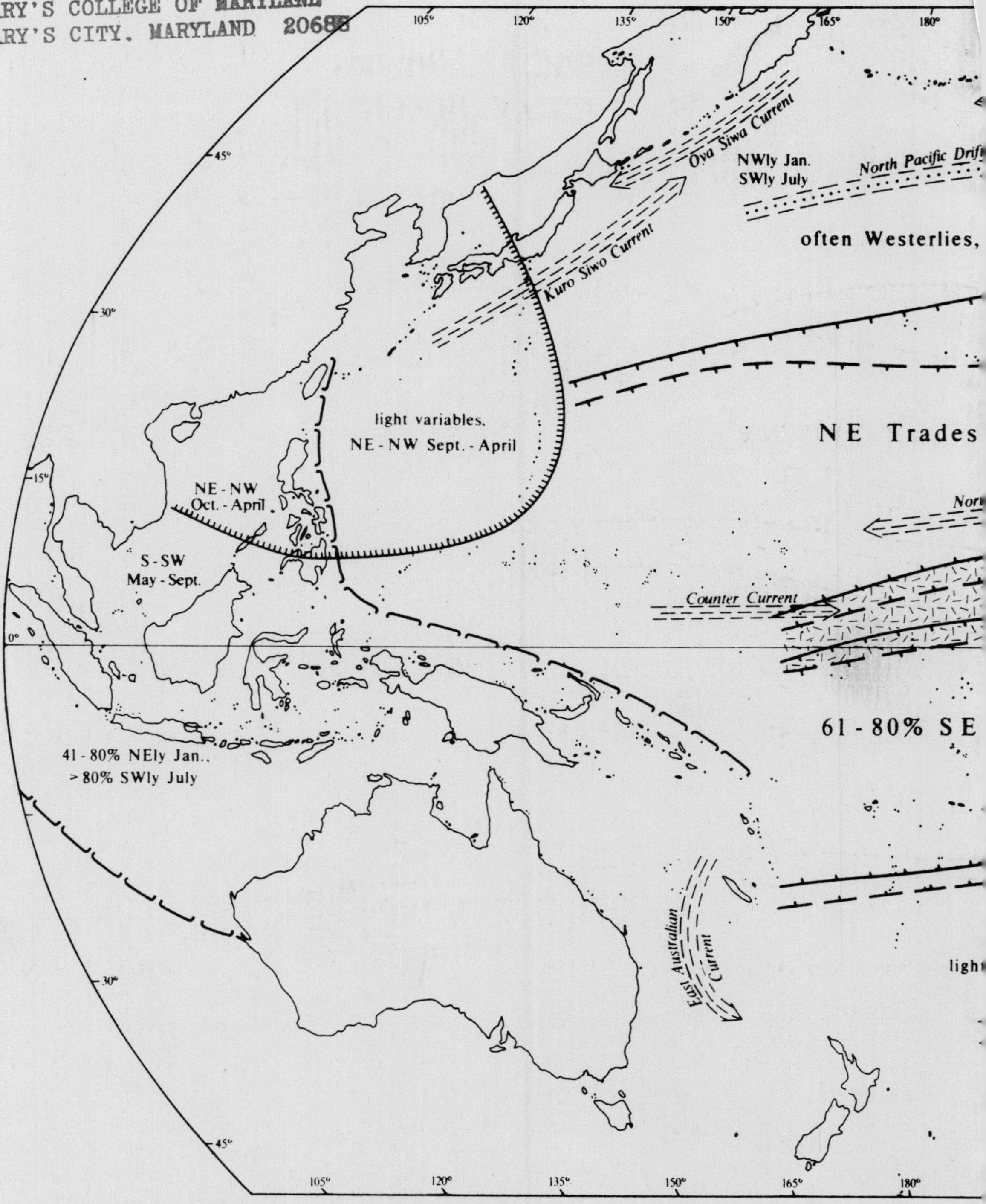

Figure 1. PACIFIC WINDS AND CURRENTS. 1, approx. limits of Trade Wind belts, April–September; 2, same in October–March; 3, approx. trend of main currents; 4, of main drifts; 5, encloses area dominated by Southeast Asian monsoons; 6, areas of high typhoon risk, especially July–October; 7, belt of calms and light airs (Doldrums). Numerals indicate frequencies of prevalent winds in total observations, excluding calms. Central meridian 165°W.